— ★ ★ ★ —

Recent America

— ★ ★ ★ —

Recent America

The United States Since 1945

Third Edition

Dewey W. Grantham

Thomas Maxwell-Long
CALIFORNIA STATE UNIVERSITY
SAN BERNARDINO

Harlan Davidson, Inc.
Wheeling, Illinois 60090-6000

Visit us on the World Wide Web at www.harlandavidson.com

Library of Congress Cataloging-in-Publication Data

Grantham, Dewey W.
 Recent America : the United States since 1945 / Dewey W. Grantham, Thomas
Maxwell-Long. — 3rd ed.
    p. cm.
 ISBN 978-0-88295-276-5 (alk. paper)
 1. United States—History—1945- 2. United States—Foreign relations—1945–1989.
3. United States—Foreign relations—1989- I. Maxwell-Long, Thomas. II. Title.
 E741.G73 2011
 973.92—dc22

                                                                    2010041390

Flag of the United States, Korean War Memorial, Battery Park, NYC. This memorial
designed by artist Mac Adams (b. 1943) was dedicated in 1991 and notable as one of the
first Korean Conflict memorials in the United States.
Credit: American Flag © Svlumagraphica | Dreamstime.com

Manufactured in the United States of America
12 11 10   1 2 3 MG

Contents

—— ★ ★ ★ ——

Preface and Acknowledgments

THIS THIRD EDITION of *Recent America* is an extensive revision that includes entirely new material to carry the coverage forward into the second decade of the twenty-first century. The emphasis is on national politics, the ever-evolving multicultural American society, the role of the United States in international affairs, economic trends, and the greater American culture. Additionally, this third edition pays particular attention to changes in American literature, fine arts, music, film, pop culture, and sports and their relationships to social, cultural, and economic trends. The incorporation of these often overlooked historical themes presents a more holistic and inclusive history of the United States.

In the pages that follow, I have brought new perspectives to bear on our recent past and to build upon the tradition set forth by the late Dewey Grantham in the first and second editions to provide student readers with a readily accessible, well-rounded narrative that reconstructs history and makes strong connections between the present and the past. I hope the result will serve as a useful and engaging introduction to American history from 1945 to the present for students and general readers alike.

I wish to acknowledge my gratitude to the people who helped make this new edition possible. I thank my colleague Professor Joyce Hanson at California State University, San Bernardino, for her careful read of my manuscript and thoughtful suggestions that assisted me tremendously.

I am grateful to Professor Cliff Trafzer of the University of California, Riverside, for his expert advice and guidance at several junctures, which made this volume a stronger work. I am most appreciative of the support that I have received from my department chair, Professor Pedro Santoni, and my college dean, Dr. Jamal Nassar, which allowed me to conduct extensive research on a variety of historical topics at archives and museums and thereby render a more balanced historical account of American life and culture.

At Harlan Davidson, Inc., Linda Gaio has provided an exceptional bevy of photos and images that fill the pages of this volume and help bring the past alive. The level of gratitude that I have for the publisher Andrew J. Davidson is of the highest order. He not only provided tremendous direction and feedback throughout the many steps in publication, but he also demonstrated exceptional patience and restraint while waiting for the finished manuscript. Furthermore, Andrew personally served as copy editor, and in this capacity he not only pressed for a better finished product but demonstrated his unique sense of humor and adherence to honest feedback for the writer.

Lastly, I am most grateful to my wife Roberta for her steadfast support throughout the entire process. I dedicate this book to her and my son, Alexander, from whom I draw all of my inspiration.

Thomas Maxwell-Long
San Diego, California

The Transition from WWII to the Cold War: Confrontation and Containment

I N THE LATE SUMMER OF 1939, a little more than two years before the United States officially entered World War II, Leo Szilard, a research physicist at Columbia University, drafted a letter for his friend, the world-renowned scientist Albert Einstein. The simple two-page letter outlined the scientists' thoughts on how the United States might realize a weapon of unprecedented destructive power, a uranium atomic bomb, recommended immediate research and development of such a weapon, and hinted that Nazi Germany had already undertaken uranium research. Einstein reviewed what Szilard had written, signed the letter, and submitted it to President Franklin Delano Roosevelt. Within two years U.S. development of nuclear weapons was in full swing. Code-named the Manhattan Project by its military director, General Leslie Groves, this remarkable scientific/military undertaking comprised more than thirty research and development (R&D) sites, with a central headquarters for building the weapons located in Los Alamos, New Mexico. There, one of the most extraordinary teams of scientists ever assembled chose the famed physicist J. Robert Oppenheimer to serve as its leader. After years of seemingly tireless labor, the project team successfully detonated a nuclear weapon on the White Sands Proving Grounds in New Mexico on July 16, 1945—the United States, and the world, had entered the atomic age.

While Nazi Germany had formally surrendered on May 8, 1945, the Empire of Japan continued to fight, even after months of intense firebombings that ultimately destroyed more than sixty Japanese cities, including Tokyo. Faced with commencing a ground assault on Japan's home islands that U.S. military leaders feared might result in the death of hundreds of thousands of American troops—this with no guarantee of a quick Japanese surrender—President Harry S. Truman, who had not been privy to any information regarding the top-secret Manhattan Project before having assumed the presidency upon the death of FDR on April 12, 1945, never wavered in his decision to use the powerful new weapons in the nation's arsenal. On August 6, 1945, the United States dropped the first atomic bomb on Hiroshima. The port city was completely destroyed, with between 100,000 and 150,000 people killed by either the blast or the ensuing radiation poisoning. President Truman issued this statement following the bombing of Hiroshima: "If they [Japan] do not now accept our terms, they may expect a rain of ruin from the air, the like of which has never been seen on this earth." Three days later, on August 9, the United States released a second atomic bomb on the city of Nagasaki, resulting in the death of at least 70,000 people. On August 15, Japan surrendered. World War II, the most destructive conflict in the history of humankind, had finally ended.

President Truman's decision to use the atomic bomb has been mired in controversy from the moment he gave the order to do so. In fact, the use of these horrific weapons has so dominated the discussion of moral behavior during war that the bombing of civilian targets with conventional bombs—by the United States as well as other combatants in World War II—has received relatively little attention. This discrepancy is easy to explain: in the case of both Hiroshima and Nagasaki only one nuclear bomb was required to destroy the entire city, and the gruesome aftereffects associated with radiation poisoning placed these bombings, and any future consideration of the use of nuclear weapons, in a new and horrific category of warfare that the world had never seen before and, fortunately, has not seen since. It is doubtful that historians will ever reach consensus on these incredible events that forever changed life on earth.

While the use of nuclear weapons did accelerate the end of World War II, it also led directly to a nuclear arms race between the U.S.A. and the U.S.S.R. that lasted for the duration of the Cold War and spawned the construction of tens of thousands of nuclear weapons at incalculable expense to both nations. In addition, other nations would either develop or purchase nuclear weapons. By the end of the Cold War, the United Kingdom, France, India, and Pakistan had joined the U.S.A. and U.S.S.R. as nations that openly admitted to having such weapons. Many believe that Israel entered the nuclear-state club by 1979, though it has not admitted to having a nuclear weapon. South Africa, which developed nuclear weapons during the 1980s and 1990s, has since dismantled its nuclear arsenal. After the dissolution of the Soviet Union in 1991, three former Soviet satellite republics, Belarus, Kazakhstan, and Ukraine, were left holding thousands of nuclear weapons that the Soviets had strategically located within their borders. By the late 1990s, however, Russia reported having received all of those weapons back from its former republics. The latest nation to claim to have built a nuclear weapon is North Korea, which reported that it conducted successful tests in 2005, though U.S. investigations concluded that it was not until the following year that North Korea produced a positive detonation.

While it is true that only a handful of nations have possessed nuclear weapons, the incredible bulk held by the United States and the Soviet Union/Russia, and their continued escalation, both in terms of quantity and technological advances, have had a considerable impact on the daily lives and thoughts of Americans and people around the globe because of one clear and inescapable fact: by the late 1960s humankind knew it possessed the power to destroy virtually all, if not all, life on the planet. U.S. foreign policy was shaped by this daunting fact for decades after World War II, as was everyday life in America. The fear of a nuclear holocaust, with which all Americans lived, was evidenced by the construction of public and private nuclear fallout and bomb shelters, as well as nuclear attack drills for schoolchildren, commonly referred to as the "duck and cover." Pop culture, literature, movies, and the fine arts were also heavily influenced by this phenomenon. Only after the Cold War ended in 1991 did American society feel a sense of relief that no nuclear conflict had taken place. We seemed to have made it through the long, dark tunnel safely.

As time continues to progress beyond the end of the Cold War (a significant and complex theme through much of this book) students in contemporary America who did not live during any portion of the Cold War have a difficult time understanding the very real fear of a nuclear holocaust with which two generations of Americans, leaders as well as ordinary citizens, lived. By the dawn of the twenty-first century, nuclear war seemed completely implausible and the majority of Americans felt secure in their daily lives. In a tragic irony, the two greatest incidents of terrorism on domestic soil occurred after the Cold War had ended and the majority of Americans believed they were safe from attack: the Oklahoma City bombing in 1995 and the 9/11 attacks of 2001. Sadly, as the United States moves through the second decade of the new century, this new fear, the threat of attack by terrorists, has replaced the old one.

When the Japanese formally surrendered to the Allies on September 2, 1945, the United States was very different from the nation that had been propelled into war by the surprise attack on Pearl Harbor on December 7, 1941. To most Americans in the late summer of 1945, the war seemed very old, its beginnings already shrouded in the mists of the retreating past. Part of this feeling was undoubtedly an illusion produced by the sacrifices and weariness of wartime, abetted by the tumultuous events of a global conflict. But the impression was also based on the reality of profound changes that had taken place in the United States during the past four years. The war led to the creation of a mighty military force, brought about a great mobilization of industry and other resources, banished unemployment, freed the economy from the grip of the Depression, helped redefine the role of government, invoked new international policies, and altered the nation's social structure. It also precipitated new social tensions and problems.

WORLD WAR II: CATALYST FOR CHANGE

The first part of the war was a grim and sobering experience for Americans, and in those dark days it sometimes seemed that it would be impossible for the Allies to stem the powerful tide of the Axis onslaught. Yet the people and their leaders set about the forbidding task in a spirit of remarkable unity. Pearl Harbor ended the great debate on foreign policy and united Americans in a common purpose. While the extravagant idealism that attended the nation's involvement in World War I was noticeably absent from American participation in World War II, most people would have agreed with Vice President Henry A. Wallace's characterization of the conflict as "a fight between a slave world and a free world." Divisions and disagreements in the United States remained, as might be expected, but there was little intolerance or hysteria compared with 1917–18, and except for the shameful treatment of Japanese Americans on the West Coast, egregious violations of civil liberties were relatively few—the persistence of Jim Crow laws in the South notwithstanding.

The war resuscitated the U.S. economy and brought a new era of prosperity in place of the devastating depression of the previous decade. In spite of serious flaws in its mobilization process, the United States became, in the phrase of the day, an "arsenal of democracy." So great was its increase in plant capacity that production almost doubled between 1939 and 1945. By late 1943 an incredible flow of tanks, airplanes, ships, and guns was pouring out of American factories, and the national output was more than twice that of the combined Axis powers. During the war, the economy was transformed in many ways: in the modernization and consolidation of industry, the growing industrialization of the South and parts of the West, the expansion of organized labor, the massive internal movement of workers, and the increase in agricultural productivity despite a substantial decline in farm population. "At the end of the war," Richard Polenberg observes, "the United States was a more urban, technological, and industrial society than when it had entered." David Brinkley remembered how the war transformed Washington, D.C.: "A languid Southern town with a pace so slow that much of it simply closed down for the summer grew almost overnight into a crowded, harried, almost frantic metropolis struggling desperately to assume the mantle of global power, moving haltingly and haphazardly and only partially successfully to change itself into the capital of the free world."

Governmental intervention during World War I appeared limited when compared to the mobilization of manpower, industry, finance, and technology during the early 1940s. Though the American home front was not subjected to the thoroughgoing controls imposed by most of the major belligerent powers, the extent of the federal government's involvement in the economy was unparalleled in U.S. history. The war enhanced the power of the president and the federal bureaucracy, thereby accustoming people to Washington's expanded role. This development was associated with a revolutionary change in the national government's fiscal policy; wartime expenditures were so enormous that they amounted to twice as much as all federal appropriations before 1941. The heightened influence of the national government centered on President Franklin D. Roosevelt, in whose deft hands the responsibility for coordinating mobilization and production rested. Roosevelt's leadership symbolized the nation at war, and his influence and personality were indelibly stamped on the great transformation of American life during those hectic years.

Although the Roosevelt administration continued to win the support of a majority of the voters, the war weakened the influence of liberals and intensified the strength of conservatives. The New Deal seemed to be waning. Power in the Democratic Party shifted in the direction of more moderate and conservative elements, and in Congress a bipartisan coalition of conservatives strongly resisted further domestic reform. "The new shape of American politics," the distinguished historian Alonzo L. Hamby has written, "included a reform-oriented presidential Democratic Party able to control presidential nominations and a moderate-to-conservative congressional Democratic Party."

No feature of the war years contrasted more sharply with the situation in the 1930s than the abandonment of isolationism in the United States. The Japanese attack on Pearl Harbor destroyed the old myth of American impregnability, and during the war the United States became the organizer and leader of the Grand Alliance in destroying the Axis powers and establishing an international organization for peace. A war-born American empire had taken shape by 1945, and at the end of the war U.S. influence had become dominant in Western Europe, Japan, Latin America, and throughout the Pacific. Most Americans seemed to think that it was both possible and desirable for the United States to use its immense power to help reshape the world along the lines of its own democratic capitalism.

The transformation of U.S. foreign policy was directly related, of course, to certain changes in the rest of the world. One such change was the decline of Europe's pre-eminence in world affairs, a development associated with the collapse of Western imperialism, the revolt of the peoples of Asia and Africa, the rise of Eastern nationalism, and the polarization of power between the United States and the Soviet Union. A second impetus for America's changing foreign policy was the end of ministration (OPA), the heart of the postwar stabilization program, was widely disliked. According to the journalist Cabell Phillips, "it inspired a devious, illicit sort of gamesmanship not unlike that of the prohibition era, with black marketeers taking the place of the bootleggers." The administration's honeymoon period soon ended, but Truman was expected both to remove wartime controls and prevent inflation.

Industrialists, businessmen, and farm representatives pressed Congress to abolish all controls. Such action, they contended, would enable the "natural forces of the marketplace" to bring about abundance and low prices within a few months. Business representatives argued that controls were delaying full production, encouraging the black market, and preventing producers from getting their rightful profits. Many trade association executives denounced the OPA as a "socialistic" bottleneck that was damaging production, employment, and the heart of the free enterprise system. Business interests mounted a concerted campaign to destroy the agency. Meanwhile, the wartime accommodation between business, labor, and the government had collapsed.

Organized labor tended to favor price controls, but only if it could secure higher wages for workers. Labor had acquired great strength and confidence during the war, but its leaders believed that workers had not shared equally with capital in the wartime prosperity. Concerned about the return to a forty-hour week and the loss of overtime pay after the war and apprehensive about the possibility of massive unemployment or drastic inflation, they were determined to protect labor's interests in the postwar era.

Labor's restiveness quickly manifested itself. Half a million workers went out on strike within a few weeks of Japan's surrender, and the following autumn and winter witnessed widespread work stoppages when union demands for wage increases and other benefits went unmet by management. The loss of worker-days reached 23 million in February 1946, and the year as a whole brought almost five thousand work stoppages involving 4.6 million workers. A series of strikes in the steel, automobile, meat-packing, and electrical industries threatened to disrupt the entire economy. Although a labor-management conference in late 1945 failed to reach agreement on reconversion wage policies, a recommendation by a presidential fact-finding board eventually provided the basis for a settlement of the great industrial strikes in the winter of

1945–46. In general, labor received a little over two-thirds of what it sought, while management was allowed substantial price increases in return. A new round of labor-management disputes began in the fall of 1946, with an agreement in April of the next year providing for an hourly wage increase of about fifteen cents. A third conflict was settled in 1948. In these and subsequent confrontations, management showed a willingness to accede to labor's demands, but with the understanding that the added costs would be passed on to the consumer in the form of higher prices.

The general settlement of 1946 did not end the Truman administration's problems with organized labor. A national emergency was created when John L. Lewis of the United Mine Workers (UMW) led 400,000 miners out of the coal pits on April 1, 1946. The strike continued until the government took over the mines. Eventually, a settlement gave the UMW most of what it wanted. Lewis made new demands in October, and when negotiations failed, the labor leader called another strike. In December 1946, Lewis and his union were fined for contempt after they disregarded a temporary restraining order. But when the mines were returned to their owners in July 1947, Lewis secured a new contract that provided virtually all he had sought.

In the meantime, the troubled spring of 1946 confronted the administration with still another labor controversy. When the railroad brotherhoods called a nationwide railroad strike in mid-May, the president seized the railroads under the provisions of the Smith-Connally Act and won a compromise settlement with most of the unions. But two of the brotherhoods—the Locomotive Engineers and the Railroad Trainmen—decided to strike anyway. "If you think I'm going to sit here and let you tie up this whole country," Truman exclaimed to the leaders of the two unions, "you're crazy as hell." When they went ahead with the strike, Truman scheduled an appearance before Congress on May 25 to request authority to prevent the paralysis of transportation and curb labor disputes in essential industries. The railroad unions gave in just before the chief executive spoke, and the crisis ended.

Many members of Congress applauded President Truman's get-tough policy toward John L. Lewis and the railroad brotherhood leaders. Yet these same legislators were often critical of Truman's economic controls in 1945 and 1946. Senator Edward H. Moore of Oklahoma declared in June 1946, "A controlled economy leads to an authoritarian psychology

THE TRANSITION FROM WWII TO THE COLD WAR

which results in the oppression and destruction of individual rights and liberties under a Gestapo system." Truman sought "continued stabilization of the national economy" through a policy of gradually relaxing the wartime regulation of prices, wages, and commodities in short supply. Most rationing was ended in the early postwar period. Unfortunately, the administration itself was divided over the implementation of its economic controls. Chester Bowles, the head of OPA, wanted to follow a more stringent program of price ceilings than did the more conservative John W. Snyder, the director of the Office of War Mobilization and Reconversion. The president leaned toward Snyder's position and allowed higher prices, a concession he described as a "bulge in the line." Bowles became discouraged and soon resigned. Nevertheless, the administration's anti-inflation record during the first ten months following the war was fairly good; wholesale prices during that period rose only 7 percent.

The brunt of the Truman administration's battle against inflation was carried by the OPA, whose statutory authority would expire on July 1, 1946. The administration urged that the agency be continued for another year, and a congressional struggle over the issue of extension ensued during the spring of 1946. A price-control bill was finally passed on June 27 providing for a one-year extension, but it gave the agency little power and ordered it to decontrol prices "as rapidly as possible." This weakness led the president to veto the measure, which he described as "a sure formula for inflation," and price controls expired on July 1. Prices immediately zoomed, climbing 25 percent in a little over two weeks—an increase almost twice as great as that of the previous three years. Congress then passed a second bill on July 25, almost as weak as the first, authorizing a one-year extension of price and rent controls. The damage had been done by that time, however, and thereafter the administration could do little to halt the inflationary spiral. Soon after the November elections, the president ended all controls over wages and prices except those on rents, sugar, and rice.

If the Democrats had won the 1946 congressional elections, President Truman might have continued the fight against inflation. As it turned out, the Republicans won a sweeping victory in 1946, taking majorities in both houses of Congress and winning control of the legislature for the first time since 1930. During the campaign they indicted the administration for inept and discriminatory price-control policies, high prices, and continuing shortages. As they put it to the voters, "Had enough? Vote Republican." The Democrats were also vulnerable in other ways. Truman was unpopular with many members of his own party—with conservatives because of his progressive domestic proposals and his economic policies, and with liberals because of certain administration appointments and his support in some instances of conservatives over liberals in the administration. The president's popularity with the public had hit a low ebb, for he seemed to present a spectacle of executive incompetence. Indeed, that year there was a rash of Truman jokes going around, including the quip that "to err is Truman."

NATIONAL DEFENSE AND WORLD AFFAIRS

In the new era, no aspect of national defense could be considered without taking the atomic bomb into account. The American monopoly on this awesome power made it imperative that policies be adopted for its control at home and abroad. Most political leaders accepted the need for governmental control over the production and use of atomic energy, but there was sharp disagreement over the nature of such regulation when Congress debated the matter in the fall of 1945. Brien McMahon of Connecticut, chairman of a special Senate committee investigating the problem, prepared a bill with the backing of the administration to establish an atomic energy commission with exclusive civilian control. Senator Arthur H. Vandenberg of Michigan, also a member of the special committee, and others insisted that military representatives be given a key role in the work of the commission. While this position won the approval of the special committee, President Truman strongly opposed it, as did much of the public, and the issue came under heated debate in the spring of 1946. A compromise was finally worked out that resulted in the Atomic Energy Act of 1946. The law created a five-member Atomic Energy Commission under civilian control but with provision for a military liaison committee to work with the commission. Complete control over fissionable materials was vested in the government, and the act stipulated that the president alone would have responsibility for ordering the use of atomic weapons in warfare.

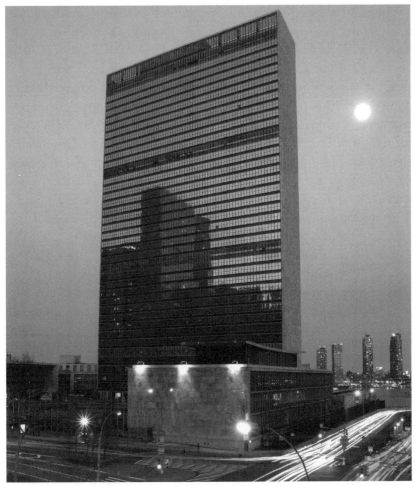

The UN dims its lights in recognition of Earth Hour in 2010. *UN photo/Paulo Filgueiras, #432321.*

In the meantime, the administration was giving thought to the need for international control. Early in 1946 the United Nations General Assembly established the UN Atomic Energy Commission, and soon afterward the so-called Acheson-Lilienthal plan for the international control and inspection of atomic energy was formulated under the aegis of the Truman administration. In mid-June 1946, the U.S. representative to the commission, Bernard M. Baruch, submitted a proposal based on this plan to the UN. Truman and his advisers hoped that it would win quick approval.

Administration leaders also made progress in solving another problem: the need to reorganize and unify the country's armed forces. The disaster at Pearl Harbor had revealed fundamental defects in military organization, and the prosecution of the war provided much more evidence of duplication, waste, and inefficiency resulting from overlapping and competing services. Many informed people urged the creation of a common command and a more streamlined organization. But a major reform of this character was not easy to effect; a bitter controversy swirled around the question for two years following war's end. Representatives of the navy were especially recalcitrant, since they feared that unification would diminish the role of sea power and eliminate the Marine Corps. President Truman actively endeavored to secure a workable arrangement, and unification legislation was enacted in July 1947. The National Security Act, as it was called, provided for a secretary of defense with cabinet rank, under whom were secretaries of the army, navy, and air force. The Joint Chiefs of Staff, representing the three services, would assist in coordinating the armed forces and be responsible for defense plans and strategy. The new legislation placed procurement, research, and intelligence in the three services under central boards in an effort to prevent duplication. The act created the Central Intelligence Agency to take charge of intelligence work at the highest level, and it established the National Security Council and the National Security Resources Board to advise the president and Congress on national security. Secretary of the Navy James V. Forrestal, who had lent his support to the unification drive, became the first secretary of defense. Although the National Security Act was a major accomplishment, it did not do away with interservice rivalry and bickering, as was demonstrated in the lengthy controversy over long-range bombers versus super aircraft carriers.

Meanwhile, the U.S. posture toward other nations was also revealed in the organization and early operation of the United Nations. The United States was, from the very beginning of its involvement in World War II, the leading advocate of a new world organization. President Truman was as enthusiastic as his predecessor had been in supporting the creation of the peace organization. Congress was also strongly in favor of the idea, and the Senate's ratification of the UN Charter by a vote of 89 to 2 on July 28, 1945, made the United States the first nation to approve the plan. The American public welcomed the new organization, whose permanent headquarters was located in New York City.

While the UN was impressive in design, experience soon showed that it could work only to the extent that its members voluntarily cooperated. Though empowered to use force against aggressor nations, the organization was unable to compel compliance over the opposition of its strongest members. Permanent members of the UN Security Council, as established by chapter six of the UN Charter, are responsible for investigating any dispute that might lead to a greater international conflict and recommend solutions. The original members of the Security Council in 1948 were France, the United Kingdom, the United States, the Soviet Union, and China. Additionally, the Security Council had the right to veto all but procedural questions, and the charter permitted "regional" agreements and agencies. The United States, despite its ardent efforts to create the new world organization, had insisted on both the veto and the legitimacy of regional defensive associations, and these two features of the UN Charter played an important part in the troubled international history of the postwar era.

During the period, the United States was a generous contributor of international aid. Its financial support was indispensable in launching the United Nations. U.S. aid, channeled through the UN and other agencies, was vitally important in bringing a measure of relief and rehabilitation to millions of starving and homeless people in war-ravaged Europe and Asia. Relief was also afforded in large amounts through the aid of private groups such as the Red Cross. The United States, moreover, made funds available to needy nations through such agencies as the Export-Import Bank, and in 1946 the American government extended Britain a $3.75-billion loan. Meanwhile, the United States worked to ease restrictions on trade, stabilize foreign currencies, and stimulate American investments abroad.

As these relief and rehabilitation efforts were being made, the United States was deeply involved in the formulation of peace treaties with the Axis Powers and in their political reconstruction. In the case of Germany, the United States occupied one of the four zones agreed on by the Allies, proceeded with the task of destroying the German military potential, and joined in the victors' policy of "denazification." The Americans were also instrumental, between November 1945 and

October 1946, in the trial at Nuremberg of a group of leading Nazi officials by the International Military Tribunal. Twelve of the Nazi leaders were sentenced to death for war crimes and atrocities. The United States alone controlled the occupation and reconstruction of Japan. General MacArthur was appointed supreme commander for the Allied powers, and under his imperious control a thoroughgoing program was carried out to demilitarize Japan, establish a system of social democracy there, and reconstruct the nation's economy. Twenty-eight top officials of war time Japan were tried before the International Military Tribunal for the Far East, and seven of these men were executed.

PEACETIME PURSUITS

International problems and matters of statecraft did not much concern the majority of Americans during the immediate postwar months. They were too preoccupied with the exhilaration of homecoming, throwing off wartime restraints, and settling down in peacetime pursuits. As jobs were found for the returning G.I.s and new business ventures were undertaken, the fears of a crippling depression in the reconstruction period soon dissipated, and most people began to achieve an unaccustomed sense of security and belief that the future might hold marvelous possibilities. "Times have changed," one labor representative remarked early in the new era. "People have become accustomed to new conditions, new wage scales, new ways of being treated." In the prosperous transition from war to peace, Americans busied themselves with the myriad plans of an energetic people in a society that still seemed uniquely open and promising.

The prosperity of the war and its aftermath expanded the middle class in the United States and raised the economic and social expectations throughout the population. As the historian Eric F. Goldman wrote a few years later, "The boom rolled out in great fat waves, into every corner of the nation and up and down the social ladder." For a time it seemed that almost all elements of American society could, if they chose, change their status and enjoy a better life than ever before. Although the reality of inequality and discrimination, not to mention inflation, soon revealed the limitations of the postwar boom, economic abundance had never before been available to such a large percentage of Americans. Incomes that went up year after year, new leisure time, regular vacations, expensive hobbies, and the spectacular development of tourism in states like California and Florida became available not merely to the privileged few but also to millions of middle-class people who had achieved new levels of well-being. The nation had never before experienced such a dynamic consumer culture.

Evidence of postwar America's social buoyancy was the sharp increase in the birthrate, resulting in the generation that came to be known as the baby boomers. There was a trend toward earlier marriages, and the marriage rate (as well as the divorce rate) rose steeply. The growing number of new households and the large crop of new babies gave a strong impetus to the economy. But they also produced social problems. For example, the veterans' return, the growth of population, and the rapid movement of people to the cities and suburbs contributed to a severe housing shortage, one not relieved for several years after 1945. The educational system also faced a major crisis during the period. Wartime neglect, the shift of many teachers from the classroom to better-paying jobs, and the crowded schools resulting from an expanding and migratory population confronted many school districts with an impossible situation. Higher education was also entering a period of remarkable expansion, caused in part by the influx of veterans studying under the G.I. Bill of Rights. The nation's campuses had never witnessed anything like this G.I. invasion, but the veterans generally proved to be serious and hard-working students who adjusted well to the requirements of academe.

Abundance in postwar America had its limits, of course. The good times did not greatly improve the condition of many disadvantaged Americans. A group of U.S. senators reported in 1944, for instance, that 20 million of their fellow citizens "dwell constantly in a borderland between subsistence and privation, where even the utmost thrift and caution do not suffice to make ends meet." Even the beneficiaries of the burgeoning economy sometimes expressed doubts. A reporter in St. Louis asked a young mother about her personal expectations. "Oh, things are going along just wonderfully," she exclaimed. "Harry has a grand job, there's the new baby—" but then she paused and asked, "Do you think it's really all going to last?" At a deeper level, affluence was tinged with anxiety, most profoundly by a pervasive awareness of the possibility of nuclear destruction.

The United States, it seemed, had entered a new and radically different stage in its historical evolution, but the conservative effects of World War II should not be overlooked. Wartime changes were often uneven and limited, and as John W. Jeffries has pointed out, the American experience "demonstrates how old patterns, old values, old ideas dominated wartime American politics and culture." One portent of the new era appeared in 1947, when the Cold War became fixed as a dominant concern in the nation's policy and consciousness. It is to that extraordinary development that we must now turn.

THE COLD WAR: CONFRONTATION AND CONTAINMENT

After the war Americans settled down to enjoy the fruits of the Allied victory, confident that the major threats to international peace and stability had been destroyed. But to their dismay they soon discovered that the United States faced a new time of testing—a far-reaching conflict with the Soviet Union that seemed ready at any moment to precipitate a worldwide holocaust. This "Cold War," as it was labeled, polarized many nations of the world into communist and anti-communist blocs, produced more than a generation of recurrent confrontations and crises, and profoundly influenced almost every consideration of foreign policy and national politics on the part of the principal protagonists. Most Americans eventually came to believe that drastic steps must be taken to counter Soviet moves, that vast amounts of aid were required by friendly allies, and that U.S. military power must be available around the globe.

America Faces Russia

The immediate origins of the momentous struggle that developed between the United States and the Soviet Union lay in the wartime relations between the Russians and the Americans and British, in the way the war changed the earlier balance of power in Europe and Asia, and in the fact that the United States and the U.S.S.R. had emerged from World War II as the two most powerful nations on earth. The two superpowers were soon at loggerheads over treatment of the occupied

The Big Three at Potsdam: Churchill, Truman, and Stalin. U. S. Army photograph. *Courtesy Harry S. Truman Library.*

countries of Eastern Europe, the fate of Germany, the economic recon-struction of Europe, conditions in the eastern Mediterranean, the future of East Asia, and control of atomic energy. In July 1945 at the Potsdam Conference, the last wartime meeting of the Big Three heads of state, the fundamental differences between the Soviet Union and the Western Allies became clear. Agreements were finally reached on the questions of reparations and the occupation of Germany, and the Russians re-luctantly conceded permission for British and American observers to move about freely in occupied countries in Eastern Europe. But these agreements were not enforceable, and even at Potsdam they scarcely concealed the deep cleavage that now divided the former allies. At the Potsdam Conference the West accepted Polish occupation of German territory as far west as the Oder-Neisse line and approved the Russian annexation of eastern Poland. President Truman and his advisers were unhappy about the Soviet spheres of influence in Eastern Europe, but they had no real alternative since the Soviet army already occupied most of those areas. They could only hope that Josef Stalin would live up to

Winston Churchill in Fulton, Missouri, on the occasion of his "Iron Curtain" address. *Courtesy Harry S. Truman Library, photograph by Terry B. Savage.*

his earlier commitments to permit free elections and minority rights in the East European nations.

At Potsdam a Council of Foreign Ministers was approved to draft definitive peace treaties with Italy and the former Axis satellites. The council held numerous conferences and struggled between September 1945 and the end of 1946 to overcome the continuing disagreement and hostility between East and West. Treaties with Italy, Finland, Hungary, Rumania, and Bulgaria were finally concluded. The Italian settlement favored the Western Allies, but in the other treaties the Western powers acquiesced in Soviet control of Hungary and the Balkans. No agreement could be reached in the case of Austria, part of which was being occupied and exploited by Russia. A Russian regime was also imposed on Albania, Marshal Josip Broz Tito's Communists controlled Yugoslavia, and a Communist movement shared power in Czechoslovakia.

The United States gradually adopted a firmer posture in its dealings with the Soviet Union. In October 1945 President Truman delivered what some officials described as a "getting tough with the Russians" speech. American policy, he declared, was "based firmly on fundamental principles of righteousness and justice." The United States would "refuse to recognize any government imposed on any nation by the force of any foreign power." In early January 1946, an exasperated Truman told Secretary of State James F. Byrnes, "Unless Russia is faced with an iron fist and strong language another war is in the making. Only one language do they understand—'how many divisions have you?' . . . I'm tired of babying the Soviets."

A series of incidents in 1946 heightened the tension between Russia and the West. While doubtless fortuitous in their timing, several of these developments appeared almost as a direct response to Truman's stiffening position and Churchill's "Iron Curtain" warning of the perils associated with Soviet expansion. The lengthy and dramatic speech Churchill gave at Westmaster College in Fulton, Missouri, shortly after receiving an honorary degree, became an iconic Cold War statement. The Russians created a crisis over Iran by refusing to withdraw their troops from that country in accordance with a previous agreement. They made demands on Turkey for naval bases and a "joint defense" of that country. They refused to become a member of the World Bank and the International Monetary Fund, agencies supported by American economic strength. They launched a new five-year plan and made a significant change in their economic policy toward East Germany. And they timed their evacuation of Manchuria in such a way as to leave there valuable matériel to benefit the Chinese Communists in their struggle with Chiang Kai-shek's Nationalist forces. The Soviet reaction to the plan for international control of nuclear energy that the United States presented to the United Nations in June 1946 was incomprehensible to Americans. The Russians refused to accept the provisions calling for international management and supervision, while vociferously demanding that the United States show its good faith by unilaterally destroying its atomic weapons. Meanwhile, as the world soon learned, the Soviet Union was rapidly completing the development of its own atomic bomb.

The major bone of contention between the Soviet Union and the West, however, was the "German question." The Russians were fearful of a reunited Germany that they could not control; the West was afraid of a Soviet-dominated Germany that would destroy the possibility of a balance of power in postwar Europe. Russia's obstructionist tactics soon produced friction within the four-power Allied Control Council, and

Atomic cloud rises in American nuclear test on Bikini Atoll, July 25, 1946. *Courtesy National Archives.*

with help from France, still uneasy about German power, the Soviet Union blocked all efforts to unite Germany economically and politically. The Russians also stripped the eastern zone of industrial equipment and exploited its economy while claiming a share of the industrial plants in the other three zones. In May 1946 the Western powers ended German reparations to the Soviet Union, and in the autumn of that year the United States gave up its attempt to secure a united Germany. Within a short time, the USSR and the Western Allies were involved in a propaganda and ideological contest to win the support of the Germans—the dreaded enemy only two years before.

Neither side fully understood the objectives of the other or appreciated the source of the other's suspicions and fears. The overriding significance of World War II for Soviet leaders was security on their country's borders and control over nearby governments. American leaders were genuinely alarmed by the Soviet Union's expansion into regions of Eastern and Central Europe formerly dominated by Germany. They expected the Russians to live up to the Yalta Conference's "Declaration on Liberated Europe," which affirmed the principles enunciated in the British-American Atlantic Charter of 1941 and pledged its signatories to self-government through free and open elections. Inspired by a vision of postwar peace and prosperity, the Americans endorsed an ambitious set of reconstruction policies and sought to encourage a revival of world trade. Although the United States was motivated by self-interest, including foreign investments and open markets in Europe, its spokespersons were also committed to traditional American values of self-determination, democracy, and humanitarianism. The central problem, Secretary of War Henry L. Stimson declared in July 1945, grew out of "the fundamental differences between a nation of free thought, free speech, [and] free elections . . . with a nation which is not basically free but which is systematically controlled from above by Secret Police and in which free speech is not permitted."

The situation that existed two years after the close of World War II was startlingly new to Americans. As Undersecretary of State Dean Acheson expressed it in June 1946, "We have got to understand that all our lives the danger, the uncertainty, the need for alertness, for effort, for discipline will be upon us. This is new for us. It will be hard for us." It proved to be a remarkably accurate forecast.

The Architects of Containment

American leaders moved to establish a policy that would restrain the expansionist tendencies of the Russians. The policy they formulated became known as "containment." The containment doctrine that President Truman urged Congress to approve in the spring of 1947 was the product of no single leader, group, or party, even though it rightly came to be identified most closely with Truman and his administration.

Harry Truman continued Roosevelt's policy of cooperation with the wartime allies and his efforts to work out an accommodation with the Soviet Union. He lent wholehearted support to the organization of the United Nations, sent Harry L. Hopkins, Roosevelt's most trusted adviser, on a special mission to talk with Marshal Stalin in May 1945, and helped arrange the conference of the Big Three at Potsdam during the following summer. But he came to the presidency with an abiding distrust of Communist ideology, and when suddenly faced with awesome responsibilities for which he had virtually no preparation, he was naturally less patient, flexible, and confident than his illustrious predecessor. Heeding the advice of U.S. Ambassador to the Soviet Union

W. Averell Harriman and other advocates of greater resistance to the Russians, the new president quickly moved to a showdown with them over the issue of Poland. Although Truman's transition from wary friend to implacable foe of the USSR was gradual, he became increasingly demanding in his relations with Moscow in 1946. In September of that year the president dismissed Secretary of Commerce Henry Wallace when he openly criticized the administration's policy toward Russia. Truman was influenced, like many other American leaders, by the assumption that the Soviet Union's great need for economic assistance in the postwar period would make Stalin more amenable to U.S. demands. His "get-tough" posture was also bolstered by the immeasurable weight of the American monopoly on the atomic bomb in all calculations involving the national interest and, perhaps, by his frustrating setbacks on domestic issues in 1946–47. Tending to personalize foreign policy and to approach international issues in terms of his own political experience, Truman was determined to avoid the trap of another failed appeasement of an aggressor, such as the infamous 1938 Munich Conference wherein Neville Chamberlain of Great Britain caved in to Hitler's demands in the vain hope of avoiding war.

The principal spokesman for the Truman administration's foreign policy during the crucial eighteen months between the Potsdam Conference and the end of 1946 was James F. Byrnes, who succeeded Edward R. Stettinius, Jr., as secretary of state in June 1945. The genial, quick-witted, and urbane Byrnes, a South Carolinian, had little experience in foreign affairs. Nevertheless, he hoped to maintain the Grand Alliance and achieve a stable world order after the war. He assumed that a quid pro quo strategy in negotiating with the Soviet Union would enable a series of acceptable compromises between the two powers. Yet like the president, he gradually adopted a harsher line in dealing with Russian leaders.

Byrnes was succeeded in January 1947 by George C. Marshall, a distinguished military officer who had served as army chief of staff during the war. While Marshall accepted the fundamental assumptions of President Truman and Secretary Byrnes about the nature of the East-West split, he was not one of the major architects of containment. Rather, his role was that of presiding over the process of transforming the doctrine into a national policy. A more important contribution to the formulation of containment was made by Under-secretary of State Dean Acheson. A diplomatic "realist," Acheson did not share Woodrow Wilson's faith in an international organization as an adequate foundation for American foreign policy or the achievement of stability in the world, nor did he agree that the purpose of U.S. policy abroad was "to carry out a 'crusade' or 'mission' to bring about equal justice or to vindicate international law." The great task in the conduct of American foreign policy, he believed, was to apply morality and power in handling international relations. As for the Soviet Union, Acheson had long been distrustful of its policies, which he termed "aggressive and expanding."

The American who provided the rationale for the containment doctrine was George F. Kennan, a Foreign Service officer who was serving in Moscow when the war ended. Kennan, who believed in "realist" diplomacy, had become convinced of the Soviet Union's deep-seated expansionist aims. In a long cable to the State Department in February 1946, the diplomat outlined the strategy that later became official national policy. In explaining Soviet behavior, he expressed the increasingly strong feeling among American observers that it was futile to seek further agreements with the Russians. Soviet leaders, Kennan warned, had a "neurotic view of world affairs. And they have learned to seek security only in patient but deadly struggle for total destruction of rival power, never in compacts and compromises with it." Yet Soviet power was "neither schematic nor adventuristic," Kennan contended. "It does not take unnecessary risks. For this reason it can easily withdraw—and usually does—when strong resistance is encountered at any point." The main element of any U.S. policy toward the USSR, Kennan later wrote in a famous article published in the journal *Foreign Affairs*, "must be that of a long-term, patient, but firm and vigilant containment of Russian expansive tendencies." This would increase "the strains under which Soviet policy must operate," force the Kremlin to show more "moderation and circumspection," and promote tendencies that "must eventually find their outlet in either the break-up or the gradual mellowing of Soviet power."

Kennan's cogent and eloquent language expressed the views and predispositions that had come to prevail among American diplomats and politicians by early 1947. The formulation of specific policies to implement the containment doctrine awaited only the formal decision of the Truman administration. The precipitant of such a decision would almost certainly be another in the recurring crises in East-West relations.

THE TRUMAN DOCTRINE AND THE MARSHALL PLAN

The crisis came in the eastern Mediterranean early in 1947. Russian pressure on Iran continued, despite the withdrawal of Soviet troops from that country in the spring of 1946. Nor had the Russian leaders given up their demands on Turkey for territorial cessions and naval bases in the Bosporus. Although the USSR was not an active force in Greece, the Greek royalist regime was encountering mounting pressure from Communist-dominated rebels in the northern part of the country. In late February 1947, the British quietly informed Washington that they could no longer bear the burden of supporting the Greek government; British troops would soon be withdrawn, thus ending Britain's historic role as a great power in the eastern Mediterranean. Now Greece and Turkey turned for economic and military assistance to the United States, which was keenly aware of the vital importance of the region in the East-West conflict. "If Greece was lost," Truman later wrote in his *Memoirs*, "Turkey would become an untenable outpost in a sea of Communism. Similarly, if Turkey yielded to Soviet demands, the position of Greece would be extremely endangered."

President Truman and Secretary of State Marshall were determined to prevent the Russians from taking advantage of the British withdrawal to move into the eastern Mediterranean. Yet public reaction to a proposal for further foreign aid might well be negative, and congressional Republicans were pushing for another tax cut and doing all they could to reduce the president's budget recommendations. Some Americans, moreover, could be expected to criticize the idea of assisting undemocratic governments in the two countries. After being informed of the British decision to withdraw from Greece, Truman conferred with congressional leaders of both parties and succeeded in gaining their backing of his plan of action. Republican Senator Arthur H. Vandenberg of Michigan, one of the most powerful members of the Senate, who had played a significant role in the establishment of the UN, was later quoted as saying at that conference, "Mr. President, if that's what you want, there's only one way to get it. That is to make a personal appearance before Congress and scare hell out of the country." Truman took Vandenberg's advice, and in an appearance before a joint session of Congress on March 12, 1947, he requested approval of a $400 million program of economic and military assistance for Greece and Turkey.

In what came to be known as the Truman Doctrine, the president described in grim words the way in which "totalitarian regimes" were threatening to snuff out freedom in various parts of the world. Truman's rhetoric transcended the call for American involvement in a local struggle. The United States must, he declared, "support free peoples who are resisting attempted subjugation by armed minorities or by outside pressures." If Americans faltered in their leadership, Truman warned, "we may endanger the peace of the world—and we shall surely endanger the welfare of this Nation." Congress approved the administration's request, and the Greek-Turkish Aid bill became law in May 1947.

It was soon evident that the Truman Doctrine was working. The United States spent over $650 million in aid to Greece and Turkey between 1947 and 1950, and the eastern Mediterranean remained within the Western sphere. Turkey was able to strengthen its economy and modernize its armed forces. The Greek problem was more difficult, but the government there succeeded in reorganizing the army and accelerating its campaign against the Communist insurgents. After Yugoslavia broke with the Soviet Union in 1948, the Greek guerrillas were deprived of a major source of support, and the civil war finally came to an end in the fall of 1949.

The Truman Doctrine cleared the way for a gigantic American aid program abroad. It was essentially a military program, and while its implications were far-reaching, its application was intended to be specific and limited. Nevertheless, it was also a natural first step in the evolution of a much more comprehensive and imaginative enterprise to relieve the misery of Europe and strengthen it against the challenge of Communist domination. This broader and more audacious undertaking emerged not only from the Kremlin's growing recalcitrance, the bitter conflict between the Western Allies and Russia over the future of Germany, and the precedent for bold American action provided by the Truman Doctrine, but also from the terrible internal conditions that existed in the countries of Western Europe following the war. Although the United States had already committed $11 billion in postwar relief, loans, and other kinds of aid to these nations, they were experi-

Acheson, Marshall, and Truman: Cold War diplomats. *Courtesy Harry S. Truman Library.*

encing massive unemployment and severe food and fuel shortages, as well as the enormous devastation caused by the war. Their leaders were haunted by the specter of social upheaval. Europe, declared Churchill, had become "a rubble heap, a charnel house, a breeding ground of pestilence and hate."

Soon after Secretary Marshall returned from Moscow, where a Council of Foreign Ministers meeting on Germany ended in failure in late April 1947, the Truman administration began to develop a program to provide further aid to Western Europe and at the same time to resist Russian expansion. Much of the work on this European aid program was done by the Policy Planning Staff in the State Department, a special committee recently created by Marshall and headed by George Kennan. This group worked at a furious pace. In May it recommended that short-term assistance be provided to arrest the deterioration of the European economy and that a long-range program be launched to encourage the economic integration of Western and Central Europe. Kennan and his colleagues developed a bold plan to contain communism by eradicating the poverty and misery that provided much of its sustenance.

The essentials of what was soon labeled the Marshall Plan were set forth in a commencement address delivered by Secretary Marshall at Harvard University on June 5, 1947. The secretary proposed the reconstruction of the European economy, to be financed largely by the United States but to be worked out as a joint plan between the United States and the European nations. Marshall spoke less in terms of anticommunism than of humanitarianism, but there was no mistaking the diplomatic and ideological objectives of the scheme. "Our policy is directed not against any country or doctrine but against hunger, poverty, desperation and chaos," Marshall asserted. "Its purpose should be the revival of a working economy in the world so as to permit the emergence of political and social conditions in which free institutions can exist."

Western Europe responded immediately. Great Britain and France took the lead in convening a European conference in Paris in July 1947. Since the American plan did not exclude Eastern Europe in this preliminary stage, Soviet leaders hesitated briefly before deciding to boycott the Paris meeting; they were joined in doing so by their satellite nations and by Finland and Czechoslovakia, where Russian influence was great. But the representatives of sixteen nations met in Paris and prepared an elaborate plan for European recovery, estimated to cost about $22 billion. In December 1947, President Truman submitted this plan to Congress, with his own recommendation for an appropriation of $17 billion over a four-year period.

The novelty of the request and the vast amount of money it called for shocked many Americans and provoked sharp criticism in Congress. The strongest congressional opposition came from Senator Robert A. Taft of Ohio and his supporters, whose ranks included some of the nation's traditional isolationists. Men of the Taft persuasion feared that the Marshall Plan would wreck the American economy and lead to a third world war. It was a huge "international WPA," one critic asserted. The support for the proposal was, however, impressively large. Liberals of both parties backed it. A powerful array of business, farm, and labor organizations endorsed the plan, recognizing the beneficial effects it would have on the national economy. Vandenberg led the bipartisan supporters of the administration measure, calling it a "calculated risk" to "help stop World War III before it starts." Events in Europe also contributed to congressional approval, particularly the Communist coup of

February 1948 in Czechoslovakia, a nation to which Americans had a strong sentimental attachment.

Congress approved the aid program in March, and it was signed by the president on April 3, 1948. Under Vandenberg's leadership the four-year commitment sought by the administration was eliminated and the first installment was reduced somewhat, from $6.8 billion to $5.3 billion. But no one could doubt that the Truman administration had won a great victory and that its foreign policy had been given an overwhelming vote of confidence. The law established a European Recovery Program to be carried out by the Economic Cooperation Administration, which in turn was supposed to work with the Committee of European Economic Cooperation.

By the end of 1952 the United States had spent about $13 billion on the program. The results were very encouraging. Industrial production in the Marshall Plan countries had increased by 64 percent within three years. An impetus was given to the economic integration and unification of Western Europe—to such eventual developments as the European Steel and Coal Community and the Common Market. Western Europeans had regained their confidence, and the Communist threats in France and Italy had been substantially lessened.

The Truman Doctrine and the Marshall Plan—described by Truman as "two halves of the same walnut"—brought a revolutionary shift in American foreign policy. For the first time in a period of peace, the United States had committed its military and economic strength to the defense of nations outside the western hemisphere. The United States had involved itself directly in the internal affairs of countries like Greece, and a host of American experts and advisers were soon swarming over Europe to help implement a huge program of reconstruction. Even more significant, perhaps, was the primary justification for these striking new policies. Their purpose, it was endlessly proclaimed, was to prevent the expansion of the Soviet Union and halt the spread of international communism.

FORGING NEW COALITIONS

The Marshall Plan exacerbated differences between the United States and the Soviet Union and, in combination with the worsening controversy over Germany, provoked the Russians into drastic action that created still another crisis in East-West relations. The Kremlin denounced the European Recovery Program as an example of American imperialism and an effort to establish continental bases for aggression against the USSR. Soviet leaders had not been idle in the face of American and Western European activities. They had consolidated their control of Hungary, forced Czechoslovakia into the Russian orbit, and set up a new Communist Information Bureau (Cominform) to promote their Marxist doctrine and exercise greater restraint on local Communist parties. In January 1949, they established the Council for Mutual Economic Assistance, an answer to the European Recovery Program and the culmination of a process designed to stimulate and guide the development of Soviet bloc nations. Nevertheless, the Russians were profoundly disturbed by the Marshall Plan and the unity it inspired in Western Europe. Meanwhile, Moscow had suffered a setback when Yugoslavia, its strongest satellite, refused to follow the Soviet line and succeeded in striking out on an independent course.

Then there was the acute problem of Germany, where the Western powers were moving rapidly to effect an economic and political consolidation of their zones. In June 1948 the three Western Allies announced the consolidation. The resulting "Trizonia" comprised a rich industrial area with a population of 50 million people, in contrast to the 17 million residents of the Soviet zone. The consolidated western region was brought into the recovery machinery of the Marshall Plan, and a drastic reform of West German currency was carried out. The Russians resisted these efforts to unify western Germany, and in the early spring of 1948 they began to obstruct traffic between the western zones and Berlin, located a hundred miles inside the eastern zone. There were violent scenes in the four-power Control Council for Berlin. When the Western powers extended their currency reform to their sectors of Berlin on June 23, Soviet leaders responded by stopping all surface traffic between the western zones and the capital city. They cited the fact that the Western Allies had never secured a written agreement guaranteeing land access to Berlin. Although the Russians maintained that they were blockading the city because of the new currency reform, it was obvious that they were trying to force the Western powers to abandon their plans for a united West Germany or, failing in that, to bring about their withdrawal from Berlin and thus to achieve a great symbolic victory in the Cold War.

American leaders refused to give ground. General Lucius D. Clay, deputy military governor of the American zone, wanted to use an armed convoy to break the blockade. "When Berlin falls, western Germany will be next," the general warned. President Truman was equally adamant, declaring, "We [are] going to stay period." But Truman did not resort to the provocative action recommended by General Clay and some other advisers. He imposed a counterblockade against the Russians in Germany and, with the British, supported the non-Communist majority on the Berlin City Council, forcing the Soviet representatives to set up a separate administration for their sector of the city. Most important of all, however, he decided to prevent the starvation of West Berliners by using air transport to supply their needs. This continuous airlift, operated by the U.S. Air Force and the British Royal Air Force, was maintained for 324 days, with 277,264 flights in all and a total cargo of 2.5 million tons of food, coal, and other supplies. The airlift was a spectacular success; it saved West Berlin and lifted the morale of its people. Early in the blockade, the Truman administration did resort to a little saber rattling: the president ordered two groups of B-29 bombers—planes designed to carry atomic bombs—sent to England.

In the end, Western resistance and the success of the airlift caused the Russians to give in. They agreed to lift the blockade if the Western powers would reopen the whole German question and discuss the Austrian peace treaty at a new meeting of the Council of Foreign Ministers. After more than ten months, the blockade came to an end on May 12, 1949, the same day on which the foreign ministers met in Paris. The Paris conference made no real progress on the German problem, but it did provide the Soviet Union with a diplomatic pretext for abandoning the Berlin blockade. In the meantime, the United States and its Western European allies were completing the formation of a West German state, the Federal Republic of Germany. The Russians also acted. In October 1949 they created the German Democratic Republic, with its capital in East Berlin. Thus, instead of a single reunited Germany, there were now two German nations.

While these developments were taking place, Western Europe and the United States formulated and adopted an extensive military alliance designed to counter Soviet expansionism. The Truman Doctrine and the Marshall Plan had pointed the way, but the Western Euro-

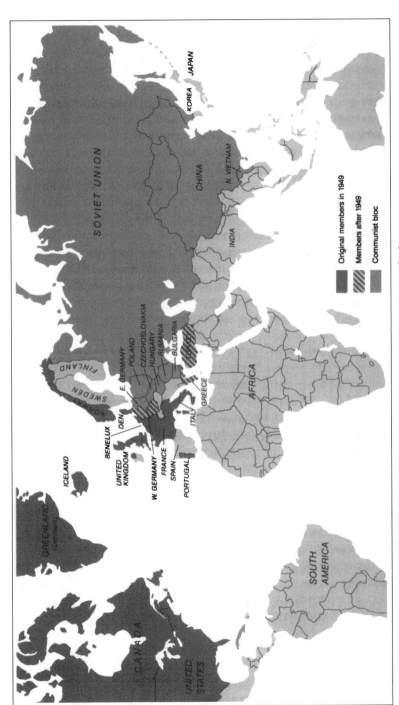

The world divided: The United States led NATO and the U.S.S.R. led Communist bloc spheres of influence.

pean nations had also done their part. France and Great Britain had
signed a mutual defense agreement in March 1947, and Britain had
indicated willingness in January 1948 to join in a Western "European Union." Meeting in Brussels soon afterward, Britain, France, and
the Benelux countries, with American encouragement, entered into a
fifty-year treaty of economic cooperation and military alliance. Early in
the following year the Council of Europe was established. The council,
which included the Federal Republic of Germany, had broader rep-
resentation than the Brussels Pact. These agreements stimulated the
interest of U.S. leaders in a still broader military alliance, for despite
this evidence of West European unity, they were dubious about the
effectiveness of military strength in Western Europe. At the time of
the Brussels agreement, there were only about a dozen inadequately
equipped and poorly trained Brussels Pact military agency divisions in
the entire region.

A significant indication of American interest and intent came from
Washington in June 1948, when Vandenberg introduced a resolution in
the Senate to encourage "the progressive development of regional and
other collective arrangements" for defense and promote the "association
of the United States" with such organizations. The Senate speedily approved the Vandenberg resolution by a vote of 64 to 4. The Truman administration, already searching for a means to this end, took advantage
of Vandenberg's resolution to begin discussions the following month
with the Western European nations. A conference of most of the Marshall Plan countries met in Washington early in 1949 and drafted the
North Atlantic Treaty. It was formally adopted on April 4, 1949, by the
United States, Canada, and ten Western European countries. Greece
and Turkey joined the North Atlantic Treaty Organization (NATO) in
1952, and three years later West Germany became a member.

The treaty constituted a twenty-year military pact. Each member
pledged itself to lend military support, which was to be jointly organized
and supervised by the North Atlantic Council, the secretary-general,
and the Military Committee. The members also agreed that

> an armed attack against one or more of them in Europe or North America shall
> be considered an attack against them all; and consequently they agree that,
> if such an armed attack occurs, each of them, in exercise of the right of in-

dividual or collective self-defense recognized by Article 51 of the Charter of the United Nations, will assist the Party or Parties so attacked by taking such action as it deems necessary, including the use of armed force, to restore and maintain the security of the North Atlantic area.

It was also assumed that, should the Soviet army move into Western Europe, the United States would respond with a nuclear attack on the Soviet empire.

The U.S. Senate ratified the treaty on July 21, 1949, by an overwhelming majority of 82 to 13. In late September, while Congress was still considering the initial appropriation for NATO, President Truman informed the public that the Soviet Union a few weeks earlier had exploded an atomic device. Within six days Congress voted $1 billion for NATO arms and equipment under the Mutual Defense Assistance Act, with an additional $211 million for Greece and Turkey.

Efforts to construct an effective military force under NATO began in earnest in 1950. Late that year General Dwight D. Eisenhower was appointed supreme commander, and soon afterward the Supreme Headquarters of the Allied Powers in Europe (SHAPE) was established near Paris. The president had also directed that the development of a more powerful nuclear weapon, the hydrogen bomb, be accelerated. American military authorities, acting within the framework of the administration's policy, were determined to build a large conventional European army, one that would include German military units. The commitment to NATO meant that the United States had abandoned its long tradition of avoiding permanent peacetime alliances. In taking this extraordinary step, the Truman administration received strong congressional support and the general approval of public opinion. America had learned, Secretary Acheson explained, "that the control of Europe by a single aggressive unfriendly power would constitute an intolerable threat to the national security of the United States."

While American leaders concentrated on European reconstruction and the containment of Russian communism on that continent, they also tried to devise policies and machinery in other parts of the world to strengthen the nation's position in the Cold War. In the western hemisphere, the United States was eager to present a united front toward the Soviet Union and the challenge of international communism.

Canada, whose relations with the United States had grown closer during World War II, became an ally in NATO. Latin America was less predictable, although the Good Neighbor Policy of the 1930s had resulted in some relaxation of tension between the United States and the twenty nations to the south, and all of the Latin American countries except Argentina had cooperated to some extent in waging war against the Axis powers.

The United States took the first step in the direction of postwar unity in Latin America by arranging a special conference in Mexico City in February 1945. The result was the Act of Chapultepec, which was eventually signed by all Latin American states; it committed the signatories to a collective security arrangement. In June 1947, after the Truman Doctrine had been announced, President Truman indicated that the United States was seeking a mutual defense agreement that would guarantee concerted hemispheric action. In the late summer, delegates from most of the American republics met at Rio de Janeiro, Brazil, to consider enforcement machinery for the Act of Chapultepec. On September 2, 1947, they adopted the Inter-American Treaty of Reciprocal Assistance. This agreement established a broad security zone around the North and South American continents, declared that an attack anywhere in this zone would constitute an attack against all American states, and provided for collective self-defense for the western hemisphere, as a regional association permitted under Articles 51 and 52 of the United Nations Charter. In the spring of 1948, at the Ninth Inter-American Conference at Bogotá, Colombia, a charter for the Organization of American States was drafted, giving full constitutional status to the inter-American system and setting up machinery for hemispheric consultation. The meeting also endorsed the principle that no state or group of states had the right to intervene in the affairs of another state. As the historian David Green has written, "All non-American military and political power had been successfully excluded from the hemisphere."

Many Latin Americans remained suspicious of the United States, which was clearly giving priority to European recovery over Latin American development. Truman's Point Four program, announced in his inaugural address in January 1949, promised U.S. technical aid to "supply the vitalizing force to stir the peoples of the world into triumphant action, not only against their human oppressors, but also against their ancient enemies—hunger, misery, and despair." This new program to make the benefits of American scientific and industrial progress available for the improvement of underdeveloped areas—and to weaken the appeal of international communism—was aimed primarily at Latin America. But one of its goals was the stimulation of private investment in the region, and, ironically, it had the effect of helping to perpetuate the colonial and extractive character of the Latin American economy.

During the early months of 1950, the National Security Council, in response to an order from the president, carried out "an over-all review and re-assessment of American foreign and defense policy." The resulting study—NSC 68—was a comprehensive statement of the nation's defense strategy. It also contained a terrible warning: "The issues that face us are momentous, involving the fulfillment or destruction not only of this Republic but of civilization itself." After reviewing the various policy alternatives in the Cold War, the authors of NSC 68 concluded that the only logical course open to the United States was the development of free-world military capabilities. They advocated an immediate and large-scale buildup in the military and economic strength of the United States and its allies in order to meet "each fresh challenge promptly and unequivocally." They were calling for what Melvyn P. Leffler has described as a "preponderance of power" for the United States in world affairs.

Although President Truman did not immediately make the document public, its recommendations were to provide a blueprint for the United States in waging the Cold War during the next two decades. Truman had been under pressure to cut the budget during the Republican-controlled Eightieth Congress, and with the launching of his so-called Fair Deal in 1949 he needed money for domestic reform. He had been able to limit federal spending for the army, navy, and air force to between $12 and $14 billion a year, less than a third of the total budget. But in 1951 he recommended that $60 billion be spent on the armed forces, almost two-thirds of federal spending for the year. The militarization of containment was well under way.

THE COLD WAR CONSENSUS

A general agreement on the containment of the Soviet Union did not emerge overnight, and several obstacles had to be overcome before such a consensus was created. At the end of the war most Americans were unprepared for the demands of the new international age—the responsibilities of world leadership, the complexities of European politics, the enormous costs of national defense and foreign aid that containment entailed, the imposition of internal security controls, and the powerful effect that foreign policy came to have on almost every domestic consideration. The idealism associated with the vision of "one world" and the strong faith in the United Nations challenged the assumptions that supported the containment program. There was also some reluctance in the United States to support reactionary governments like that of Greece in the name of democracy and morality.

The most spectacular dissent from the Truman administration's hardening opposition to the Russians was led by Henry A. Wallace, who, as mentioned, had been dismissed from the cabinet after calling for a softer line toward the Soviet Union. Wallace and his supporters saw no reason why the wartime collaboration with the Russians could not continue. They discounted the charges of Soviet aggression and contended that the USSR would cooperate with the Western powers if the West recognized the Russian sphere of influence in Eastern Europe and otherwise showed that it had no intention of "encircling" the Soviet Union. Wallace lost much of his support when he attacked the Marshall Plan, and as a Progressive Party nominee for president in 1948 he was tellingly assaulted by Democratic spokesmen, including the Americans for Democratic Action, for opposing the containment policies and allegedly making common cause with Communist groups within the United States.

Meanwhile, there was also some conservative opposition to the Truman policies. At the beginning of 1947, just before the Truman Doctrine was made public, East-West tensions seemed to ease somewhat following the completion of the Big Three peace treaties with Germany's former puppet states, Bulgaria, Hungary, and Rumania. The Republicans, led by such economy-in-government advocates as Robert Taft, controlled Congress. The Taft wing of the party was suspicious not only of costly foreign aid programs but also in general of aggressive foreign policies that were sponsored by the administration.

A series of events, plus the deep division over foreign policy in the Republican Party, played an important part in undermining potentially powerful opposition to the containment doctrine. These developments included Russian pressure on Iran and Turkey in 1946, the Soviet Union's chronic obstructionism in the UN Security Council, the atmosphere of crisis that surrounded the eastern Mediterranean early in 1947, the Communist coup in Czechoslovakia in 1948, the Berlin blockade of 1948–49, the fall of Nationalist China in 1949, the Russian explosion of an atomic bomb in 1949, and the mounting fear of a Communist conspiracy in the United States. These events provided the Truman administration with several dramatic issues, cleared the way for the announcement of the containment policy, and contributed mightily to the emergence of American solidarity in sentiment and belief on the Cold War. Truman's startling electoral victory in 1948 also strengthened the emerging American consensus on foreign policy. The administration, frustrated in its domestic policies, made skillful use of foreign policy to increase its support during the campaign, and such alarming developments as the Czech coup and the Berlin blockade enhanced its credibility. Forced by expediency to cooperate with the Russians during the war, U.S. leaders soon accepted the idea that it would be necessary, in John Gaddis's words, "to prevent the Soviet Union from using the power and position it won as a result of that conflict to reshape the postwar international order."

The national consensus on the Cold War was one of the remarkable aspects—and manifestations—of the revolution in American foreign policy in the 1940s. Even so, this consensus had its limits. It did not extend to China and East Asia. Also, the bipartisanship of the late 1940s began to break down by 1950, as Republicans mounted an attack on the Democratic administration's foreign policies. In 1950, for example, Senator Taft and former president Herbert Hoover strongly criticized the Truman administration for its plans to use American ground troops in Europe, its relative neglect of the western hemisphere, and the heavy financial burden of its foreign programs. Other critics, including George Kennan and political commentator Walter Lippmann, deplored what they regarded as the excessive moralism and legalism of U.S. policy and the growing preoccupation with military affairs.

Despite such complaints, the broad agreement on the policies adopted to contain the expansion of Russian communism continued well after the end of Democratic control in 1952. The consensus did not break down until the late 1960s, when bitter divisions over the war in Vietnam brought a reassessment of American policy. In the long interim, the radical transformation that had occurred in American attitudes and policies soon after the end of World War II largely determined the role of the United States in international affairs.

——————— ★ ———————

SUGGESTIONS FOR FURTHER READING

The best general works on the American side of the Cold War are John Lewis Gaddis, *Strategies of Containment: A Critical Appraisal of Postwar American National Security Policy* (1982); Warren I. Cohen, *America in the Age of Soviet Power, 1945–1991* (1993), vol. 4 in *The Cambridge History of American Foreign Relations*; Thomas J. McCormick, *America's Half-Century: United States Policy in the Cold War and After* (2nd ed., 1995); Walter LaFeber, *America, Russia, and the Cold War, 1945–1992* (8th ed., 1997); and H. W. Brands, *The Devil We Knew: Americans and the Cold War* (1993). Ralph B. Levering's *The Cold War: A Post–Cold War History* (2nd ed., 1995) provides an interpretive overview of the long struggle between the two superpowers. Other useful general studies include Thomas G. Paterson, *Meeting the Communist Threat: Truman to Reagan* (1988).

An extensive literature exists on the beginnings and early years of the Cold War. Three studies are particularly noteworthy: John Lewis Gaddis, *The United States and the Origins of the Cold War, 1941–1947* (1972); Daniel Yergin, *Shattered Peace: The Origins of the Cold War and the National Security State* (1977); and Melvyn P. Leffler, *A Preponderance of Power: National Security, the Truman Administration, and the Cold War* (1992). But see also Robert A. Pollard, *Economic Security and the Origins of the Cold War, 1945–1950* (1986); David S. Painter, *Oil and the American Century: The Political Economy of U.S. Foreign Oil Policy, 1941–1954* (1986); and Bruce Robellet Kuniholm, *The Origins of the Cold War in the Near East: Great Power Conflict and Diplomacy in Iran, Turkey, and Greece* (1980). Gregg Herken's *The Winning Weapon: The Atomic Bomb in the Cold War, 1945–1950* (1980) is a fine study of the bomb as a factor early in the East-West confrontation. Herbert Feis, *From Trust to Terror: The Onset of the Cold War, 1945–1950* (1970), is an illuminating older work.

By the mid-1960s, the earlier, orthodox view of U.S. involvement in the Cold War was being challenged by a more critical interpretation of the American role in the ongoing struggle. Among the significant revisionist studies are William Appleman Williams, *The Tragedy of American Diplomacy* (2nd rev. ed., 1972); Diane Shaver Clemens, *Yalta* (1970); and Joyce Kolko and Gabriel Kolko, *The Limits of Power: The World and United States Foreign Policy, 1945–1954* (1972).

Critical evaluations of Cold War revisionism are Robert W. Tucker, *The Radical Left and American Foreign Policy* (1971), and Robert James Maddox, *The New Left and the Origins of the Cold War* (1973).

A moderate revisionist, Lloyd C. Gardner, presents a series of enlightening biographical studies in *Architects of Illusion: Men and Ideas in American Foreign Policy, 1941–1949* (1970). Among other important interpretations of American leadership are Robert L. Messer, *The End of an Alliance: James F. Byrnes, Roosevelt, Truman, and the Origins of the Cold War* (1982); Gaddis Smith, *Dean Acheson* (1972); Forrest C. Pogue, *George C. Marshall: Statesman, 1945–1959* (1987); Walter L. Hixson, *George F. Kennan: Cold War Iconoclast* (1991); and Walter Isaacson and Evan Thomas, *The Wise Men: Six Friends and the World They Made* (1986). For the views of several key actors in the drama of recent U.S. foreign policy, see Dean Acheson, *Present at the Creation: My Years in the State Department* (1969); George F. Kennan, *Memoirs, 1925–1950* (1967); Arthur H. Vandenberg, Jr., ed., *The Private Papers of Senator Vandenberg* (1952); and Harry S. Truman, *Memoirs* (2 vols., 1955–56).

The German problem in the early postwar period is dealt with in John Gimbel, *The American Occupation of Germany: Politics and the Military, 1945–1949* (1968), and W. Phillips Davison, *The Berlin Blockade: A Study in Cold War Politics* (1958). Joseph M. Jones, *The Fifteen Weeks (February 21–June 5, 1947)* (1955), is an absorbing if uncritical account of the formulation of the Truman Doctrine and the Marshall Plan. Especially important for the latter are Michael J. Hogan, *The Marshall Plan* (1987), and Alan S. Milward, *The Reconstruction of Western Europe, 1945–1951* (1984). For NATO, see Timothy P. Ireland, *Creating the Entangling Alliance: The Origins of the North Atlantic Treaty Organization* (1981). William Whitney Stueck, Jr., *The Road to Confrontation: American Policy toward China and Korea, 1947–1950* (1981), examines the beginnings of the Cold War in East Asia. In *American Cold War Strategy: Interpreting NSC 68* (1993), Ernest R. May reprints the document and presents a wide-ranging commentary on it.

William L. O'Neill provides a fresh and stimulating treatment of World War II in *A Democracy at War: America's Fight at Home and Abroad in World War II* (1993). O'Neill integrates diplomatic and military developments into his discussion of American mobilization, politics, and society. Michael C. C. Adams offers a critical evaluation of the "good war" concept in his extended essay, *The Best War Ever: America and World War II* (1994). A third study, John W. Jeffries's *Wartime America: The World War II Home Front* (1996), is stimulating and useful. Two older works remain indispensable: Richard Polenberg, *War and Society: The United States, 1941–1945* (1972), and John Morton Blum, *V Was for Victory: Politics and American Culture during World War II* (1976). See also the more impressionistic accounts by Geoffrey Perrett, *Days of Sadness, Years of Triumph: The American People, 1939–1945* (1973), and Paul D. Casdorph, *Let the Good Times Roll: Life at Home in America During World War II* (1989). The range of individual American experiences is suggested in the vivid recollections assembled by Studs Terkel, *"The Good War": An Oral History of World War Two* (1984).

The Proud Decades: America in War and Peace, 1941–1960 (1988), by John Patrick Diggins, is a useful general history. Important economic dimensions are treated in Harold G. Vatter, *The U.S. Economy in World War II* (1985); Lester V. Chandler, *Inflation in the United States, 1940–1948* (1951); and Nelson Lichtenstein, *Labor's War at Home: The CIO in World War II* (1982). For illustrations of the war's effects upon particular cities and regions, see David Brinkley, *Washington Goes to War* (1988), and Neil R. McMillen, ed., *Remaking Dixie: The Impact of World War II on the American South* (1997).

———— ★ ————

2

Harry Truman, the Korean War, and the Politics of Stalemate

Politics in the United States had been transformed in the age of Franklin D. Roosevelt. The thirty-second president dominated the political culture of his day as had none of his predecessors. He established an extraordinary identification with the mass of voters, fashioned strong organizational support, and helped bring about a fundamental realignment in the political system. Roosevelt made the Democratic Party an instrument of progressive change, and he was the major contributor to a new liberal tradition of social reform and international involvement. His legacy was destined to have a profound influence on the course of American politics in the postwar period.

The 1930s had witnessed the coming of political age of the urban minorities, the emergence of organized labor as a powerful factor in politics, the shift of a majority of black voters into the Democratic column, and the development of strong loyalties to Roosevelt and the Democratic Party on the part of millions of white-collar workers and middle-class Americans. The results of this political revolution were spectacular. FDR had been elected president four times, and the Democrats had ended the one-party domination that had long prevailed in many parts of New England, the Midwest, and the Far West and had won control of both houses of Congress in every election since 1930.

But all of this had changed—or appeared on the verge of changing—by the end of World War II. Bereft of the magnetic and compelling

Roosevelt, the Democrats appeared to be leaderless and confused. Harry S. Truman, the new president, seemed woefully unprepared to assume the mantle of Roosevelt's leadership. The Democrats, moreover, had been in power a long time, were badly divided along ideological and regional lines, and faced the inevitable discontents and irritations that accumulated with lengthy tenure. A conservative coalition, led by Southern Democrats and Midwestern Republicans, had emerged in Congress in the late 1930s, and while Roosevelt's foreign policies and war programs had served to unite the Democratic Party in later years, the coalition asserted itself effectively on many domestic issues. There was also another discouraging prospect. The Democratic administration in Washington was confronted in the postwar period with the threat of rampant inflation rather than severe depression and deflation as in the 1930s. The politics of inflation, unlike the politics of depression, made it difficult to attract and retain the support of major interest groups.

Although the Republicans were themselves divided, they stood united in their determination to recapture control of the national government, which they confidently expected to do by winning the midterm elections of 1946 and the presidential election two years later. The unanswered question was: How durable was the Roosevelt coalition?

THE RISE OF HARRY S. TRUMAN

The symbol of the Democrats' declining fortunes in the aftermath of the war and the natural target of Republican attacks was Harry Truman, the thirty-third president of the United States. Succeeding to the presidency after the death of FDR on April 12, 1945, Truman was immediately faced with a multitude of perplexing problems and momentous decisions, including the use of the atomic bomb, the most effective approach to demobilization and reconversion of the national economy, and the question of how best to deal with the Soviet Union. Few American presidents have encountered greater pressures and strains in time of peace.

Harry Truman seemed in many ways to be an ordinary man, a small-town, middle-class American. He was a friendly, direct, and practical man, unpretentious, sincere, and uncomplicated. Devoted to his family, he liked the simple things of life—a visit with friends, an occasional drink, and a little poker with the boys. He played the piano and liked to read history. Bespectacled and scholarly in appearance, he spoke in a voice that was flat and monotonous. As Truman himself once said, "I look just like any other fifty people you meet in the street." Truman could be petty and pugnacious, he sometimes acted impulsively, and he was not above name-calling in public. A fierce partisan, he tended to accept Democrats as he found them, and his unswerving loyalty to friends did not always serve him well. But he also possessed many excellent and unusual qualities. He worked hard and studied diligently. The journalist Eric Sevareid, in commenting on the press coverage of the president from Missouri, recalled that Truman's "simplicity, his honesty and his self-discipline were so obvious as to be non-arguable, however much we disagreed about some of his actions and appointments." While somewhat awed by the enormous responsibilities that confronted him in the White House, Truman never doubted his ability to handle them. He displayed courage and boldness in the presidency, and he soon demonstrated a capacity for making decisions. A sign on his desk read: "The buck stops here."

During his eighty-two days as vice president, Truman had little contact with Franklin Roosevelt and almost no tutelage from the White House. That fact no doubt helps explain a certain confusion and vagueness as to direction in the first part of the Truman administration. Conservatives hoped that the new president's moderate views would bring him into their camp, but Truman did not commit himself to the conservatives' cause. In fact, he did just the opposite. In a comprehensive message to Congress on September 6, 1945, only three weeks after V-J Day, he revealed his progressive inclinations and expressed a determination to add to the structure of New Deal reforms. He presented a twenty-one-point reform program. Among his recommendations were the extension of economic controls in the postwar period, an increase in the minimum wage from 40 to 65 cents an hour, extension of the Social Security system, a full-employment program, more slum clearance and public housing projects, a public works program, regional development of "the natural resources of our great river valleys," reorganization of the executive branch of the federal government, and establishment of a permanent Fair Employment Practices Commission. Soon afterward, Truman recommended the national control of atomic energy, a national health insurance system, federal aid to education, and U.S. approval of the St. Lawrence Seaway.

Although Truman had put himself on record as favoring a broad program of domestic reform, few of his recommendations were approved during the next two years, except for the Employment Act and Atomic Energy Act of 1946. He seemed to desire a continuation of the New Deal but also the maintenance of harmonious relations with Congress, now in a conservative mood and clearly determined to assert its independence of executive restraint. A series of labor crises and the losing struggle to control prices and maintain economic stability dominated the domestic scene in 1945 and 1946. The president also experienced a succession of personal difficulties with executive subordinates, leading to the resignation of such men as Harold L. Ickes and Henry Wallace and helping to alienate many liberals from the administration. Then, in November 1946, the resurgent Republicans captured control of Congress.

Seemingly overnight, Truman's administration ran aground after months of drift and vacillation. Harry Truman, people were saying, was certainly no Franklin Roosevelt! His leadership appeared to be designed to promote a politics of stalemate. Truman himself, Samuel Lubell observed in 1952 in *The Future of American Politics*, was "a product of political deadlock." Lubell pictured Truman as "the man who bought time," as a leader whose role was "to raise all issues but to settle none." While this harsh judgment contains a good deal of truth, it is not the whole truth. It does not adequately take into account the turbulent times, the bitter partisanship, and the conflicting pressures of the early postwar years.

THE EIGHTIETH CONGRESS, 1947–1948

Republican leaders interpreted their thumping congressional victory in 1946 as a repudiation of Democratic reformism, and they turned with alacrity to the task of reducing taxes, passing legislation to control labor unions, and freeing business from governmental restraints. If Senator Arthur Vandenberg was the most influential Republican spokesman on foreign affairs, Senator Robert Taft was the most powerful party leader in the domestic arena. The son of William Howard Taft—the younger Taft had come to the Senate in 1939—contended for his party's presidential nomination in 1940 and 1944, and he headed the Republican policy committee in 1947. A man of ability, integrity, and intelligence, the Ohio senator was frequently referred to as "Mr. Republican." Although he was willing to support federal programs to develop public housing and to aid education, Taft was basically a conservative, a spokesman for economic conservatism. "We have got to break with the corrupting idea that we can legislate prosperity, legislate equality, legislate opportunity," he declared.

The most important domestic statute enacted during the Eightieth Congress was the controversial Taft-Hartley Act of 1947. The Republicans were determined to curb the power of organized labor, and under the circumstances it was probably inevitable that Congress would pass some kind of labor-control law. The Wagner Act of 1935, the basic labor policy statute, had long been criticized in some quarters as one-sided and unfair to employers. Wartime labor strife had led to the imposition of restrictions on labor unions' right to strike, if such work stoppages would affect the supply of materials essential to the prosecution of the war, with the passage of the Smith-Connally Labor Disputes Act of 1943. The legislation, which was passed over President Roosevelt's veto, was a wartime act that became null and void at the conclusion of World War II. A long series of strikes following the war, as well as John L. Lewis's contemptuous defiance of the government during the war and again in 1946, brought mounting public pressure for congressional action. Congress responded by passing the Case bill in 1946, which proposed excessively strict regulations that virtually outlawed the right of laborers to strike. President Truman disagreed with the content and spirit of the bill and promptly vetoed it, referring publicly to the proposed legislation as "punitive."

When the Eightieth Congress assembled, legislators introduced a large number of regulatory bills aimed at labor that heavily favored corporate interests and the expansion of the national economy, including one with severe restrictions presented by Fred L. Hartley, Jr., of New Jersey, the chairman of the House Committee on Education and Labor. The congressional issue involved more than public pressure for curbs on labor militancy, more than management's determination to maximize profits, more than labor's demand for higher wages to counter the effects of inflation and losses in real income. The larger issue was the place of labor unions in American society: whether the labor movement would continue to grow, its role in controlling the workplace, its influence as a political action group, and the specter of a movement dominated by social democracy or even communism.

Representative Hartley's bill was rushed through the lower house and passed by a large majority on April 17. Action in the Senate was led by Taft, chairman of the Labor and Public Welfare Committee. Under his direction, a more carefully drafted and less vindictive labor bill was developed and eventually adopted, after additional compromises, by both houses in June. The measure outlawed the closed shop (an arrangement to prevent the hiring of nonunion workers); prohibited several "unfair" labor practices by unions, including secondary boycotts, jurisdictional strikes (by one labor organization to exclude another from a given company or field), and "featherbedding" (pay for work not done); permitted employers to sue unions for breaking contracts, to petition the National Labor Relations Board to hold elections, and to speak freely during union campaigns; forbade campaign contributions by labor unions; required loyalty oaths from union officers; and authorized the issuance of injunctions to halt strikes and "cooling-off" periods for as long as eighty days in strikes that threatened to create a national emergency.

Sponsors of the Taft-Hartley bill described it as "the first step toward an official discouragement" of a trend that had "permitted and encouraged" labor "to grow into a monster supergovernment." Truman responded with a sharp veto on June 20. He charged that the strike procedures provided in the bill were impractical, that the measure was biased against labor, and that it would "reverse the basic direction of our national labor policy." The Republicans, with notable help from southern Democrats, swiftly overrode the veto—by a vote of 331 to 83 in the House and 68 to 25 in the Senate. The Taft-Hartley Act was a milestone in recent American history, not only for the legal restrictions it imposed on labor unions, but as the labor historian Nelson Lictenstein remarks, "as a climax to and a symbol of the shifting relationship between government and unions during the 1940s." It hurt weak unions in some industries, made organizing more difficult, and encouraged many states to enact stronger "right to work" laws, particularly in the South, where the Congress of Industrial Organization's (CIO's) "Operation Dixie"— a campaign to strengthen the labor movement in the region—became a victim of the new statute. Union leaders denounced Taft-Hartley as a "slave labor law," and with its passage they rallied their forces behind the Truman administration.

Truman renewed and sharpened his demands for domestic reforms early in 1948. Among his recommendations was a group of civil rights measures. But the administration got little from Congress. Rent controls were extended for another year, a severely limited housing program was approved, and an agricultural bill providing for a continuation of price supports at 90 percent of parity through 1949 and thereafter on a flexible basis was passed. Congress also extended the Reciprocal Trade Agreements Act, though for only one year rather than the three recommended by the president. In addition, the lawmakers authorized the creation of a commission on the reorganization of the executive branch of the government. Truman appointed Herbert Hoover to head this inquiry, and after an extensive study the Hoover Commission in 1949 issued eighteen comprehensive reports recommending the consolidation and streamlining of numerous executive departments and agencies. Many of these recommendations were put into effect during Truman's second term. Congress followed Truman's recommendation in passing a new Presidential Succession Act, placing the speaker of the House and the president pro tempore of the Senate ahead of the members of the cabinet in the line of presidential succession after the vice president. And in 1947 Congress adopted the Twenty-second Amendment to the Constitution, limiting the president's tenure to two terms. It was ratified by the requisite number of states in 1951.

The Republican-controlled Congress won most of the battles over domestic issues in 1947 and 1948. But in opposing Taft-Hartley and the conservatism of the Eightieth Congress, Truman developed a sense of purpose and the image of a fighter for the people, thereby putting himself and his party in position to challenge the Republicans in the campaign of 1948.

THE ELECTION OF 1948

As the presidential campaign of 1948 got under way, the Democratic Party was badly split. Henry Wallace, around whom critics of the Truman administration's Cold War policies were rallying, had announced his intention of running for president on an independent ticket. The president's strong advocacy of a civil rights program had spurred a group of southern governors to begin laying plans for a regional opposition movement against the national Democratic Party. Truman's popularity in all parts of the country had dropped to a low level. "People are restless, dissatisfied, fearful," one administration member explained. "They want someone who can 'take over' and solve everything." A new liberal organization known as Americans for Democratic Action (ADA) wanted to dump Truman and nominate a more attractive standard-bearer in 1948.

Although Truman had earlier given some thought to the possibility of stepping aside in favor of the universally admired General Dwight D. Eisenhower, he had decided by the end of 1947 to run in his own right. He made his decision public on March 8, 1948. Truman designed various reform proposals during the early months of 1948 to provide him with a coherent program and a tactical advantage over his Republican opponents in the forthcoming campaign. Moreover, Clark Clifford, the president's special counsel, and other advisers had begun to develop a strategy for the next presidential campaign soon after the disastrous congressional elections of 1946. In a confidential memorandum to Truman on November 19, 1947, Clifford summed up the views of the president's counselors on "the politics of 1948." He urged Truman to stake out a liberal position in dealing with the next session of Congress, to exploit his conflicts with his congressional opponents, and to move forward in the field of civil rights. He should consider the South "safely Democratic."

The Republican National Convention held its convention in Philadelphia beginning on June 21. The front-runner in the contest for the presidential nomination was New York Governor Thomas E. Dewey, who in late May had won an impressive primary victory in Oregon over Harold E. Stassen, a former governor of Minnesota. Senator Taft was also an aspirant for the honor, and party regulars seemed to prefer him to Dewey. The senator's isolationist record, outspoken conservatism, and unexciting campaign style, however, made him a less attractive possibility than the internationalist and progressive governor. The delegates unanimously nominated Dewey on the third ballot and selected Governor Earl Warren of California as the vice-presidential nominee. The platform, to the chagrin of some extreme conservatives, was a moderate document that, by implication at least, accepted the main features of Roosevelt's New Deal and Truman's foreign policy.

Three weeks later the Democrats convened in Philadelphia to choose their national ticket. The convention was steeped in gloom. A movement by the ADA, labor leaders, and city bosses to draft General Eisenhower had failed shortly before the convention when Eisenhower unequivocally rejected the overtures made to him. Thus the nomination went to Truman almost by default, although Senator Richard B. Russell of Georgia received most of the southern delegates' votes. Senator Alben W. Barkley of Kentucky, whose old-fashioned keynote address had roused the convention out of its lethargy, was made the vice-presidential nominee. The platform praised the Truman administration's international policies and called for the enactment of most of the president's progressive recommendations. The forthright endorsement of civil rights was made only after a bitter floor fight in which the young mayor of Minneapolis, Hubert H. Humphrey, and other northern liberals demanded that the rather vague plank proposed by the administration be strengthened. "I say the time has come to walk out of the shadow of states' rights and into the sunlight of human rights," Humphrey declared.

President Truman brought the Democratic delegates to life when he appeared before them at two o'clock in the morning to deliver his acceptance speech. "Senator Barkley and I will win this election," he asserted. As the climax to his fighting address, Truman announced that he was calling the Eightieth Congress—the worst Congress in American history, he charged—into special session on July 26, the day turnips were planted in Missouri. He wanted to give the Republicans a chance to carry out their campaign pledges immediately, explained the president, and thus enable the voters to "decide on the record." The Republicans accused Truman of resorting to petty politics. The "turnip Congress" remained in session for almost two weeks, but it accomplished nothing of importance, which was what Truman expected.

Meanwhile, however, the Democratic Party seemed to be breaking apart as a result of insurgency on the right and the left. A revolt by southern Democrats, which had been brewing for months, was precipitated by the action of the party's national convention in Philadelphia and the dramatic walkout of the Mississippi and Alabama delegates.

A conference of the southern rebels met in Birmingham on July 17. The bolters proceeded to organize the States' Rights Democratic Party, nominate Governor J. Strom Thurmond of South Carolina for president and Governor Fielding L. Wright of Mississippi as his running mate, and draft a platform that emphasized states' rights and opposition to the Democratic Party's civil rights proposals. The Dixiecrats, as they were dubbed, conducted a vigorous campaign during the following months in an effort to unite the South against the regular Democratic ticket. Since they controlled the Democratic Party machinery in several states, the Dixiecrats were able to place their electors on the ballot as the regular Democrats. The States' Righters hoped to prevent either of the major parties from obtaining a majority in the electoral college, thus throwing the election into the House of Representatives, where they might become the deciding factor.

In some respects the threat to the Democratic ticket from the left appeared even more ominous. At the end of 1947, Henry Wallace had announced his willingness to run for president on a third-party ticket sponsored by the Progressive Citizens of America. Many radicals and disgruntled liberals were expected to support Wallace in demanding a more conciliatory approach to the Soviet Union and a domestic program described by the former vice president as "progressive capitalism." Representatives of the Wallace movement met in Philadelphia on July 23 to launch their campaign. They organized the Progressive Party, nominated Wallace and Senator Glen Taylor of Idaho as their standard-bearers, and drafted a platform that blamed the Truman administration for the Cold War, condemned its containment policies, and urged a variety of domestic reforms, including the nationalization of basic industries and equal treatment of all minority groups. Although some old-time New Dealers and a wide assortment of radicals took part in organizing the new party, it was apparent that Communists were extremely active in its campaign. Even so, the Wallace movement seemed to pose a formidable challenge to the Democrats in the key northern states.

President Truman's chances of winning the election looked hopeless. Many Democratic leaders had a defeatist attitude, the party was disorganized, and it badly needed money. The Republicans, meanwhile, were conducting an efficient and well-financed campaign. Traveling in his "Victory Special" train, Governor Dewey toured the country, talking

Truman versus Dewey.
*Courtesy Harry S.
Truman Library.*

confidently and a bit smugly about efficiency and good government. He emphasized the need for an administration that would promote national unity and the cause of peace. Dewey's magisterial campaign, avoiding specifics somewhat in the manner of Franklin Roosevelt's approach in 1932, seemed calculated to ensure a Republican victory. But it made the GOP nominee appear rather remote to the voters—a machine with a cellophane cover, in the opinion of one contemporary. Near the end of the campaign, some of Dewey's advisers expressed concern over the damage Truman might do between election day and January 20, which prompted one reporter to ask ironically: "How long is Dewey going to tolerate Truman's interference in the government?"

Nevertheless, the Democrats under Truman's leadership breathed life into their own campaign. The president's decision to convene the "turnip Congress" revealed an important part of his campaign strategy. He would make the Eightieth Congress rather than the more progressive Dewey his principal target, blaming the Republicans in Congress for the failure of his anti-inflation recommendations, his civil rights proposals, and such social welfare measures as additional public housing and an increase in the minimum wage. "I'm going to fight hard," Truman told Senator Barkley at the outset of the campaign. "I'm going to give them hell." And fight hard he did! Harry Truman, acting as if he expected to win, made one of the most strenuous campaigns in modern history. He traveled 22,000 miles, mostly by train, gave 271 speeches, and was heard directly by approximately 12 million Americans. Speaking extemporaneously at "whistle-stops" across the country, where his friendliness and warmth of personality came through, Truman hammered away at the record of what he called the "do-nothing, good-for-nothing" Eightieth Congress, charging it with the responsibility for high prices and rents, the housing shortage, and cutting back on such programs as national resource conservation and water reclamation. The crowds that gathered to hear the president grew in size, and people increasingly voiced admiration for his plucky fight in the face of apparent defeat.

Despite Truman's gallant effort, most informed observers agreed that he would lose the election. All of the leading polls, political analysts, and important newspapers predicted a Dewey victory. After checking with its correspondents shortly before the balloting, the *New York Times* concluded that Dewey would receive 305 electoral votes to Truman's 105. *Life* magazine carried the New York governor's picture on its cover the week before the election, describing him as the "next president." And in a banner headline on the night of the election, the *Chicago Daily Tribune* announced that "DEWEY DEFEATS TRUMAN"!

The election results surprised almost everyone, and Truman's sensational victory has to be characterized as one of the most extraordinary in American history. The outcome revealed that the public opinion polls had failed to detect a swing to President Truman late in the campaign. The Democratic success also suggested that the political experts had underestimated the extent to which the party of Roosevelt and Truman had become the normal majority party in the United States. In an election marked by a low voter turnout, Truman received 24,105,812 popular votes (49.5 percent) and 303 electoral votes to Dewey's 21,970,065 (45.1 percent) and 189. Thurmond received 1,169,021 popular votes and carried four southern states (with 39 electoral votes), while Wallace had a popular vote of 1,157,172 and won no electoral votes. The Democrats recaptured both houses of Congress, gaining seventy-five seats in the House of Representatives and nine in the Senate. They won twenty of the thirty-two gubernatorial contests that year. Dewey carried sixteen states, most of which were in New England, the Middle Atlantic region, and the Plains belt.

In the immediate aftermath of Truman's surprising victory, George Gallup, the well-known pollster, admitted, "I just don't know what happened." Whatever the explanation, liberals were jubilant. The *New Republic* exuberantly declared that "nothing less than a new era of reform has been demanded by America." Basically, Truman's triumph resulted from his success in maintaining the old Democratic coalition. He ran well among labor voters, ethnic groups, and farmers. General satisfaction among farmers with the administration's agricultural programs strengthened Truman's position, as did the favorable response of particular groups to the veto of the Taft-Hartley bill, the recognition of the new nation of Israel, the president's civil rights proposals, and his executive order calling for desegregation of the armed forces. The country was at peace, the economy was doing well, and there was widespread approval of the Truman administration's Cold War initiatives. Finally, Truman's own role must not be overlooked, for he was his party's greatest campaign asset.

Ironically, the Progressive Party and the Dixiecrat movement probably had ensured Truman's election. The Wallace party, by attracting Communists and other radicals, removed the taint of their support from the mainstream Democrats. Indeed, Truman took advantage of Wallace's Communist support by implying that the former vice president was disloyal. The States' Righters failed to bring about the defection of the whole South, and by undertaking a racist campaign against the Truman administration, they persuaded black voters in the North to rally behind the president's banner. Another contribution to the Democrats' success in 1948 was the fact that the party had a considerable number of strong local candidates, among them G. Mennen Williams in Michigan, Robert S. Kerr in Oklahoma, Hubert Humphrey in Minnesota, and Adlai E. Stevenson, who was elected governor of Illinois.

THE FAIR DEAL, 1949–1952

In his annual State of the Union message on January 5, 1949, President Truman outlined what came to be called the Fair Deal. "Every seg-

ment of our population and every individual," he declared, "has a right
to expect from our Government a fair deal." Truman recommended an
increase in the minimum wage from forty to seventy-five cents an hour,
the broadening of the Social Security system, national health insurance,
federal aid to education, low-cost housing and slum clearance, repeal of
the Taft-Hartley Act, and an increase of $4 billion in federal taxes to
help finance the new programs and reduce inflationary pressures. As the
commentator Elmer Davis once said, "It was roses, roses all the way for
Harry Truman when he rode in the bright sunshine to be inaugurated.
But a good deal of the rest of the way . . . was poison ivy."

Although the Democrats controlled Congress throughout Truman's second administration, the president's legislative proposals were
subjected to continual congressional assault and subterfuge. As the
Eighty-first Congress began its work in January 1949, Truman had
high hopes, most of which were dashed. On the repeal of the Taft-
Hartley Act, Senator Taft was willing to make some concessions, and
the administration might have obtained a compromise revising certain provisions of the 1947 law. But the president was not enthusiastic
about such a compromise, and a measure that got through the Senate
bogged down in the House of Representatives. The administration's
health insurance plan called for prepaid medical, dental, and hospital
care to be financed by employee and employer contributions through
a payroll tax and government subsidies. The American Medical Association conducted a frenzied lobbying and advertising campaign
against the proposed legislation, which it condemned as "national-
ized, bureaucratic, governmental or socialized medical care." Congress
bowed before this onslaught. Truman was no more fortunate with his
recommendation for federal aid to education. Although the Senate
passed a bill appropriating $300 million to the states for the support
of education, the legislation died in the House as a result of a Prot-
estant-Catholic conflict over whether federal aid should go to private
and parochial schools as well as to public institutions.

On the agricultural front, the administration in April 1949 presented the Brannan Plan, named for Secretary of Agriculture Charles F.
Brannan. This proposal sought to maintain a "farm income standard"
comparable to that of the previous decade, to hold food prices at reasonable levels, and to reduce the government's storage expenses if possible. The plan would have retained high fixed support prices for basic

commodities. The novel feature of the scheme was a recommendation that the prices of perishable commodities be determined by the free market, with the government compensating producers for the difference between the market price and a price considered fair by the Department of Agriculture. Critics, including the major farm organizations, charged that the plan would cost too much and lead to the regimentation of American farmers. Congress refused to pass the proposed legislation. Only the heavy demands for food and textiles at home and abroad—demands underwritten by the Marshall Plan and the Korean War—prevented an acute agricultural problem from emerging before the end of Truman's term.

President Truman's worst defeats came in his fight for civil rights legislation. During his second administration, Truman repeatedly tried to get Congress to establish a permanent FEPC, to enact anti-lynching and anti–poll tax laws, and to give legislative sanction to the other recommendations contained in the 1947 report of his Commission on Civil Rights. Southern Democrats, with strong Republican assistance, stymied all these efforts. Truman had to resort to executive action in order to make any immediate headway in the civil rights struggle. He issued executive orders in 1948 providing for an end to discrimination and segregation in the armed forces and in government departments. He established a special committee in 1951 to bar the awarding of defense contracts to companies practicing discrimination. He strengthened the civil rights section of the Justice Department, named the first African American to a federal judgeship, and appointed another as governor of the Virgin Islands. Truman was the first president in modern times to proclaim the equality of blacks, to assail discrimination and violence against them, and to identify his office with the broad objectives of the civil rights movement.

The Eighty-second Congress, elected in 1950, proved even less cooperative its predecessor in responding to Truman's domestic reform proposals. Although the Democrats retained nominal control of both houses, the conservative coalition was stronger in 1951 and 1952 than it had been in the previous Congress. Exploiting the fears and frustrations growing out of the Korean War, internal subversion, and corruption in government, the Republicans made a good showing in the midterm elections; they gained twenty-eight House seats, five Senate seats, and seven governorships.

Republican charges that corruption was rampant in the Truman administration served the interests of the president's opponents in other ways than the ballot box; they helped destroy any lingering hopes Truman had for his unfinished program of social reform. The "mess in Washington" never involved Truman personally, but there was enough evidence of "five percenters"—expediters who sold actual or pretended influence with government officials—and irregularities in various government agencies to lend some credence to the charges. Truman's military aide, General Harry H. Vaughan, was shown to have been given a $520 deep-freeze unit under somewhat cloudy circumstances, while the wife of a Reconstruction Finance Corporation (RFC) official was the beneficiary, for practically nothing, of a $9,540 mink coat. Irregularities in the Internal Revenue Service forced the resignation of several officials and the overhaul of the agency. The RFC was also reorganized. Truman had apparently lost the confidence of a majority of Americans, and one Gallup poll gave him an approval rating of only 23 percent.

It would be a mistake, however, to say that the Fair Deal was a complete failure. In 1950 Congress increased the Social Security benefits by an average of 80 percent, extended the system's coverage to an additional 10.5 million people, and liberalized many federal–state public assistance programs. It raised the minimum wage to 75 cents an hours, extended rent controls, and gave the chief executive more power to deal with the problem of inflation. The National Housing Act of 1949, passed with the help of Senator Taft, authorized the construction of 810,000 subsidized low-income housing units over the next six years, as well as grants for slum clearance and rural housing. Congress also increased appropriations for power development and water reclamation in the West, the TVA, and the Farmers' Home Administration, which was carrying on some of the work of the Farm Security Administration. While Congress rejected Truman's national health insurance plan, it did pass the Hill-Burton Act, which authorized matching federal and state grants for the construction of public and nonprofit hospitals and clinics. In 1950 it set up the National Science Foundation. And at Truman's insistence, Congress in the same year passed the Displaced Persons Act. This statute increased the number of such persons permitted entry into the United States to 415,000 over the next three years and remedied some of the defects the president had complained about in earlier legislation. Nevertheless, the politics of stalemate continued, reflecting the powerful conservative coalition in Congress, the internal conflict within the majority party, and the ambivalence of the public mood.

"The Truman Administration," Richard O. Davies has written, "established no radically new programs, but it performed remarkably well in updating and expanding existing programs and, especially, in serving to assimilate the New Deal into American life." If Truman's record as a social reformer represented an extension of New Deal concepts rather than the inauguration of new programs, the thirty-third president's domestic leadership was nonetheless far more significant than most of his contemporaries supposed. Truman not only successfully defended and strengthened the New Deal, but he also established the agenda that would reach fruition in the social reforms of the 1960s. He was one of the architects of a liberal persuasion that went beyond the New Deal.

As he left office, Harry Truman's standing in history seemed dubious. In 1952 Samuel Lubell could not find "a single, decisive breakthrough" in the whole Truman record. Truman's reputation brightened with the passage of time, however, and by the 1970s he had become something of a folk hero. People admired him, the historian John Lukacs wrote, because he was viewed as "a man of the older American type: outspoken, courageous, loyal to his friends, solidly rooted in his mid-American past, and *real*—a self-crafted piece of solid wood, not a molded plastic piece." David McCullough, in his prize-winning biography, concludes that "The homely attributes, the Missouri wit, the warmth of his friendship, the genuineness of Harry Truman, however appealing, were outweighed by the larger qualities that made him a figure of world stature, both a great and good man, and a great American president." Today, despite his limitations and failures, the Missourian's place in history seems secure, as scholarly polls during the last two decades have consistently ranked him as "near great," and typically in the top ten among all U.S. presidents.

THE KOREAN WAR

In its early stages the Cold War between the United States and the Soviet Union was centered in the eastern Mediterranean and Europe, and the American containment policy, while worldwide in its implications, was largely confined to Europe. But the conflict soon shifted to the Far

East, and the outbreak of the Korean War in June 1950 precipitated a major change in America's East Asian policy. The fall of Nationalist China and the beginning of the Korean War, moreover, heightened a wave of anti-Communist hysteria within the United States. The stage was thus set for the extraordinary rise to power of Senator Joseph R. McCarthy, the frustration of the hapless Truman administration, and the election of Dwight D. Eisenhower as president in 1952.

On the mainland of East Asia the key country was China, whose political independence and territorial integrity had been American objectives for almost half a century. During the war U.S. leaders tried to elevate China to the status of a great power. They helped persuade Josef Stalin to sign a treaty of alliance and friendship with China, recognizing the Nationalist government rather than the Communist forces under Mao Tse-tung. But the fact was that China was deeply divided, and Chiang Kai-shek's Kuomintang Party was too corrupt, inefficient, and reactionary to unify the country. Hoping to end the Chinese civil war and effect a coalition government, President Truman dispatched General George C. Marshall to China in December 1945. Marshall secured a cease-fire and other tentative agreements, but neither side wanted to give up its major political objectives and they failed to reach a settlement.

Before long the Nationalists and the Communists were locked in an all-out military struggle. At first the Nationalists appeared to have the advantage, since they held the most territory, had the larger army, and were better equipped than their adversaries. But Chiang's government had alienated the great majority of the populace, including business people and intellectuals. When General Albert C. Wedemeyer visited China in the summer of 1947 to report on the situation for General Marshall, who had become secretary of state, he was dismayed at the political and military ineptitude of the Kuomintang. The Nationalist armies were soon in retreat everywhere, and by early 1949 Chiang had lost half of his troops and 80 percent of the equipment given to him by the United States. Before the end of 1949, he fled with the remnants of his army to the island of Taiwan (Formosa). Meanwhile, in September 1949, Mao Tse-tung announced the formation of the People's Republic of China, with its capital at Beijing.

With the breakdown of Nationalist control, the Truman administration faced the task of explaining the failure of its China policy. This was not an easy undertaking, for there had long been a group of "Asia-firsters" in the United States who believed that their government had neglected American interests and obligations in Asia, first by giving priority to the defeat of Hitler in the early 1940s and later by concentrating its energies on the defense of Europe in the Cold War. On August 5, 1949, with the collapse of Nationalist authority clearly imminent, the State Department issued a lengthy White Paper that sought to explain American policy in China. The United States had extended more than $2 billion in grants and credits to the Kuomintang—representing far greater resources than those available to the Chinese Communists—and the Nationalists' failure, the document contended, was the result of a great internal change within China, a genuine revolution over which Americans had no control. The United States could have attempted a "full-scale intervention" with troops, Secretary of State Dean Acheson declared, but it "would have been resented by the mass of the Chinese people, would have diametrically reversed our historic policy, and would have been condemned by the American people."

During the winter of 1949–50, the Truman administration's foreign policy received one blow after another. The "loss" of Nationalist China and a divisive debate over NATO had apparently destroyed bipartisanship. The Russians had exploded an atomic bomb, and early in 1950 a Sino-Soviet pact had been concluded between the two Communist powers. The United States had begun to negotiate a peace treaty with Japan, but there was growing uneasiness and even open hostility among the Japanese because of the American desire to retain military bases on the islands. At about this time the National Security Council was completing its reassessment of U.S. foreign and defense policies; NSC 68 forecast "an indefinite period of tension and danger" and recommended that the United States undertake "a bold and massive program" to meet the Soviet challenge. A new issue emerged in June 1950 when North Korean troops crossed the 38th parallel and began an invasion of the Republic of South Korea.

Korea had been dominated by Japan during most of the twentieth century. At a conference in Cairo in 1943, Allied leaders promised the Koreans their freedom "in due course." Russian troops moved into the northern part of the peninsula just before the Japanese surrender in August 1945, and a short time later American soldiers occupied South Korea. The victorious powers decided rather arbitrarily that the occupation zones would be divided at the 38th parallel, and they assumed that an independent Korean government would eventually take over throughout the peninsula. But that was not to be, for with the beginning of the Cold War the division of Korea became permanent.

In late 1947 the United States took the Korean question to the United Nations Assembly, requesting that body to sponsor free elections throughout Korea. United Nations representatives were denied entry into North Korea, but elections were held under UN auspices in South Korea. The Soviet Union proceeded to establish a Communist "people's government" and to train and equip a strong army in North Korea. In South Korea the American military government aligned itself with conservative elements and on occasion resorted to repressive measures that alienated many people. It also gave support to a reactionary leader named Syngman Rhee, who was elected president following the adoption of a republican constitution in 1948. In 1949 American and Russian troops were withdrawn from their respective zones. Meanwhile, there were frequent border clashes between the two Koreas, neither of which recognized the legitimacy of the other's government.

Communist leaders probably thought there was a good chance that the United States would not come to South Korea's defense, for American officials had defined their nation's line of defense in the western Pacific without including Korea. In the calculation of Soviet leaders, the unification of Korea under their control might intimidate Japan, where the United States hoped to retain military bases and anchor its Far Eastern security system. A Korea united under the USSR might also serve to undermine the role of Mao Tse-tung as an exemplar of nationalist revolutions in Asia, a matter of concern to the masters of the Kremlin even this early. Nevertheless, North Korea's assault on June 25, 1950, brought a decisive response from the United States. President Truman, with the concurrence of his advisers, immediately instructed General MacArthur to furnish arms and supplies to the hard-pressed South Koreans. The Truman administration also moved swiftly to bring the matter before the United Nations. In an emergency session on the afternoon of June 25, the Security Council adopted a resolution by a vote of 9 to 0 condemning the invasion and demanding the withdrawal of North Korean troops from South Korea.

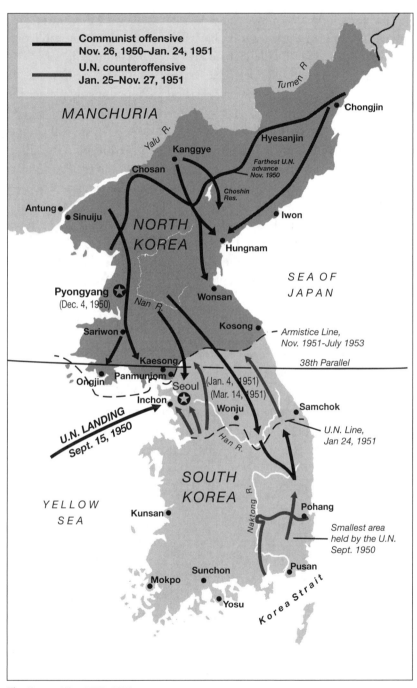

Communist offensive
Nov. 26, 1950–Jan. 24, 1951

U.N. counteroffensive
Jan. 25–Nov. 27, 1951

MANCHURIA

Tumen R.

Chongjin

Yalu R.

Kanggye

Hyesanjin

Chosan

*Farthest U.N.
advance
Nov. 1950*

*Choshin
Res.*

Antung

Sinuiju

NORTH
KOREA

Iwon

Hungnam

SEA OF
JAPAN

Pyongyang ✪
(Dec. 4, 1950)

Nan R.

Wonsan

Sariwon

Kosong

*Armistice Line,
Nov. 1951-July 1953*

Kaesong

38th Parallel

Ongjin

Panmunjom

Seoul ✪

(Jan. 4, 1951)
(Mar. 14, 1951)

U.N. LANDING
Sept. 15, 1950

Inchon

Wonju

Samchok

*U.N. Line,
Jan 24, 1951*

Han R.

YELLOW
SEA

SOUTH
KOREA

Kunsan

Naktong R.

Pohang

*Smallest area
held by the U.N.
Sept. 1950*

Mokpo

Sunchon

Pusan

Yosu

Korea Strait

The Korean War, 1950–1953

The North Korean advance could not be halted by the South Koreans, and within three days the invaders had captured the capital city of Seoul. Truman began to send American air and naval forces into the fray. "The attack upon the Republic of Korea," the president declared, "makes it plain beyond all doubt that the international Communist movement is prepared to use armed invasion to conquer independent nations." On June 27 the UN Security Council, with the Soviet delegate still absent, adopted by a vote of 7 to 1 an American-sponsored resolution calling on member nations to provide all necessary assistance to the Republic of Korea. Three days later Truman made the difficult decision to send two divisions of American ground troops from Japan to Korea. He also authorized a naval blockade of North Korea. Soon afterward the Security Council recognized the United States as the leader of the UN forces in Korea, and Truman named General MacArthur to head the defending army. While these developments took place, the nation rallied behind the president's decision to resist North Korea's aggression. Truman had acted "with a magnificent courage and terse decision," declared the *New York Herald Tribune* in a front-page editorial.

For a time the South Korean situation looked hopeless. The North Korean army advanced down the peninsula for almost six weeks, overrunning most of the south and pushing the Republic of Korea and U.S. Eighth Army soldiers to a perimeter around the southern port of Pusan. There the defenders finally held their ground, their position strengthened by heavy reinforcements and crucial support from American air operations. On September 15 MacArthur launched a brilliant amphibious operation with a successful landing at Inchon near the western end of the 38th parallel. At the same time the UN forces broke out of the Pusan encirclement and began a drive northward. A large number of North Korean soldiers were trapped, over half of them were soon captured or killed, and the rest were driven out of South Korea. Seoul was recaptured on September 26, and MacArthur's men were soon at the 38th parallel.

Having driven the Communist invaders out of South Korea, the UN forces had to make a tough decision: should they undertake an invasion of the north? Would such action bring the Chinese Communists into the war? Should American objectives be reconsidered? President Truman first approved military operations north of the 38th degree of latitude on September 11, unless there was, as he later wrote, "indication

Leathernecks use scaling ladders in amphibious invasion of Inchon, September 15, 1950. *Defense Department (Marine Corps), photograph by Sgt. W. W. Frank.*

or threat of entry of Soviet or Chinese Communist elements in force." The UN General Assembly also gave its approval. MacArthur's forces crossed the 38th parallel on October 7 and began a rapid advance up the peninsula. By the end of the month they were within fifty miles of the Yalu River, the boundary between North Korea and Manchuria. Although the Truman administration did not believe the Chinese would intervene in the Korean War, it wanted to make sure that air strikes were confined to the Korean peninsula. This concern was a major reason for Truman's decision to travel to Wake Island in mid-October to confer with MacArthur. The general assured the president repeatedly "that the Korean conflict was over and that there was little possibility of the Chinese coming in." MacArthur soon began what he thought would be the final great offensive of the war.

By the time Truman left Wake Island on his long flight back to Washington, however, the first military units of Chinese "volunteers" were crossing the Yalu River into Korea. Mao Tse-tung and his associates had evidently decided that a reunited Korea under American control would be intolerable—a powerful opponent at China's very doorstep. But the large-scale Chinese intervention did not come until after MacArthur had commenced his last great offensive. On November 26, thirty-three Chinese divisions hit the middle of the UN line. MacArthur's armies had advanced along two widely separated routes, which left the center wide open. The Communists exploited this mistake, forced the UN soldiers into a retreat, and within two weeks had isolated MacArthur's units into three bridgeheads. The Chinese and North Koreans quickly cleared most of the northern peninsula, sent MacArthur's forces reeling across the 38th parallel, and once more forced the abandonment of Seoul. When Communist China moved into Korea, historian John L. Gaddis has written, the assumption that "there existed significant differences between varieties of Communism, and that these could be turned to the advantage of the United States" largely disappeared from the thinking of U.S. leaders in Washington. This exceptional misunderstanding of the highly strained relationship between Red China and the Soviet Union by U.S. Officials and politicians did not change until the early 1970s, when President Richard Nixon began to implement his foreign policy, one that recognized the competitive and mutually distrustful nature of Chinese-Soviet relations.

The month of December 1950 was a grim time for Americans. U.S. and South Korean military units suffered a series of humiliating defeats. The UN soldiers during the cruel winter of 1950–51 faced both a ferocious enemy equipped with Russian tanks and aircraft and the hardship of coping with bitter cold, numerous storms, and an exceedingly rugged terrain. The mood in Washington was jittery, and talk of another world war swept the country. General MacArthur importuned Washington for permission to bomb "the privileged sanctuary of the adjacent Manchurian border." President Truman and his advisers considered MacArthur's proposals too risky. They were acutely aware of the Soviet Union's obligation to China under the mutual security pact of February 1950. They were afraid of getting trapped in a large land war in China and precipitating a global war in the Far East.

U.S. Marine tanks and South Koreans direct North Korean prisoners to nearest stockade. *Defense Department (Marine Corps), photograph by Sgt. John Babyak, Jr.*

In January 1951 the U.S. Eighth Army, under the command of General Matthew B. Ridgway, finally halted the Communist advance in South Korea. The UN forces slowly resumed the offensive, and by March they had reoccupied Seoul and reached the 38th parallel once more. As General MacArthur's men moved northward, the question of crossing the parallel was again raised. With the Republic of Korea largely cleared of Communist troops, President Truman and many United Nations spokespersons believed the time was ripe for a negotiated settlement. MacArthur was informed by Washington on March 20 that Truman was about to seek a settlement of the war through diplomatic means. At this point the general openly challenged the president. On March 24 MacArthur defiantly threatened mainland China with an attack. In Truman's opinion, this threat killed any hope of an early truce. In a letter to Representative Joseph W. Martin (R-MA), which the congressman read in the House of Representatives on April 5, MacArthur expressed his views freely and vigorously. He wanted to unify Korea, unleash Chiang for an attack on mainland China, and fight communism in Asia rather than in Europe.

Truman could no longer brook such insubordination, and on April
10 he relieved MacArthur of his command, replacing him with General
Ridgway. The dismissal of MacArthur created a furor, and the White
House received a flood of vituperative letters and telegrams—more than
27,000 within twelve days. Flags were flown at half-mast in Massachusetts and Ohio, Truman was burned in effigy in towns across the
country, and several state legislatures condemned him for his "irresponsible and capricious action." Republican leaders in Washington urged a
congressional investigation and talked of impeaching the president. A
Gallup poll showed that the public favored MacArthur over Truman by
a margin of 69 to 29 percent.

In a few days Douglas MacArthur flew into San Francisco and began
a triumphant tour of the United States. He was accorded great ovations.
In a moment of high drama he appeared before a joint session of Congress on April 19. "I address you," the general began, "with neither rancor nor bitterness in the fading twilight of my life, with but one purpose
in mind: To serve my country." MacArthur described the frustration
and humiliation he had suffered in trying to win a war in Korea under
the restrictions imposed by his Washington superiors. He rejected the
concept of limited war. His views were endorsed by such prominent Republicans as Robert Taft and Herbert Hoover, and the controversy that
swirled around his dismissal whipped up the GOP assault on Truman
and Acheson. But the reaction to the MacArthur affair went beyond
politics. It revealed the dissatisfaction with containment as a strategic
concept in the conduct of American foreign policy. Containment ran
counter to the nation's historical approach to international conflict, to
the American expectation of quick solutions and total victories in foreign disputes and wars.

A joint Senate committee under the chairmanship of Senator Richard B. Russell held extensive hearings on the MacArthur case between
May 3 and June 25, 1951. MacArthur presented his case, but so did the
Truman administration, whose position began to elicit more public understanding and backing as the hearings continued. Many Americans,
probably a majority of them, came to agree with the administration's
contention that Europe was the crucial theater in the Cold War and
that it would be a terrible mistake for the United States to become involved in a full-scale war with China in Asia. General Omar N. Bradley,

speaking as chairman of the Joint Chiefs of Staff, put the administration's case succinctly when he stated that MacArthur's approach would "involve us in the wrong war, at the wrong place, at the wrong time, and with the wrong enemy." MacArthur's challenge did not reverse American policy in the Far East, but it did cause the administration to adopt a more inflexible posture toward Beijing and nonrecognition became an established policy, as did an increase of aid to the Chinese Nationalists on Taiwan.

By the spring of 1951, the Korean conflict had become deadlocked. In April and May the American forces and their UN allies repulsed two major Communist offensives, with the enemy suffering heavy losses. The United Nations had branded China as an aggressor in February 1951, and on May 18 the United States secured UN approval of an embargo against the shipment of munitions and critical war materials to China. Still, the military action had bogged down in the general vicinity of the 38th parallel. When the Soviet delegate to the UN suggested in June that an armistice be arranged, with mutual withdrawal of the two sides behind the 38th parallel, Washington welcomed the move. Leaders of the opposing forces began discussions on July 10 looking toward an armistice, only to have the talks break down two days later; they continued in an on-again, off-again fashion during the rest of the year. A truce was held up because of disagreement over an exact boundary and the disposition of the prisoners of war.

The Korean War was the first war ever fought by a world peace organization with an international army. Technically, the war was "a police action by the United Nations." But its consequences—for Korea and the United States—were profound. Sixteen nations eventually sent military units to Korea or provided other assistance to the UN forces there. The United States, however, bore the burden of the war, along with the South Koreans. The former provided half of the ground forces, 86 percent of the naval units, and 93 percent of the air power. American losses numbered 54,246 dead and 103,284 wounded, and the monetary costs climbed into the billions of dollars. Korean and Chinese battlefield casualties were far greater than those suffered by the Americans. At home Congress authorized various economic controls and in September 1950 passed the Defense Production Act, which sought to increase military production and give priority to war orders. Rigid price controls and rationing were not necessary, but taxes were increased and efforts were made to prevent price increases and large wage hikes. In December 1950, following the Chinese intervention in the war, President Truman declared a state of national emergency and outlined a vast new mobilization program.

A sharp increase in American military preparedness and an extension of containment were set in motion by the Korean conflict. Indeed, the Cold War was soon "globalized." In the second half of 1950, while America was fighting in Korea to contain the Communist expansion in Asia, the nation saw its defense budget triple and its armed forces grow substantially. At the same time, Washington was actively aiding Chiang on Taiwan and the French in Indochina. American leaders also committed themselves to the rearming of West Germany and the stationing of four divisions of their own troops in Western Europe. Meanwhile, they were working hard to develop the hydrogen bomb. "Because of these American initiatives," historian Walter LaFeber observes, "the six months between June and December 1950 rank among the most important of the Cold War era." During the next year, the United States completed a treaty with Japan that allowed it to retain military bases in the islands. Mutual defense treaties were worked out with Australia, New Zealand, and the Philippines, and NATO was strengthened. By 1955 the United States had about 450 bases in thirty-six countries around the world and had negotiated political and military pacts with some twenty nations outside Latin America. When Truman left office early in 1953, containment had been institutionalized in East Asia, it had undergone a process of militarization, and NSC 68 was rapidly being implemented.

INTERNAL SECURITY AND THE POLITICS OF FEAR

By the time the shooting war began in Korea in mid-1950, the American people had succumbed to an irrational fear of disloyalty and subversion within the United States, an outbreak of distrust and hysteria that was to last until about 1954. Many factors were involved in the development of America's second Red Scare: the exigencies and setbacks of the Cold War, the Truman administration's loyalty program, a series of sensational spy cases, the Korean War, the Republican Party's desperate search for a viable issue to use against the Democrats, and the emergence of a remarkable demagogue. During the late 1940s and early 1950s, suspicion destroyed habitual trust, and guilt by association tactics damaged the lives and reputations of many men and women.

In the quest for security, teachers were required to sign loyalty oaths, the courts and Congress assumed a harshly punitive attitude toward Communists, and liberals and reformers of every kind were criticized. Between 1948 and 1954 Hollywood released more than forty anti-Communist films. Radicals in the communications and entertainment industries began to be blacklisted. In 1950 an anti-Communist group called "Counter-Attack" published *Red Channels: The Report of Communist Influence in Radio and Television*, a book that contained the names of 151 people described as "potential subversives." Meanwhile, a large number of states enacted legislation denying public employment to individuals who advocated violent overthrow of the government or belonged to suspect organizations, while others adopted Communist-control laws.

Following World War II, the Federal Bureau of Investigation (FBI) began the first comprehensive scrutiny of government workers, and the federal departments undertook their own loyalty checks. In November 1946 the president created the Temporary Commission on Employee Loyalty to study the whole question, and its major recommendations were embodied in Truman's Executive Order No. 9835 of March 21, 1947. This order instituted a thorough investigation of all federal civil servants. The administration's loyalty inquest was conducted with some procedural safeguards and through the establishment of a Loyalty Review Board, but procedures differed among agencies. In many cases employees received little notice of the charges against them, were denied the right to confront their accusers, or were questioned about matters having nothing to do with their loyalty. About half of the cases appealed from lower-level boards were reversed. More than 4 million individuals were eventually checked. Charges were brought against 9,077 employees, some 2,500 of whom resigned under suspicion, and by March 1952 the government had dismissed about 380 persons, not as spies but as security risks. In 1948 the Truman administration began the prosecution of the top Communist party leaders under the Smith Act of 1940, which made it a crime to conspire to advocate the violent overthrow of the government even if no overt act was committed. After the Supreme Court upheld the conviction of the Communist leaders, the government proceeded to prosecute dozens of lesser figures in the party. The administration's actions and rhetoric doubtless helped develop the framework for the extravagant anticommunism of later years.

The first public awareness of Soviet wartime espionage came well before the introduction of Truman's loyalty program. Early in 1945, FBI agents discovered a large number of classified State Department documents when they raided the offices of *Amerasia*, a small left-wing magazine specializing in Far Eastern affairs. The following year, in February 1946, a Canadian Royal Commission disclosed that several local spy rings had given military information and atomic secrets to the Russians during the war. Meanwhile, the House Un-American Activities Committee (HUAC) was engaged in a search for subversives. Two of the witnesses who appeared before HUAC in the summer of 1948 provided information that led to one of the most bizarre and sensational cases in American history. Elizabeth Bentley and Whittaker Chambers—both former Communists—described the existence of two independent espionage rings operating in Washington for the Soviet Union in the 1930s.

Chambers, a senior editor of *Time* magazine, identified Alger Hiss, the highly respected president of the Carnegie Endowment for International Peace and a former State Department official, as a member of a Communist cell in Washington during the 1930s. Later, in the fall of 1948, Chambers broadened his charges, asserting that Hiss had given him copies of State Department documents to be turned over to Soviet agents. To prove his charges, Chambers escorted government agents to his farm near Westminster, Maryland, where he removed microfilm copies from a hollowed-out pumpkin. He claimed that the documents had been given to him by Hiss in 1938. Hiss, appearing before a federal grand jury in New York, denied that he had ever given State Department documents to Chambers or anyone else. But the grand jury indicted Hiss on two counts of perjury; the statute of limitations prevented him from being tried for treason. The trial began in May 1949 and ended six weeks later in a hung jury. A second trial was concluded in late January 1950, with Hiss being found guilty and sentenced to five years in prison.

Many liberals felt that Alger Hiss was being persecuted by a vindictive congressional investigating committee, and some men in high places, like Dean Acheson, refused to turn their backs on him. For others, the Hiss case confirmed their darkest fears and suspicions. Representative Richard M. Nixon (R-CA), one of the most aggressive HUAC members in the whole affair, described the case as "the most treasonable conspiracy in American history." Nixon's success in the Hiss case brought him national attention and helped catapult the second-term representative into the Senate. For his party, Hiss became the symbol of all that had gone wrong in the United States and the world.

The espionage in which Hiss was implicated had occurred before the war, but other cases soon produced evidence of Communist infiltration in more recent years. In March 1949 a young New Yorker named Judith Coplon, a former political analyst in the Department of Justice, was arrested with her Russian lover on the charge of stealing classified documents for Soviet agents. The case of Dr. Klaus Fuchs, revealed to the public early in February 1950, was much more important. Fuchs, a German-born scientist employed in the British nuclear energy establishment, had worked during the war at Los Alamos, New Mexico, on the development of the first atomic bomb. When arrested by the British, he confessed to having transmitted important atomic secrets to the Russians between 1942 and 1947. The story Fuchs told led to the arrest of Harry Gold, an accomplice in the United States, and four other Americans: Julius and Ethel Rosenberg, Morton Sobell, and David Greenglass, all of whom were charged with passing atomic secrets to Soviet agents during and after the war. They were tried and convicted in 1951. The Rosenbergs were sentenced to death, and their execution in June 1953 was broadcast live on radio across the nation.

Hiss, Fuchs, and the Rosenbergs seemed to explain many of the disappointments and setbacks the United States had suffered since the end of World War II. At a time when the president was asking Congress to vote billions of dollars to halt the Communist expansion in Europe and Asia, how else could one explain the fall of China, the loss of America's atomic monopoly, and its inability to win the war in Korea? Disloyalty, subversion, and trickery at home—by intellectuals, left-wingers, and New Deal internationalists—must be at the root of the nation's difficulties. As Republican Senator Homer Capehart of Indiana exclaimed, "How much more are we going to have to take? Fuchs and Acheson and Hiss and hydrogen bombs threatening outside and New Dealers eating away the vitals of the nation. In the name of Heaven, is this the best America can do?"

Men like Capehart had earlier tried to cope with the threat of internal subversion by adopting strong antisubversive legislation. They had been denied a new law in 1948, when President Truman successfully vetoed the Mundt-Nixon bill on subversive activities. But the shocking developments of 1949, the rising tide of anticommunism, and the sensational charges made by Republican congressmen smoothed the path for the McCarran Internal Security Act of September 1950, which was passed overwhelmingly over Truman's veto. The McCarran Act required Communist and Communist-front organizations to register with the attorney general, forbade entry into the United States of anyone who belonged or had belonged to a totalitarian organization, and provided for the internment of such persons in the event of national emergencies. The new law broadened the definition of espionage and sabotage, extended the statute of limitations for prosecution, and made it illegal to conspire to perform any act that would "substantially contribute" to the establishment of a totalitarian government in the United States. In the McCarran-Walter Act, which passed over Truman's veto in 1952, Congress provided for the screening of undesirables seeking entry into the United States and struck at communism through various exclusion and registration clauses.

The Truman administration's containment policy, its comprehensive loyalty program, and the defection of Henry Wallace shielded the Democrats from a Republican attack invoking the Communist issue in the campaign of 1948. But the loss of that election left the Republicans frustrated and embittered, and the events of 1949 and 1950 finally brought them to the employment of anticommunism as a principal weapon in their political war against the Democrats. What came to be known as McCarthyism emerged as a powerful political dynamic.

The man most successful in demonstrating the political possibilities of the Communist issue was a first-term senator from Wisconsin named Joseph R. McCarthy. A lawyer and former circuit judge, McCarthy had narrowly defeated Senator Robert M. La Follette, Jr., in the Republican primary of 1946 and had gone on to defeat his Democratic opponent in the November election. The Wisconsin senator violated the Senate's rules and customs from the beginning of his tenure, made immoderate claims, and engaged in questionable dealings with lobbyists for special interests. By 1950 he had displeased powerful senators from both parties, lost his only major committee assignment, and was worried about his chances of re-election in 1952. At this point, while casting about for an issue—any issue—that might revive his political fortunes, he adopted anti-communism.

McCarthy first came to the attention of the American public as a result of a speech he made to the Republican Women's Club of Wheeling, West Virginia, on February 9, 1950. Asserting that the United States had been the greatest power in the world on V-J Day, he explained that the country's strength had been diminished "because of the traitorous actions of those who have been treated so well by this Nation." McCarthy's precise words on this occasion will probably never be known, but according to the radio and newspaper journalists who followed his rough draft, he held up a sheaf of papers and shouted: "I have here in my hand a list of 205—a list of names that were made known to the Secretary of State as being members of the Communist Party and who nevertheless are still working and shaping policy in the State Department." The senator was hard to pin down, but his charges were swiftly carried by the media from one end of the country to the other.

Back in Washington the Democrats sought to deal with McCarthy by having a subcommittee of the Senate Foreign Relations Committee make a thorough investigation of his accusations. The subcommittee, under the chairmanship of Senator Millard E. Tydings of Maryland, began a series of extensive hearings on March 8, 1950. McCarthy soon stated that he would rest his case on his contention that Professor Owen Lattimore of Johns Hopkins University, a Far Eastern expert who had served as a consultant to the State Department on several occasions, was the "top Russian espionage agent" in the United States. Lattimore denied under oath that he was a Communist or a "follower of the communist line." When he was later indicted for perjury, his case was thrown out by the court. When the Tydings committee reported in July 1950, its Democratic majority called the McCarthy charges "a fraud and a hoax" on the Senate and on the American people.

Most Republicans in Congress defended McCarthy. Many GOP members echoed the then-current phrase, "I don't like some of McCarthy's methods, but his goal is good." McCarthy became the most popular campaigner for his party and probably contributed to the defeat of Senator Tydings in Maryland and Governor Chester Bowles in Connecticut. The Wisconsin senator took advantage of the social strains of the time and became a forceful articulator of simple answers to complex and baffling questions arising from the Cold War. While McCarthy was fundamentally a product of the anti-Communist consensus that existed before 1950, he was a talented demagogue who skillfully manipulated the media and built up a network of informers within the government itself.

The Korean War also strengthened McCarthy by refueling anti-Communist extremism, and in the early 1950s his influence increased spectacularly. He fought off all efforts in the Senate to restrain him, and throughout 1951 he added his reckless voice to the China inquest and continually sought to discredit the Truman administration. His accusations and innuendos resulted in a long succession of charges and countercharges. Few public figures in American history have matched McCarthy's intemperate and vituperative attacks on his adversaries. The senator denounced all the "egg-sucking phony liberals" whose "pitiful squealing . . . would hold sacrosanct those Communists and queers" who had sold China into "atheistic slavery," and he committed himself to driving out the "prancing mimics of the Moscow party line in the State Department."

McCarthy was not the only practitioner of McCarthyism—he was joined by many Republican politicians and some anti-Communist Democrats—but the Wisconsin senator was the star of the show. He dominated the channels of mass communication. He intimidated government officials and private citizens, and while many Washington politicians deplored his methods, few of them would openly challenge him at the height of his power. By 1953 McCarthy was given credit for having won almost a dozen Republican Senate seats and a "myth of political invincibility" had grown up about him. This estimate was exaggerated, but he was unquestionably an influential force in American politics.

"I LIKE IKE": THE ELECTION OF 1952

The frustration and rancor that spread through American society during the final years of Harry Truman's presidency brightened Republican prospects in the election of 1952. Truman's popularity dropped sharply, and in the public mind his administration was associated with a wide assortment of national setbacks and threatening problems: the involvement in Korea, Chinese aggression, internal communism, corruption in government, high taxes, and inflation. Republican leaders were determined not to let electoral success slip from their grasp as they had done in 1948, and that determination was one reason for the most vigorous intraparty struggle the GOP had experienced in a generation.

This fight over the Republican nomination in 1952 reflected a division in the party that had existed for many years. The more conservative faction championed Senator Taft, who had announced his candidacy in October 1951. The conservative wing, strongly supported by party leaders and business interests in the Midwest and Mountain West, urged a real and easily discernable alternative to the Democrats. The liberal-internationalist wing of the Republican Party, strongest in the East and the Far West, viewed Taft's position on foreign and domestic questions with suspicion, and men like Governor Dewey doubted that Taft could win if nominated. Liberal Republicans pinned their hopes on General Dwight Eisenhower, then on leave from the presidency of Columbia University to serve as supreme commander of NATO forces in Europe. A draft-Eisenhower movement began to take shape by the late summer of 1951, and in January 1952 the general finally agreed to accept the nomination if it were offered to him. He seems to have been motivated in part by a desire to save his party and the country from the policies of Taft and McCarthy.

Eisenhower won the New Hampshire primary in March and went on to prevail in several other primaries. Meanwhile, Taft was campaigning hard and obtaining a large number of delegate commitments, particularly in the Middle West and the South. As the preconvention campaign proceeded, Eisenhower's representatives charged that the Taft-controlled state organizations in the southern states were disqualifying pro-Eisenhower delegates chosen by local and state conventions. By the time the Republican National Convention opened in Chicago

Eisenhower at the
Republican National
Convention, 1952.
*Courtesy Dwight D.
Eisenhower Library.*

on July 7, 1952, Taft probably had a slight lead over Eisenhower in the number of committed delegates, although it was clear to most observers that the general was far more popular than the senator with rank-and-file Republicans.

When the convention began, the Eisenhower forces succeeded in passing by a vote of 658 to 548 the so-called Fair Play Amendment, which provided that the contested delegates seated by the national committee during the previous week could not vote on the credentials of other delegates. This victory foreshadowed Eisenhower's nomination, for the Eisenhower delegations challenging the regular slates in Texas, Georgia, and Louisiana were later seated by convention vote, and the general was nominated on the first ballot. Senator Richard Nixon was selected for the vice-presidential nomination. The Republican platform was strongly critical of the Democratic administration, charging that in seven years it had "squandered the unprecedented power and prestige which were ours at the close of World War II" and that it had "lost the peace so dearly earned" by the war.

There were several aspirants for the Democratic nomination, but most of them were handicapped at first by uncertainty over President Truman's possible candidacy. This was not true of Senator Estes Kefauver of Tennessee, who had won a Senate seat in 1948 by defeating the machine of Edward H. Crump of Memphis. Kefauver had attracted national attention as chairman of a special Senate subcommittee created to investigate interstate crime, but he was unpopular with the big-city Democratic bosses because his investigations had disclosed links between organized crime and local politics. Nor was he acceptable to Truman, whose administration, he declared, should be doing more to clean up corruption in government. Nonetheless, the Tennessee senator entered the New Hampshire Democratic primary and, to the surprise of the nation, defeated the president in the preferential vote on March 11. This startling development no doubt hastened Truman's announcement that he himself would not be a candidate for re-election, which he made on March 29 at a Jefferson-Jackson Day dinner in Washington. In order to stop Kefauver, who went on to win a series of other primaries, Truman turned to Adlai E. Stevenson, who had made a fine record as governor of Illinois. When Stevenson insisted that he had no interest in running for president, Truman and other party leaders endorsed seventy-four-year-old Alben Barkley, the vice president, who eventually retired from the race because of opposition from several labor leaders.

At the Democratic National Convention, also held in Chicago that year, party leaders again sought to persuade Governor Stevenson to seek the nomination; now he reluctantly agreed. Although Kefauver led on the first two ballots, his brave fight was unavailing against the power and influence of the administration and other Democratic leaders, who nominated Stevenson on the third ballot. Senator John J. Sparkman of Alabama, one of the architects of a compromise civil rights plank designed to prevent a southern bolt, was chosen as Stevenson's running mate. The platform committed the party to the repeal of the Taft-Hartley Act, maintenance of high price supports for agriculture, and continuation of the Fair Deal. Adopting the theme of "peace with honor," the assembled Democrats endorsed American intervention in Korea and praised the Truman administration's foreign policies.

The Republican campaign did not get off to a fast start, for General Eisenhower was rather fumbling and uninspiring in his early speeches. In September, however, Eisenhower's "great crusade" began to pick up momentum. The GOP candidate began to stress the formula Senator Karl E. Mundt called K1C2: Korea, communism, and corruption in government. Eisenhower pledged his support to all Republican candidates, including extreme conservatives and such rabid anti-Communists as Senator McCarthy. He made a genuine effort to assuage the bitterness of the Taft faction, arranging a special conference with the senator in New York City on September 12. As a result of that meeting, the two Republican leaders reached an agreement on the importance of fiscal responsibility in the conduct of the national government, the need to reduce federal expenditures and balance the budget, and the necessity of defending "liberty against creeping socialism."

The Republicans had a popular candidate, they were united in supporting him, and their campaign was abundantly financed. Republican strategists made extensive use of television, which assumed importance for the first time in a presidential campaign, and they used the advertising and public relations techniques of Madison Avenue to give their candidates a good "image." Party campaigners, including McCarthy and Nixon, did not neglect the Communist issue. They spoke scornfully of the "egghead" support that Stevenson was receiving. As the campaign developed, Eisenhower began to emphasize the Korean War. He described the negotiations as a "swindle," a "Soviet trap" designed to enable the North Koreans to renew their strength. At Detroit on October 24, the general made a sensational announcement that if elected, "I shall go to Korea" to seek an early and honorable end to the war.

Eisenhower's campaign ran into real trouble only once—the dramatic episode of the secret Nixon fund. The public learned on September 18 that Senator Nixon, the GOP vice-presidential nominee, had benefited from a private fund of about $18,000 contributed by California businessmen. Now Eisenhower, who had said that his administration would be as "clean as a hound's tooth," faced a dilemma. Some of the general's advisers urged him to remove Nixon from the ticket, but Eisenhower hesitated. Meanwhile, Nixon fought back, presenting his case to the people in a national television broadcast on September 23. The speech was melodramatic but effective. The senator emphasized his own relatively limited personal assets, remarked that his wife, Pat, "doesn't have a mink coat," and said of his cocker spaniel, Checkers—a gift from a Texan who had heard that his children wanted a dog—"regardless of what they say about it, we're going to keep it." The response was all that Nixon could have wished; nearly 200,000 telegrams poured into the party's national committee urging Nixon's retention on the ticket. Eisenhower accepted that verdict.

In the meantime, the Democrats had launched their campaign. Stevenson—articulate, thoughtful, and witty—quickly emerged as something of a television personality. Indeed, he had a special way with words, assuring his audiences that "if the Republicans will stop telling lies about us, we will stop telling the truth about them." It was clear to Stevenson that in some respects the Truman administration would be a liability to his campaign, and he sought, with only limited success, to establish his independence of President Truman. The Democratic nominee laid out his position in a series of extraordinary addresses during the campaign. Basically he wanted to continue the New Deal–Fair Deal line.

Both major parties waged vigorous and comprehensive campaigns. The Democrats, remembering the miracle of 1948, hoped the voters would respond to their campaign slogan that Americans had "never had it so good." But the election returns dashed their hopes. Eisenhower won 33.8 million popular votes (55.4 percent) to Stevenson's 27.3 million (44.4 percent) in the heaviest turnout since 1908. The electoral vote was 442 to 89, with the Democratic ticket carrying only nine southern and border states.

The defections from the Democratic coalition were numerous, including white southerners, Catholics, certain ethnic groups, and even low-income voters. In the South, where Governors James F. Byrnes of South Carolina, Robert F. Kennon of Louisiana, and Allan F. Shivers of Texas actively supported Eisenhower and Nixon, the Republican ticket obtained 48.9 percent of the popular vote and carried Virginia, Florida, Tennessee, Texas, and Oklahoma. Eisenhower had disrupted the solid South and given the minority party in that region a new respectability, particularly among affluent and middle-class urbanites and suburban dwellers. Almost one-fourth of Eisenhower's national vote came from people who had voted for Truman in 1948, and many new voters cast their ballots for the Republicans. Blacks were the only group that gave Stevenson as high a percentage of its vote as it had given Truman four years earlier. Yet the election was fundamentally a personal victory for Dwight Eisenhower; he ran an astonishing 19 percent ahead of other GOP candidates in 1952.

Only the general's immense popularity enabled the Republicans to win control of Congress. They gained twenty-two House seats—three more than the 218 needed to give them control—and only one Senate seat, just enough to make it possible for them to organize that body. In

84
CHAPTER 2

spite of preferring the Republican presidential candidate, it was clear that a majority of the voters still thought of themselves as Democrats. Nevertheless, after having endured twenty years of Democratic control, the Republicans were moving back to 1600 Pennsylvania Avenue as well as to supremacy on Capitol Hill.

———— ★ ————

SUGGESTIONS FOR FURTHER READING

Gary W. Reichard's *Politics as Usual: The Age of Truman and Eisenhower* (2nd ed., 2004) provides an authoritative and balanced introduction to national politics in the postwar period. Important aspects of the political scene in the United States following the New Deal are described in Herbert Parmet, *The Democrats: The Years after FDR* (1976); William E. Leuchtenburg, *In the Shadow of FDR: From Harry Truman to Bill Clinton* (2nd ed., 1993); Michael Barone, *Our Country: The Shaping of America from Roosevelt to Reagan* (1990); James T. Patterson, *Grand Expectations: The United States, 1945–1974* (1996); and Alonzo L. Hamby, *Liberalism and Its Challengers: From F.D.R. to Bush* (2nd ed., 1992). Hamby's *Beyond the New Deal: Harry S. Truman and American Liberalism* (1973) is a valuable study of the relationship between Truman and postwar liberalism.

Truman himself has attracted a great deal of attention from biographers and interpreters. The most impressive biography is Alonzo L. Hamby, *Man of the People: A Life of Harry S. Truman* (1995), a work characterized by solidity, balance, and insightful interpretation. Robert H. Ferrell, *Harry S. Truman: A Life* (1994), is informative, readable, and reliable. William E. Pemberton has written a good brief study: *Harry S. Truman: Fair Dealer and Cold Warrior* (1989). David Mc-Cullough won the Pulitzer Prize for biography with *Truman* (1992), a detailed, approving, and unusually readable treatment of the thirty-third president. The best scholarly history of Truman's presidency is Donald R. McCoy, *The Presidency of Harry S. Truman* (1984). The most comprehensive study of the Truman administration is the two-volume work by Robert J. Donovan, *Conflict and Crisis* (1977) and *Tumultuous Years* (1982). These volumes by an outstanding journalist are informative but not very interpretive. *Public Papers of the Presidents of the United States* (1961) is an invaluable source for the addresses, public statements, and press conferences of U.S. presidents beginning with Truman. Eight volumes are devoted to the Truman administration. See also Merle Miller, *Plain Speaking: An Oral Biography of Harry S. Truman* (1974), and Robert H. Ferrell, ed., *Off the Record: The Private Papers of Harry S. Truman* (1980).

Susan M. Hartmann, *Truman and the 80th Congress* (1971), is an informative study. James T. Patterson's *Mr. Republican: A Biography of Robert A. Taft* (1972) is an important study of a key figure. For other congressional leaders, see Gilbert C. Fite, *Richard B. Russell, Jr., Senator from Georgia* (1991), and Richard O. Davies, *Defender of the Old Guard: John Bricker and American Politics* (1993). The election of 1948 is analyzed in Irwin Ross, *The Loneliest Campaign: The Truman Victory of 1948* (1968); Richard Norton Smith, *Thomas E. Dewey and His Times* (1982); Nadine Cohodas, *Strom Thurmond and the Politics of Southern Change* (1993); Robert A. Garson, *The Democratic Party and the Politics of Sectionalism, 1941–1948* (1974); and Norman D. Markowitz, *The Rise and Fall of the People's Century: Henry A. Wallace and American Liberalism, 1941–1948* (1973).

Fiscal and economic policies are examined in Edward S. Flash, Jr., *Economic Advice and Presidential Leadership: The Council of Economic Advisers* (1965), and Francis H. Heller, ed., *Economics and the Truman Administration* (1981). For the labor scene and labor policy, see R. Alton Lee, *Truman and Taft-Hartley: A Question of Mandate* (1966); Arthur F. McClure, *The Truman Administration and the Problems of Postwar Labor, 1945–1948* (1969); Kevin Boyle, *The UAW and the Heyday of American Liberalism, 1945–1968* (1995); and Robert H. Zieger, *The CIO, 1935–1955* (1995). Other political questions are considered in William H. Moore, *The Kefauver Committee and the Politics of Crime, 1950–52* (1974), and Andrew J. Dunar, *The Truman Scandals and the Politics of Morality* (1984).

Burton I. Kaufman, *The Korean War* (2nd ed., 1996), is notable for its balance and reliability. Glenn D. Paige, *The Korean Decision* (1968), is a detailed account of decision making between June 24 and June 30, 1950. Bruce Cumings, *The Origins of the Korean War, 1945–1950,* 2 vols. (1981–1990), and Rosemary Foot, *The Wrong War: American Policy and the Dimensions of the Korean Conflict, 1950–1953* (1985) are useful. For military action, consult David Rees, *Korea: The Limited War* (1964); Max Hastings, *The Korean War* (1987); Francis H. Heller, ed., *The Korean War: A 25-Year Perspective* (1977); and Michael Schaller, *Douglas MacArthur: The Far Eastern General* (1989). Allen S. Whiting's *China Crosses the Yalu: The Decision to Enter the Korean War* (1960) throws light on an important aspect of the war. John W. Spanier, *The Truman-MacArthur Controversy and the Korean War* (rev. ed., 1965) stresses the concept of "limited war." Mobilization and the home front are considered in Arthur A. Stein, *The Nation at War* (1980), and Maeva Marcus, *Truman and the Steel Seizure Case: The Limits of Presidential Power* (1977).

Richard M. Fried, *Nightmare in Red: The McCarthy Era in Perspective* (1990), and Ellen Schrecker, *The Age of McCarthyism: A Brief History with Documents* (1994), are good introductions to the second Red Scare and both contain helpful bibliographies. Serious students should also consult Albert Fried, *McCarthyism, the Great American Scare: A Documentary History* (1996). Earl Latham, *The Communist Controversy in Washington: From the New Deal to McCarthy* (1966), provides a good discussion of the rising Communist issue, which is explained in terms of a conservative drive for power. Alan D. Harper, *The Politics of Loyalty: The White House and the Communist Issue, 1946–1952* (1969), is a balanced treatment of the Truman administration's loyalty program and its response to the anti-Communist issue. For other good studies, see Richard M. Freeland, *The Truman Doctrine and the Origins of McCarthyism: Foreign Policy, Domestic Politics, and Internal Security, 1946–1948* (1972); Michal R. Belknap, *Cold War Political Justice: The Smith Act, the Communist Party, and American Civil Liberties* (1977); and Stanley I. Kutler, *The American Inquisition: Justice and Injustice in the Cold War* (1982). Thomas C. Reeves, *The Life and Times of Joe McCarthy: A Biography* (1982), and David M. Oshinsky, *A Conspiracy So Immense: The World of Joe McCarthy* (1983), are major studies. Robert Griffith's prize-winning *The Politics of Fear: Joseph R. McCarthy and the Senate* (1970) focuses on the senatorial stage upon which the Wisconsin senator operated. Robert Griffith and Athan Theoharis, eds., *The Specter: Original Essays on the Cold War and the Origins of McCarthyism* (1974), is useful for McCarthyism and American institutions.

For the election of 1952, begin with Herbert S. Parmet, *Eisenhower and the American Crusades* (1972), and Charles C. Alexander, *Holding the Line: The Eisenhower Era, 1952–1961* (1975). Also consult Stephen E. Ambrose, *Eisenhower: Soldier, General of the Army, President-Elect, 1890–1952* (1983); John Bartlow Martin, *Adlai Stevenson of Illinois: The Life of Adlai E. Stevenson* (1976); Jeff Broadwater, *Adlai Stevenson and American Politics: The Odyssey of a Cold War Liberal* (1994); and Joseph Bruce Gorman, *Kefauver: A Political Biography* (1971).

———★———

3

Politics of Moderation: Eisenhower, the New Look, and Brinksmanship

D
WIGHT DAVID EISENHOWER, the nation's thirty-fourth president, suited the 1950s singularly well. Coming to office at a time of confusion, division, and bitterness, the immensely popular "Ike" rendered the decade's politics less acrimonious, eased the accumulated tensions of a generation of crisis, and helped to restore a sense of national unity. The new president's moderate Republicanism and restrained approach to government appealed to millions of Americans who had grown weary of great public enterprises and social conflict. The purposes and style of the Eisenhower administration blended comfortably into a national mood of complacency, well-being, and self-indulgence.

Eisenhower's two terms in the White House contained their full share of setbacks and unexpected difficulties, including two serious illnesses the president suffered in 1955 and 1956. Many of the general's early supporters were disappointed with the results of his executive leadership, in some cases because the administration did not challenge the New Deal, in others because it did not undertake fresh programs and a more venturesome course in domestic affairs. Yet there were some notable accomplishments during Eisenhower's presidency, and there can be no doubt that he greatly influenced the course of our recent history. Thus he ended the Korean War without being labeled an appeaser, and his administration helped to establish the New Deal as an enduring feature of our national government.

EISENHOWER AND THE NEW ADMINISTRATION

Dwight D. Eisenhower's long years of military service gave him a unique background among twentieth-century presidents. Born in 1890 in Denison, Texas, into an economically pressed family of Pennsylvania Dutch descent, young "Ike" Eisenhower spent his boyhood in Abilene, Kansas, which was still something of a frontier town at the turn of the century. In some ways, Ike never left home, for his world would always retain traditional American values and virtues he had assimilated as a boy in Abilene. In other respects, however, his world soon broadened. He received an appointment to West Point and graduated from the military academy in 1915. After serving as an officer in the tank training program at Camp Colt during World War I, he held a variety of assignments at army posts and service schools during the next two decades and served as an aide to General MacArthur for several years. He came to know his way around Washington and learned to deal with politicians and the press. He distinguished himself in army maneuvers held in Louisiana in 1941 and was subsequently assigned to the war plans division of the War Department. General Marshall soon recommended Eisenhower to command American forces in Europe, and he served as commander of the Allied invasion of North Africa, Sicily, and Italy. Then President Roosevelt selected him as supreme commander of the Allied forces in Europe, and in that role Eisenhower directed the momentous "D-Day" invasion of France and the subsequent conquest of Germany. He emerged from the war as a five-star general and an authentic military hero.

The general had demonstrated a remarkable talent for leadership. His military success had come not as a result of genius as a strategist or brilliance as a field commander, but as a result of his unusual personal qualities and his capacity as a coordinator and conciliator. He knew how to direct large projects, was willing to shoulder vast responsibilities, and was familiar with the operation of modern bureaucracies. Eisenhower was also at home in the realm of international relations, and he was firmly committed to a policy of internationalism.

In other ways, however, he was ill-equipped for the task of presidential leadership. Though deeply involved in civil-military relations in earlier years, he was not well acquainted with the way the political system worked in the United States and knew little about the problems and complexities of American society. His ideas, embodying such basic values as self-reliance and faith in free enterprise, were widely shared by his fellow Americans, but they tended to be cast in the simplistic and somewhat romantic mold of an earlier day. Still, he took ideas seriously, was a quick learner, and communicated easily. The new president was also a man of great warmth, personal charm, and becoming modesty. He liked people and expected them to like him. As Arthur Krock of the *New York Times* wrote in 1957:

> His manner is genial; his ways and reflexes are kindly. His bearing is soldierly, yet his well-tailored civilian clothes never seem out of character. His smile is attractively pensive, his frequent grin is infectious, his laughter ready and hearty. He fairly radiates "goodness," simple faith and the honorable, industrious background of his heritage.

Eisenhower's view of the presidency differed sharply from that of his immediate predecessors. He had no taste for the ordinary ways of the politician: the rough-and-tumble of active partisanship, haggling over matters of patronage, and involvement in the details of government. This "least partisan president," as the former New Dealer Rexford G. Tugwell called him, seemed to stand above the political battles, to preside over his administration rather than to be actively involved in it. Especially at first, before the death of Senator Taft in the summer of 1953, he approached Congress with great deference. Eisenhower seemed to desire a less active role than Roosevelt and Truman, to be more respectful of the separation of powers, and to prefer working quietly behind the scene. Yet his concept of the presidency was expansive, especially in foreign affairs, and he saw it as an office of vital moral leadership. Disliking controversy, he stressed persuasion, patience, moderation, and flexibility. He also relied heavily on a carefully organized staff and departmental system. Sherman Adams, a former governor of New Hampshire, became the "assistant to the president." His task was to direct a staff in serving as a clearinghouse on policy.

While Adams shielded Eisenhower from many troublesome details and, as a trusted assistant, supervised important governmental functions in the White House, the members of the cabinet also assumed larger roles in the operation of the executive branch. The most prominent cabinet official was Secretary of State John Foster Dulles. The second most influential department head was Secretary of the Treasury George M. Humphrey, an Ohio industrialist and financier. "In cabinet meetings I always wait for George Humphrey to speak," Eisenhower once said, because "I know . . . he will say just what I am thinking." Another businessman, Charles E. Wilson, president of the General Motors Corporation, was appointed secretary of defense. Ezra Taft Benson of Utah, a farm marketing specialist and an apostle of the Mormon Church, became secretary of agriculture. The other departments were also directed by businessmen or Republican politicians, except for the Department of Labor, which was headed by Martin P. Durkin, a Democrat, a Catholic, and the president of the United Association of Journeyman Plumbers and Steamfitters. According to one pundit, the new cabinet contained "eight millionaires and a plumber." Eisenhower had, in fact, surrounded himself with business executives, financiers, and corporate lawyers.

Once in office, Eisenhower adopted a distinct style of leadership. He also revealed considerable skill in the arena of domestic politics. He went to great lengths to conceal his political motivations, since he believed that a president who was viewed largely in terms of his prowess as the nation's highest political executive would lose public support by appearing to neglect his role as chief of state. Thus his was what the political scientist Fred Greenstein has called "the hidden-hand presidency." Although he was an active practitioner of "the controversial politics of leadership," Eisenhower presented himself as a "guileless folk hero," leaving what Greenstein describes as "a public impression that he was not a political strategist, but rather a head of state who was above politics."

Increasing federal intervention, Eisenhower had warned before his nomination, would turn "the American dream into an American nightmare." He saw the business community as a major source of responsible leadership. Determined to reverse the growth of big government, he sought a "middle way" in which business would voluntarily make concessions and governmental interference could be kept to a minimum.

He intended to balance the federal budget and remove as many economic controls as possible. The thirty-fourth president also hoped to heal the sharp division in the Republican Party, curb its strong isolationist tendencies, and modernize it in certain other respects. At a more fundamental level he wanted to promote social harmony, stability, and consensus among Americans.

THE EISENHOWER POLICIES

Dwight Eisenhower's concept of a limited role for the federal government in the economic life of the nation, a concept he labeled "dynamic conservatism," was quickly put into effect by the new administration. The president and his advisers cut back on the recommended expenditures in the Truman budget for foreign aid and military equipment. Some 200,000 civilian workers were removed from the federal payroll during Eisenhower's first term. The administration ended most of the Korean War controls over rents, wages, and prices. Eisenhower and Congress allowed the Reconstruction Finance Corporation to expire in 1953, and Washington made efforts to sell or close down government establishments that competed with private enterprise. The new federal plan also included the formation of commissions and orders to wipe out duplication, increase efficiency, and reduce expenditures throughout the government service.

The economic conservatism of the administration was manifested in other ways as well. Presidential appointments soon weakened several of the independent regulatory commissions. The new chairman of the Federal Trade Commission had spent his entire career defending corporate clients before the FTC. Secretary of Commerce Sinclair E. Weeks, a Massachusetts manufacturer, had scarcely taken office before he fired Dr. Allen V. Astin as head of the Bureau of Standards for not being mindful of the "business point of view." The furor that resulted caused Weeks to restore Astin to his position. When a measure was introduced in Congress in the spring of 1955 to have the government provide Dr. Jonas Salk's polio vaccine free to American children, Secretary of Health, Education, and Welfare Oveta Culp Hobby strongly opposed it on the ground that it would lead to "socialized medicine" by the "back door." Eisenhower himself took a firm stand against so-called socialized medicine proposals, and he spoke out against medical insurance amendments to Social Security bills.

Republican candidates had promised in 1952, as in earlier campaigns, to undo the "excesses" of the Roosevelt and Truman administrations: to balance the budget, reduce federal spending, cut taxes, check inflation, and restore an "unregulated" economy. Nevertheless, Eisenhower's proposed budget for fiscal year 1953–54 contained a deficit of $5.5 billion (a considerable improvement over the $9.9 billion projected by the Truman administration). This so shocked Senator Taft, when he learned of it in a conference with the president, that the senator exclaimed with great emotion, "You're taking us down the same road Truman traveled." The administration finally managed, with the ending of the Korean War, to pare the deficit down to $3.1 billion. But the next fiscal year ended with a deficit in excess of $4 billion, and Eisenhower was able to avoid deficits in only three of his eight years in office. By 1956 the administration's non-defense expenditures were higher than those under Truman, and Eisenhower's proposed budget of $71.8 billion for fiscal 1957–58 set a peacetime record. The expenditures for national defense, foreign aid, and social welfare along with such annual outlays as farm subsidies constituted a major portion of the budget and could not easily be reduced. When the economy experienced trouble, as it did in 1954 and 1958, it seemed wise to resort to the fiscal remedies provided by the New Deal and the Fair Deal.

The dimensions of Eisenhower's "dynamic conservatism" were fully revealed in the administration's proposals in the areas of natural resources and the production of electrical power. An early indication of Eisenhower's approach came in the disposition of tidelands oil—the rich offshore oil deposits claimed by California and the gulf states. President Truman had vetoed a measure in 1952 designed to turn these rights over to the claimant states, and the Supreme Court, in 1947 and 1950, had decided that the federal government had "paramount rights" to the offshore lands. Eisenhower pledged his support to the states during the campaign of 1952, and as president he promoted the adoption of the Submerged Lands Act of May 1953. This law invalidated earlier arrangements and granted the states title to the coastal lands within their "historic" boundaries.

Eisenhower regarded federal control of electrical power as a menace to private enterprise, a danger to local autonomy, and "a threat deadly to our liberties." He wanted to replace "exclusive dependence on Federal bureaucracy" with "a partnership of state and local communities, private citizens, and the Federal Government, all working together." In some cases, the administration conceded, the federal government had to assume major responsibility, as in river development projects. Thus Eisenhower agreed to large federal expenditures for the construction of hydroelectric, irrigation, and other water-supply facilities on the upper Colorado River. He also supported the St. Lawrence Seaway, signing a bill in 1954 that created a self-financed public corporation to finance, construct, and develop the American portion of the long waterway connecting the Atlantic Ocean and the Great Lakes.

In many other cases the Eisenhower administration worked hard to curtail federal involvement in stream development and power projects. The president cut the budget of several federal power projects and abandoned certain undertakings already approved by Congress. The administration strongly opposed a Democratic plan, carried over from the Truman period, for the federal construction of a high multipurpose dam and hydroelectric plant in Hell's Canyon along the Snake River. Instead, Eisenhower and Secretary of the Interior Douglas McKay endorsed the proposed construction of three smaller dams by private concerns, and the Federal Power Commission eventually granted the Idaho Power Company a license for this purpose. Republicans were then able to beat back a movement in Congress to authorize the building of the Brownlee Dam by the federal government. Eisenhower also won some concessions for his partnership approach in the Atomic Energy Act of 1954, which authorized the operation of new atomic energy plants by private companies.

Although the president referred to the Tennessee Valley Authority (TVA) as an example of "creeping socialism," he did not attack the agency directly. Opposing the TVA's request for funds to build a new steam-generating plant to serve the power needs of the Memphis area, Eisenhower and his advisers sponsored a proposal for the private construction of a steam-generating plant in West Memphis, Arkansas, which would contract with the Atomic Energy Commission (AEC) to feed its power into the TVA system, thus enabling the Authority to meet its obligations to the AEC and serve the needs of Memphis. The new plant would be built and operated by a syndicate headed by Edgar H. Dixon of Middle South Utilities, Inc., and Eugene A. Yates of the Southern Company. Despite the opposition of the TVA board of directors and many political leaders in the Tennessee Valley, the AEC, following Eisenhower's wishes, signed a long-term contract with the Dixon-Yates combine in October 1954. The terms were exceedingly generous to the private utilities.

Eisenhower accepted the necessity for some social welfare programs, and like Truman he had difficulty in securing congressional approval of his social and economic proposals, modest as they were. His successes in the domestic arena owed a good deal to Democratic support, and in some ways the Republican president got along better with opposition members of Congress than with members of his own party. A series of amendments broadened the Social Security system, including an act in 1954 that extended the system's coverage to include millions of workers and self-employed people. The minimum wage was raised in 1956 from seventy-five cents to $1 an hour. The Refugee Relief Act of 1953 provided for the admission to the United States of more than 200,000 refugees and displaced persons. The administration continued the liberal trade policies begun during the New Deal. It supported the Federal Aid Highway Act of 1956, under which a 41,000-mile interstate highway system was launched, largely at federal expense. Eisenhower also endorsed a modest proposal for federal aid to the states for public education. Despite its business orientation and its conservative rhetoric, the Eisenhower administration adopted many of the policies of its opposition; it supported the welfare state that had developed by mid-century and used federal authority to manage the economy.

THE CLIMAX OF McCARTHYISM

Many observers assumed that the election of a Republican president would cause Joseph McCarthy and other vociferous anti-Communists to lose influence and fade from the headlines. But McCarthyism did not disappear. The administration was zealous in its own search for subversives in government, broadening the definition of "security risk" to include behavior quite unrelated to disloyalty. Almost 3,000 such "security risks" were dismissed from government positions in 1953 and

1954, although none of them were charged with subversion or brought to trial in a court of law. The most publicized security case was that of J. Robert Oppenheimer, who had played a major role in the development of the atomic bomb during World War II. President Eisenhower, following the initiative of Chairman Lewis L. Strauss of the Atomic Energy Commission, directed officials in late 1953 to place "a blank wall between Oppenheimer and all Government secrets." The FBI had prepared a report that detailed the scientist's prewar associations with Communists, and the president acted against him because of alleged "fundamental defects in his character." (Oppenheimer was exonerated several years later.)

It was soon apparent that the administration's security program and anti-Communist activities did not satisfy Joe McCarthy. Senator Taft had hoped, in organizing the upper house in the Republican-controlled Eighty-third Congress, to sidetrack McCarthy by giving the chairmanship of the Senate Internal Security Committee to the colorless William E. Jenner. McCarthy was made chairman of the Senate Government Operations Committee, and he also assumed the chairmanship of that committee's Permanent Subcommittee on Investigations. The Wisconsin senator quickly asserted the subcommittee's claims to at least a share of the jurisdiction over the campaign against communism in government. He loudly objected to Eisenhower's appointment of Charles E. Bohlen as ambassador to the Soviet Union, charging that Bohlen, a career diplomat who had been at the Yalta conference, was "Acheson's architect of disaster." In March 1953 McCarthy announced that he had "negotiated" an agreement with Greek ship owners to stop all trade with mainland China and North Korea. McCarthy's subcommittee carried out a search for Communists in the Voice of America program, demoralizing the staff of that agency in the process. In the spring of 1953, two of the senator's assistants, chief counsel Roy M. Cohn and "consultant" G. David Schine (the latter was conscripted into the army as a private in November of that year), made a whirlwind trip through Western Europe searching for "subversive" literature in U.S. Information Agency libraries. The trip was widely covered by the press—and widely ridiculed by McCarthy detractors. The State Department also issued a new directive banning from American information activities all "books, music, paint-

ings, and the like . . . of any Communists, fellow travelers, et cetera."
Throughout 1953 and the first part of 1954, McCarthy made one wild
charge after another, dramatically announced numerous "disclosures"
of Communist infiltration, and conducted a series of widely publicized investigations.

Eisenhower refused to be drawn into a direct confrontation with
McCarthy, and the administration seemed to go out of its way to please
him. Thus R. W. Scott McLeod, a McCarthyite, was made security officer for the State Department, and Secretary Dulles allowed McCarthy
a strong voice in the department's personnel policy. Eisenhower was privately contemptuous of McCarthy, but he was quoted as saying, "I will
not get in the gutter with that guy." In any case, Eisenhower thought
the best way to deal with McCarthy was to ignore him. This was not
always possible, and on occasion, as in the book-burning controversy
that erupted in the summer of 1953 in the wake of McCarthy's attacks
on the overseas information program, the president spoke out against
McCarthyism. He did so reluctantly and gingerly, however, and his administration appeared to vacillate between appeasing and opposing the
Red-hunting senator.

The McCarthy committee's investigation of alleged subversion
among scientists working for the Army Signal Corps center at Fort
Monmouth, New Jersey, led the senator, in February 1954, to launch
a direct attack upon the army. A New York dentist named Irving
Peress, who had been inducted into military service in 1952, subsequently refused to sign an army loyalty certificate. When called before
the McCarthy committee, he had invoked the Fifth Amendment. The
army had then released Peress, giving him an honorable discharge.
McCarthy was incensed. He brought General Ralph W. Zwicker before his committee to explain what had happened. Conceding that the
army had mishandled the case, Zwicker promised to see that it did
not happen again. But under orders from his superiors, the general
would not reveal the names of those persons who had processed Peress's release. McCarthy proceeded to browbeat and humiliate Zwicker,
accusing him of being "ignorant," of "shielding Communist conspirators," and of being "a disgrace to the uniform." Secretary of the Army
Robert T. Stevens, under strong pressure from the Pentagon, defended
Zwicker and ordered him and other officers not to testify further before the McCarthy committee.

Senator McCarthy (*R-WI*) and Army Counsel Joseph Welch square off during the Army-McCarthy hearings. *Appleton Library.*

When a meeting between Stevens and McCarthy resulted in a "memorandum of agreement" between the two, it was widely regarded as an administration surrender to the high-flying senator. But McCarthy had finally overreached himself. On March 11, 1954, the administration counterattacked. The army charged that McCarthy and Cohn had persistently and flagrantly sought preferential treatment for David Schine after his induction into the armed forces. The senator from Wisconsin met this challenge by making forty-six charges against the army. To investigate these charges and countercharges, the Permanent Subcommittee on Investigations voted to make its own inquest, with Senator Karl Mundt temporarily replacing McCarthy as chairman.

The committee began its inquiry on April 22, and for the next five weeks its proceedings were closely followed by a nationwide television audience. McCarthy himself was the center of the hearings, bullying and haranguing Secretary Stevens for thirteen days. McCarthy constantly interrupted witnesses, made insinuating comments and veiled threats, and shouted "point of order, Mr. Chairman." Some members of the committee, such as Senator Stuart Symington of Missouri, stood up to him, and Joseph N. Welch, the counsel for the army, was more than a match for the Wisconsin senator in most of their verbal encounters. The hearings revealed McCarthy to millions of Americans as uncouth, brutal, unscrupulous, and contemptuous of decent men and women. Technically, neither McCarthy nor the army won in the committee hearings, but in reality the senator lost because the inquiry contributed greatly to his own self-destruction. A Gallup poll revealed, at the end of the hearings, that McCarthy's standing had dropped to an approval rating of 35 percent, while that of the opposition to him had risen to 49 percent. He had become a liability to the Republican Party.

Finally, the Senate bestirred itself to deal with McCarthy. On June 11, 1954, Ralph Flanders, an elderly Republican from Vermont, introduced Senate Resolution 261, calling for McCarthy's removal from the chairmanship of the Committee on Government Operations and its Permanent Subcommittee on Investigations. Flanders later changed the resolution to one of censure. A struggle over the resolution followed, but eventually the senators agreed to have the matter considered by a select committee of six members headed by Arthur V. Watkins, a respected Republican from Utah.

The Watkins committee considered five general categories of charges against McCarthy. The Wisconsin senator testified at length in his own behalf. In September the committee adopted a unanimous report recommending that McCarthy be censured on two counts. The Senate slowly moved to consider the censure report in the fall of 1954, and after a good deal of debate and maneuvering the first vote was taken on December 1. All efforts to head off censure by McCarthy's defenders were defeated, and on March 2, 1955, the upper house voted by a margin of 67 to 22 to condemn McCarthy on two counts: for contempt and abuse of the Subcommittee on Privileges and Elections in 1952, and for contempt and abuse of the Senate and its select committee in 1954. McCarthy's decline thereafter was rapid. Long before he died in May 1957, at the age of forty-nine, he had become just another member of the Senate, a man of some lingering notoriety but no longer a figure of any real consequence.

CHANGE AND CONTINUITY IN NATIONAL POLITICS

By the middle of 1955 Eisenhower could afford to be optimistic about the progress and prospects of his administration. The new Democratic Congress had proved surprisingly cooperative, the economy was once more booming, and the president had apparently achieved notable success at the summit conference held in Geneva during the summer. But the administration's optimism was suddenly dispelled on September 24, 1955, when Ike suffered a heart attack while vacationing in Colorado. The nation held its breath as his doctors, including the eminent Boston cardiologist Paul Dudley White, attended him at the Fitzsimons Army Hospital in Denver. Press secretary James C. Hagerty kept the news media fully informed of the president's medical condition during the next several weeks. There were no complications, and in mid-November Eisenhower was moved to his Gettysburg farm, where he assumed an increasing portion of his normal executive duties. During earlier weeks Vice President Nixon had presided over meetings of the cabinet, and the efficient White House staff had continued to function smoothly.

Although Eisenhower had not, prior to his illness, indicated whether he would run for a second term, he came under mounting pressure to do so as his convalescence progressed. The president was cautious, however, postponing a final decision and talking often about his desire to retire to a quieter life back at Gettysburg. Meanwhile, his message to Congress in January 1956 hardly sounded like that of a leader contemplating early retirement; it was a comprehensive and generally progressive set of recommendations for the building of "an ever-stronger, ever-better America." In mid-February 1956, Eisenhower's doctors reported, after a thorough examination of the president, that in view of his "good recovery" he would be able to "carry on an active life for another five to ten years." Two weeks later Eisenhower announced, in a nationwide television address, that he would accept renomination. The chief executive's decision was influenced by his doubt that the Republican Party could replace him with a winning candidate in 1956 and his determination to prevent the Democrats from regaining the White House.

Eisenhower's re-nomination was now only a formality to be completed by the party's national convention, which would be held in August 1956. But before that meeting there was another moment of shock and dismay involving the president's health. He underwent a serious operation on June 9 for ileitis (an intestinal obstruction), but his recovery was rapid, and any uncertainty about his ability to campaign in 1956 was soon removed. He was quickly re-nominated when the Republican delegates convened in San Francisco. Richard Nixon was re-nominated for vice president, although Eisenhower had been somewhat slow in endorsing him for the position. A "stop Nixon" movement launched on

July 25 by Harold E. Stassen, Eisenhower's adviser on disarmament, suffered an ignominious collapse.

In the meantime, the Democrats had held their convention in Chicago early in August, following a long and hard-fought struggle between Adlai Stevenson and Estes Kefauver for a nomination that appeared, for a time following Eisenhower's heart attack, to be worth a good deal more than it had in 1952. The Tennessee senator, employing a folksy campaign style and prodigious energy, made a fast start early in the year by winning the New Hampshire and Minnesota primaries. Stevenson also conducted a strenuous campaign, attracting broad support from party regulars and capturing important Democratic primaries in Oregon, Florida, and California. Stevenson's lead was so great by summer that Kefauver withdrew on July 16, endorsing the former Illinois governor for the nomination. This left Governor W. Averell Harriman of New York as Stevenson's only challenger, and despite former President Truman's last-minute endorsement of Harriman, Stevenson was easily nominated on the first ballot at the convention in Chicago. In a surprising move, Stevenson asked the delegates themselves to select the party's vice-presidential nominee. A spirited contest resulted between Senator Kefauver and Senator John F. Kennedy of Massachusetts, with the Tennessean winning a narrow victory on the second ballot.

The presidential campaign of 1956 was a dull and uninspiring affair. Democratic speakers found it difficult to combat Republican boasts of having brought peace, prosperity, and unity at home. The Republican Party, Eisenhower asserted in his acceptance speech, "is again the rallying point for Americans of all callings, ages, races and incomes," and the millions of "I Like Ike" buttons seemed to bear him out. Unlike 1952, Eisenhower spoke mainly in lofty terms—"leave the yelling to the opposition," he advised.

Eisenhower won by a landslide. His plurality was more than 9 million votes (out of 62 million cast), and he received 457 electoral votes to Stevenson's 73. The Democratic ticket carried only seven states—Missouri and six southern states. Democratic support among black voters dropped to 61 percent and among Catholics to 51 percent. Eisenhower did well everywhere, even in the South, and he captured such Democratic strongholds as Chicago and Jersey City. Yet Eisenhower's victory was an anomalous one. The Democrats, however, won Congress—49 to 47 in the Senate and 234 to 201 in the House—making Eisenhower the first president since Zachary Taylor in 1849 to begin a term with both houses of Congress in the hands of the opposing party. Republican congressional fortunes declined even further in the midterm elections of 1958. Eisenhower still held the public's affection, but talk of a "lack of leadership" was heard more often as his second administration unfolded. New problems and perplexities had begun to confront Ike in his second term.

President Eisenhower dominated the national political scene in the 1950s. He shattered the Democratic majority in presidential elections. He appealed to the new white-collar elements, the residents of the mushrooming suburbs, and the growing number of independent voters. He was able to exploit the great economic and social changes taking place in the southern states, whose political solidarity his candidacy disrupted in 1952 and 1956. Nevertheless, Eisenhower proved unable to transfer his own popularity to other Republican candidates; that is, he was unable to create a new majority coalition to replace the one he had defeated. The New Deal party system persisted through his presidency. Although Eisenhower did a good deal to unify his party and went some distance in transforming it in the field of foreign policy, he faced a formidable obstacle in the Republican right wing. Eisenhower's own political ideas—his belief in free enterprise and rugged individualism, balanced budgets, and governmental noninterference—had led him to the Republican Party, but the GOP was heavily freighted with reactionary and frustrated elements bent on overcoming Democratic control through politics of provincialism and revenge.

SECOND TERM: PROBLEMS AND PORTENTS

The second Eisenhower term was far more troubled and in some ways less successful. A series of controversies over administration budget requests, national defense, welfare policies, and school desegregation, in addition to new international crises, marked Ike's final years in the White House. The Eisenhower equilibrium was upset. The economy went into a severe recession in the latter part of 1957 and continued weak during most of 1958. A long steel strike in the summer and fall of 1959 helped disrupt the recovery that began late in 1958. Eisenhower's principal advisers changed in his second term: Humphrey and Wilson left the cabinet in 1957, Chief of Staff Sherman Adams resigned in September 1958, and Dulles had to retire because of illness in the spring of 1959. The president experienced another serious illness himself when he suffered a small stroke on November 25, 1957. Although he was pronounced "completely recovered" on March 1, 1958, his leadership appeared to become less effective thereafter. In the late 1950s, as pressure mounted for greater federal involvement in such areas as education, public works, and African American rights, Eisenhower's domestic policies seemed increasingly inadequate.

One of the issues that came to the fore early in Eisenhower's second administration was the enforcement of the federal courts' school desegregation orders. The issue was related to the broader struggle for black equal rights in America. The elaborate structure of Jim Crow, an odd mixture of legal and extralegal discrimination, remained intact throughout the South, and African Americans in all parts of the country were still the daily victims of social prejudice and discriminatory treatment in employment, housing, and education. Yet what would become an organized civil rights movement was beginning to take shape. African Americans enthusiastically, heroically, and patriotically aided the war effort, both domestically and in the military. As the irony of fighting to "preserve democracy" abroad while still being treated as second-class citizens at home became too glaring for African Americans to ignore, black leaders urged their people to conceive of a "Double V" campaign, meaning that their genuine commitment to victory in the war would lead to victory at home—an end to racial discrimination. The hoped-for victory at home was far from realized at war's end. While this disheartened African Americans, it galvanized like nothing before it the resolve of those who would lead the climactic post–World War II civil rights movement. Meanwhile, the ideological conflict between the United States and the Communist powers caused U.S. policymakers to become more sensitive to the status of African Americans. At the same time, the emergence of new nations from colonialism in Asia and Africa, under the direction of nonwhite leaders, had a profound influence on blacks in the United States.

A dramatic starting point of black protest in the 1950s was the simple act of a forty-two-year-old African American seamstress, activist, and advisor to the National Association for the Advancement of Colored People (NAACP) Youth Council in Montgomery, Alabama: her name was Rosa Parks. Mrs. Parks on December 1, 1955, decided that she would not surrender her bus seat to a white person, as the segregation system required. She was promptly arrested. The response of the black community could scarcely have been predicted. Under the leadership of the Montgomery Improvement Association, the city's African Americans rallied overwhelmingly to support a crippling boycott of the local bus company. For 381 days, the African American community of Mobile maintained the boycott, which ended in an impressive victory for blacks after the federal courts invalidated Alabama's segregation laws. The Montgomery bus boycott was a portent of things to come. Its church meetings, singing of old religious hymns, frequent reference to American ideals, nonviolent tactics, and black unity and discipline would characterize the "movement" during the years ahead. The leader of the Montgomery Improvement Association was an eloquent young Baptist minister named Martin Luther King, Jr.

Meanwhile, the Supreme Court had become the main instrument for reform in race relations, and its decisions sparked the equal rights movement in the 1950s. A series of cases initiated by the NAACP culminated in the historic decision of *Brown* v. *Board of Education of Topeka* on May 17, 1954, which overturned the approval of segregation in public schools as enunciated in 1896 in *Plessy* v. *Ferguson*. Speaking for a unanimous court, Chief Justice Earl Warren declared that "in the field of public education the doctrine of 'separate but equal' has no place."

Resistance to the court's decision soon developed in the southern states. The opposition movement was strongest in the eight South Atlantic and Gulf Coast states—from Virginia to Louisiana—where advocates of white supremacy formed groups such as the White Citizens' Council to defend segregation, and school desegregation became an absorbing issue in southern politics. Beginning in the lower South, state legislatures passed dozens of laws designed to frustrate the enforcement of desegregation and maintain segregated schools. Additionally, the tactic of closing public schools and then reopening them as private ones took place, particularly in Virginia. A striking indication of the South's mounting political defiance came in March 1956, when 101 of the 128 congressmen from the ex-Confederate states issued a

Elizabeth Eckford being taunted by whites as she tries to enter the Little Rock Central High School, September 4, 1957. *Courtesy UPI/Corbis-Bettmann.*

"Southern Manifesto" denouncing the *Brown* decision and pledging to resist its implementation.

Then, in September 1957, Governor Orval E. Faubus of Arkansas dramatically and theatrically confronted President Eisenhower with a constitutional crisis by ordering the state National Guard to prevent nine black students from attending Central High School in Little Rock. After a federal court decreed the removal of the National Guardsmen and angry demonstrators made it impossible for the black children, who became known as the "Little Rock Nine," to attend the school, Eisenhower ordered federal troops sent into Little Rock to enforce the court's order. "Mob rule," the president said when he dispatched the troops to Little Rock, "cannot be allowed to override the decisions of our courts." The entire nation watched the drama unfold on television as the nine black high school students, escorted by paratroopers from the famed 101st Airborne Division, endured jeers from the phalanxes of angry white protestors who lined the walkways. While this one instance of forced desegration was a step forward and away from Jim Crow society, Eisenhower had done little to encourage compliance with the federal courts' desegregation decrees or to help make Americans sensitive to their legal and moral implications. He considered the *Brown* ruling a mistake and seemed to feel that action in this field by the courts or Congress would only create discord and slow progress. In civil rights he preferred to act administratively, with as little publicity as possible.

The Eisenhower administration was unwilling, for philosophical and partisan reasons, to move beyond symbolism to an open confrontation with racial inequality in areas like basic human services, employment, and housing. Eisenhower did approve the barring of racial discrimination in the armed forces, federal hiring, and the public services of the District of Columbia. And he lent his support to the modest civil rights legislation of 1957 and 1960, which created a Civil Rights Commission and sought to prevent interference with the right to vote. But the president would not publicly endorse the *Brown* decision, opposed authorizing the attorney general to bring school desegregation suits, and made little effort to use the Justice Department to investigate southern white interference with black voting.

The record of the Eighty-fifth Congress (1957–1958) was one of moderate achievement—a compromise between the "mildly conservative" president and the "mildly liberal" congressional leadership of Texas Democrats Lyndon B. Johnson in the Senate and Sam Rayburn in the House. Several issues relating to national defense received attention during the second session of this Congress. The president worked hard and successfully in 1958 to secure the passage of a military reorganization bill, and Congress established a civilian-controlled National Aeronautics and Space Administration (NASA). The Soviet Union's launching in October 1957 of *Sputnik I,* a manmade satellite that orbited the earth, no doubt had encouraged the creation of NASA. Although the Eisenhower administration gave greater priority to the development of new, complex defense systems than to the development of space technology, a succession of space probes was carried out following the launching of the first successful American satellite, *Explorer I,* from Cape Canaveral, Florida, on January 31, 1958.

The administration's major accomplishment in the field of education in 1958 was the National Defense Education Act, which included a provision for $295 million in low-interest loans to college students, special inducements for those who would agree to enter elementary or secondary school teaching after having earned their degrees, and grants for the establishment of facilities in languages, mathematics, and the sciences. The second session also brought passage of the Alaskan statehood bill; emergency housing and highway construction legislation to help combat the recession; the Transportation Act of 1958, designed to resuscitate the failing railroads; a low-support farm bill with few controls and generally in line with Eisenhower's recommendations; and an unprecedented four-year extension of the chief executive's power to negotiate reciprocal trade agreements. A $280-million area redevelopment bill providing loans for new industries in economically depressed regions was vetoed by the president, who wanted a measure requiring more local responsibility.

Eisenhower seemed to become more active in seeking the realization of his objectives during his last two years in office. Following the Democratic congressional victory of 1958, he set himself to prevent the large appropriations for domestic programs urged by liberal Democrats. He made greater use of the veto and, employing press conferences and public appeals, tried to dramatize the issue of "lavish spending." Thus he was able, with the powerful assistance of the conservative coalition in Congress, to frustrate such Democratic proposals as a comprehensive program of aid for school construction and teachers' salaries, a higher minimum wage, and increased medical care for the aged under Social Security. But liberals soon discovered a new issue on which to base their demands for more extensive social welfare legislation: the need for more rapid growth in the national economy. Meanwhile, there was increasing evidence of partisan divisions between the executive and legislative branches. A $750-million pay increase for federal employees was passed over the president's veto, and the Democrats, anticipating success in the approaching elections, refused to approve a measure creating a large number of new, badly needed federal judgeships.

The Eisenhower administration was identified with the enactment of some significant legislation in the Eighty-sixth Congress (1959–60). Perhaps the best example on the domestic side was the relatively conservative revision of the Taft-Hartley Act completed in 1959. Hearings held in 1957 by a select Senate committee had revealed widespread racketeering and corruption in the International Brotherhood of Teamsters and other labor unions. In 1958 the Senate passed a mild anticorruption bill sponsored by Senator John F. Kennedy, but it died in the House of Representatives. During the closing days of the 1959 session, Congress approved a stronger measure known as the Landrum-Griffin Act. The law contained a number of anticorruption features, and it increased the Taft-Hartley Act's limits on boycotts and picketing and guaranteed a secret ballot in union elections. In another act of 1959, Congress established the Labor Pension Reporting Service to compel unions to publish an accounting of the pension and welfare funds under their control.

STRATEGIES OF CONTAINMENT
IN THE EISENHOWER YEARS

The major theme in world affairs during the 1950s continued to be the Cold War and the wide-ranging efforts of the Soviet Union and the United States to counter each other's moves and win the support of other nations. Although the Americans maintained a decided superiority over the Russians in nuclear striking power, the two nations had become locked in a nuclear arms race. By this point the two superpowers had nuclear weapons that were vastly more powerful than the Hiroshima-type bombs of 1945 and had established, as one contemporary aptly put it, a "nuclear balance of terror."

Many Americans expected President Eisenhower to adopt a bold new approach that would turn back the advances of international communism, and they were encouraged in their expectations by the rhetoric of administration leaders. Eisenhower had run on a platform that attacked "the negative, futile and immoral policy of containment," and Secretary of State Dulles had denounced the Truman-Acheson approach as "treadmill policies which, at best, might perhaps keep us in the same place until we drop exhausted." Eisenhower thought the nation needed "a new, positive foreign policy," one that would recapture the initiative from the Communist aggressors, "make the free world secure," and rest on a form of military strength that did not weaken the economy. But the new president had hardly moved into the Oval Office before his administration encountered a series of difficult international problems: the persistence of the East-West conflict over Germany; belligerent confrontation with the People's Republic of China (PRC); Communist expansion in Indonesia and Indochina; and a Soviet peace offensive that culminated in a high-level conference in 1955. In the meantime, Eisenhower's international leadership was challenged at home by the virulence of McCarthyism and a constitutional proposal that threatened his conduct of foreign policy.

Rhetoric and Reality in Foreign Affairs

John Foster Dulles was a dominant figure in the conduct of the Eisenhower diplomacy. A prominent Presbyterian layman, Dulles seemed to have a sense of predestination about his role as secretary of state; his family background, long experience in foreign affairs, abundant energy, and supreme confidence surely encouraged such a feeling. While Dulles shared Eisenhower's broad internationalist outlook, he was even more passionately committed to the reform of U.S. foreign policy than was his chief. He believed that the nation needed to reassert its traditional moral mission and identify itself with the universal longing for peace. Eisenhower and Dulles were sensitive to the deep division in the Republican Party over international issues, and their support of the "reform" movement in foreign policy was no doubt intended in part as a means of reassuring the Taft wing. It also reflected the administration's need to find ways of differentiating its policy objectives from those of the Democrats. Yet Eisenhower and Dulles soon found their freedom of action circumscribed by a variety of stubborn realities, and in practice they continued most of the containment policies of their predecessors.

The Eisenhower administration proclaimed a "new look" in its management of national defense and foreign affairs, and for a time there was an appearance of novel approaches and techniques. One example was the doctrine of "liberation," which was to apply to the "captive peoples" behind the Iron Curtain. Another was the effort to revamp national defense policy in order to get what Secretary of Defense Charles Wilson called a "bigger bang for the buck"—cutting expenditures for conventional warfare and placing greater reliance on air power and nuclear weapons. In resisting localized Communist aggression, the United States would employ as a first line of defense American-equipped and trained indigenous troops. The new defense strategy rested heavily on nuclear deterrence, on what Dulles described as "the deterrent of massive retaliatory power." According to the secretary, it would "depend primarily upon a great capacity to retaliate, instantly, by means and at places of our own choosing." The "new look" also featured the art of "brinkmanship." In an interview published in *Life* magazine on January 16, 1956, Dulles spoke of his approach to foreign affairs:

> The ability to get to the verge of war without getting into the war is the necessary art. If you cannot master it, you inevitably get into wars. If you try to run away from it, if you are scared to go to the brink, you are lost. We've had to look it square in the face—on the question of enlarging the Korean War, on the question of getting into the Indo–China war, on the question of Formosa. We walked to the brink and we looked it in the face.

On January 7, 1953, two weeks before Eisenhower entered the White House, Senator John W. Bricker, a Republican from Ohio, presented a constitutional amendment, first introduced in 1951, that would prohibit the negotiation of executive agreements, which did not require the approval of Congress, in place of treaties; render the provisions of treaties conflicting with the Constitution null and void; and require that any treaty, to become effective as internal law in the United States, must have supporting legislation that "would be valid in the absence of a treaty." The Bricker amendment was backed by senators who charged that the executive branch had usurped legislative functions, and it enjoyed powerful support from such organizations as the American Bar Association. Eisenhower and Dulles tried for almost a year to work out a compromise, but this proved impossible, and the president eventually declared that he was "unalterably" opposed to the measure in its existing form. By curtailing executive discretion in the conduct of foreign relations, Eisenhower argued, Bricker's proposal would take away the maneuvering room the president must have in foreign affairs. The amendment was finally defeated on February 26, 1954, but it had come within a single vote of obtaining the necessary two-thirds majority in the Senate.

One aspect of the administration's new design in foreign relations was its plan to make extensive changes in the military establishment. Eisenhower rejected the premise of NSC 68 that the United States could spend up to 20 percent of its gross national product on arms, but he worked hard to reconcile defense needs with budget constraints.

President Eisenhower and Secretary of State Dulles. *National Park Service photo, courtesy Dwight D. Eisenhower Library.*

Defense expenditures were reduced in both fiscal 1954 and 1955, in part as a result of the ending of the Korean War. The ground forces were diminished by one-third between 1953 and 1955, and the size of the army was cut from about 1.5 million in 1953 to 873,000 in 1960. The navy also suffered some reductions in this period.

Eisenhower gave a good deal of time to the task of modernizing the military establishment. The Defense Reorganization Acts of 1953 and 1958 were meant to coordinate and centralize the vast enterprises of the Department of Defense. The administration sought to replace an obsolescent military apparatus with "highly mobile naval, air, and amphibious units" in combat readiness, prepared to strike quickly, and in some cases equipped with tactical atomic weapons. Even so, the new defense policies resulted in reliance on strategic air power and nuclear weapons, for this course seemed to promise maximum destruction at minimum cost. The whole approach was epitomized by the doctrine of "massive retaliation" enunciated by Dulles in January 1954.

The European Focus

Despite the spread of the Cold War to all parts of the globe, the most important theater for American policymakers remained Europe. By 1953 the North Atlantic Treaty Organization (NATO) had provided an integrated command system for Western Europe, and the United States had contributed large stockpiles of weapons and equipment for the alliance's military needs. But NATO's troop strength was far below the projected levels, and the European members of the organization appeared reluctant to undertake large-scale rearmament when the United States was concentrating its energies on the Korean War. Then, in the spring of 1952, France, Italy, the Benelux countries, and West Germany signed treaties for the establishment of the European Defense Community (EDC), which American leaders regarded as a means of rearming Germany and bolstering NATO.

The EDC quickly encountered opposition, especially from the French, who began to have second thoughts about the proposed rearmament of Germany and were disturbed by the specter of foreign control over France's internal affairs. While the French delayed, Secretary Dulles did his best to bring them into line, threatening in late 1953 an "agonizing reappraisal" of American policy in Europe. The problem of strengthening NATO, however, was more fundamental than French recalcitrance. The Soviet peace offensive encouraged a more relaxed atmosphere in Western Europe, while the growing fear of a thermonuclear holocaust simultaneously raised doubts among Europeans about the real benefits of NATO. In August 1954 the French Assembly finally acted, decisively defeating ratification of the EDC.

American leaders were stunned and keenly disappointed. But it was Britain and not the United States that rescued the situation. Prime Minister Anthony Eden took the lead during the following weeks in arranging a compromise that was formally approved in Paris in October 1954. Using the Brussels Pact of 1948, Eden and other Western European leaders created an alliance to be called the Western European Union. The arrangement ended the Allies' military occupation of West Germany except for a small garrison in West Berlin, restored sovereignty to the Federal Republic of Germany, and provided for West Germany's admission to NATO in 1955. The Russian response to these developments was the Warsaw Pact of May 1955, which bound the East European satellites to the USSR in a tight military alliance. In the meantime, other developments were encouraging changes in the relationship between the two superpowers. The end of the war in Korea and a compromise peace in Vietnam in 1954 contributed to a relaxation of international tensions. Following the Soviet Union's explosion of a hydrogen bomb in August 1953, President Eisenhower turned to the question of renewing international efforts to control atomic energy. In an address to the United Nations on December 8, he dramatically proposed that the major scientific nations of the world jointly contribute to a UN pool of nuclear power to be used solely for peaceful purposes. Nothing came of this "atoms for peace" proposal, but it was soon apparent that the American allies in Western Europe, fearing nuclear devastation in case of war between the United States and the Soviet Union, welcomed the prospect of a détente between the rival powers. In mid-May 1955 the Foreign Ministers Conference was finally able, after years of controversy and delay, to agree upon an Austrian peace treaty. The treaty signed in Vienna ended the four-power occupation of Austria and created an independent, neutral state.

Plans for a summit were worked out in the spring of 1955, and the top leaders of the Soviet Union, the United States, Great Britain, and France opened the conference in Geneva on July 18. Eisenhower quickly sounded a note of hope and goodwill by urging a new approach to the problem of German unification, free communication between East and West, peaceful use of atomic power, and some practical contributions to disarmament. The warmth of Eisenhower's personality made a tremendous impact on the conference. At one point he turned to Soviet Premier Nikolai Bulganin and declared, "The United States will never take part in an aggressive war." To which Bulganin responded, "Mr. President, we believe that statement." It was this atmosphere that produced the "spirit of Geneva."

But when it came to more concrete matters, the conference made little or no progress. In the case of Germany, the United States demanded free elections and suggested that a reunited Germany be given the right to join NATO. Russia advocated a general European security pact that would include the withdrawal of all foreign troops from Germany. Neither side would retreat from its basic position. As Walter LaFeber has written, "The United States had successfully armed and tied West Germany to the Western alliance, while at the same time pushing on the Soviets the blame for blocking reunification through free elections." The Americans did present a new disarmament scheme at Geneva—an "open skies" plan calling for the exchange of information on each nation's military facilities and allowing planes to photograph each nation's territory to prevent any possible surprise attack. The Soviet leaders rejected this proposal on the ground that it would infringe Russia's territorial sovereignty.

Still, the early optimism of the Geneva meeting did not disappear completely. Certain developments within the Soviet Union helped sustain the thaw in the Cold War. For one thing, following Josef Stalin's death in March 1953, the new Soviet leaders accelerated their de-Stalinization campaign. At the Twentieth Communist Party Congress, held in Moscow in February 1956, Nikita S. Khrushchev denounced Stalin and his use of terror. Although still critical of capitalist states, he declared that "war is not a fatalistic inevitability." Later developments in 1956, however, provided little comfort to those people who hoped for a Soviet–American rapprochement. In October, after Polish Communists had succeeded in easing the grip of Soviet control, Hungarians staged an uprising against Russian domination. In short order, 200,000 Soviet soldiers and hundreds of tanks swept into Hungary and ruthlessly put down the revolt. Eisenhower could do nothing to help the rebels. Meanwhile, Russian leaders aggressively challenged the Western nations in a new Middle East crisis. These events seemed to reveal the illusory nature of the administration's doctrine of "liberation." They also dispelled whatever remained of the "spirit of Geneva." While these ups and downs in the Cold War were taking place in Europe, Eisenhower and Dulles were grappling with a different set of international challenges in East Asia.

Containment in Asia

The Eisenhower administration's East Asian diplomacy was, in considerable part, an inheritance from and a natural outgrowth of the Truman period. This was evident in such policies as the support of Nationalist China (on Taiwan), non-recognition of the People's Republic of

China (mainland China), the strong commitment to the defense of South Korea, and the aid given to the French in Indochina. But the new administration's determination to go beyond the Truman-Acheson policies in Asia was also a corollary of its broader indictment of the Truman administration's handling of foreign affairs and a concession to the extreme nationalist, Asia-oriented right wing of the Republican Party. Thus when Eisenhower announced, soon after entering the White House, that the U.S. Seventh Fleet would "no longer be employed to shield Communist China," he was suggesting that the doctrine of "liberation" might be applicable to the Far East.

President Eisenhower's first diplomatic problem in East Asia was ending the Korean War. In mid-December 1952, after returning from Korea, Eisenhower had warned that unless the war could be brought to an end quickly, the United States might retaliate "under circumstances of our own choosing." During its first months in office, the Eisenhower administration not only "unleashed" Chiang Kai-shek, but also hinted that if the war continued the United States would bomb Chinese bases, blockade the mainland of China, and use tactical atomic weapons. For whatever reason, the Communists indicated their willingness in the early spring of 1953 to resume the Korean truce talks, and on July 27 of that year an armistice was finally signed. It provided for a cease-fire, a demilitarized zone that coincided with the military line and generally followed the 38th parallel, and a possible conference within three months to consider the withdrawal of all foreign forces from the peninsula and "the peaceful settlement of the Korean question." The Korean War was over at last, but a permanent settlement failed to emerge in the aftermath of the armistice. Instead, Korea was divided, like Germany, into Communist and non-Communist states.

By the early months of 1954, the focus of the American containment policy in East Asia had shifted to Indochina, where French colonialism had encountered mounting resistance following World War II. A strong nationalist movement had developed in Vietnam, led by Ho Chi Minh, a longtime Communist and professional revolutionary. War in Vietnam had dragged on for years, with the resistance forces employing Mao Tse-tung's tactics of peasant guerrilla warfare. The Chinese Communists, having overcome Chiang's forces, recognized Ho's Vietminh early in 1950 and began to send it arms. The United States, still shocked over the "loss" of China and increasingly obsessed with a resolve to contain the Communists in the Far East, began to provide the French in Indochina with military and economic supplies in the spring of 1950. By 1952 the Americans were bearing about a third of the cost of the French war on the Vietminh (Ho's Communist force). The war went badly for the French, however, and by 1954 they were on the verge of military collapse. Thousands of their best troops were surrounded in a military garrison at Dien Bien Phu, an ill-advised defensive site near the Laotian and Chinese borders. On March 20, 1954, the French chief of staff arrived in Washington to plead for American intervention.

Eisenhower and his advisers were fully aware of the implications of a French defeat in the Indochinese war. As the president warned early in April, "You have a row of dominoes set up, you knock over the first one, and what will happen to the last one is that it will go over very quickly. So you have the beginning of a disintegration that would have the most profound influence." Dulles was convinced that the United States could not permit the loss of Vietnam to the Communists, and he joined Admiral Arthur W. Radford, chairman of the Joint Chiefs of Staff, in urging Congress to consider passing a resolution authorizing an air strike to save the French at Dien Bien Phu. Other leaders suggested a more cautious approach. Public opinion also proved to be critical of such a venture, and British leaders, in spite of American appeals, would not endorse any kind of joint support of the French in Indochina. In the end Eisenhower decided against intervention. Although the doctrine of massive retaliation seemed to call for decisive action, the United States followed a course the *London Economist* described as "vociferous inaction."

Dien Bien Phu fell on May 7, and the French, facing the prospect of further military losses in other parts of Indochina and domestic disenchantment with the war, gave up the struggle and accepted a compromise, which was signed at Geneva in July 1954. The Geneva Agreements provided for a cease-fire in Vietnam, recognized the independence of Laos and Cambodia, and divided Vietnam along the 17th parallel, with the Communists under Ho Chi Minh in control of the north and the French puppet emperor Bao Dai and his new prime minister, Ngo Dinh Diem, dominant in the south. One provision stipulated that internationally supervised elections to determine the reunification of Vietnam be held in 1956. Although the major powers, including the PRC, worked out the Geneva Accords, the United States was not a formal party to the arrangement. But when South Vietnam refused to take part in the elections called for at Geneva, the United States supported the Saigon-based regime.

The United States moved to strengthen its East Asian position in other ways. Secretary Dulles took the lead in creating the Southeast Asia Collective Defense Treaty, which was signed in Manila on September 8, 1954, by representatives of the United States, Great Britain, France, Australia, New Zealand, Pakistan, Thailand, and the Philippines. The Southeast Asia Treaty Organization (SEATO) would, if any of its members were threatened with armed aggression, "meet in order to agree on the measures which should be taken for common defense." In a separate protocol the SEATO allies later agreed to defend the independence of South Vietnam, Laos, and Cambodia. Dulles praised SEATO as a vital part of the American defense system in the Far East—an Asian counterpart of NATO—but the two alliances were not all that analogous. SEATO had no armed forces of its own and possessed no permanent command structure or standing military organization. In addition, the major neutral nations of the region refused to join the alliance.

Another area in which the U.S. policy of containment in East Asia collided with the aims of mainland China was Taiwan. The question of the "two Chinas" persisted from the beginning to the end of the Eisenhower administration, and the malignant character of the Chinese Communists became an *idée fixe* in American thought. The immediate area of confrontation between the United States and the People's Republic of China was not Taiwan and the nearby Pescadores Islands, however, but the small offshore islands of Quemoy, Matsu, and the Tachens, which were also occupied by Nationalist forces. In September 1954 the Chinese Communists began to bombard Quemoy and Matsu, apparently as a prelude to assaulting them. Near the end of 1954 the United States signed a mutual defense treaty with the Nationalist government, pledging itself to defend Taiwan and the Pescadores and station American land, naval, and air forces "in and about" the area. The Communists soon began to move into the Tachen Islands, causing the evacuation of the Nationalist forces with U.S. assistance. Eisenhower resisted a drastic response, but he went to Congress on January 24, 1955, to request authority for the use of American forces in protecting the Nationalists. Congress responded swiftly by passing a joint resolution on January 28, authorizing the president to use whatever means he considered appropriate to defend Taiwan and the Pescadores, as well as "such related positions and territories" as he found necessary. A war scare followed, but the crisis gradually eased when the attackers relented in their bombardment of the islands.

In August 1958 PRC forces resumed their heavy shelling of the offshore islands, and the United States was faced with another crisis in the Far East. Secretary Dulles declared that the joint congressional resolution of 1955 might apply to Quemoy and Matsu, and he implied that the United States would defend the islands if they were invaded. Meanwhile, a powerful American striking force was assembled in the Taiwan area, and U.S. naval units escorted supply ships to the beleaguered Nationalist outposts. It was a time of enormous tension, when many observers fearfully anticipated the outbreak of Sino-American hostilities. Eisenhower combined firmness with restraint, and the administration hinted that the offshore islands might be demilitarized and even abandoned by Chiang if the PRC attacks were ended. The bombardment was reduced, and the acute crisis slowly passed, though the status of Quemoy and Matsu remained uncertain through the remainder of the Eisenhower presidency.

The Eisenhower administration had decided soon after the signing of the Geneva Accords in the summer of 1954 to make South Vietnam a bulwark against Communist expansion in the region. Between 1955 and 1961, the United States provided Vietnam with more than a billion dollars in economic and military assistance. Early in 1956 the U.S. Military Assistance and Advisory Group (MAAG) assumed from the French full responsibility for training the (South) Vietnamese army. Eisenhower and Dulles were undertaking an experiment in nation-building and the creation of a proving ground for democracy in East Asia. The task, however, proved extremely difficult. Although American leaders suggested the desirability of introducing certain domestic reforms in South Vietnam, Prime Minister Diem followed his own course. He eliminated Bao Dai in 1955 and made himself president. He refused to permit the general elections scheduled for 1956, and his government became increasingly repressive. Diem's Communist opponents occasionally resorted to terrorism, but North Vietnam did not publicly announce a war of liberation against the south until 1960. At the end of that year Communists, still in South Vietnam, established the National Liberation Front of South Vietnam (NLF) and within a short time men and supplies were being sent from North Vietnam to the Vietcong, the name of the NLF's military force.

The American position in East Asia was little if any better at the end of the decade than it had been in 1953. To be sure, the Eisenhower administration had ended the Korean War, and a settlement of sorts had been brought to that troubled peninsula. But the focus of the containment policy had shifted to Indochina, where, in spite of large amounts of U.S. aid, conditions were perilous and prospects for non-Communist states were uncertain. The Chinese Nationalists still survived on Taiwan—thanks to American power—but the illusions surrounding their reconquest of the mainland had long since disappeared. While SEATO gave the United States a defensive alliance in Asia, it was little more than a paper organization. At the same time, Americans were increasingly identified as imperialists in the minds of anti-colonialists in the Far East.

The Middle East, Latin America, and the Third World

During the years after 1953 the Cold War was altered in several respects, but none was more dramatic than the growing involvement of the underdeveloped countries of the world. By the mid-1950s the Cold War had moved from Europe and the Far East to the Middle East, a vast and strategic area embracing some twelve countries and stretching from the Dardanelles to the Caspian Sea and from Egypt to the Gulf of Oman. Long dominated by Western colonialism, this "bridge of three continents" contained the richest oil resources in the world along with masses of desperately poor people, a feudal society, and backward and unstable governments. An upsurge of nationalism and independence movements had swept over the Middle East following World War II, and by mid-century the populations of the various states were infused with an ardent Arab nationalism, a strong hatred of colonialism, and a fierce hostility toward the Jewish state of Israel.

Egypt's emergence as the leader of the Arab nations and the eager champion of Arab nationalism complicated Western diplomacy in the Middle East. A revolution led by young, nationalistic army officers had deposed the inefficient and corrupt regime of King Farouk in 1953 and resulted in the establishment of an Egyptian republic. General Gamal Abdel Nasser, who emerged as head of the revolution, became the premier of the new republic. Nasser set about improving the internal conditions of his country and uniting the Arab nations. In October 1954 he completed an agreement with Great Britain providing for the withdrawal of British troops from the Suez Canal within twenty months. Nasser secured economic aid from the United States and the Soviet Union, signed an arms agreement with Czechoslovakia, and formed a close military alliance with Syria, Saudi Arabia, and Yemen. He proposed the construction of a huge dam at Aswan, on the upper Nile River, to increase the nation's arable land and encourage its industrialization and economic growth.

In 1955 American leaders indicated their willingness to provide Nasser with a substantial part of the funds needed to construct the Aswan Dam. They also moved to create the equivalent of NATO and SEATO in the Middle East, although the United States would not formally be a member of this alliance. In February 1955 Secretary Dulles was instrumental in bringing Turkey and Iraq into a defensive alliance, which was soon broadened to include Britain, Iran, and Pakistan. In effect, the NATO line had been extended from Turkey to India. This Baghdad Pact was very upsetting to Nasser, who viewed it as an effort to split the Muslim world and as a means of enhancing the influence of Iraq as a rival of Egypt for Arab leadership in the Middle East.

In the meantime, the recurrent truce violations and border clashes between Egypt and Israel resulted in a large-scale Israeli raid on the Egyptian territory of Gaza in February 1955. The success of this attack spurred Nasser's determination to strengthen Egypt's armed forces, and after the signing of the Baghdad Pact, he found Russian leaders quite willing to supply him with arms. The Egyptian premier also intimated that the Soviet Union might finance the building of the Aswan Dam on more favorable terms than the Western powers. In the spring of 1956, Egypt withdrew its diplomatic recognition of Nationalist China and extended recognition to the People's Republic of China.

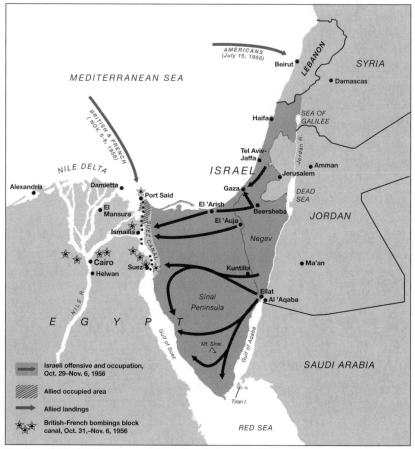

The Suez Crisis, 1956

These actions no doubt influenced Secretary Dulles' abrupt announcement, in July 1956, that the United States had decided not to advance funds for the Aswan Dam.

Nasser responded to this rebuff within a week by nationalizing the Suez Canal on July 26, 1956. The British and French protested Nasser's seizure of the canal, but a compromise resolution in the United Nations that would have satisfied the European allies was blocked in the Security Council by a Russian veto. Eisenhower and Dulles stated publicly that the United States would not be a party to armed intervention in settling the Middle Eastern crisis. Nevertheless, there was a small war in the fall of 1956. Israel, provoked by the repeated conflicts along its border with Egypt, convinced of the desirability of a preventive strike against the Egyptians, and probably secretly encouraged by the British and French, suddenly attacked Egypt. The Israeli forces drove swiftly across the Sinai Peninsula, scattering a much larger Egyptian army and approaching the canal within a few days. Meanwhile, the British and French, after issuing an ultimatum to the two sides to stop the fighting on the ground that the conflict was endangering the operation of the canal, moved against the Egyptians themselves on October 31. Egyptian forces managed to obstruct the canal with sunken ships, however, and Syrian saboteurs succeeded in cutting British oil pipelines from Iraq, thus making the Western nations dependent on the United States for petroleum.

The Anglo-French intervention came as a surprise to the Eisenhower administration, which was preoccupied with the approaching national election. Angry and embarrassed over their allies' action, the Americans strongly endorsed the cease-fire resolution overwhelmingly passed by the UN General Assembly on November 2. Three days later the UN agreed to create an international emergency force to "secure and supervise the cessation of hostilities." The speedy arrival of the UN emergency force permitted the invaders to withdraw with a modicum of dignity, but no one could doubt the extent of the British and French setback. Their prestige and influence in the region had been dealt a devastating blow. Nor was that all. The Suez crisis had separated and almost shattered the Western alliance. To add to the irony, it was the Soviet Union rather than the United States that received most of the credit among Arab nations for the peaceful settlement of the conflict.

Eisenhower and Dulles sought some means, in the wake of the Suez crisis, of countering the Soviet Union's growing influence and Nasser's continuing adventurism in the Middle East. On January 5, 1957, the president asked Congress, in a move reminiscent of his approach to the Quemoy-Matsu crisis of 1954–55, for authority to deal with the threat of Communist infiltration in the region. Two months later Congress passed a joint resolution approving the extension of economic and military aid to nations in the area "requesting assistance against armed aggression from any country controlled by international communism." The success of this Eisenhower Doctrine in halting Soviet penetration of the region was limited, but it was used as a pretext for U.S. intervention in Middle Eastern affairs during the years that followed.

When King Hussein of Jordan was confronted by an anti-Western revolt in the spring of 1957, Eisenhower sent the Sixth Fleet to the eastern Mediterranean and provided him with $20 million in American aid. Hussein's government managed to survive the crisis. More severe crises developed as Nasser's influence and intrigue spread through the Middle East. In the late spring of 1958, the pro-Western government of Lebanon came under heavy pressure from Nasser supporters, and when Lebanese leaders were unable to obtain help from the United Nations and the Arab League, they turned to the United States. Eisenhower was reluctant to intervene with force, fearing the Russian and Arab reaction, but when the friendly government of Iraq was overturned by a Nasserite revolt in mid-July, he decided to act. He repositioned the Sixth Fleet in the eastern Mediterranean and dispatched more than 14,000 troops to Lebanon. At the same time, the British moved about 3,000 troops into Jordan in response to King Hussein's plea for support.

Despite the protests and warnings from Egypt and the Soviet Union, the situation in the Middle East gradually improved. The United States recognized the new regime in Iraq, thus easing Arab fears considerably. Dag Hammerskjöld, secretary-general of the United Nations, helped work out arrangements that led to the withdrawal of American and British troops from Lebanon and Jordan in November 1958. Prospects for long-range stability, however, were not bright. Nasser remained powerful. The enmity between Arabs and Jews was as bitter as ever. The United States and the Soviet Union were still locked in a Cold War that had come to involve every nation in the Middle East. Unable to come to terms with the forces of Arab nationalism, American leaders resorted to the expediency of wooing reactionary monarchies such as that of Saudi Arabia.

As the Cold War moved into the Middle East in the 1950s, it also began to manifest itself in Latin America. The region was vulnerable to such conflict. In 1953 and 1954 the radical regime of President Jacobo Arbenz Guzmán of Guatemala, encouraged by Communist elements in that country, began to expropriate foreign holdings and promote subversive movements in neighboring states. This threatened to give the Communists their first foothold in the western hemisphere. Secretary Dulles attempted to contain the threat through diplomatic channels, persuading the Tenth Inter-American Conference, meeting in Caracas in March 1954, to condemn "any dominion or control of the political institutions of any American state by the international Communist movement." That did not stop Guatemalan leaders, who obtained a shipment of military equipment from Czechoslovakia in May and proclaimed martial law early in June, claiming that a foreign plot had been devised to overturn the government. In fact, the United States did provide support to an opposition force in Honduras, and the Central Intelligence Agency (CIA) engineered a successful coup by Guatemalan exiles. Arbenz appealed to the United Nations, where Russia sparked a bitter debate and a call for an end to hostilities was approved by the Security Council. But the council deferred action, Arbenz soon fled to Czechoslovakia, and a strong anti-Communist government came to power in Guatemala.

Evidence of deteriorating U.S.–Latin American relations was dramatically revealed in the spring of 1958 when Vice President Nixon and his wife undertook an eighteen-day goodwill tour of leading South American countries. They were met by radical, populist demonstrators, mobs that went so far as to attack the Nixons' motorcade, throwing rocks, glass bottles, eggs, and fruits and vegetables at the vice president's car. While Richard and Pat Nixon were unharmed, the vice president had to tell his Secret Service agents not to respond to the protesters with any degree of force. Nixon's advice to the young men proved sage, as a handful of agents were no match for thousands of anti-American radicals, who evidently had been organized by Communists and other enemies of "Yankee imperialism." Some changes in American policies had been made by this time, and others were gradually initiated. In 1955 the United States had agreed to a liberalization of its treaty with Panama. Washington promoted regional free-trade agreements in Latin America and backed an international program to stabilize the price of coffee. The United States agreed in the late 1950s to supply almost half the capital for a new $1-billion Inter-American Bank to make development loans. Eisenhower visited South America in 1960. "We are not saints," he said in Santiago, Chile. "We know we make mistakes, but our heart is in the right place."

Near the end of the Eisenhower period, a perplexing situation developed in Cuba. When the repressive regime of Fulgencio Batista was overthrown and a new government headed by Fidel Castro took control on January 1, 1959, public opinion in the United States was highly favorable to the change. It soon became evident, however, that Prime Minister Castro was no ordinary liberal. He undertook an extensive program of agrarian reform and began to confiscate foreign assets, including over $1 billion of American holdings. In February 1960 Castro signed a five-year trade agreement with the Soviet Union, and he soon extended diplomatic recognition to the People's Republic of China. In May the United States ended all economic aid to Cuba, and in July the president, on the recommendation of Congress, virtually ended the importation of Cuban sugar. When the West Indian nation complained of American action to the UN Security Council, Russia's Khrushchev could not refrain from a shrill denunciation of the United States, warning that "Soviet artillerymen can support Cuba with rocket fire" if America attacked the island. In the fall of 1960 the Unites States imposed an embargo on all exports to Cuba except food and medicine and began a naval patrol in the Caribbean to stop any possible invasion of Nicaragua and Guatemala by Castro's forces.

It became apparent in the 1950s that there were three large groups of nations in the world: the Western bloc, the Communist bloc, and a growing number of neutral states. The Bandung Conference of 1955 revealed the increasing importance of the "Third World" of the nonaligned nations. While that conference mounted a vehement attack on colonialism, its most significant action was its formulation of the doctrine of "neutralism," an affirmation that much of Asia and Africa would not ally itself with either side in the Cold War and that its major goal was to liberate the underdeveloped nations of the world from dependence upon the economically advanced powers. In part because of the exigencies of its conflict with the Soviet Union, the United States frequently resisted change in the Third World, thereby provoking the distrust of anti-colonial nationalists. Secretary Dulles was quoted as saying in 1956 that neutrality had "increasingly become an obsolete conception and, except under very exceptional circumstances, it is an immoral and short-sighted conception."

THE HEIGHTENING OF COLD WAR TENSIONS

Following his triumphant re-election in 1956, Dwight Eisenhower began his second term with high expectations and the great approbation of the American people. Emmet John Hughes, one of Eisenhower's assistants in 1953–54, was struck by the president's commanding presence when he visited the White House in August 1956. "His vitality seemed undiminished, the eyes as brightly alert and intense as ever, the excited stride around the office still as brisk and assured. Every gesture, every response, seemed to speak for a man astonishingly strong." As it turned out, the thirty-fourth president's second administration was filled with domestic and international challenges: a constitutional crisis over school desegregation, prosperity giving way to a severe recession, the Soviet Union's apparent superiority in the development of long-range missiles, and a series of controversies over the budget, farm subsidies, foreign aid, and space policy. Criticism of the chief executive increased, and doubts were openly expressed about the effectiveness of his leadership. Thus an administration that began on a note of assurance and optimism was confronted with what seemed to be an endless number of challenges and crises.

The comfortable assumption most Americans held about the U.S. military advantage over the Soviet Union was suddenly upset in the late summer and fall of 1957. The Russians announced in August that they had successfully fired the world's first intercontinental ballistic missile (ICBM). On October 4 they launched the first artificial earth satellite—*Sputnik* ("traveling companion" in Russian), a 184-pound vehicle, propelled into orbit by a powerful booster rocket. A month later they launched *Sputnik II*, six times heavier than *Sputnik I* and carrying aboard a live dog. During the next few years the Russians made other spectacular ventures into space. The Soviet Union also possessed the most powerful army in the world, was developing a navy second only to that of the United States, and had an unexcelled submarine fleet.

News of Russia's sensational accomplishments in the development of long-range missiles and the launching of powerful satellites into space coincided with its diplomatic gains in the Middle East and its growing intransigence in the on-again, off-again disarmament negotiations. *Sputnik* created a crisis of confidence for the American people, and it precipitated a debate on the adequacy of American education, science, space exploration, and national security. The lesson of *Sputnik*, as historian Robert A. Divine has noted, was that the Soviet Union "had won a sweeping propaganda victory by upstaging the United States and placing the first artificial satellite into orbit around the globe."

Echoing the charges of "missile gap," many U.S. military spokespersons and political leaders urged a concentrated effort to overtake the Russians, but the Eisenhower administration did not immediately surrender to the advocates of a large increase in military spending. Nor was the public altogether prepared to undertake yet another forward leap in the arms race. A *New Yorker* cartoon in September 1957, poking fun at a much-publicized Ford Motor Company flop, showed a middle-aged, middle-class woman saying to her husband, "It's a great week for everybody. The Russians have the intercontinental ballistic missile, and we have the Edsel."

Torn between its commitment to economy and the pressure for greater military preparedness, the administration followed a middle course in the years after 1957. Military expenditures for missiles and other new devices were increased, although not as much as many critics wanted. The United States placed its first satellite into orbit early in 1958 and fired its first ICBM in the autumn of that year; by 1960 each branch of the armed forces had designed and put into operation its own missiles. The American nuclear stockpile tripled (from 6,000 to 18,000 weapons) between 1958 and 1960, and by the latter year the United States had fourteen Polaris nuclear submarines, each with sixteen missiles.

The threat of a terrible nuclear conflict haunted the minds of people everywhere. The Joint Congressional Committee on Atomic Energy reported in August 1959 that an attack on this country might kill 50 million people and seriously injure an additional 20 million, while destroying or making uninhabitable half of all the nation's dwellings. By 1958 disarmament talks had begun to focus on the possibility of formulating an agreement to halt the testing of nuclear weapons, a proposal Prime Minister Jawaharlal Nehru of India had urged as early as 1954. Recognizing an opportunity for a propaganda coup, Soviet leaders announced in March 1958 a unilateral suspension of nuclear testing. The United States countered with a proposal for joint technical studies of feasible means to detect violations of such a test ban, and in August, Washington and London suggested a one-year moratorium on testing. Negotiations for a more permanent disarmament settlement were resumed in Geneva at the end of October, but in spite of the hundreds of sessions held during the next two years, no agreement could be reached. Meanwhile,

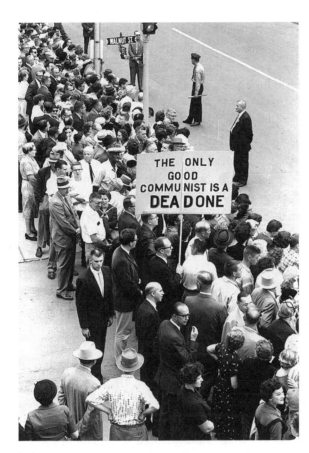

The Anti-Communist Persuasion: Crowds line the streets of Des Moines, Iowa, for a glimpse of the Soviet leader Nikita Khrushchev during his tour of the United States. *Courtesy Library of Congress.*

however, the three nuclear powers voluntarily adhered to the cessation of tests begun in 1958.

Germany continued to be an incendiary issue in East-West relations. The United States had followed the twofold policy of urging the reunification of the two Germanies through free elections and rearming West Germany. The Soviet Union had urged German reunification under various guises but had adamantly opposed free elections, while linking the settlement of the German question to a general European security arrangement, including the withdrawal of American forces. Soviet leaders were especially concerned about the status of West Berlin, which not only provided the Western powers with a ready source of intelligence concerning the Communist world, but also served as an avenue of escape for East Germans, some 3 million of whom had fled to the West since 1945. Furthermore, the contrast between the prosperous and brightly lighted western zones of Berlin and the depressed and drab eastern part of the city served as a constant reminder to Germans and Russians alike of the economic recovery and vitality of West Germany and its allies.

In November 1958 Khrushchev suddenly announced a six-month deadline for a settlement of the West Berlin problem; if an agreement was not reached by May 27, 1959, he threatened to sign a separate peace treaty with East Germany and relinquish to it the control of Berlin. Another nerve-tingling crisis now enveloped the Cold War antagonists. But the Western allies took a firm stand in the face of this Soviet harassment. The Berlin crisis subsided during the early months of 1959, and the Russians began to reveal their interest in another high-level meeting. In September 1959 the ebullient Khrushchev made a two-week tour of the United States that culminated in a visit with President Eisenhower at his Camp David retreat in Maryland. During the meeting the Soviet premier canceled his Berlin ultimatum, while Eisenhower conceded that the troublesome question of West Berlin should be resolved in the near future. Later in the year, Eisenhower and other Western leaders agreed to invite Khrushchev to a top-level conference in May 1960.

A few days before the summit was to convene in Paris, the Soviet Union announced that an American plane had been shot down over Russia on May 1. The United States indicated that the aircraft was a weather plane that had wandered off course. Soviet leaders then revealed that the American plane had been downed more than 1,200 miles inside Russia, the aircraft was a high-flying photoreconnaissance plane, and the pilot, Francis Gary Powers, had conceded the "spy" character of his mission. The CIA had inaugurated these reconnaissance flights over Soviet territory in 1956, employing high-altitude, lightweight planes known as U-2s. Khrushchev bitterly attacked the United States for its "aggressive acts," denounced Eisenhower, demanded an apology for the invasion of Soviet territorial sovereignty, and threatened to destroy those "accomplices" in Europe and Asia that provided bases for the U-2 flights. Acutely embarrassed, Eisenhower then admitted the validity of Khrushchev's accusations; he described the U-2 flights as "a distasteful but vital necessity."

It is clear that Khrushchev used the U-2 incident as a pretext to destroy a meeting that he no longer wanted. He was under pressure in the

Eisenhower and
Khrushchev at Camp
David, September 1959.
*Courtesy U.S. Naval Photo
Center, Washington, D.C.*

Kremlin, and his caustic public statements on the Berlin situation during the weeks before the summit suggested the difficulties that would have attended the Paris negotiations. American prestige did suffer as a result of the incident. Khrushchev announced that Eisenhower's scheduled visit to Russia later in the year must be canceled, and he soon made it evident that no serious negotiations would be undertaken with the United States until the advent of a new presidential administration.

Despite Eisenhower's dedicated search for peace during the last years of his presidency, he found it an elusive goal. He made three goodwill trips between December 1959 and the summer of 1960, the first to India, the Middle East, and Southern Europe; the second to Latin America; and the third to the Far East. "Our basic aspiration," he declared on one of these tours, "is to search out methods by which peace in the world can be assured with justice for everybody." Ironically, the last six months of Eisenhower's tenure were among the most trying of his eight years in the White House: the Paris summit was a fiasco, the long-continued disarmament negotiations in Geneva soon broke down, anti-American demonstrations caused the cancellation of the president's trip to Japan, a new crisis developed in the Congo, and the Russians appeared to have found in Cuba an ally only ninety miles from United States soil.

In a farewell address delivered on the eve of his retirement from the presidency, Dwight Eisenhower warned against the military-industrial complex—against the "conjunction of an immense military establishment and a large arms industry." In view of the swollen defense budgets of the postwar period, the close ties that linked the nation's industrial society and the military, and the immense power concentrated in the Pentagon and the giant corporations that dominated the business of defense procurement, it was a prescient warning. The military-industrial complex included, in addition to military and business leaders, members of Congress eager to secure defense contracts for their districts, universities and new institutions like the Rand Corporation interested in federal research funds, as well as veterans' groups, labor organizations, and cities dependent on defense expenditures. The complex was, in reality, a vast, loosely organized pressure group working for an active foreign policy based on military power.

Accepting the basic assumptions of the Truman administration, Eisenhower and Dulles supported and even extended its Cold War commitments and objectives. By 1955 the United States had about 450 bases in thirty-six countries and was linked by political and military pacts with some twenty counties outside Latin America. Eisenhower's greatest success as president came in dealing with foreign and military affairs. Robert R. Bowie, who directed the State Department Policy Planning Staff during Eisenhower's first term, believes that "the course Eisenhower set assured security while avoiding major conflict in a turbulent decade when both sides were learning to live with nuclear plenty. To a large extent, his strategy established the guidelines for the long haul leading to the ultimate ending of the Cold War." He held down the pace of defense spending, was skeptical of military adventurism, and kept the United States from involvement in another war. He left office as one of the nation's most popular presidents, and in later years a flowering revisionism among biographers and other writers elevated his reputation from one of mediocrity to a standing well above average.

SUGGESTIONS FOR FURTHER READING

For an introduction to the international scene and American foreign policy in the 1950s, readers can turn to Brands, *The Devil We Knew*; LaFeber, *America, Russia, and the Cold War*; Gaddis, *Strategies of Containment*; and Cohen, *America in the Age of Soviet Power*, all mentioned earlier. Volume 2 of Ambrose's biography, *Eisenhower: The President*, contains a detailed and balanced treatment of the thirty-fourth president's foreign policies. Among other good studies are Pach and Richardson, *The Presidency of Dwight D. Eisenhower*, cited before, and Robert A. Divine, *Eisenhower and the Cold War* (1981). Two collections of essays are important: Richard A. Melanson and David Mayers, eds., *Reevaluating Eisenhower: American Foreign Policy in the 1950s* (1987), and Bischof and Ambrose, eds., *Eisenhower: A Centenary Assessment*.

For the contributions of John Foster Dulles, see Townsend Hoopes, *The Devil and John Foster Dulles* (1973), and Richard H. Immerman, ed., *John Foster Dulles and the Diplomacy of the Cold War* (1990). H. W. Brands, Jr., *Cold Warriors: Eisenhower's Generation and American Foreign Policy* (1988), is a revealing study of Dulles and other key figures in the Eisenhower administration. See also Stephen E. Ambrose, *Nixon: The Education of a Politician, 1913–1962* (1987), and Douglas Brinkley, *Dean Acheson: The Cold War Years, 1953–71* (1992).

The Eisenhower defense policies are discussed in Richard A. Aliano, *American Defense Policy from Eisenhower to Kennedy* (1975); Douglas Kinnard, *President Eisenhower and Strategy Management* (1977); and E. Bruce Geelhoed, *Charles E. Wilson and Controversy at the Pentagon, 1953 to 1957* (1979). Seymour Melman, *Pentagon Capitalism: The Political Economy of War* (1970), throws light on the military-industrial complex. The role of the CIA during the Eisenhower years is evaluated in Christopher Andrew, *For the President's Eyes Only: Secret Intelligence and the American Presidency from Washington to Bush* (1995).

American involvement in the Middle East following World War II is considered in H. W. Brands, *Into the Labyrinth: The United States and the Middle East, 1945–1993* (1994); Robert W. Stookey, *America and the Arab States: An Uneasy Encounter* (1975); and Peter L. Hahn, *The United States, Great Britain, and Egypt, 1945–1956* (1991). For the Suez crisis, see especially Cole C. Kingseed, *Eisenhower and the Suez Crisis of 1956* (1995); William Roger Louis and Roger Owen, eds., *Suez 1956* (1989); and Donald Neff, *Warriors at Suez: Eisenhower Takes America into the Middle East* (1981).

Among the useful books on U.S. involvement in the Far East during the 1950s are Gordon H. Chang, *Friends and Enemies: The United States, China, and the Soviet Union, 1948–1972* (1990), and Ellen J. Hammer, *The Struggle for Indo-China, 1940–1955* (1966). For the early phases of the struggle over Vietnam, see Andrew J. Rotter, *The Path to Vietnam: Origins of the American Commitment to Southeast Asia* (1987); Robert D. Schulzinger, *A Time for War: The United States and Vietnam,*

1941–1955 (1997); Melanie Billings-Yun, *Decision Against War: Eisenhower and Dien Bien Phu, 1954* (1988); and Robert F. Randle, *Geneva 1954* (1969).

U.S. policy in Latin America is discussed in Stephen G. Rabe, *Eisenhower and Latin America: The Foreign Policy of Anticommunism* (1988). More specialized studies include Richard H. Immerman, *The CIA in Guatemala: The Foreign Policy of Intervention* (1982); Richard E. Welch, Jr., *Response to Revolution: The United States and the Cuban Revolution, 1959–1961* (1985); and Thomas G. Paterson, *Contesting Castro: The United States and the Triumph of the Cuban Revolution* (1994).

Several books are helpful in understanding international problems during Eisenhower's last years in office, among them James L. Richardson, *Germany and the Atlantic Alliance: The Interaction of Strategy and Politics* (1966); Jack M. Schick, *The Berlin Crisis, 1958–1962* (1971); Robert A. Divine, *The Sputnik Challenge* (1993); and Michael R. Beschloss, *Mayday: Eisenhower, Khrushchev and the U-2 Affair* (1986).

The best place to begin a study of the Eisenhower administration is Herbert S. Parmet, *Eisenhower and the American Crusades* (1972), the first scholarly assessment; Chester J. Pach, Jr., and Elmo Richardson, *The Presidency of Dwight D. Eisenhower* (rev. ed., 1991); and Gunter Bischof and Stephen E. Ambrose, eds., *Eisenhower: A Centenary Assessment* (1995). Carl N. Brauer, *Presidential Transitions: Eisenhower Through Reagan* (1986), is also helpful. The second volume of Stephen E. Ambrose's biography, *Eisenhower: The President, 1952–1969* (1984), is of central importance.

For Eisenhower's own views, read his comprehensive but rather bland narrative of events, *The White House Years: Mandate for Change, 1953–1956* (1963), and *The White House Years: Waging Peace, 1956–1961* (1965). The thirty-fourth president's thinking is also revealed in Robert H. Ferrell, ed., *The Eisenhower Diaries* (1981). Among the best personal accounts are Arthur Larson, *Eisenhower: The President Nobody Knew* (1968); Emmet John Hughes, *The Ordeal of Power: A Political Memoir of the Eisenhower Years* (1963); Sherman Adams, *Firsthand Report: The Story of the Eisenhower Administration* (1961); Richard M. Nixon, *Six Crises* (1962); and Milton S. Eisenhower, *The President Is Calling* (1974).

Gary W. Reichard, *The Reaffirmation of Republicanism: Eisenhower and the Eighty-third Congress* (1975), is an impressive study of Eisenhower's relations with his first Congress. For other policies and programs, see Iwan W. Morgan, *Eisenhower versus "the Spenders": The Eisenhower Administration, the Democrats and the Budget, 1953–60* (1990); Willard W. Cochrane and Mary E. Ryan, *American Farm Policy, 1948–1973* (1976); Mark H. Rose, *Interstate: Express Highway Politics, 1939–1989* (1990); David A. Frier, *Conflict of Interest in the Eisenhower Administration* (1969); Elmo Richardson, *Dams, Parks and Politics: Resource Development and Preservation in the Truman-Eisenhower Era* (1973); Barbara Barksdale Clowse, *Brainpower for the Cold War: The Sputnik Crisis and the National Defense Education Act of 1958* (1981); Elizabeth A. Fones-Wolf, *Selling Free Enterprise: The Business Assault on Labor and*

Liberalism, 1945–60 (1995); and R. Alton Lee, *Eisenhower and Landrum-Griffin: A Study in Labor-Management Politics* (1990). James L. Sundquist, *Politics and Policy: The Eisenhower, Kennedy, and Johnson Years* (1968), is valuable for congressional action in the domestic field.

Jeff Broadwater's *Eisenhower & the Anti-Communist Crusade* (1992) throws light on the Eisenhower administration's handling of the Communist issue and McCarthyism. For the climax of McCarthyism and the downfall of its most visible exemplar, see the works cited in chapter 4. Robert F. Burk, *The Eisenhower Administration and Black Civil Rights* (1984), is the best book on that topic. See also E. Frederic Morrow, *Black Man in the White House* (1963); Richard Kluger, *Simple Justice: The History of* Brown v. Board of Education *and Black America's Struggle for Equality* (1976); Taylor Branch, *Parting the Waters: America in the King Years, 1954–63* (1988); and Elizabeth Huckaby, *Crisis at Central High, Little Rock, 1957–58* (1980).

———★———

———— ★ ★ ★ ————

CHAPTER

4

Leading the World: Economic Expansion, Affluence, and Social Change

OST AMERICANS IN THE POSTWAR PERIOD WERE CHEERED
by the reality of good times and a vigorous economy that
heightened their expectations and only occasionally faltered with a downturn in the business cycle. The ascendancy of the U.S.
economy was evident in its remarkable productivity, its structural and
technological changes, the ingenuity of its business practices, and the
profits of its domestic and international commerce. These developments
were accompanied by rapid population growth, the emergence of a new,
buoyant middle class, and the ongoing assimilation of the nation's most
distinctive ethnic groups. In addition, the civil rights movement promised to end discrimination against African Americans. Yet, even with
the new prosperity and the reforms of the 1960s, the United States remained a segmented and unsettled society—in the gap between rich and
poor, the persistence of poverty, the separate lives of inner-city and suburban dwellers, the isolation of many rural and small-town people, and
the white "backlash" against reform measures designed to assist African
Americans and other minorities. Meanwhile, the cultural scene revealed
the influence of an expansive economy, the Cold War, and increasing
reliance on science and technology. Growth, vitality, and a good deal
of innovation characterized such cultural institutions as education and
religion. What had been called the "fine arts" experienced their own sea-

sons of creativity and recognition. Finally, a dynamic and broad-based U.S. popular culture captured the attention of not only Americans but much of the outside world as well.

Emerging from the depression that racked the nation in the pre–World War II years, the United States entered the greatest and most sustained period of prosperity in its history. Although the passage from war to peace proved difficult, the economy did not revert to the hard times of the 1930s. Instead, Americans enjoyed an almost uninterrupted boom that raised production, incomes, and standards of living to heights that would have seemed incredible a short time earlier. Despite several recessions, the gross national product (GNP), in constant dollars, increased more than twice the rate of the population growth. By 1960 the GNP had reached $500 billion, and within little more than another decade it had climbed to the trillion-dollar level. By 1980 it had reached $2.6 trillion.

THE MIRACLE OF PRODUCTION

So expansive was the American economy that the output of goods and services doubled and then redoubled during the twenty-five years after 1945. World War II revivified the nation's industrial and business system, brought a sharp rise in purchasing capacity, created a huge backlog of consumer demand, and made the United States the dominant economic power in the world. Prosperity in the years that followed was also promoted by the growth of population, the vital role government had come to play in the economy, and the increase in production resulting from technological innovations. The federal government's enormous military budgets (they reached $50 billion a year in the early 1960s), foreign aid programs, and far-reaching welfare and entitlement programs constituted profoundly important elements in the national economy. The expenditures of federal, state, and local governments after the mid-1950s made up about one-fifth of all purchases in the private sector, dwarfing those of any other "industry." Federal support for research and development (R&D) bolted ahead in the late 1950s, following *Sputnik*, and by the mid-1960s had reached $15 billion a year—two-thirds of the total national expenditures for R&D. Increasing horsepower per worker, advances in production techniques and mechanical efficiency, and growing reliance on scientific and technological research gave a dynamic impetus to productivity, which increased by 35 percent during the first postwar decade.

Theoretical knowledge provided the foundation for a vast increase in technological and scientific expertise. One manifestation of this "knowledge revolution" was automation, the talisman of the new productivity in the 1950s. Simply put, automation involved the use of machines to operate other machines, more technically, "the introduction of self-regulating devices into the industrial sequence through the feedback principle whereby electronic sensing devices automatically pass information back to earlier parts of the processing machine, correcting for tool wear or other items of control." The result was increased production and output per employee-hour, improved quality and uniformity of products, more efficient management, and greater speed in decision making. Automation not only affected industrial work in factories but also rapidly altered many jobs in office, administrative, and service occupations. The trend toward automation was encouraged by the invention and commercial production of the electronic digital computer. First developed in 1944 and rapidly perfected in the 1950s, the computer was perhaps the most far-reaching and significant of the nation's postwar technological achievements.

Computers were introduced commercially in the 1950s to process data. Their capacity for analysis, synthesis, and memory soon led to other uses. They transformed the manufacturing and processing of many products and revolutionized numerous business operations. By 1970 the number of computers in the United States had increased to an estimated 100,000. The declining price and expanded memory of the newer models combined to put these devices in the hands of millions of individuals and small businesses. More than 6 million personal and home computers were sold in the United States in 1983. By that time, computer technology had begun to affect almost every facet of American life. But its greatest impact occurred in the workplace, where computers were used to design products, control the flow of materials on production lines, and operate robots that painted cars and welded metal. Even more significant, perhaps, was their employment in the service area—the banks, insurers, utilities, and other businesses that made up half of the U.S. economy. Meanwhile, education was being reshaped by the computer, which also became a household tool. People used it, one journalist noted, "to play games, prepare tax returns, monitor investments, write resumes, and trace their family trees." The computer seemed to symbolize a nation moving from an industrial to a scientific society.

Another trend in postwar production was the decline of certain old industries, including coal, textiles, and public transportation. Railroads made some progress after 1945 but faced increasing competition from trucking and a steadily shrinking demand for passenger train service. The American steel industry produced 60 percent of the world's output of crude steel at the end of the war, but its share had dropped to about 25 percent by 1960 as a result of foreign competition, aging plants, and lagging expenditures for research and development in the industry. Other mature industries expanded in the postwar period—sometimes in spectacular fashion, as in the case of automobiles. One of the traditional industries that played an important part in the peacetime prosperity was housing, which usually represented at least 20 percent of all private investment. Construction of all kinds flourished following the war, but residential housing, held back for a decade and a half by depression and war (the value of all U.S. housing was less in 1945 than in 1929), enjoyed a phenomenal advance in the new era. Government support, through G.I. loans, the Federal Housing Administration, and public housing appropriations, augmented the large investments from private sources to create a great housing boom in the 1950s. During some years, over a million new units were constructed.

Automobiles continued to be crucially important to the well-being of the national economy. The industry went through a temporary time of rebuilding immediately after the war, but it soon entered a flush period that surpassed even the 1920s. Factory sales of motor vehicles averaged almost 7 million a year in the 1950s, and by 1956 some 75 million cars and trucks were operating in the United States. Dominated by the "Big Three," General Motors, Ford, and Chrysler, the industry profited from new developments in automobile engineering such as automatic transmissions and power brakes. It also made use of a type of product innovation known as "dynamic obsolescence" or "planned obsolescence," in which annual new models featured increasingly powerful engines and more and better features than "last year's" model. The advent of the small car—the so-called compact—from abroad in the mid-1950s brought a sharp jump in the import of Volkswagens and other foreign makes, so American producers belatedly introduced their own compacts. The auto industry sustained a vast network of enterprises: dealerships, garages, filling stations, a giant interstate highway system, and the manufacture of tires and other accessories, in addition to a multitude of services catering to the motoring public like motels and drive-in restaurants.

Chemicals became one of the most spectacularly successful of the nation's industries after World War II. Chemicals and petrochemicals encompassed many subgroups, having great variety and manifesting divergent trends. Du Pont, Monsanto, Dow, and other large corporations produced a large number of synthetic materials, drugs, and detergents. The industrial chemicals market grew at an annual rate of 10 percent between 1947 and 1960. Profits were enormous. Meanwhile, the petroleum industry remained vitally important. In 1957 Standard Oil of New Jersey ranked as the largest American industrial corporation, and in that year five of the nation's ten biggest industrial firms were in the oil business.

The extraordinary increase in the consumption of electrical power in the United States in the 1940s and 1950s both reflected and contributed to the growth of three giant industries: electrical power utilities and the related electrical machinery and equipment industry, electrical appliances, and electronics. Growing at a rate of 15 percent a year, electronics had become the nation's fifth largest industry by 1960, exceeded only by automobiles, steel, aircraft, and chemicals. One major category of the industry included such products as computers, testing and measuring machinery, industrial control equipment, microwave communications systems, television sets, radios, phonographs, tape recorders, and high-fidelity components. The use of transistors rather than vacuum tubes in radios, television sets, and other electronic devices eliminated time-consuming and bulky hand-wiring. Transistors, which underwent miniaturization spurred by space-vehicle research in the 1960s, contributed to a far-reaching electronics revolution in the 1970s and 1980s.

Other relatively new arrivals as major components of the U.S. economy included the aircraft and air transport industries. Following the war, aircraft became larger and faster, and in the 1950s the first American-built jet-propelled planes—the Boeing 707 and the Douglas DC-8—went into passenger service. The commercial jet age had arrived by the end of the decade. The development and production of ballistic missiles and the emergence of the space industry also had a significant effect on the economy. Among the metal industries, aluminum developed rapidly in the postwar era, as did fuel industries such as natural gas. Nuclear power, an energy source of great potential, developed more slowly. Although the advantages of large, electricity-generating nuclear plants seemed to have been established by the late 1960s, a wide-ranging environmental controversy, stimulated by mounting concern over health and safety risks, checked the progress of nuclear power during the 1970s. In the mid-1980s the industry began to recover, by which time more than eighty nuclear plants were operating in the United States.

By the 1970s, Americans outside the South had begun to view the region in a new and more appreciative light. This changing perspective was related to the South's burgeoning economy, population growth, racial change, and political transformation. Commentators identified the South with the so-called Sunbelt, a dynamic area stretching from the South Atlantic states to Southern California, with a casual and inviting lifestyle, a favorable climate, and conservative politics increasingly inclined toward the Republican Party. One consequence of the Sunbelt South was the growing convergence of South and non-South—in income and material prosperity, the character of their economies, the configuration of their cities, and the nature of the work done by their inhabitants. Although the concept of the Sunbelt was not applicable to many depressed and stagnant parts of the region, a new southern economy had taken shape in the postwar period.

Postwar economic growth was also dramatic in the Pacific Coast states and particularly in California, where a distinctive style of life furnished one of the incentives for westward migration. By 1963 California had surpassed New York as the wealthiest and most populous state in the union; it was now first in both industrial and agricultural production. The Great Lakes and Middle West regions, long the country's agricultural and industrial heartland, basically held their position in the national economy—no mean feat in itself. Some other leading industrial and business centers, such as Pennsylvania, faced serious stagnation in certain industrial lines. Much of New England fought a rearguard action to prevent a lag in economic growth compared with other parts of the country. Large depressed areas such as Appalachia, as well as numerous centers of declining industry and hundreds of depopulated counties and small towns throughout the country, failed to participate directly in the economic expansion.

Agricultural productivity following World War II was even greater than that of industry. A revolution swept over American farms. One feature of this revolution was the rapid mechanization of farm operations: larger tractors and bigger and better machines for preparing the soil, planting, cultivating, and harvesting came into use. The agricultural transformation was also furthered by the genetic research of plant and animal breeders; the use of chemical fertilizers and insecticides, fungicides, and herbicides; and increasing specialization of production and greater emphasis on modern management. The production of huge surpluses and a cost-price squeeze resulting from mounting operating costs and falling agricultural prices during many years encouraged the shift toward highly organized and highly capitalized farm units characterized as "agribusiness." These developments placed great pressure on poor and marginal farmers, and the celebrated family farm seemed headed for extinction.

Changes in Farming: 1950–1983

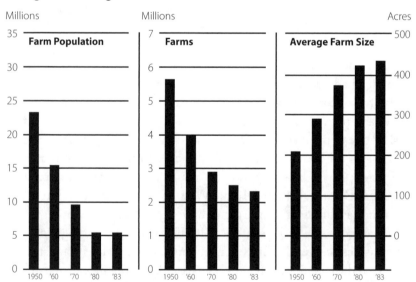

Source: U.S. Bureau of the Census, *Statistical Abstract of the United States, 1985* (Washington, D.C., 1984), p. 628.

COMPETITION AND STRUCTURE

No aspect of the American economy was more prominent than the continuing trend toward large-scale corporate enterprise. The growing concentration of economic power in the United States went far beyond the combination movement at the turn of the twentieth century and the big holding companies and business consolidations of the 1920s. By the 1950s and 1960s giant corporations dominated almost every area of the nation's industrial life, and a few hundred large concerns exerted a preponderant influence on the economy as a whole. In 1960, 600 corporations had annual earnings in excess of $10 million. These 600 companies made up only .5 percent of all U.S. corporations, but they accounted for 53 percent of total corporate income. The emerging super-corporations were national and even international in operation, integrated in their organization, and increasingly diversified in the range of their products and services. While the percentage of the total labor force classified as self-employed dropped from 26 to 11 percent between 1940 and 1960, small business enterprise did not disappear.

Oligopoly, or the dominance of an industry or business by a few large firms, became common. Three automobile companies produced 95 percent of the new cars manufactured in the United States, three aluminum companies produced 90 percent of all the aluminum, and three radio and television networks monopolized the nation's airwaves. Bank deposits increased fourfold between 1940 and 1960, but the number of banks declined by more than a thousand during the two decades, and branch banking became prevalent. In aircraft production in the mid-1950s, ten firms employed 94 percent of all workers in the industry; in petroleum, fifteen firms employed 86 percent; in steel, thirteen corporations hired 85 percent; in office machinery, four concerns employed 71 percent; and in electrical machinery, six companies employed 50 percent of those working in the industry.

Ownership and management in large corporations were now almost completely separate, and a new managerial class directed the great business units. Since most of the new capital for the operation of the super-corporations was generated internally from profits and depreciation accounts, the large concerns no longer were very dependent upon banks, insurance companies, and individual investors. The great corpo-

Harvesting the corn crop on an Iowa farm. This machine cuts and shells six rows of corn at a time. *Courtesy USDA.*

ration was a complex organism, with its own personality, an interest in the well-being of its employees, and other "human attributes." Because most of the giant firms competed in a broad consumers' market, they were increasingly concerned about their "public image" and very attentive to the requirements of public relations. They sought long-run security in a variety of ways, including diversification through product innovation and merger. With the strategy of diversification came a new, decentralized structure in large-scale business.

The trend toward bigness in the U.S. economy was evident in hundreds of mergers every year. Holding-company pyramids came into vogue again, as they had been before the Great Depression, and a new form of consolidated firm known as the conglomerate—a company comprising a group of unrelated operating units—emerged. The goal of the conglomerate was to minimize risks and maximize profits through industrial and commercial diversification, and also, no doubt, to avoid prosecution under the antitrust statutes. Combinations and acquisitions were a widely chosen alternative to the creation of new capacity and additional output, which might be attended by price reductions. Mergers were encouraged as well by the tax deductions afforded profitable acquiring companies. In addition, new technology contributed to the growth of industrial concentration, since the costs of research, retooling, and development in an age of faster-than-sound transport, atomic power, and intercontinental missiles were simply prohibitive for smaller firms. During the years 1950–61, the 500 largest American corporations merged with and absorbed no fewer than 3,404 smaller companies in a wide variety of production and distribution areas. The peak year 1968 witnessed 2,500 mergers in the United States, many of them involving conglomerates.

Big business in the United States tended to become "multinational" as well as diversified. A multinational corporation owned and managed businesses in two or more countries. Companies of this kind flowered in the postwar period, and American petroleum firms led the trend in this direction. Huge international corporations such as General Motors, International Business Machines (IBM), Eastman Kodak, and Exxon launched extensive operations in foreign countries. In the early 1970s the International Telephone and Telegraph Company, to take a striking example, employed over half a million people in ninety-three countries and owned more than 330 subsidiary corporations around the world. Direct foreign investments by U.S. corporations had reached $78 billion by 1970.

Economic concentration clearly led to a decline in traditional competition, increased the incidence of so-called administered prices, and made for instability in the economy. Nevertheless, a good deal of competition continued to exist in several economic sectors, including construction, services, and the distribution of products at the retail level, where a large number of producers or service units prevailed. The removal of international trade barriers also promoted competition and, ironically, concentration in certain industries appeared to shrink as a result of the conglomerate movement.

The record of the federal government's antitrust suits since 1945 reveals its recurrent attempts to halt the trend toward ever-greater economic concentration. In a case against the Aluminum Company of America, decided in 1945, the government secured the dissolution of the corporation. The following year, in a suit against three giant tobacco companies for conspiring to control the price of leaf tobacco and cigarettes, the government won another important decision. Significantly, the Supreme Court in this case declared that monopoly consisted as much in the possession of power to suppress competition and raise prices as in the commission of unlawful acts. The Celler-Kefauver Act of 1950, an amendment to the Clayton Antitrust Act of 1914, seemed to discount monopolistic intent and emphasize a corporation's actual size and market share in lessening competition. The Justice Department, under this authority, initiated a number of successful suits to prevent mergers or acquisitions in the milk, steel, paper, and sugar industries. In one of the most famous court actions of the postwar period, Du Pont was forced in 1957 to divest itself of its 23 percent stock interest in General Motors.

Americans were shocked in 1960 when twenty-nine leading electrical equipment companies and forty-four of their officers were brought to trial for conspiring to rig bids and fix prices on $1.75 billion worth of equipment sold between 1955 and 1959. The government won the case, and the guilty firms were fined a total of $1.9 million. In a series of decisions during the immediate postwar years, the Supreme Court invalidated the notorious basing-point pricing system, which had long been used in such industries as steel and cement to avoid price competition. In other decisions the courts opened patents to more liberal licensing arrangements, prohibited tying contracts, required the sale rather than the mere leasing of equipment, and in general assured greater access to technological knowledge. The Justice Department filed an antitrust suit against AT&T in the mid-1970s that led to the signing of a divestiture agreement early in 1982. The agreement broke the monolithic Bell System into eight independent corporations.

Yet none of the postwar administrations in Washington pursued a determined antitrust policy, and the government's occasional successes in the courts did little to counter the increasing concentration in the economy. The Justice Department's somewhat desultory approach to monopolistic practices reflected the public's ambivalence on the question. Polls suggested that most people were suspicious of businesspeople and thought the government should keep a sharp eye on their important decisions. On the other hand, relatively few Americans seemed concerned by the threat of monopoly and such matters as restraint of trade and administered prices. Critics of the big corporations appeared to be more interested in the social implications of corporate power than disturbed by its economic consequences. Thus William H. Whyte's widely read book, *The Organization Man* (1956), emphasized the malign effects of big-business bureaucracy. He lamented the way in which it smothered individuality and caused the new businessman to abandon the "Protestant ethic" and assume the "social ethic."

There was still much talk in America about "free enterprise," and Washington lawmakers were not unresponsive to the precarious position of many small businesspeople. The House of Representatives set up a Small Business Committee as early as 1941, and the Senate created its own Select Committee on Small Business in 1950. The Small Business Administration was established in the 1950s to absorb the remaining functions of the Reconstruction Finance Corporation and the Small Defense Plants Administration and render aid "to small business concerns, including financial, procurement and technical assistance."

The link between government and business was most conspicuously manifested in the defense and space programs. A community of interest developed between the Pentagon and the giant corporations that received the bulk of the procurement funds, and the defense contractors were frequently able to avoid competition or to secure payment for billion-dollar cost overruns, as in the case of Lockheed's C-5 transport plane. Early in 1969 some 2,072 retired military officers of high rank were employed by one hundred of the major defense contractors. In 1966 a single firm—General Dynamics—received government contracts totaling $2.2 billion. Lockheed, the recipient of $2 billion in defense contracts in 1968, faced bankruptcy in 1971. But Congress came to its aid, authorizing a $250-million loan to rescue the company. One scholar has used the term "military Keynesianism" in referring to the economic effects of U.S. defense expenditures. In 1958, for instance, the military purchased virtually all of the nation's ordnance production, 94 percent of its aircraft, 61 percent of its ships and boats, and 21 percent of its electronic equipment.

PATTERNS OF TRADE AND DISTRIBUTION

The domestic commerce and foreign trade of the United States in the postwar years revealed the extent to which the economy had shifted to a mass-consumption base at home and how dominant the nation had become in the international sphere as the world's industrial and financial center. The domestic market seemed to be almost insatiable, and it was sustained year in and year out by accumulated savings and rising incomes, large annual crops of new babies, a vast network of credit, new technology, huge government expenditures, and enormous advertising outlays. The country's pre-eminent position in the world economy reflected its importance as a market for goods and as a source of goods and savings.

In the new "affluent society," the business world was drawn as if by a magnet to the needs and desires of the almighty consumer. The consumer orientation was evident in the growing importance of the service industries and trades, ranging from fast foods to data processing. By the late 1950s the service industries employed more than half of all U.S. wage-earners, an indication of the nation's shift from an industrial to a "post-industrial" economy. Expenditures for services had risen by 1983 to 50 percent of all consumer spending (the figure for 1950 was 36.9 percent), as compared with 13 percent for durable and 37 percent for nondurable goods.

The consumer market not only spread into all manner of personal services but also came to encompass an endless array of durable goods: television sets, stereos, tape recorders, dishwashers, home freezers, boats, sporting goods, and so on, not to mention new houses and automobiles. New technology and efficient systems of national distribution facilitated this development. By 1958, 96 percent of the nation's families owned refrigerators, 89 percent had washing machines, and 81 percent had television sets. The "youth market" developed rapidly in the 1960s, with a host of its own special products. Americans spent increasing amounts of money for entertainment, recreation, and travel. The commercialization of athletics proceeded apace, as was strikingly illustrated in the rise of televised sports. This far-flung consumer culture spawned a variety of institutions, such as gourmet food stores, art centers, record stores, and pet shops. Franchise businesses—in fast foods, motels, coin-operated laundries, and other enterprises—became widespread, enabling small owners to benefit from mass-purchasing discounts and use of the name and corporate image of a giant national firm.

Novel forms of retail enterprise appeared, such as variety and drug stores, grocery chains, and discount stores, the number of which increased dramatically in the 1960s. One of the most impressive new retail institutions was the supermarket, whose spacious and glistening rows of well-displayed merchandise included virtually any item the customer might fancy. Shopping centers sprang up, usually in suburban areas, and many of them eventually became enclosed, air-conditioned malls. Taking advantage of depreciation allowances, James W. Rouse, a Maryland developer, constructed and operated dozens of shopping centers in the 1960s and 1970s, as well as the new town of Columbia, Maryland. Accompanying the new consumerism was the growth of an "underground economy" involving illegal goods and services like bookmaking, illegal drugs, and prostitution.

Economic prosperity had become dependent in considerable degree upon the creation of what John Kenneth Galbraith called a "synthesis of desire"—the contrived creation of demand—in which advertising and salesmanship played an indispensable part. Advertising in such traditional media as newspapers and periodicals enjoyed a substantial increase, but the most spectacular new medium for this purpose was television. One development in this field was the popularization of depth psychology (that is, the study of the unconscious mind) and the use of motivational research in an effort to discover what would have a favorable effect on the consumer's ego and libido. The public relations expert became a prominent figure in the postwar business world, and every corporation of any size had its own public relations department, where such schemes as "press junkets" and newsworthy activities were conceived. Frederic Wakeman's popular novel, *The Hucksters,* drew public attention to the existence and influence of the advertising business—"Madison Avenue"—and alerted many readers to the cynicism of some advertising methods. Another writer suggested that "the giant corporation, in alliance with the most efficacious advertising medium ever invented, the television screen, had done more than anything else to establish our present habits of consumption and thus to a great extent set the style and pattern of our lives."

There was, however, a sobering side to rampant consumerism. The flourishing enterprise involving consumer goods and services was also stimulated by the ready availability of credit. Total private debts in the United States increased from $73 billion to $196 billion during the 1950s. Consumer credit at the end of 1963 amounted to almost $70 billion, eight or ten times what it had been in 1945. Credit was available for nearly every kind of purchase, and consumer buying was facilitated by checking accounts, credit cards, home mortgages, auto loans, installment buying, and finance companies. The credit card, valid throughout much of the world, became a symbol of U.S. affluence and consumerism. Meanwhile, a whole new industry emerged based on the need to investigate, report, and maintain records on the credit rating of individuals.

While a large number of Americans customarily spent more than they earned, many others were able to save money. Personal savings contributed directly to the striking growth after 1945 of life insurance companies, savings and loan associations, mutual savings banks, investment firms, and credit companies, in addition to commercial banks. A great increase took place in private pension funds—from a total of $11 billion in 1950 to $44 billion in 1959 and $453 billion in 1980. The stock market also reflected the mounting volume of savings and investments in the United States. There were at least 20 million individual stockholders in 1965, in contrast to only 6.5 million in 1952. Some so-called growth stocks, such as IBM, doubled their assets every four or five years beginning in the late 1940s and were traded at 60 to 70 times their earnings in the 1960s.

American leaders worked to reduce international economic barriers during and after the war. They pursued a liberal tariff policy, particularly during the years 1946–50, entering into the General Agreement on Tariffs and Trade (GATT) in 1947–48 and extending the reciprocal trade program every few years. Making use of the GATT formula, America and other major trading nations achieved substantial tariff reductions in six rounds of negotiations between 1948 and 1967. The United States also contributed to the internationalization of foreign lending. It took the lead in 1944 in creating the International Monetary Fund, to avoid drastic fluctuations in exchange rates and competitive currency devaluations following the war, and the International Bank for Reconstruction and Development (the World Bank) to provide long-term investment funds to Europe and less-developed countries.

The United States was a leading global supplier of goods and services, accounting in 1961 for nearly one-fourth of the total world exports of manufactures and almost one-third of the world exports of capital goods. It also exported large amounts of military equipment and many agricultural goods, especially cotton, wheat, tobacco, soybeans, and poultry. The Marshall Plan and other foreign aid programs had obviously been designed with an eye to the support of U.S. economic interests overseas. Foreign trade and investment were likewise promoted through liberal tax policies and such agencies as the International Cooperation Administration, established in 1948. In the mid-1960s foreign markets accounted for 29 percent of IBM's business, 40 percent of Coca Cola's, and 45 percent of that of Caterpillar Tractor. Eleven of the top twelve American industrial corporations each had foreign sales exceeding $1 billion in 1970.

American corporations and citizens in the postwar era made large investments abroad. Those investments totaled more than $12 billion in Europe alone by the mid-1960s. Direct U.S. private investment abroad rose from $11.8 billion in 1950 to $54.6 billion in 1966, with an additional $32 billion in portfolio holdings in the latter year. By 1963, U.S. firms controlled over half of the British automobile industry, 40 percent of the German petroleum industry, and 40 percent of the French telegraph, telephone, electronics, and statistical equipment business. One estimate fixed the gross value of products manufactured by American companies abroad in 1967 at over $100 billion.

Reversing a longtime trend, the United States after 1945 became a major importer of industrial and consumer goods. Americans were increasingly attracted to the efficient, low-priced cars, cameras, stereo equipment, and other products produced by Germany and Japan, national economies that the United States had played a significant role in rebuilding following World War II. The United States had also become more dependent on foreign raw materials such as iron ore, bauxite, and crude oil. In addition to payments for imports, the U.S. government had spent almost $100 billion in economic and military aid to other countries by the late 1960s. Large foreign investments also affected the balance of payments adversely, as did American travel abroad, interest on foreign investments in the United States, foreign transportation, and the like. Accelerating foreign investments in the United States represented another aspect of the international economy. Foreign direct investment in the United States increased from $7.7 billion in 1950 to $20.7 billion in 1974, with the growing presence of foreign multinationals.

THE WORKER'S WORLD

One manifestation of the sustained prosperity in postwar America was the general security enjoyed by most workers. The civilian labor force expanded enormously, from 57.5 million workers in 1946 to 82.7 million in 1970 and 111.5 million in 1983. Labor's share of national income rose appreciably. Average nonagricultural weekly earnings increased from $45.58 in 1947 to almost $120.00 in 1970; real weekly earnings of factory workers went up 50 percent between 1945 and 1970. American workers were better off than ever before, and they increasingly took on a bourgeois appearance. Organized labor, having grown to maturity, assumed a place of great power in the economy and politics.

The composition of the work force changed dramatically in the postwar era. The number of farmers declined steadily and by 1960 made up only 8.7 percent of the nation's workers. At some point in the 1950s the number of persons engaged in goods-producing activities dropped below 50 percent of all civilian labor, and by 1960 the blue-collar percentage of all workers had fallen to 45, as compared to 59 in 1929. The great increase in employment occurred in the ranks of white-collar workers, including business and personal services, finance, distribution, education, and government. An important aspect of this white-collar domination was the accelerated movement of women into positions of gainful employment. Between 1940 and 1960, approximately 9.4 million women joined the labor force as against only 7.5 million men. During the same years the percentage of married women working outside the home doubled, and by 1970 about half of all married women were gainfully employed. In the 1960s two out of every three clerical workers were women (only one out of four had been in 1900). Women began for the first time to enter such fields as finance, public relations, and computer programming. Nevertheless, American women achieved only a token presence in many occupations

Trends in the Labor Force: 1950–1983

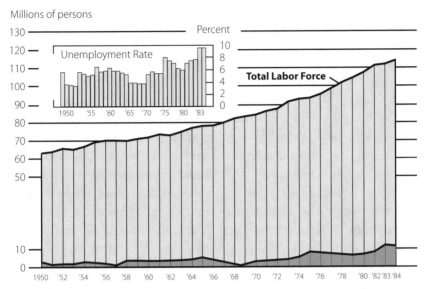

Source: U. S. Bureau of the Census, *Statistical Abstract of the United States, 1985* (Washington, D.C., 1984), p. 386.

and professions, and they continued to suffer discrimination in pay, promotions, and recognition.

Organized labor, moving ahead on the basis of the expansion of the New Deal years and World War II, was stronger than ever before. The number of union members in the United States climbed from 14.7 million in 1945 to 18 million (about 35 percent of total nonagricultural employment) in the mid-1950s. Having secured legal safeguards to ensure its right to organize and bargain collectively, labor enjoyed marked success in gaining its specific economic objectives. "Big labor" had also become a power center in the nation's politics. By mid-century the American Federation of Labor (AFL) and the Congress of Industrial Organizations (CIO) were prepared to cooperate in their efforts to advance labor's interests in Congress, and they took an active part in national political campaigns. After the merger of the two organizations in December 1955, the AFL-CIO established a new Committee on Political Education (COPE), and in later years the giant labor federation became a major component of the Democratic coalition.

Labor-management relations became far less antagonistic and much more orderly than in the 1930s. The 116-day steel strike of 1959 demonstrated how disruptive national strikes in vital industries could be, but in general the interaction between labor and management had become peaceful and stable. Most unions and corporations negotiated mutually acceptable contracts without strikes or with only brief work stoppages. A key factor in labor's cooperative attitude was the fact that workers won so many benefits in the new era. The scope of labor-management negotiations came to include a wide range of "fringe benefits," among which were pension plans, paid vacations and holidays, sickness and hospitalization benefits, and supplementary unemployment insurance. Growing use was made of what was termed the "annual improvement factor," through which a portion of the gains in productivity was transferred to the wage earner each year. Another innovation was the "package settlement" that combined a cost-of-living adjustment with so many cents per hour for fringe benefits, to which was frequently added a separate productivity increment.

Still another example of labor progress was the merger of the AFL and CIO into one great federation. Although the differences and the rivalry between the two national organizations had been acute in the 1930s and 1940s, the situation changed considerably during the first decade after the war. The Taft-Hartley Act of 1947 tended to unify labor against the common enemy, and the old industrial-versus-craft distinction had become less significant as a source of friction. The new AFL-CIO brought the great majority of American unionists into one organization, with George Meany of the AFL as president and the dynamic Walter P. Reuther of the CIO as senior vice president. But it soon became evident that the merger had not solved all problems of jurisdictional rivalry and internal friction. Nor did the AFL-CIO show much initiative in trying to bring in unorganized workers. While union bureaucracy increased and organized labor became more centralized, the movement lost its old militancy. Trade unionism in the 1950s seemed to be hardening, to be growing stodgy and conservative. The labor movement's interest in social reform dwindled. Union strength began to experience a relative decline in the late 1950s, and between 1954 and 1962 actually lost more than a million members. Organized labor's percentage of the nation's nonfarm workers fell to 31 percent in 1960 and to 26 percent in 1970.

Massive structural changes in employment were a significant factor in organized labor's loss of vitality. Technological changes sharply reduced the available jobs in many areas where unions were traditionally strong. Between 1947 and 1961, for example, approximately two-thirds of the jobs in bituminous coal mining disappeared, two-fifths of those in railroading, and almost one-fifth of those in steel, copper, and aluminum production. Containerization, to take another example, revolutionized the loading and unloading of ships, drastically reducing the need for dockside labor (the "longshoremen" that had traditionally run the nation's big ports). Few developments in the postwar period were more disturbing to labor than the rapid progress of automation, which eliminated an estimated 1.5 million blue-collar workers between 1953 and 1959. When new machinery and technological advances forced middle-aged and older workers out of jobs, it was frequently impossible for them to find substitute employment or secure the training and expertise necessary for more sophisticated work. School dropouts and young people from disadvantaged groups were doubly handicapped, for many of them were financially unable or insufficiently motivated to acquire the education and training needed to compete for good jobs.

New jobs in the labor market were increasingly created in such areas as sales, services, and government rather than manufacturing, where some older industries were declining and automation was taking its toll on workers. The white-collar sector was difficult to organize, having a traditional aversion to unionization. Labor organizations faced still other impediments, including powerful opposition from many employers and the hostility of local authorities, the absence of a union tradition in the South and Southwest, where much of the new economic expansion was occurring, and a number of strong political barriers. The Taft-Hartley Act, with its list of "unfair labor practices," reduced union power in several respects. A wave of state right-to-work laws was enacted at about the same time, striking at the union shop and tending to favor nonunion workers. Meanwhile, the anti-Communist struggle proved disruptive for some labor organizations—for the general public had long associated labor organizers with "radicals" or socialists—and the labor movement's high hopes of using political influence to further its objectives were not often realized. The growing fear that labor organizers were "pinko" Communists became political blustering that far exceeded the reality that a very slim minority of subversives had actually influenced American labor unions.

Behind the legislatures and the courts was a public that had become more and more critical of organized labor's "excesses." Many people disliked union encouragement of "featherbedding"—the retention of useless positions. Basically, however, a large number of Americans, perhaps even a majority, had begun to feel that big labor had grown too powerful and irresponsible. This attitude was broadened and reinforced by congressional revelations in the late 1950s. Early in 1957 a special Senate committee under the chairmanship of John L. McClellan of Arkansas launched an extensive investigation of corruption and other "improper activities" in the labor and management fields. The McClellan committee found evidence of widespread bribery, graft, and misuse of union funds and expense accounts by labor leaders, as well as racketeering, corrupt practices, and undemocratic internal politics in many unions. The publicity resulting from this inquest contributed to the passage of the Landrum-Griffin Act of 1959 and spurred the more responsible labor leaders to set about putting their own house in order.

One industry that clearly had a surplus of labor in the postwar era was agriculture, in which production increased as the number of workers declined. The total number of farm workers dropped from 10.3 million in 1946 to 7 million in 1960 and only 3.7 million in 1980. By this time, the federal government's expensive price support system principally aided large commercial farmers. According to the *Economic Report of the President* in 1959, "More than 2.5 million farmers—whose annual sales are less that $2,500 and who produce each year only about 9 percent of our marketed farm products—receive only very small supplements, or none at all, to their incomes from Government expenditures for price support." Unable to expand and modernize their operations, many of the smaller and poorer farmers dropped out of agriculture after 1945. The industrialization of agricultural regions, such as parts of the South, enabled some of these disadvantaged farmers to find a more productive life in the towns and cities. But a goodly number of small farmers held on, continuing to eke out a subsistence livelihood on the land. In 1968 at least one-fifth of the nation's farm families received less than $5,000 a year from farming. Even more discouraging was the tragic plight of about 200,000 migrant farm workers (predominantly Mexican or Mexican American), who provided much of the seasonal labor for the orchards and truck farms of California and other areas specializing in the production of fruits and vegetables. Their low wages, inadequate housing, and social deprivation gave most of them and their families a status little better than peasantry.

The great majority of Americans were more fortunate. They had jobs and, equally important, opportunities for new jobs and occupational advancement. They shared in the postwar prosperity. Millions of men and women, moreover, used their jobs and professions as escalators not only to a higher standard of living but also to a social status within the nation's dynamic middle class.

SOCIAL CHANGE AND THE SOCIAL ORDER

If the nation's population continued to be dynamic and mobile in the postwar era, it also grew at an impressive rate. The total population increased from 139.9 million in 1945 to 151.3 million in 1950, and over the next decade it grew by more than 24 million people, an extraordinary increase of almost 19 percent in that decade. The 200-million mark was reached in 1967. An important factor in this growth was a reversal of the declining birthrate of the prewar period. The birthrate, which stood at 19.4 per thousand in 1940, rose to 23.3 in 1946, and to 25 or above during the years 1951–57. The rate began to drop after 1956. Meanwhile, the death rate declined and some 4 million immigrants entered the United States during the years 1945–60.

The marrying age for men and women dropped at the end of the war, as millions of G.I.s came home and thousands of "Rosie the Riveters" left the war plants. Americans in the 1950s married at an earlier age, had more children, and were less frequently divorced than during and just after the war. The number of newborns began to increase during the war, but the "nesting" phase really began with the end of the conflict. From 1947 to about 1960 the United States enjoyed the greatest "baby boom" in its modern history. In 1947 there were 3.5 million births, a jump of 800,000 in one year, and the number of new babies increased with every change of the calendar, reaching 4.3 million in 1960. The baby boom of the 1940s and 1950s had a telling effect on the age distribution of the American people. Young Americans—those aged fourteen and under—increased from 33.5 million (23 percent of the total population) in 1945 to 56 million (31 percent of the population) in 1960. In 1970 there were twice as many four-teen-year-olds as there were people forty years of age.

Paradoxically, Americans were growing older as well as younger. The death rate declined from 10.6 per thousand in 1945 to 9.6 per thousand in 1960. Almost 10 percent of all Americans were sixty-five or older in 1970, as compared with 8.1 percent in 1950 and only 4.1 percent in 1900. In 1960 for every 100 children under the age of five, there were only eighty-one persons aged sixty-five or over. Better diets made possible by a higher standard of living contributed to this im-provement in the health of the American people. The most important factor, however, was the spectacular progress in medical science. Many dreaded diseases, including diphtheria, typhoid fever, and poliomy-elitis, were virtually eliminated. Tuberculosis and syphilis in the early 1960s caused only one-tenth as many deaths per hundred thousand people as in 1939. Infection-fighting drugs made possible tremendous

The Elderly Population Boom

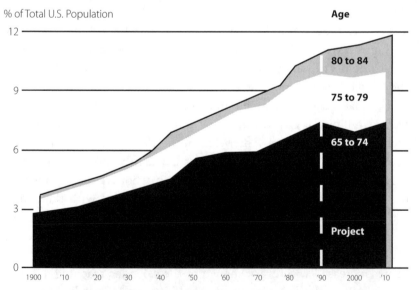

Source: Sam Roberts, *Who We Are: A Portrait of America Based on the Latest U.S. Census* (New York: Times Books, 1994), p. 233.

advances against bacterial and viral disease: penicillin during World War II, streptomycin in 1945, and, in the following years, aureomycin and other antibiotics, the Salk and Sabin Polio vaccines, cortisone, oral antidiabetic drugs, and an array of tranquilizing agents. Impressive gains were also made in the reduction of infant mortality, the perfection of heart surgery, the techniques of organ transplants, and the development of psychiatry. Increasing evidence that death and a number of serious diseases were associated with the heavy use of tobacco encouraged nearly 8 million Americans to quit smoking between 1965 and 1970, years in which the incidence of cigarette smoking declined from 41.6 to 36.7 percent. As people lived longer, however, the ravages of heart disease, cancer, and mental illness increased.

Americans had always been characterized as a people on the move, and in the postwar years the open road beckoned them as never before. In the age of the automobile, the jet airliner, and the expense account, people traveled constantly for business and pleasure. One out of every five Americans changed his or her place of residence each year. Among the more notable aspects of this geographic mobility was the continued movement of people from the farm to the town and city. Over two-fifths of the counties in the United States lost population during the 1960s, and more than two-thirds of all counties experienced a net out-migration during that decade. The most striking feature of this urbanization was the extraordinary growth of the suburbs.

A regional redistribution of population, beginning in the early 1940s, significantly altered the appearance of the national map in the postwar decades. The rapid movement of African Americans out of the South, a phenomenon that began during World War I, accelerated during and after World War II. The number of African Americans living outside the southern states increased from 3 million in 1940 to over 7 million in 1960 and to 12.4 million in 1980. Some regions grew much more rapidly than others after 1945. The population of the Pacific Coast, for example, increased 40.2 percent in the 1950s and that of the Mountain States 35.1 percent in the same decade.

The massive redistribution of population in the period following the war blurred the old regional identities in the United States; yet regionalism persisted and in some respects found new expression as a result of demographic trends and economic development. The growing importance of the service sector of the economy and the emergence of new "footloose" industries in search of locations with climatic, scenic, and recreational advantages contributed to the regional pattern of growth. The rapid influx of people into these areas and the dynamic quality of their economies combined with a distinctive lifestyle to give some of them a peculiar kind of regional character and eventually led to talk of the "Sunbelt." At the same time, the most clearly identified section in modern America—the South—lost some of its homogeneity and distinctiveness.

CITY AND SUBURB

While regionalism became less important as a distinguishing feature of American life, urbanization grew increasingly vital as a powerful force in the nation's social order. By the 1980s three-fourths of all Americans were living in what the Census Bureau referred to as Standard Metropolitan Statistical Areas (SMSAs), that is, cities of 50,000 or more people and the surrounding county or counties economically integrated with such places. The number of SMSAs increased from 168 in 1950 to 284 in 1980, and during that period the "metropolitan" portion of the population rose from 56.1 percent to 74.8 percent. The most spectacular example of metropolitan growth was the supercity, or "megalopolis"— great concentrations or clusters of cities so closely situated as to constitute one enormous urban area. The region from Boston to Washington formed one such "conurbation," and by the 1970s there were ten or twelve others, such as the area stretching from San Francisco and Oakland south to San Jose. It was truly the age of the Metro-American.

Most large American cities after World War II were hard hit by the separation between the central city and the mushrooming suburbs that surrounded them. A mighty exodus from the inner cities to the peripheral areas was soon afoot, with the middle class leading the way. Fourteen of the fifteen U.S. cities with more than a million inhabitants actually lost population during the 1950s. Of 13 million dwelling units erected in nonfarm areas between 1946 and 1958, 85 percent were constructed outside the central cities. The suburban trend reflected the great increase that was simultaneously taking place in social mobility. Much of the young, active, and better-educated population left the old parts of the metropolis for the new suburbia. The development of suburbia involved not only the attraction of open and unsettled country, where badly needed homes could be bought or built at reasonable cost, but also a flight from the "pathology" of the inner city—its crime, disease, and disorder. Still other factors encouraged the growth of the new suburbs: the role of housing and land developers, the mortgage policies of federal agencies like the Federal Housing Administration (FHA), the use of the automobile as a major means of transportation, the construction of new highways and freeways, the mass production of houses, and the decentralization of business and the workplace. California, with its millions of automobiles and sprawling freeways, became the symbol of the postwar suburban culture.

Some of the suburban developments were so-called mushroom communities built seemingly overnight. One of the best-known builders and merchandisers of new homes in bulk was William J. Levitt, whose firm built and sold 17,500 houses in Levittown, Long Island, in the postwar years, using mass production techniques. "No man who owns his own house and lot can be a Communist," Levitt asserted. "He has too much to do." Other Levittowns were constructed in Pennsylvania and New Jersey. The first batch of 16,000 houses on 1,100 streets "cut through acreage where but a few months ago local farmers raised only spinach."

Whatever one thought of the new suburbia, the flight from the inner city continued and the urbanization of the "crabgrass frontier" went on apace. Suburban institutions such as schools, churches, civic organizations, shopping centers, and organized "culture" groups flourished. By 1960 there were 3,840 suburban shopping centers. In time, moreover, some of the defects of unattractive subdivisions were remedied. Trees and shrubs were planted, houses were repaired and enlarged, and even the tract housing usually escaped the fate of becoming new slums. No matter how ordinary their houses or how stultifying their lives may have seemed to outside observers, most suburban dwellers did have more room, better living accommodations, more fresh air, and more independence than they would have had in the old parts of the metropolis. The suburbs varied, and while they tended to be internally homogeneous, they were typically differentiated along social and economic lines—a circumstance that created obstacles to the development of area wide governments and planning authorities. Though ethnic attachments became more tenuous in the suburbs, suburbanization did encourage the growth of a racially segmented society.

The term *suburban* had formerly implied a relationship with the city, but increasingly it represented a distinction from the city. Meanwhile, the decay and disorganization in blighted neighborhoods of the great cities grew progressively worse as the middle class continued to move out, the cost of social services mounted, the tax base shrank, and violent crime became more prevalent. Many of the commercial and cultural institutions also left the central areas. Downtown decline, inner-city deterioration, and exurban development became characteristic of most large population centers in the United States. In the early 1970s cities were reporting the abandonment of houses, despite a housing shortage.

Deconcentration and fragmentation characterized the urban landscape in recent America, as the modern metropolis responded to the pressures of social and ethnic separatism. Suburban growth tended to lock nonwhite and poor people into the urban ghettos and in effect create two cultures. Some big cities became "black" cities. The population of Washington, D.C., was 60 percent African American by the early 1970s, while Newark, Gary, Richmond, and Atlanta also had an African American majority by that time. The terrible conditions in the ghettos and the nonwhite concentrations in the nation's large cities were of central importance in the great riots of the 1960s in Watts (a neighborhood of Los Angeles), Detroit, Newark, and other places. Most metropolitan authorities tried to deal with urban blight by bulldozing the slums and building huge high-rise apartments. Critics like Jane Jacobs, in *The Death and Life of Great American Cities* (1961), and Martin Anderson, in *The Federal Bulldozer* (1964), spoke out against the wholesale destruction of neighborhoods and architectural treasures, called attention to the profit motive that inspired many of the projects, and protested the instrumental role of the federal government in such "urban reform."

Still, notable efforts were made to arrest the decay of the inner city and rejuvenate the metropolis. Urban renewal was usually the focus of these efforts, and the number of urban-renewal projects multiplied in the 1950s. In city after city new skylines arose, comprising office buildings, apartment complexes, public housing, and downtown shopping centers. Some attempts were made to retain and restore old buildings that were still basically sound, although modern, functional but uninspiring buildings often replaced the older, more elegant structures. In an effort to eliminate what had become a perennial traffic problem, most cities constructed huge freeways and hundreds of parking lots. A few metropolises, including San Francisco and Atlanta, laid plans in the 1960s for elaborate new rapid transit systems. There was also evidence of a cultural revival in many American cities. A new breed of mayors appeared, better educated, more sophisticated, and more dedicated to improving the city than the average prewar mayor. In some cases cities made genuine progress. Pittsburgh, for instance, achieved marked success under the leadership of Mayor David Lawrence and an urban reform coalition. The city's central business district was revitalized, and its accomplishments in such activities as housing renewal and pollution control were impressive. Other cities, including Miami, Florida, and Nashville, Tennessee, combined overlapping county and municipal governments by creating new metropolitan systems.

In an environment of "urban catacombs and suburban cellblocks," a few bold spirits dreamed of constructing entirely new cities. A scattering of "new towns," somewhat reminiscent of the Greenbelt towns of the New Deal period, appeared in the 1960s. Perhaps the best-known of these communities was Reston, Virginia, near Washington, D.C. Officially opened in December 1965, Reston attracted attention for its imaginative arrangement of clustered "town houses," situated on plazas that were grouped around an artificial lake and opened on acres of wooded and terraced land. The houses were reached by walkways inaccessible to automobiles, and the shops and other community facilities were all within easy walking distance.

The small town did not entirely disappear from the contemporary scene. The census of 1970 identified almost 21,000 incorporated and unincorporated places, only some 7,000 of which were classified as urban. More than half of the nation's non-metropolitan municipalities grew during each of the first three postwar decades. The President's Commission on Population and the American Future reported in the early 1970s that, when asked where they would prefer to live, respondents indicated a pronounced preference for small towns and rural areas. Nevertheless, the traditional community based on local attachments, a web of personal relationships, and identification with a particular place was declining.

The small town and countryside were steadily being absorbed into a broader national framework.

SOCIAL CLASS AND STATUS

The long period of prosperity that began in the early 1940s enabled most Americans to make steady advances in occupational status, income, and standard of living. Although the benefits of prosperity were widely shared in American society after 1945, a decided concentration of wealth at the top continued, albeit at a slightly reduced level. Studies of stratification in postwar America showed the presence of marked differentials in wealth and income and in social participation, authority and power, education, health, safety, and legal protection. While lacking an established aristocracy, the United States possessed a discernible upper class, set apart not only by income and wealth but also by position, elegant lifestyle, membership in exclusive clubs, patronage of private schools, extensive travel, and, in some older regions, connection with old, locally prominent families.

Organized blue-collar workers made dramatic gains in economic security and well-being in the years following the war, leading some observers to conclude that the American working class was disappearing. This was a myth, compounded from the reality of 1950s prosperity, the exigent tensions of the Cold War, and what British journalist and historian Godfrey Hodgson has called the ideology of "the liberal consensus"—the assumption that Keynesian economics made it possible for the government to guarantee low and declining unemployment without inflation and the belief that the remarkable growth of the economy would benefit all segments of society and promote equality of opportunity. While there was substantial working-class social mobility in this period, the most impressive economic and social leveling was the broadening of the middle class.

A substantial majority of the population had apparently entered the middle class, and by the mid-1950s three out of five Americans were enjoying a "middle-class" standard of living. The steady increase in per-capita income, the extensive changes in the structure of employment, and the great expansion in the number of college graduates all helped swell the ranks of the middle class. Since white-collar employment was widely associated with upward mobility, the numerical superiority of such workers by the late 1950s seemed to mark the triumph of the middle class.

If the middle register of the American social order was expanding, it also appeared to be increasingly homogenized. Americans, particularly the white-collar employee and the suburban dweller, seemed to conform not only in dress, food, and housing, but even in their ideas. Novels such as Sloan Wilson's *The Man in the Gray Flannel Suit* (1956) and sociological studies like C. Wright Mills's *White Collar: The American Middle Classes* (1951) called attention to the loss of individuality, the stuffiness, and the mindless materialism that characterized contemporary middle-class living. The psychologist Erich Fromm, for instance, wrote of the prevalence of individuals with a "marketing orientation" who wanted to avoid having to make choices and eagerly accepted values imposed by the group. In *The Status Seekers* (1959), Vance O. Packard described the incongruity between what he pictured as an increasingly stratified society and millions of Americans struggling to display the visible evidence of the social status they wanted to achieve. Social scientist David Riesman noted how the consumer-oriented economy reinforced the old American tendency to conform to the tastes and attitudes of one's neighbors. Riesman suggested, in *The Lonely Crowd: A Study of the Changing American Character* (1950), that the national character had changed from an "inner-directed" type, responding to a sort of internal gyroscope, to an "other-directed" personality, basically attuned to the mass values of one's neighbors.

The greatest split within the middle class was that between its white-collar and blue-collar elements. Millions of industrial workers had become, by any objective measure, members of the middle class, and many skilled workers now earned more than office workers, schoolteachers, and some people in the service trades. Yet the entry of skilled and semiskilled workers into the economic middle class did not lead to wholesale adoption of middle-class manners and tastes—middle-class values and attitudes, social life, methods of rearing children, gender roles, and the like. Even so, the absence of militant class consciousness on the part of Americans in this period was striking. Part of the explanation, one suspects, is the fact that social mobility demonstrated great vitality in the years following World War II, and economic opportunity brought more comfortable and secure lives for many—though by no means all—Americans. Public-opinion polls showed that at least three-fourths of U.S. adults labeled themselves as middle class. Education continued as a powerful vehicle of social equality. The treatment of minority and ethnic groups improved, and certain vestiges of social inequality, such as high society and the servant class, disappeared. As the nation's consumer culture became ever more pervasive, Americans looked, dressed, and acted more like one another than ever before.

RACE AND ETHNICITY

American society in 1945 was divided along racial and ethnic lines as well as by class distinctions. Racial prejudice and hostility in their harshest forms were directed at African Americans, Hispanics, Asians, and American Indians. Despite regional variations, the color line was a fact of life everywhere in terms of economic subordination, legal insecurity, and social inferiority. The elaborate structure of Jim Crow proscription was intact throughout the South, and African Americans in all parts of the nation were the daily victims of social prejudice and discriminatory treatment in employment, housing, and education. Nevertheless, World War II had a notable effect on the nation's African Americans, giving them new experiences, new skills, and new confidence in themselves. The ideological conflict between the United States and the Communist powers caused U.S. policymakers to become more sensitive to the status of African Americans and other minority groups at home. At the same time, the emergence of new nations from colonialism in Asia and Africa, under the direction of nonwhite leaders, had a profound influence on African Americans in the United States. Things were changing—even in the South. Following the Supreme Court's invalidation of the white primary in 1944, African Americans began to take part in that crucially important part of the electoral process in the one-party South. Another kind of change occurred in New York in 1947 when a talented baseball player named Jackie Robinson joined the Brooklyn Dodgers and thus became the first African American to play in major league baseball.

Sports in post–World War II America began a period of growth that has continued to the present, though in 1945 baseball, football,

Jackie Robinson breaks
the color barrier in
major league baseball.
*Courtesy Library of
Congress.*

and basketball were, unlike professional boxing, segregated sports.
The following year, however, the so-called "color barrier" that prevented African Americans from directly competing with or playing
on the same teams as whites started to erode. In 1946, Kenny Washington and Woody Strode became the first African American NFL
players when the Cleveland Rams moved to Los Angeles to play in
that city's famed Coliseum. Before the war, more than a dozen African American men had played in the NFL, yet from 1933 to 1945,
not one roster included a black athlete. By 1952 all NFL teams, with
the exception of the Washington Redskins under the ownership of
well-known racist George Marshall, had at least one African American player. Marshall eventually acquiesced when President John F.
Kennedy threatened to revoke Marshall's use contract for the publicly held D.C. stadium in 1962.

Baseball moved faster than did football in the development of African American players, and in many ways the baseball players bore the
brunt of the negative reaction spawned by whites associated with desegregation. Rude fans routinely shouted racial epithets at black play-

ers, both in their home stadiums and on the road. Anticipating such social challenges, Brooklyn Dodgers manager Branch Rickey chose Jackie Robinson to become the first African American Dodger (and thereby the first black player in the major leagues) not just because of his remarkable athletic prowess, but also because Rickey believed that Robinson had the fortitude of character needed to endure the jeers and other slights he knew Robinson would face. Within ten years of Robinson's entry into Major League Baseball, more than twenty other African Americans, including Willie Mays, Ernie Banks, and Hank Aaron, had made their way from the Negro Leagues into the big leagues. The year 1950 marked the first season in which African Americans were permitted to play in the NBA, as Earl Lloyd, Nat "Sweetwater" Clifton, and Chuck Cooper broke the color barrier in that popular sport. Just like their counterparts in football and base-ball, these African American professional athletes faced racist crowds and restricted hotels that did not permit black boarders. The impact of the desegregation of professional sports on the greater U.S. society was significant, because it was one of a growing number of changes within the nation that played a role in the solidification of the civil rights movement as African Americans steadily began to achieve higher levels of status and acceptance. The struggles and hardships these black athletes endured along the way were remarkable, yet their efforts and courage paid great dividends in that they affected not just professional sports but society, politics, and eventually the laws that governed the nation.

The major manifestations of these new currents emerged in the are-na of national politics and were dramatized in the civil rights program sponsored by the Truman administration. In the 1950s the Supreme Court became a vital source of reform in race relations. It would be hard to exaggerate the influence of the *Brown* v. *Board of Education* decision as a dynamic factor in the development of the modern civil rights move-ment. Although the progress of school desegregation in the Sunbelt was slow in the late 1950s, the civil rights movement entered a new and highly dynamic phase during the second half of that decade, in response to the *Brown* decision and the development of new leaders, new organi-zations, and new tactics that went far beyond the NAACP's legal chal-lenges to racial discrimination.

Without question, the most heralded of the new civil rights leaders was Martin Luther King, Jr. The son of a successful Atlanta preacher, King was a doctoral graduate of Boston University. He developed a program of nonviolent resistance during the long months of the Montgomery bus boycott; it was based on the evangelical Christianity in which King had been nurtured and Mahatma Gandhi's satyagraha philosophy, to which the minister had been attracted for some time. King would use "nonviolent direct action" to provoke crisis and "creative tension," which would force the white community to confront its racism. "If we are arrested every day, if we are exploited every day, if we are trampled over every day," he declared at one of the Montgomery mass meetings, "don't ever let anyone pull you so low as to hate them. We must use the weapon of love. We must have compassion and understanding for those who hate us." In 1957 King organized the Southern Christian Leadership Conference (SCLC), with headquarters in Atlanta, and the influence of his leadership soon spread throughout the South.

Protest took still another turn on February 1, 1960, when four students from North Carolina Agricultural and Technical College, an all-black institution in Greensboro, took seats at a Woolworth lunch counter and refused to move when they were denied service. This new tactic, based on King's nonviolent ethic, quickly caught on; the result was a wave of "sit-ins" at lunch counters and restaurants, "kneel-ins" at churches, and other nonviolent but pointed challenges to segregated facilities in the South. The sit-ins also produced a new civil rights group, the Student Nonviolent Coordinating Committee (SNCC), and during the next year more than 50,000 people—mostly young men and women, both black and white—took part in demonstrations in nearly one hundred cities.

In the spring of 1961 the Congress of Racial Equality (CORE) sponsored "freedom rides" through the South to challenge the continued segregation of interstate buses and terminals. The primary thrust of the freedom rides was to test the 1960 U.S. Supreme Court decision *Boynton* v. *Virginia*, which held that racial segregation in public transportation was illegal, as it violated the Interstate Commerce Act. CORE carefully selected volunteers who would be willing to risk great bodily injury, even death, without fighting back or retaliating in any way. The first set of riders who departed from Washington, D.C., on May 4,

Martin Luther King, Jr. (fourth from left), participates in the March on Washington for Jobs and Freedom, August 28, 1963. *Courtesy National Archives.*

1961, comprised a diverse group of thirteen people that included blacks and whites, men and women, and young and old. The oldest two were a white couple, Walter and Frances Berman, a 61-year-old retired school administrator from Michigan and his 57-year-old wife, who had been an elementary school teacher and assistant principal. The riders would flaunt southern mores simply by sitting together on the buses and using restroom and waiting facilities in bus terminals without regard to race. In response to the freedom rides, tensions and white backlash in the South escalated. Angry white mobs, sometimes backed by or ignored by local law enforcement agents—sometimes at the direction of the KKK—intimidated and used brutal violence against the riders as well as local black citizens, this as the as the Kennedy administration was getting underway. Ultimately, the freedom rides and the response to them became highly media-covered civil rights actions, shocking events that helped convince the federal government to take action.

By the summer of 1963 the equal rights movement had almost reached flood tide. School desegregation had, to some degree at least, breached the defenses even of Mississippi and Alabama. Protests and demonstrations, often accompanied by white retaliatory beatings and bombings, flickered over the South like heat lightning. In April 1963 Martin Luther King, Jr., led a giant demonstration in Birmingham to protest the city's segregated businesses and institutions. Millions of Americans saw what happened on their television screens when the Birmingham police, under the notorious segregationist T. Eugene "Bull" Connor, turned on the demonstrators with clubs, police dogs, and high-pressure water hoses. A different kind of demonstration took place in Washington, D.C., on August 28, 1963, when over 200,000 black and white marchers gathered before the Lincoln Memorial in a dramatic gesture of protest against the federal government's long indifference to the plight of African Americans in the United States. Dr. King's eloquent address—his inspiring dream of racial equality and brotherhood some day—was a fitting climax to this stirring demonstration. Meanwhile, the work at the grassroots level continued. SNCC, for example, initiated voter registration drives in Mississippi in 1962 and 1963 and joined other equal rights organizations in planning a great "Mississippi Summer" in 1964.

Ironically, the legal and political progress of the early 1960s served to heighten black expectations that all too often went unrealized, leading to greater frustration in the African American community. Nothing revealed the growing mood of frustration, bitterness, and anger among blacks more dramatically than the explosion of ghetto riots between 1964 and 1967. These uprisings were largely unplanned, unorganized, and unscheduled, but much of the violence that attended them was directed at such symbols of white power as the police and white-owned businesses. The four-year period of ghetto rebellions began in New York's Harlem in July 1964, with an outburst of arson, looting, and attacks on whites. But it was the following summer's riot in Watts, a black community in Los Angeles, that first aroused the country to the danger of large-scale ghetto violence. Watts erupted five days after President Johnson signed the Voting Rights Act of 1965, and it resulted in the deaths of

thirty-four people, the arrest of almost 4,000 others, and an estimated
$35 million in property losses. In the midst of the riot there were cries
of "burn, baby, burn" and "kill whitey." The climax came in 1967, when
forty-one major outbreaks occurred, including terrible riots in Newark
and Detroit. Joseph Boskin, a historian who studied the revolt of the urban ghettos, concluded that "the revolts of the mid-1960s—more than
the nonviolent movement of Dr. Martin Luther King and the extraordinarily powerful civil rights movement of the early 1960s—directed attention to the anguished plights of millions of Negroes, Puerto Ricans,
and Mexican Americans living in the urban centers of the country."

The ghetto riots were also related to an accelerating shift in the
direction and control of the equal rights movement from interracial
collaboration to separatism and black domination. The white liberal
response to racism seemed to many young blacks to be inadequate,
paternalistic, and even hypocritical. "White liberal," as August Mei-
er and Elliott M. Rudwick observed, thus joined "black bourgeoisie"
and "Uncle Tom" as "an epithet of opprobrium in the vocabulary of
many Negro militants." As the radicalization of the civil rights movement proceeded, as its more militant spokesmen began to emphasize
the economic, housing, and educational inequalities oppressing the
masses, the demands for "Freedom Now!" became more strident. Dr.
King, the most charismatic leader of the civil rights crusade during
its nonviolent phase, faced a growing challenge from more militant
black leaders. It was this challenge, in part at least, that caused the
SCLC leader to become steadily more critical of the American war in
Vietnam, which was infused with racial meaning, and to plan a mighty
"poor people's" march on Washington in the spring of 1968. The minister was murdered in Memphis before he could lead the Washington
march, and his death as much as any other single event of the late
1960s symbolized the end of a reform movement that had already lost
its direction, its unity, and much of its momentum.

One expression of the new African American militancy was the
slogan "black power," which seems to have been used first by Stokely
Carmichael in 1966. Carmichael, the chairman of SNCC, asserted that
the black masses suffered from both class exploitation and white racism. He and his successor, H. Rap Brown, rapidly became more radical, more hostile toward whites, and more committed to the concept of

black power. Some of the more moderate separatists advocated "black capitalism," the creation of industries and retail businesses operated by African Americans. Others, like Carmichael, urged the establishment of separate political parties. A more revolutionary group known as the Black Panther Party was organized in Oakland, California, by Huey P. Newton and Bobby Seale. Many of the Black Panthers and black ideologues among college students praised revolutionaries like Ernesto "Ché" Guevara, subscribed to a Marxist or Maoist theory of class struggle, and supported the alignment of American blacks with Third World peoples. The Black Muslims were still another black nationalist group. The most magnetic Black Muslim leader was Malcolm X, whose influence grew in the 1960s despite his break with Elijah Muhammad in 1963 and Malcolm's assassination in 1965.

The black power movement nourished the growth of racial consciousness, promoted the development of black pride and black culture (including Afro hair styles, soul food, and African American history), and helped complete a revolution in the thinking of black Americans. But it also did much to fragment the movement for racial reform. Most of the older, established civil rights organizations and African American leaders, including King and Roy Wilkins, opposed the separatism of the black power approach and continued to espouse nonviolent methods, integration, and political and economic reforms. The new black militancy also encouraged a white backlash and frightened many white liberals, who interpreted black power to mean black supremacy, reverse racism, and another form of apartheid.

Although the United States in the 1970s remained in many fundamental respects a racist society, a profound social upheaval and a great change in race relations had occurred during the previous quarter-century. For the first time since Reconstruction, the U.S. government had used its authority to stamp out racial discrimination and integrate African Americans into the larger community. While this precipitated a new crisis in federalism, it resulted in the destruction of the legal structure of segregation, discrimination, and political proscription. Jim Crow—the laws, policies, and practices providing for racially segregated public facilities—was legally banished from the South, and by the spring of 1971 all but seventy-six of the region's 2,700 school districts had at least begun the desegregation of their pupils and teachers.

The percentage of American blacks who had completed high school rose from 38 in 1960 to 58 in 1970. By the early 1980s black students accounted for 10 percent of all college enrollments, as compared with only 4.8 percent in 1965. The black presence in politics assumed increasing importance. Meanwhile, the black middle class was expanding. A growing number of African Americans were employed as skilled laborers, managers, and white-collar workers. Twenty-eight percent of all black employees were white-collar workers in 1970, as compared with only 10 percent in 1950.

Nevertheless, the situation for most black Americans was far less encouraging than that of other minority groups, including those with ethnic identities. World War II had sharpened ethnic self-awareness in the United States but at the same time had softened ethnic divisions and animosities. Following the war many people with immigrant backgrounds moved up the occupational ladder, entering white-collar employment and the professions, taking advantage of educational opportunities, and steadily improving their economic and social status. White Americans who traced their ancestry to northern and western Europe continued to possess more power and prestige than other ethnic groups, but people of recent immigrant stock were rapidly being assimilated. For example, Italians and Jews, the largest of the white ethnic groups originating in southern, central, and eastern Europe, moved into the major institutions of American society. In the meantime, the Cold War improved the image of the newer immigrant elements from Europe. Anti-Semitism, which seemed to increase during the war, declined sharply in the years that followed.

As the postwar period unfolded, it became clear that ethnic and religious identification remained vitally important in shaping the fabric of American society. "Ethnicity," Nathan Glazer and Daniel Patrick Moynihan wrote of New York City in 1963, "is more than an influence on events; it is commonly the source of events. Social and political institutions do not merely respond to ethnic interests; a great number of institutions exist for the specific purpose of serving ethnic interests." Much the same could be said of other great cities in the Northeast and Midwest.

In 1965 Congress completed a major reform of the nation's immigration policy. The act abolished the quota system and adopted a policy based on criteria such as labor skills, the reunification of families, and humanitarian concerns like the provision of asylum for political refugees. The statute established an annual limit of 170,000 immigrants, with no more than 20,000 to come from any one country. The act also set an annual limit of 120,000 per year on western hemisphere immigration, which had previously been unrestricted. This legislation changed the composition of the immigrant stream. By the middle 1970s, persons of Latin American and Asian origin made up almost three-fourths of the legal immigration to the United States. This new immigration was part of a "backward" flow from developing to developed nations.

The changing character of immigration to the United States after 1965 no doubt contributed to a heightened ethnic awareness on the part of Americans generally. This awareness sometimes revived declining ethnic communities, as in the case of San Francisco's Chinatown. But the new ethnicity also reflected a substantial increase in the number of native-born Americans who had become more conscious of their national origins. This awareness was evident in the activities of organizations formed to further ethnic interests, the popularity of visits to ancestral homelands, and a burgeoning literature devoted to ethnic themes. In 1972 Congress took note of these developments by passing the Ethnic Heritage Studies Act, described by its supporters as "a new federal effort to legitimize ethnicity and pluralism in America." Although the public mood seemed to accept the lasting role of ethnicity as a force in American life, it also strongly supported a policy of limiting foreign immigration.

Ethnicity and race were interrelated in various ways. One sign of this relationship was the resentment expressed by white Americans, particularly members of white ethnic groups, over urban renewal projects, affirmative action, labor reforms, and other social uplift efforts. Among the consequences of the black revolution was a broader ethnic crisis that involved demands by other submerged groups for entrance into the main institutions of U.S. society. Many of these groups assumed a more militant position in the 1960s, manifested renewed interest in cultural nationalism, and began to advocate brown or yellow or red power. This was the case with Mexican Americans, who constituted the nation's second largest minority. While comprising only 2.3 percent of the national population in 1960, they numbered almost 3.5 million and made up 12 percent of the population in California, Texas, New Mexico, Arizona, and Colorado. By 1980 the Hispanic population of those five states had increased to almost 9 million. The postwar period witnessed continued migration from Mexico to the United States, increasing self-awareness and recognition among the newcomers of the cultural value of their heritage, some improvement in the social conditions of "*la raza,*" and eventually the development of campaigns by Mexican Americans for a greater share in the American way of life through an insistence on equality of economic opportunity, education, and full civil rights.

The Mexican organizations and programs that sprang up in the 1960s were known collectively as the Chicano movement. It was given direction by a number of new leaders, ranging from moderate advocates of nonviolence to fiery militants. The first Chicano to achieve national recognition was Cesar Chavez of California, who organized the National Farm Workers' Association in 1963. Chavez led a boycott of California grape growers between 1965 and 1969 that forced the producers to recognize the union and bargain with it. The "huelga" drive and other strikes led by Chavez in the vineyards and vegetable fields symbolized and helped mobilize the Chicano revolt. Meanwhile, Reies López Tijerina of New Mexico organized the separatist and millennial *Alianza Federal de Mercedes* (Federal Alliance of Land Grants), while Rodolfo "Corky" Gonzales led the Crusade for Justice in Colorado and José Angel Gutierrez established a new political party in Texas known as *La Raza Unida.* A separatist cultural wing of "la Causa" also emerged, demanding bilingual education in the public schools, Chicano courses, and the like. Gradually Mexican Americans began to exert greater influence in local and state politics.

The plight of the oldest of all Americans, the Indians, represented a tragic and poignant national wrong. By the early 1970s, over 300,000 "urban" Indians had left the reservations and were living in the nation's cities, often in wretched poverty. Approximately 477,000 American Indians remained on the reservations, occupying a kind of no-man's-land, subject to the guardianship of the Bureau of Indian Affairs (BIA) as a kind of "dependent nation" and excluded from many rights held by other Americans. The reservations lacked industries and good schools, and the Indian unemployment rate frequently exceeded 50 percent. During the late 1960s and early 1970s Indian protests over the problem of alienated lands and the policies of the BIA mounted, to the accompaniment of renewed interest in Indian culture and heritage.

Books like Vine Deloria's *Custer Died for Your Sins* (1969) deplored the sad condition of American Indians. Other works pointed to Indian demands for the retention of a separate culture. The seizure of Alcatraz Island in San Francisco Bay, the capture of Wounded Knee, South Dakota, and the occupation of the BIA offices in Washington, D.C., by Indian militants provided dramatic evidence of yet another minority's rebellion. While the protests were not very fruitful, American Indians did regain some of their ancestral lands, and by the mid-1970s the federal government seemed to recognize that many of them did not want to be assimilated into American society.

Minorities, *U.S. News & World Report* noted in 1984, "are putting their imprint on every aspect of American life." The writer went on to say that "blacks, Japanese, Puerto Ricans, Koreans, West Indians and Chinese Americans mingle in what were once all-white neighborhoods. . . . Sushi bars sit next to taco stands. Oriental and Mexican eateries are among the fastest-growing segments of the restaurant business." These comments reflected a new openness in American society and a wide range of new options available to ethnic and religious groups in the United States. The old melting-pot idea had given way to the concept of ethnic and religious pluralism, the kind of society Senator Hubert H. Humphrey once described as "a rich tapestry of separate strands woven together." "Out of many, one" was an ideal that Americans had never fully achieved. But since the end of World War II, the social critic Charles E. Silberman wrote in the mid-1980s, "the gap between ideal and reality has been substantially narrowed, and for some groups almost completely closed, for . . . the United States has become a genuinely multiethnic, multireligious, and, increasingly, a multiracial society."

THE SEARCH FOR COMMUNITY

If the period following the war engendered a spirit of exhilaration and optimism, it also brought an undercurrent of anxiety and insecurity. The mood of social well-being and "togetherness" in the 1950s did not altogether conceal a broad uneasiness about the disintegration of the family as an organic and healthy institution. Among the disruptive trends in the postwar years were earlier marriages, more births out of wedlock, evidence of a revolution in sexual manners and morals, and growing numbers of women working outside the home. Families became more decentralized, and the nation's prosperity encouraged a phenomenon demographers called "uncoupling." Despite the great cultural emphasis on the role of women as housewives and mothers, this traditional sphere became steadily less fulfilling to American women, a tendency that millions of men found difficult to comprehend.

Family stability was also threatened by the challenges of child-rearing. One of the most daunting aspects of this challenge was coping with dramatic changes in teenage behavior, including an upsurge in juvenile delinquency. Various explanations were offered by sociologists and other experts, one of which stressed the influence of a new peer culture disseminated by movies, television, radio, and comic books. According to some social analysts, these so-called mass media had managed to assume a position between the parent and the child. In any case, relations between parents and children became less certain, as the young developed their own values in a rapidly changing society.

One of the traditional sources of community that remained important was the voluntary group, which continued to serve as a primary institution for maintaining (or reforming) American society. The ordinary citizen was likely to belong to voluntary associations of several types, and these associational enterprises performed substantial cultural, social, civic, and economic functions. There were hundreds of thousands of such private groups—trade associations and chambers of commerce; agricultural and horticultural federations; labor unions; professional societies; associations of scholars, scientists, engineers, civil servants, and military officers; groups involved in public health and social welfare; athletic associations; leagues of lobbyists; and so forth. Service clubs flourished in the postwar decades as the older fraternal societies and secret orders declined. At the same time, voluntary associations tended to become special-interest groups primarily concerned with defending the rights of their members rather than working for the good of society.

American society remained essentially conservative in the years after 1945, but the social conflict growing out of racial prejudice, ethnic and minority discrimination, and extensive poverty, as well as the disappearance of older forms of community, left their scars. Furthermore, the upheaval of the 1960s and the Vietnam War produced alienation, confron-

NBC's *Father Knows Best,* with Robert Young (center), Elinor Donahue, Lauren Chapin, Jane Wyatt, and Billy Gray. *Courtesy Photofest.*

tation, and fragmentation. Although people talked about the need for citizen involvement, the complexity of modern society frequently overwhelmed them. A great many Americans no longer thought they could make a difference in a complex society. Still, the nation's society exhibited remarkable continuity, stability, and resilience. Finally, one could see evidence of a broader acceptance of a social order based on cultural diversity and mutual respect among many distinctive social groups.

———— ★ ————

SUGGESTIONS FOR FURTHER READING

John F. Walker and Harold G. Vatter, eds., *History of the U.S. Economy since World War II* (1995). Also see John Kenneth Galbraith, *American Capitalism: The Concept of Countervailing Power* (1952); Thomas C. Cochran, *American Business in the Twentieth Century* (1972); and Keith L. Bryant, Jr., and Henry C. Dethloff, *A History of American Business* (2nd ed., 1990). Thomas S. Dicke, *Franchising in America: The Development of a Business Method, 1840–1980* (1991), deals with a notable innovation.

Robert Sobel, *The Age of Giant Corporations: A Microeconomic History of American Business, 1914–1992* (3rd ed., 1993), and Martin J. Sklar, *The Corporate Recon-*

struction of American Capitalism: The Market, the Law, and Politics (1989), are important studies. Another good, concise, overview is Thomas K. McCraw's American Business Since 1920: How It Worked (2nd ed., 2009). For particular industries, see Emma Rothschild, Paradise Lost: The Decline of the Auto-Industrial Age (1973); John B. Rae, Climb to Greatness: The American Aircraft Industry, 1920–1960 (1968); and J. Harry Du Bois, Plastics History U.S.A. (1972). Energy and the environment are considered in Martin V. Melosi, Coping with Abundance: Energy and Environment in Industrial America (1985). For research and technology, see Walter Buckingham, Automation: Its Impact on Business and People (1963); William Aspray and Martin Campbell-Kelly, Computer: A History of the Information Machine (1996); and David F. Noble, Forces of Production: A Social History of Industrial Automation (1984). Cultural dimensions are explored in Neil Harris, Cultural Excursions: Marketing Appetites and Cultural Tastes in Modern America (1990), and Jackson Lears, Fables of Abundance: A Cultural History of Advertising in America (1995). A new and engaging overview of consumerism is Regina Lee Blaszczyk, American Consumer Society, 1865–2005: From Hearth to HDTV (2009).

The distribution of income and wealth in the postwar period is analyzed in Gabriel Kolko, Wealth and Power in America: An Analysis of Social Class and Income Distribution (1962), and Herman P. Miller, Rich Man, Poor Man (1964). See also John Kenneth Galbraith's stimulating essay on The Affluent Society (1958).

Kim McQuaid, Uneasy Partners: Big Business in American Politics, 1945–1990 (1994), provides an overall treatment of the interaction of large-scale business and the federal government in the period since World War II. For a useful related study, read Richard H. K. Vietor, Contrived Competition: Regulation and Deregulation in America (1994). Economic and fiscal policies are considered in Herbert Stein, The Fiscal Revolution in America (rev. ed., 1990); Edward S. Flash, Jr., Economic Advice and Presidential Leadership: The Council of Economic Advisers (1965); Herbert Stein, Presidential Economics: The Making of Economic Policy from Roosevelt to Reagan and Beyond (1984); Robert M. Collins, The Business Response to Keynes, 1929–1964 (1981); and David P. Calleo, The Imperious Economy (1982).

A fresh treatment of organized labor since 1920 is offered by Robert H. Zieger in American Workers, American Unions (2nd ed., 1994). For a survey history see Melvyn Dubofsky and Foster Rhea Dulles, Labor in America: A History (8th ed., 2010). Among other helpful accounts are Zieger, The CIO, 1935–1955, referred to earlier; Nelson Lichtenstein, The Most Dangerous Man in Detroit: Walter Reuther and the Fate of American Labor (1996); and Kevin Boyle, The UAW and the Heyday of American Liberalism, 1945–1968 (1995). Opposition to organized labor is examined in Gilbert J. Gall, The Politics of Right to Work: The Labor Federations as Special Interests, 1943–1979 (1988), and Barbara S. Griffith, The Crisis of American Labor: Operation Dixie and the Defeat of the CIO (1988). See also Bert Cochran, Labor and Communism: The Conflict That Shaped American Unions (1977), and Studs Terkel, Working (1972).

Gilbert C. Fite, *American Farmers: The New Minority* (1981), is a solid general history that emphasizes the postwar period. Also consult Fite, *Cotton Fields No More: Southern Agriculture, 1865–1980* (1984), and Willard W. Cochrane and Mary E. Ryan, *American Farm Policy, 1948–1973* (1976).

Richard Polenberg's *One Nation Divisible: Class, Race, and Ethnicity in the United States since 1938* (1980) illuminates recent American society and culture by focusing on significant patterns of division. See also Jennifer L. Hochschild, *Facing up to the American Dream: Race, Class, and the Soul of the Nation* (1994). Three general works are helpful on many aspects of postwar society: James Gilbert, *Another Chance: Postwar America, 1945–1985* (2nd ed., 1986); William L. O'Neill, *American High: The Years of Confidence, 1945–1960* (1986); and David Mark Chalmers, *And the Crooked Places Made Straight: The Struggle for Social Change in the 1960s* (2nd ed., 1996). Postwar social trends are discussed in David Halberstam, *The Fifties* (1993), and Douglas Miller, *On Our Own: Americans in the Sixties* (1996). Statistical information at particular points is contained in Ben J. Wattenberg, *This U.S.A.: An Unexpected Family Portrait of 194,067,296 Americans Drawn from the Census* (1965), and E. J. Kahn, Jr., *The American People: The Findings of the 1970 Census* (1974).

For the persistence of regionalism as manifested in the contemporary American South, see Numan V. Bartley, *The New South, 1945–1980* (1995); David R. Goldfield, *Promised Land: The South Since 1945* (1987); Dewey W. Grantham, *The South in Modern America: A Region at Odds* (1994); and Peter Applebome, *Dixie Rising: How the South Is Shaping American Values, Politics, and Culture* (1996).

Incisive introductions to postwar urbanization and metropolitan life are provided by Carl Abbott, *Urban America in the Modern Age: 1920 to the Present* (2nd ed., 2007), and Jon C. Teaford, *The Twentieth-Century American City* (2nd ed., 1993). Among the most instructive of the many books on the urban crisis are Scott A. Greer, *Urban Renewal and American Cities: The Dilemma of Democratic Intervention* (1966), and Sam Bass Warner, *The Urban Wilderness: A History of the American City* (1972). Mark I. Gelfand, *A Nation of Cities: The Federal Government and Urban America, 1933–1965* (1975), is indispensable for federal urban policy in the postwar era. Kenneth T. Jackson's *Crabgrass Frontier: The Suburbanization of the United States* (1985) is the best book on suburbia. Other illuminating studies are Robert Fishman, *Bourgeois Utopias: The Rise and Fall of Suburbia* (1987), and Scott Donaldson, *The Suburban Myth* (1969). David B. Danborn, *Born in the Country: A History of Rural America* (1995), offers a contrast.

Important dimensions of class and status in recent America are considered in Peter M. Blau and Otis Dudley Duncan, *The American Occupational Structure* (1967); Loren Baritz, *The Good Life: The Meaning of Success for the American Middle Class* (1989); James T. Patterson, *America's Struggle Against Poverty, 1900–1994* (1996); and Carole Haber and Brian Gratton, *Old Age and the Search for Security: An American Social History* (1993).

Good introductions to race and black protest are provided by C. Vann Woodward, *The Strange Career of Jim Crow* (3d rev. ed., 1974), and Harvard Sitkoff, *The Struggle for Black Equality, 1954–1992* (rev. ed., 1993). Richard Kluger, *Simple Justice: The History of* Brown v. Board of Education *and Black America's Struggle for Equality* (1976), is a splendid account. A different kind of black struggle is recounted in Jules Tygiel, *Baseball's Great Experiment: Jackie Robinson and His Legacy* (expanded ed., 1997).

For Martin Luther King, Jr., see David L. Lewis, *King: A Critical Biography* (2nd ed., 1978); David J. Garrow, *Bearing the Cross: Martin Luther King, Jr., and the Southern Christian Leadership Conference* (1986); and Adam Fairclough, *To Redeem the Soul of America: The Southern Christian Leadership Conference and Martin Luther King, Jr.* (1987). Other notable studies include Michael Eric Dyson, *Making Malcolm: The Myth and Meaning of Malcolm X* (1995); Gerald Horne, *Fire This Time: The Watts Uprising and the 1960s* (1995); and John Dittmer, *Local People: The Struggle for Civil Rights in Mississippi* (1994).

Thomas J. Archdeacon, *Becoming American: An Ethnic History* (1983), is a fine study of immigration and assimilation in the American experience. For other instructive books on immigration and ethnicity, see Reed Ueda, *Postwar Immigrant America: A Social History* (1994); John Bodnar, *The Transplanted: A History of Immigrants in Urban America* (1985); Roger Daniels, *Coming to America: A History of Immigration and Ethnicity in American Life* (1991); Stanley Lieberson and Mary C. Waters, *From Many Strands: Ethnic and Racial Groups in Contemporary America* (1988); Ronald Takaki, *Strangers from a Different Shore: A History of Asian Americans* (1989); Frederick E. Hoxie and Peter Iverson, eds., *Indians in American History: An Introduction* (2nd ed., 1998); and Iverson's *"We Are Still Here": American Indians in the Twentieth Century* (1998). See also Lawrence H. Fuchs, *The American Kaleidoscope: Pluralism and the Civic Culture* (1989).

An outstanding work on the postwar family is Elaine Tyler May, *Homeward Bound: American Families in the Cold War Era* (1988), which approaches the family in the context of Cold War containment. Arlene Skolnick, *Embattled Paradise: The American Family in an Age of Uncertainty* (1991), is also helpful. William H. Chafe's *The Paradox of Change: American Women in the 20th Century* (1991) is illuminating. Other perspectives are explored in James Gilbert, *A Cycle of Outrage: America's Reaction to the Juvenile Delinquent in the 1950s* (1986); Landon Jones, *Great Expectations: America and the Baby Boom Generation* (1980); John Modell, *Into One's Own: From Youth to Adulthood in the United States, 1920–1975* (1989); and Howard P. Chudacoff, *How Old Are You? Age Consciousness in American Culture* (1989).

──────── ★ ────────

CHAPTER

5

Inspiration, Crises, and Tragedy: John F. Kennedy and the New Frontier

B Y 1960 THE POSTWAR WORLD APPEARED TO HAVE ACHIEVED A kind of fragile stability, and in the United States there were indications that the next decade would bring some major shifts in the nation's politics. John Fitzgerald Kennedy, the youngest man ever to be elected to the presidency, succeeded the elderly Eisenhower, making himself the spokesman for "a new generation of Americans." Many people were hopeful that, under Kennedy's leadership, the United States would not only undertake a more resourceful foreign policy but turn resolutely to the solution of social problems that had been neglected or postponed in the 1950s.

THE ELECTION OF A NEW PRESIDENT, 1960

There was a spirited contest for the Democratic nomination in 1960. Four U.S. senators became active candidates: Lyndon B. Johnson of Texas, Hubert H. Humphrey of Minnesota, Stuart Symington of Missouri, and John F. Kennedy of Massachusetts. Adlai E. Stevenson still had strong support and seemed to be waiting in the wings for a possible third call. Johnson, who was strong in the South, saw his best chance in the gratitude and loyalty he had won from virtually all Democratic senators in his skillful role as majority leader. Kennedy had launched a well-organized drive for the nomination immediately after the election of 1956, when he first came to national attention as a surprisingly strong contender for his party's vice-presidential nomination. Kennedy's prestige was further enhanced when he was overwhelmingly re-elected to the Senate in 1958. He was challenged by Humphrey in a series of primary contests early in 1960. The two key primaries turned out to be those in Wisconsin and West Virginia. Most observers thought that Humphrey had an advantage in Wisconsin, which adjoined his home state and seemed to reflect his brand of Midwestern liberalism, but Kennedy won a surprising victory there on April 5. The struggle then shifted to West Virginia, where the Massachusetts senator's Catholicism became a major though largely silent issue in a state dominated by Protestants. The outcome was a stunning triumph for Kennedy by a 61 to 39 percent margin. Humphrey dropped out of the race.

When the Democratic National Convention met in Los Angeles in July, Kennedy was nominated on the first ballot, receiving 806 votes to 409 for Johnson and 86 for Symington. Kennedy's 65,000 miles of travel in two dozen states, his impressive primary victories, and his skillfully organized and well-financed campaign had paid off. Having secured the nomination, the Massachusetts senator moved at once to strengthen the ticket by persuading Senator Johnson to accept the vice-presidential nomination.

Meanwhile, the Republican Party managed to avoid the kind of heated and divisive nomination fight through which the Democrats had gone. The principal reason for this situation was the powerful position Vice President Richard M. Nixon had established by the late 1950s. The vice president encountered only one significant challenger along the road to his presidential nomination. That challenge came from Nelson A. Rockefeller, who was elected governor of New York in 1958 in a sweeping victory over Averell Harriman. Handsome, hard-driving, and immensely wealthy, the ambitious Rockefeller sought to attract moderate and liberal Republican support as a fresh, exciting alternative to Nixon. But the vice president had far more political experience and know-how than the governor, was identified with the popular Ike's presidency, and was favored by most party leaders. In December 1959 Rockefeller withdrew from what was obviously a hopeless contest.

Nevertheless, in June 1960 Governor Rockefeller challenged the GOP and its platform committee, then at work in Chicago, in effect to repudiate the Eisenhower administration on a long list of national security, civil rights, and social welfare issues. Determined to avoid a bitter platform fight and hold the party together for the November election, Nixon flew to New York for a secret meeting with Rockefeller. The two men agreed upon a detailed program that reflected the governor's views on a number of domestic and foreign policies. The "Compact of Fifth Avenue" infuriated conservatives like Senator Barry Goldwater, who characterized the agreement as the "Munich of the Republican Party." The Nixon forces managed to secure approval of the main features of the agreement in the national convention, and the vice president was easily nominated on the first ballot. Nixon selected Henry Cabot Lodge, Jr., ambassador to the United Nations, for the vice-presidential nomination.

Kennedy, being in effect the challenger, took the initiative in developing campaign issues. He emphasized the need for positive leadership, public sacrifice, and vigorous action to "get America moving again." He frequently referred to an alleged "missile gap" between the United States and the Soviet Union, challenged the American commitment to defend certain offshore islands in the Formosa Strait, and criticized the Eisenhower administration for its handling of Castro's Cuba. Concentrating on the large industrial states, Kennedy also hammered away at unemployment, the worsening economic slump, and the need to stimulate economic growth. Nixon emphasized his own knowledge, experience, and long association with Eisenhower. "The major test to which the people of the country are putting the candidates," he declared, "is which by experience, by background, by judgment, by record . . . can best continue the leadership of Dwight D. Eisenhower and keep the peace without surrender for America and extend freedom throughout the world." A Gallup poll taken immediately after the two conventions gave Nixon a 50 to 44 percent lead over Kennedy, with only 6 percent of those questioned being undecided.

The "Catholic issue" reminded worried Democrats of Al Smith's disastrous campaign in 1928, and it was soon evident that, despite Nixon's refusal to invoke it, the matter of Kennedy's religion had become the focus of widespread uneasiness as well as scurrilous attack. In early September a highly publicized Washington convocation of conservative Protestant clergymen accused the Catholic Church of openly intervening in political affairs, and they ascribed this and other evils to candidate Kennedy. The Democratic leader decided, as he had done in the West Virginia primary, to meet the issue directly. He did so in a bold and dramatic appearance on September 12 before a group of 300 Protestant ministers in Houston. In his frank discussion of his religion he declared:

> I believe in an America where the separation of Church and State is absolute— where no Catholic prelate would tell the President (should he be a Catholic) how to act, and no Protestant minister would tell his parishioners for whom to vote—where no church or church school is granted any public funds or political preference—and where no man is denied public office merely because his religion differs from the President who might appoint him or the people who might elect him.

Kennedy's speech in Houston did not silence the anti-Catholic faction, but it offered reassuring answers to many reasonable questions on the subject. It also pointed up the Democratic leader's ability to sell himself in a variety of ways. "One of the most impressive aspects of the Kennedy campaign," historian Alonzo L. Hamby suggests, "was its calculated use of imagery on a level of sophistication that was still unusual in American politics."

A series of four television "debates" between the two major candidates gave Kennedy an opportunity to demolish the notion of his youthful inexperience and to force Nixon into the role of defending a passive administration. For the first time in the nation's history, Americans from coast to coast would be able to see the presidential candidates debate live. While the substance of the debates played a significant role in a race in which up to 30 percent of the voters had yet to decide, image had a major impact. Kennedy, a handsome, photogenic man, wore a suit that contrasted nicely with the background of the television stage set, while Nixon, who refused to wear makeup to conceal his heavy "five o'clock shadow," wore a suit that blended into the backdrop. Ironically, Nixon's chief advance man, H. R. Haldeman, was an advertising executive with the firm J. Walter Thompson, but Kennedy, not Nixon, appeared to have been properly prepped for the relatively new medium. An estimated 70 million adult Americans viewed the first of the hour-long confronta-

The Kennedy-Nixon televised debates, 1960. Copyright *Washington Post. Reprinted by permission of D.C. Public Library.*

tions on September 26. Most people thought Kennedy appeared to best advantage during the initial encounter. The following three debates were more even, but Kennedy benefited from the favorable impression he already had made on millions of viewers. According to a Roper poll, of 4 million voters who were decisively influenced by the debates, 3 million of them voted for Kennedy.

As the campaign went on, Nixon's relationship with President Eisenhower was both a source of strength and a continuing problem for the GOP nominee. Although Nixon privately disagreed with the administration's position on a number of issues, he found it necessary to endorse the Eisenhower policies as a whole. Eisenhower's own entry into the campaign was somewhat delayed, but he delivered several hard-hitting speeches in the closing weeks of the contest, attracting great crowds and enthusiastic responses wherever he appeared. Meanwhile, Nixon crammed into those weeks an extraordinarily full traveling and speaking schedule. The Republicans also launched a massive television effort in the final days of the campaign.

In an election that set a record for voter participation (more than 10 percent higher than in 1956), Kennedy had a popular margin of only 119,450 votes out of 68.8 million cast, although his electoral advantage was 303 to 219. Kennedy carried twelve states by margins of less than

2 percent of the two-party votes, and if 4,500 more voters in Illinois and 28,000 more in Texas had gone against him, he would have lost the election by two electoral votes. The Democrats carried Congress handily, however, winning a 65 to 35 majority in the Senate and a superiority of 262 to 174 in the House.

THE KENNEDY APPROACH TO FOREIGN POLICY

The new president made no mention of domestic affairs in his moving inaugural address on January 20, 1961, concentrating instead on the challenges that confronted American pre-eminence in the world. He called upon the nation's citizens to join him in developing new frontiers to achieve greatness. "Let the word go forth from this time and place, to friend and foe alike," he declared, "that the torch has been passed to a new generation of Americans—born in this century, tempered by war, disciplined by a hard and bitter peace, proud of our ancient heritage— and unwilling to witness or permit the slow undoing of those human rights to which this nation has always been committed, and to which we are committed today at home and around the world." The United States must be "the watchman on the walls of world freedom."

John F. Kennedy had come to maturity during the years of Franklin D. Roosevelt's burgeoning internationalism and wartime diplomacy. Born on May 29, 1917, in Brookline, Massachusetts, Kennedy was part of an Irish Catholic family that was rapidly moving up in the world as he himself grew up. He was educated in private schools and graduated with honors from Harvard College in 1940. During the war he served in the navy and was seriously injured in 1943 when the PT boat he commanded was sunk by a Japanese destroyer off the Solomon Islands. He was elected to the House of Representatives in 1946 and was twice returned to his seat before moving up to the Senate in 1952.

There was a bit of the scholar and writer in the politician. His senior thesis at Harvard, an examination of the reasons for Britain's refusal to oppose Hitler's challenge in the 1930s, had been published as *Why England Slept* (1940). He wrote a second book during his early Senate tenure while convalescing from a serious operation on his injured back. This work, *Profiles in Courage* (1956), surveyed the careers of several courageous senators who, in times of crisis, stood against the prevailing sentiment of their colleagues and the public. It won the young senator a Pulitzer Prize. Indeed, Kennedy's intellectual qualities and political instincts were impressive. His mind was practical, ironic, skeptical, and remarkably curious. He tended toward understatement. When asked on one occasion how he became a wartime hero, Kennedy replied, "It was involuntary. They sank my boat."

In some respects, however, the thirty-fifth president's background and character were troubling. Notwithstanding his heroism as a naval officer, he had sometimes shown poor judgment in the service and on occasion had subjected his men to unnecessary risk. In Congress he acquired something of a playboy reputation and even after his marriage to the beautiful Jacqueline Bouvier in 1953 seemed unable or unwilling to give up his philandering ways. He had a cynical view of women and marriage. For all his admirable qualities, Kennedy was innately ambiguous, complex, and inscrutable. Though thoroughly committed to anticommunism, he was not driven by ideology. Yet his thinking about public service was altogether positive. Kennedy was convinced of the need for active, pragmatic government.

In the beginning, Kennedy made few changes in the established U.S. approach to the containment of communism. He bypassed such frequently mentioned possibilities as Adlai E. Stevenson and Senator J. William Fulbright in selecting a secretary of state. Instead, Kennedy chose Dean Rusk, a soft-spoken and urbane southerner who had served as assistant secretary of state for Far Eastern Affairs in the Truman administration and, since 1952, as president of the Rockefeller Foundation. Robert S. McNamara took over as Kennedy's secretary of defense. McNamara, who had been president of the Ford Motor Company, was an expert in applying statistical analysis to management problems. Distrusting professional diplomats, Kennedy surrounded himself with a group of bright young advisers, known as "the best and the brightest." Several of these aides were academic intellectuals, such as McGeorge Bundy, special assistant for national security affairs, and Arthur M. Schlesinger, Jr., an adviser on Latin American affairs. The new chief executive made little use of cabinet meetings. He dismantled the elaborate National Security Council structure developed by Eisenhower and relied on the small, efficient staff directed by Bundy in the White House.

Assuming that the thermonuclear power of the United States and the Soviet Union was so awesome as to constitute a "balance of terror" or a "mutual deterrent," Kennedy and McNamara adopted a strategy of "flexible response" in place of the Eisenhower-Dulles doctrine of "massive retaliation." Searching for a wider range of options and greater flexibility in meeting aggression, the administration emphasized a balanced and diversified defense establishment, one that would include not only strategic and tactical nuclear weapons, but also conventional arms and guerrilla forces. The emphasis on a more sophisticated and diversified defense was accompanied by an increase in military expenditures. The defense budget rose by $7 billion during the first year of Kennedy's tenure. The airborne-alert capacity of the Strategic Air Command was extended. The submarine-launched Polaris missile program was accelerated, as were the intercontinental Minutemen (which could be launched from underground silos). The army's combat divisions were increased from eleven to sixteen and modernized in various ways. The tactical wings of the air force were expanded from sixteen to twenty-one. The Marine Corps was enlarged. McNamara wanted to build up NATO's ground forces to the long-sought thirty divisions, and while that goal was never reached, about 400,000 American troops were stationed in Europe by 1963. Kennedy, a committed cold warrior, had entered one of the greatest arms races in history.

The strategy of "controlled and flexible response" was conceived as a means of preventing Communist subversion in the Third World and bolstering the American capacity to deter local aggression. While expanding and diversifying the defense establishment, the Kennedy team sought to control nuclear forces more closely and thus reduce the chances of accidental war. McNamara opposed the proliferation of nuclear arsenals within the NATO alliance, and the administration canceled plans to provide Britain with a nuclear air-to-ground missile called Skybolt.

Although the ideology of the Cold War framed President Kennedy's view of the world and he shared the conventional American view of communism as a monolithic force, he also realized that the key to world peace was improved relations between the United States and the Soviet Union. He hoped to relax Cold War tensions. While his own public statements were not devoid of militant rhetoric, he abandoned some of the clichés of the Cold War, particularly in references to the Third

Peace Corps volunteer Elaine Willoughby teaching in the Highgate area of St. Mary's Parish, Jamaica. *Courtesy Peace Corps Press Office.*

World, where he claimed to be willing to accept neutralism and even socialism. In writing his inaugural address, he decided to use the word "adversary" rather than "enemy"—and he continued to make that distinction in later statements. "Let us never negotiate out of fear," he had declared on that January day in 1961, "but let us never fear to negotiate." By taking the lead in strategic weapons and building mobile strike units to suppress wars of national liberation, America would bargain with the USSR from a position of strength.

Kennedy thought that important changes should be made in the U.S. approach to Latin America and other underdeveloped areas, whose social problems and revolutions seemed to provide a fertile breeding ground for political extremism and international communism. The administration expanded and reorganized the foreign aid program, reorienting it toward the Third World. It established the Agency for International Development (AID) to manage the aid program. Congress approved the president's proposals for the Development Loan Fund to help underdeveloped countries, the Alliance for Progress to assist Latin America, and U.S. membership in the Organization for Economic Co-operation and Development (OECD), in which Canada and eighteen Western European countries collaborated to improve world trade and help underdeveloped nations.

The most successful of the Kennedy foreign aid programs was the Peace Corps, an idea JFK borrowed from others but pledged himself to sponsor during the campaign of 1960. Kennedy announced the formation of the Peace Corps by executive order on March 1, 1961. Congress passed legislation in September 1961 putting the program on a permanent basis and appropriating $30 million for its operation during the first year. During the next few years, Peace Corps volunteers, primarily young adults, served two-year stints in scores of underdeveloped countries, making significant contributions in such fields as education, sanitation, irrigation, and agriculture. By early 1963, five thousand volunteers were enrolled. The Peace Corps proved to be immensely popular in the United States and brought an overwhelmingly favorable response from other parts of the world.

The first year and a half of Kennedy's foreign policy struck many contemporaries as ambiguous and disappointing. He brought renewed vigor and innovation to the handling of international relations, and he appealed successfully to the idealism and altruism of his fellow citizens, especially young Americans. But the globalism of earlier years continued to hold sway, manifesting itself in a dangerous tendency to react indiscriminantly to every international crisis without regard to national capability. Twice during the first twenty months of its tenure the Kennedy government was confronted with a crisis that threatened to plunge the world into nuclear war.

A TROUBLED BEGINNING

One of the problems Kennedy inherited from Eisenhower was Fidel Castro's revolution in Cuba. In the summer of 1960 the conflict between Cuba and the United States was drawn into the vortex of mounting U.S.-USSR hostility in the wake of the U-2 affair. While the United States and Cuba attempted to discredit each other in the Organization of American States and the United Nations Security Council, Premier

Nikita S. Khrushchev denounced the Monroe Doctrine and pledged Soviet support of Cuba in its struggle with the American colossus. As president-elect, Kennedy first learned of a secret plan, approved by Eisenhower in the spring of 1960, for the invasion of Cuba by anti-Castro refugees. Kennedy's military advisers endorsed the scheme, and the Central Intelligence Agency assured him that the attack would likely succeed. Although Senator William Fulbright and a few others opposed the undertaking and the president himself had some qualms about it, he acquiesced in the venture. Not only was Kennedy basically hostile to a Cuban revolutionary government like Castro's, but he had criticized the Eisenhower administration during the campaign of 1960 for not being tough enough with Castro. The invasion took place on Cuba's southern coast at the Bay of Pigs on April 17, 1961. The invading forces included fewer than 1,500 troops who were never able to establish a defensible beachhead along the swampy terrain selected for the operation. Lacking U.S. naval and air support as promised them by their CIA advisers, they were quickly pinned down by Castro's military forces. There was no popular uprising, and the invasion was completely crushed within three days.

The whole affair was an appalling and humiliating disaster for the United States and the Kennedy administration. The project was poorly planned, the size of the invading force totally inadequate, and the operation filled with tactical blunders and miscalculations. Kennedy, who was badly shaken by this early mishap in foreign policy, took the blame for the debacle. "There is an old saying that victory has one hundred fathers and defeat is an orphan," he said. "I'm the responsible officer of the government and that is quite obvious." The abortive invasion made Kennedy look weak and enabled his Republican opponents to criticize him for failing to defend the Monroe Doctrine. Meanwhile, the Bay of Pigs gave Castro an enormous propaganda victory, strengthened the relationship between Cuba and the Soviet Union, and convinced American leaders that Cuba was now a Soviet satellite "ninety miles from our shores." It gave Khrushchev a pretext to bluster and threaten. It outraged many Latin Americans, revived fears of Yankee imperialism in the southern hemisphere, and set back Kennedy's promising attempts to identify the United States with anti-colonialism. The urgency in the minds of administration leaders in contemplating the Cuban problem in the 1960s reflected a convergence of international pressures: the bitter rivalry with the Soviet Union, the history of difficult relations with Latin America, and the U.S. response to social revolution in various Latin American nations and other parts of the Third World.

President Kennedy was prodded by the Bay of Pigs setback to agree to a meeting with Premier Khrushchev in which he could test the Russian leader's mettle. Kennedy and Khrushchev held a series of private meetings in Vienna on June 3 and 4, 1961. They did not get along well. The two leaders did agree to stop the growing conflict in Laos, but there was no accord in their other discussions. Kennedy's position was that efforts to impose communism by force of arms in any country would threaten the balance of power all around the globe. Khrushchev would not agree to stop supporting what he termed "wars of liberation." He was even more militant about Berlin, renewing his demand of the late 1950s for an "immediate" peace treaty with Germany and an end to the current four-power occupation of the city. Kennedy was deeply disturbed by his confrontation with the Soviet premier.

At Vienna Kennedy emphasized his determination to defend West Berlin, but Khrushchev seemed to take these warnings lightly, and he insisted throughout the following summer that the problem of Berlin would have to be resolved before the end of 1961. If the West would not sign a treaty turning Berlin into a "free city," the Soviet Union would sign a separate peace treaty with East Germany, thereby automatically abrogating the right of the Western powers to be in Berlin. The Russians wanted a satisfactory settlement in Germany before the effects of Kennedy's military buildup could be felt. But they were also concerned over another matter—the enormous success of West Berlin as a "showcase of democracy" behind the Iron Curtain. In the late spring of 1961 a thousand refugees a day, including many technicians, skilled workers, and young people, were flocking into West Berlin. The very economic survival of the East German state, to say nothing of its prestige, was at stake in this swelling exodus. Fearful of appearing weak, Kennedy resolved to make the Berlin crisis not only a question of West Berlin's rights, but, in the words of Kennedy's adviser, Theodore Sorensen, "a question of direct Soviet-American confrontation over a shift in the balance of power."

During the weeks after the Vienna conference, Khrushchev heightened the tension over Berlin by increasing his demands for concessions from the Western powers and strengthening his military posture. Kennedy, bolstered by advice from such stout cold warriors as Dean Acheson, was prepared to engage in a "conflict of wills" with his Soviet adversary. By July a war of words and of nerves had developed. On July 25 Kennedy announced that he was speeding up draft calls, extending enlistments, and mobilizing some reserve and National Guard units; he eventually increased the size of the armed forces by 300,000 men. At the same time, he requested an additional defense appropriation of $3.25 billion. Congress voted for the president's new defense budget by overwhelming majorities. Encouraged in part by a presidential recommendation, a wave of fallout-shelter building swept the nation. Then, suddenly, the climax came in Berlin.

Before dawn on August 13, 1961, the East German government closed the border between East and West Berlin, and during the next few days the Communists began constructing an elaborate wall of concrete and barbed wire throughout the city, a barrier they ultimately extended along the entire western border of East Germany. The Western powers protested sternly but did not use force against the barricade. President Kennedy dispatched a battle force of U.S. troops down the 100-mile autobahn from West Germany through the Communist zone into Berlin as a gesture of defiance and a test of Soviet intentions. The Communists did not halt the convoy. Kennedy also sent Vice President Johnson and General Lucius D. Clay (the commander of the American forces in Germany during the Berlin blockade of 1948–49) to West Berlin as evidence of continuing American support of the Western position.

The Berlin crisis finally dissipated in the fall and winter. Khrushchev's wall was a brilliant and dramatic stroke, and it removed a running sore on the Soviet Union's western flank. But the wall was also a confession of Russian frustration and bankruptcy in dealing with the German question.

THE CUBAN MISSILE CRISIS AND THE TEST BAN TREATY

The most crucial event of the Kennedy years and the most dangerous of all Cold War confrontations was the Cuban missile crisis of October 1962. After the Bay of Pigs, Fidel Castro's hostility toward the United States understandably grew. He built up a large army, renewed a trade

Executive Committee of the National Security Council during the Cuban Missile Crisis. *Courtesy John F. Kennedy Library.*

pact with the Soviet Union early in 1962, and boasted of his Communist ideology. Khrushchev, frustrated in the face of American nuclear superiority, unable to get the Western powers out of Berlin, and irritated by Chinese criticism of Soviet weakness, sought an opportunity to alter the strategic balance. In May 1962 he decided on a daring move: to deploy intermediate-range ballistic missiles in Cuba, the first Soviet commitment of nuclear weapons outside of the Soviet Union. This Russian effort was altogether a very large undertaking, involving many months of planning, 175 ships, 6,000 men, and a cost of about three quarters of a billion dollars. The success of this scheme would make the Soviet strategic force more credible, weaken the United States in the eyes of its NATO allies, possibly enable Khrushchev to reopen the Berlin negotiations, and undermine the U.S. position in the Americas. Installation of nuclear missiles ninety miles off the U.S. coast would, at the very least, give the appearance of Soviet power.

But Premier Khrushchev was unable to achieve strategic surprise. U.S. officials were well aware of the heavy movement of arms and military equipment, including surface-to-air missiles, from Soviet-bloc countries into Cuba. Even if these materials were defensive in nature, as the

American intelligence community assumed, they helped create a political crisis for President Kennedy, who had already been sharply criticized by congressional Republicans for neglecting the Monroe Doctrine and failing to remove the Communist presence from Cuba. Then, on October 14, U.S. photographic surveillance revealed that Soviet missile sites were being constructed on the island, which precipitated an around-the-clock search by Kennedy and his advisers for a way to remove any missiles that had reached Cuba, if possible without going to war. During the next few days, until October 22, secret White House discussions within a special "Executive Committee" explored alternatives. The atmosphere was tense but businesslike. Quick action was imperative since additional missiles were on the high seas and the missile sites would become operational within a matter of days. During the lengthy sessions of ExComm, a variety of options was considered, but gradually two possible courses of action came to the fore. One group of advisers, including the military spokesmen and Dean Acheson, argued vigorously for a "surgical" air strike against the missile sites, even though such an attack would probably kill Soviet technicians working on the project. A second group of the president's lieutenants supported Undersecretary of State George Ball's recommendation that some kind of blockade be instituted against Cuba. This represented a flexible arrangement that would give the Russians the maximum opportunity to back down without humiliation. Ball's position won the support of Secretary of Defense McNamara and Attorney General Robert F. Kennedy, who became a key figure in the formulation of the American response to the situation.

It was the president, however, who dominated the secret meetings and made the ultimate decision. The discovery of the missiles put the administration in a difficult position. A "war party" had already begun to develop in the United States as rumors of Soviet military penetration of Cuba spread. The midterm congressional elections were less than three weeks away, and Republicans could be expected to make the most of any administration weakness in responding to new Cold War challenges. Sensitive to any appearance of weakness, Kennedy was prepared to act; but he chose the more moderate course of imposing a blockade instead of an immediate attack on Cuba. At the same time, he decided upon a public confrontation in order to dramatize and reverse Khrushchev's aggression. Having made these critical decisions, the president acted swiftly to put the plan into effect. On October 22, he briefed the cabinet and congressional leaders, informed the other NATO nations of the situation, and called a meeting of the Organization of American States for the next day. He also assumed the task of defining the crisis for the public. At 7:00 P.M. on October 22 JFK delivered a nationwide television address to the American people.

Kennedy described the rapid pace of work on the missile sites and the American response to the challenge. The presence of "these large, long-range, and clearly offensive weapons of sudden mass destruction," he declared, represented "an explicit threat to the peace and security of all the Americas." It was "a deliberately provocative and unjustified change in the status quo which cannot be accepted by this country, if our courage and our commitments are ever again to be trusted by either friend or foe." The American leader proclaimed a "strict quarantine"— actually a blockade—on "all offensive military equipment under shipment to Cuba." He issued a stern warning to the Soviet Union and demanded that Khrushchev remove the missiles already in Cuba. Even as the president spoke, the Strategic Air Command was beginning a massive airborne alert, 156 intercontinental ballistic missiles were in combat readiness, a fleet of Polaris submarines was on guard at sea, the navy was establishing a 2,100-mile ring around Cuba (eventually employing 180 ships), and hundreds of thousands of men were placed in combat readiness.

The world shuddered as the two great powers confronted each other at the brink. What would happen when the Russian missile-carrying freighters were intercepted by the American blockading units? The Soviet Union's immediate reaction was to denounce the U.S. blockade as illegal. But finally, after two of the most anxious days in modern times, the crisis began to ease. A dozen Soviet vessels headed for Cuba suddenly reversed course or were diverted, prompting Secretary Rusk to remark, "We're eyeball to eyeball and I think the other fellow just blinked." Conditions remained dangerous and uncertain, but it was soon evident that Khrushchev had overplayed his hand.

On October 26 a solution began to emerge. First through an unofficial emissary and then in a long, emotional letter, Khrushchev began to back down. The letter seemed to imply that the Soviet Union would remove the missiles if the United States would end its blockade and promise not to invade Cuba. Before Kennedy and his colleagues could reply to this offer, a second Soviet message reached Washington on October 27, offering to dismantle the missile sites in Cuba if the United States would withdraw its missile bases from Turkey. Faced with this perplexing situation, American leaders adopted Robert Kennedy's suggestion that they respond to the first message and ignore the second. This ingenious expedient worked. The United States promised not to invade Cuba if the missiles were quickly withdrawn and if a number of Russian medium-range bombers were returned to the USSR. The United States also made an oral promise, delivered by Attorney General Kennedy to Soviet Ambassador Anatoly Dobrynin, that the U.S. missiles in Turkey would be removed. Khrushchev agreed to this arrangement, and the crisis ended.

The crisis over Cuban missiles in the autumn of 1962 turned out better than Kennedy and his advisers had dared to hope. The missile crisis set the stage for a gradual improvement in Soviet-American relations. The most notable evidence of this relaxation of tensions during the Kennedy administration was the agreement reached in the summer of 1963 to restrict the testing of nuclear weapons. The antecedents of this so-called test ban were numerous and diverse. They included Kennedy's new confidence and the more moderate approach he began to employ toward Russia. There was also Khrushchev's desperate need to ease the military pressure on his slumping economy, the possibility that a diplomatic coup would restore his fading reputation, and the widening rift between Moscow and the People's Republic of China. Both China and France coveted nuclear weapons, and the Russians and the Americans were by no means happy over the prospect of such nuclear dispersion. Still another consideration was the growing concern over the large amounts of radioactive materials being released into the atmosphere as a result of nuclear testing, which the Soviet Union had resumed in the fall of 1961 and the United States in the spring of the following year.

Disarmament talks had dragged on fruitlessly for years when Kennedy made the decision, in the spring of 1963, that the United States would not be the first nation to carry out further atmospheric tests. In a conciliatory address at American University on June 10, 1963, the president disclosed that representatives of Britain, the Soviet Union, and the United States would soon meet in Moscow to discuss the question of a nuclear test ban treaty. If the United States and its adversaries could not now end all differences, he declared, "at least we can help make the world safe for diversity. For, in the final analysis, our most basic common link is that we all inhabit this small planet. We all breathe the same air. We all cherish our children's future. And we are all mortal."

To emphasize the importance the administration attached to the Moscow deliberations, Kennedy selected Averell Harriman, perhaps the most experienced and formidable American who had dealt with the Russians, to represent the United States. Harriman proved to be a skillful negotiator, and he had a large part in fashioning the treaty concluded by the three powers on July 25. Although the agreement did not provide for on-site inspection or ban underground testing, it did prohibit all nuclear tests in the atmosphere, in outer space, on land, and underwater. The Nuclear Test Ban Treaty was quickly signed by about a hundred other nations, though neither the People's Republic of China nor France ratified it. While the treaty encountered some opposition in the United States, including that of a few scientists like Dr. Edward Teller who were concerned about the maintenance of American nuclear deterrence, the Senate ratified the agreement, under strong administration pressure, on September 24 by a vote of 80 to 19.

A few weeks after the treaty was signed, Kennedy proposed a joint Soviet-American expedition to the moon. He also approved the sale of $250-million worth of surplus wheat to the Russians, who were suffering from a grain shortage. Washington and Moscow soon agreed to the installation of a "hot line" between the White House and the Kremlin. Although there was little evidence of progress in the resolution of fundamental differences between the two superpowers, a mild thaw in the Cold War had begun.

GLOBAL CONNECTIONS AND THIRD WORLD POLICIES

John F. Kennedy's foreign policies reflected the United States' growing interest during the late 1950s and early 1960s in the underdeveloped nations or the so-called Third World. Indeed, the Kennedy administration was apprehensive about Communist gains in these areas and afraid that time was running out in the competition for their ideological support. The president's concern over the emerging nations, many of which had only recently won their independence, stemmed both from his desire to halt the spread of international communism and his belief that those countries constituted the real arena of competition between the United States and the Soviet Union. While convinced of the indispensable requirement of military and economic power in that struggle, the American leader also understood that the underdeveloped countries desperately needed economic and technical assistance and that it was desirable to encourage internal change and social reform in the Third World.

Although the United States generally remained aloof from the conflict between the new nations of Africa and their erstwhile European colonizers, it was impossible not to take some part in the Congo, which was plunged into civil war almost as soon as it received its independence from Belgium in 1960. Hoping to avoid a confrontation with the Soviet Union in the Congo, where the Russians were backing one of the contending factions, Kennedy supported the military efforts of the United Nations to suppress the Katanga secession movement led by Moishe Tshombe. The President persuaded Congress to purchase $100-million worth of UN bonds as a means of strengthening United Nations operations, which managed to reunite the country by early 1963. One of the tragedies of the conflict was the death of UN Secretary-General Dag Hammarskjöld, who died in an airplane crash while trying to arrange a settlement in the Congo. His death precipitated a struggle in which the Soviet bloc tried to change the nature of the Secretariat into a "troika," or three-horsed harness arrangement, composed of Communist, Western, and neutralist representatives, each with a veto. This scheme, which would have rendered the UN utterly powerless, was defeated in November 1961, with strong U.S. help, and U Thant of Burma was chosen as acting secretary-general.

In the meantime, the Kennedy administration was taking a keen interest in Latin America, a region that had long felt neglected by the United States. While Kennedy's Latin American diplomacy was designed to counter Castroism and win the support of the nations to the south in the Cold War, the American chief executive seemed to sense the pressure for social change and the urge for a better life in this vast underdeveloped area. In mid-March 1961, he urged that a partnership be undertaken between the United States and the various Latin American nations in order "to satisfy the basic needs of the American peoples for homes, work and land, health and schools." The idea was received with enthusiasm in Latin America, and in August 1961 representatives of the OAS meeting in Punta del Este, Uruguay, formulated a blueprint for the Alliance for Progress.

The Act of Punta del Este called for a massive development program during the next decade, with the United States agreeing to provide more than half of the $20 billion to be obtained outside of Latin America. In return the Latin American nations would make an immense investment of their own, while committing themselves to important land and tax reforms. Although Congress appropriated funds to help inaugurate the program and every American republic except Cuba joined it, the Alianza got off to a poor start and did little to change the lives of the Latin American masses.

Kennedy never questioned the need to support American commitments to contain communism in East Asia. As historian George C. Herring has written, "Kennedy and most of his advisers accepted, without critical analysis, the assumption that a non-Communist Vietnam was vital to America's global interests, and their rhetoric in fact strengthened the hold of that assumption." One trouble spot was Laos, an isolated mountain country that bordered the People's Republic of China on the north and stretched southward roughly parallel to the divided Vietnam. The pro-Western Laotian government was weak and unstable, and by the beginning of the 1960s it was under increasing attack from the Pathet Lao, a revolutionary movement modeled on Ho Chi Minh's Vietminh. By early 1961, the Communist-assisted Pathet Lao had captured the strategic Plain of Jars and was pushing south along the Vietnam border. In March Kennedy warned Moscow, Beijing, and Hanoi that the United States would not tolerate a Communist takeover in Laos. The president decided against large-scale American intervention, however, and, at the urging of Averell Harriman, sought a diplomatic solution that would preclude a Pathet Lao victory, avoid an armed confrontation with the Soviet Union, and establish a "neutral and independent Laos."

A neutralization formula was finally agreed to on July 21, 1962. Although the agreement prevented a superpower confrontation over Laos, the Pathet Lao soon resumed the civil war and received military support from North Vietnam so that the Ho Chi Minh Trail, the supply route for the Communist military, could be kept open as a means of supplying the National Liberation Front in South Vietnam. In May 1962 the United States sent troops into Thailand, which borders Laos on the west, in order to counter gains by the Pathet Lao. Thailand, disturbed over the pending neutralization of Laos, had signed a treaty with the United States in March 1962 permitting the American government to come to the Thais' rescue, even if other SEATO members should object (thereby transforming the multilateral nature of the original SEATO pact). The neutralist government of Prince Souvanna Phouma was still trying to govern Laos at the end of 1963, with the continuing, if grudging, support of the United States.

Kennedy set about strengthening the South Vietnamese Diem regime. At the suggestion of American experts, for example, Diem instituted a plan to deal with insurgency known as the strategic hamlet program, as a means of securing the countryside and protecting friendly peasants. In the spring of 1961 Kennedy sent Lyndon Johnson to investigate conditions in South Vietnam, and the vice president brought back some ominous impressions. Johnson recommended an increase in U.S. assistance to Diem, whom he brashly characterized as the "Winston Churchill of Asia." In the fall the president sent another mission to Saigon, headed by General Maxwell D. Taylor and presidential aide Walt Whitman Rostow. They reported that South Vietnam had enough vitality to justify a major American effort, and their recommendations pointed toward a military solution. In a later report the Defense Department and the Joint Chiefs of Staff urged the desirability of using U.S. troops if necessary to preserve the Diem government. They estimated that the force needed would not exceed six divisions. After returning from Vietnam in June 1962, Secretary McNamara asserted that "every quantitative measurement we have shows we're winning the war."

Vietnam seemed to offer the kind of situation in which the new Kennedy-McNamara flexible response approach could be employed successfully. In fact, Kennedy thought he had found a way to overcome the incongruity between the goal of victory in Vietnam and the reality of a limited U.S. involvement. It was the political-military program of counterinsurgency. The Cuban missile crisis probably accelerated American intervention in Vietnam by encouraging the administration to assume that it could manage crisis situations. In any event, Kennedy steadily expanded the U.S. training program in South Vietnam and American assistance to the Diem government. By early 1962 there were over 4,000 U.S. military "advisers" in the country, compared to about 650 when Eisenhower left office. Many Europeans found it difficult to comprehend the choice of South Vietnam as a proving ground for democracy.

Ultimately, American success in Vietnam would rest upon the effectiveness of the Saigon government in resisting the challenge of the Vietcong and its political arm, the National Liberation Front. Although the United States made sporadic efforts to persuade Diem to carry out land reform and other needed domestic changes, the South Vietnam leader showed little interest in such programs. The ruling Catholic minority encountered mounting dissent from the large Buddhist population, and in May 1963 Diem brutally suppressed a series of Buddhist protests. Such blatant repression not only played into the hands of the Vietcong but provoked outcries in the United States and eventually undermined the Kennedy administration's confidence in Diem. On November 1, 1963, a military conspiracy, with the acquiescence of Washington, overthrew the Diem regime and assassinated the president and his brother. Unfortunately, however, the new leaders came from the same conservative elements that had produced Diem.

By the end of Kennedy's first thousand days (in office), 16,000 American military men were stationed in South Vietnam, and they were increasingly involved in the actual fighting there. The president failed to give sufficient weight to the fact that the struggle in Vietnam was in considerable part a civil war and that the opponents of the pro-Western government in Saigon reflected nationalist sentiment as well as Communist ideology.

Kennedy's international objectives also included a stronger trans-Atlantic partnership. Through the Grand Design for Europe, JFK hoped to strengthen the unity and effectiveness of the Western alliance. He envisioned a Western Europe united in the Common Market, and moving toward political federation, and cooperating with the United States and Britain in freer trade agreements, which would promote the economic growth of non-Communist countries everywhere. To lend American support to this development, Kennedy persuaded Congress to pass the

Trade Expansion Act of 1962, empowering the chief executive to lower tariff barriers in return for trade concessions. On the military front, the Kennedy administration opposed President Charles de Gaulle's plan to build an independent French nuclear deterrent. Kennedy wanted the nations of Western Europe to spend more for their own security, and he hoped to broaden NATO's defense options by having them place renewed emphasis on conventional, non-nuclear forces. These proposals met with little favor from his European allies.

Furthermore, the easing of Cold War tensions that followed the Cuban missile crisis encouraged European leaders to assert greater independence in their relations with the United States. Thus de Gaulle prepared a Franco-German treaty of friendship, worked to improve relations with the Warsaw Pact nations, and stepped up the pace of French nuclear development. He withdrew his country's naval forces from NATO and made a bold bid for European independence from American international domination. Early in 1963, in characteristically dramatic fashion, de Gaulle rejected Britain's request for membership in the Common Market, repudiated the U.S.-sponsored "multilateral nuclear force" (MLF), and declared that France would provide itself with necessary nuclear defenses. Kennedy soon abandoned the MLF plan, and while he and other American spokespersons continued to talk about a stronger and more unified Europe, it had become clear that many of the NATO countries were no longer willing to follow United States leadership unquestioningly.

Perhaps the most distinctive characteristic of Kennedy's foreign policy was its ambiguity. Even so, the young president demonstrated an ability to learn and grow in dealing with international problems. His record in foreign affairs was promising in many respects. Had he lived and served a second term in the presidency, there is at least a chance that recent American history would have been significantly different.

NEW FRONTIERS AND THE RESURGENCE OF LIBERALISM

The fourth postwar recession in the United States had not yet ended when Kennedy entered the White House, and during February and March of that winter more men and women were out of work than at any previous time in the postwar period. Kennedy's State of the Union message drew a bleak picture. "We take office," the new president said, "in the wake of seven months of recession, three and one-half years of slack, seven years of diminished economic growth, and nine years of falling farm income." He declared that his administration did not intend "to stand helplessly by." He urged Congress to enact a series of measures designed to promote employment and counter the economic slowdown. He also recommended the approval of health care for the elderly, federal aid to schools, a conservation program, housing and community development, and the strengthening of national defense and foreign aid.

Although Kennedy's major reform proposals did not fare well in 1961, the administration enjoyed some success in its efforts to end the recession. It expanded government expenditures in a variety of ways, tried to stimulate residential construction by lowering interest rates, and dealt adroitly with the balance of payments problem. Congress liberalized Social Security benefits, raised the minimum wage to $1.15 an hour (and authorized a further increase to $1.25 two years later), passed legislation enabling the states temporarily to extend unemployment benefits for an additional thirteen weeks, approved an expanded public works program, and passed a $4.88 billion omnibus housing bill.

The administration's major congressional triumph in 1962 was the Trade Expansion Act, which Kennedy hailed as the most significant advance in U.S. foreign policy "since the passing of the Marshall Plan." Designed to improve the U.S. economy by stimulating competition and trade with the nations of the European Economic Community and Japan, the act included the largest tariff-cutting power ever granted an American president. The United States then launched a major campaign of trade liberalization—the "Kennedy Round." In the meantime, Congress had enacted the administration's Manpower Development and Training Act, which appropriated $435 million to be spent on a matching basis with the states for the training of the unemployed in new skills.

Kennedy's new approach to the agricultural problem emphasized tighter production controls. The president and his secretary of agriculture, Orville L. Freeman, advocated adoption of the "supply management" technique, which was intended to prevent farm products from becoming surplus-storage inventories while keeping farm income up and

Caroline and John dance in the Oval Office. *Courtesy John F. Kennedy Library.*

helping to preserve small farmers. The proposed legislation encountered strong opposition in Congress, particularly from southern Democrats and Midwestern Republicans, some of whom cited the notorious case of Billie Sol Estes, the Lyndon Johnson contributor who fraudulently reported growing and storing massive amounts of cotton that never existed in order to use the crop as collateral for loans, to buttress their arguments. Although some of the administration's land-use proposals were approved in the Farm Act of 1962, stringent production controls were rejected and the existing program was continued.

Another of the administration's proposals in the second session of the Eighty-seventh Congress turned out better. This was the president's request for authority to establish a privately owned and financed corporation to administer a communications-satellite system capable of relaying telephone and telegraph messages and television programs throughout the world. Despite the spirited attack on the measure in the Senate led by Paul H. Douglas of Illinois and Estes Kefauver of Tennessee, who labeled the bill a giveaway to the communications industry and urged that the system be owned and controlled by the government, the Communications Satellite Act was approved in 1962.

The "Telstar" bill reflected Kennedy's enthusiastic commitment to the U.S. space program. On May 5, 1961, soon after the Russian cosmonaut Yuri Gagarin had circled the earth in a space vehicle, Commander Alan B. Shepard, Jr., made a 300-mile suborbital flight from Cape Canaveral. During the same month Kennedy urged Congress to commit the United States "to achieving the goal, before this decade is out, of landing a man on the moon and returning him safely to the earth." No single space project in this period, he declared, "will be more impressive to mankind, or more important for the long-range exploration of space; and none will be so difficult or expensive to accomplish." Congress responded by doubling NASA appropriations in 1962 and again in 1963. Within five years almost half a million people were employed in the aerospace facilities that sprang up from Southern California to Texas to Florida. Project Apollo and other NASA plans soon began to pay off. On February 20, 1962, Lieutenant Colonel John H. Glenn flew around the earth three times in his Mercury space capsule, *Friendship 7*, and landed in the Caribbean on the same afternoon.

One of Kennedy's rising concerns, as the recession lifted in the second part of 1961, was the danger of inflation. Relying mainly on "jawboning," he tried to persuade labor and management to keep wages and prices down. Thus he and Secretary of Labor Arthur J. Goldberg worked hard in March 1962 to avoid a strike in the steel industry and to negotiate a non-inflationary labor contract. It was tacitly understood that the steel manufacturers would not raise their prices, but ten days later, on April 10, Roger M. Blough of the United States Steel Corporation informed the president that his company was increasing its prices by about $6 a ton. Five other large firms announced identical increases on the following day. Kennedy, feeling betrayed, denounced the steel companies' action as "a wholly unjustifiable and irresponsible defiance of the public interest." He quickly mobilized the power of the federal government against the offending firms. The Defense Department announced that it would award new contracts only to those companies that refrained from raising prices. The steel executives capitulated within seventy-two hours.

This incident increased business distrust of the Kennedy administration, which many businesspeople already regarded as "anti-business." When the stock market, on May 28, 1962, experienced its most precipitate drop since the crash of 1929, the setback was attributed in business circles to "lack of confidence" in Kennedy's leadership. Bumper stickers soon appeared with such messages as "I Miss Ike—Hell, I Even Miss Harry." It is true that Kennedy was provoked into attacking the steel companies in 1962. He also fostered Justice Department suits against Chrysler Corporation executives for conflict of interest activities and against General Electric and Westinghouse officials for price-fixing conspiracies. On the other hand, there were many indications of Kennedy's economic conservatism, including his backing of AT&T on the Telstar bill, his successful efforts to obtain the Trade Expansion Act, his refusal to move against the oil depletion allowance, and his support of a measure in Congress that gave a special tax break to shareholders of the Du Pont Company several years after the Supreme Court had decreed that Du Pont must divest itself of ownership of 63 million shares of General Motors stock.

Although the economy had improved, it was still hindered by certain basic underlying problems. Unemployment remained at a disappointing 5.5 percent. The annual increase in the gross national product for the period 1960–62 was only about 3.6 percent, as compared with a growth rate in Western Europe of from 4 to 6 percent. These trends eventually helped persuade the president to follow the recommendations of Walter W. Heller, chairman of the Council of Economic Advisers, and other liberal economists who favored a substantial reduction of taxes, even in a time of relative prosperity, as a means of quickening growth. JFK thus combined the conservatives' desire for a reduction in taxes with the Keynesian faith in the power of fiscal policy. He had come to believe that a large tax cut would stimulate demand, promote economic growth, and increase federal revenue to support foreign initiatives and domestic reforms.

When the new Congress convened in January 1963, Kennedy presented a comprehensive proposal calling for a reduction in taxes of over $10 billion during a three-year period. While the president set out to win the support of sophisticated businesspeople for his tax-cut plan and to educate Americans generally as to the advantages of the "new economics," his proposal encountered criticism from several directions. Congress was extremely slow in responding to the administration's request, and the House did not pass the bill until late September. In the Senate, Harry Flood Byrd and other conservatives prevented a vote on the measure during the first session of the Eighty-eighth Congress. Meanwhile, Americans were enjoying a robust economic boom, and the annual rate of growth between 1962 and 1964 had risen to 5.3 percent.

SOCIAL REFORM AND LOSING BATTLES

John F. Kennedy came to the presidency by taking advantage of the vague discontents that had begun to spread through American society and identifying himself with the growing desire for a renewed sense of national purpose, the restoration of U.S. prestige in the world, and a more dynamic administration in Washington. Emerging from this orientation were not only the demands for a revitalization of the economy and a stronger and more flexible defense program but also an increasing concern over the quality of American life and measures to enhance it. Although Kennedy persuaded Congress to enact several of his domestic reform bills, his efforts to win approval of major social welfare measures often proved to be losing battles.

One of the Kennedy administration's most disappointing setbacks during the Eighty-seventh Congress was the fate of its ambitious education program. Unlike earlier federal programs such as the National Science Foundation and the National Defense Education Act, the educational reforms of the 1960s were intended to offer particular assistance to those disadvantaged as a result of low incomes, physical handicaps, and discrimination. Kennedy's proposed legislation in 1961 provided for a federal grant of $2.3 billion over a three-year period for school construction and teachers' salaries, plus another $3.3 billion for the support of higher education over a five-year period. After passing the Senate in May, the measure was killed in the House Rules Committee by a vote of 8 to 7. Catholic leaders insisted that parochial schools should share in the federal aid program, a demand the president opposed, and the resulting controversy played into the hands of opponents of the bill. Many southern congressmen were suspicious of federal aid because they viewed it as an instrument, in the hands of aggressive blacks like

Representative Adam Clayton Powell, for the advancement of school desegregation. Kennedy's education assistance legislation, which had been broadened to include provisions for combating adult illiteracy and training handicapped children, fared no better in 1962. The administration was, however, largely responsible for the passage of the Higher Education Facilities Act of 1963, which President Johnson signed after Kennedy's death.

The administration was dealt another reversal in 1962 when Congress rejected its proposal for the creation of a cabinet-level Department of Urban and Housing Affairs. The lawmakers also refused to act on the president's recommendation for a federally assisted mass transportation program, and administration measures such as the liberalization of the immigration law, youth employment legislation, general aid to medical schools and medical students, and a bill to assist migrant workers all bogged down in Congress.

Kennedy was no more successful in his fight for the so-called Medicare program. He had cosponsored a federal medical assistance bill while in the Senate, but it had been sidetracked in favor of the Kerr-Mills Act of 1960. President Kennedy's health care proposal was embodied in the King-Anderson bill, which was introduced in 1961. The American Medical Association led a powerful attack on the measure, characterizing it as "socialized medicine." Although public hearings were held by the House Ways and Means Committee, a majority of the committee's members opposed the legislation, and the same was true in the Senate Finance Committee. Many critics contended that Medicare would be too expensive, that it would exclude millions of people not covered by Social Security, and that the Kerr-Mills Act was adequate for the nation's needs. In February 1962, the president renewed his recommendation to Congress, urging approval of a program that would provide medical insurance under the Social Security Act for retired workers over sixty-five. The administration marshaled all of its forces for the Medicare battle, helping devise a compromise bill and launching a grassroots campaign to promote it. But the bill was tabled in the Senate by a vote of 52 to 48, with twenty-one Democrats—mostly southerners—joining thirty-one Republicans in defeating the proposal. Most Americans, apparently, were not yet convinced that a national health care system was needed.

Chief Counsel Robert F. Kennedy and Senator John F. Kennedy (D-MA) question a witness during the Hearing of the Select Committee to Investigate Improper Activities in Labor-Management Relations ("McClellan Committee"), in May, 1957. *Photograph by Douglas Jones, Library of Congress, Prints and Photographs Division, LOOK Magazine Collection (PX-65-105:185).*

Most of the thirty-fifth president's domestic reforms—federal aid to housing, liberalization of Social Security, expanded public works, a higher minimum wage—represented extensions of the New Deal and Fair Deal. His boldest domestic proposals, including federal programs for education and medical care, were defeated. Still, JFK grew as a social reformer during his three years in the presidency, and under his leadership critical beginnings were made in such fields as area redevelopment, manpower training, and ways of dealing with water and air pollution. During his last year in office, Kennedy began to consider an "unconditional war on poverty in America." Several of the administration's earlier programs, such as the Area Redevelopment Act, the Manpower Development and Training Act, the Public Welfare Amendments, and the President's Committee on Juvenile Delinquency and Youth Crime, had emphasized job training, social services, and rehabilitation for the unemployed and deprived. Kennedy shared the growing awareness among Americans of economic inequality and deprivation in the United States.

KENNEDY AND THE CIVIL RIGHTS MOVEMENT

Although the Democratic platform of 1960 contained the most far-reaching civil rights pledges that had yet been made by a major political party in the United States, the Kennedy administration demonstrated great reluctance in sponsoring a broad civil rights program in Congress. Martin Luther King, Jr., later concluded that JFK had "waged an essentially cautious and defensive struggle for civil rights." The reason was not hard to find: Kennedy feared that administration pressure for such legislation would jeopardize the enactment of other important measures, known collectively as the "New Frontier," especially among powerful southern Democrats. The White House did exert its influence to help secure a two-year extension of the Civil Rights Commission in 1961, and during the following year it endorsed two voting rights initiatives. One of these proposals, a constitutional amendment outlawing the poll tax as a prerequisite for voting in federal elections, was approved by Congress.

In sharp contrast to its relative inactivity in the legislative field, the Kennedy administration proved to be vigorous in its use of executive action to promote greater equality in such areas as voting rights, employment, transportation, and education. Kennedy increased the appointment of blacks to high office. Carl Rowan became ambassador to Finland, Andrew Hatcher served as White House associate press secretary, and five African Americans were appointed to federal judgeships. The president gave firm support to the civil rights division in the Department of Justice, which emerged under Robert F. Kennedy's leadership as the strategic center of the administration's early efforts to advance the cause of African American rights. The younger Kennedy was perhaps more deeply committed to the civil rights movement than any other top administration leader, and he brought into his department a remarkable group of talented and dedicated young people to work on the civil rights frontier.

Among the administration's achievements was its part in desegregating interstate transportation, including terminal facilities. Following the Freedom Rides in the spring of 1961, the Justice Department obtained from the Interstate Commerce Commission an order integrating interstate buses and railroads and the terminals they used. The department also moved against discrimination in airport facilities, securing voluntary desegregation in most cases and in a few instances resorting to litigation to effect changes. In addition, the administration integrated the Army Reserves and National Guard, and it sought to desegregate facilities surrounding military camps. Meanwhile, the president conferred at the White House with delegations of southern businesspeople, theater owners, and newspaper editors in the interest of voluntary desegregation, and administration members like Secretary of Commerce Hodges of North Carolina worked to persuade southern leaders to cooperate with the government.

Administration officials did their best through private conversations and behind the scenes work to smooth the way for school desegregation in southern cities such as Memphis and New Orleans. In Virginia the Justice Department cast itself as the plaintiff in requesting the federal courts to compel the reopening of schools in Prince Edward County, which had been closed to forestall desegregation. Abraham A. Ribicoff, secretary of health, education, and welfare, announced in the spring of 1962 that only integrated schools would qualify for federal aid to "impacted" school districts and that the government was making plans to establish on-base schools where no desegregated public institutions existed in the vicinity of military bases.

The administration's greatest emphasis and its chief success in the civil rights struggle was voting reform. The right to vote was basic, Robert Kennedy declared, "and from it all other rights flow." Whereas the Eisenhower administration had filed only six voting suits, the Justice Department under Kennedy brought thirty-two suits in less than two years. The Democratic administration emphasized the ballot in part because it seemed to offer a safer alternative to the more volatile direct-action campaigns being waged by such organizations as CORE and SNCC. While the Justice Department sent several hundred federal marshals to protect the beleaguered Freedom Riders in Alabama in May 1961, such intervention troubled the president and his aides, who wanted to avoid alienating local and state leaders in the South. Attorney General Kennedy, asking for a "cooling-off period," encouraged civil rights groups to undertake large registration drives rather than protest demonstrations in the southern states.

As the pressure for change in racial practices mounted, the White House was eventually drawn into a dramatic confrontation with intransigent white supremacists in the Deep South. The spirit of defiance in Mississippi, the citadel of white supremacy, came to a climax early in the fall of 1962, with the impending desegregation of the state university. The federal courts had ordered the admission of James H. Meredith, a black Mississippian who had served eight years in the air force. Governor Ross Barnett, who had been elected with strong support from the Citizens' Council and other resistance elements, aroused the state with demagogic rhetoric and talk of nullification. The governor defied the court orders and denied Meredith's enrollment in the university. The White House tried persuasion at this point, but Barnett proved to be a devious adversary, and he secretly encouraged the gathering mob to attack Meredith and his escort of federal marshals when they appeared on the Ole Miss campus.

With a crisis at hand, the president addressed the nation over television, urging the students and people of Mississippi to comply with the court ruling. "The eyes of the nation and all the world are upon you and upon all of us," Kennedy said, "and the honor of your university and state are in the balance." Such pleas were to no avail. Meredith's appearance was greeted by an outbreak of violence, and only after a night of terror and a pitched battle involving thousands of students and segregationist sympathizers, on the one hand, and 400 federal marshals and a contingent of army troops, on the other, was the lone African American enrolled. Kennedy moved to quell the riot by sending in regular troops and federalizing the state's National Guard. Two people were killed and 375 were injured in the melee. Meredith was registered under federal bayonets, and some of the troops remained on the campus until the university's first black student finally graduated.

The force of events in the South, the rising tide of discontent in the black community, and increasing sympathy for the equal rights crusade among white Americans combined to bring about a decided alteration in President Kennedy's position. Among the developments that influenced the administration was a series of demonstrations beginning in early April 1963 against the segregated institutions and business places of Birmingham, Alabama. The demonstrations were led by Dr. King and the Reverend Fred Shuttlesworth. When the Birmingham police, under the leadership of the outspoken segregationist "Bull" Connor, met the peaceful demonstrators with clubs, fire hoses, guns, and police dogs, Americans across the country saw vivid pictures of the brutal repression in the news media and on their television screens. The president eventually sent federal troops to restore order in the city. In June 1963, when Governor George C. Wallace threatened to "bar the entrance" of two black students whom the federal courts had ordered admitted to the University of Alabama, Kennedy federalized part of the state's National Guard in order to guarantee the enrollment of the students.

In an eloquent television address on June 11, immediately after the Alabama episode, Kennedy declared that America was confronted "primarily with a moral issue." Continuing, he warned that "the fires of frustration and discord are burning in every city, North and South, where legal remedies are not at hand."

> One hundred years of delay have passed since President Lincoln freed the slaves, yet their heirs, their grandsons are not fully free. . . . They are not yet freed from social and economic oppresion. And this Nation, for all it boasts, will not be fully free until all its citizens are free.

Kennedy's address represented a critical turning point that moved him from the periphery to the center of the civil rights controversy. On the night of the same day the president spoke, Byron De La Beckwith ambushed and murdered Medgar Evers, the field secretary of the NAACP in Mississippi, as he entered his home in Jackson.

On June 19 Kennedy sent Congress a comprehensive civil rights bill. Since a focal point of recent equal rights demonstrations had been the exclusion of blacks from lunch counters, restaurants, theaters, and the like, a public accommodations provision was said to be the "symbolic heart" of the administration's bill. The chief executive proposed a limited ban on discrimination in public places, requested power to enable the Justice Department to sue for school desegregation when an aggrieved citizen asked its help, and called for a vital provision authorizing the government to withhold funds for federal assistance programs in cases of discrimination. Administration leaders moved energetically to develop grassroots support for the proposed legislation and to rally backing for it in Congress.

The struggle for black equality now seemed to be moving inexorably toward enactment of a broad civil rights law. The Birmingham demonstrations in the spring had sparked one black protest after another, and by the end of the year demonstrations involving growing numbers of whites had taken place in more than 800 cities and towns. The culmination came when 200,000 blacks and whites staged a great March on Washington on August 28, which the president praised for its "deep fervor and quiet dignity." When Martin Luther King delivered his powerful address on that occasion, he warned of the "whirlwind of revolt" that would sweep over the country if the rights of African Americans were delayed any longer. But it was soon apparent that Congress was in no hurry to pass the civil rights bill. The Senate Judiciary Committee, under the chairmanship of Mississippi's James O. Eastland, held hearings on the proposed legislation but took no further action during the session. The most significant activity took place in the House, where the groundwork was laid for ultimate success as a result of intensive negotiations between White House spokesmen and congressional leaders of both parties.

Kennedy became a full-fledged supporter of the equal rights movement only hesitantly and under considerable pressure. Nevertheless, no previous president had made more determined efforts to enforce the Constitution with regard to blacks. The Kennedy administration contributed substantially to the advancement of the nonviolent phase of the equal rights revolution. Despite the likelihood of losing several southern states in 1964 and signs of a "white backlash" in northern suburbs, Kennedy continued until his death to fight for civil rights legislation.

THE DEATH OF A PRESIDENT

In the fall of 1963 the president and his advisers were devoting more attention than usual to politics. In September Kennedy made a tour of eleven western states, and he later made a number of appearances throughout the East. Democratic prospects in the South were of particular concern to administration leaders, and Texas was especially critical because of a widening cleavage between a liberal Democratic faction identified with Senator Ralph W. Yarborough and a more conservative element associated with Governor John B. Connally. Following a visit to Florida in mid-November, Kennedy flew to Texas for appearances in several cities, an inspection of space installations, and an effort to patch up differences between the feuding factions in the state's Democratic Party.

In Dallas on November 22, Kennedy and the other dignitaries set out that sunny Friday morning in a motorcade from Love Field to the Dallas Trade Mart, where the president was to make a luncheon address. The people of Dallas, a dynamic city of modern commerce, greeted JFK warmly, despite some recent rhetorical outbursts by local critics of the administration and several displays of violence by the radical right during the past few weeks. As the president's open car moved through the cheering crowds in downtown Dallas, shots were fired and Kennedy was hit in the neck and the head; Governor Connally, sitting in front of the president, was also wounded, though not fatally. Kennedy's car sped to nearby Parkland Memorial Hospital, but efforts to save the chief executive proved futile, and he died half an hour later, at 1:00 P.M. Shortly afterward, Lyndon B. Johnson took the oath of office as president; the oath was administered on board Air Force One, as the jet plane prepared to take the body of the fallen leader back to Washington.

Within an hour of Kennedy's death, an employee of the Texas School Book Depository named Lee Harvey Oswald was arrested, after having allegedly shot a Dallas policeman, and was charged with the assassination. Oswald, a twenty-four-year-old former marine, was a self-styled Marxist who had lived for a while in the Soviet Union and married a Russian woman. Unstable and frustrated, probably psychotic, the young man was at one time a member of the Fair Play for Cuba Committee. He maintained his innocence through several hours of questioning, and then, in a bizarre sequel two days after the president's assassination, Oswald himself was shot and killed while being moved to another jail. His assailant was a Dallas nightclub operator with Mafia connections named Jack Ruby.

One of President Johnson's first official acts was to appoint a special seven-member commission headed by Chief Justice Earl Warren to investigate the assassination. The commission presented a report and a twenty-six-volume supplement in September 1964. The report concluded that Lee Harvey Oswald, "acting alone and without advice or assistance," had shot President Kennedy. Unfortunately, the Warren Commission's findings, which were meant to reassure the public and put to rest the many rumors and suspicions surrounding the president's murder, left a good deal to be desired. Despite its bulk, the report was not a thorough and careful piece of research. Critics of the commission

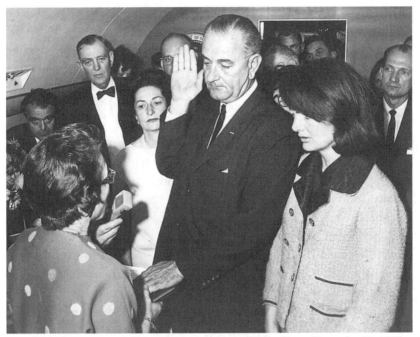

A new president assumes office aboard *Air Force One*, Dallas, Texas, November 22, 1963. *Courtesy Lyndon B. Johnson Library.*

soon challenged its lone assassin and "one bullet" theories. A variety of hypotheses about the assassination was given currency in scores of articles and books, including one that pictured Oswald as only a decoy set up by the real assassin and another that attributed the murder to some U.S. agency like the CIA. In *JFK* (1991), the filmmaker Oliver Stone presented an elaborate conspiracy theory that involved the CIA, the FBI, the Pentagon, and even Vice President Johnson in the assassination. To this day, conspiracy theories surrounding Kennedy's assassination continue to evolve.

The slain president's admirers spoke of the glowing prospects his leadership had kindled and the great progress that would have come in 1964 and later years had he lived. In *A Thousand Days* Arthur M. Schlesinger, Jr., wrote movingly of how Kennedy had "re-established the republic as the first generation of our leaders saw it—young, brave, civilized, rational, gay, tough, questing, exultant in the excitement and potentiality of history." Kennedy's youth, vitality, and modernity made him, in Adlai Stevenson's phrase, the "contemporary man." He understood better than most Americans the challenge of change, and he had a feeling for the way the world was going. Critics, by contrast, depicted a man of flaws and limitations, noting that, in spite of its outward brilliance, Kennedy's presidency achieved few of its major goals. According to the journalist I. F. Stone, "Kennedy, when the tinsel was stripped away, was a conventional leader, no more than an enlightened conservative, cautious as an old man for all his youth, with a basic distrust of the people." In later years commentators identified other weaknesses. The young president was perhaps too obsessed with imagery, he was not very sensitive to the conditions and needs of women, and in his private life his self-indulgence was evident in sexual excesses and macho behavior. Even so, John F. Kennedy's leadership was quite remarkable. He prepared the way for several of his successors' important reform programs, and no public figure since Franklin D. Roosevelt did as much to stimulate the idealism and self-sacrifice of his fellow citizens, particularly the young. At the time of his death, he seemed to be in the process of capturing the imagination of the American people as had few of his predecessors.

A NEW PRESIDENT AND A DEMOCRATIC LANDSLIDE

"Let us continue" was the advice the new president gave to Congress in his first address on November 27, 1963. Lyndon Baines Johnson took over the Oval Office in the White House confidently and with a firm hand. He conducted himself well, moving through the difficult days of Kennedy's funeral and memorial services with dignity and tact. Taking advantage of a more sober and supportive mood in Congress and throughout the country, Johnson adroitly maneuvered to break the long congressional deadlock. During the first hundred days of his administration the legislative logjam began to break up; the foreign aid bill was approved, the Higher Education Facilities Act was passed, the tax reduction bill was enacted, and the Kennedy civil rights legislation was passed by the House of Representatives. In 1964 during the second session of the Eighty-eighth Congress, Johnson's legislative accomplishments were still more impressive. The chief executive also succeeded, in the spring of 1964, in arranging a labor-management agreement for the nation's railroads, thereby preventing a serious national strike and a possible resort to compulsory arbitration.

While Johnson was consolidating his national leadership, the two major political parties were making preparations for the presidential election of 1964. The Republicans, racked by internal conflict and frustrated by the resurgence of Democratic strength in the late 1950s and early 1960s, turned abruptly from the moderate course followed by their presidential nominees since 1940 and launched a militantly conservative campaign for control of Washington. A variety of right-wing organizations had sprung up, among them the John Birch Society, the Christian Anti-Communist Crusade, the Citizens' Council, and the Minutemen. A kind of intellectual "new conservatism" found expression in the *National Review*, edited by William F. Buckley, Jr., and news commentators such as Fulton Lewis, Jr., Clarence Manion, and Dan Smoot added their voices to the "radical right" refrain. In general these zealous antiliberals stressed economic freedom; opposition to governmental intervention, social democracy, and heavier taxes; and unrelenting hostility toward international communism, which they interpreted as a pervasive and subversive threat within the United States.

The radical right found a political figure to rally around in Senator Barry M. Goldwater of Arizona. Goldwater, a millionaire department-store owner who was first elected to the Senate in 1952, had been a staunch supporter of Senator Joseph R. McCarthy. By 1960, when he made a strong impression on conservatives at the Republican National Convention, the senator had become an aggressive spokesman for right-wing elements. He was a popular after-dinner speaker and wrote a newspaper column carried by scores of papers. Goldwater summed up the tenets of his conservative Republicanism in *The Conscience of a Conservative* (1960), which had sold 3.5 million copies by 1964. He urged a sharp cutback in federal power and spending; a reassertion of state rights, including those involving school desegregation decisions; an end to farm subsidies and the restoration of agriculture to free-market conditions; and restrictions on organized labor. He believed that America's objective in foreign policy should be "total victory" over "the all-embracing determination of Communism to capture the world and destroy the United States."

While the conservative revival during the early 1960s was facilitating the emergence of Barry Goldwater as a national figure, a group of little-known Republicans was working to convert the movement into an effective political organization. Beginning in 1961, skillful GOP organizers such as Clifton F. White of New York (head of the Young Republicans), Peter O'Donnell of Texas, and John Grenier of Alabama began to take over the party machinery for the senator from Arizona. The leaders of the Goldwater movement aimed at both securing the Republican nomination in 1964 for the senator and remaking the party as a vehicle of militant conservatism. Bitterly resentful of the long domination of Republican presidential nominations by the moderate, eastern wing of the party, they were convinced that the "me too" leadership of men like Thomas E. Dewey had led to disaster and that a vast silent vote would respond to a nominee who presented "a choice, not an echo." Goldwater himself was tireless in his campaigning.

At the Republican convention in San Francisco, July 13–16, the conservatives completed their long-awaited conquest of the Grand Old Party. Tightly controlled by Goldwater partisans, the convention rejected moderate, internationalist Republicanism and revenged itself with verbal abuse of Governor Rockefeller and others who advanced anti-extremist positions. Goldwater was easily nominated on the first ballot, and William E. Miller, a conservative congressman from upstate New York and chairman of the GOP National Committee, was selected as the vice-presidential nominee. The platform was forthright in its conservatism. In his acceptance speech Goldwater asserted that "extremism in the defense of liberty is no vice!" and that "moderation in the pursuit of justice is no virtue!"

The situation in the Democratic Party was far simpler than that of the Republican. While Republican factionalism was threatening to destroy the GOP, President Johnson was preparing the way for the greatest Democratic victory since the days of Franklin D. Roosevelt. Johnson, as William S. White has observed, was a "compulsive competitor," and he set out to win the presidency in his own right—and to win big. His remarkable success with Congress and his impressive performance as executor of Kennedy's political legacy made him all the more formidable. Public opinion polls in the preconvention period showed him far in front of any Republican candidate. There were few surprises and not much drama in the Democratic National Convention, which met in Atlantic City, New Jersey, August 24–27. Johnson was nominated by acclamation. His running mate, whose identity the president revealed only at the last minute, was Senator Hubert H. Humphrey of Minnesota, whose choice reassured the party's liberal-labor component. The convention's placidity had earlier been disturbed briefly by a fight over the seating of the all-white Mississippi delegation and the later walkout of most of the Mississippi and Alabama delegates. Otherwise, the convention seemed to be united behind the president and his program.

In spite of the ideological contrast between the candidates and platforms, the presidential campaign of 1964 was a dull contest, one filled with strenuous campaigning and a plethora of platitudes. A leading theme of Goldwater's campaign was that "something basic and dangerous is eating away at the morality, dignity and respect of our citizens." The Republican standard-bearer continued to urge the need for a more militant foreign policy and to assert that the United States was pursuing "no win" policies abroad. In one campaign speech he declared: "I charge that this Administration is soft on Communism . . . I charge that this Administration has a foreign policy of drift, deception, and defeat."

Goldwater's campaign gave Johnson the great advantage of running as a social reformer and still seeming less "radical" than his opponent. When Goldwater tried to associate violence in the streets with civil rights demonstrations, the Democrats accused him of seeking a white backlash, anti-black vote. When the GOP nominee said he wanted to strengthen Social Security, the Democrats recalled his earlier statements about making the system "voluntary." Over and over Goldwater demanded, "What kind of country do we want to have?" To which Johnson replied, "The kind we've made it," and then proceeded to talk about prosperity, progress in education, and the goals of his Great Society. Charging that Goldwater was "trigger-happy" and would endanger world peace if elected, Democratic partisans reminded the voters that he had earlier recommended that NATO commanders be given control of tactical nuclear weapons and that he had once said, "I'd drop a low-yield atomic bomb on the Chinese supply lines in North Vietnam or maybe shell 'em with the Seventh Fleet." Johnson, following the adoption of the Gulf of Tonkin Resolution in late August, played down the war in Vietnam and urged a prudent course in foreign affairs.

The election returns on November 3 confirmed the opinion polls' forecast of a Democratic landslide. The Johnson-Humphrey ticket received a total of 43.1 million popular votes (61.4 percent) to 27.1

million for Goldwater and Miller. The Democrats carried forty-four states and the District of Columbia, with 486 electoral votes, while the Republicans won only five Deep South states and Goldwater's home state of Arizona, with 52 electoral votes. Only an unusual amount of ticket splitting saved the Republicans from greater losses in the congressional races, in which the Democrats added to their existing majorities by gaining 38 seats in the House and two in the Senate. Republican candidates in state legislative races experienced numerous defeats, with the GOP losing more than 500 seats it had previously held. Since almost all state legislatures were faced with the compulsory reapportionment of their own bodies and congressional redistricting as a result of *Baker* v. *Carr* (1962) and *Wesberry* v. *Sanders* (1964), the Democrats were in a good position to draw the new lines to their own long-range advantage. Kennedy's assassination made a Democratic victory in 1964 almost inevitable. At the same time, the Democratic triumph owed a good deal to Johnson's emergence as a genuine national leader and his record of accomplishment as president.

———————★———————

SUGGESTIONS FOR FURTHER READING

Politics and domestic reform during the Kennedy years are examined in Irving Bernstein, *Promises Kept: John F. Kennedy's New Frontier* (1991); David Mark Chalmers, *And the Crooked Places Made Straight: The Struggle for Social Change in the 1960s* (2nd ed., 1996); and Allen J. Matusow, *The Unraveling of America: A History of Liberalism in the 1960s* (1984). The previously cited general works by Blum, Gilbert, and Patterson are also useful. Three other important books, all mentioned before, focus on Kennedy as president: Parmet, *JFK: The Presidency of John F. Kennedy*; Giglio, *The Presidency of John F. Kennedy*; and Reeves, *President Kennedy*. Tom Wicker's *JFK and LBJ: The Influence of Personality upon Politics* (1968) is a revealing comparison of the two Democratic presidents.

Economic reforms, regulations, and trends during the early 1960s are considered in Jim F. Heath, *John F. Kennedy and the Business Community* (1969), and Kim McQuaid, *Uneasy Partners: Big Business in American Politics, 1945–1990* (1994). See also Collins, *The Business Response to Keynes*; Calleo, *The Imperious Economy*; Stein, *The Fiscal Revolution in America*; and Stein, *Presidential Economics*, all referred to before. The steel crisis of 1962 is discussed in Grant McConnell, *Steel and the Presidency—1962* (1963). Walter A. McDougall, *The Heavens and the Earth: A Political History of the Space Age* (1985), illuminates the politics of the space program.

The best studies of the Kennedy administration and civil rights are Carl M. Brauer, *John F. Kennedy and the Second Reconstruction* (1977), and Hugh Davis Graham, *Civil Rights and the Presidency: Race and Gender in American Politics, 1960–1972* (1992), an abridgement of Graham's *The Civil Rights Era: Origins and Development of National Policy* (1990). Mark Stern, *Calculating Visions: Kennedy, Johnson, and Civil Rights* (1992), is also useful. Examples from the extensive literature on the Second Reconstruction include Richard H. King, *Civil Rights and the Idea of Freedom* (1992); John A. Salmond, *"My Mind Set on Freedom": A History of the Civil Rights Movement* (1997); Clayborne Carson, *In Struggle: SNCC and the Black Awakening of the 1960s* (1981); and Michael R. Belknap, *Federal Law and Southern Order: Racial Violence and Constitutional Conflict in the Post-Brown South* (1987).

Specific social reforms advocated by the Kennedy administration are considered in Graham, *The Uncertain Triumph*, and Barbara Kellerman, *The Political Presidency: Practice of Leadership* (1984), on federal aid to education; Edward D. Berkowitz, *America's Welfare State: From Roosevelt to Reagan* (1991); Sheri I. David, *With Dignity: The Search for Medicare and Medicaid* (1985); and Patterson, *America's Struggle Against Poverty*, cited above.

William R. Manchester, *The Death of a President, November 20–November 25, 1963* (1967), is an absorbing but controversial account of Kennedy's assassination. Among many other treatments, see DeLloyd Guth and David R. Wrone, *The Assassination of John F. Kennedy: A Comprehensive Historical and Legal Bibliography, 1963–1979* (1980); Henry Hurt, *Reasonable Doubt: An Investigation into the Assassination of John F. Kennedy* (1985); and Michael L. Kurtz, *Crime of the Century: The Kennedy Assassination from a Historian's Perspective* (2nd ed., 1993). Art Simon's *Dangerous Knowledge: The JFK Assassination in Art and Film* (1996) is interesting.

For the campaign and election of 1960, read the absorbing popular account by Theodore H. White, *The Making of the President, 1960* (1961), and the scholarly work edited by Paul T. David, *The Presidential Election and Transition, 1960–1961* (1961). On the presidential election of 1964 is Theodore H. White, *The Making of the President, 1964* (1965). For a more scholarly work, see Milton C. Cummings, ed., *The National Election of 1964* (1966). Barry Goldwater and the Republican campaign are analyzed in Bernard Cosman and Robert J. Huckshorn, *Republican Politics: The 1964 Campaign and Its Aftermath for the Party* (1968). The revival of the extreme right is discussed in David W. Reinhard, *The Republican Right Since 1945* (1983), and Mary C. Brennan, *Turning Right in the Sixties: The Conservative Capture of the GOP* (1995).

The most satisfactory biography of John F. Kennedy is Herbert S. Parmet's two-volume study: *Jack: The Struggles of John F. Kennedy* (1980) and *JFK: The Presidency of John F. Kennedy* (1983). Thomas Brown, *JFK: History of an Image* (1988), is a useful bibliographical essay. Thomas C. Reeves, *A Question of Character: A Life of John F. Kennedy* (1991), portrays Kennedy as a morally stunted man. Arthur M. Schlesinger, Jr., *Robert Kennedy and His Times* (1978), is a valuable source for the

Kennedy administration as well as a moving biography. See also Edwin O. Guthman and Jeffrey Shulman, eds., *Robert Kennedy in His Own Words: The Unpublished Recollections of the Kennedy Years* (1988).

James N. Giglio's *The Presidency of John F. Kennedy* (1991) is a good introduction to the Kennedy administration, with a comprehensive bibliography. Richard Reeves, *President Kennedy: Profile of Power* (1993), contains a detailed chronological summary of JFK's paper trail. Arthur M. Schlesinger, Jr., *A Thousand Days: John F. Kennedy in the White House* (1965), and Theodore C. Sorensen, *Kennedy* (1965), are notable contributions. Garry Wills, *The Kennedy Imprisonment: A Meditation on Power* (1982), is a critical assessment. Scholarly perspectives are offered by Hamby, Heath, Patterson, and Leuchtenburg—all mentioned before—and by John Morton Blum in *Years of Discord: American Politics and Society, 1961–1974* (1991). Kennedy's advisers are evaluated in Warren I. Cohen, *Dean Rusk* (1980); George W. Ball, *The Past Has Another Pattern: Memoirs* (1982); David Halberstam, *The Best and the Brightest* (1972); and Deborah Shapley, *Promise and Power: The Life and Times of Robert McNamara* (1993).

Roger Hilsman's *To Move a Nation: The Politics of Foreign Policy in the Administration of John F. Kennedy* (1967) is still one of the best general accounts of Kennedy's diplomacy. Among other important studies are Thomas G. Paterson, ed., *Kennedy's Quest for Victory: American Foreign Policy, 1961–1963* (1989); Michael R. Beschloss, *The Crisis Years: Kennedy and Khrushchev, 1960–1963* (1991); Richard J. Walton, *Cold War and Counterrevolution: The Foreign Policy of John F. Kennedy* (1972); Montague Kern and others, *The Kennedy Crises: The Press, the Presidency, and Foreign Policy* (1983); and Joseph F. Berry, Jr., *John F. Kennedy and the Media: The First Television President* (1987). Also consult the books by Ambrose, Brands, Cohen, Gaddis, Levering, McCormick, and Paterson cited in earlier chapters.

A potpourri of other foreign affairs studies is useful for the Kennedy years, including John W. Evans, *The Kennedy Round in American Trade Policy: The Twilight of the GATT?* (1971); Gerald T. Rice, *The Bold Experiment: JFK's Peace Corps* (1985); Richard B. Mahoney, *JFK: Ordeal in Africa* (1983); and Timothy P. Maga, *John F. Kennedy and the New Pacific Community, 1961–63* (1990).

Background and setting for U.S.–Latin American relations are provided in David Green's *The Containment of Latin America: A History of the Myths and Realities of the Good Neighbor Policy* (1971); Cole Blazier's *The Hovering Giant: U.S. Responses to Revolutionary Changes in Latin America* (1976); and Gaddis Smith's *The Last Years of the Monroe Doctrine, 1945–1993* (1994). The Alliance for Progress is the subject of Jerome Levinson and Juan de Onis, *The Alliance That Lost Its Way: A Critical Report on the Alliance for Progress* (1970). Trumbull Higgins, *The Perfect Failure: Kennedy, Eisenhower, and the CIA at the Bay of Pigs* (1987), describes that fiasco. For the background of the missile crisis of 1962, see Morley, *Imperial State and Revolution*, and Paterson, *Contesting Castro*, referred to earlier. The crisis itself is examined in Mark J. White, *Missiles in Cuba: Kennedy, Khrushchev, Castro, and the 1962 Crisis* (1997); Graham T. Allison, *Essence of Decision: Explaining the Cuban Missile Crisis* (1971); Robert F. Kennedy, *Thirteen Days: A Memoir of the Cuban Missile Crisis* (1969); Raymond L. Garthoff, *Reflections on the Cuban Missile Crisis* (1989); and James G. Blight and David A. Welch, *On the Brink: Americans and Soviets Reexamine the Cuban Missile Crisis* (1989).

The conflict over Berlin is discussed in Robert M. Slusser, *The Berlin Crisis of 1961: Soviet-American Relations and the Struggle in the Kremlin, June–November 1961* (1973), and Peter Wyden, *Wall: The Inside Story of Divided Berlin* (1989). The nuclear buildup and disarmament efforts are considered in Glenn T. Seaborg, with the assistance of Benjamin S. Loeb, *Kennedy, Khrushchev, and the Test Ban* (1981), and Bernard J. Firestone, *The Quest for Nuclear Stability: John F. Kennedy and the Soviet Union* (1982).

In *America's Longest War: The United States and Vietnam, 1950–1975* (3rd ed., 1995), George C. Herring offers a reliable and balanced history of the United States in Vietnam. See also Charles E. Neu, *America's Lost War: Vietnam, 1945–1975* (2005); William J. Rust, *Kennedy in Vietnam* (1985); David L. Anderson, ed., *Shadow on the White House: Presidents and the Vietnam War, 1945–1975* (1993); George McT. Kahin, *Intervention: How America Became Involved in Vietnam* (1986); and R. B. Smith, *An International History of the Vietnam War* (1986). For valuable primary sources, see *The Pentagon Papers: The Defense Department History of United States Decisionmaking on Vietnam*, Senator Gravel edition, 5 vols. (1971), esp. vol. 2, and *Foreign Relations of the United States, 1961–1963*, vol. 1: *Vietnam 1961* (1988).

★

CHAPTER

6

The Culture of Affluence
and Anxiety: Postwar America

NOT SURPRISINGLY, AMERICAN CULTURE WAS STRONGLY influenced by the long-sustained prosperity of the postwar period. At the same time, the cultural effects of a pervasive but seldom articulated anxiety induced by the Cold War and an awareness of living under the shadow of a nuclear holocaust were scarcely less compelling. Many traditional values persisted in the new era, while longtime trends such as the commitment to public education and faith in organized religion continued and were frequently strengthened. There were also powerful new forces that affected the nation's culture, including the development of the mass media, particularly television. None of the new trends was more remarkable than the rise of science, which swiftly attained a position of almost universal prestige and popular faith. On the other hand, in the 1960s a much-publicized counterculture savagely attacked established cultural patterns and sought alternative lifestyles and values. Meanwhile, the literary scene changed drastically in the quarter-century following the war, reflecting not so much the realities of the evolving American society as the subtle shifts in fundamental assumptions and outlook.

EDUCATION: THE TROUBLED CRUSADE

At the end of World War II, education in the United States faced a number of pressing problems, including low salaries and a shortage of teachers, a desperate need for new buildings and equipment, overcrowded colleges and universities, and uncertainty about funding sources. In the absence of broad federal support, there was no effective means of equalizing educational resources, and thousands of small, poorly equipped schools continued to hobble along as best they could. The onset of the Cold War put new constraints on the education system in the form of censorship and loyalty oaths. While engaging in a spirited debate over the nature of these problems and possible solutions to them, Americans set out to expand and improve their schools. Their efforts rested on the traditional American belief in the social utility of education, a conviction that the school could "cure society's ills" as well as provide an essential vehicle for self-improvement. There were, in addition, more tangible factors: continuing prosperity, the broadening middle class, the baby boom, the G.I. Bill of Rights, and the demands of an increasingly complex society in a technological age.

Almost every year witnessed more people in attendance at every level of education. The number of children attending public schools increased from 25 million in 1945 to almost 45 million in 1975. Expenditures for public schools during the 1950s rose from $6 billion to $15 billion a year, and the proportion of the gross national product devoted to education steadily increased. Teachers' salaries enjoyed marked improvement, the average expenditure per pupil went up substantially, the school term was lengthened, and facilities were gradually improved. College and professional school enrollments boomed. By 1970 almost 60 million students were attending schools in the United States, and the nation's expenditures for education totaled more than $78 billion annually. Three out of every four American youths were completing high school, two out of every five were going to college, and nearly a million people were earning a college or university degree every year.

These gains resulted in part from the fact that during the 1950s the public schools became the subject of extensive criticism, much of it by educators. The criticism centered on the charges that the educational system lacked intellectual vitality and discipline, that it emphasized mediocrity at the expense of excellence, and that it promoted athletics and social activities rather than basic academic work. A spate of books and articles challenged the rationale of a "child-centered" school system and pointed out the essential mindlessness of the "life adjustment" doctrine associated with "progressive education." Such books as historian Albert Lynd's *Quackery in the Public Schools* (1953) and historian Arthur E. Bestor's *Educational Wastelands* (1953) proclaimed their themes in their titles. Bestor was scathing in his criticism of the educationists, and he urged the establishment of more rigorous standards, teacher involvement in professional scholarship, and greater academic freedom. Less searching was English professor Rudolf Flesch's *Why Johnny Can't Read,* a best seller published in 1955. Later in the decade James B. Conant, former president of Harvard University, wrote a widely read volume, *The American High School Today* (1959). Conant recommended the elimination of the small high school, the need to enhance the intellectual foundation of the curriculum, and the desirability of raising the minimum standards for high school students.

The Soviet Union's spectacular success in launching the two *Sputnik* satellites in the autumn of 1957 precipitated a new crisis in American education. The events dramatized the apparent superiority of Russian scientists, highlighted the fact that the USSR spent a larger percentage of its income on education than did the United States, and increased the influence of the critics of the school system at home. Admiral Hyman G. Rickover, for instance, asserted that the schools had endangered national security by letting American students fall behind the Russians in science, mathematics, and engineering. Most people now agreed that the national interest depended upon improvements in the quality of U.S. schools, and the demands for meaningful federal action grew more intense. One result was the passage of the National Defense Education Act (NDEA) of 1958. This legislation provided for low-interest loans to college students as well as fellowships for advanced study in new and expanded programs. The NDEA also offered special inducements to college students who entered teaching, and it sought to strengthen instruction in mathematics, the sciences, and foreign languages at the elementary and secondary school levels. Federal aid, as well as the grants made by such private foundations as the Fund for the Advancement of Education, encouraged reforms in teacher training, updated facilities, and innovative courses in the natural sciences, foreign languages, and other fields. Meanwhile, innovators like Jerome S. Bruner were demonstrating novel approaches to learning, and the school curriculum soon began to include the "new math," the "new biology," and so forth.

Educational successes in the 1960s and 1970s were impressive. The promise of education was extended to virtually all of the nation's children, regardless of race or national origin. A much larger proportion of students of high ability was admitted to colleges and universities. Significant modifications were made in the educational preparation of teachers, and important changes were introduced in school curricula. Increased federal aid to education became a reality, and noteworthy congressional statutes were adopted in 1965 and 1972. State agencies assumed greater responsibility in the operation of the public schools, states began to define standards of school performance, and statewide testing programs sought to achieve greater accountability among teachers and administrators for the instruction they provided. Education acquired unprecedented importance as a national resource, and the federal government made use of the schools in waging the Cold War and helping to solve pressing social problems at home.

Nevertheless, there were limits to this educational progress, and new, perplexing problems soon emerged. During the 1960s, in an era of curriculum reform and increasing federal involvement, the nation's schools were buffeted by social unrest. Schools and colleges were subjected to new political pressures and found themselves having to deal with new responsibilities such as affirmative action programs that directly impacted both student recruitment and admission policies. In the late 1960s and early 1970s, city after city rejected bond issues designed to finance the schools, and the courts in California and several other states struck down the heavy reliance on property taxes in educational expenditures. At the same time, the performance of many schools left much to be desired. The writer Charles E. Silberman, in conducting a three-year investigation of the schools in the late 1960s, found overwhelming evidence of repressive and arbitrary rules, the dehumanizing of learning, and what he called the "killing of dreams and the mutilation of spirits." He was dismayed to discover "what grim, joyless places most American schools are, how oppressive and petty are the rules by which they are governed, how intellectually sterile and aesthetically barren the atmosphere, what an appalling lack of civility obtains on the part of teachers and principals, what contempt they unconsciously display for children as children." In 1975 the College Entrance Examination Board revealed that scores on the Scholastic

Aptitude Test (SAT), taken each year by more than a million high school seniors, had declined steadily since 1964. And several reports over the next few years identified alarming deficiencies in the school system. While the growing and demographically changing K–12 student population presented great chalenges to teachers and administrators, the expansive numbers of high school graduates made a positive impact on the nation's colleges and universities.

The development of higher education in the United States after 1945 was nothing less than spectacular. College and university enrollment more than doubled between 1940 and 1960, climbing to almost 4 million by the latter year and to more than 8 million by 1970. The number of the nation's graduate students increased from 120,000 in 1946 to 900,000 in 1970. The growth of community and junior colleges, once scorned as "high schools with ashtrays," was especially notable in the 1960s. By 1980 approximately 4.5 million students were attending institutions of this type. Adult education also flourished, with millions of people being involved in continuing education programs. The inundation of the campuses in the postwar years created numerous problems, including the need for more classrooms, dormitories, library facilities, and laboratory equipment. But the needs were somehow met, and state and private support of higher education grew rapidly. The federal government also contributed indispensable assistance, first in the form of the G.I. Bill and various foreign exchange programs and later through the NDEA legislation and the education measures of the 1960s.

Higher education's democratization, paralleling the growth of the middle class, went a long way toward ending the old exclusivity of the nation's colleges. University professors after mid-century were increasingly drawn from new-stock Americans and other new additions to the middle class. With the expansion of higher education, a college degree became a prerequisite for a growing number of occupations. One study found, for example, that almost 60 percent of the big business leaders of 1952 were college graduates, as compared with 30 percent a generation earlier. Meanwhile, the universities became more intimately involved in the larger community: in the social application of their scientific and social science investigations, in their cultural programs, and in big-time football and other athletic events. Collectively, the president of the Carnegie Corporation of New York observed in 1971, "American universities, colleges, and two-year institutions prepare young people for an extraordinary range of professions, subprofessions, and occupations." They also served "an indispensable purpose as *custodians of our cultural heritage.*"

The remarkable growth of higher education did, however, lead to new problems. Many educational institutions became huge "multiversities"—impersonal, mechanical in approach, bureaucratic. Student demonstrations at the University of California, Berkeley, in 1964 and on many other campuses in later years were, in part at least, protests against large classes, a highly structured approach to learning, a sterile lecture system, and the neglect of individual student development. The ferment of the 1960s, including opposition to the Vietnam War, had a pronounced effect on colleges and universities. Students seemed to have become more socially conscious, and they began to demand a greater voice in the operation of the universities. Indeed, a student rebellion swept the nation during the late 1960s. Even though it shocked many older Americans, the student movement ultimately resulted in greater student involvement in academic decision making, the relaxation of in loco parentis rules, the introduction of new courses, and increased enrollment from minority groups. Still, the student movement did not radically transform American institutions of higher education. As the campus upheavals subsided after 1970, there was mounting concern over the "new depression in higher education," a consequence of the leveling off in the rate of growth of the college-age population and the economic downturn of the seventies.

No aspect of contemporary intellectual progress can compare with the dramatic emergence of science in American life. By 1965 a million Americans held scientific degrees, and the annual output of new Ph.D.s in science was about 8,000. Whereas the federal government spent a paltry $50 million for scientific research and development in 1939, it was allocating approximately $15 billion for such work by the mid-1960s. An incredible proliferation of scientific literature resulted from the publication of hundreds of thousands of scientific papers every year. Employment opportunities continually increased for scientists, engineers, and technicians. The university was central to this "knowledge revolution," which proved to be a major factor in the dynamism of the U.S. economy and in reshaping the nation's society, including its occupational structure.

The remarkable accumulation of new scientific knowledge involved basic research, the application of scientific findings to new processes and products, and the commercial development of new technology. Among the more notable developments by American scientists were advances in nuclear physics, the progress of medical science, the rise of jet air transportation, spectacular successes in exploring outer space, and perfection of the electronic computer. Americans won more than their share of the prestigious Nobel Prizes in science and medicine.

THE CHANGING SHAPE OF AMERICAN RELIGION

Religion prospered in the post–World War II era. Church membership increased from 64.5 million (49 percent of the total population) in 1940 to 125 million (64 percent) in 1965. Almost all religious bodies added to their membership during this period, the Pentecostal groups, Southern Baptists, and Roman Catholics being especially noteworthy for their rates of growth. By 1972 the membership of the Roman Catholic Church stood at 48.2 million. The various Baptist churches counted 27 million members, the Methodists 13 million, and the Lutherans 8.8 million. Jewish congregations comprised 5.6 million members. Most Americans were prepared, in response to an inquiry of the mid-1950s, to identify themselves in religious terms: 68 percent as Protestants, 23 percent as Catholics, and 4 percent as Jews. Gallup polls taken in 1975 and 1976 indicated that on Sundays 41 percent of the nation's adult population went to church, that 94 percent of those questioned expressed a belief in God, that 69 percent believed in life after death, and that 34 percent had undergone a "born again" experience. Millions of Americans—particularly among evangelicals, fundamentalists, and Pentecostal Protestants—accepted the inerrancy of the apocalyptic passages in the Scriptures, believing that the course of history and the sequence of events leading to the end of the world had been foretold in the Bible.

Among the more remarkable aspects of the religious landscape in the early postwar years was the vogue of a "peace of mind" religion that seemed to result, in some measure, from the shadow of the atomic bomb, the frustrations of the Cold War, and the search for relief from social problems. This "cult of reassurance" was evident in a rash of inspirational books such as Fulton J. Sheen's *Peace of Soul* (1949) and Norman Vincent Peale's *The Power of Positive Thinking* (1952), in epic films such as *The Ten Commandments*, in religious songs like "I Believe" and "The Man Upstairs," and in "Religion in American Life" programs that were popular on college campuses. Even theologians seemed to foster the idea that the church's role was, as one scholar has said, "to translate the Gospel into the pieties of contemporary culture." Will Herberg, a professor of Judaic Studies and Social Philosophy at Drew University, suggested that religion for the typical American "is something that reassures him about the essential rightness of everything American, his nation, his culture, and himself."

Closely related to these developments was a new interest in revivalism and evangelism, a point illustrated vividly by the postwar phenomenon of Billy Graham's mass conversions. Graham, a clean-cut and eloquent young Baptist minister from North Carolina, spoke with passionate sincerity and powerful effect, reasserting fundamentalist doctrine in a modern idiom. Fearing both internal subversion and the external threat of the Soviet Union, he also proclaimed a brand of Christian Americanism in the struggle to win the Cold War. Graham led one great crusade for Christ after another, speaking, for example, to 100,000 people at one time in New York's Yankee Stadium in 1957. His name became synonymous with mass evangelism. He displayed organizational skill and sophistication in leading the Billy Graham Evangelistic Association, made effective use of radio and television in his popular evangelism, and in a long career preached to more people than any other Christian in the world.

Religion in America clearly reflected but was also part of the popular culture. It was also boosted by politicians, including top leaders in Washington, which led writer William Lee Miller to speak of "piety on the Potomac" in describing the 1950s. President-elect Eisenhower declared late in 1952, for instance, that "our government makes no sense unless it is founded on a deeply felt religious faith—and I don't care what it is!" In 1954 Congress lent its support to the new piety, adding the phrase "under God" to the pledge of allegiance and during the next year making it mandatory that all U.S. currency bear the inscription

The New Revivalism: Billy Graham addresses a large crowd in Trafalgar Square, London, April 1954. *Courtesy Library of Congress.*

"In God We Trust." Some contemporaries lamented the fact that all creeds appeared to be submerged in a kind of "civil religion," which might be called the "American Way of Life." The emphasis seemed to be humanistic and secular.

In *Protestant—Catholic—Jew,* an influential book published in 1955, Will Herberg argued that the impressive growth of religion following World War II was part of a search for identity, especially by third-generation Americans in a rapidly changing social order where ethnic and other distinctions seemed to be disappearing. Thus, while the church enabled Americans to maintain some nominal distinctions, it also contributed to the homogenizing of the society. A kind of "national religion" had emerged, one based on good fellowship and good works. "By and large," Herberg wrote, "the religion which actually prevails among Americans today has lost much of its authentic Christian (or Jewish) content." Much of the church growth took place in the suburbs, and to a considerable extent the new institutional strength of the churches was a product of suburbia. The expansion of the middle class was particularly significant for American Catholics, whose rapid economic and social advancement ended the class disparity that in earlier times had often set them apart from mainstream Protestants.

In spite of these trends, religious division and conflict had by no means disappeared from the American scene. Catholics might be more fully assimilated into the national culture than ever before, but they were still resented and distrusted by many Americans. Organizations like the Protestants and Other Americans United for Separation of Church and State focused their attention on Roman Catholics, as did a stream of anti-Catholic publications that included books such as Paul Blanshard's *American Freedom and Catholic Power* (1949) and *Communism, Democracy, and Catholic Power* (1952). The question of federal aid to education and public support of parochial schools became a bitterly divisive issue among U.S. churches, with both sides sometimes resorting to name-calling.

No development of the postwar period provoked such a storm of protest and anguished condemnation as did the U.S. Supreme Court decision in *Engel* v. *Vitale* (1962), which held that compulsory prayer in public schools violated the First Amendment to the Constitution. The House of Representatives Committee on the Judiciary held hearings on the matter, many bills were introduced in Congress to restore prayer to the schools, and one congressman presented Emanuel Celler, the chairman of the committee, with a petition containing 170,000 signatures asking that God be returned to his rightful place in the classroom. The court's ruling was frequently disregarded, and many schools carried on with prayers as usual, seldom receiving any interference from local officials. In the meantime, another series of Supreme Court decisions, those involving school desegregation and civil rights, resulted in much controversy in religious circles, especially in the South, where rank-and-file church people tended to divide along racial lines in debating the court's decrees.

The social gospel had not been abandoned by American churches, despite the peace of mind emphasis and the somber views of the neo-orthodox. Most churches continued to perform good works in society, but a broader and stronger social reform impulse began to course through U.S. churches in the late 1950s and early 1960s. One example of this religious involvement in social amelioration was the role of the black church in the equal rights movement, most notably the leadership of Martin Luther King, Jr., in making the African American church a powerful lever in the fight for racial justice and equality. White ministers and lay leaders, particularly outside the South, soon began to take an active part in the struggle for civil rights, desegregation, and social justice in other areas.

In the 1960s American churches encountered new developments and new controversies. Traditional Christian theology, long challenged by science and rationalism, faced fresh assaults in the cultural rebellion of the decade. The churches, in part no doubt because of their participation in the social reform movements of the time, seemed to be increasingly inadequate—in a state of crisis. Existential doctrines were gaining adherents, and a situational ethics was postulating that people should be guided by internal human urges in dealing with a constantly changing and often irrational universe.

The religious upheaval of the 1960s was particularly evident among the young, some of whom now believed that mysticism or astrology or even magic was a more helpful guide to ultimate truth than either science or religion. Yet the dissent of American youth and their counterculture contained a strong appeal to faith. Jesus, whose ministry had stressed love and resistance to unjust institutions, attracted many of the young dissenters, as was evident in the popular musical *Jesus Christ Superstar*. The new supernaturalism was apparent in the antiwar movement, and many of the peace demonstrations in the late 1960s were filled with religious symbolism. Some of it was absorbed by the established churches in the form of happenings, rock masses, light shows, and readings from Eastern mystics. The meditation and transcendentalism of Zen Buddhism and other Oriental religions attracted thousands of youthful followers. A movement of "Jesus freaks," who were Bible-oriented but employed the language of the counterculture, began in California and spread across the country. Among Americans generally, the fundamentalist religion of Billy Graham, Oral Roberts, and other revivalists elicited an enthusiastic and broad-based response in the late 1960s and early 1970s.

In some ways the nation's Catholics experienced an even more profound upheaval. This eruption was to some extent a consequence of the extraordinary influence of Pope John XXIII, who died in mid-1963. But the reforms associated with Pope John proved upsetting to many conservative Catholics in the United States, the more traditional policies of his successor, Paul VI, aroused the opposition of numerous liberals and moderates in the American Catholic Church. Thus Pope Paul's long-awaited encyclical on birth control, *Humanae Vitae* (*Of Human Life*), reaffirming the church's ban on artificial contraception, was widely challenged and opposed by a majority of the younger priests in the United States. Many Catholics had begun to reassess the church's position on such questions as divorce, abortion, and the celibacy of the priesthood.

A new surge of religious fervor and revivalism marked the 1970s. Although the phenomenon of "Jesus freaks" began to lose strength early in the decade, more durable Jesus movements developed in the conservative denominations. Meanwhile, the Pentecostal movement broadened its appeal and grew rapidly. There was also a boom in conservative Protestantism in the form of neo-evangelicalism. By the late 1970s these groups claimed the loyalty of every third church member in the United States, and a survey in 1977 found that 70 million Americans described themselves as "born again" Christians. The remarkable appeal of evangelical, fundamentalist, and Pentecostal religions was promoted by television personalities and best-selling authors. Out of these movements and conservative political interests came organizations that were soon identified as the New Christian Right. One of the most prominent representatives of the New Christian Right was the Reverend Jerry Falwell, a Virginia evangelist and television superstar. Falwell led what he called the "Moral Majority," working with other fundamentalist groups and nonreligious right-wing organizations to register voters, campaign for political candidates like Ronald Reagan, and work to outlaw abortion and restore prayer to the public schools.

These movements may have grown at the expense of "mainline" Protestantism, but the established religious groups retained their own vitality in the 1970s and 1980s. Approximately 100 million Americans remained in the membership of Protestant and Catholic churches. Many Protestant churches underwent a process of spiritual reinvigoration. With ethnic diversity being more highly valued, Roman Catholicism demonstrated a renewed sense of "peoplehood." Judaism also experienced a spiritual recovery, an "inward journey" similar to that of other religious groups in the 1970s. At the same time, some older causes such as ecumenism lost ground. Yet polls suggested that the American people had become more tolerant of each other, and progress had been made in facilitating closer relations between and better understanding among Catholics, Protestants, and Jews.

POPULAR CULTURE

In a society characterized by enormous production, widespread prosperity, and increasing leisure, the stage was set for the emergence of a national culture that was more democratic and more homogeneous than it used to be. The economy was oriented toward the consumer as never before, and the insatiable appetite for middle-class amenities constantly reinforced the mass-production and mass-consumption business system. As technology made more leisure available for the average citizen, it also created the means for the use of that leisure, including the mass media, especially television, radio, and film. In addition, the cultural boom made the arts, literature, and high culture in general more available to ordinary people.

Any realistic characterization of the consumer culture in the United States must stress the sheer volume and variety of items purchased by Americans in their supermarkets, department stores, specialty shops, and shopping malls. An incredible array of products was consumed, which an earlier generation, one more circumscribed by the need to buy basic necessities, would have considered unattainable luxuries—art objects, stereo sets, jewelry, exotic foods, wine, camping and boating equipment, swimming pools, outdoor cooking equipment, power tools, and sporting goods, not to mention houses, appliances, and automobiles. Vacation travel became almost universal, and the motel became as ubiquitous as the automobile. Teenagers in the affluent society following World War II comprised an important part of the new consumerism, with their patronage of television, movies, records and phonograph equipment, and distinctive youth clothes. The attention given to the adolescent market was obviously influenced by the increasing number and purchasing power of the young. Though described by some observers as the "silent generation," many teenagers became dissatisfied with the sterile version of life projected by American music and television. They were attracted instead to the theme of rebellion in films like *Across the River* and *Rebel Without a Cause*, and some of them turned to the black subculture for an alternative to a homogenized America.

The Golden Age of Television was central to mass culture, as the small, glittering screen soon made its way into virtually every American house and apartment. "The most striking thing about the arrival of television on the American scene," John Brooks wrote, "was certainly the almost apocalyptic suddenness with which it became a fully established part of our national life, complete with a huge audience and an established minority opposition, affecting not only all our other communications media and the whole world of our popular arts but also our manners, morals, habits, ways of thinking." Television was almost unknown at the end of the war, and only a few thousand sets had been sold by 1947. But between 1948 and 1955, TV sets were installed in nearly two-thirds of the nation's homes, and by 1960 almost 90 percent of U.S. households had at least one receiver. By that time the average viewer spent about five hours a day in front of the "home screen." By the 1970s television reached more people than all the other media combined. Few Americans, the journalist David Halberstam observed, "doubted the essential goodness of their society. After all, it was reflected back at them not only by contemporary books and magazines, but even more powerfully and with even greater influence in the new family sitcoms on television."

Almost everyone quickly accepted the idea that television was the new medium. Art historian Karal Ann Marling put it well: "As seen on TV, everything suddenly looked new to the 1950s." Technical developments played an important part in the success of the new industry. The East and West Coasts were soon linked by coaxial cable and microwave relay. Transmission in color became prevalent within a few years. Satellite transmission, beginning in 1962, enabled people in Europe and other parts of the world to enjoy simultaneous reception of U.S. programs and televised events. Cable television, advancing rapidly in the 1970s, made it possible for subscribers to gain access to a larger number of channels.

In the meantime, television broadcasting in the United States was monopolized by three national chains or networks—ABC, NBC, and CBS. By the 1970s, their hegemony was formidable, even though they faced new competition from individual stations, public broadcasting, and cable systems. About 90 percent of the nation's TV viewers typically watched a network program in the seventies. Dominating the field of mass entertainment, the three networks presented numerous programs designed to attract a mass audience. Most of this fare, including the soap operas, family sitcoms, westerns, quiz programs, and variety shows, was incredibly insipid and uninspiring. The live coverage of athletic events soon became a TV staple, and by the 1960s television audiences for professional and college football, basketball, and baseball were enormous. There were some holdouts among academics and other intellectuals, who complained about the superficiality of most programs and the tyranny TV exercised over children, but their criticisms did little to stem the tidal wave of enthusiasm for the new medium. Still, the low level and trivial character of many of the network programs did provoke criticism, and the revelation of rigged quiz shows, highlighted by the dramatic case of Charles Van Doren in 1959, increased the adverse opinion of TV's performance. From January to March 1957, Charles Van Doren enjoyed a winning streak on the top-rated game show *21*, a question-and-answer based quiz show on NBC that pitted two contestants against one another in a battle over command of trivia. Two years after completing his legendary run and after a short stint on NBC's *Today show*, in response to affidavits filed by other former *21* contestants, a congressional hearing assembled in response to allegations that the game show had been rigged. During the course of his testimony, Van Doren revealed that the producers of the show had given him the answers to the questions he would be asked on the show. The revelation that this former Columbia University instructor and celebrity intellectual, who had even made the cover of *Time*, had committed fraud shocked the nation. In 1961 Newton Minow, the chairman of the Federal Communications Commission, described television programming as "a vast wasteland."

Few people doubted the tremendous potential of television. It appeared to offer great hope, for example, as an educational medium and a means of easing the loneliness and brightening the lives of older people, slum dwellers, and rural households. No other communications medium could compare with television in its capacity to make distant places an immediate experience and dramatize individual events, to etch them indelibly into the viewer's mind. Thus it seemed that the whole nation focused its attention on the Kefauver crime hearings, the quadrennial political conventions beginning with 1952, the Army-McCarthy hearings, the events following the assassination of John F. Kennedy, and the urban riots and peace marches of the 1960s. The historian Daniel J. Boorstin has suggested that "just as the printing press democratized learning, so the television set has democratized experience." TV's impact was apparently both protean and profound. It was a powerful agent in shaping the popular culture, celebrating what someone has called a kind of "classless prosperity," and in nationalizing and homogenizing American society. It also contributed to the "revolution of rising expectations" among the poor and disadvantaged.

The attack of the critics had some effect, for the networks cautiously began to introduce greater variety in their programming. Some high-caliber classical music, ballet, and drama programs were presented, as well as excellent documentaries, public affairs forums, and news commentaries. Educational television eventually made a place for itself, and National Educational Television became a real force in the early 1970s, stimulated by a $150-million contribution from the Ford Foundation. In time, television programming was diversified and enriched by the rise of cable systems and the decline of the long-dominant networks and by such developments as the video revolution. These changes did not, however, go far toward displacing the vast array of vapid and inferior programs that had become the staple of American television.

Given television's dominance of mass culture, the other major media—radio, movies, newspapers, and magazines—were forced into the position of secondary services, struggling to retain a share of the mass audience. Radio stations and the film industry, for instance, began to cultivate the teenage market. While losing the central place they had enjoyed in the entertainment field during the 1930s and 1940s, both remained indispensable components of popular culture. Radio had two huge constituencies: the millions of Americans on the highway at any given time and the millions of teenagers who listened to it as a source of current popular music. The wisecracking disc jockey became a cultural hero to the younger generation. Improvements resulted from the application of the new electronics to high fidelity and stereophonic sound and from the introduction of frequency modulation (FM). FM stations attracted older listeners by playing classical music and presenting cul-

Marilyn Monroe in
*Gentlemen Prefer
Blondes. Courtesy
Photofest.*

tural programs. Some radio stations also provided excellent news reports
and commentaries.

With the dramatic growth of television, Hollywood's voice became
less powerful. Average weekly movie attendance dropped by about half
between 1948 and 1958, and many movie theaters were forced out of
business. One response by the moviemakers to the box-office decline
was the production of high-priced extravaganzas like *The Ten Commandments, Exodus,* and *Cleopatra*—the last, a colossal flop. Some Hollywood
pictures such as *Dial M for Murder* and *Born Yesterday* achieved a high
level of technical excellence, and others, particularly such popular musicals as *The Music Man, My Fair Lady,* and *The Sound of Music,* proved
to be smashing box-office attractions. But a great number of inferior
pictures were made during the 1950s. Toward the end of that decade,
Hollywood capitulated to television by making available for showing on
the home screen most of its huge library of films. The industry soon be-

gan to produce motion pictures especially for TV, and by the mid-1960s it was once again prospering.

The sixties brought new vitality to American movies, in part because of the growing importance of small, independent film companies. Another factor was the importation of creative foreign films and their influence on American producers. Censorship, once a major problem for U.S. filmmakers, had become less burdensome. Some noteworthy movies resulted, among them *The Graduate, Patton, M*A*S*H, Dr. Strangelove, Easy Rider, Midnight Cowboy,* and *Z.* Meanwhile, the star system declined, although celebrated performers like Clark Gable, Bette Davis, Gary Cooper, Spencer Tracy, Humphrey Bogart, and John Wayne, as well as such younger stars as Elizabeth Taylor, Marlon Brando, Grace Kelly, William Holden, Gregory Peck, Paul Newman, Marilyn Monroe, George C. Scott, and Jane Fonda, continued to attract large followings. With the liberalization of obscenity laws, X-rated films became common. Movies became sexier than ever in the late 1960s and early 1970s. They also featured unprecedented violence and brutality, as shown in such popular films as *Bonnie and Clyde, True Grit, A Clockwork Orange,* and *The Godfather.*

Popular music, a vital part of contemporary mass culture in the United States, attracted the largest audiences in history through the media of radio, television, record, and tapes. Although the more conventional music forms represented by such varied performers as Guy Lombardo, Duke Ellington, Count Basie, and Louis Armstrong remained popular, a new style known as bebop or modern jazz emerged in the mid-1940s. Looser in rhythm and more advanced in harmony than earlier jazz, the new genre was played by small ensembles mainly for listening rather than dancing. It was best exemplified in the music of the saxophonists Charlie Parker and John Coltrane, the trumpeter Dizzy Gillespie, and the "smooth jazz" of the Dave Brubeck Quartet. A new urban music identified with the African American community and known as rhythm and blues also gained popularity in the late 1940s and early 1950s.

"Rock 'n' roll" was a reaction against the prevailing popular music and a powerful attraction to young Americans. A rhythm and blues variant, it drew upon black, country, and folk music. Featuring a strong beat and amplified guitars, it was audacious, defiant, and sexy. The his-

Elvis Presley, the "king" of rock 'n' roll, in a publicity shot from the movie *King Creole,* 1959. *Courtesy Photofest.*

torian William L. O'Neill suggests that in some ways rock 'n' roll was "the working-class equivalent of the Beat Generation." It erupted in 1954 with Bill Haley's recording of "Rock Around the Clock," which eventually sold 16 million copies. Singers like Chuck Berry, Fats Domino, and Carl Perkins prepared the way for rock 'n' roll's tremendous success, but its most popular performer proved to be Elvis Presley, a young white truck driver from Tupelo, Mississippi, with a wild vocal style and a potent combination of country music, gospel, and rhythm and blues. During the "golden era" of rock 'n' roll, between 1956 and 1958, Presley had ten number-one hit records, including "Heartbreak Hotel," "Don't Be Cruel," "Love Me Tender," and "All Shook Up." His succession of hit recordings continued during the next decade. Folk music also grew in popularity, especially after it became identified closely with the civil rights movement in the early 1960s. Pete Seeger, Bob Dylan, and Joan Baez attracted large audiences wherever they performed. The rise of country music also was noteworthy. *Country* was a generic term applied to such musical varieties as "hillbilly," "mountain," "cowboy," and "western." Nashville, with its Grand Ole Opry, became known as the country music capital of the United States.

A new form of music known simply as rock, introduced in England by the Beatles, the Rolling Stones, and other groups, was based on the older rock 'n' roll, employing a system of intensely amplified electric guitars and other instruments. The Beatles, who appeared on Ed Sullivan's Sunday evening TV show in 1964, soon became the premier musical phenomenon of their time. During the years that followed, innovators such as Bob Dylan, John Sebastian, Procol Harum, Paul Butterfield, Janis Joplin, and Frank Zappa elaborated the new rock music into folk rock, country rock, classical motif rock, blues rock, and jazz-based rock. Groups like the Who, the Yardbirds, and Led Zeppelin revealed the range of hard-rock sounds. As many of these bands and performers had migrated across the Atlantic from the United Kingdom, their dominant impact on American popular music came to be known as the "British Invasion." Rock also stimulated new ideas and new forms in other kinds of music. It was an important element in the musicals *Hair* and *Jesus Christ Superstar.*

Meanwhile, Frank Sinatra, who began as a big band singer, became a bobby-soxer idol, and then emerged as the "saloon singer" supreme. He continued to perform for many years, surviving the years of changing tastes and cultural upheaval. Sinatra's firm, pure baritone voice made him one of the greatest singers in the history of American popular

Scene from the Broadway production of the musical *Hair. Courtesy Photofest.*

The Rat Pack on the set of *Oceans 11,* 1960. Frank Sinatra, Dean Martin, Joey Bishop, and Sammy Davis, Jr. *Courtesy Warner Bros. Pictures/Photofest.*

music. Other stellar performers in the field of popular music included Bing Crosby, Perry Como, and Nat "King" Cole, all of whom recorded extensively and were perennial favorites. Among the most popular female pop vocalists in the postwar era were Peggy Lee, Billie Holiday, Judy Garland, Rosemary Clooney, Diana Ross, and Barbra Streisand.

The consumer culture in postwar America was nourished by old as well as new media. Newspapers were still widely read, although the daily papers were hit hard by rising costs, labor strikes, and increasing competition from radio and television. Newspaper publishing more than ever became a species of big business, and the trend toward consolidation proceeded steadily. The quality of the newspapers was not very high, except for a few first-rate papers like the *New York Times*, the *Washington Post*, and the *Los Angeles Times*. Most papers had a more or less standardized assortment of features and departments—sports, home furnishings, food, comics, finance, editorial, and the like—and the great emphasis was on the highest possible display of advertising. One interesting new trend that became noticeable in the 1960s was the rapid growth of small-town and suburban newspapers.

Mass media magazines were threatened by the emergence of television in the 1950s, but a number of them enjoyed huge circulations during the first two postwar decades. Henry Luce's *Time* claimed almost 14 million readers in the mid-1960s, as did *McCall's*, while *Ladies' Home Journal* enjoyed a readership of almost 12 million. *Reader's Digest* was even more successful. Nevertheless, ruinous competition for circulation, chronic management upheavals, and poor editorial quality contributed to the demise of many famous magazines, among them *Collier's, Saturday Evening Post, Look,* and *Life.* At the same time pulp magazines, including the romance periodicals, comics, and pornographic magazines, continued to prosper. Aside from the pulps, most of the magazines that seemed to fare best were those aimed at special audiences, periodicals as varied as *National Geographic, Psychology Today, Ebony, Playboy, Esquire,* the *New Yorker,* and numerous hobby and sports publications.

The popular book, in a variety of forms, was another agent of mass culture in the United States. Boosted by the "paperback revolution," the sale of books more than doubled between 1952 and 1961. By 1966, at least 38,000 titles were available in paperback editions, many of them serious works and even classics, and in the mid-1960s paperbacks were selling almost a million copies a day. Dr. Benjamin M. Spock's *Common Sense Book of Baby and Child Care* (1946) went through 167 printings within ten years and sold 23 million copies of the pocket edition by 1976, making it second only to the Bible as the best-selling book in American history. Books that reached a huge market, however, were often ephemeral, popular fiction like westerns, sexual novels, and detective stories, much of which appealed to the romanticism and nostalgia in the American mind. Thus Harold Robbins's series of sexual novels, beginning with *The Dream Merchants* (1949), enjoyed tremendous success, as did Grace Metalious's sexual epic of a small New England town, *Peyton Place* (1956), and Jacqueline Susann's stories of sexual conquest and ennui among the jet set, *Valley of the Dolls* (1966) and *The Love Machine* (1969). Even more remarkable was the popularity of Mickey Spillane's books, which had sold over 50 million copies by 1969. The spy novel, a detective variant, was widely read by Americans. Ian Fleming's *James Bond* (Secret Agent 007) adventures proved especially popular in the 1950s and 1960s and resulted in a series of lucrative movies. The popular book also included humor books, of which 650 titles, with a combined circulation of 100 million a month, were in print in 1953–54.

Possible consequences of America's extraordinary consumer cul-ture—its penchant for the cheap and sensational, its homogenizing tendencies, its vulgarization of the older, established culture, and its threat to rigorous standards—provoked severe criticism from guard-ians of "high" culture. The offensive was led by a group of New York intellectuals associated with the *Partisan Review* and other magazines; these critics argued that the more culture spreads, the more it tends to become corrupted and commercialized. Mass culture did not lack for defenders, however. Marshall McLuhan, a Canadian writer, argued that modern communications had transformed life and created a "global village." He believed that the old intellectual and aesthetic standards had been made anachronistic by technological innovation, particularly in electronic media, and that society was being reordered. Content was far less important than the experience of seeing and hearing, ac-cording to McLuhan. Others suggested that popularity and value were not mutually exclusive, and that there had been accomplishments of genuine merit in the popular arts.

A very different challenge to the consumer culture came from the cultural rebellion of the 1960s and the search for an alternative lifestyle by the young radicals of that decade. Like the beatniks of the 1950s, the adherents of the so-called counterculture criticized the values of the consumer society and resisted many traditional cultural patterns. Skeptical of the nation's vaunted technological achievements, they con-demned its unbridled materialism and manipulative social structures. The counterculture assumed various forms: absorption in rock music, adoption of distinctive clothing and hair styles, creation of a new vo-cabulary, acceptance of a more liberal code of sexual behavior, use of hallucinogenic drugs, and an interest in mystical experiences. Although most of the youthful radicals of the late sixties sooner or later rejoined the mainstream culture, what they did in their youth left a significant cultural residue.

ART AND AMERICAN LIFE

The cultural boom that developed in the United States by mid-century extended to the fine arts as well as the popular culture. Not only were more and more Americans financially able to patronize artistic endeavors, but the number of well-educated people with an interest in the arts had reached substantial size. Cultural centers, arts councils, and local art museums multiplied. The number of symphony orchestras in the United States more than doubled between 1950 and 1965, and virtually every American city with more than 50,000 inhabitants had such an orchestra. Hundreds of chamber music groups, "art" cinema houses, FM radio stations, and community theaters made their appearance. In spite of the public's heightened interest in the arts and increasing private support of artists, the continuing need for more adequate financial backing eventually resulted in greater government involvement at all levels in the promotion of art and "high culture." Thus in the 1960s New York City completed its Lincoln Center for the Performing Arts, an impressive complex for concerts, opera, ballet, and drama. In 1964 Los Angeles inaugurated its huge music center pavilion, and in 1971 the John F. Kennedy Center for the Performing Arts opened in Washington, D.C. In 1965 Congress passed the National Arts and Humanities Act, which provided, among other things, federal grants-in-aid to groups and individuals concerned with creative and performing arts.

The American response to operatic and other forms of classical music was most noteworthy in people's enthusiasm for performing artists. There were also some outstanding American composers of "serious" music, including Aaron Copland, Charles Ives, Kurt Weill, Elliot Carter, Samuel Barber, Roger Sessions, and Hugo Weisgall. Many universities attracted composers such as Walter Piston and Douglas Moore as permanent residents. The versatile Leonard Bernstein, conductor of the New York Philharmonic Orchestra, produced operas, symphonies, chamber music, and musical comedies. Ballet enjoyed considerable support in the United States, not only in the widespread interest in famous foreign groups but also in the support of numerous local organizations. Ballet, as well as other artistic endeavors, benefited from the contributions of European émigrés. The Russian choreographer George Balanchine, for example, played a vital role in the great postwar success of the New York Ballet.

This period was also characterized by a good deal of experimentation in architecture. Perhaps the most conspicuous evidence of "modern" architecture in America was the growing popularity of the so-called international style, exemplified in the work of men like Ludwig Mies van der Rohe and in such structures as the Lever Building and the UN Secretariat in New York City. Employing new building materials such as stainless steel, aluminum, and enormous quantities of glass, the international style had the great virtue of simplicity and sweeping, geometric lines. All too often, however, the new public and commercial buildings designed in this style were simply glass-walled, rectilinear structures.

If new artistic movements did not often originate in the United States, they seemed to flourish there more exuberantly than in any other country. The art movement was stimulated by an expansive economy, art galleries, art schools, and art publications, as well as private and public foundations. In these years artists were blessed by an unprecedented level of support, instruction, and access to a public hungry for knowledge and novelty. Perhaps the greatest artistic renaissance in the postwar years occurred in the field of painting. American painters began to move away from the realism and socially conscious themes and mood of the 1930s—regionalism in painting, folk art, and the WPA artists' projects—toward abstraction, surrealism, and new art forms. To be sure, the more traditional realism of some painters remained influential, including Georgia O'Keefe's desert landscapes and Edward Hopper's portrayal of lonely city dwellers. Yet even the realistically oriented Andrew Wyeth, the single most popular American painter of modern times, considered himself an abstractionist. Like some other realists, his pictures projected a haunting quality of fantasy and dreaminess.

The movement that dominated American art in the postwar era was called "abstract expressionism." Rejecting representational art and traditional symbols of visual communication, the expressionists sought, whatever their particular emphasis, to create a mood or feeling, not a figure as it actually existed. Their great concern was with feeling at the moment paint touched the canvas. These painters, sometimes identified as the New York School, were unconcerned with perspective or objects except as they might be used to symbolize powerful life forces. They seemed to paint without plan or precision—with great splashes of color, crude shapes, and gobs of paint slapped or dripped on huge canvases. Much of this work could be characterized as "action painting." As art critic Harold Rosenberg wrote in an essay on the expressionist movement:

At a certain moment the canvas began to appear to one American painter after another as an arena in which to act—rather than as a space in which to reproduce, re-design, analyze or "express" an object, actual or imagined. What was to go on canvas was not a picture but an event . . . . What matters always is the revelation contained in the act . . . the way the artist organizes his emotional and intellectual energy as if he were in a living situation.

Traditionalists were frequently shocked and offended by the new art, while those without artistic knowledge often found it uninteresting, chaotic, or unintelligible. Yet abstract expressionism mirrored contemporary American society surprisingly well. It reflected the estrangement of the artist from the world of the atomic bomb and embodied a revolt against the materialism and novelty-for-novelty's-sake attitude of contemporary mass culture. By the late 1950s, abstract expressionism dominated painting in the United States, and it was accepted as the movement that had propelled American art to a leading position in the international avant-garde.

Jackson Pollock was the most famous of the abstract expressionists. He laid his huge canvases on the floor, working from four sides, walking around on the canvas, literally in the painting. Pollock produced a number of extraordinary works, such as his *Blue Poles*, notable for its use of brilliant color. Among the other well-known abstract expressionists was Mark Rothko, who painted great pools or vaguely defined planes of color. Franz Kline's paintings consisted of wide black strokes at seemingly random angles on a white background, conveying a generalized sense of modern tension. Large, gaudy slashes of paint characterized much of the work of Willem de Kooning, who was most famous for *The Women*, a series of paintings completed in the early 1950s. Robert Motherwell and Clyfford Still were other talented artists who painted in this mode.

In the late 1950s, some American painters began to emphasize a new approach that led to a movement dubbed "pop art," a blend of commercialism and realism, with a dash of dadaism. Its antecedents may also have included such works as Picasso's *Plate with Wafers* (1914). Possessing clearly defined, hard-edged forms, this new art lacked quality of movement or a sense of duration. Pop art began with the most common of the arts that surrounded people—comic strips, billboards, magazine

Jackson Pollock's *Echo*, 1951. Oil on canvas, 7′ 7-¹/₈″ x 7′2″. *Courtesy the Museum of Modern Art, New York. Acquired through the Lillie P. Bliss Bequest and the Mr. and Mrs. David Rockefeller Fund.*

advertisements, display windows, and in the words of one critic, "any mass-produced vulgarity." Pop artists painted such mundane objects as soup cans and packing cases. They sometimes seemed to be satirizing the nation's mass-production, consumer-oriented society. At times their work contained an element of social realism and a statement about the deteriorating human environment. Robert Rauschenberg, one of the new mode's originators, created a successful object work in 1955 simply entitled *Bed*. It consisted of a real quilt and pillow on a stretcher, with other designs and objects added. Jasper Johns produced a celebrated work he called *Painted Bronze* (1960), a casting of two Ballantine Ale cans with the labels painted on. Roy Lichtenstein, Andy Warhol, Claes Oldenburg, James Rosenquist, and Tom Wesselmann, among others, made pop art the vogue during the following few years. Critics such as Hilton Kramer of the *New York Times* charged that these "unserious" painters were offering easy-to-read, cheap thrills in place of the more difficult, less amusing works of modernism. Although many observers found it hard to tell whether pop art was a significant art movement, a diverting novelty, or perhaps only a running gag, in the 1960s it demonstrated all of the characteristics of a genuine art movement.

To the horror of traditionalists, the pop art movement proved resilient and incredibly popular. In New York City's Metropolitan Museum of Art, curator Henry Geldzahler assembled arguably the most influential special exhibit in the twentieth century in 1969 with the New York Painting and Sculpture: 1940–1970 exhibition. While some critics continued to rail against the new movements, no one could dispute the fact that Geldzahler's exhibition was a financial success beyond anyone's anticipation. Additionally, once the regal, encyclopedic, though stodgy "Met" validated pop art with this exhibit, widespread acceptance followed. Museums and galleries across the nation began to organize contemporary art exhibits in the wake of the Met's great success at drawing enormous patronage with contemporary art.

By the 1970s Americans were confronted with a variety of artistic movements and styles that was baffling in its diversity. Indeed, the conceptual range of art in the United States had become so great that once-familiar distinctions and terminology no longer applied. Words like "figurative" and "abstract" became meaningless as art took in all reaches of the mind and senses. Writing in 1979, the art historian Joshua C. Taylor suggested that, "with bases from scientific experiments in perception to drug-induced imagery, art represented too wide an exploration of human activity to be encompassed in a single set of terms or aligned in a particular direction."

THE LITERARY IMAGINATION

Unlike the aftermath of World War I, the years following World War II failed to produce a noteworthy literary renaissance in America. Several of the major literary figures of the interwar period continued to be productive in the 1940s and 1950s, including Ernest Hemingway, John Dos Passos, Eugene O'Neill, John Steinbeck, and William Faulkner. Few of these writers, however, added to their earlier reputations, and none was closely identified with any important new development in creative writing. Hemingway produced only two major works after the war, and one of those, *Across the River and into the Trees* (1950), proved a great disappointment. The other was a short novel entitled *The Old Man and the Sea* (1952), a compelling story of individual heroism in the face of relentless adversity. Faulkner, who wrote steadily until his death in 1962, was perhaps the most talented of all modern American writers. He turned out a succession of novels in the postwar period, among them *Intruder in the Dust* (1948), a Pulitzer-Prize winner concerned with race relations. *The Town* (1957) and *The Mansion* (1959) completed his trilogy on the Snopes clan. The human drama that Faulkner unfolded had a southern setting, but his artistic genius transcended regionalism and at its best achieved a powerful universality in its depiction of the contingency and precariousness of the human condition.

A series of war novels published between 1945 and 1952 marked the literary transition from war to peace. The most widely acclaimed of these novels was Norman Mailer's *The Naked and the Dead* (1948), a work obviously influenced by the examples of Hemingway and Dos Passos. It described the adventures of a combat platoon in the Pacific theater. Many of the war novels focused on the relationship between the individual and the impersonal military machine. Thus Private Prewitt, in James Jones's *From Here to Eternity* (1951), tries to maintain his individuality in the prewar army.

The postwar novel of manners was illustrated in the work of such writers as John O'Hara and John Gould Cozzens, who ably portrayed well-to-do groups in small-town settings; but this literature became steadily less characteristic of the literary scene. The social tragicomedies of John Marquand, usually set against the relatively fixed society of New England, began to seem parochial. John Cheever, author of *The Wapshot Chronicle* (1957), *The Wapshot Scandal* (1964), *Bullet Park* (1969), and other novels, revealed a vision of everyday life that was anything but normal. Cheever seemed less interested in exposing the fatuities and self-deceptions of his suburban New York and Connecticut world than he was in understanding the compromises and repressions of the "upwardly dispossessed," people whose very material success had removed them from all that was genuinely vital in life. As for postwar novelists in general, life seemed to have become too threatening, tenuous, and ambiguous to give social comment in fiction the fixed moral background that traditional storytelling requires. Saul Bellow's character in *Henderson the Rain King* (1959) summed up the mood: "Nobody truly occupies a station in life any more. There are displaced persons everywhere."

Novelists and poets turned to the individual human experience. Their writings reflected a deep-seated anxiety that mass society and modern technology would destroy the individual entirely. So strong was this sense of alienation—this feeling that people were strangers even to themselves—that writers found it almost impossible to create order in their imaginary worlds. Heroes and heroines disappeared from modern fiction, or they assumed absurd dimensions like Yossarian in Joseph Heller's *Catch-22* (1961), or they were simply antiheroes. The compelling focus became the individual's search for his or her own identity. American fiction also revealed a new preoccupation with the bizarre and grotesque and with satire and black humor, evident in such works as Ken Kesey's *One Flew Over the Cuckoo's Nest* (1962), Thomas Pynchon's *V* (1963) and *Gravity's Rainbow* (1973), and Kurt Vonnegut's *Slaughterhouse Five* (1969). In *Giles Goat-Boy* (1966), John Barth explored and satirized the human condition by making his hero the offspring of a woman and a computer. John Hawkes, Joyce Carol Oates, and other promising young writers explored horror and nightmares in their novels.

Many of the new writers departed radically from the conventional format of the American novel. The "beatnik school," which emerged in the 1950s and grew out of New York's Greenwich Village, included the novelist Jack Kerouac and the poet Allen Ginsberg. The "beats" were in tune with existentialism and Buddhism, and they attacked mainline literature, literary scholarship, and established criticism. They presented a picture of violence, perversion, and madness in their work. Vladimir Nabokov, a Russian émigré, produced one of the best fictional portrayals of contemporary America: the novel *Lolita* (1955), the story of an automobile tour of the United States taken by a seedy and depraved refugee scholar and a rudderless and sexy American adolescent. The book is funny and sad, and its evocation of the social and moral aspects of postwar America is curiously unforgettable. J. D. Salinger, a favorite of high school and college students in the 1950s, was concerned in *Catcher in the Rye* (1951) with the inner rebellion of Holden Caulfield and his search for identity and self-awareness. Salinger examined the same theme in *Franny and Zooey* (1961). A more prolific writer, John Updike, illustrated the use of unconventional form in *The Centaur* (1963), while revealing the modern concern with individual character and the antihero in such novels as *Poorhouse Fair* (1959), *Rabbit, Run* (1960), *Couples* (1968), and *Rabbit Redux* (1971).

One of the striking features of the American literary scene after World War II was the emergence of a new group of talented writers from the South. Its members included Carson McCullers, Eudora Welty, Walker Percy, Peter Taylor, Reynolds Price, and Elizabeth Spencer, in addition to more established writers such as Robert Penn Warren and Caroline Gordon. Two of the most gifted of the new southern authors were William Styron of Virginia and Flannery O'Connor of Georgia. Styron's major books include *Lie Down in Darkness* (1951), *Set This House on Fire* (1960), *The Confessions of Nat Turner* (1967), and *Sophie's Choice* (1975). The first is a powerful depiction of a tormented family in a small southern town. *The Confessions of Nat Turner* is a moving recreation of the life of the famous slave insurrectionist. O'Connor, who died in 1964 at an early age, provides an illustration of Southern Gothic at its best. Her novels and short stories—*Wise Blood* (1952), *A Good Man Is Hard to Find* (1955), and *The Violent Bear It Away* (1960)—are tragicomic allegories on humanity's fall, redemption, and faith, written from the perspective of a devout Catholic. This second generation of modern southern writers had, as Louis D. Rubin has observed, a strong awareness of the "inroads of time," a special feeling for landscape and place, a "relish for rhetoric," and an "uninhibited commitment to the full resources of the language both spoken and written."

Some southern writers were black, and the African American experience provided the focus for another significant group of postwar novelists and poets. In a sense these authors perpetuated the socially conscious literature of the prewar years, since they were intent upon showing what it was like for an African American to live in white America. Yet even they were forced to resort to symbols, and Ralph Ellison, in *The Invisible Man* (1952), the most celebrated African American novel of the period, adopted an oblique approach in order to suggest how it felt to be a sophisticated and sensitive black man in a white-dominated society. In his book, Ellison used the metaphor of "invisibility" to show that the black person in America was living in the midst of a society that refused to recognize his humanity. The best-known black writer of the 1950s and 1960s was James Baldwin, whose first novel, *Go Tell It on the Mountain* (1953), was about the great African American migration from the South to the urban slums of the North. As the black revolt intensified, Baldwin spoke out eloquently and sometimes bitterly in support of the drive for racial equality. *The Fire Next Time* (1963), a work of nonfiction, is an anguished and deeply moving indictment of white racism in the

United States. Among a number of gifted younger black writers were Ernest J. Gaines, John A. Williams, Alice Walker, and Toni Morrison. In *The Third Life of Grange Copeland* (1970), *Meridian* (1976), *The Color Purple* (1982), and other novels, Walker wrote in moving language and with profound insight about the inner life and character of black people. Alex Haley's prize-winning novel *Roots* (1976) recreated the history of his family in America.

In 1967 Norman Podhoretz, the editor of the Jewish journal *Commentary*, expressed the opinion that Jews were replacing southern writers as "the leading school of novelists." There was unquestionably an outburst of creativity among Jewish writers in the United States in the postwar era. Saul Bellow, Bernard Malamud, Philip Roth, Isaac Bashevis Singer, and several other writers produced notable novels, some of which dealt with American-Jewish life. Bellow, perhaps the most impressive of the group, in *The Adventures of Augie March* (1953), *Herzog* (1965), and other works not only provided a brilliant commentary on the confusion and sordidness of modern life, but also helped enrich the modern novel with his understanding of American manners, his instinct for the texture of urban life, and the tension he created between feeling and character in his novels. It was not clear, however, whether this literature signaled the reawakening of Jewish consciousness or the literary climax of assimilation and the weakening of Jewish self-awareness.

Norman Mailer was not primarily concerned with ethnic and religious consciousness, and his literary imagination seemed to transcend that theme. *Advertisements for Myself* (1959) suggested that Mailer was developing a literary genre peculiar to himself; the book included essays, doggerel, fictional experimentation, and a great deal of self-exposure. In the late 1960s Mailer turned to reporting, a shift also evident in the work of writers such as Truman Capote, and in a series of nonfiction books he wrote about the Democratic National Convention of 1968, the moon landing of 1969, and American involvement in Vietnam. His novel *The Executioner's Song* (1979), an imaginative and exhaustive re-creation of a real case in which capital punishment was resumed following its abolition by the Supreme Court, won the Pulitzer Prize. As the critic Richard Poirier has written, "More than anyone else of his time, Mailer is implicated, in every sense of that word, in the way we live now."

American poetry also entered into new directions and showed evidence of considerable vitality in the postwar period. A number of established poets from earlier years such as Robert Frost, Carl Sandburg, Archibald MacLeish, W. H. Auden, Conrad Aiken, e. e. cummings, Marianne Moore, Wallace Stevens, and William Carlos Williams continued to be productive. Frost, the grand old man of American poetry, became more abstract in his old age. Another of the older poets, Ezra Pound, was declared insane and committed to a hospital in 1946. He continued to write, however, and ironically his *Pisan Cantos,* based on his experiences in an army prison camp in Pisa, won the Library of Congress' Bollingen Award in 1948. The newer poets were preoccupied with psychological and mythological themes, humanity's alienation, and its quest for individual identity. Robert Lowell's *Lord Weary's Castle* (1946), for instance, was the exploration of a ruined world and an illustration of the conflict of opposites in Lowell's cosmography. Many of these younger poets demonstrated great technical ability, new and intricate styles, and philosophical subtlety. Among the more impressive of these writers, in addition to Lowell, were John Berryman, Elizabeth Bishop, Randall Jarrell, Karl Shapiro, Theodore Roethke, Richard Wilbur, Phyllis McGinley, William Meredith, Louis O. Coxe, Sylvia Plath, and James Merrill.

When they thought of the theater, most Americans thought of Broadway and such famous musicals as *Oklahoma, South Pacific,* and *My Fair Lady.* (The last, based on Bernard Shaw's *Pygmalion,* ran on Broadway for over five years.) But there were also more serious dramas produced in the post–World War II period. Eugene O'Neill, the most famous American playwright, while demonstrating less vitality and originality than in earlier years, wrote several plays after 1945, including The *Iceman Cometh* (1946) and *Long Day's Journey into Night* (1956). Of the newer dramatists, the most prolific was Tennessee Williams, who produced a long series of plays. The best of these—such works as *The Glass Menagerie* (1945), *A Streetcar Named Desire* (1947), and *Cat on a Hot Tin Roof* (1955)—were powerful dramas with great psychological penetration. Arthur Miller, in plays like *Death of a Salesman* (1949), *The Crucible* (1953), and *A View from the Bridge* (1955), protested the fate of the individual in a society dominated by materialism and conformity, while demonstrating his belief that tragedy was still possible in the modern theater and that its proper hero was the common man and woman. Other talented playwrights included William Inge, Lillian Hellman, and Edward Albee. Inge, with plays like *Come Back, Little Sheba* (1950), *Picnic* (1953), *Bus Stop* (1955), and *The Dark at the Top of the Stairs* (1957), was the representative American playwright of the 1950s. In *Who's Afraid of Virginia Woolf?* (1960), Albee exposed the illusions that people use to get along in modern life. *Raisin in the Sun* (1959), by a young black playwright named Lorraine Hansberry, was a poignant portrayal of a black family's struggle in an unfriendly white environment. During the years that followed, other playwrights came to the fore, among them Ronald Ribman, Sam Shepard, Jules Feiffer, and Lanford Wilson.

New groups, largely unrepresented in the past, were beginning to gain recognition in the American literary world. These included, in addition to women and African Americans, Latin Americans, and Asian Americans. Meanwhile, critics and other informed observers could no longer doubt that American culture was wonderfully dynamic and full of life in the years following 1945. The rest of the world could no longer ignore the cultural dimensions of the western colossus—such manifestations as the expressionism of Jackson Pollock, the literature of Faulkner and Mailer, the scientific achievements of U.S. Nobel Prize winners, and the continuing American efforts to develop a workable system of universal education. In that sense, at least, American culture had achieved its independence.

------ ★ ------

SUGGESTIONS FOR FURTHER READING

Norman Cantor, *The American Century: Varieties of Culture in Modern Times* (1997), considers the arts, philosophy, science, and political movements. Stephen J. Whitfield, *The Culture of the Cold War* (2nd ed., 1996), ingeniously examines the impact of the domestic Cold War on the movies, television, the press, and several other cultural institutions. Richard H. Pells, *The Liberal Mind in a Conservative Age: American Intellectuals in the 1940s and 1950s* (1985), surveys liberal thought in the postwar years. Among the more interesting studies that probe the cultural meaning of the 1950s and 1960s are W. T. Lhamon, Jr., *Deliberate Speed: The Origins of a Cultural Style in the American 1950s* (1990); William L. O'Neill, *Coming Apart: An Informal History of America in the 1960s* (1971); and Morris Dickstein, *Gates of Eden: American Culture in the Sixties* (1977), which gives special attention to fiction and rock music in showing the shift in cultural sensibilities during the 1960s.

The 1950s: American Popular Culture through History (2004), by William H. Young and Nancy K. Young presents a highly nuanced look into the social changes in the 1950s and their lasting effect on American society.

The best history of education in the United States since 1945 is Diane Ravitch, *The Troubled Crusade: American Education, 1945–1980* (1983), and it is especially helpful on the politics of education. For other books on educational developments, see Charles E. Silberman, *Crisis in the Classroom: The Remaking of American Education* (1970); David Riesman and Christopher Jencks, *The Academic Revolution* (1968); and Hugh Davis Graham, *The Uncertain Triumph: Federal Education Policy in the Kennedy and Johnson Years* (1984). Other themes are considered in Richard King, *The Party of Eros: Radical Social Thought and the Realm of Freedom* (1972), and Lary May, ed., *Recasting America: Culture and Politics in the Age of the Cold War* (1989). *Sex Goes to School: Girls and Sex Education before the 1960s* (2008) by Susan Freeman is a compelling study of the changing social mores of the era as reflected by female sex education practices.

For the main contours of American religious history in the postwar era, consult Martin E. Marty, *Protestantism in the United States: Righteous Empire* (2nd ed., 1986); Robert Wuthnow, *The Restructuring of American Religion: Society and Faith Since World War II* (1988); and Philip Gleason, ed., *Contemporary Catholicism in the United States* (1969). Other important studies include David Edwin Harrell, Jr., *All Things Are Possible: The Healing & Charismatic Revivals in Modern America* (1975); Nathan Hatch, *The Democratization of American Christianity* (1989); and Carol V. R. George, *God's Salesman: Norman Vincent Peale and the Power of Positive Thinking* (1993), Modern revivalism is examined in William G. McLaughlin, Jr., *Billy Graham: Revivalist in a Secular Age* (1960); David Edwin Harrell, Jr., *Oral Roberts: An American Life* (1987); Jeffrey K. Hadden and Anson D. Shupe, *Televangelism, Power, and Politics on God's Frontier* (1988); Steve Bruce, *Pray TV: Televangelism in America* (1990); and R. Laurence Moore, *Selling God: American Religion in the Marketplace of Culture* (1994). See also Paul Boyer, *When Time Shall Be No More: Prophecy Belief in Modern American Culture* (1992), and Alan Crawford, *Thunder on the Right: The "New Right" and the Politics of Resentment* (1981). *Televangelism and American Culture: The Business of Popular Religion* (2003), by Quentin Schultze, is an examination of the origins, growth, and impact of televangelism.

Russel B. Nye has written a sprightly history of popular culture entitled *The Unembarrassed Muse: The Popular Arts in America* (1970). Helpful context is provided by Lawrence W. Levine, *Highbrow/Lowbrow: The Emergence of Cultural Hierarchy in America* (1988), and Joan Shelley Rubin, *The Making of Middle-Brow Culture* (1992). Among other useful studies are Alvin Toffler, *The Culture Consumers: A Study of Art and Affluence in America* (1964), and Philip Olson, ed., *America as a Mass Society: Changing Community and Identity* (1963). *Hide in Plain Sight: The Hollywood Black-listees in Film and Television, 1950–2002* (2004), by Paul Buhle and Dave Wagner, is a revealing study of the lasting impact of the Hollywood Blacklist.

The best place to begin a study of the mass media in recent America is James L. Baughman's incisive history, *The Republic of Mass Culture* (2nd ed., 1997). Other evaluations of the mass media and mass culture are provided by Daniel J. Boorstin in *The Image: A Guide to Pseudo-Events in America* (1964), and James L. Baughman, *Henry R. Luce and the Rise of the American News Media* (1987).

Filmmaking, one of the major mass media, is described in Robert Sklar, *Movie-Made America: A Cultural History of American Movies* (1975), and Garth Jowett, *Film: The Democratic Art* (1976).

Television has been the subject of many books. Two volumes by Erik Barnouw are authoritative and useful: *The Image Empire: A History of Broadcasting in the United States* (1970) and *Tube of Plenty: The Evolution of American Television* (1975). Among other helpful books are David Marc, *Demographic Vistas: Television in American Culture* (1984); Lynn Spigel, *Make Room for TV: Television and the Family Ideal in Postwar America* (1992); Karal Ann Marling, *As Seen on TV: The Visual Culture of Everyday Life in the 1950s* (1994); Craig Allen, *Eisenhower and the Mass Media: Peace, Prosperity, & Prime-Time TV* (1993); and Mary Ann Watson, *The Expanding Vista: American Television in the Kennedy Years* (1990). Still other themes are pursued in Ella Taylor, *Prime-Time Families: Television Culture in Post-War America* (1989), and Ron Powers, *Supertube: The Rise of Television Sports* (1984).

Popular music of the postwar period is discussed in R. Serge Denisoff and Richard A. Peterson, eds., *The Sounds of Social Change: Studies in Popular Culture* (1972), and R. Serge Denisoff, *Solid Gold: The Popular Record Industry* (1975). For the development of rock 'n' roll, see Charlie Gillett, *The Sound of the City: The Rise of Rock and Roll* (rev. and expanded ed., 1983); David P. Szatmary, *Rockin' in Time: A Social History of Rock-and-Roll* (2nd ed., 1991); and E. Ann Kaplan, *Rocking Around the Clock: Music, Television, Postmodernism, and Consumer Culture* (1987). Other varieties of music are considered in Bill C. Malone, *Country Music U.S.A.: A Fifty-Year History* (rev. ed., 1985); John Rockwell, *Sinatra: An American Classic* (1984); Albert Goldman, *Elvis* (1981); and Mark Herlsgaard, *A Day in the Life: The Music and Artistry of the Beatles* (1995).

American art in the postwar period is dealt with in Oliver W. Larkin, *Art and Life in America* (1949); Matthew Baigell, *A Concise History of American Painting and Sculpture* (1984); and Barbara Rose, *American Art Since 1900* (1967). See also Charles Jencks, *Post-Modernism: The New Classicism in Art and Architecture* (1987); Joshua C. Taylor, *The Fine Arts in America* (1981); and Harold Rosenberg, *Discovering the Present: Three Decades in Art, Culture, and Politics* (1985). Abstract expressionism is described in Michael Leja, *Reframing Abstract Expressionism: Subjectivity and Painting in the 1940s* (1993); Irving Sandler, *The New York School: The Painters and Sculptors of the Fifties* (1978); Stephen Polcari, *Abstract Expressionism and the Modern Experience* (1991); and Erika Doss, *Benton, Pollock, and the Politics of Modernism: From Regionalism to Abstract Expressionism* (1995). See also Christin J. Mamiya, *Pop Art and Consumer Culture: American Super Market* (1992).

The broad expanse of American literature since World War II is surveyed in Leslie Fiedler, *Waiting for the End: The American Literary Scene From Hemingway to Baldwin* (1964); Alfred Kazin, *Bright Book of Life: American Novelists and Storytellers from Hemingway to Mailer* (1973); and Daniel Hoffman, ed., *Harvard Guide to Contemporary American Writing* (1979). The beatniks are discussed in Bruce Cook, *The Beat Generation* (1971). Poetry is considered in Robert von Hallberg, *American Poetry and Culture, 1945–1980* (1985). For southern writers, see John M. Bradbury, *Renaissance in the South: A Critical History of the Literature, 1920–1960* (1963), and Fred Hobson, *The Southern Writer in the Postmodern World* (1991).

———★———

$$\star\,\star\,\star$$

CHAPTER

7

Great Changes, Great Failings: LBJ, the Great Society, and the Vietnam War

L YNDON B. JOHNSON MOVED EASILY INTO THE ROLE of domestic reformer, working energetically and skillfully to advance first the Kennedy program and then his own more ambitious legislation. Johnson wanted desperately to be "president of all the people," and during his first years in the White House he seemed to succeed in creating a national consensus. The new president hoped to improve the quality of American life and thus achieve a "Great Society," which "asks not only how much, but how good; not only how to create wealth, but how to use it." Johnson repeatedly assured the American people that "we have the power to shape the civilization that we want." There was irony—indeed, tragedy—in the presidency of Lyndon Johnson. For in spite of his impressive record of domestic reforms and an overwhelming mandate in the election of 1964, Johnson soon began to lose the support of the public and to have a serious "credibility" problem. The Great Society lost its momentum and the administration virtually collapsed before LBJ left office.

THE THIRTY-SIXTH PRESIDENT

Lyndon Baines Johnson's ascent to the pinnacle of national politics was quite as remarkable, in its own way, as that of Harry Truman or Dwight

Eisenhower. Born near Stonewall, Texas, on August 27, 1908, Johnson grew up in the bleak Hill Country surrounding Johnson City, which his grandfather had founded. The Johnsons, sturdy and self-reliant, were influential in the local community, and both Lyndon Johnson's father and grandfather had served in the state legislature. But the rural economy was depressed and times were hard as Lyndon grew up, and in order to complete Southwest Texas State Teachers' College at nearby San Marcos, he was forced to work at a variety of jobs. After teaching school for a time following his graduation, he went to Washington late in 1931 as secretary to the congressman from his district. In 1935 the young Texan was appointed director of the National Youth Administration (a New Deal agency) in his home state, a position in which he flourished. Meanwhile, he had married Claudia "Lady Bird" Taylor. In 1937 he won a special election to fill a congressional vacancy and was regularly reelected thereafter. He was an ardent New Dealer. After losing a bid for the U.S. Senate in 1941, he ran again in 1948 and managed to win (by 87 votes) in an extraordinarily close election.

Johnson's success in the Senate was meteoric, and his qualities of leadership so impressed powerful Democrats like Richard B. Russell of Georgia that he was chosen as Senate minority leader in 1953. After the Democrats won the congressional elections of 1954, Johnson became majority leader in the upper house. Although he suffered a severe heart attack in 1955, the Texas senator made a good recovery and by the late 1950s had become perhaps the most dominant Democrat in Washington. Johnson became a master of parliamentary maneuver, made effective use of "unanimous consent" agreements to limit debate, and was adept at applying and relaxing pressure on senators who were undecided or opposed on a particular question. "By political background, by temperament, by personal preference," one contemporary wrote, the senator was "the riverboat man. He was brawny and rough and skilled beyond measure in the full use of tricky tides and currents, in his knowledge of the hidden shoals." By avoiding conflict and promoting compromise, he was able to control others and enhance his own power. He had an unlimited capacity for courtesies, flattering attentions, and small favors in his personal relations with his colleagues and in applying what some observers called "the treatment." Journalists Rowland Evans and Robert Novak described the majority leader in action: "He moved in close, his

LBJ giving "The Treatment" to Sen. Richard Russell, Jr., (D-GA), 1963. *LBJ Library photo by Yoichi Okamoto (W98-30).*

face a scant millimeter from his target, his eyes widening and narrowing, his eyebrows rising and falling. From his pockets poured clippings, memos, statistics. Mimicry, humor, and the genius of analogy made The Treatment an almost hypnotic experience and rendered the target stunned and helpless."

The Texan's record in the Senate was neither liberal nor conservative, although he revealed some pronounced conservative leanings in supporting Taft-Hartley, opposing Truman's civil rights program, and manifesting special concern for the oil and gas interests of the Southwest. On these and other issues, he was no doubt reflecting the conservatism of his most powerful constituents. At the same time, he was not basically ideological. He was, first and foremost, a professional politician. Still, his fundamental outlook had been enduringly shaped by his background and formative experiences. For one thing, he was a southerner—a white man who had grown up in a depressed regional economy and society; his own experiences and observations as well as the attitudes and stereotypes he encountered among non-southerners in Washington made him sensitive to his regional and cultural disadvantages. Whether or not he was influenced by southern populism, Johnson was imbued with real concern for the poor and the deprived, and he accepted the Populist prescription of positive governmental action as a means of restoring opportunity. The New Deal reinforced these convictions, and Franklin Roosevelt provided him with a model. Though strongly influenced by his regional heritage, the Texan moved steadily toward a wider perspective. In seeking his party's presidential nomination in 1960, he endeavored to portray himself as a westerner as well as a southerner, and his role as a conciliator and harmonizer in the Senate served to broaden his views.

A tall, powerfully built man, Johnson presented a marked contrast to John F. Kennedy; LBJ's rural, southwestern background, small-college education, drawling speech, and backslapping demeanor seemed the antithesis of Kennedy's northeastern, metropolitan youth, Harvard training, eloquence, and urbanity. Johnson lacked his predecessor's graceful style on the speaker's platform, and his unadorned language and effusive rhetoric caused some sophisticated liberals to wince. But Johnson had a flair for the dramatic, and he was a man of enormous energy, drive, and determination. He was also a vain man, eager for approval and sensitive to criticism.

Johnson entered the White House with a great deal of congressional support and goodwill. Relishing his own role from 1600 Pennsylvania Avenue, Johnson seemed to know every detail of the administration's program and every pressure that would affect its disposition. He made a point, especially during his first year in office, of stressing his commitment to the realization of Kennedy's New Frontier. Congress and the public responded positively to the administration's articulation of these reform goals, as they did to the president's announcement of his own Great Society. Following his electoral triumph in 1964, Johnson amplified the Great Society and explained it in greater detail. Presenting his State of the Union message to Congress early in 1965, he outlined a far-reaching and unprecedented program of domestic reform.

Having achieved a series of spectacular successes during his first year in office, President Johnson proceeded to guide through Congress the most impressive array of domestic reforms since the 1930s. The first session of the Eighty-ninth Congress (1965) was particularly productive for liberal Democrats; during that year the lawmakers passed eighty of

Senators James O. Eastland (left) and Richard Russell (right), southern opponents of civil rights legislation. *Courtesy U.S. Senate Historical Office.*

the administration's eighty-three major proposals. The coalition of Republicans and conservative Democrats, when it did appear in the House of Representatives roll call votes, was victorious only 25 percent of the time in 1965, as compared with 67 percent in 1963 and 1964 and 74 percent in 1961. Gallup and Harris polls showed that two-thirds of the American people liked LBJ's performance in the White House.

THE QUEST FOR EQUALITY

In his first address to Congress, in late November 1963, President Johnson urged the lawmakers to complete action on the Kennedy administration's tax-cut proposal. He also called for "the earliest possible passage" of Kennedy's civil rights bill, which had recently been reported favorably by the House Judiciary Committee. The new chief executive soon made it clear that he was totally committed to the enactment of this broad equal rights measure and that he was prepared to push on boldly to advance the cause with additional legislation and executive action. "We have talked long enough in this country about equal rights," Johnson declared. "We have talked for one hundred years or more. It is time now to write the next chapter, and to write it in the books of law." Civil rights represented a test of Johnson's credentials as a reformer and national leader. "If I didn't get out in front on this issue," he recalled, the liberals would "throw up my background against me, they'd use it to prove I was incapable of bringing unity. . . . I had

to produce a civil rights bill that was even stronger than the one they'd
have gotten if Kennedy had lived."

When the second session of the Eighty-eighth Congress began its
work in January 1964, the Johnson administration mobilized all its powers behind the effort to enact an omnibus civil rights statute. The threat
of a discharge petition to force action persuaded the House Rules Committee, by late January, to clear H.R. 7152 for floor action, and the bill
was passed with strong bipartisan support on February 10, by a vote of
290 to 130. In steering the measure through the lower house, Emanuel
Celler, the floor manager, was greatly assisted not only by liberal party
members identified with the Democratic Study Committee but also by
such Republican leaders as William H. McCulloch of Ohio, the ranking minority member of the House Judiciary Committee. Thousands of
people poured into Washington in early 1964 to press for congressional
approval, and scores of national organizations participated in the movement through the Leadership Conference on Civil Rights.

Prospects for the passage of such far-reaching civil rights legislation
in the Senate were much less encouraging, given the strategic positions
of southern leaders in that body and the difficulty of overcoming filibusters. Southern senators hoped to bury the House-approved bill in
James Eastland's Judiciary Committee, but administration leaders skillfully avoided that trap and got the Senate on February 26 to place the
measure directly on the upper chamber's calendar. Hubert Humphrey,
who managed the drive for Senate passage, and other supporters of the
proposed law succeeded in creating a sturdy coalition and in preventing its disruption as a result of partisan politics, an ever-present danger.
Senate leaders of both parties and administration spokespersons carried
on intensive negotiations in an effort to work out an agreement that
would make it possible to halt debate and enact the bill. The pivotal
figure in these negotiations was minority leader Everett M. Dirksen of
Illinois. The administration undertook painstaking conferences with
Dirksen, and so intense were the discussions that, in the words of one
White House aide, Johnson "never let him alone for thirty minutes." The
Illinoisan slowly moved toward a compromise, and in mid-May, during
the seventh week of floor debate, a package of compromise amendments
was agreed to in these negotiations and incorporated into a "clean bill"
to be offered as a substitute for H.R. 7152.

On June 10 the Senate adopted a cloture resolution by a vote of 71 to 29, and for the first time in its history the upper house had voted to close debate on a civil rights bill. Senator Richard B. Russell and his southern colleagues had made a strategic error in demanding unconditional surrender. Had they sought an agreement with Republican moderates earlier in the debate, they might well have obtained significant concessions and seriously weakened the final enactment. Yet as Dirksen said, quoting words attributed to Victor Hugo, "Stronger than all the armies is an idea whose time has come." After cloture the Senate approved a few minor amendments, voted down a large number of others designed to weaken the measure, and passed the bill on June 19 by a roll call vote of 73 to 27. The House accepted the Senate version, and President Johnson signed it on July 2.

The Civil Rights Act of 1964 was the most sweeping affirmation of equal rights and the most comprehensive commitment to their implementation ever made by a U.S. Congress. The law assured access to public accommodations such as motels, restaurants, and places of amusement; authorized the federal government to bring suits to desegregate public facilities and schools; extended the life of the Civil Rights Commission for four years and gave it new powers; provided that federal funds could be cut off if programs were administered unfairly; required most private companies and labor unions to offer equal employment opportunities; and authorized the Justice Department to enter into pending civil rights cases. Compliance was not universal, but the act was generally obeyed throughout the South, in part because of careful preparations by federal and local officials. A startling change in the daily behavior if not the thinking of millions of southerners took place with incredible swiftness.

Johnson soon decided to take advantage of the reform impulse in civil rights by seeking additional legislation in the field of voting rights, an area where the 1964 law was considered weak. Such ancient obstructions as literacy tests, discriminatory treatment by local officials, economic pressure, and intimidation were still prevalent in much of the South, particularly in the lower part of the region. The ballot, it was widely assumed, would provide the most practical means of changing the status of southern blacks. With this in mind, hundreds of students—black and white—came to Mississippi in 1964 to participate in the Freedom Summer project—known nationally as the Mississippi Summer Project—an undertaking that concentrated on the voter registration of African Americans. White resistance was bitter. White supremacists burned churches, beat many civil rights workers, and killed several of the students.

As those who organized the drive had predicted, the violent response of the local white supremacists attracted the national media. The media coverage reached a crescendo when three young male activists, James Chaney, a local black CORE member, CORE organizer Michael Schwerner, and Andrew Goodman, both of whom were white New Yorkers, went missing on June 21. President Johnson, now embarrassed by the administration's refusal to protect Mississippi civil rights activists, ordered the FBI to investigate the case actively and closely monitor the Klan; he also ordered hundreds of U.S. Navy personnel to look for the missing men. Saddened but undaunted, the activists continued their efforts—and local whites continued to inflict violence, some of it lethal, on them and local black residents. On August 4, the bodies of Goodman, Chaney, and Schwerner were discovered buried in the Olen Burrage Dam in Neshoba County. (The facts of the case became known many years later.) When local law enforcement failed to investigate the murders, the Department of Justice took over, ultimately convicting seven white men and sentencing them to three to ten years for their respective roles in the crimes. While the number of newly registered voters never reached the hoped-for 20 percent mark, the greater effect that Freedom Summer had on the national civil rights movement is undeniable, as it galvanized and energized activists across the nation as well as opened the eyes of many Americans of all races and walks of life.

Early in 1965 Martin Luther King, Jr., launched a series of demonstrations centered in Selma, Alabama, to dramatize the absence of black voting rights in the Deep South. Dallas County, in which Selma is located, had a black majority, but only 325 African Americans were registered to vote as compared with 9,800 whites. In some other Black Belt counties not a single black man or woman was enfranchised. King announced plans for "a march on the ballot boxes throughout Alabama," moving from Selma to Montgomery, the state capital, fifty-four miles away. Governor George Wallace refused to permit such a march, and when the demonstrators tried to proceed without his approval, they were met by legal law enforcement with clubs and tear gas. The president finally stepped in, federalizing the Alabama National Guard, and the march was completed between March 21 and 25. The violent clashes that took place in the Selma area provoked national outrage and set the stage for congressional action on voting rights legislation.

Having become committed to the passage of a strong voting rights statute, the Johnson administration sent Congress a carefully developed proposal on March 17, 1965. From March until August, the voting rights coalition never lost its momentum. It was a bipartisan effort, with solid administration support and powerful assistance from the Leadership Conference on Civil Rights and other groups. After a compromise anti–poll tax provision was approved, the Senate adopted a cloture motion on May 25—the second one in two years. The bill was passed on the following day. The House passed a similar measure on July 9, and after a conference committee reconciled the differences between the two houses, the revised measure was approved early in August. The president signed it on August 6. "They came in darkness and they came in chains," he said of the first American blacks. "Today we strike away the last major shackle of those fierce and ancient bonds."

The Voting Rights Act of 1965 authorized direct federal action to enable blacks to register and vote. It empowered the attorney general to appoint federal examiners to supervise voter registration in states or voting districts where a literacy test or similar qualifying devices existed and where fewer than 50 percent of the voting-age residents were registered or had cast ballots in the 1964 presidential election. Stiff penalties were provided for interference with voter rights, and the Department of Justice moved quickly to implement the new statute. The act of 1965 invalidated the poll tax, and the "one man, one vote" principle handed down by the Supreme Court went a long way to democratize southern—and American—politics.

Meanwhile, the Johnson administration brought many blacks into important government jobs, and Johnson became the first chief executive to appoint African Americans to his cabinet and to the Supreme Court. Robert C. Weaver was named to head the new Department of Housing and Urban Development, while the famous NAACP attorney Thurgood Marshall was elevated from the federal circuit court to the nation's highest court. Johnson also pressed on, along with many civil rights leaders and organizations, to secure still more congressional action. In his State of the Union message of January 1966, the president urged the passage of legislation to prevent discrimination in jury selection, to guarantee the physical security of all citizens, and to outlaw discrimination in housing. The House of Representatives passed this legislation, though by a narrow margin in the case of the housing title, but the proposals failed in the Senate when efforts to adopt a cloture resolution were twice unsuccessful.

Black impatience and white resistance mounted even as the structure of legal segregation was being dismantled. Equality, many black leaders had come to realize, would be only a mirage unless tangible opportunities for self-improvement were created. This awareness was reflected in the growth of black militancy, declining white participation and leadership in the movement for equal rights, and a mood of disappointment and bitterness among African Americans over conditions in the urban ghettos, which were increasingly segregated and victimized by economic blight and inadequate public services. Frustration and rage found expression in "black power," a new rallying cry and an angry reaction against nonviolence as a tactic and integration as a goal. Advocates of black power envisaged self-determination for African Americans based on political and economic power, an improved self-image, and the development of more militant black leadership. As this unfolded, white and black attitudes became more polarized, and the civil rights coalition began to splinter. By the summer of 1966, a white backlash was evident in many Northern and Midwestern areas, open-housing demonstrations were causing violent racial conflicts, and "law and order" was emerging as a key political issue.

Some of the basic problems facing African Americans were touched upon in a controversial memorandum on the black family written in 1965 by Daniel Patrick Moynihan, an official in the Johnson administration. The Moynihan report, while pointing out that perhaps half of the nation's African Americans could be classified as middle class in socioeconomic terms, emphasized the disintegration of the black family in the great urban centers. The report angered many blacks and depressed many whites. A more comprehensive treatment of racial problems was contained in *The Report of the National Advisory Commission on Civil Disorders* (1968). The work of a special commission appointed by President Johnson and headed by Otto Kerner, a former governor of Illinois, the report stated that "white racism is essentially responsible for the explosive mixture which has been accumulating in our cities since the end of World War II." The commission cited the growing concentration of blacks in cities; the chronic discrimination and segregation in employment, education, and housing; the oppressive effects of ghetto life on the young and the increase in crime, drug addiction, and welfare dependency; and the fact that 2 million "hard-core disadvantaged" urban blacks were making no significant economic gains.

Members of the militant Black Panther party participate in a close order drill at the 1968 funeral for Bobby James Hutton, a party member shot by police during a gun battle. A speaker at the funeral called the shooting "a political assassination." *Courtesy UPI/Corbis-Bettmann.*

On February 21, 1965, forty-year-old African American civil rights leader Malcolm X was murdered in the Audubon Ballroom in Manhattan by members of the Nation of Islam (NOI). Born Malcolm Little, he had converted to Islam while in prison for burglary and, upon his parole in 1952, became an active member of the NOI and an outspoken critic of the white establishment. After a split with NOI leader Elijah Muhammad, Malcolm X departed the NOI but retained his Muslim faith. Malcolm X regularly stated views in support of the separation of blacks and whites in society and denounced the code of nonviolence espoused by King and other, better-established civil rights leaders. Then, following his 1964 pilgrimage to Mecca, Malcolm X moved toward more inclusive racial views. Despite his short life, he had a tremendous influence on what became the Black Power movement, as his refusal to embrace Martin Luther King's pacifist platform attracted support from more radical, militaristic civil rights movements.

With a growing rift between younger and older civil rights activists and the attention of the American people turning more fully to the war in Vietnam, by early 1967 the civil rights movement appeared to have collapsed. While the urban riots raged out of control during the summer of 1967, the House of Representatives voted down rent subsidy and rat control legislation. Then Americans' eyes were opened still wider by yet another act of racial violence. On April 4, 1968, Dr. Martin Luther King, Jr., was standing on the second-story balcony of the Lorraine Hotel in Memphis, having come to the city to support striking sanitation workers. The sound of a single rifle shot rang out and felled him. Within an hour, King was pronounced dead following an emergency operation to try to save him. His assailant, a white supremacist named James Earl Ray, was apprehended two months later at London's Heathrow Airport while attempting to board a plane bound for Rhodesia.

The assassination of King touched off widespread rioting in African American areas throughout the nation and contributed further to black disillusionment and alienation—but it also helped bring about the enactment of an important additional civil rights measure during the Johnson years. The Civil Rights Act of 1968, which had been pending for more than two years, outlawed racial discrimination in the sale and rental of 80 percent of all U.S. houses and apartments. The statute charged the executive branch with acting "affirmatively" to bring about integrated housing.

It also gave the federal government its first effective weapon with which to control all forms of racial brutality. With the passage of the act, the right of black Americans to equal treatment in most aspects of the national life was—almost a century after the end of the Civil War—finally established in law. While all of the brutality that took place during the post–World War II civil rights movement had pushed Congress to act, the assassination of Martin Luther King, Jr., was perhaps the single most compelling tragedy that compelling tragedy that guaranteed Congressional support of the new civil rights legislation.

Lyndon Johnson was, as the black novelist Ralph Ellison said, "the greatest American president for the poor and for the Negroes." LBJ, much more than JFK, contributed to the quickening pace of the civil rights movement during the 1960s and to the great progress made since World War II toward the goal of equal rights for all citizens. Even so, the task of converting equal rights into truly equal opportunity was far from finished. Most white Americans were still opposed to open housing, the urban ghettos remained volatile, millions of blacks worked menial jobs or remained mired in unemployment, and the nation in the 1970s and 1980s seemed to have lost a sense of urgency about the terrible condition in which so many of its minorities lived.

THE WAR ON POVERTY

Like all modern American presidents, Lyndon Johnson was continually concerned with the effort to promote the nation's economic growth and security. He quickly embraced the Kennedy administration's tax reduction plan, which had passed the House of Representatives in September 1963, and pushed it through the Senate in February 1964, though without many of the tax reforms Kennedy had originally recommended. Johnson's sympathetic attitude toward business, as well as his early budgetary restraint, appealed to the business community, and for a time he succeeded in bringing the business class into his broad-gauged coalition. The tax cut of 1964 seemed to work brilliantly. The continued expansion of the economy during 1964 and 1965, the steady decline of unemployment, and the marked increase of sales and profits lent support to the claims of the administration for its fiscal policy and justified the slash in excise taxes enacted by Congress in June 1965.

The Johnson administration moved to help less fortunate Americans in more direct ways. In 1966 the administration persuaded Congress to raise the minimum wage from $1.25 to $1.60 an hour, effective in 1968. The Manpower Development and Training Act of 1964 was designed to train the unskilled or technologically displaced worker in new skills. Congress established a permanent food stamp program in 1964. Poverty, LBJ asserted in his first State of the Union message, was a national problem against which his administration "here and now declares unconditional war." At the University of Michigan a few months later, the president declared that "the Great Society rests on abundance and liberty for all. It demands an end to poverty and racial injustice, to which we are totally committed in our time."

The Economic Opportunity Act of 1964 established ten separate programs to be administered by an Office of Economic Opportunity (OEO), which was given broad discretionary powers. The president appointed Sargent Shriver, director of the Peace Corps, to head the OEO. The act authorized funds for job training, small farm and business loans, work-training programs and part-time employment to help thousands of young men and women stay in college, assistance to urban and rural communities in fighting poverty and illiteracy, and much more. Many of the new undertakings were designed to help the young and to do so primarily by giving them opportunities for further education and training. Thus Head Start was a program for preschoolers, while Upward Bound was devised for college students. VISTA (Volunteers in Service to America) was intended to function as a domestic peace corps on behalf of the poor and disadvantaged. The most innovative and controversial part of the legislation was Title II, which called for community action programs to develop employment opportunities and improve performance and motivation by providing for "maximum feasible participation" of the poor themselves in developing and operating the projects.

In 1965, with the administration vigorously pursuing the realization of the Great Society, the war on poverty was stepped up still further. Congress passed amendments to the 1964 legislation that more than doubled the first year's authorization. By 1966 the OEO was devoting about two-fifths of its budget to an assortment of community action programs, another two-fifths to its youth programs, and most of its remaining funds to work experience projects. One of Johnson's major congressional accomplishments in 1965 was the passage of the Appalachian Regional Development Act, which had passed the Senate but failed to win House approval in 1964. Emphasizing economic development rather than welfare support, the act provided $1.1 billion in subsidies for highway construction, resource development, and health centers in a depressed region stretching from Pennsylvania to Alabama. Another 1965 statute, the Public Works and Economic Development Act, extended the same concept to other depressed areas.

The war on poverty began to slow down in 1966, as Johnson became more engrossed in the struggle over Vietnam and growing inflationary pressure resulted from the sharp increase in defense expenditures and the Great Society programs. Congressional Republicans found new Democratic allies in their efforts to curb the administration's social reform spending. A measure to overhaul the unemployment compensation system, for instance, was left languishing in conference as the session ended in 1966. The OEO expected to receive $3.5 billion in its second year but was given only half that amount. Its budget for the following year was slashed to $1.5 billion.

For all its call to arms and good intentions, the war on poverty during the 1960s was never given more than a fraction of the funds it needed. Its entire cost during the years of its most active support, 1964–67, was only $6.2 billion. Much of this money went to landlords and construction companies; big corporations like International Telephone and Telegraph and Litton Industries that received contracts for antipoverty projects; and construction of highways, airports, and other facilities that benefited the middle class and the affluent much more than the needy (who, of course, use highways much less and airports rarely, if ever). In the end, the Great Society did little for the central cities and their inhabitants, and the depressed rural areas received even less help from Washington. Many of the antipoverty projects were hastily initiated, there was the usual bureaucratic inertia and inefficiency, and the control exercised by established agencies and local officials frequently limited success. There was also waste in the OEO undertakings, as well as a substantial amount of pork-barrel funds in such programs as those begun in Appalachia. The rent supplement provisions of the housing legislation of the mid-1960s were never really implemented.

Rather than seeking to organize the poor to combat alienation, the war on poverty might have been more effective in the long run with legislation providing for public employment and an income program guaranteeing a minimum standard of living. Though audacious in some respects, the struggle against poverty was not a radical undertaking; it set out to provide the poor with opportunities as individuals to break the cycle of poverty and climb the social ladder. There were some gains, not all of which resulted from action by the national government. By the end of the 1960s, only 11 percent of the nation's families received an annual income of less than $4,000, as compared with 22 percent at the beginning of the decade (this does not take into account the losses resulting from inflation). The antipoverty programs, as well as Medicare and increased Social Security benefits, did help many poor people, young Americans, and the elderly. In 1965, 25 percent of the federal budget was devoted to social programs. The effort to involve the poor in community action programs, while alarming to many local leaders and the subject of much criticism, did represent a new approach by government to the problem of poverty. Finally, the war on poverty represented a beginning, even if a limited one, in the search for a solution to a great social ill in the United States.

BREAKTHROUGHS IN EDUCATION AND HEALTH

One of the goals of the Great Society, proclaimed President Johnson early in 1965, was to improve the quality of American life. "We begin with learning," he said. "Every child must have the best education our nation can provide." Johnson was fond of saying that all young Americans should have as much education as they could absorb. Several factors had served to obstruct direct federal support of education: the historic church-state issue, the conservative suspicion of increased federal involvement in this area, and southern congressional fear that a national program would become an instrument of school desegregation. The Kennedy administration had mounted a new attack on the problem but without much immediate success. Johnson's efforts in 1964 to secure the passage of direct federal aid to education legislation were also unsuccessful.

The Elementary and Secondary Education Act of 1965 was the first general federal aid to education law in U.S. history. The act authorized the expenditure of over $1 billion in federal funds for textbooks, library materials, special educational programs for adults and the handicapped, and the strengthening of state educational agencies. While little money was provided for teacher salaries and school construction, large sums were earmarked for improving the teaching of students in the urban slums and impoverished rural areas. Private schools, whether religious or not, could benefit from this federal support in several ways, including the use of library materials and educational television.

Another feature of the Great Society was a wide-ranging program of aid to higher education. The Higher Education Act of 1965 expanded federal assistance to colleges and universities, authorizing scholarships and low-interest loans for students, aid to struggling colleges and community service programs, and grants for college libraries. The law made scholarships available to more than 140,000 capable but needy students and approved a National Teacher Corps to work in poverty-stricken areas. This federal support contributed to the remarkable growth of American colleges and universities in the postwar period.

By mid-1965 resistance to federal aid to education had been shattered, and Congress was pouring more than $4 billion a year into all

LBJ signs the Medicare bill. *Courtesy Lyndon B. Johnson Library.*

branches of the national education system. In 1966 Congress provided further infusions of federal aid, including $3.9 billion over a three-year period for colleges and universities and $6.1 billion for public schools in a two-year extension of the Elementary and Secondary Education Act. Meanwhile, the U.S. Office of Education issued broad new guidelines for the desegregation of schools, hospitals, and other medical facilities under Title VI of the Civil Rights Act of 1964. Lyndon Johnson liked to be called "the education president," and he deserved the appellation.

President Johnson achieved another dramatic breakthrough with the approval of Medicare in 1965. The final legislation was the product of fifteen years of liberalization and refinement since the first comprehensive medical care proposal was made by the Truman administration. But like the educational enactments of the mid-1960s, it reflected the special circumstances and pressures associated with Johnson's Great Society. By the early 1960s, polls indicated that over two-thirds of the American people favored national medical care for the elderly. Organized labor, senior citizens, and other groups increased the pressure for congressional approval. In February 1964 the president delivered a major address to Congress on the nation's health needs, calling for passage of Medicare and several other measures providing health benefits to older Americans. Although a number of laws, including Hill-Burton hospital legislation, were extended and broadened that year, Medicare was defeated once again.

The Democratic landslide of 1964 went a long way toward settling the question. Practically the entire Democratic "class of '64" in the House—numbering sixty-five—was committed to Medicare. Johnson made the issue his top legislative measure in 1965, and the administration's bill, introduced by Representative Cecil R. King and Senator Clinton P. Anderson, was appropriately numbered H.R. 1 and S. 1. The American Medical Association (AMA), sensing the rising tide of support for congressional action, endorsed a legislative plan of its own known as Eldercare, which called for a voluntary program to be financed through private insurance companies, with the government paying the premiums for the indigent. Congressional Republicans also introduced comprehensive medical care legislation, based on the voluntary concept but covering some doctors' services as well as hospital bills. Congress effectively resisted the lobbying of the AMA and other opponents of Medicare, in part by incorporating

Spending on Health: 1965–1984

Total public and private spending on health care for each year in billions of dollars and as percentage of the gross national product.

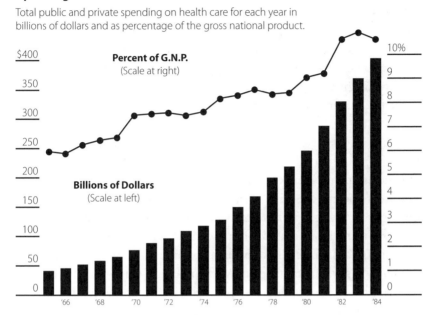

Source: Department of Health and Human Services

some features of the other proposals into the King-Anderson bill, which was considerably broadened in scope during the process. Both houses passed the bill by large majorities.

Two major health care programs for persons sixty-five and older were established by the $6.5 billion Medical Care Act of 1965. The basic plan, typically referred to as Medicare, would cover most hospital and some nursing home costs, diagnostic studies, and home health care visits. It was to be compulsory, financed mainly by a payroll tax and administered by the Social Security system. The second health care program, called the supplementary plan, would be voluntary and was to be financed by monthly premiums from participants and general revenue. It was designed to cover about 80 percent of the costs of a variety of health services, including doctors' bills. A third feature of the Medical Care Act was the provision authorizing Medicaid, a program making federal funds available to the states to help cover medical expenses of the needy, regardless of age. The new law also provided a 7 percent increase in Social Security benefits.

Medicare had its flaws. The program it established helped only the elderly, and then in a cumbersome and limited way. The federal government turned over many of its administrative responsibilities to the states and Blue Cross and Blue Shield plans. It gave control over fees to physicians, some of whom abused the system. Nevertheless, Medicare was a landmark in the history of American social reform, and it eased the burden of the unbearable costs of health care to the elderly.

LBJ AND THE URBAN NATION

The increasing problems of American cities provided a major focus for the Great Society. The crisis of the city grew steadily worse with the continuing middle-class flight to the suburbs and the subsequent shrinking tax base in the inner city. During the 1960s the Kennedy and Johnson administrations pushed hard for such programs as urban renewal, public housing, mass rapid transit, and water pollution control, and following the election of 1964 Congress approved an unprecedented number of urban-oriented reforms.

Although the assault on the slums drew the most attention, Washington's response to the urban crisis was broad and diversified. One approach was the community-centered character of the antipoverty programs. This approach sought to meet the criticism of the traditional urban renewal process—charges, for example, that it involved haphazard and undemocratic destruction of communities, the forced relocation of families, and the replacement of older houses and buildings with high-rise apartment complexes.

The most striking feature of the administration's urban program was the Demonstration Cities and Metropolitan Area Redevelopment Act of 1966. This so-called Model Cities Act was concerned with the "total environment" of the slum resident. The statute authorized the expenditure of $1.2 billion in slum areas for the improvement of housing, health, education, job training, recreational facilities, welfare, and transportation. Calling for an intensive attack on urban blight, the act sought to encourage slum clearance and rehabilitation by covering up to 80 percent of the costs of planning and construction, to foster metropolitan area planning, and to underwrite the building of new model communities. A demonstration program, the undertaking was designed to use public resources to improve selected neighborhoods and enhance the efficiency and quality of urban life throughout the nation.

Part of the trouble in urban America was the result of inadequate, inefficient, and expensive transportation. Although public transit was cheaper, safer, and more efficient for the user, it was costly to provide and much less central to the economy than the automobile system, in which a huge investment existed. In 1964 Congress enacted a $375-million mass transit bill to aid in planning and developing area-wide urban transit systems. The federal grants aimed at relieving the heavy traffic congestion in major metropolitan areas were supplemented by appropriations in the Urban Mass Transportation Act of 1966. Congress also responded to another administration request that year by creating a cabinet-level Department of Transportation, with responsibility for the development of a coordinated transportation system for the United States.

A growing consumer movement in the second half of the 1960s spurred the Johnson administration to sponsor other measures related to its urban programs. One response was the establishment of the Highway Safety Act and the Traffic Safety Act of 1966, which allocated federal funds for state and local traffic safety programs and applied safety standards to automobile manufacturers. Ralph Nader's muckraking book, *Unsafe at Any Speed* (1965), and his research and lobbying played an important part in the enactment of these laws. Nader, a young lawyer, soon became a full-time advocate of the public interest, investigating and criticizing numerous products, industries, and government agencies. Congress also took action in 1966 to broaden federal controls over the labeling and packaging of foods, drugs, cosmetics, and household supplies. The Consumer Credit Protection Act of 1968 established a Commission on Consumer Finance to oversee the operations of the consumer finance business and consumer credit transactions in general. The Truth in Lending Act, as it was popularly called, did not limit the charge for credit, but it did require lenders and creditors to give their customers full, honest, and comparative information on the interest rates they were paying—and on a uniform, annual basis.

"A prime national goal," the president told Congress in 1965, "must be an environment that is pleasing to the senses and healthy to live in." During the early postwar years little was said in Washington to suggest that the purity of air and water, the pressure of population on outdoor open space, and the beauty of countryside and city were national concerns. Yet there was a growing awareness of the environmental implications of industrial and postindustrial patterns of growth in the United States. Writers such as Rachel Carson and Barry Commoner warned of increasing ecological dangers, and groups like the Sierra Club began to attract political support in their battles for conservation and an end to the wholesale destruction of the environment. President Kennedy endorsed the idea of more federal spending for conservation and environmental controls. By the time Johnson sent Congress the first presidential message ever devoted to natural beauty, in February 1965, the federal government had adopted or was in the process of adopting a long list of measures designed to protect the environment.

According to President Johnson and Secretary of the Interior Stewart L. Udall, the Eighty-eighth Congress was a "conservation Congress." Among the conservation measures it passed was the National Wilderness Preservation Act of 1964, which incorporated federally held wilderness areas into a national wilderness system. Congress also set up a Land Conservation Fund in 1964 to provide for future state and federal recreation area needs. Each year thereafter brought new legislation and increased appropriations for conservation and environmental protection, an enlargement of federal responsibility in this field, and an intensified attack on the problem through the formation of regional control agencies and planning commissions. In 1965 Senator Edmund S. Muskie of Maine and other congressional advocates of conservation cooperated with the administration in securing passage of the important Water Quality Act, The Clean Air Act, and the Solid Waste Disposal Act of 1965, the Clean Water Restoration Act of 1966, and a variety of other statutes that provided federal support for the establishment of air and water purification programs by state and local governments, the construction of sewage and waste treatment plants, and the establishment of mandatory standards and enforcement procedures.

Lyndon Johnson sponsored the most advanced program of social reform in the history of the republic. Congress responded to his leadership by enacting an extraordinary array of social legislation: civil rights, the war on poverty, Medicare, federal aid to education, housing and urban development, increased Social Security benefits, conservation measures, a new immigration law, and even the subsidization of American "culture." The Great Society was intended to correct old racial wrongs, provide badly needed educational and medical services, advance social justice by mounting a broad-based attack on poverty and urban blight, and demonstrate people's capacity to master their environment. There were genuine successes in moving toward greater racial equality, offering expanded educational opportunities and better health care, and launching federal programs to combat poverty and protect the environment. A leader of uncommon ability and impressive accomplishments, Johnson had a vision of presiding over an era of historic social reform that would ensure his rank as a great president. It is not surprising that he made mistakes and that some of his programs failed. Much more critical was his attempt to wage both a comprehensive campaign of social reform at home and a divisive and debilitating war in Southeast Asia, for in the process he lost the confidence and trust of a majority of the American people.

THE DOMINO THEORY AND INTERNATIONAL AFFAIRS

An internationalist schooled in the struggles of World War II and the Cold War, Johnson accepted implicitly the threat of international communism, the wisdom of containment, the need to live up to commitments to one's allies, and the special obligation to maintain an American presence in the Far East. He believed that American foreign policy "must always be an extension of our domestic policy," that the nation's best guide "to what we do abroad is always what we do at home." The Texan was not well prepared by political experience, personal preference, or temperament to meet the challenges of international leadership. His instinct was to seek consensus in waging the Cold War abroad just as he did in creating the Great Society at home. Following his overwhelming victory at the polls in 1964, Johnson's consciousness of the immense power at his disposal and his faith in his capacity to use it nourished his global pretensions and determination to master intractable problems in the international arena.

Although the U.S. conflict with the Soviet Union and international communism was no longer quite such an obsession by the mid-1960s, it was still the single most important international factor in shaping

American policy. There was some concern in Washington when Nikita Khrushchev was suddenly deposed in October 1964, but his successors, Leonid Brezhnev and Alexei N. Kosygin, soon revealed their desire for a continuation of peaceful coexistence. A conciliatory spirit was evident in a number of treaties and understandings worked out between the two superpowers during the Johnson years: a formal agreement not to place nuclear weapons in space; a cultural exchange program involving teachers, researchers, and artists; the inauguration of direct air service between New York and Moscow; and a new treaty establishing additional consulates in both nations.

The Johnson administration also took up the cause of a nonproliferation treaty with the Soviet Union in 1964. Years of effort to reach an agreement to prevent the spread of nuclear arms culminated in July 1968 with the signing of a nonproliferation treaty by the United States, the Soviet Union, Great Britain, and fifty-eight non-nuclear nations. The treaty forbade the transfer of nuclear weapons to any country not possessing such devices; the non-nuclear nations agreed not to manufacture or receive nuclear weapons. In 1967, the two superpowers began Strategic Arms Limitations Talks, which became known as SALT and eventually led to the treaty of 1972. The spirit of détente persuaded Soviet leaders to invite President Johnson to a summit in Russia, an invitation Johnson eagerly accepted but then postponed. One reason for his decision was the invasion and occupation of Czechoslovakia by Russian troops in August 1968 in order to crush the liberalization program of Czech party leader Alexander Dubcek. That action provoked strong criticism in the United States, including its denunciation by the president. But even those events failed to disrupt the improved relations between the two great powers. The United States was now less concerned with a policy of "liberation" in Eastern Europe than with efforts to encourage more independent Communist governments in that region through greater trade and cooperation.

This relaxation of tension did not mean that the United States and the Soviet Union had abandoned their rivalry for the support of the unaligned nations and the Third World. The explosive situation in the Middle East made that clear. The fierce animosity between the Arab nations and Israel, aggravated by Egypt's provocative behavior, burst into hostilities on June 5, 1967, when the Israelis suddenly attacked the Egyptians and their Syrian allies. Within six days Israeli forces had won a series of spectacular victories and occupied large areas belonging to Egypt, Syria, and Jordan. The war was effectively over. Although the Russians had encouraged the aggressiveness of their client states in the region and the Americans had long provided Israel with vital military and diplomatic support, the two superpowers had tried unsuccessfully to restrain their allies and prevent war. But they did not intervene in the hostilities once they began, and they sought to help fashion a satisfactory armistice. The Six Day War did not contribute to stability in the Middle East. The Suez Canal had been blocked, the Arab states had imposed an embargo on petroleum, and at the end of hostilities Israel refused to withdraw from the territories it had occupied, creating an enduring source of conflict with its neighbors.

Meanwhile, the Russians denounced Israel's "aggression," provided new military aid to their Arab friends, and dispatched naval forces into the eastern Mediterranean to counter the U.S. Sixth Fleet. Thus the war strengthened the Soviet position in the Middle East, while it weakened that of the United States, since the Arabs associated Israeli assertiveness with U.S. aid. The UN was unable to bring the Arab-Israeli dispute much closer to a permanent settlement, and in later years the problem was further complicated by the guerrilla attacks carried out by bands of Palestinian refugees against the Israelis. President Johnson and Premier Kosygin made no real progress in dealing with the Middle East crisis when they held a series of friendly conversations at Glassboro State College, New Jersey, June 23–25, 1967.

In western and central Europe, Johnson hoped to carry forward the Kennedy administration's plans to strengthen defense and trade relations within the Atlantic community. He made little progress, however, and the NATO alliance continued to lose cohesiveness as its members grew more independent of Washington. Franco-American relations were exacerbated in 1964 when France extended diplomatic recognition to Communist China, and U.S. annoyance with Charles de Gaulle grew as a result of the French leader's loud overtures to Eastern Europe and criticism of U.S. policies. Early in 1966 de Gaulle announced that France would formally withdraw from the NATO military organization within three years, and the alliance's commands and installations were thus forced to leave French soil. A bitter quarrel between Greece and Turkey over the relative political status of their respective nationals on the island of Cyprus also strained the Atlantic alliance.

American leaders encountered similar difficulties in their endeavor to promote further economic integration of the Atlantic community. France blocked British membership in the European Economic Community, and the tariff negotiations made possible by the Trade Expansion Act of 1962 failed to produce the hoped-for trading area stretching from West Germany to Japan, in which goods and services could move with relative freedom. In the bargaining preliminary to the so-called Kennedy Round negotiations within the General Agreement on Tariffs and Trade, the United States and the Common Market nations engaged in sharp debate over certain issues. Nevertheless, the completion of the Kennedy Round in 1967 resulted in tariff reductions averaging 35 percent between the United States and the Common Market.

During the campaign of 1964 Lyndon Johnson portrayed himself as a peaceful and prudent president, this in contrast to his campaign's highly exaggerated illustration of Barry Goldwater as a trigger-happy warmonger. The president talked about strengthening the United Nations, reducing Cold War tensions, expanding economic aid to underdeveloped countries, increasing world trade, and employing patience and

Kosygin and Johnson confer at Glassboro State College, June 1967. *Courtesy Lyndon B. Johnson Library.*

moderation in dealing with international crises. Yet Johnson also urged a powerful military system for the United States.

U.S. IDEALS AND SELF-INTEREST IN LATIN AMERICA

While the United States had emerged in the twentieth century as one of the world's major power centers, the vast region to its south remained a power vacuum. Lacking political stability and a tradition of self-government, much of Latin America was backward, agrarian, and undiversified in its economic life. Despite some notable exceptions, it tended to be a land of mass illiteracy, grinding poverty, and inadequate social services. Long dominated by foreign capitalists, local elites, and right-wing military dictatorships, most of the region faced an enormous task of modernization. At the same time, millions of Latin Americans resented the long record of U.S. intervention in their affairs; they were also both envious of their powerful neighbor to the north and unhappy over its relative neglect of them in the post-1945 period. It was the challenge of the "revolution of rising expectations" in Latin America that eventually had resulted in Kennedy's Alliance for Progress.

Lyndon Johnson was determined to prevent a recurrence of Castroism in the western hemisphere, not only because of his commitment to the containment of communism but also because of his keen awareness of the political use the Republican Party had made of the Cuban situation during the early 1960s. Johnson's ambassador to Chile later recalled the president's "romantic, Tex-Mex view of Latin America." One indication of the administration's approach to the nations to the south came with the appointment of Thomas C. Mann as assistant secretary of state for inter-American affairs. Mann, a Texas lawyer and former ambassador to Mexico, wanted above all else to stabilize Latin American politics, protect the private interests of the United States in the area, and wage a vigorous struggle against communism. Johnson and Mann took a hard line toward Castro's regime. They resisted Cuban pressure on the U.S. naval base at Guantánamo and maintained the economic boycott of the island.

The major crisis in Johnson's Latin American diplomacy came with his decision in the spring of 1965 to send a contingent of U.S. Marines into the Dominican Republic, ostensibly to protect American lives and property. The government of Juan Bosch, a non-Communist intellectual and nationalist reformer, had been overthrown by a military coup in September 1963. In April 1965 an odd coalition of democrats, radicals, and junior military officers launched a countercoup with the objective of restoring constitutional government under Bosch. A bloody struggle ultimately broke out in the streets of Santo Domingo. The American embassy in Santo Domingo and the State Department in Washington, which from the beginning had sided with the conservative military elements against the Bosch rebels, hastily urged the use of U.S. troops to stop the fighting.

On April 28, four days after the revolt began, Johnson sent in the marines. They were followed during the next few weeks by more than 20,000 army troops. The president defended the intervention by charging that the rebels had carried out mass executions, which proved not to have been the case. He also asserted that "people trained outside the Dominican Republic are seeking to gain control." Fearing that the revolt was part of a larger challenge from international communism and Soviet expansion, Johnson had acted decisively. "We don't expect to sit here on our rocking chairs with our hands folded and let the Communists set up any government in the western hemisphere," he explained. On May 2, 1965, he announced that the "American nations cannot, must not, and will not permit the establishment of another Communist government in the western hemisphere." Once the American troops had restored some order, Washington sought to broaden the basis of its intervention by securing OAS support. The two sides finally accepted a cease-fire, and an interim government was agreed upon. More than a year after the rebellion, Joaquin Balaguer, a moderate, was chosen president in a peaceful election on June 1, 1966.

Johnson's police action and diplomatic moves had seemingly accomplished their purpose. A strife-torn Caribbean republic had been stabilized, and the possible establishment of another Castro-like government in the western hemisphere had been prevented. Johnson could also claim to have supported the cause of free elections. Furthermore, the venture in the Dominican Republic appeared to confirm the promise of the Kennedy-McNamara strategy of flexible response. LBJ's apparent success in the Caribbean almost certainly encouraged him to push forward with his military involvement in Vietnam. On the other hand, the intervention raised serious doubts throughout Latin America about U.S. intentions as well as Johnson's capacity for the wise and restrained exercise of power. It led to new charges of United States imperialism and support of right-wing dictatorships. It also reinforced many long-standing Latin American fears and placed new strains on the relations between the United States and the nations to its south. It created Johnson's first credibility crisis at home, as well.

The Johnson administration's gunboat diplomacy in the Dominican Republic threatened the good that might have been accomplished through the Alliance for Progress. Indeed, virtually all students of the Dominican intervention agree with political scientist Jerome Slater's conclusion that the American action dealt "a death blow to the Alliance for Progress and the policy of non-revolutionary democratic change that underlay it." United States support of the Alianza began to decline in the mid-1960s. As American fears of Castro declined, U.S. appropriations for Latin American aid dropped, especially those earmarked for economic development. Non-revolutionary democratic change now seemed less urgent to American leaders, as was demonstrated by U.S. acceptance and in some cases backing of military coups in Brazil, Bolivia, and Argentina. Furthermore, Alliance aid was not predicated, as originally intended, on local reforms. Little land reform was undertaken, and income distribution throughout Latin America remained virtually unchanged. Although the United States had spent $9.2 billion on the Alliance by 1969, the program had done relatively little to improve the conditions of the masses or advance social change in the region.

VIETNAM: INTO THE QUAGMIRE

When Lyndon Johnson entered the White House in late November 1963, he hoped to continue JFK's policies in Southeast Asia, as in other parts of the world. His experts assumed that this would require only a limited American involvement, largely in the form of military advisers to instruct the South Vietnamese, and that the Communist threat in the region could be blunted with economic and military aid. Having made South Vietnam (the Republic of Viet Nam) a client state, the United States reorganized, equipped, and trained that country's army. It also provided the South Vietnamese with a great deal of economic assistance. Late in 1963, when South Vietnam's National Liberation Front (the political wing of the Vietcong, or Communists, in South Vietnam) made overtures to General Duong Van Minh, head of the new Saigon government, for the possible negotiation of a cease-fire and a coalition government, Johnson asserted that the "neutralization of South Vietnam would only be another name for a Communist take-over." He promised Minh "American personnel and material as needed to assist you in achieving victory." Johnson had earlier declared, "I am not going to be the president who saw South Vietnam go the way China went."

The situation in South Vietnam became more uncertain in 1964 as the Vietcong enlarged its operations and political instability in Saigon continued. In June of that year, when the Pathet Lao fired upon American planes making reconnaissance flights over Laos, Johnson ordered retaliatory air strikes against the rebel positions. American advisers continued to assist the Army of the Republic of Viet Nam (ARVN) in carrying out raids and acts of sabotage in the north. Furthermore, the U.S. Navy had begun to send destroyers on reconnaissance missions off the North Vietnamese coast.

Early in August 1964, the U.S.S. *Maddox* came under attack while on such a mission in the Gulf of Tonkin by North Vietnamese PT boats, and two days later the *Maddox* and a second destroyer were allegedly fired upon during a night so dark and rainy that the two U.S. ships could not even see each other. President Johnson seized upon this encounter to broaden his discretionary authority in the Vietnam conflict, ordering retaliatory air strikes against three North Vietnamese torpedo boat bases and an oil storage depot. More important, he asked Congress for blanket authorization to use military force to defend the American position in Southeast Asia. Congress speedily complied with the president's request. By August 25 the House and the Senate had passed the Gulf of Tonkin Resolution with only two opposing votes in the Senate and none in the House. The resolution authorized the chief executive "to take all necessary measures to repel any armed attack against the forces of the United States and to prevent further aggression." It also stated that the United States was prepared, "as the president determines," to take "all necessary steps, including the use of armed force," to assist any nation covered by SEATO that requested assistance "in defense of its freedom."

Having rejected negotiations, Johnson was left with the problem of how to win the war in Vietnam. The position of South Vietnam had steadily deteriorated. The Vietcong, receiving supplies and some military reinforcements from North Vietnam by way of the Ho Chi Minh Trail through Laos, controlled great sections of the southern countryside. In Saigon seven different governments came to power in 1964 as one coup followed another. While the generals feuded in Saigon, there were student demonstrations, Buddhist protests, and other evidence of disunity among the South Vietnamese peoples. Virtually all of the president's close advisers recommended an expansion of American military force in Vietnam. They believed that Hanoi was directing and controlling the Vietcong insurgency, and they were convinced that a demonstration of U.S. military power north of the 17th parallel—roughly the dividing line or demilitarized zone (DMZ)—would persuade the North Vietnamese to abandon their plans to take over the south and unify Vietnam. They also assumed that a Communist victory in South Vietnam would result in the collapse of all Southeast Asia and dominance of the area by the People's Republic of China. Once again, as so often in the past, American policymakers talked about the Munich appeasement analogy, the test-of-will hypothesis, and the need to maintain "our credibility vis-à-vis the Communists." Furthermore, North Vietnam was, in LBJ's pungent phrase, only a "raggedy-ass little fourth-rate country."

Following a Vietcong attack on February 6, 1965, Johnson made a fateful decision. Guerrillas struck an American military advisers' compound in Pleiku and a nearby helicopter base in the central highlands, inflicting heavy casualties. Johnson ordered an immediate reprisal on a North Vietnam barracks forty miles north of the DMZ. New incidents provoked similar reprisals later in the month, and on March 2 the Americans began a systematic campaign of bombing the north. Within a week Operation Rolling Thunder, as this campaign was called, began dropping powerful bombs on military bases and supply depots in North Vietnam. "We seek no wider war," the president declared in a nationwide television address following the attack on Pleiku. "We want nothing for ourselves, only that the people of South Vietnam be allowed to guide their own country in their own way."

When Operation Rolling Thunder had no perceptible effect on the position of North Vietnam or that of the National Liberation Front, the Johnson administration made another critical decision: to commit

U.S. ground troops to the war in Vietnam. On March 8, 3,500 marines came ashore near Danang, and by late April, Johnson authorized the dispatch of 40,000 additional combat troops. These ground forces were expected to help implement the "enclave strategy" devised by General Maxwell D. Taylor. By the summer of 1965, the "advisory" role of the American military units had been abandoned, and the mission of U.S. ground forces in Vietnam had changed from defense to offense. In mid-July, Secretary of Defense Robert McNamara, pressed by the Joint Chiefs of Staff, urged Johnson to send an additional forty-four battalions to South Vietnam, and during the last days of July LBJ decided on that course. More than 184,000 U.S. troops were stationed in Vietnam by the end of the year. Johnson's decisions in the summer of 1965 represented an open-ended commitment to deploy U.S. military forces as the situation might demand. Between November 1964 and late July 1965, a crucial period in the so-called Americanization of the war, the president misled Congress and the public about several of his decisions, apparently in an effort to avoid what he thought would be "a mean and destructive debate."

While the United States was doing its best to force North Vietnam to end its support of the NLF and recognize the independence of South Vietnam under an anti-Communist government, American leaders talked of peace. Thus, in an important address at Johns Hopkins University on April 7, 1965, Johnson urged an end to the war on the basis of self-determination for the south and a massive U.S. investment of a billion dollars for the development of the rich Mekong Valley, a development in which North Vietnam would share. Reiterating the American commitment to the independence of South Vietnam, the chief executive made it clear that the United States would not withdraw, "either openly or under the cloak of a meaningless agreement." From time to time in the years that followed, beginning with a cessation in the bombing of North Vietnam at Christmas in 1965 that lasted thirty-seven days, Washington launched other peace offensives. There was a missionary consideration in Johnson's approach to Vietnam. He genuinely seemed interested, if American intervention was accepted and communism could be halted, in improving the lot of its people, perhaps with a kind of New Deal for Southeast Asia. He declared in 1966, "I want to leave the footprints of America in Vietnam. I want them to say when the Americans come,

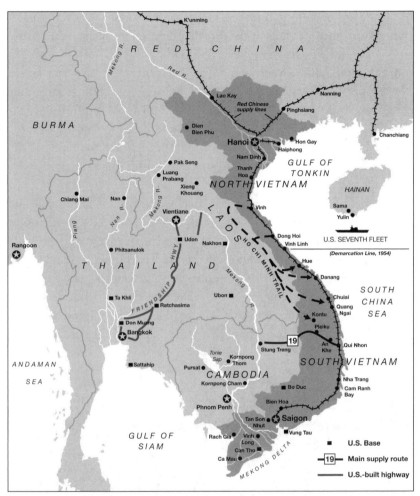

The Vietnam conflict, 1966

this is what they leave—schools, not long cigars. We're going to turn the Mekong into a Tennessee valley." But despite such rhetoric, Johnson increasingly relied on military pressure in dealing with the Vietnamese problem.

Meanwhile, the tempo of the war continually increased. By the spring of 1966, B-52 bombers were regularly conducting large-scale raids on military bases, industry, and transport in North Vietnam, and in June of that year their strikes were extended to include oil installations and other targets near the major cities of Hanoi and Haiphong.

The tonnage of bombs dropped in South Vietnam was even greater than that dropped earlier in the North. The total number of American troops in Vietnam had grown to 385,000 by the end of 1966 and to more than 485,000 a year later. But escalation was a two-way street. North Vietnam responded to the U.S. buildup by sending additional forces to the south, leading General William C. Westmoreland, the American commander in South Vietnam, to plead for more and more troops. By October 1967, 40 percent of America's combat-ready divisions, half of its tactical air power, and a third of its naval strength were involved in the Vietnam War.

American experts had assumed that their nation's industrial and technological superiority would enable U.S. and ARVN forces to subdue the enemy relatively quickly and with relative ease. The marvels of United States technology were evident on every hand: B-52 bombers, helicopter gunships, mobile armor, chemical weapons, napalm, and herbicides like Agent Orange. Yet the war had developed into a costly stalemate. As American soldiers and equipment poured into South Vietnam, it became clear that North Vietnam lacked the

U.S. Marines on a search and destroy mission, South Vietnam, October 1967. *Courtesy Defense Department (Marine Corps), photograph by Cpl. Randolph.*

military power to drive the United States out of Southeast Asia; on the other hand, it eventually became equally apparent that the United States, for all its military and industrial predominance, could neither prevent Communist infiltration into the south nor force the North Vietnamese to enter into what U.S. leaders considered genuine negotiations. The United States carefully avoided an invasion of North Vietnam, fearing large-scale Chinese intervention—as had happened in Korea—as a consequence; but the American air assault above the 17th parallel was unprecedented in its severity. Still, even the massive air war failed either to break the enemy's morale or to stop the flow of supplies to the Vietcong from the north.

General Westmoreland's ground strategy was no more successful than the U.S. air bombardment. His basic purpose was to debilitate his adversaries and drain their will to resist through a war of attrition. In addition to protecting the urban areas of South Vietnam, the general periodically sent "search and destroy" missions through the countryside in an effort to demolish pockets of the Vietcong. The Americans also carried on a general "pacification campaign" intended to win the loyalty of the South Vietnamese peasants. These tactics sometimes worked, but neither the military operations nor the pacification programs achieved their real objective. The Vietcong guerrillas would habitually fade away (into the jungle or back among the "peasants" of any given village) in the face of search and destroy sweeps, only to reappear and resume control as soon as American and ARVN forces withdrew. In fact, the United States never developed an appropriate strategy for the war it was waging in Vietnam. Washington found some satisfaction in the greater stability of the Saigon government that resulted from Air Marshal Nguyen Cao Ky's accession to power as premier in 1965. In 1967 a new South Vietnam constitution was approved, and in an effort to display its democracy, the Saigon government held national elections in which Nguyen Van Thieu and Ky were selected as president and vice president, respectively.

Still, the war went on, month after month, year after year. The employment of bombs, napalm, and defoliants wiped out whole villages and created thousands of refugees. In the absence of established battle lines, American officials measured progress not in the amount of territory won but in the number of Vietcong killed. By 1968 the "body count" in this numbers game had exceeded 400,000 of the enemy—surely an exaggerated figure. For U.S. policymakers, American involvement had a certain incremental character. Each step along the way seemed no more than a modification of past practice and thus obviated the need for a full-scale reassessment of basic policies.

Americans—most of whom were horrified to watch televised coverage of the brutal and bloody conflict on the evening news—had never experienced anything quite like the Vietnam War. As one historian has written:

> It was a bizarre struggle, in which correspondents could drive or helicopter into the countryside, film or watch an engagement, come home, change clothes, open a cold beer, and report it all—uncensored—to the people at home. Americans, gathered around their television sets, saw unforgettable scenes from this "living-room war"—bound and frail-looking Viet Cong captives, equipment-burdened Americans setting fire with PX cigarette lighters to hootches, screaming wounded being lifted into choppers, piles of anonymous dead that were the stuff of body counts, sweating men pinned down in tall grass by fire from invisible machine guns, black-and-red billowing explosions of a tactical air strike on the enemy.

Then, on January 30, 1968, came a surprise offensive in which the enemy launched powerful, simultaneous attacks against dozens of key cities and towns in South Vietnam. Days and even weeks of bitter fighting ensued before the opposition forces were finally dislodged. This "Tet offensive"—which took place during the celebration of Tet, the lunar New Year—was the most destructive enemy attack of the war. The offensive inflicted heavy losses on U.S. and ARVN forces as well as the Vietcong and North Vietnamese who waged it. Although Westmoreland described the all-out offensive as the "last gasp" of the enemy, he also requested that an additional 206,000 American troops be sent to Vietnam. The Tet offensive was, as historian Townsend Hoopes remarked, "the eloquent counterpoint to the effusive optimism" that had long held sway in the White House and the Pentagon. It appeared that Lyndon's War had run out of steam. After years of heavy fighting in Vietnam, victory for the Americans and their allies seemed as remote as ever.

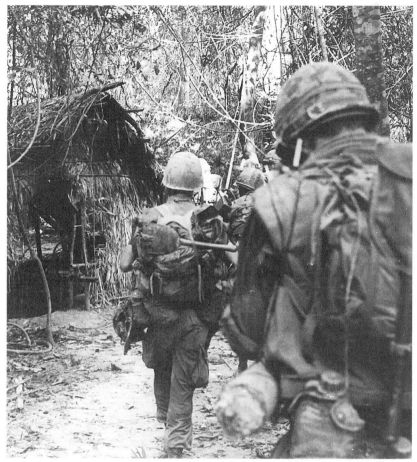

U.S. infantrymen enter an enemy sanctuary during Operation Dewey Canyon, 1968.
Courtesy Defense Department (Marine Corps), photograph by Cpl. Randolph.

ANTIWAR PROTEST: AMERICA DIVIDES

The war in Vietnam disrupted the political consensus that Lyndon Johnson prized so highly and eventually created profound suspicion and disillusionment among the American people. Indeed, the war became the most divisive issue in the modern history of the United States. It provoked a far-reaching protest movement, shattered Johnson's presidency, crippled the Democratic Party, damaged the U.S. position in international affairs, and encouraged a critical reappraisal of the nation's political institutions, culture, and values. The mounting violence in Vietnam was closely paralleled by the heightened turmoil and social disorder at home—urban riots, black militancy, campus unrest, and a strident antiwar movement. The very legitimacy of the national government came into question, and there was, as Senator Eugene J. McCarthy said, a "growing sense of alienation from politics." The war, observed the journalist Godfrey Hodgson, "became the organizing principle around which all the doubts and disillusionments . . . all the deeper discontents hidden under the glossy surface of the confident years coalesced into one great rebellion."

Defenders of Johnson's policies (many of whom were veterans of World War II or the Korean War) generally believed that the United States must contain Communist expansion in every part of the world. Accepting the logic of the domino theory, they endorsed the administration's promise to contain the far-flung Communist aggression by fighting in Southeast Asia. They stressed Johnson's often-expressed willingness to negotiate a general withdrawal of "foreign" forces from the south, which the Communists continued to reject. Some "hawks," as supporters of the war were dubbed, disapproved of the president's approach as too limited and urged that America should instead pursue a quick and total victory. Most Americans were no doubt ambivalent in their attitudes toward the war, believing that international communism should be halted but doubting that it could be turned back in Southeast Asia, at least not without the loss of thousands of U.S. soldiers.

Liberal critics of the American war in Vietnam, who were called "doves," pictured Johnson as too quick to resort to force. They tended to view the Vietnam conflict as fundamentally another nation's civil war, and they questioned the administration's assumption that the North Vietnamese, given their traditional distrust of the Chinese, were pawns of Beijing. They scoffed at the domino theory as too simplistic; charged the administration with exaggerating the Communist threat in Vietnam; called attention to the repressive, reactionary character of the Saigon government; objected to the massive aerial bombing throughout Vietnam; deplored the mounting loss of American life (as the number of American military deaths jumped from a total of 9,000 to nearly 15,000 from 1967 to 1968); decried the enormous cost of the war (over

$20 billion by 1968); and denied that the United States was advancing the cause of democracy or a stable peace. Questioning the official explanation of the war, Johnson's critics expressed doubts about the sincerity of his peace efforts and accused him of rejecting opportunities for negotiation and stiffening his demands on North Vietnam.

Much of the antiwar protest in the United States was based on moral considerations, including traditional pacifism and revulsion at the war's brutality. The corrupt and repressive regimes of Ky and Thieu seemed to make a mockery of American intervention in support of democracy and self-determination in Vietnam. Photography (in newspapers and magazines) and television brought daily, often graphic, images of the war's inhumanity into American homes: the death and maiming of U.S. soldiers, the killing of civilians by American military operations, the wholesale destruction of Vietnamese villages, the use of napalm and defoliants to destroy forests and crops, and the savage spoliation of an ancient culture by modern warfare. In March 1968, for example, a war-weary platoon led by Lieutenant William Calley, Jr., indiscriminately machine-gunned and bayoneted several hundred old men, women, and children in the South Vietnamese hamlet of My Lai. Opposition slowly increased in both houses of Congress following the major escalation of 1965. The most important defector from Johnson's policy was Senator J. William Fulbright of Arkansas. Early in 1966, Fulbright's Foreign Relations Committee commenced televised hearings on the Vietnam situation, and this inquiry was followed by another set of hearings that probed the war's effects on Chinese affairs.

Nevertheless, most of the lawmakers seemed to accept President Johnson's theory of the war-making power—that the role of Congress was not to sanction but to support the war. This attitude became characteristic of Johnson's presidency. Yet grumbling and dissatisfaction, in and out of Congress, increased with the president's growing preoccupation with the war. Many liberals feared that the war would jeopardize the Great Society, while many conservatives were disturbed by the economic consequences of the conflict. Military spending had risen to $55 billion in 1965 and a whopping $80 billion in 1968. The rising cost of the war encouraged inflation, which cut into export growth and worsened a balance of payments problem. Spiraling war costs also made it more difficult for the administration to get its foreign aid proposals through

Support for the Vietnam War

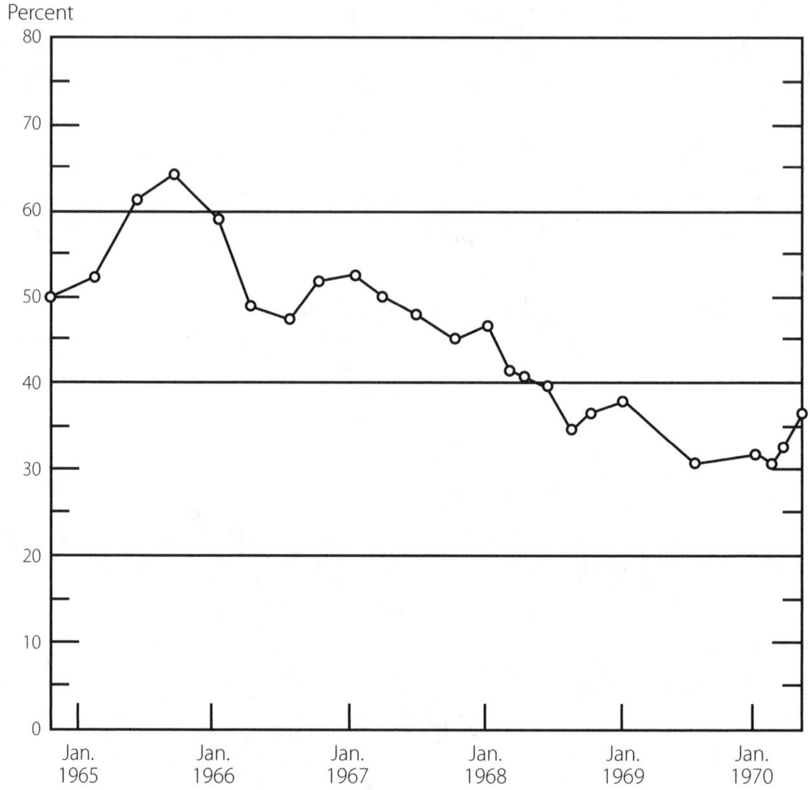

Source: Herbert Y. Schandler, *The Unmaking of a President: Lyndon Johnson and Vietnam* (Princeton, NJ: Princeton University Press, 1977), p. 195.

Congress. "If we didn't have Vietnam . . ." became a preamble to almost any congressional consideration. Despite the inflationary pressures, Johnson resisted a tax increase. He finally recommended an income tax surcharge in his 1967 State of the Union message, but his formal proposal to Congress later that year set off months of wrangling before being approved. Congressional conservatives demanded large domestic spending cuts in return for their support of the tax increase.

University students and professors were among the earliest critics of the American military escalation, and antiwar protests called "teach-ins" were held on various campuses in the spring of 1965. Beginning at the University of Michigan in late March, the teach-ins quickly spread. During a two-day demonstration at Berkeley, California, 12,000 students heard such speakers as Dr. Benjamin Spock, the noted authority on baby care, Socialist leader Norman Thomas, and comedian-activist Dick Gregory condemn the government's policy in Vietnam. In mid-May a national teach-in was held in Washington, D.C., and during the following August representatives of several peace, civil rights, and church groups organized a National Coordinating Committee to End the War. This committee sponsored a series of mass demonstrations during the fall of 1965. The teach-ins and other campus demonstrations, while initially supported by only a small minority of students, were important because they helped make dissent respectable. In the meantime, the Free Speech Movement of 1964–65 at the University of California, Berkeley, an early manifestation of campus protest, helped radicalize college and university students and served as a bridge between the civil rights and antiwar movements.

The political radicalism of the young was expressed most forcefully on the campuses of the nation's major universities. Strongly influenced by the civil rights movement, what became known as the New Left was concerned with individual freedom, the decentralization of power, moral protest, and an activism free from conventional politics. It called for "participatory democracy" and the reconstruction of American society. The Students for a Democratic Society (SDS), formally organized in 1962 at Port Huron, Michigan, embodied the main tenets of the new radicalism, which it distinguished from the radicalism of the previous generation—the Old Left of labor unions, Marxist convictions, and emphasis on dogma. The organization was soon involved in community action programs and social protest campaigns, including the antiwar movement. SDS and other New Left groups regarded the war in Vietnam as an expression of fundamental ills in American society, such as political hypocrisy, the oppression of nonwhite people, imperialism, and the capitalist drive for raw materials, markets, and investment opportunities.

In 1969, the most radical SDS faction left the organization and formed the Weather Underground with the expressed desire of overthrowing the U.S. government. The so-called Weathermen went well beyond protesting, as they undertook actual bombings of selected national-interest targets from 1969 through the mid-1970s, including even the Pentagon, which they attacked in 1972. The Weathermen quickly became a focus of the FBI, and the members began to operate in a very clandestine, "underground" manner. By 1976 the Weathermen had lost their drive, as the Vietnam War had concluded, and within a year they dissolved. Ultimately, the members of the Weather Underground escaped prosecution following a decision by the Supreme Court that held that the FBI and the CIA had failed to get a court order to install electronic surveillance devices to spy on the Weathermen, rendering evidence obtained through such methods unusable. In an ironic twist of fate, former associate FBI director W. Mark Felt and his deputy, Edward Miller, were convicted in 1980 in a federal court of having authorized and carried out the illegal wire taps on the Weathermen and other radical groups organizations; none other than former President Richard M. Nixon testified on their behalf during the trail. While both Felt and Miller were convicted, President Ronald Reagan later pardoned the two men. Twenty-five years later, on May 31, 2005, Felt revealed to the world that he had been the infamous "Deep Throat" informant who had played such a significant role in disclosing damaging facts about the Nixon administration to the *Washington Post* reporter Bob Woodward during the Watergate scandal.

Another stream of youthful radicalism was primarily cultural rather than political in nature. Rejecting an established culture resting on authoritarian, fundamentalist, and puritanical principles, as well as the desirability of technological progress, the cultural rebels sought an alternative lifestyle. Commonly referred to as "hippies," both internally and externally, they idealized nature, formed communes, experimented with drugs and sex, and discovered in rock music the promise of a revolution in consciousness and culture. They felt part of a larger rebellion. Though not primarily interested in politics, most of them condemned America's use of its immense power against a small, struggling country. Not surprisingly, the counterculture contributed to the polarization of U.S. society and the increasing disillusionment with the war. Many of the same people passed from cultural rebellion to political activism and back again.

Some civil rights leaders, including Martin Luther King, Jr., also joined the peace ranks. King argued that African Americans were being called upon to make disproportionately large sacrifices in Vietnam and that the conflict there was undermining badly needed reforms at

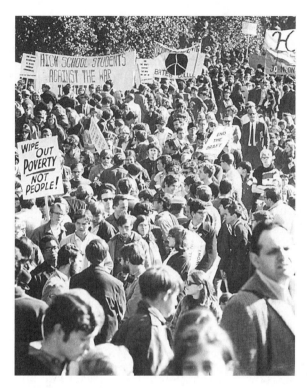

Antiwar demonstrators
march on the Pentagon,
October 1967. *Courtesy
Library of Congress.*

home. In April 1967 King led a march of over 100,000 people from
New York's Central Park to United Nations headquarters in an antiwar demonstration. A few days earlier he had characterized the United
States as "the greatest purveyor of violence in the world today." His role
in the antiwar movement caused a break in the black leader's friendly
relations with President Johnson. The assassination of Martin Luther
King, Jr., in the early spring of 1968 completed the disillusionment that
many African Americans had begun to feel over the American war
in Vietnam. Black leaders and organizations faced increasing pressure
after 1965 to oppose the war.

One of the effective forms of antiwar protest was the draft-resistance
movement. The government's increasing reliance on the Selective Service System imposed an enormous burden of uncertainty, coercion, and
risk upon young American men, especially those from the lower and
lower-middle classes who were unable to attend college and thereby obtain educational deferments. In *Chance and Circumstance: The Draft, the*

War and the Vietnam Generation (1978), attorney Lawrence M. Baskir
and historian William A. Strauss discuss avoiders, evaders, deserters,
and exiles. Draft card "turn-ins" began to occur, and the public burning
of such cards became a dramatic means of resisting the war in Vietnam.
Thousands of young men exiled themselves to Canada or Europe in
order to avoid military duty. Mass protests were held outside induction centers. In October 1967 some 60,000 demonstrators conducted a
spectacular march on the Pentagon, hated symbol of the U.S. war machine. Resistance eventually began to appear within the military itself.
The desertion rate from the armed forces mounted, and sizable numbers
of American deserters moved to Canada, Mexico, Sweden, and other
western European countries. By the time the war finally ended for the
United States in March 1973, it had produced 570,000 draft offenders
and 563,000 less than honorable discharges from the service. They all
were part of "the Vietnam generation"—the 27 million draft-age men in
the United States—and the 25 million men who did not fight.

The continuing escalation of the war tended not only to polarize
public opinion on the issue but also to radicalize a significant proportion of the antiwar protesters. The country seemed to be coming apart,
both because of the wide-ranging opposition to the Vietnam War and
intense political and social divisions. All of this complicated Lyndon
Johnson's efforts to win the war. During the second half of the 1960s, the
non-violent phase of civil rights movement began to disintegrate, Black
Power intensified interracial discord, the Great Society encountered
rising opposition, and a "backlash" developed against the radical youth
insurgency of the late 1960s and the attacks on "establishment" values
and traditions. In addition, alienation and resentment were evident in
the inner-city ghettos during the outbreak of urban riots, and anger and
frustration characterized the behavior of many black militants. Consensus, which had been such a pronounced feature of the years following
World War II, was no longer a feature of the national scene.

THE LOST CRUSADE

Plagued by ghetto riots, campus unrest, an overheated economy, and
sharp divisions over the Vietnam War, Lyndon Johnson lost popularity
rapidly after 1965. While 63 percent of the public approved of Johnson's

handling of the presidency at the beginning of 1966, his approval rating had dropped to slightly more than 40 percent by November. In the mid-term elections that year, the Democrats lost 47 House seats and three Senate seats. The president's problems were complicated by what many Americans began to perceive as his duplicity—his "credibility gap." Johnson, hoping and believing that every new increase in American military effort in Vietnam would bring victory into sight, persisted on his course for a long time. He lashed out at his critics, contemptuously referring to "some Nervous Nellies and some who will become frustrated and bothered and break ranks under the strain."

In the fall of 1967 the White House launched an energetic campaign to win renewed support for the war, and the Pentagon reiterated its confidence in an early military victory for the United States. But the administration's problems were steadily exacerbated. The president's neglect of the ambitious reform programs of the mid-1960s weakened his support within the United States. The economy was in trouble by 1967, with the cost of the war going up drastically and the resulting inflation becoming more and more acute. Some of the administration's ablest Great Society architects, including Secretary John W. Gardner of the Department of Health, Education, and Welfare (HEW), resigned because of the president's absorption in Vietnam. Secretary of Defense McNamara, who had been instrumental in formulating the strategic and technological rationale for the American escalation, left office in November 1967, having become unhappy over U.S. policy in Vietnam and dubious as to its effectiveness.

Early in 1968 the administration was dealt a series of heavy blows. First came the seizure by North Korea of the U.S.S. *Pueblo*, an intelligence ship cruising off the North Korean coast. This incident created a new American crisis in the Far East and led to drawn-out negotiations that finally secured the release of the crew (but not the ship) almost a year later. The Tet offensive followed hard on the heels of the *Pueblo* affair, and for many Americans that psychological setback was the last straw. Then, on March 12, Senator Eugene McCarthy, an announced candidate for the Democratic presidential nomination in 1968, made a surprisingly strong showing in the New Hampshire primary, winning 42.2 percent of the votes to President Johnson's 49.4 percent. Private polls indicated that McCarthy would defeat Johnson in the approaching

Wisconsin primary. Four days after the New Hampshire primary, Robert F. Kennedy entered the Democratic presidential race as an active candidate. It was obvious that the president's renomination would be bitterly challenged and that the Democrats would be confronted with a bruising intraparty fight in the coming months. The nation was deeply fragmented, its mood had become intensely bitter, Johnson's popularity had sunk to a new low, and the chief executive himself had become a virtual prisoner in the White House.

Nevertheless, the administration's most difficult problem was not that a majority of the people opposed the war in 1968. The real problem was that Johnson had lost the confidence of much of his political coalition, of the members of Congress, and of the nation's trendsetters. As Clark Clifford explained, "Major elements of the national constituency—the business community, the press, the churches, professional groups, college presidents, students, and most of the intellectual community have turned against this war." The president could no longer govern effectively. He also feared that the "loss" of Vietnam would lead to a fierce controversy, one that would "shatter my presidency, kill my administration, and damage our democracy." Johnson's greatest failure was his inability to be honest with the American people—and with himself—about the war in Vietnam.

Johnson finally heeded those who contended that the United States must abandon the search for a decisive victory in Vietnam. A high-level review of U.S. policy, brilliantly conducted by Clark Clifford, the new secretary of defense, convinced the president that further expansion of the war would not guarantee greater success. By 1968 the conflict in Vietnam had become the longest war in American history. (By 1969 it became the bloodiest in terms of U.S. casualties.) It had cost almost $100 billion, brought incalculable losses to the Vietnamese people, and become the least popular war in the nation's experience. In a major address to a national television audience on March 31, Johnson announced that he was restricting the bombing of North Vietnam and inviting Hanoi to discuss a settlement of the war. At the end of his speech, the chief executive made an even more startling announcement. "I have concluded," he said, "that I should not permit the presidency to become involved in the partisan divisions that are developing in this political year. . . . Accordingly, I shall not seek, and I will not accept, the nomination of my party for another term as your president."

U.S. Battle Deaths in Vietnam

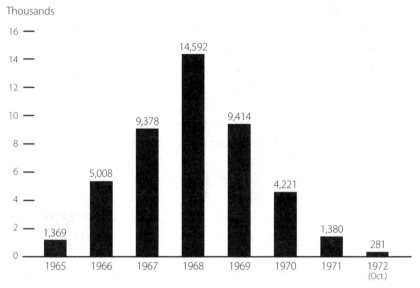

Source: Robert Warren Stevens, *Vain Hopes, Grim Realities: The Economic Consequences of the Vietnam War* (New York: Franklin Watts, 1976), p. 3.

The Tet offensive and the decisions U.S. leaders made in its aftermath proved to be a turning point in American policy on Vietnam. The decisions Johnson and his advisers reached in March finally imposed some limits on American participation in the war and helped pave the way for the withdrawal of U.S. troops from Vietnam. Intervention by the United States in that distant land ultimately became a lost crusade. Lyndon Johnson must bear much of the blame for that misadventure, but many other leaders were also responsible, and for a time most Americans seemed willing to seek a military solution to the problem in Vietnam. Johnson had tried to carry out a responsible policy in waging the war and to follow a moderate course without abandoning what he considered vital American interests. He was never able, however, to justify his policy satisfactorily either to the press or to the people.

POLITICS AND RESOLUTION: THE ELECTION OF 1968

The struggle going on in the Democratic Party became a focus of political interest following President Johnson's dramatic announcement that he would not run for re-election. Three contestants for the party's presidential nomination dominated the center of the stage in the hectic spring of 1968: Eugene McCarthy, Robert Kennedy, and Hubert Humphrey. McCarthy, a handsome, soft-spoken congressional liberal with a sharp wit and an intellectual bent, brought thousands of students actively into his campaign. As the "peace candidate," he appealed to many elements of the New Left, as well as to various other groups calling for a "new politics" eschewing special interests and backroom deals and emphasizing a more moral and intellectual approach to national problems.

In announcing his candidacy on March 16, Senator Kennedy told a press conference in the Senate caucus room where his older brother had declared his candidacy eight years earlier: "I run to seek new policies, policies to end the bloodshed in Viet Nam and in our cities, policies to close the gap that now exists between black and white, between rich and poor, between young and old in this country and around the rest of the world." Kennedy plunged into a characteristically energetic campaign. Hard-driving, charismatic, and ambitious, "Bobby" aroused either passionate approval or intense dislike; he appealed strongly not only to those who venerated the memory of his martyred brother but also to African Americans, the lower-middle classes, and urban ethnic groups, many of whom looked on him as a zealous champion.

Vice President Humphrey announced his candidacy on April 27. Having the tacit support of President Johnson, Humphrey could count on the backing of party leaders throughout the country. While the two Democratic senators fought it out in the primaries between April and early June, the vice president proceeded to gather a large number of convention delegates in the non-primary states. He avoided all primaries and most public appearances. A reluctant defender of the administration's foreign policies, Humphrey was closely identified with the civil rights acts of the mid-1960s and other reforms of the Great Society. His strength lay squarely in the old Democratic coalition.

Kennedy's vigorous and well-financed campaign soon began to pick up steam. In May the New York senator defeated his Minnesota opponent in Indiana and Nebraska, but he received a setback at the end of the month when McCarthy won the Oregon primary. The two candidates turned to California for a final showdown in the June 4 primary in which 174 convention votes were at stake. The Kennedy forces were elated when they won a narrow victory in California with a 46 to 42 percent edge in primary votes. Then another bizarre and incredible act of violence occurred, which seemed almost more than the American people could bear. Robert Kennedy was fatally shot early on June 5 as he was leaving a victory celebration being held in Los Angeles' Ambassador Hotel. The assassin was a young Jordanian immigrant named Sirhan Bishara Sirhan, a confused Arab zealot who probably resented the New York senator's support of Israel. Once again the nation paused, stunned and saddened, as funeral rites were held for a second Kennedy.

The Democratic Party never really recovered in 1968 from the shock of Robert Kennedy's assassination. McCarthy attracted many, though by no means all, of Kennedy's more than 300 delegates, and he consistently led the vice president in the public opinion polls. Yet McCarthy's quest for delegates was attended by many handicaps, including his own introspective and enigmatic personality, the image of his campaign as a "children's crusade," the fact that professional politicians tended to distrust him, and the success Humphrey achieved among party regulars in lining up delegates.

Democratic delegates met in Chicago late in August for their party's national convention. The sessions were held in the Amphitheater in an atmosphere of controversy and strain. Humphrey's supporters controlled the convention. After an angry debate, a "peace" plank calling for "an unconditional end to all bombing in North Vietnam" was voted down in favor of an endorsement of the president's efforts to achieve "an honorable and lasting settlement." Humphrey was easily nominated on the first ballot. He decided upon Edmund S. Muskie, a respected senator from Maine, as his running mate. The Democrats adopted a platform in keeping with their traditional liberalism, and in spite of the steamroller tactics sometimes employed by the Humphrey managers, the delegates abrogated the long-established unit rule, refused to seat the segregationist Mississippi delegation, and initiated an unprecedented democratization of delegate selection to take effect in 1972.

In the meantime, a drama of street violence unfolded in downtown Chicago. Some 10,000 youthful protesters had descended upon the city, including such elements of the New Left as the National Mobilization to End the War in Vietnam and the less-serious Youth International Party (Yippies), to demonstrate against Johnson's Vietnam policy. This setting led to a series of acrimonious and bloody clashes between the demonstrators and the fully mobilized city police, who operated under the tight control of Mayor Richard J. Daley, a powerful old-time political boss and strong Humphrey partisan. Given orders to restrict the organized activities of the protesters and whipped into a frenzy by taunts, obscenities, and showers of stones, the police went berserk and turned brutally on their tormentors with clubs, tear gas, and mace. A nationwide television audience watched in fascinated horror as scenes of party warfare in the Amphitheater and mayhem in the streets followed each other. For the moment it seemed as if the Democratic Party had simply imploded.

Republicans were spared such divisive differences and fierce intra-party struggles as they prepared for the campaign of 1968. The party's leading candidate at the outset was Governor George W. Romney of Michigan, a dynamic businessman who had built the failing American Motors Company into a going concern before entering politics. Although a series of forthright but undiplomatic statements on Vietnam and other issues had hurt Romney's reputation, he formally announced his candidacy in November 1967. New York's Governor Nelson A. Rockefeller, who in 1965 had forsworn future presidential ambitions, once more became interested in heading the national ticket following his election to a third gubernatorial term in 1966. A third aspirant from the ranks of the Republican governors was Ronald Reagan of California, who had defeated Governor Edmund G. "Pat" Brown in 1966 by more than a million votes.

The fourth major candidate was Richard M. Nixon, who, despite having been twice pronounced politically dead—the first time after his narrow loss to JFK for the presidency in 1960 and the second time following his humiliating defeat in the California gubernatorial race against Pat Brown in 1962—had undergone a remarkable rehabilitation. Nixon left California after failing to win the governorship and joined a prominent New York law firm. Nevertheless, he remained active in Republican affairs, speaking frequently and attending party meetings all over the country. He had loyally supported Barry Goldwater in 1964 and had won the gratitude of hundreds of Republican candidates and party leaders with his extensive efforts in the campaign of 1966. Nixon did not formally announce his candidacy until February 1, 1968, but he had determined long before to undertake a strenuous campaign in most of the party primaries in order to demonstrate his popular support and erase his loser's image. The New Hampshire primary brought forth the "new Nixon"—relaxed and confident, gracious and unhurried, seemingly without bitterness or rancor.

Nixon quickly established his dominance in the Republican contest for the presidential nomination. Romney abandoned his campaign two weeks before the New Hampshire primary, while Rockefeller had entered the race too late to mount an effective challenge to Nixon. Meanwhile, the former vice president won a number of significant primaries and steadily added to his delegate strength in non-primary states. Nixon was concerned over the threat that Governor Reagan posed in the South and other conservative quarters, but he dealt with that potential obstacle by holding private talks with a number of important southern Republicans in Atlanta on May 31 and June 1. Nixon enacted his "southern strategy," as he assured Senator J. Strom Thurmond of South Carolina and other Republican as well as Democratic leaders of his sympathy for their position on questions like school busing and law and order.

When the Republican National Convention was held in Miami Beach, Florida, in early August, Nixon won the nomination on the first ballot. To the surprise of most observers, he chose Governor Spiro T. Agnew of Maryland for second place on the ticket. Agnew was acceptable to conservatives like Thurmond, and the selection of the governor, rather than a representative of the liberal wing of the party, was another indication of Nixon's southern strategy. The GOP platform emphasized an "all-out" campaign against crime, reform of the welfare laws, an end to inflation, and a stronger national defense. On Vietnam, the platform promised to "de-Americanize" the war, to engage in "clear and purposeful negotiations," and not to accept "a camouflaged surrender."

By early September, the national campaign was well under way. Republicans, confident that they would be able to smash the divided Democrats, unleashed the most elaborate and expensive presidential campaign in United States history. Nixon campaigned at a deliberate, dignified pace, seeking to dramatize the nation's decline at home and abroad under two Democratic administrations. The Democratic campaign, by contrast, started very badly. The disastrous Chicago convention still hung like a pall over the party. Humphrey and Muskie also faced a serious challenge from the third-party candidacy of former governor George C. Wallace of Alabama.

Increasingly unhappy with the Democratic Party's national policies, Wallace finally organized what he labeled the American Independent Party; he selected General Curtis E. LeMay, former chief of the Strategic Air Command, to run with him on a national ticket. Supported by wealthy conservatives and many grassroots donations, the new party was able to get itself listed on the ballots of all fifty states. Wallace developed surprising strength not only among white southerners but also among blue-collar groups and the lower-middle class in other regions, where rising tension was evident between white and black America. While denying the centrality of race in his campaign, the Alabamian adroitly used that issue and exploited the fears and grievances of white voters with telling effect. A short, pugnacious man with a quick wit and a folksy speaking style, Wallace liked to assert that there was not "a dime's worth of difference" between the two major parties. He promised a policy of victory in Vietnam and tough measures at home against dope users, hippies, and Communists. The feisty governor titillated his audiences by declaring, "If any demonstrator ever lays down in front of my car, it'll be the last car he'll ever lay down in front of." He condemned federal "meddling," the "coddling" of criminals, and forced desegregation of the schools.

Nixon, in a subtle way, appealed to many of the same anxieties and prejudices that Wallace was exploiting, but the Republican nominee's basic strategy was to seize the middle by stressing peace and healing in contrast to the demagogic Wallace and the divided Democrats, whose failings Nixon promised to repair. Offering himself as a harmonizer, Nixon pledged to bring Americans together and achieve "peace with honor" in Vietnam. Agnew, on the other hand, was given the task of capturing as much of the right from Wallace as possible. Emphasizing the "social issue," the Maryland governor fulfilled this assignment with a series of blunt speeches, attacks on left-wing dissident groups, and racial slurs.

For the Republican Party, Humphrey appeared to be an ideal opponent: he could not dissociate himself from his party's record in Washington without provoking opposition within the Democratic organization itself. Nevertheless, from the rock-bottom position his campaign had reached in September, Humphrey began to move upward. During October the vice president's aggressive, underdog campaigning began to catch fire. Senator Muskie's low-key personality and calm but forceful style made him a distinct asset to the Democratic cause. The Democrats were also encouraged by Senator McCarthy's reluctant endorsement of their ticket on October 29. Humphrey was searching for a way in which to take an independent line without actually repudiating Johnson. He made what seemed to be a significant move in that direction with a televised speech in Salt Lake City on September 30. "As president," he declared, "I would stop the bombing of the North as an acceptable risk for peace." On November 1, just before the election, President Johnson made a dramatic effort to get the stalled peace talks moving and to help his party win. He proclaimed a complete halt in the bombing of North Vietnam on that day.

By early November the Humphrey surge had brought the Democrats almost abreast of the Republican ticket in the public opinion polls. Some experts even predicted a Democratic victory. Nixon won a narrow victory, however, receiving 31.8 million votes (43.4 percent) to 31.3 million (42.7 percent) for Humphrey and 9.9 million (13.5 percent) for Wallace. Nixon carried thirty-two states and 301 electoral votes, while Humphrey was successful in thirteen states with 191 electoral votes. Wallace carried five southern states and received 46 electoral votes. Both houses of Congress remained in Democratic hands.

The Republicans took advantage of the disarray and division in the Democratic Party. Vietnam was clearly both an immediate cause of Democratic enervation and a symbol of more widespread dissatisfaction with the party's programs and policies. Race was a powerful underlying issue, and many "middle Americans" associated liberal Democrats with the social protests of the 1960s. At the same time, a good many liberals failed to vote at all, support from various of the traditional Democratic components declined somewhat, and even the usually reliable African American vote dropped 11 percent from the 1964 level. The Democrats suffered losses among southerners, blue-collar workers, and those on the left. Vietnam, race, and the cultural civil war provoked the defection of white voters in the South to Wallace and in other regions to Nixon. The Republicans conducted a well-organized and well-financed campaign.

Nixon solidified the "law and order" tendencies of the GOP, and his southern strategy enabled him to divide the South with Wallace, without subtracting much from his support in the Midwest and West.

Yet the result was hardly conventional from the point of view of the Democratic Party and the Johnson administration. In four years a Democratic presidential plurality of 16 million votes had evaporated. From 1965 on, the Johnson consensus had declined in a steady curve, its structure shattered by war, inflation, racial strife, and widespread disillusionment with the leadership and performance of the president. Thus the election of 1968 was the final scene in the tragedy of Lyndon Johnson. It also introduced changes that would have a profound effect on the American political system.

———— ★ ————

SUGGESTIONS FOR FURTHER READING

Lyndon B. Johnson: Portrait of a President (2005), by Robert Dallek, is one of the strongest works ever published on LBJ's presidency. The best introduction to Johnson's foreign policies is H. W. Brands, *The Wages of Globalism: Lyndon Johnson and the Limits of American Power* (1995), which places the Vietnam War in the context of accumulating U.S. problems around the world. An older book, Philip L. Geyelin, *Lyndon B. Johnson and the World* (1966), remains useful. Also important are works already cited by Ambrose, Blum, Bornet, Cohen, Conkin, Divine, Gaddis, LaFeber, Levering, McCormick, Paterson, and Patterson. Walt W. Rostow, *The Diffusion of Power: An Essay in Recent History* (1972), presents a comprehensive defense of the Johnson policies.

United States relations with Latin America are surveyed by Samuel Baily in *The United States and the Development of South America, 1945–1975* (1976) and Smith in *The Last Years of the Monroe Doctrine*, previously mentioned. More specialized works include Phyllis Parker, *Brazil and the Quiet Intervention, 1964* (1979); Morley, *Imperial State: The United States and Cuba*, cited earlier; and Robert A. Packenham, *Liberal America and the Third World* (1973). For the U.S. intervention in the Dominican Republic, see Theodore Draper, *The Dominican Revolt: A Case Study in American Policy* (1968), and Abraham Lowenthal, *The Dominican Intervention* (1972). *Reaching for Glory: Lyndon Johnson's Secret White House Tapes, 1964–1965* (2002), by Michael Bechloss, is a most revealing look at life and policy development inside the White House.

The literature on Vietnam is vast and still growing. The best overview of U.S. involvement is provided by Herring in *America's Longest War*, referred to earlier. For other important general studies, consult George Donelson Moss, *Vietnam: An*

American Ordeal (1990); James S. Olson and Randy Roberts, *Where the Domino Fell: America and Vietnam, 1945–1995* (2nd ed., 1996); and Gary R. Hess, *Vietnam and the United States* (1990). Among the critical studies of American intervention is Gabriel Kolko's massive volume, *Anatomy of a War: Vietnam, the United States, and the Modern Historical Experience* (1985). See also Marilyn B. Young, *The Vietnam Wars, 1945–1990* (1991); James Pinckney Harrison, *The Endless War: Fifty Years of Struggle in Vietnam* (1982); Andrew J. Rotter, ed., *Light at the End of the Tunnel: A Vietnam War Anthology* (1991); and Michael Charlton and Anthony Moncrieff, *Many Reasons Why: The American Involvement in Vietnam* (1978). *Vietnam: The History of an Unwinnable War, 1945–1975,* by John Prados, is an insightful and accessible study of the complexities of the Vietnam War, as is Charles Neu's *America's Lost War: Vietnam, 1945–1975* (2005).

President Johnson's role in the war is analyzed in John Galloway, *The Gulf of Tonkin Resolution* (1970); Larry Berman, *Planning a Tragedy: The Americanization of the War in Vietnam* (1982); Brian VanDeMark, *Into the Quagmire: Lyndon Johnson and the Escalation of the Vietnam War* (1991); Michael H. Hunt, *Lyndon Johnson's War: America's Cold War Crusade in Vietnam, 1945–1968* (1996); Herbert Y. Schandler, *The Unmaking of a President; Lyndon Johnson and Vietnam* (1977); and David M. Barrett, *Uncertain Warriors: Lyndon Johnson and His Vietnam Advisers* (1993). The diverse pressures that Johnson faced in waging the war are illustrated in David L. Anderson, ed., *Shadow on the White House: Presidents and the Vietnam War, 1945–1975* (1993); Kathleen J. Turner, *Lyndon Johnson's Dual War: Vietnam and the Press* (1985); and Townsend Hoopes, *The Limits of Intervention: An Inside Account of How the Johnson Policy of Escalation in Vietnam Was Reversed* (rev. ed., 1973).

A good beginning place for the military side of the war is Dave Richard Palmer's *Summons of the Trumpet* (1978). See also Shelby L. Stanton, *The Rise and Fall of an American Army: U.S. Ground Forces in Vietnam, 1965–1973* (1985); Mark Clodfelter, *The Limits of Air Power: The American Bombing of North Vietnam* (1989); John B. Nichols and Barrett Tillman, *On Yankee Station: The Naval Air War Over Vietnam* (1987); William C. Westmoreland, *A Soldier Reports* (1976); and Bruce Palmer, Jr., *The 25-Year War: America's Military Role in Vietnam* (1984).

Various aspects of the American military experience are described in Tony Fuller, *Charlie Company: What Vietnam Did to Us* (1983), and Ronald H. Spector, *After Tet: The Bloodiest Year in Vietnam* (1993). The brutality and horror of the war are revealed in Seymour M. Hersh, *My Lai 4: A Report on the Massacre and Its Aftermath* (1970); Michael Herr, *Dispatches* (1977); and Robert Pisorn, *The End of the Line: The Siege of Khe Sanh* (1982). For the media's coverage of the war, see Daniel C. Hallin, *"The Uncensored War": The Media and Vietnam* (1986).

Within the United States, the range of social protest in the 1960s is shown in Terry H. Anderson's important study, *The Movement and the Sixties* (1995). For other helpful accounts, see Todd Gitlin, *The Sixties: Years of Hope, Days of Rage* (1987); Thomas Powers, *The War at Home: Vietnam and the American People, 1964–1968*

(1973); Cyril Levitt, *Children of Privilege: Student Revolt in the Sixties* (1984); W. J. Rorabaugh, *Berkeley at War: The 1960s* (1989); and David Farber, *The Age of Great Dreams: America in the 1960s* (1994). *The Sixties* (2003), by Paul Monaco, is a dramatic and revealing look at the arts and pop culture of the decade.

The new radicalism is discussed in Christopher Lasch, *The Agony of the American Left* (1969); Maurice Isserman, *If I Had a Hammer: The Death of the Old Left—And the Birth of the New Left* (1988); Edward J. Bacciocco, *The New Left in America* (1974); and James Miller, *"Democracy Is in the Streets": From Port Huron to the Siege of Chicago* (1987). See also William L. Van Deburg, *New Day in Babylon: The Black Power Movement and American Culture, 1965–1975* (1992). Cultural manifestations of the new radicalism are considered in Theodore Roszak, *The Making of a Counter Culture* (1969); Charles Perry, *The Haight-Ashbury: A History* (1984); Jay Stevens, *Storming Heaven: LSD and the American Dream* (1987); and Charles Kaiser, *1968 in America: Music, Politics, Chaos, Counterculture, and the Shaping of a Generation* (1988).

Antiwar protest is analyzed in two notable volumes: Charles DeBenedetti, with Charles Chatfield, *An American Ordeal: The Antiwar Movement of the Vietnam War* (1990), and Tom Wells, *The War Within: America's Battle over Vietnam* (1994). Among other good studies are David W. Levy, *The Debate over Vietnam* (2nd ed., 1996); Murray Polner and Jim O'Grady, *Disarmed and Dangerous: The Radical Lives and Times of Daniel and Philip Berrigan* (1997); Melvin Small, *Johnson, Nixon, and the Doves* (1988); and William C. Berman, *William Fulbright and the Vietnam War: The Dissent of a Radical Realist* (1988). See also Kenneth J. Heineman, *Campus Wars: The Peace Movement at American State Universities in the Vietnam Era* (1993); David Farber, *Chicago '68* (1988); and Lawrence M. Baskir and William A. Strauss, *Chance and Circumstance: The Draft, the War, and the Vietnam Generation* (1978).

Several studies explore the cultural reception of the war. Among these are Albert Auster and Leonard Quart, *How the War Was Remembered: Hollywood and Vietnam* (1988); Andrew Martin, *Receptions of War: Vietnam in American Culture* (1993); and H. Bruce Franklin, ed., *The Vietnam War in American Stories, Songs, and Poems* (1995).

1960—LBJ vs. JFK vs. Nixon: The Epic Champaign That Forged Three Presidencies (2010), by David Pietrusza, is the definitive account of the 1960 presidential election and its historical impact. Lewis L. Gould's *1968: The Election That Changed America* (1993) is a perceptive and incisive introduction to the presidential contest of that year. The campaign and election are described in Theodore H. White, *The Making of the President, 1968* (1969), and Lewis Chester, Godfrey Hodgson, and Bruce Page, *American Melodrama: The Presidential Campaign of 1968* (1969). See also Dan T. Carter, *The Politics of Rage: George Wallace, the Origins of the New Conservatism, and the Transformation of American Politics* (1995); William H. Chafe, *Never Stop Running: Allard Lowenstein and the Struggle to Save American Liberalism* (1993); and Kevin Phillips, *The Emerging Republican Majority* (1969).

Several books are valuable sources for an understanding of the domestic politics and policies of the Johnson years, including Blum, *Years of Discord;* Heath, *Decade of Disillusionment;* Matusow, *The Unraveling of America;* Sundquist, *Politics and Policy;* Chalmers, *And the Crooked Places Made Straight;* Hamby, *Liberalism and Its Challengers;* and Patterson, *Grand Expectations,* all cited before. Other previously mentioned volumes worth consulting are Leuchtenburg, *In the Shadow of FDR;* O'Neill, *Coming Apart;* and Stein, *Presidential Economics.*

Perhaps the best one-volume biography is Paul K. Conkin's *Big Daddy From the Pedernales: Lyndon Baines Johnson* (1986), a lively and revealing portrait. Robert Dallek's two magisterial works, *Lone Star Rising: Lyndon Johnson and His Times, 1908–1960* (1992) and *Flawed Giant: Lyndon Johnson and His Times, 1961–1973* (1999), along with Robert Caro's LBJ trilogy, *The Path to Power: The Years of Lyndon Johnson,* volume 1 (1990), *Means of Ascent: The Years of Lyndon Johnson,* volume 2 (1991), and *Master of the Senate: The Years of Lyndon Johnson,* volume 3 (2003) are considered the definitive biographical accounts of LBJ. Vaughn Davis Burnet, *The Presidency of Lyndon B. Johnson* (1983), is informative and useful. For other worthwhile studies, see Bruce J. Schulman, *Lyndon B. Johnson and American Liberalism: A Brief Biography with Documents* (1995); Irving Bernstein, *Guns or Butter: The Presidency of Lyndon Johnson* (1995); and Doris Kearns, *Lyndon Johnson and the American Dream* (1976). Robert A. Divine, ed., *Exploring the Johnson Years* (1981), is the first of several collections of essays devoted to Johnson and his administration.

Johnson's own views on public policy are presented in his *The Vantage Point: Perspectives of the Presidency, 1963–1969* (1971) and in *Public Papers of the Presidents of the United States: Lyndon B. Johnson* (12 vols., 1965–1970). Michael R. Beschloss, ed., *Taking Charge: The Johnson White House Tapes, 1963–1964* (1997), is fascinating and suggestive. See also Ladybird Johnson, *A White House Diary* (1970), and Harry McPherson, *A Political Education* (1972). The British journalist Louis Heren wrote an impressive contemporary book on Johnson entitled *No Hail, No Farewell* (1970).

For the civil rights movement and national policy during the Johnson years, readers should begin with the books cited in Chapter 7. See also James C. Harvey, *Black Civil Rights During the Johnson Administration* (1973); Rhoda Lois Blumberg, *Civil Rights: The 1960s Freedom Struggle* (1984); Manning Marable, *Race, Reform and Rebellion: The Second Reconstruction in Black America, 1945–1982* (1984); David J. Garrow, *Protest at Selma: Martin Luther King, Jr., and the Voting Rights Act of 1965* (1978); and *The Report of the National Commission on Civil Disorders* (1968), an indispensable document for the urban riots of the 1960s. Also consult William L. Van Deburg, *New Day in Babylon: The Black Power Movement and American Culture, 1965–1975* (1993).

The war on poverty is examined in Berkowitz, *America's Welfare State;* Patterson, *America's Struggle Against Poverty;* David Zarefsky, *President Johnson's War on Poverty: Rhetoric and History* (1986); and Edward D. Berkowitz and Kim Mc-

Quaid, *Creating the Welfare State: The Political Economy of Twentieth-century Reform* (rev. ed., 1992). For various aspects of the war on poverty and welfare reform, see J. David Greenstone and Paul E. Peterson, *Race and Authority in Urban Politics: Community Participation and the War on Poverty* (1973); Karen Davis and Cathy Schoen, *Health and the War on Poverty: A Ten Year Appraisal* (1978); Kellerman, *The Political Presidency*, mentioned above; Barbara C. Jordan and Elspeth D. Rostow, eds., *The Great Society: A Twenty Year Critique* (1986); and Gareth Davies, *From Opportunity to Entitlement: The Transformation and Decline of Great Society Liberalism* (1996). Charles Murray, *Losing Ground: American Social Policy, 1950–1980* (1984), presents a biting critique of national welfare policy.

Johnson's educational reforms are considered in Graham, *The Uncertain Triumph*, and Ravitch, *The Troubled Crusade*, both referred to earlier. See also Joel Spring, *The Sorting Machine: National Education Policy Since 1945* (1976). Among other helpful studies are Theodore R. Marmor, *The Politics of Medicare* (1973); Robert Stevens and Rosemary Stevens, *Welfare Medicine in America: A Case Study of Medicaid* (1974); and Karen Davis, *National Health Insurance: Benefits, Costs, and Consequences* (1975).

Urban social policy is illuminated by Gelfand, *A Nation of Cities*; Greer, *Urban Renewal and American Cities*; Bernard Frieden and Marshall Kaplan, *The Politics of Neglect: Urban Aid from Model Cities to Revenue Sharing* (1975); and Robert Fishman, *Bourgeois Utopias: The Rise and Fall of Suburbia* (1987). For other aspects of the urban crisis, see Jackson's *Crabgrass Frontier*, referred to earlier; Jon C. Teaford, *City and Suburb: The Political Fragmentation of Metropolitan America, 1850–1970* (1979); and John Mollenkopf, *The Contested City* (1983).

The environmental movement is treated in an accessible and readable volumes by Philip Shabecoff, *A Fierce Green Fire: The American Environmental Movement* (1994); Thomas R. Wellock, *Preserving the Nation: The Conservation and Environmental Movements, 1870–2000* (2007); and a more scholarly work by Samuel P. Hays, with Barbara D. Hays, *Beauty, Health, and Permanence: Environmental Politics in the United States, 1955–1985* (1987). Craig W. Allin, *The Politics of Wilderness Preservation* (1982), is among other important works. The First Lady's contributions are described in Lewis L. Gould, *Lady Bird Johnson and the Environment* (1988).

———————★———————

8

The End of Innocence: National Limits, Richard Nixon, and Watergate

LTHOUGH RICHARD NIXON PROMISED during the campaign of 1968 to "bring Americans together," his policies failed to halt "the unraveling of America." As president he paid lip service to a negotiated peace in Vietnam, but Nixon continued the war and employed secret and unlawful means in the process. His administration was also confronted with an economy out of control and a serious energy crisis. Nonetheless, Nixon changed the direction of the Cold War by establishing détente with the Soviet Union and negotiating a rapprochement with the People's Republic of China. And he did, finally, bring an end to the Vietnam War. He was overwhelmingly re-elected in 1972. That electoral triumph, however, led to Watergate, a political scandal that gradually consumed Nixon's presidency and eventually forced him from office. While the American system survived that constitutional crisis, it was, in the words of one political leader, "a symptom of political decadence." Other developments added to the traumatic and disillusioning effects of Vietnam and Watergate, among them the erratic performance of the economy, its declining competitiveness in international markets, and the relative loss of U.S. productivity. During this period Americans lost much of their confidence and became uncharacteristically apprehensive about their future prospects. Though still an economic and military superpower, the United States had become less central and less dominant on the world stage than in the early postwar decades. Jimmy Carter and other American leaders tried without much success to find solutions to these troubles, and the 1970s ended with a convergence of seemingly intractable problems and setbacks.

THE NIXON YEARS BEGIN

Richard M. Nixon's victory in the election of 1968 and his inauguration as the nation's thirty-seventh president on January 20, 1969, seemed to mark the beginning of a new era in American politics. Yet the meaning of the transfer of power in Washington was far from clear, and the prospects for the new Republican era remained uncertain. Nixon had not won a clear-cut mandate, he was a minority president facing a Congress controlled by the opposition party, and American society was still caught in the grip of racial division, cultural conflict, and the polarizing effects of the war in Vietnam. The center Nixon represented was apparently holding, but widespread discontent existed over the national welfare system, the implementation of school desegregation, and the future of the economy, as well as the challenge to law and order and the breakdown of authority. It was not clear what changes the Nixon administration would seek in the reform policies of the New Frontier and the Great Society. Foreign affairs reflected a similar ambiguity involving such developments as the emergence of the People's Republic of China as a third great power center, continued improvement of relations with the Soviet Union, the increasing opposition to foreign aid programs, and the pressing problem of ending the Vietnam War.

The Return of Richard Nixon

Richard Milhous Nixon, the second of five sons in a hard-working Quaker family, was born on January 9, 1913, in Yorba Linda, California, a farming community in the southern part of the state. He grew up in nearby Whittier, graduated from Whittier College, and attended the Duke University Law School in North Carolina, where he worked hard and compiled an impressive academic record. After receiving his degree, he returned to Whittier to practice law and in 1940 married a local schoolteacher named Thelma "Pat" Ryan. During World War II the young lawyer served as a naval supply officer in the South Pacific. The war years gave him valuable personal and administrative experience. After the war Nixon was presented with an opportunity to enter politics, and he made the most of his chance, unseating Representative Jerry Voorhis with a hard-hitting and somewhat demagogic campaign in 1946. In Washington Nixon soon made a name for himself as a hard-hitting, rabidly anti-Communist member of the House Committee on Un-American Activities. He moved up to the Senate in 1950 by defeating Helen Gahagan Douglas in another campaign in which he charged his opponent with radicalism and used guilt by association tactics. Two years later Senator Nixon was selected by General Eisenhower as his running mate on the Republican national ticket.

Nixon was a controversial figure during his eight years as vice president. His loss of the presidency by an eyelash in 1960 and his devastating defeat in the California gubernatorial election of 1962 set the stage for an incredible recovery and political vindication in 1968. Totally absorbed in political affairs, this intensely ambitious and rigorously disciplined man was determined to succeed. There was a streak of ruthlessness in his character, a tendency toward arrogance and moral self-righteousness, and self-made man's emphasis on the ethical value of success. A somewhat shy and introverted person, Nixon was also secretive, sensitive, and rather lonely—easily hurt, prone to lash back at his critics, always careful not to reveal too much of himself. Although not especially athletic, he was attracted to football, with its combination of discipline and violence, in part one suspects because that sport encouraged his tendency to view combat as a metaphor for life. The Californian was neither charismatic nor eloquent, but in the troubled late 1960s he appealed to more and more Americans because he gave expression to—indeed, he embodied—traditional American virtues and aspirations that millions of people continued to cherish and hoped to maintain.

During the interim between his election and his inauguration, Nixon and Johnson cooperated in effecting a smooth transition in the presidency. The president-elect announced the makeup of his cabinet in December. William P. Rogers, an urbane New York lawyer who had served as attorney general under Eisenhower, was appointed secretary of state. David M. Kennedy, a Chicago banker, was named secretary of the treasury, while Representative Melvin R. Laird, a hawkish member

"Buzz" Aldrin walks on the moon. *Courtesy NASA, photograph by Neil A. Armstrong.*

of the House Armed Services Committee from Wisconsin, took over as secretary of defense. Nixon's New York law partner and campaign manager, John N. Mitchell, became attorney general. The other cabinet members did not alter the conventional character of the collective portrait. Two Harvard University professors were brought into the new administration as presidential advisers: Henry A. Kissinger in the area of national security and foreign affairs and Daniel Patrick Moynihan in the field of urban affairs and domestic policies. H. R. "Bob" Haldeman, who had been a member of Nixon's campaign team, became the president's chief of staff.

President Nixon sought to foster a spirit of moderation, and he pledged to put an end to inflated rhetoric and exaggerated promises in his conduct of the presidency. Stressing organization with clearly defined lines of authority and areas of responsibility, Nixon established an elaborate array of assistants and counselors in the executive branch. At the same time, he went to extraordinary lengths to centralize authority in the White House and make sure that the levers of power remained in his own hands, particularly in the case of foreign affairs. He carefully set about defusing the explosive controversy surrounding U.S. involvement in Vietnam. Even so, there were signs that the Nixon administration would not drastically change Johnson's policies in Southeast Asia. The selection of Henry Cabot Lodge as chief U.S. negotiator in Paris and the retention of Ellsworth Bunker as ambassador to Saigon were straws in the wind. Nixon's increasing reliance on the tough-minded Henry Kissinger, who emphasized stability as the goal of policy and military power as its most trusted instrument, provided another clue to the president's basic ideas on foreign policy.

Nixon's restrained and prudent course elicited general approval in the United States. Tension subsided and the public mood changed, not to one of optimism as much as one of relief over the passing of the bitter divisions associated with Lyndon Johnson's handling of Vietnam. People seemed prepared to give Nixon a chance to end the war, unify the country, and formulate policies for the solution of troublesome social problems. In July 1969, while this mood persisted, *Apollo 11* landed on the moon after a long and dramatic flight. Americans everywhere experienced a feeling of exuberance as Commander Neil Armstrong and Colonel Edwin E. Aldrin made a perfect landing on the Sea of Tranquility and became the first earthlings to walk on the moon.

The Persistence of Vietnam

The Nixon administration's most pressing task was to end the war in Vietnam. The president had committed himself to solving the Vietnamese problem, and his failure to end it, or at least to remove most American combat forces before 1972, might well have dashed Nixon's hope for re-election. The U.S. position was that all outside forces should be withdrawn from South Vietnam and that the voters of that country should decide their future in internationally supervised elections. The North Vietnamese and the National Liberation Front insisted on a complete withdrawal of American forces and the installation in Saigon of a coalition government that would include the NLF. The regime of President Thieu was fiercely resolved to continue as the dominant element in any postwar government, and the United States, while trying from time to time to persuade South Vietnam to moderate its position, was unwilling to sacrifice the existing government, which Washington associated with the right of self-determination for the South Vietnamese. Its survival thus became, in the calculation of Nixon and his advisers, an essential requirement for a peace settlement.

Numerous proposals and counterproposals were presented as the peace talks dragged on in Paris. The formal discussions frequently stalled and sometimes broke down completely, only to be resumed after a few weeks. The United States sought to convince the other side of its error in two ways. One was the process of "Vietnamization"—gradually withdrawing American ground troops from Vietnam, building up the ARVN forces, and preparing them to take over an increasingly large part of the fighting. Vietnamization was accompanied by unprecedented U.S. support of the South Vietnamese—arms, matériel, and training assistance. The second feature of the Nixon approach to the enemy in Vietnam was the massive use of American air power, tactical and strategic, in direct support of ground operations and attacks on North Vietnamese supply routes, bases, and production centers. In March 1969 American planes began "Operation Menu," a long series of secret raids on Communist bases in Cambodia. In all their talk about "peace with honor," Nixon and Kissinger apparently envisaged a settlement that would guarantee an independent, non-Communist South Vietnam.

The administration hoped that a systematic reduction of U.S. combat troops in Vietnam would disarm its critics and ease the antiwar pressures at home. The president announced in June 1969 that 25,000 men were being sent home without replacements, and in December 1969 he ordered the withdrawal of an additional 50,000 soldiers. The process continued until the number of American troops had declined from a high of 543,000 in the spring of 1969 to approximately 255,000 in May 1971. Meanwhile, monthly draft quotas were reduced, and the administration eventually reorganized the Selective Service System and replaced its unpopular director. In late July 1969 Nixon enunciated what came to be known as the Nixon Doctrine. The United States, he declared, would remain a Pacific power safeguarding Asia's peace, but the principal responsibility for Asian security and development must rest with the

Asians themselves. America would honor its treaty commitments and provide its Asian allies with economic assistance, nuclear reassurance, and moral support. Nixon seemed to be suggesting that the world was changing and that there were limits to the role the United States could play on the world stage.

Despite the general disposition in the United States to give the administration time in which to work out a settlement in Vietnam and the widespread approval of troop reductions and such pronouncements as the Nixon Doctrine, antiwar feeling remained strong. In the autumn of 1969 a number of antiwar demonstrations erupted throughout the country. Hundreds of rallies and almost a million demonstrators took part in a national "moratorium" on October 15, and a second round of protests staged a month later drew still larger crowds. Some 250,000 persons participated in a three-day demonstration in the national capital, with a "March against Death" proceeding from Arlington National Cemetery to Capitol Hill.

President Nixon denounced the demonstrators in a television address on November 3, 1969, stated that he planned to remove all American ground forces from Vietnam (though he failed to be specific about such plans), and pleaded for support from "the great silent majority of my fellow Americans." Vice President Agnew also spoke out caustically against the peace demonstrators, condemning them on one occasion as "an effete corps of impudent snobs who characterize themselves as intellectuals." The public response to the administration's actions was encouraging. Fifty thousand telegrams and thirty thousand letters, most of them favorable to the president, poured into the White House, and a few days later Nixon's approval rating climbed to 68 percent. American troops were coming home, the draft had become less threatening, and the financial costs of the war were beginning to decline.

To secure the kind of settlement he wanted, Nixon was prepared to take risks and use massive force. He was also willing to employ secrecy in moving toward his objective. Thus he failed to consult Congress or inform the public about his decision to bomb Cambodia, in order to avoid provoking further antiwar protest and possibly to shield himself from congressional charges of violating the Constitution. Nixon later arranged for Kissinger to hold secret talks with the North Vietnamese in Paris, and when the talks began in February 1970, the South Vietnamese (and the State Department) were excluded from the discussions. In dealing with North Vietnam, Nixon and Kissinger intended to apply pressure on Hanoi by linking the Vietnam problem and the desire of the Soviet Union and possibly the People's Republic of China to move toward détente with the United States and the resolution of other issues. The American leaders assumed that Moscow and Beijing were in a position to persuade the North Vietnamese to moderate their demands in the peace negotiations.

Then came the shock of Cambodia. Late in April 1970, in a step long urged by American military leaders, U.S. and ARVN troops invaded Communist staging areas in Cambodia. This Cambodian "incursion" was also justified as necessary to prevent Communists from taking over all of Cambodia. Addressing the American people on the evening of April 30, the president called the military move "indispensable" for the continuing success of his withdrawal program. "If when the chips are down," he declared, "the United States acts like a pitiful helpless giant, the forces of totalitarianism and anarchy will threaten free nations and free institutions throughout the world." The advancing troops, supported by powerful air forays, destroyed extensive supply centers and huge stores of materials but failed to uncover the elusive command headquarters of the enemy.

The Cambodian invasion triggered an outbreak of protest and violence in the United States. Just when Nixon was supposedly winding down the war, he had extended it to a neutral country in the region. The contradictions between Nixon's earlier claims for Vietnamization and his alarmist statements about powerful enemy forces threatening South Vietnam were disturbing to many Americans. Reaction to the president's announcement was especially turbulent on college and university campuses. In one of the demonstrations, at Kent State University in Ohio, a confrontation between students and national guardsmen ended on May 4 with four students fatally shot and eleven others wounded. Three days earlier, on May 1, the day after President Nixon announced the move into Cambodia aimed at stopping the North Vietnamese supply lines, more than 500 protestors held a demonstration on Kent State's campus. Later that evening, several businesses in town were severely vandalized and after midnight, widespread looting began to take place. A state of emergency was declared by Mayor Leroy Satrom, who requested that Ohio governor James Rhodes send in the National Guard. Rhodes honored the mayor's request. Over the next two days tensions between protestors and law enforcement increased, in particular on the Kent State campus, reaching a climax on Monday, May 4. Just after noon on that day, Guardsmen began to open fire on a hostile crowd that had grown to over 2,000 persons. Of the seventy-seven National Guard troops at the scene, it is believed that approximately thirty opened fire on the civilians. Of the four students whom they killed that day, Jeffrey Miller and Allison Krause had been among the protestors; the other two, William Schroeder and Sandra Scheuer, had merely been walking to their next class meetings. The response to "Kent State" was swift and emotionally charged. Student protests soon forced more than 400 colleges and universities to close, and many of these institutions did not reopen until summer or fall.

Criticism of the Cambodian invasion and the upheaval it provoked on college campuses shook Nixon. He agreed to talk to six Kent State students who had traveled to Washington, conferred with the presidents of eight universities, and asked Chancellor Alexander Heard of Vanderbilt University to serve as a special liaison between the universities and the White House. Still, Nixon's interest in placating his critics did not last long, partly perhaps because a good many Americans seemed to approve of his Cambodian policy and to oppose the antiwar protests. On May 8, 1970, for example, a group of protesting students in New York City was brutally attacked by helmeted construction workers who bludgeoned them with wrenches and clubs. Shouting "all the way, U.S.A.," the hard hats then marched on City Hall and raised the American flag. Similar backlash incidents as well as rallies in support of the administration took place during the next few weeks. Peter Brennan, head of the construction workers' union, visited the White House, presented the president with a hard hat, and pinned an American flag on his lapel.

Nixon had not consulted or even informed Congress prior to announcing his move into Cambodia, and the congressional response to the invasion was sharp and critical. A bipartisan amendment to a military bill, sponsored by Senators Frank Church of Idaho and John Sherman Cooper of Kentucky, sought to require the chief executive to withdraw all American troops from Cambodia by July 1, 1970, and to forbid any new U.S. strikes into that country. Although the measure was adopted by the Senate, it was defeated in the House of Representatives. The Senate repealed the Gulf of Tonkin Resolution, and the House followed suit later in the year. Meanwhile, many of the lawmakers were incensed when they learned for the first time of the administration's secret air attacks on Cambodia. Senators Mark Hatfield of Oregon and George S. McGovern of South Dakota presented an unsuccessful amendment that would have required the withdrawal of all United States troops from Vietnam by the end of 1971.

The progress of Vietnamization was tested in February 1971, when South Vietnamese troops invaded Laos, which had long been subjected to heavy air bombardment by U.S. bombers. By that time Congress had specifically forbidden the use of American ground troops in Cambodia and Laos. Assuming that a major offensive by the South Vietnamese army was finally feasible, American leaders approved a large-scale ARVN offensive, with strong U.S. air support, in an attempt to sever the Ho Chi Minh Trail in eastern Laos, the vital supply route for men and materials flowing south from North Vietnam. The offensive went badly for the invaders. Communist forces outflanked the South Vietnam units, destroying some of them and forcing others into headlong retreat. In the meantime, the Vietcong challenged the pacification efforts in South Vietnam, shelling cities and raiding villages that U.S. forces had assumed invulnerable to attack.

New antiwar protests quickly followed in the United States, and in April 1971 demonstrators were back in Washington. Among the protesters was a group that called itself Vietnam Veterans Against the War. The reaction against the Laotian venture was heightened when Americans began to learn that approximately 25,000 South Vietnamese civilians had been killed and 100,000 wounded during the past two years of fighting. Public awareness of the massacres of Vietnam civilians by U.S. servicemen was intensified by the military trial of Lieutenant William Calley, which began at Fort Benning, Georgia, in November 1970. On March 29, 1971, a court composed of six army officers found Calley personally guilty of the premeditated murder of at least twenty-two unarmed civilians in the Vietnamese hamlet of My Lai. He was sentenced to life imprisonment.

Nixon countered the antiwar protests and criticisms of his policies in Vietnam with a combination of rebuffs to the peace advocates and a continuation of troop withdrawals. The president's reaction to the demonstrators reflected his siege mentality: he was caught up in a struggle he defined as "us against them." He could take some satisfaction in his efforts to discredit the antiwar movement, particularly its more radical elements. The New Left, torn apart by its own mistakes and militant tactics, was in complete disarray. Most of the Weathermen, who had set out to assist the National Liberation Front by bringing "the war to Amerika," had gone underground by the end of 1969. Yet as the war ground on, there was a growing loss of credibility in the Nixon administration's policies and pronouncements on Vietnam. These doubts were increased by the *New York Times'* publication, in June 1971, of excerpts from the so-called Pentagon Papers. Daniel Ellsberg, a military analyst who had worked for the Defense Department, photocopied a secret documentary history of U.S. involvement in Vietnam that had been commissioned by officials at the Pentagon. Ellsberg made these documents available to the press. The Pentagon Papers not only suggested that the Kennedy and Johnson administrations had made a fairly steady effort to widen the American role in the Vietnam War, but they also revealed the government's lack of candor in explaining certain details of this policy to the public. Polls now revealed that 71 percent of those questioned thought it had been a mistake for the United States to go to war in Vietnam.

On March 30, 1972, the North Vietnamese and the Vietcong launched their heaviest offensive since the Tet campaign four years earlier. With most of the American ground forces gone and the burden of defense on the South Vietnamese troops, the enemy soon overran Quangtri Province in the north, made substantial advances in the central and southern sections, and inflicted heavy losses on the ARVN units before the situation was stabilized and some of the lost ground had been recovered. His Vietnamization program in jeopardy, Nixon again resorted to drastic action. Contending that the Communist offensive violated the implicit understanding under which President Johnson had halted the bombing of North Vietnam in 1968, Nixon ordered renewed attacks north of the DMZ, first with sporadic retaliatory raids and then with sustained air bombardments. In a television address on May 8, the president announced an even bolder move—the mining of Haiphong and other North Vietnamese ports, along with a naval blockade of North Vietnam.

Although Richard Nixon had promised to end the war, on it went. Fifteen thousand Americans had lost their lives in Vietnam during the first three years of the Nixon administration alone. In 1971 the United States dropped 800,000 tons of bombs in Indochina—an amount equal to that of 1967. By this point the war had assumed a surrealistic quality. As one staff officer remarked, "Often it reminded me of the caucus race in 'Alice in Wonderland.' Everyone runs in circles, no one really gets anywhere, and when the race is over, everybody gets a medal."

In the Domestic Arena

President Nixon was also confronted with pressing problems on the domestic front. Although he felt more at home in the realm of foreign affairs, the thirty-seventh president intended to pursue an active domestic agenda. During his first year in office, he sent more than forty proposals to Congress, including a tax-reform package, a plan to revamp the welfare system, and measures to control crime and introduce electoral changes. The new president made a special effort to identify his administration with the "silent majority" and "middle America," and against militants, radicals, and youthful dissenters. While leaning to the right, Nixon assumed a centrist position on many issues and adopted a "neoconservatism" that clearly differed from established Republican doctrine. After a brief period of amicability, Nixon's relations with Congress worsened as partisan friction increased and recurrent deadlocks occurred. The chief executive frequently succeeded in dominating the Democratic-controlled Congress by good timing, skillful maneuvering, and effective presentation of his case through television and other media. One of Nixon's first triumphs was approval of the antiballistic missile program originally sponsored by the Johnson administration. Despite strong opposition, Congress authorized an ABM system by a narrow margin in the summer of 1969.

Another area in which Nixon hoped to effect substantial change was the composition of the Supreme Court. Eager to add "strict constructionists" to the tribunal and overcome the liberal majority that had dominated the Warren Court, Nixon's first appointment to the Supreme Court was Warren E. Burger, who was named chief justice when Earl Warren retired in June 1969. Burger, a respected conservative who had served as a court of appeals judge, was readily confirmed by the Senate. This was not the case with Clement F. Haynsworth, Jr., whom Nixon appointed to replace Abe Fortas in 1969. Haynsworth, a federal circuit court judge from South Carolina, was strongly opposed by several civil rights groups and labor organizations. He was also charged with having owned stock in a company involved in litigation before his court. A heated debate broke out over the nomination, and in November 1969 the Senate voted 55 to 45 against his confirmation. Much annoyed by this rebuff, Nixon then submitted the name of G. Harrold Carswell, a Floridian who had recently been appointed to the Fifth Circuit Court of Appeals. Carswell's record on the bench was decidedly mediocre, he had frequently been overruled on appeal, and some said he had been a racist earlier in his career. The Senate rejected Carswell by a vote of 51 to 45. Nixon was furious, but in his next effort he was successful. The Senate, in May 1970, unanimously approved the nomination of Harry A. Blackmun, a federal judge from Minnesota known for his judicial scholarship.

The conservatism of the Burger Court was further strengthened in the fall of 1971 when Justice Hugo L. Black died and Justice John Marshall Harlan resigned. President Nixon replaced them with two staunch conservatives: Lewis F. Powell, a well-known Virginia lawyer, and Assistant Attorney General William H. Rehnquist of Arizona. Thus within three years Nixon was able to transform the high court, and before the end of his first term the new conservative majority had begun to chip away at some of the Warren Court's rulings, particularly in criminal law cases.

Nixon also tried in other ways to identify himself as a champion of law and order. His administration made greater use of wiretapping and other electronic surveillance of organized crime, obtained increased support for the Law Enforcement Assistance Administration, and in a bid for symbolic leadership sponsored a special District of Columbia Criminal Justice bill, which Congress passed in 1970. Other new statutes, including the organized crime law of 1970, limited immunity under the Fifth Amendment, permitted a judge to lengthen the sentence of a dangerous criminal, and authorized the death penalty for bombings involving loss of life. It was ironic, given this emphasis on law and order, that the Nixon White House itself should have condoned extensive lawbreaking by government agencies in the campaign to discredit and destroy dissidents and opponents.

In promising to "get tough on crime" and condemning drugs and pornography, the Nixon administration sought to take advantage of the backlash against rising crime rates, antiwar protests, campus disorders, black militancy, and moral permissiveness. Middle Americans, the president and his advisers believed, were moving to defend the flag, traditional authority, and older values. Among the administration's concerns were the so-called white ethnics, whose new self-consciousness and distrust of the social ferment of the 1960s made them sensitive to the "social issue." A broader group of people became what the administration referred to as "middle" Americans—some 55 percent of the population—included families with annual earnings between $5,000 and $15,000. Many of these people, feeling neglected, resented the civil rights and welfare programs sponsored by liberals and reformers; they often felt victimized for the advantage of others who had not struggled as they had to make good and abide by the rules. There was also a pervasive sense of crisis in cultural values that manifested itself in apprehension over such traditions as the sanctity of marriage and the morality of work.

Richard Nixon's approach to civil rights and the condition of African Americans was clearly part of his southern strategy designed to appeal to white southerners and outflank Alabama's Governor George Wallace. It would also elicit the support of many middle Americans outside the South. The Department of Justice, in sharp contrast to its position under Kennedy and Johnson, opposed the extension of the Voting Rights Act of 1965, tried to persuade Congress to defeat the fair-housing enforcement program, and attempted to slow the pace of school desegregation in the South. In 1969 the Department of Health, Education, and Welfare relaxed its policy against five school districts in South Carolina and flip-flopped in handling litigation involving thirty-three Mississippi school districts (after having earlier approved desegregation plans for the fall term). In January 1971 the president announced his firm opposition to federal efforts to "force integration of the suburbs," calling such measures "counterproductive, and not in the interest of race relations." Meanwhile, Nixon adopted a hard line on the courts' use of school busing (sending students to schools outside their home districts) to achieve racial balance. For a time he advocated a constitutional amendment to ban such busing, and in March 1972 he urged Congress to establish a moratorium on the practice. He continued to make political use of the issue.

Nixon approved the Equal Employment Opportunity Act of 1972, which gave the Equal Opportunity Commission power to enforce antidiscrimination laws through the courts. He also strongly supported Secretary of Labor George Shultz's version of affirmative action, based on precedents in the Johnson administration, implementing what became known as the Philadelphia plan. Though avoiding the establishment of quotas, the plan was intended to put pressure on employers and labor unions in the construction industry, notorious for its discrimination against blacks, to introduce fair employment practices that would increase the percentages of African Americans as apprentices, skilled workers, and union members in the industry.

Rapidly expanding welfare rolls and rising costs challenged President Nixon to make drastic changes in the federal welfare system. The number of Americans on public assistance had increased from 7.8 million in 1965 to 11.1 million in 1969. Tutored by Daniel Patrick Moynihan, Nixon sent Congress a message in August 1969 recommending "the transformation of welfare into 'workfare,' a new work-rewarding system." Instead of the existing federal welfare grants, the government under the Family Assistance Plan (FAP) would guarantee a minimum income level—$1,600 a year (disregarding earnings of $720) for a family of four. Such a family could also receive food stamps valued at $820 a year. In some states, particularly in the South, the plan would have tripled the income of impoverished blacks and whites. The proposal would have made the welfare system a federal rather than a state responsibility. Nixon and Moynihan hoped to promote work by requiring able-bodied recipients to accept employment or vocational training and providing benefits to those with low-paying jobs. The president was also attracted by the idea of combining conservatism with social activism.

Nixon's welfare reform proposal created quite a stir, and during the controversy that followed the measure's introduction it came under attack by both the right and the left. The House passed a bill containing the basic features of FAP in April 1970, but the Senate Finance Committee rejected the plan and later voted to recommit it. The administration resumed the struggle in the Ninety-second Congress, and in June 1971 the House passed a revised bill, which the Senate Finance Committee voted (early in 1972) not to report. Nevertheless, part of FAP was salvaged when Congress approved the Supplemental Security Income (SSI) legislation, which guaranteed a minimum annual income to the elderly, the blind, and the disabled.

The president and his advisers looked to the midterm elections of 1970 for popular endorsement and legislative support of his program. Nixon believed that a major party realignment was taking place, and he accepted journalist Kevin P. Phillips's thesis that a new conservative majority of "middle" Americans might be emerging—a majority that would come from the suburbs, the U.S. heartland, and "the Sunbelt" stretching from Florida through the Southwest to southern California. Nixon's southern strategy was calculated to win support from many Wallace sympathizers, while his attempts to exploit the more conservative aspects of cultural politics were aimed at middle-class Americans throughout the country. Nixon and Agnew joined other Republican leaders in conducting a strenuous campaign in 1970. Agnew had earned a reputation as an outspoken and controversial champion of the administration, and in numerous speaking engagements he lashed out at dissident college students, critics of American involvement in Vietnam, radicals, hippies, and network television commentators, whom he described as "a tiny and closed fraternity of privileged men" biased toward the eastern establishment. Nixon took a more elevated road, but he too assumed the familiar role of partisan campaigner. The outcome of the elections of 1970 was disappointing to the administration: while the Democrats lost two seats in the Senate, they gained nine in the House.

The thirty-seventh president demonstrated considerable interest in and support for the environmental movement, which gained momentum during his presidency. In 1969 he signed the National Environmental Policy bill, an important measure he had initially opposed but later supported. He submitted an executive reorganization plan that established the Environmental Protection Agency (EPA), which Congress authorized in 1970. This action brought together in a single department various agencies charged with regulating air and water quality, automobile exhaust emissions, nuclear radiation, toxic waste disposal, and pesticides. Nixon also proposed and signed the Occupational Safety and Health Act (OSHA) of 1970. He appointed Walter J. Hickel of Alaska as secretary of the interior, and surprisingly Hickel became something of an environmentalist. The secretary halted drilling in California's Santa Barbara Channel after a severe oil spill there, persuaded the Justice Department to prosecute the Chevron Oil Company for polluting the Gulf of Mexico, moved against the Cross-Florida Barge Canal on environmental grounds, took firm action to protect the Florida Everglades from a proposed jet airport, and held up construction of a trans-Alaskan oil pipeline that threatened the tundra. Nixon fired Hickel in 1970, and in other ways as well the administration's commitment to environmental protection became weaker. The Nixon presidency had a pro-business orientation, and the principal polluters were large corporations in such industries as automobiles, aviation, and petroleum. Nixon vetoed a bill appropriating almost $25 billion to clean up the nation's rivers and lakes, although in this case the Democratic-controlled Congress passed the measure over his veto. By 1972 the White House had serious doubts about environmentalism, and the president was openly attacking "the environmental lobby."

Nixon's New Economic Policy

Perhaps the most pressing domestic problem facing Nixon was mounting inflation, which had intensified during the late 1960s as a result of the overexpansion of demand and President Johnson's attempt to continue the Great Society while waging a war in Vietnam without a major tax increase. The inflation rate was almost 5 percent when Johnson left office, and it continued to rise. Nixon realized the importance of halting inflation, and he was sensitive to the political consequences of worsening economic conditions, but he opposed direct federal intervention and the imposition of economic controls. The new president first tried to reduce the budget deficit by cutting expenditures and raising taxes, but congressional Democrats were not cooperative and the administration's own support of the ABM program, space exploration, and the Vietnam War wiped out any economies it was able to make in health, education, and housing. Nixon then encouraged the Federal Reserve Board to raise interest rates and reduce the money supply, a tight money policy that proved counterproductive. Signs of economic trouble only increased.

In May 1970 the Dow Jones average of industrial stocks dropped from almost 1,000 to below 700. The Penn Central Railroad and several other big corporations went bankrupt. Corporate profits, industrial production, automobile sales, and new construction all slipped markedly. Even still, inflation was higher than it was when Nixon took office. Someone coined the term *stagflation* to describe the strange combination of lagging output and rising prices. Meanwhile, the inflated dollar price of American goods in overseas markets slowed U.S. exports, and in 1971 America ran its first trade deficit of the twentieth century. The dollar came under pressure in international exchanges, although the United States continued freely to convert dollars to gold at the traditional fixed rate. By the fall of 1970, the economy was in a recession. Perplexing economic problems and their political implications finally forced the president to take more drastic action.

In a nationally televised address on August 15, 1971, Nixon unveiled a "New Economic Policy," whose formulation owed a great deal to Secretary of the Treasury John B. Connally. The president announced that, under authority previously given him by Congress (which he had vowed never to use), he was freezing all wages, prices, and rents for ninety days. In an effort to strengthen the position of the dollar abroad and to improve the trade balance, he cut the dollar's tie with gold and permitted it to "float" freely in foreign exchange. This abruptly ended the convertibility of the dollar into gold, which had long served as an important source of stability and predictability for world currencies. The plan also imposed a 10 percent surtax on dutiable imports, a bargaining mechanism for use against foreign resistance or retaliation. Nixon established a Cost of Living Council headed by Secretary Connally to administer the new program. At an international monetary conference held in Washington in December 1971, the United States agreed to reduce the exchange value of the dollar by about 12 percent and to drop the 10 percent import surtax in return for increases in the exchange rate of foreign currencies and other trade concessions. Phase II of the plan was initiated in November 1971, with the introduction of a system of mandatory guidelines for subsequent price and wage increases under the supervision of a federal agency.

Annual Growth Rate in GNP per Employed Worker

Percentage

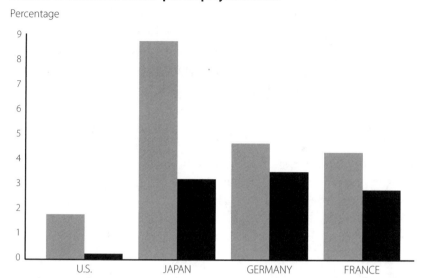

Source: Michael J. Boskin, *Reagan and the Economy: The Successes, Failures, and Unfinished Agenda* (San Francisco: ICS Press, 1987), p. 12.

Earlier in the year, Nixon had sent Congress a "full employment budget" and had labeled himself a Keynesian. With that extraordinary turnaround, the administration became an unrestrained practitioner of countercyclical spending. Nixon urged Congress to fund new projects, moved quickly to spend money already appropriated, and supported larger transfer payments for people receiving Social Security checks and veterans' benefits. Millions of Americans shared directly in this increased cash flow. The Nixon administration also implemented an investment tax credit and a personal income tax exemption scheduled for later application. Federal spending rose by almost 11 percent during calendar year 1972. In the meantime, the Federal Reserve Board did its part by easing credit and increasing the supply of money. There was obviously a political aspect in this activity, and the president always had his eye on the election of 1972. His economic policies seemed to be working. The economic controls kept the rate of inflation to about 3.2 percent during the first year of the policy's operation. In 1972 the real gross national product (GDP) rose by 5.7 percent, unemployment declined to 5.6 percent, and the balance of payments in foreign trade improved dramatically. Indeed, the economy was booming by 1972, and it took a notable upturn just in time for the presidential campaign in the fall.

Nevertheless, the success of Nixon's New Economic Policy was limited; its long-term effects were disappointing. Inflation became an even more serious problem during Nixon's second term, and stagflation again cast its baleful shadow over the economic landscape.

Détente and Triangular Diplomacy

Although Nixon seemed to recognize the need to change the nation's overextended international posture, his basic impulses were those of the cold warrior. As the *New York Times* observed after two years of the Nixon administration, "President Nixon has labored to protect and to perfect the foreign-affairs concepts of the last two decades against the widespread disenchantment with Vietnam and against the allure of insular doctrines." Nixon moved quickly to centralize the most critical aspects of foreign policy formulation within the White House. With the passage of time, it became apparent that he had brought to the Oval Office a new and more realistic outlook on world affairs. Despite his Cold War instincts, he understood that the conflict between the superpowers had undergone great change, the old polarity had broken down, and power had become multidimensional. Nixon proved to be more flexible than his predecessors in his perception of global interests and less concerned with ideology as the chief criterion by which to identify threats. He recognized, as the Nixon Doctrine suggested, there were limits to American power, and he seemed to be willing to endorse "sufficiency" rather than the traditional U.S. insistence on nuclear "superiority."

Nixon and his national security adviser, Henry Kissinger, accepted the fact that conflict in international affairs was inevitable. They believed in great power politics and worked out a grand strategy based on the concept of "linkage." The goal in dealing with an adversary such as the Soviet Union was to seek a general settlement rather than a series of ad hoc, piecemeal agreements. The idea was to link the bilateral consideration of troublesome issues like the Vietnam War, instability in the Middle East, and the nuclear arms race with progress toward a larger objective, such as détente. Nixon and Kissinger wanted to maintain an overall balance of power and achieve a "structure of peace" in the world.

As Nixon declared in an interview early in 1972, "I think it will be a safer world and a better world if we have a stronger, healthy United States, Europe, Soviet Union, China, Japan, each balancing the other, not playing one against the other, an even balance."

Although the continuation of the war in Vietnam and the volatile situation in the Middle East endangered the path toward a more harmonious relationship between Russia and America, Nixon hoped to bring the two superpowers closer together through a mutual agreement to limit strategic nuclear weapons. He expressed great satisfaction over the Senate's approval of the Nuclear Nonproliferation Treaty in March 1969, and during the following November he unilaterally renounced American use of biological warfare and chemical weapons except for defense. The Strategic Arms Limitation Talks (SALT) were resumed in Helsinki, Finland, in November 1969, and the chief executive kept a close eye on those negotiations. Russian and American leaders agreed in 1971 to modernize and strengthen their hotline communications link. More important was the breakthrough that came in August 1971, when the Soviet Union offered new guarantees to keep the access routes open into West Berlin from West Germany, in exchange for an Allied promise to reduce the city's political significance for the West and allow a Soviet consulate in West Berlin. While moving to ease the conflict over Berlin, Soviet leader Leonid Brezhnev suggested the possibility of a general settlement in Europe under which NATO and the Warsaw Pact allies would reduce their forces. Nixon responded positively to this overture.

In the Middle East the Russians had begun to supply the Arab nations with new military equipment soon after the Israeli triumph in the Six Day War of 1967. Egyptian leaders began what they called a war of attrition against Israel in 1969, a step that brought Israeli reprisals. Though committed to the defense of Israel, the Nixon administration delayed sending additional arms to that country, while negotiating with Egypt and the Soviet Union on a plan calling for Israeli withdrawal from the occupied territories in return for recognition of Israel's right to exist and use the Suez Canal and other waterways. The United States did help obtain an Israeli-Egyptian cease-fire along the Suez, but little came of Secretary of State William P. Rogers' efforts to secure a more permanent settlement.

Farther to the east, the United States suffered a diplomatic setback when it became involved in a new crisis between India and Pakistan. When the Pakistani government attempted to suppress a nationalist rebellion in East Bengal, India intervened on behalf of the Bengali rebels. Washington supported Pakistan, hoping that India would be deterred from going to war against Pakistan, while the Soviet Union demonstrated its sympathy for India and the rebels. After the Bengali nationalists won their independence and forged the new state of Bangladesh, the USSR brandished an enhanced prestige in South Asia.

In general, the United States under Nixon showed little tolerance for political change in the developing nations. The limits of its tolerance were determined by the expected consequences of such change. The administration's Latin America policy illustrates Nixon's approach to the Third World. Governor Nelson Rockefeller, who made a special investigation for the president in 1969, emphasized serious problems and deficiencies in the Latin American economies and called for greater U.S. assistance in strengthening them. Nixon, like his predecessors, counted on private American investments in developing regions, but Washington could not control the investment policies of the large multinational corporations, which became relatively less interested in such uncertain areas. Terrorism and guerrilla activity increased in Venezuela, Colombia, Guatemala, and Bolivia, and in 1970 Salvador Allende, who headed the Socialist party in Chile, won the presidency of that country as a coalition candidate of the left-wing parties. The United States used its influence against his election. Allende was the first avowed Marxist to come to power in the western hemisphere through free elections. He soon began to nationalize the large U.S. investments in Chile (eventually taking over properties worth almost $1 billion), opened diplomatic relations with Cuba, and signed a trade agreement with the Soviet Union. Nixon and Kissinger regarded his regime as a second Cuba and a potential Soviet satellite. Allende's government was overthrown in 1973, a result the United States had covertly encouraged for the past two years.

In 1971 Nixon arranged a startling new departure in American policy toward the People's Republic of China. For two decades the United States had refused even to concede the legitimacy of Communist China. It was hard to imagine Richard Nixon, the quintessential cold warrior, as the architect of such a novel policy. The turnabout in Sino-American relations came as the People's Republic was emerging from a prolonged period of political and social upheaval. It was also related to strained relations between China and the Soviet Union and the concern the Chinese had over Russian decisions in Europe and Asia. Nixon had concluded as early as 1969 that U.S. relations with the People's Republic should be improved and that China should be brought out of its isolation. Nixon and Kissinger wanted Beijing to help end the war in Vietnam, and they hoped closer relations with China could be used as a lever in negotiations with the USSR. But their objectives went beyond these considerations to include a more stable balance of power in East Asia. Thus the China card became an essential part of the triangular diplomacy they pursued.

The United States approached the People's Republic through intermediaries in 1969, indicating its interest in developing a more amicable relationship, and representatives of the two nations later began secret talks in Warsaw. The talks proved inconclusive, partly because of differences within the Chinese leadership, but in December 1970 Mao Tse-tung and his associates let the Americans know that they were willing to receive a special U.S. envoy to the People's Republic. In January 1971, they invited Nixon himself to visit China. Over the next few months, Washington and Beijing publicly signaled their desire for an end to their long enmity; an American table tennis team traveled to mainland China, and the United States relaxed trade and travel restrictions against Communist China. Early in July, Kissinger made a secret trip to the Chinese capital to discuss the most difficult issues separating the two powers and make plans for the president's visit. Nixon, speaking on national television on July 15, 1971, informed the American people about Kissinger's trip and announced his own intention to visit China during the first part of 1972 "to seek the normalization of relations" between the United States and the People's Republic. The State Department soon indicated that the United States would no longer oppose the admission of the People's Republic to the United Nations.

President and Mrs. Nixon, accompanied by a large number of advisers and journalists, began their spectacular visit to the Far East by landing at the Beijing airport on February 21, 1972. They remained in China for a crowded week of ceremonial functions, high-level talks, and visits to other parts of the country. Nixon's series of conferences with Premier Chou En-lai generally confirmed the agreements Kissinger had already worked out with Chinese leaders. While the concrete results were not especially impressive, the meetings were extremely significant as a symbolic event in the search for more normal Sino-American relations. Nixon seemed to agree that Taiwan really was part of China and that U.S. forces would eventually leave the island, as tension "in the area" subsided. In a joint statement following their discussions, Nixon and Chou discussed other areas of agreement and wider contacts in such fields as science, sports, and culture. A delegation of Chinese physicians soon visited the United States, the Chinese bought ten Boeing 707 transport planes and $50-million worth of American grain, and early in 1973 the two nations agreed to exchange diplomatic missions.

Playing the China card accomplished most of what Nixon wanted. It showed the Chinese the advantages of cooperating with the United States, moved the People's Republic more securely into the realm of world affairs, and did provide leverage the Americans could use against the Russians. It also promised to be a major asset in the president's campaign for re-election. The rapprochement with the People's Republic facilitated Nixon's and Kissinger's pursuit of détente with the Soviet Union, a process they had set in motion with the SALT meetings, the agreement on Berlin, and the search for a settlement in the Middle East. Nixon continued his triangular diplomacy by making his second sensational trip abroad in 1972—a visit to the Soviet Union in May. Preparations for the Moscow summit had been in progress for many months, and they involved back-channel methods and Kissinger's clandestine travel to Moscow.

After several days of talks with Brezhnev and other Russian leaders, Nixon came home with a number of signed agreements. The Moscow meeting focused on an arms limitation treaty and a series of agreements concerning trade, scientific and space cooperation, and environmental problems. The arms treaty represented the consummation of the first phase of SALT I efforts. One document dealt with defensive weapons, limiting the building of antiballistic missile systems to two sites in each country. The issue of anti-satellite weapons was not covered. On the more difficult question of offensive weapons, an interim agreement was

President and Mrs. Nixon
at the Great Wall during
the American trip to
China in 1972. *Courtesy
Nixon Presidential
Materials Staff.*

signed placing a five-year ceiling on the number of strategic offensive
weapons in both arsenals, including ICBMs, modern ballistic missile
submarines, and submarine-launched missiles.

Nixon had agreed to recommend that Congress give the Soviet
Union the status of most favored nation for trade purposes. Though unable to negotiate a comprehensive trade agreement, the two nations did
establish a joint commission to discuss that question in detail, and the
American leader arranged credit for the Russians to buy $750 million of
grain over three years. Finally, the two signatories promised to "do their
utmost to avoid military confrontations and to prevent the outbreak
of nuclear war." Senator Henry M. Jackson (D-WA) charged that the
nuclear arms agreements conceded too much to the Russians, and he
succeeded in securing a proviso that in any future accords the United
States would not accept any inferiority to the Soviet Union. Otherwise,
the Nixon arms limitation agreements won overwhelming congressional
approval. Public reaction was equally favorable.

By the late summer of 1972, the Nixon administration had reason to be pleased with its foreign policy initiatives of the past year. Détente represented a new approach to, not a retreat from, the implementation of containment policy. Although triangular diplomacy had not done much to end the Vietnam War, American leaders were hopeful that the war would soon come to an end. In August 1972 the last U.S. ground combat unit in Vietnam was deactivated, leaving fewer than 40,000 American military personnel in the country. Secret meetings between Kissinger and the principal North Vietnam diplomats, Xuan Thuy and Le Duc Tho, were continuing. On October 8, Tho made a significant concession in these talks. No longer insisting on a new government in Saigon, he offered to accept an internationally supervised cease-fire and promised to release American prisoners of war in return for the withdrawal of all U.S. forces from Vietnam. Kissinger quickly accepted these terms. The Hanoi government then announced that a nine-point agreement would shortly be signed.

NIXON'S TRIUMPH: THE ELECTION OF 1972

Despite the president's initiatives on the economic front and in the international sphere, his political prospects were not altogether favorable as election year 1972 opened. Nixon and other Republican leaders could not forget their party's relatively poor showing in the congressional elections of 1970. The Vietnam War dragged on, inflation had not yet been brought under control, and although public discourse had become less strident, controversy and division continued to disrupt American life.

The leading presidential possibility among most Democrats during the early part of Nixon's presidency was Senator Edward M. Kennedy of Massachusetts, the surviving Kennedy brother and the recently chosen party whip in the Senate. Not only did Kennedy have the advantage of his famous family name, but he had also proved, to the surprise of many observers, to be an able senator, a strong campaigner, and a popular figure with party regulars as well as Democratic liberals. While driving back from a party on Chappaquiddick Island, off Martha's Vineyard, on the night of July 18, 1969, Kennedy was involved in a tragic accident that suddenly altered his prospects for 1972. The car he was driving ran off a bridge and his young female passenger, Mary Jane Kopechne, drowned in the submerged vehicle. These circumstances and Kennedy's inexplicable failure to report the accident until the following morning raised many questions in the public mind, damaged the senator's reputation, and removed what seemed to be the Democrats' best hope for 1972.

After Kennedy became unavailable, Senator Muskie emerged as the Democratic front-runner. But the senator from Maine was forced to share the Democratic center with Hubert Humphrey, who had re-entered the Senate in January 1971. A third aspirant from the Senate was George S. McGovern of South Dakota, a liberal and an early opponent of the war in Vietnam. One other Democrat cast a long shadow over the contest for the party's presidential nomination in 1972—Governor George C. Wallace. There were several minor candidates: Senator Henry Jackson of Washington, Congresswoman Shirley A. Chisholm of New York, and Mayor John V. Lindsay of New York City (who had recently left the Republican Party to affiliate with the Democrats).

Senator Muskie continued to lead the field of Democratic hopefuls until early 1972, when his drive lost momentum and the middle ground he had cultivated so well suddenly became untenable. Although Muskie won the New Hampshire primary, his bland performance there was unimpressive, and during the next few weeks his campaign failed to arouse genuine enthusiasm. With Muskie's decline, Humphrey's prospects brightened somewhat, even though he suffered in many quarters as a result of his identification with the Johnson administration and the ill-fated Chicago convention of 1968. The most noteworthy primary campaigns were those of McGovern and Wallace, the candidates of the left and right, respectively. Starting from far back in the pack, the South Dakota senator won a series of primary victories in states like Wisconsin, Massachusetts, and New York. Wallace likewise demonstrated impressive strength, sweeping several southern primaries as well as such northern states as Michigan and Maryland. Then, as he rattled "the eyeteeth of the Democratic party," fate intervened: Governor Wallace was critically wounded by a gunman on May 15 while campaigning in Maryland. Left paralyzed from the waist down, he was unable to continue his campaign for the Democratic nomination. Thereafter, McGovern advanced rapidly to a dominant position, defeating Humphrey in the important California primary and winning that state's 271 delegate votes.

New party rules democratized the Democrats' selection of a presidential nominee in 1972. Senator McGovern, as chairman of the party's reform committee, had taken a leading part in liberalizing the choice of delegates to the national convention. The new rules stipulated that the makeup of each delegation must "reasonably" reflect that state's relative proportion of women, minorities, and young people—all groups that leaned toward McGovern. At the Democratic National Convention, which convened in Miami Beach, Florida, on July 10, the reform faction took control of the proceedings. One experienced politician observed that "there is too much hair and not enough cigars at this convention." McGovern was easily nominated on the first ballot. He selected Senator Thomas F. Eagleton of Missouri, a liberal, a Catholic, and a friend of organized labor, as his running mate. In his acceptance speech the South Dakotan pleaded with Americans to "come home"—to abandon their imperialistic ambitions, subordinate their differences, devote their energies to pressing domestic problems, and renew their idealism and faith in the American dream.

Republicans were spared the harsh conflict that took place in the Democratic Party during the first half of 1972. President Nixon was in an unassailable political position by the spring of that year, and the GOP convention, opening on August 21 in Miami Beach, brought few surprises. Although Nixon had been challenged in the primaries by Representative Paul N. "Pete" McCloskey, Jr., of California, a liberal who opposed the Vietnam War, and Representative John M. Ashbrook of Ohio, a conservative who was unhappy with the administration's economic policies and critical of détente with the Communist powers, he was overwhelmingly renominated on the first ballot. Vice President Agnew was also nominated for a second term. The president, in the midst of much pageantry, rhetorical acclaim, and a galaxy of movie stars and other celebrities, called for "a new America bound together by our common ideals." For Nixon the convention was like a coronation.

Although Nixon was strongly favored to win in November, McGovern's preconvention appeal seemed to reveal a widespread desire among Americans for new approaches and new solutions to national problems. Unfortunately for Democratic hopes, the party's national campaign failed to capture the public imagination or carry forward the momentum of the Miami Beach convention. McGovern ran into bad luck soon after his nomination when it was revealed that his attractive young running mate, Senator Eagleton, had been hospitalized in the 1960s for "nervous exhaustion and fatigue" and had twice voluntarily received shock treatment for depression. McGovern, who had not known about Eagleton's hospitalization, at first supported the Missouri senator, but as the pressure for his removal from the ticket mounted, the Democratic leader capitulated and asked his colleague to withdraw. McGovern then selected Sargent Shriver, a former head of the Office of Economic Opportunity and a brother-in-law of Senator Kennedy, to replace Eagleton. McGovern's inept handling of the Eagleton incident damaged his campaign.

McGovern and Shriver campaigned hard, but they made little headway. Acting as if he were conducting a religious crusade, the Democratic standard-bearer urged the need for many reforms such as changes in the tax laws to ease the burden on disadvantaged groups and stronger programs in education, health, and welfare. The senator also hit hard at the alleged corruption associated with the Nixon administration. Some McGovernites suspected that a large contribution to the Nixon campaign by the International Telephone and Telegraph Company was linked to the favorable settlement of an antitrust suit against ITT in 1971, and that a sizable sum contributed by the dairy interests was related to an increase in the price support of milk. McGovern and his associates cited the break-in, on June 17, at the Washington headquarters of the Democratic national committee. Five men had been apprehended in the party headquarters located in the office and apartment building known as the Watergate: the security coordinator of the Committee to Re-elect the President (CRP) and four members of the anti-Castro Cuban community in Miami. Several of them had formerly been connected with the CIA. They were later indicted and charged with breaking and entering, planting wiretaps and electronic bugging devices, and stealing and photographing documents. Administration spokespersons dismissed the Watergate break-in as a "third-rate burglary attempt" of little importance. Later disclosures revealed a pattern of "dirty tricks" perpetrated by Nixon's campaign lieutenants, including efforts to exacerbate the disarray in the Democratic Party, destroy Senator Muskie's candidacy by spreading false rumors about his behavior and beliefs, and prevent Governor Wallace from getting on the ballot in California.

The election results confirmed the polls, which had shown President Nixon ahead all the way. In fact, Nixon won by a landslide, receiving 47.1 million popular votes to McGovern's 29.1 million and carrying every state except Massachusetts (and the District of Columbia). With 60.7 percent of the popular vote (a percentage surpassed only by Lyndon Johnson in 1964) and 520 electoral votes, Nixon made the best showing of any Republican presidential nominee in history. He captured 65 percent of the votes of middle-income Americans, who comprised over half of the electorate. The once-powerful Democratic coalition was left in a shambles. Whereas Humphrey had won 59 percent of the Catholic vote in 1968, McGovern received only 47 percent of that vote four years later. Jewish voters continued to support the party of Franklin Roosevelt but by a declining majority. Another Democratic constituency, African American voters, maintained their longtime party loyalty in the presidential election.

In spite of the president's one-sided margin, the Democrats retained control of both houses of Congress. Richard Nixon thus became the first president in U.S. history to begin two terms with an opposing Congress. Concentrating on a great personal triumph in 1972, he had neglected the role of party leader and the task of working for a genuine party realignment. Nevertheless, in Nixon's eyes, the voters had given him a strong mandate to govern as he wished. The polls revealed, as 1973 began, that almost 70 percent of the people approved of his performance, and in February *Time* magazine chose Nixon and Kissinger as its "men of the year."

LAUNCHING THE SECOND NIXON ADMINISTRATION

At the outset of his second term, Nixon reorganized his cabinet and made new appointments to many other upper-level positions in the executive branch. Henry Kissinger continued to play a leading role in the administration's foreign policy, and when Secretary of State Rogers resigned in the fall of 1973, Nixon replaced him with Kissinger. Relying heavily on such aides as H. R. Haldeman and John Ehrlichman, the president appeared to increase his isolation in the White House, much to the displeasure of some Republican leaders. He held few press conferences, preferring to deliver prepared addresses to national television audiences.

Nixon's second administration got off to a good start in foreign affairs. A formal settlement of the Vietnam War was finally negotiated. In mid-December 1972, with the agreement so confidently predicted in late October still unrealized because of South Vietnam's opposition, Nixon ordered the resumption of massive bombing attacks on North Vietnam. He ended this heavy aerial assault after eleven days, and in January the peace discussions were resumed in Paris. After several days of intensive negotiations, Kissinger and Le Duc Tho worked out an agreement—one very similar to the draft agreement of the previous October—and on January 27 representatives of the United States, South Vietnam, North Vietnam, and the Provisional Revolutionary Government (formerly the National Liberation Front) signed the formal accord. The treaty provided for a cease-fire; the complete withdrawal of all American troops and military advisers from Vietnam within sixty days; the dismantling of all U.S. military bases; the return of all prisoners of war held by both sides; and the maintenance of a demilitarized zone at the 17th parallel to serve as a provisional dividing line between North and South Vietnam, with the reunification question to be settled by peaceful means. While the agreement left the Thieu government intact, it also allowed North Vietnamese troops to remain in the south. Nguyen Van Thieu, under great pressure from the United States, reluctantly accepted the treaty, this after Nixon assured him of continued U.S. support and promised to "respond with full force" if North Vietnam violated the agreement.

Meanwhile, fighting in Vietnam continued, and U.S. bombers, operating out of Thailand, kept up their raids on Cambodia until Congress adopted an amendment prohibiting the use of any funds for military action in either Cambodia or Laos. Nixon assisted South Vietnam in every way he could, but by the end of 1973 the president was preoccupied with the growing Watergate scandal and had lost much of his autonomy in foreign affairs. In November, for instance, Congress passed, over Nixon's veto, the so-called War Powers Act, which required the chief executive to inform Congress within forty-eight hours of the deployment of U.S. military forces abroad and obligated him to terminate hostilities or withdraw the troops after sixty days in the absence of explicit congressional approval.

The administration's domestic policies reflected the president's sweeping electoral conquest of 1972. Although Nixon refrained from attacking directly the reform programs instituted by Kennedy and Johnson, he made clear his intention of eliminating numerous Great Society programs, including the Office of Economic Opportunity, and restricting federal spending. He gave up altogether on his own programs for welfare reform and health insurance. He dismissed the liberal Theodore M. Hesburgh as chairman of the Civil Rights Commission. He used his veto power more freely, disapproving congressional measures providing for environmental control, hospital construction, and the establishment of child day-care centers. The administration's budget proposals, while providing generously for defense and aerospace development, slashed funds for welfare, medical services, housing, and training programs.

Nixon now assumed a tough stance in dealing with Congress. One of his tactics was to impound billions of dollars appropriated by Congress for social services; that is, the president simply refused to spend congressional appropriations larger than he wanted, contending that it was his prerogative to exercise this kind of executive discretion. By 1973 Nixon's impoundments had reached the level of about $15 billion, affecting more than a hundred federal programs. The courts eventually ruled that the chief executive had exceeded his authority in impounding federal funds and eliminating some federal programs. Another source of presidential-congressional conflict was the administration's assertion of the doctrine of executive privilege—the right to refuse to make its documents accessible to Congress or to testify before congressional committees.

The erratic performance of the economy confronted the administration with a continuing problem in 1973 and 1974. On January 11, 1973, Nixon terminated most wage and price controls and substituted reliance on "voluntary cooperation." Food prices skyrocketed, and the cost of such items as rents, fuel, and durable goods rose rapidly. In June the president changed course by imposing a sixty-day ban on all price increases except for food products at the farm level. But prices continued to rise, and the administration soon introduced a system of moderate controls that permitted price adjustments. The cost of living rose by almost 9 percent in 1973. Meanwhile, the Federal Reserve System followed a tight money policy. The president signed a new price support measure designed to increase domestic farm production, thus reversing the restrictive programs introduced in the 1930s. The economic situation worsened during the winter of 1973–74, when the country suddenly found itself in the midst of a fuel crisis. Inflation during the first half of 1974 increased at an annual rate of over 11 percent, unemployment mounted once more, and the gross national product for the first quarter actually declined. Stagflation was in the saddle. As for inflation, it was part of a global problem, sparked by heavy demands for agricultural products, petroleum, and other commodities.

WATERGATE: A CANCER IN THE PRESIDENCY

To the surprise of most Americans, the burglary of the Democratic National Committee headquarters in mid-June 1972 did not fade out of public consciousness, despite the limited effect it had on the election of 1972. The trial of the defendants early in 1973 set off a startling chain of developments showing that Watergate was part of a larger pattern of covert and illegal activities fomented by the Nixon administration. It also came to light that a systematic effort had been made to cover up the administration's involvement in the Watergate affair. By the spring of 1973, the outlines of an unprecedented political scandal were emerging.

The Watergate trials began in the Federal District Court in Washington on January 8, 1973. Five of the defendants pleaded guilty to all charges. The other two, G. Gordon Liddy and James W. McCord, maintained their innocence and were tried and convicted. The presiding judge, John J. Sirica, was suspicious of the eagerness of five defendants to plead guilty, and during the trial he made it clear that he thought they were withholding information. In late March, shortly before Sirica handed down sentences in the case, he revealed that McCord had informed him that perjury had been committed during the trial, that the defendants had been under pressure to plead guilty and divulge nothing, and that persons in the White House or higher up in the re-election committee had been involved in the Watergate break-in. It was later discovered that the defendants were paid hush money, at least $400,000 during the first eight months after the break-in.

McCord's revelations exposed the cover-up and set off a succession of further disclosures in the Watergate affair. Much of the story was brought to light through the probing inquiries of persistent journalists, particularly Bob Woodward and Carl Bernstein of the *Washington Post*. It was soon apparent that some of the president's aides and former advisers were willing to divulge information in the hope that they could gain immunity or partial immunity from prosecution. Jeb Stuart Magruder, a former special assistant to Nixon and later deputy director of CRP, was reported to have implicated John N. Mitchell and John W. Dean III, counsel to the president, in the Watergate intrusion and subsequent efforts to buy the silence of the convicted conspirators. Dean himself informed the press that the Nixon administration had decided to make him the "scapegoat" in the cover-up, and he charged that Haldeman and Ehrlichman had supervised the concerted effort to conceal the administration's involvement. On May 10, 1973, a New York grand jury indicted Mitchell and Maurice H. Stans, a former secretary of commerce, for conspiracy to defraud the United States and to obstruct justice. Meanwhile, a Senate committee considering the nomination of L. Patrick Gray for director of the Federal Bureau of Investigation uncovered evidence linking presidential aides with Watergate. Gray, who eventually asked that his name be withdrawn from consideration, admitted that as acting director of the FBI he followed an order from John Ehrlichman and destroyed incriminating documents relating to the Watergate incident.

In late April 1973, Judge W. Matthew Byrne, who was presiding at the trial of Daniel Ellsberg for stealing and making public the Pentagon Papers, reported that two of the men convicted in the Watergate case had burglarized the office of Ellsberg's psychiatrist in an attempt to obtain the physician's files on Ellsberg. On May 11 Judge Byrne dismissed all charges against Ellsberg and his codefendant, Anthony Russo, on grounds of improper government conduct. John Ehrlichman later stated that Nixon had ordered him to reinforce the FBI investigation of the leaks that led to the publication of the Pentagon Papers in June 1971. Ehrlichman then assembled the White House Special Investigations Unit, later dubbed the "plumbers," to stop such leaks, and some of its members were subsequently involved in the Ellsberg case and the Watergate burglary. The plumbers also bugged the telephones of several journalists and government officials suspected of giving sensitive information to the press.

When the Watergate disclosures began early in 1973, the administration tried to ignore the rising furor; but it soon became defensive and gradually acknowledged the involvement of certain White House aides. Nixon finally conceded that "major developments" had led him to make a new inquiry into the case. On April 30 the president made a nationwide television address on Watergate. Flanked by a bust of Lincoln and a photograph of his family, Nixon accepted official "responsibility" for the Watergate events and asserted that "there can be no whitewash at the White House." Yet he denied any foreknowledge of these events or any part in their cover-up, declaring that there had been an effort "to conceal the facts both from the public—from you—and from me." He announced the resignations of Attorney General Richard G. Kleindienst, John Dean, and his close aides Ehrlichman and Haldeman, whom he described as "two of the finest public servants it has been my privilege to know." Nixon implied that Dean had, for reasons of his own, masterminded the entire Watergate cover-up and kept the chief executive in the dark about the whole affair. He denied any personal involvement or knowledge in all areas except certain limited "national security" matters, which he clearly tried to distinguish from Watergate.

In the meantime, Nixon was under pressure to authorize the appointment of a special prosecutor, one independent of the Justice Department and armed with subpoena power. On May 1 the Senate voted unanimously in favor of such a prosecutor, and the president agreed to follow that course. Attorney General Elliot L. Richardson then chose Professor Archibald Cox of the Harvard Law School for the position. While Cox set about his work, another inquiry into Watergate—its political phase—was getting under way on Capitol Hill. The Senate had voted on February 7 to establish a seven-member select committee to investigate the Watergate break-in and other campaign election violations. The committee, headed by Senator Sam J. Ervin, Jr., of North Carolina, began its public hearings on May 17. During the weeks and months that followed, the Ervin committee heard a parade of witnesses, including Mitchell, Stans, Dean, Haldeman, Ehrlichman, McCord, and Magruder. J. Fred Buzhardt, special counsel to the president, presented a memorandum in which he falsely claimed that John Dean was "the principal actor in the cover-up." The committee hearings, televised by the national networks, assumed the character of a great dramatic spectacle in the summer of 1973.

Americans soon learned that various individuals connected with the Nixon administration and the presidential campaign committee had been involved in raising illegal campaign funds, burglary, bugging, spying on the sex lives of political opponents, destruction of evidence, blackmail, perjury, and pledges of executive clemency to buy silence. It was also disclosed that an attempt had been made after the initial Watergate arrests to put the FBI off the trail by implying that secret CIA activities might be uncovered if the search were continued. Senator Howard H. Baker of Tennessee posed the essential question: "What did the president know and when did he know it?" Dean told the committee that the president had known of the cover-up almost from the beginning. Dean had warned Nixon on March 21, 1973, that "there was a cancer growing on the presidency." It was also learned from Dean's testimony that the White House had maintained a "Political Enemies Project" and that the "enemies" on this list were to be subjected to income tax audits and other kinds of harassment.

Another sensational discovery was that the Secret Service, on Nixon's orders, had installed a secret tape-recording system in the presidential offices, presumably to provide the chief executive with a reliable record of what was said in his offices and on the telephone. The Ervin committee sought access to these presidential tapes for several specified days, as

Sam Ervin,
chairman of the Senate's select
committee on Watergate. *Courtesy
U.S. Senate Historical Office.*

did special prosecutor Cox. The White House denied these requests, and the Watergate tapes became the focus of intense legal maneuvering. After Judge Sirica ordered that the disputed White House tapes be turned over to him for review, a presidential assistant told the judge that two of the tapes (possibly the most important ones) had never existed.

Early in the fall of 1973, another crisis in Washington momentarily diverted attention from the Watergate scandal, but this new development represented an additional blow to the reeling Nixon administration. Vice President Agnew, who had not been implicated in Watergate, was informed in August 1973 that a federal grand jury in Baltimore was probing his connection, as governor of Maryland, with certain alleged kickbacks to state and Baltimore County officials. The vice president vigorously denied these allegations, and as rumors of his probable indictment spread, he spoke out sharply in maintaining his innocence. But in a dramatic move on October 10, Agnew resigned the vice presidency and pleaded nolo contendere to a charge of income tax evasion. His lawyers had earlier engaged in plea bargaining with the prosecutors. The judge fined Agnew $10,000 and gave him a suspended prison sentence, thus bringing down the most outspoken "law and order" champion in the administration. President Nixon, following the provisions of the Twenty-fifth Amendment, nominated Gerald R. Ford of Michigan, Republican leader in the House of Representatives, to succeed Agnew, and both houses readily confirmed Ford's nomination.

Shortly after Agnew's resignation, another major development occurred in the Watergate case. It grew out of the efforts by the Ervin committee and Archibald Cox to subpoena nine presidential tapes. When the president refused to comply with the subpoenas, Ervin and Cox sought an order from Judge Sirica to force their release, and after hearing arguments from both sides, the judge in late August ordered Nixon to turn over the tapes and related documents to him for review, after which he would decide whether the tapes were protected by the doctrine of executive privilege or whether they should be turned over to the Ervin committee and the special prosecutor. The White House appealed Sirica's decision to the circuit court, which upheld the district judge on October 12. Seeking to avoid an appeal to the Supreme Court, Nixon and his advisers then sought a "compromise" with the Ervin committee and the special prosecutor. They offered to provide a summary of the nine tapes, which Senator John C. Stennis of Mississippi could "authenticate" after listening to the tapes in question. Senator Ervin apparently agreed to this proposal at first, but Cox rejected it on the ground that no trial court would accept summaries of evidence when the full evidence existed. On October 19 Nixon directed Cox "to make no further attempts by judicial process to obtain the tapes, notes, or memoranda of presidential conversations." Cox refused to accept this order, at which point the president ordered Attorney General Richardson to fire the special prosecutor. Richardson resigned rather than carry out this order, as did Deputy Attorney General William D. Ruckelshaus. But the next man down the line, Solicitor General Robert Bork, fired the special prosecutor as asked.

What became known as the "Saturday night massacre," coming only hours before the deadline for filing an appeal with the Supreme Court, shocked the country and provoked talk of impeachment in Congress. One White House spokesman described the reaction to the president's defiant action as a "firestorm." This widespread disapproval was doubtless one reason Nixon soon abandoned his adamant position on the White House tapes and directed his attorneys to inform Sirica that the White House would comply with the judge's order. The chief executive's credibility had sunk so low that some people interpreted the alert as a desperate ploy to divert attention from Nixon's domestic difficulties. The president held a televised press conference in an effort to improve his standing in the eyes of the public. In it, he named Leon Jaworski, a respected Houston lawyer, to succeed Cox as special prosecutor and Senator William B. Saxbe of Ohio to replace Richardson as attorney general.

As the year ended, Watergate remained very much alive in the news. Although the Ervin committee had completed most of its investigation, its final report had not yet been made. Jaworski and his staff were continuing their quiet but methodical probe, including an effort to obtain access to additional White House tapes. Perhaps of even greater significance was the full-fledged impeachment inquiry being undertaken by the House Judiciary Committee. George Gallup's polls indicated that Nixon's popularity had dropped from a high of 68 percent early in 1973 to a mere 27 percent a year later.

THE ENERGY CRISIS AND THE ENVIRONMENT

Most Americans were worried and exasperated during the winter of 1973–74 by a more immediate problem than Watergate. The United States was suddenly hit by an acute fuel shortage, particularly of gasoline. The possibility of inadequate fuel supplies first became meaningful to Americans soon after Egypt and Syria attacked Israel on the Jewish holiday of Yom Kippur, October 6, 1973. Within two weeks of the resumption of war in the Middle East, the Arab petroleum-producing nations announced an outright ban on oil exports to countries supporting Israel. The boycott was clearly aimed at the United States, the major supplier of arms to Israel, and it would apparently remain in effect until the Israeli forces withdrew from the territories occupied in 1967 and 1973. This boycott would deprive the United States of more than a million barrels of oil a day.

Neither President Nixon nor Congress had done much to anticipate the energy shortage, but in November 1973 Congress passed the Emergency Petroleum Allocation Act. It provided for a mandatory allocation program of available fuel supplies within thirty days. Early in December, William E. Simon took over as director of the administration's new omnibus energy agency. While warning of higher fuel prices, Simon stated that gasoline rationing would be employed only as a last resort. Congress adopted other energy legislation in late 1973, including the Trans-Alaska Oil Pipeline bill. The act cleared the way for the construction of a 789-mile-long pipeline, to be built by a consortium of seven oil companies at an estimated cost of $4.5 billion. The pipeline was designed to carry oil from the North Slope to the southern Alaskan port of Valdez, whence it would be transported by tanker to West Coast ports. By 1980, the sponsors of the bill predicted, the pipeline would be supplying the United States with 2 million barrels of oil a day. In December Congress completed action on a measure instituting daylight saving time on a year-round basis, an innovation expected to save as much as 1.5 percent of the nation's fuel consumption during the winter months.

Both the legislative and executive branches of the national government were preoccupied with the energy crisis during the winter of 1973–74. A large number of proposed laws descended upon Congress, and in his State of the Union message on January 30, 1974, President

Nixon declared that "the number one legislative concern must be the energy crisis." He urged the development of "reliable new energy sources," but he also cautioned Americans to adjust "to the fact that the age of unlimited supplies of cheap energy is ended." The administration proposed a five-year research program costing $10 billion, which Senator Henry Jackson, the Senate's chief authority in the energy field, criticized as altogether inadequate. In late February, Congress passed the Emergency Energy bill, only to have the president veto the measure. The legislation would have resulted in a substantial rollback in domestic crude oil prices. Opponents of this provision argued that it would discourage petroleum companies from exploring and drilling for new wells. While the debate continued, fuel prices rose dramatically. The cost of gasoline to the average American driver rose from 36 cents to over 60 cents a gallon in a few weeks.

The Federal Energy Office under William Simon moved clumsily to allocate gasoline and other scarce fuels among the states and regions of the country. Several states resorted to programs for the rationing of their gas supplies, but the Nixon administration, continuing to blame the Arab oil embargo for the crisis, steadfastly opposed federal rationing. Gradually, by the early spring of 1974, the fuel shortage began to ease. One of the contributing factors was the success of voluntary efforts to conserve heating fuel, which made it possible to begin refining more gasoline. The winter in most parts of the country providentially proved to be exceedingly mild. And the Arab oil-producing countries ended the embargo on March 18.

There was widespread suspicion in the United States that the giant petroleum concerns were reaping inordinate profits from the energy crisis and that they might even have conspired to cause it. The big oil companies operated with the advantage of concentrated economic resources and technological expertise. They maintained powerful political lobbies in Washington and the state capitals. The National Petroleum Council, made up entirely of industry representatives, served as the Department of Interior's official advisory body on all aspects of oil policy. The industry enjoyed a 22 percent depletion allowance on domestic and foreign operations. For the past fourteen years U.S. oil producers had demanded and obtained restrictive import quotas on petroleum products, and in addition American companies were permitted by the federal government to use the royalties they paid to foreign producing countries to off-

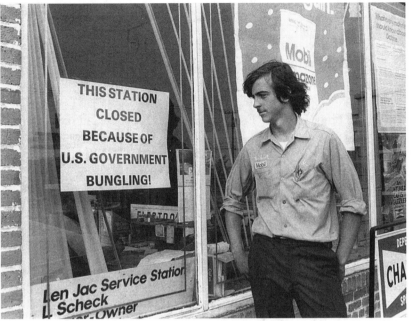

Long Island, New York, service station during gas shortage of 1973. *Courtesy UPI/Corbis-Bettman.*

set, dollar for dollar, their U.S. taxes. The profits of American petroleum companies were up 61 percent in the last quarter of 1973, as compared with a similar period the prior year.

The energy crisis of the 1970s evoked the image of an economic catastrophe. Some Americans expressed fear that economic growth would soon have to be curtailed, that it might be necessary to place limits on the nation's historic industrial and business expansion. The crisis aroused concern about the need for energy conservation and led to much discussion of "alternative energy." A boom in coal and domestic fuel production seemed certain during the next few years. National policy apparently assumed that increased energy use was desirable. By sponsoring long-term investment to meet expected needs, government action would probably reinforce existing patterns of energy demand.

Americans were becoming disturbed by the increasing evidence of decline in the quality of their air and water, the proliferation of toxic chemicals, the accumulation of hazardous wastes, and a series of human-made disasters. The industrial and urban atmosphere was filled with sulfur, carbon, lead, and a perilous mixture of gases. Waterways were fouled with detergents, fertilizer, and sewage. In its first report, the Council on Environmental Quality observed that the Santa Barbara oil spill early in 1969 showed the nation how one accident could temporarily devastate a large area. "Since then," the report continued, "each environmental issue—the jetport project near Everglades National Park, the proposed pipeline across the Alaskan wilderness, the worsening blight of Lake Erie, the polluted beaches off New York and other cities, smog in mile-high Denver, lead in gasoline, phosphates in detergents, and DDT—flashed the sign to Americans that the problems are everywhere and affect everyone." *U.S. News & World Report* estimated in 1970 that it would cost $71 billion within the next five years to clean up the American environment.

Although the movement to protect the environment had deep roots in the American past, it began to take shape and gather momentum in the 1960s. Rachel Carson, a scientist and nature writer, helped to spotlight the perils of ecological imbalance in her influential book *Silent Spring* (1962). Concentrating on the massive and often careless use of chemical pesticides, she showed the disastrous effects of the synthetic pesticide DDT. At one point in her book, she remarked that "the early mornings are strangely silent where once they were filled with the beauty of bird song." Ralph Nader, the most prominent of the new public-service lawyers, encouraged the environmental movement with his work for consumer protection and corporate responsibility. His exposé of the automobile industry, *Unsafe at Any Speed,* aimed in part at air pollution, contributed to the passage of the National Traffic and Motor Vehicle Safety Act of 1966 and other legislation designed to protect consumers from unsafe and inferior products. "Nader's Raiders," volunteer teams that began in the late 1960s to investigate various industries and government regulatory agencies, were strong advocates of environmental protection. As the consumer movement spread, it exerted greater influence on business, Congress, and state legislatures.

By the early 1970s the new environmentalism had emerged as a compelling public concern and a national movement. Television brought pictures of ecological disaster into every American home, politicians began to discuss the problems of environmental collapse, and a new vocabulary of words like *population explosion* and *ecology—*

derived from a term in biology referring to the interaction of living organisms with their physical and biological environment—entered everyday speech. An outpouring of articles and books described the phenomenon, and authorities such as biologist Barry Commoner began to argue that "the proper use of science is not to conquer nature, but to live in it." The movement was promoted by established groups like the Sierra Club and the Wilderness Society, as well as new organizations and recruits who were often young, aggressive, and more politicized than older members. An environmental lobby became a major force in the national capital, while grassroots groups sprang up throughout the country. A citizens' group in Santa Barbara, California, for example, drew up a "Declaration of Environmental Rights," a manifesto that attracted more than local attention. In April 1970 about 20 million Americans took part in the first Earth Day, a remarkable symbol of the enthusiasm for environmental matters. "Ecology," remarked a California politician, "has become the political substitute for the word 'mother.'"

Not all Americans joined the environmental crusade. An opposition movement arose to challenge the reformers, and it, too, became strong and vocal. The business community tended to resist new regulations, fearing that they would cut into profit margins, while many conservatives opposed such federal intrusion and the great cost of cleaning up toxic waste sites and other projects. Farmers, labor union members, and minority representatives often opposed protective measures that might jeopardize or limit jobs. One popular labor union bumper sticker asserted, "If You're Hungry and Out of Work, Eat an Environmentalist." Many professionals in science, economics, and planning were inclined to think the environmentalists were pushing their reform proposals too hard and too fast. Other opposition arguments included the claim that environmental programs would limit economic growth and material well-being, lead to high unemployment, lower food production, increase disease, and adversely affect poor people. Opponents wanted to reduce federal regulations, encourage a vigorous search for petroleum deposits, promote nuclear power as a source of energy, open vast areas of public lands—including national forests—to private development, and place greater reliance on local and state governments and the marketplace in dealing with environmental problems.

Despite forceful resistance in the media, public relations campaigns, Congress and state legislatures, and the struggle over administrative and judicial rulings, the environmental movement made notable gains, including more effective regulation of effluents and pollution, stronger protection of the remaining wilderness and wildlife, and tighter controls on the usage and disposal of pesticides, toxins, and hazardous wastes. The Nixon years brought the National Environmental Policy Act, the Environmental Protection Agency, the Clean Air Amendments of 1970, the Endangered Species Act, and other landmark legislation.

FEMINISM: REFORM IN A DIFFERENT MODE

If the civil rights movement was losing its momentum, one group complaining about its discriminatory treatment showed signs of new vitality. The civil rights movement, student protests, and antiwar demonstrations, as well as the new "sexual revolution," stimulated a resurgent movement in women's rights that gathered strength in the 1960s. It was evident in a variety of feminist organizations, protests, and campaigns. Female activists demanded equal employment opportunities in professional associations, spoke out against the oppression of "sexual politics," sat in at the editorial offices of *Newsweek* and *Ladies' Home Journal,* picketed the Miss America contest, and even forced their way into male-only bars and restaurants. Feminism suddenly became a national concern and a topic of absorbing interest in the media. On August 26, 1970—the fiftieth anniversary of the ratification of the Woman Suffrage Amendment—feminists conducted a "Strike for Equality," with a big parade in New York City and smaller demonstrations in numerous other cities. The demonstrators emphasized such objectives as equal opportunity for women in jobs and education, free child-care centers, and free abortions on demand.

The "objective" conditions and attitudes of American women had undergone considerable change between 1940 and 1960. The broad social changes flowing from the nation's industrialization, urbanization, and consumer economy contributed to a situation in which increasing numbers of women were members of middle-class and professional families, attended college, enjoyed greater longevity, remained single longer, and had access to improved methods of contraception. Millions of women entered the work force during World War II, and the number of women working outside the home increased in the 1950s. The number of married women with jobs almost doubled during the two decades after 1940. But most of these workers were concentrated in traditional "female" jobs, were paid less than men, and made no real challenge to the dominant attitudes on sex roles and the place of women. However, a new form of feminist activism developed in reaction to the inequality and second-class status.

The new ideological perspective was articulated in feminist activist Betty Friedan's brilliant polemic, *The Feminine Mystique* (1963), which identified an invisible culture that pervaded women's lives and continually reaffirmed their traditional roles. Reacting against the "sterility" of the consumer culture, Friedan described the plight of the middle-class woman trapped in a daily routine of housework and child care. In the 1960s many American women were attracted to the civil rights movement, since they were increasingly sensitive to the theme of social inequality, and they soon adopted much of the message, moral commitment, and tactics of the so-called Second Reconstruction. The equal rights struggle had also given many women valuable experience, including, ironically, being subjected to sexual discrimination when participating in groups such as SNCC and SDS.

While feminists agreed that men were the dominant sex and that women as a group were oppressed, they differed in their analysis of causes and solutions. During the movement's early years, one activist group included many professional, well-educated, and experienced women who emphasized women's rights within established institutions. Another group, generally made up of younger women, many of whom had participated in the civil rights or other social protest movements, stressed women's liberation and the politics of confrontation. The mainstream of the movement, represented by the National Organization for Women (NOW), founded by Friedan and others in 1966, launched a broad attack on sexual discrimination and sought legal equality through legislation and the courts. The National Women's Political Caucus, organized in 1971, concerned itself with politics and government, lobbying for women's rights within both major parties.

Feminist activists quickly turned their attention to legislation. Some gains had been made during the Kennedy administration, including the enactment of a measure to outlaw discrimination in the civil service, the enactment of an equal pay law, and the administration's support of a civil rights bill intended primarily for women. Title 7 of the Civil Rights Act of 1964, which prohibited discrimination in the workplace based on sex as well as race, religion, or national origin, became the cornerstone in the drive for economic equality. It resulted in a flood of complaints about sexual discrimination. President Johnson had issued an executive order in 1968 forbidding federal contractors from discriminating against women, and two years later the Office of Federal Contract Compliance, under heavy pressure from women's groups, promulgated guidelines to strengthen the antidiscrimination ban. In 1972 Congress passed the Equal Pay Act, prohibited sexual discrimination in federally supported educational programs, and enlarged the jurisdiction of the Equal Employment Opportunity Commission to include local government agencies and educational institutions. Under Title 9 of the Educational Amendments of 1972, colleges and universities were required to establish programs of "affirmative action" to ensure equal opportunity for women. Meanwhile, NOW, the Women's Equity Action League (WEAL), and other organizations had been working at the state and local levels. By 1972 all fifty states had enacted legislation to prevent sexual discrimination in employment. Congress overwhelmingly approved the Equal Rights Amendment (ERA) in 1972, and American feminists spent the next decade in an intensive campaign to secure its ratification by three-fourths of the state legislatures. The amendment provided that equality of rights under the law should not be denied or abridged by the United States or by any state "on account of sex" and that Congress should have the power to enforce its provisions.

By the mid-1970s, affirmative action programs were helping white women even more than men of racial minorities. Universities, business institutions, and the professions began to employ more women, in part because of pressure exerted by Washington. Women assumed high-level positions in government, business, labor, the judiciary, and the military. They moved into new roles such as television commentators, airline pilots, and police officers—to mention only a few—and they began to make their way into the skilled trades and other formerly restricted areas of employment. The number of women workers increased dramatically, and by 1980 about half of all adult females were working outside the home. Women also began to play a more conspicuous part in politics. Several states, including New York, liberalized their abortion laws, and in 1973 the Supreme Court, in *Roe* v. *Wade*, upheld a woman's right to have an abortion during the first three months of pregnancy and set up guidelines for abortion during the remaining six months. Being more financially independent, freer from traditional sexual constraints, and with ready access to effective contraceptives, middle-class white women in particular were marrying later, having fewer children, and getting more education.

Although the movement for women's liberation accomplished many of its objectives and brought notable changes to American society, it encountered powerful opposition and suffered major setbacks. The

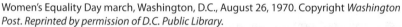

Women's Equality Day march, Washington, D.C., August 26, 1970. Copyright *Washington Post. Reprinted by permission of D.C. Public Library.*

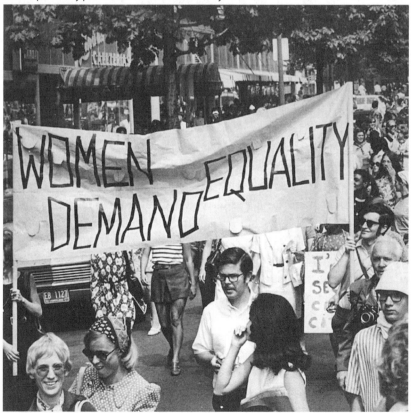

ideology of domesticity and traditional family values retained great strength, and the new feminism seemed threatening to millions of women as well as men. In 1970 a Gallup poll revealed that 70 percent of American women believed they were treated well by men. Five years later a Harris poll showed that, while 63 percent of women questioned favored most changes improving the status of women, some of them insisted that they were not "women's libbers." Though gender had become a unifying force among women, they were divided by class, race, ethnicity, education, and occupation. Most feminists were middle-class, white, and college-educated. In the battle over the ratification of the ERA, women tended to divide along lines of social class, with middle-class and professional women providing most of the support for the amendment. Conservatives like Phyllis Schlafly, an Illinois lawyer who headed the Eagle Forum, attracted broad support with fervent appeals to older values and traditional ideas about women's place in society. When the ERA failed to gain ratification in 1979 by a narrow margin, the women's movement had been dealt a huge symbolic defeat.

One of the most controversial issues in the politics of anti-feminism was abortion, especially after the *Roe* decision. Most feminists were confident that technological advances now enabled physicians to detect fetal abnormalities and carry out medically safe abortion procedures. They believed in the right of every woman to control her own body. Opponents of abortion bitterly denounced the practice. The very success of the drive to liberalize abortion statutes encouraged a determined "right to life" movement, particularly among Catholics and conservative Protestants. Feminism was also identified in the public mind with another polarizing issue—homosexuality and the gay rights movement. In addition, the split between gays and "straights" racked women's organizations in the late 1960s and the 1970s over questions of ideology and tactics. Meanwhile, as gays and lesbians came out of the closet, they formed the National Gay Task Force and other organizations, openly worked to establish their political and legal rights, and argued against the idea that heterosexuality and marriage should be given privileged status in law and custom.

There was much evidence of tokenism in the acceptance of women, just as there was in the case of African Americans and other minorities. Despite the tangible gains made in the economic sphere, about 80 percent of all working women in the early 1980s were still concentrated in gender-segregated, low-paying occupations. The gap between male and female income actually widened in the 1970s. Women earned only about two-thirds as much as men. Even so, the movement to liberate and empower women had a profound effect on recent America. Beyond the opening of doors and the creation of more equitable opportunities in the economic, legal, and institutional spheres, the movement brought to millions of American women a new feminist consciousness, an understanding of the social context of being female, an appreciation of the personal nature of political action, and a commitment to the redefinition of gender roles in the United States. Feminism also influenced the outlook and behavior of American men, many of whom accepted and supported women's liberation. One example of institutional change, often unnoticed, was the way sex roles and child-rearing practices evolved to accommodate families in which both husband and wife had full-time jobs outside the home, as well as the fact that men began to do a lot more work inside the home, especially as it related to child care.

THE DOWNFALL OF A PRESIDENT

The succession of dramatic revelations and confrontations in the Watergate controversy dominated public affairs in the United States in 1973 and 1974. By the beginning of the latter year, the issue of overwhelming importance in the Watergate affair had become President Nixon's possible involvement in the scandal. The focus of the Watergate inquiry had become a movement to impeach the president. What had seemed unthinkable during the early stages of the various investigations into the incident had become a realistic possibility, especially in the aftermath of the notorious Saturday night massacre in October 1973. The House Judiciary Committee, under the chairmanship of Peter W. Rodino, Jr., of New Jersey, had begun to consider impeachment charges against the chief executive.

Public reaction to the firing of special prosecutor Cox in the fall of 1973 was so hostile that the president had agreed to turn over the disputed tapes to Judge Sirica. But a week later the White House informed the court that two of the nine subpoenaed tapes were missing and that another of the specified conversations had never been recorded. One of the other tapes contained an eighteen-minute gap in a conversation between Nixon and Haldeman on June 20, 1972—three days after the Watergate break-in. Embarrassed White House spokesmen tried to explain the gap as resulting from an accidental erasure by the president's secretary, Rose Mary Woods, but a panel of electronics experts reported to Sirica, after studying the tape, that someone had deliberately erased it in at least five attempts.

With scarcely more than one-fourth of the American people approving his performance as chief executive, Nixon launched "operation candor" in November 1973. This bid for public support through speeches and travel to various parts of the country served only temporarily to improve the president's image. Even the traditional bases of his support—the business community, conservative Republicans, and the South—seemed to be eroding. Congress had grown less willing to approve executive initiatives. The *Congressional Quarterly* reported that the administration had won only 50.6 percent of the votes on legislative issues upon which it expressed its wishes in 1973, as compared with 66 percent in 1972 and 77 percent in 1970.

Both Leon Jaworski and the House Judiciary Committee requested further evidence from the White House, including a large number of recorded conversations between the president and his subordinates. Nixon adamantly refused to provide this information, arguing that to do so would infringe upon executive privilege and interfere with the stability and authority of the presidency. Nixon's strategy was to delay, assert that the president was unimpeachable in the absence of explicit proof of serious criminality, and refuse to surrender evidence that could either provide such proof or demonstrate his innocence. On April 11 the Judiciary Committee voted 33 to 3 to issue a subpoena ordering the chief executive to deliver the tapes of forty-two presidential conversations within two weeks. A week later the special prosecutor subpoenaed sixty-four White House tapes for his own use.

Nixon then counterattacked. He decided, in a carefully staged move, to make public edited transcripts of thirty-one of the forty-two tapes demanded by the House committee. After providing the committee with what he described as voluminous materials, the president made it clear that there would be no further White House disclosures concerning Watergate. Before the transcripts were released, James D.

St. Clair, Nixon's top lawyer, gave the press an account of the documents; presidential aides also approached key Republican leaders and lined up television programs in an effort to blitz the media. The chief executive took his case for the Watergate transcripts directly to the people in a televised speech on April 29, 1974. He projected a forceful and controlled image, and as a TV presentation his address seemed to be a success. The bulky transcripts—1,308 pages from forty-six taped conversations—were made public on May 1. Although cleansed of profanity ("expletive deleted") and filled with sections marked "unintelligible," the transcripts were published in several editions and read by millions of people. They did not have the effect the president had evidently intended, for at crucial points such as the conversation involving Nixon, Haldeman, and Dean on March 21, 1973, they contained talk of extortion, blackmail, cover-ups, hush money, and other desperate measures.

Still, Nixon held on. His recalcitrance finally led Jaworski to point out that he had been personally assured by General Alexander M. Haig, Jr., Nixon's chief of staff, that the White House recognized his right as special prosecutor to seek any evidence he considered necessary, including that in the president's personal possession. On May 20, 1974, Judge Sirica ordered the president to turn over to the court the sixty-four tapes subpoenaed by the special prosecutor. Nixon appealed Sirica's ruling to the Court of Appeals, but Jaworski petitioned the Supreme Court to take immediate jurisdiction. The high court announced on May 31 that it would do so. The court would test the constitutionality of Nixon's claim of executive privilege as the basis for his refusal to deliver the tapes. The public learned that the grand jury that indicted those persons involved in the Watergate cover-up had also named the president as an "un-indicted co-conspirator." At about the same time, the House Judiciary Committee voted 37 to 1 to issue still another subpoena for tapes, calling on Nixon to produce, by June 10, forty-five Watergate-related conversations held between November 15, 1972, and June 4, 1973. Nixon refused to comply.

The beleaguered president was apparently determined to ride out the worsening Watergate storm. His tactics were those of fighting, counterattacking, toughing it out, and resorting insistently to his international role in an effort to vindicate himself at home. In mid-June, hard on the heels of Secretary of State Kissinger's successful negotiations in arranging a military disengagement between Syria and Israel, Nixon made a well-publicized visit to the Middle East in search of a more lasting peace. The Nixon entourage was delighted with the reception given their chief, and it almost seemed that the exhilarating pre-Watergate days had returned. In late June and early July of 1974, the president made another spectacular visit to the Soviet Union, where he signed a limited underground nuclear test-ban treaty.

Nixon's chances of escaping impeachment appeared to be improving, but there was a pattern in the continuing drama of Watergate: every time the outlook for Nixon brightened, a series of new developments renewed the storm. The second week of July brought a spate of new disclosures and setbacks for the White House. John Ehrlichman was convicted by a federal court of having authorized the 1971 burglary of Ellsberg's former psychiatrist. The House Judiciary Committee released a mass of evidence indicating that the transcripts approved and released by Nixon with such fanfare in the spring had been edited to make the president's involvement appear less extensive than it was. A 2,500-word segment of a March 22, 1973, conversation had been left out entirely. In that conversation Nixon had told his aides, "I want you all to stonewall it, let them plead the Fifth Amendment, cover up or anything else, if it'll save it—save the plan."

The Senate Watergate committee published its final report at about this time. While refraining from making charges that would interfere with the impeachment procedure or the Watergate trials, the Ervin committee expressed alarm over indications that people in high office were indifferent to public morality and operated "on the belief that the end justifies the means, that the laws could be flouted to maintain the present administration in office." The committee recommended broad legislative reforms "to safeguard the electoral process and to provide the requisite checks against the abuse of executive power." A few days later, on July 24, the Supreme Court ruled 8 to 0 (Justice Rehnquist recused himself) that the president must turn over the sixty-four subpoenaed tapes to Judge Sirica so that whatever relevant material they contained could be used by the special prosecutor.

The final scenes of the Watergate drama now unfolded. The House Judiciary Committee held six days of nationally televised debate in late

July, and the committee members adopted three articles of impeachment. The committee recommended that the president be impeached
by the House of Representatives for obstruction of justice in the Watergate cover-up, general abuse of his powers, and refusing to comply with
its subpoenas for White House tapes. Several Republican members
voted for impeachment, and virtually all informed observers agreed that
the chief executive would be impeached by the House. In a surprise
move on August 5, Nixon made public the transcripts of three of the
tapes recently surrendered to Sirica. The three conversations took place
between Nixon and Haldeman on June 23, 1972—six days after the
Watergate burglary—and they showed that the president had sought
to use the CIA to halt the FBI investigation of the crime. This was the
"smoking gun" long sought by investigators. It proved that Nixon was
involved in the cover-up almost from the beginning and that he had lied
about his involvement. Many influential Republicans now joined the
call for Nixon's resignation or impeachment. It was clear that he would
have to stand trial in the Senate for "high crimes and misdemeanors."

While the nation waited, Richard Nixon made a decision. Addressing Americans by nationwide television on the evening of August 8,
1974, Nixon announced that he would resign the presidency on the
following day. At noon on August 9, Vice President Gerald Ford was
sworn in as the nation's thirty-eighth president. "Our long nightmare
is over," Ford declared, "Our Constitution works. Our great republic is
a government of laws and not of men." Indeed, Americans could take
some satisfaction in the constructive role of the press, Congress, the
courts, and an aroused public opinion in responding to the challenge
of Watergate.

Most Americans were relieved that the ordeal was over and that their
constitutional system had worked. Watergate provoked a reappraisal of
the "imperial presidency," the excesses of intelligence activities, and the
need for a more ethical politics and a deeper commitment to the rule of
law. It seemed that Congress might be moving to reassert its authority.
One such step was the passage over Nixon's veto of the War Powers Act,
which limited presidential authority to commit troops abroad by executive action. Congress also passed the Federal Election Campaign Act of
1974, setting campaign contribution and spending limits for candidates
in federal elections and providing for public financing of presidential

campaigns. In addition, the lawmakers strengthened the Freedom of Information Act to prevent the government from denying access to official documents "arbitrarily or capriciously." There were signs of reform vigor at the grassroots level as well, and public interest groups such as Common Cause pressured Congress and the state legislatures to adopt campaign and lobbying reforms.

Watergate is an American story of hubris and tragedy, of a flawed protagonist whose abuse of power, refusal to speak candidly to the American people, and failure to understand the moral dimensions of U.S. politics were the acts of a man haunted by insecurity and the delusion that powerful enemies were determined to obstruct his presidency. The Watergate crimes represented an attempt to use government power to subvert the political process in the broadest sense of the term. The scandal revealed Richard Nixon's deep-seated weaknesses: his siege mentality and tendency to demonize his adversaries, his resort to secrecy and a pattern of "dirty tricks" in his political career, and his willingness to make full use of the imperial presidency to protect the national security as he viewed it. The record made it clear that Nixon shared in the guilt of liege men who followed his instructions, "implied or not."

———— ★ ————

SUGGESTIONS FOR FURTHER READING

The best biography of the thirty-seventh president is Stephen E. Ambrose's balanced and readable narrative. The second of his three volumes, *Nixon: The Triumph of a Politician, 1962–1972* (1989), is of major importance. Two other studies are helpful in the absence of a solid history of Nixon's presidency: A. James Reichley, *Conservatives in an Age of Change: The Nixon and Ford Administrations* (1981), and John Robert Greene, *The Limits of Power: The Nixon and Ford Administrations* (1992). See also Garry Wills, *Nixon Agonistes: The Crisis of the Self-Made Man* (1970). Nixon's own views are presented in *RN: The Memoirs of Richard Nixon* (1978) and the various volumes of *Public Papers of the Presidents*. *President Nixon: Alone in the White House* (2002), by Richard Reeves, is the most recent authoritative work on Nixon and is worth a look. *Reinventing Richard Nixon: A Culture History of an American Obsession* (2008), by Daniel Frick, is a masterful examination of the evolution of historical perspectives on Nixon that have developed over the years.

Two studies by Hugh Davis Graham, *The Civil Rights Era* and *Civil Rights and the Presidency*, both referred to before, are indispensable. See also Steven A. Shull, *The Presidency and Civil Rights Policy: Leadership and Change* (1989); Leon E.

Panetta and Peter Gall, *Bring Us Together—The Nixon Team and the Civil Rights Retreat* (1971); and J. Harvie Wilkinson III, *From* Brown *to* Bakke: *The Supreme Court and School Integration, 1954–1978* (1979). *The Rehnquist Choice: The Untold Story of the Nixon Appointment that Redefined the Supreme Court* (2002), by John W. Dean, Nixon's former White House counsel, is a behind the scenes account of the nomination of Rehnquist, who subsequently played a significant role on the high court.

Nixon's approach to public welfare is discussed in two works already cited: Berkowitz, *America's Welfare State,* and Patterson, *America's Struggle Against Poverty.* The Family Assistance Plan is described in Vincent J. Burke and Vee Burke, *Nixon's Good Deed: Welfare Reform* (1974), and Daniel P. Moynihan, *The Politics of a Guaranteed Income: The Nixon Administration and the Family Assistance Plan* (1973). The administration's sudden shift in economic policy is examined in Stein's *Presidential Economics* and Calleo's *The Imperious Economy,* both referred to earlier. See also Roger L. Miller, *The New Economics of Richard Nixon: Freezes, Floats, and Fiscal Policy* (1972), and Wyatt C. Wells, *Economist in an Uncertain World: Arthur F. Burns and the Federal Reserve, 1970–78* (1994).

For Vietnam and Southeast Asia, readers should consult the suggested readings listed in Chapter 7. See also William Shawcross, *Sideshow: Kissinger, Nixon, and the Destruction of Cambodia* (1979); Jonathan Schell, *The Time of Illusion* (1976); and I. F. Stone, *The Killings at Kent State: How Murder Went Unpunished* (1971).

Nixon and Kissinger: Partners in Power (2007), by Robert Dallek, is the strongest study published that analyzes how these two men developed and implemented foreign policy. *No Peace, No Honor: Nixon, Kissinger, and Betrayal in Vietnam* (2002), by Larry Bergman, and *Nixon, Kissinger, and Allende: U.S. Involvement in the 1973 Coup in Chile* (2010), by Lubna Z. Qureshi, are strong criticisms of the Nixon-Kissinger foreign policies.

An important source for Richard Nixon's foreign policy is Raymond L. Garthoff's *Détente and Confrontation: American-Soviet Relations from Nixon to Reagan* (1985), a comprehensive, authoritative, and elegantly constructed study. Good treatments include, in addition to the general works suggested in earlier chapters, Richard C. Thornton, *The Nixon-Kissinger Years: Reshaping America's Foreign Policy* (1989); Franz Schurmann, *The Foreign Policies of Richard Nixon: The Grand Design* (1987); and Tad Szulc, *The Illusion of Peace: Foreign Policy in the Nixon Years* (1978). For more focused studies, consult Robert Sutter, *China Watch: Sino-American Reconciliation* (1978); Robert S. Litwak, *Détente and the Nixon Doctrine* (1984); and Harland B. Moulton, *From Superiority to Parity: The United States and the Strategic Arms Race, 1961–1971* (1973). Henry Kissinger's influential role is considered in John G. Stoessinger, *Henry Kissinger: The Anguish of Power* (1976), and Walter Isaacson, *Kissinger: A Biography* (1992). Kissinger's own *The White House Years* (1979) is revealing.

The election of 1972 is described in Theodore H. White, *The Making of the President, 1972* (1973), and Ambrose, *The Triumph of a Politician.* Other aspects of the campaign are covered in Byron E. Shafer, *Quiet Revolution: The Struggle for the*

Democratic Party and the Shaping of Post-Reform Politics (1983); Mary C. Brennan, *Turning Right in the Sixties: The Conservative Capture of the GOP* (1995); Ronald Radosh, *Divided They Fell: The Demise of the Democratic Party, 1964–1996* (1996); Richard Krickus, *Pursuing the American Dream: White Ethnics and the New Populism* (1976), and Michael Schaller and George Rising, *The Republican Ascendancy: American Politics, 1968–2001* (2002).

The best history of Richard Nixon's second administration is the third volume of Stephen E. Ambrose's biography: *Nixon: Ruin and Recovery, 1973–1990* (1991). See also Gerald S. Strober and Deborah R. Strober, *Nixon: An Oral History of His Presidency* (1994).

Comprehensive and informative accounts of the Watergate scandal can be found in Fred Emery, *Watergate: The Corruption and Fall of Richard Nixon* (1994); J. Anthony Lukas, *Nightmare: The Underside of the Nixon Years* (1976); Theodore H. White, *Breach of Faith: The Fall of Richard Nixon* (1975); and Stanley I. Kutler, *The Wars of Watergate: The Last Crisis of Richard Nixon* (1990). See also Leon Friedman and William F. Levantrosser, eds., *Watergate and Afterward: The Legacy of Richard Nixon* (1992), and the *Congressional Quarterly's Watergate: Chronology of a Crisis* (1973–1975). Among fine recent works are *Watergate: The Presidential Scandal that Shook America* (2003), an insightful scholarly examination by Keith W. Olson; *The Secret Man: The Story of Watergate's Deep Throat* (2006), by Bob Woodward, which reveals the former *Washington Post* reporter's relationship with the legendary shadow figure of Watergate; *Watergate: A Brief History with Documents* (2009), by Stanley I. Kutler, is a sturdy reference volume; and *Watergate and the Resignation of Richard Nixon* (2004), by Harry P. Jeffrey and Thomas Maxwell-Long, eds., is an outstanding scholarly anthology that examines the crisis through several distinct disciplinary lenses.

Personal accounts and memoirs of participants make up a sizable collection of Watergate materials. Among the best of these are John W. Dean, III, *Blind Ambition: The White House Years* (1976, 2009); John J. Sirica, *To Set the Record Straight: The Break-in, the Tapes, the Conspirators, the Pardon* (1979); Samuel Dash, *Chief Counsel: Inside the Ervin Committee—The Untold Story of Watergate* (1976); and Richard Ben-Veniste & George Frampton, Jr., *Stonewall: The Real Story of the Watergate Prosecution* (1977).

The relationship between energy and the environment is discussed in a good general history by Martin V. Melosi, *Coping with Abundance: Energy and Environment in Industrial America* (1985). See also Richard H. K. Vietor, *Energy Policy in America since 1945: A Study of Business-Government Relations* (1984); Frank R. Wyant, *The United States, OPEC, and Multinational Oil* (1977); Richard H. K. Vietor, *Environmental Politics and the Coal Coalition* (1980); and S. David Aviel, *The Politics of Nuclear Energy* (1982).

Four outstanding books provide historical background and social context for an interpretation of the modern feminist movement: Carl N. Degler, *At Odds:*

Women and the Family in America from the Revolution to the Present (1980); Nancy F. Cott, *The Grounding of Modern Feminism* (1987); John D'Emilio and Estelle Freedman, *Intimate Matters: A History of Sexuality in America* (1988). The organization and politics of the women's rights movement are considered in Sara Evans, *Personal Politics: The Roots of Women's Liberation in the Civil Rights Movement and the New Left* (1979); Cynthia Harrison, *On Account of Sex: The Politics of Women's Issues, 1945–1968* (1989); and Anne N. Costain, *Inviting Women's Rebellion: A Political Process Interpretation of the Women's Movement* (1992). For other themes, see Susan Estabrook Kennedy, *If All We Did Was to Weep at Home: A History of White Working-Class Women in America* (1979); Kristin Luker, *Abortion and the Politics of Motherhood* (1984); *Finding the Movement: Sexuality, Contested Space, and Feminist Activism* (2004), by Anne Enke and Daniel J. Walkowitz, is a fascinating scholarly examination of the feminist and gay movements; *The Trouble Between Us: An Uneasy History of White and Black Women in the Feminist Movement* (2007), by Wini Breines, is a powerful study of the complex relationship between white and black women in the feminist movement; and *Moving the Mountain: The Women's Movement in America Since 1960* (1999), by Flora Davis, is a well-researched work well worth reading.

———— ★ ————

CHAPTER

9

The Search for Solutions in a "Crisis of Confidence"

T HE MAN SUDDENLY ELEVATED TO THE PRESIDENCY on August 9, 1974, was a successful but undistinguished politician from Michigan. Gerald Ford was born in Omaha, Nebraska, on July 14, 1913. He grew up in Grand Rapids, Michigan, graduated from the University of Michigan, where he was a varsity football player, and worked his way through the Yale Law School. He served in the navy during World War II and was elected to Congress as a Republican in 1948. A conservative on domestic issues, Ford was something of an internationalist, though of an aggressive, interventionist type. As the representative gained seniority, he moved slowly up through GOP ranks, and in 1965 he defeated Charles Halleck to become minority leader of the House. Ford was thoroughly familiar with the workings of the political system but somewhat limited in his broader view of politics. His greatest ambition was to become speaker of the House of Representatives. During the Nixon years, he was a staunch administration supporter, an important factor in his selection as vice president in 1973. Most people liked Ford. He was a warm, open, and unpretentious man, a collegial person devoid of his predecessor's sense of insecurity and distrust of people.

THE PRESIDENCY OF GERALD FORD

Ford's first weeks in the White House were reassuring. The press and the public welcomed the new president's low-key approach and his promise of an "open, candid" administration. He made no changes in the cabinet and delayed bringing in his own personal aides. Ford's honeymoon lasted only a short time, however. One reason it ended was his announcement on September 8 that he had granted Nixon a full pardon, apparently because of the virtual certainty that the former president would be indicted and tried for obstruction of justice. The media then turned on Ford, many people questioned his judgment and motives, and his popularity dropped precipitately, declining to an approval rating of only 50 percent by the end of September. Ford seemed to view Watergate as an unfortunate incident and a tactical political problem, and he may not have been sensitive to its broader implications. He was probably influenced by his fear that the trial and possible conviction of a former president would slow the country's needed healing. His agreement to give Nixon custody of the disputed presidential tapes and papers, which was subsequently invalidated by Congress, also damaged the new chief executive's standing, as did the controversy that arose over his choice of Nelson Rockefeller as vice president. November brought another setback, with substantial Democratic gains in the midterm congressional elections.

Basically, Ford was even more strongly opposed than was his predecessor to vigorous action by federal regulatory agencies that might prevent "maximum freedom for private enterprise." Nor was Ford a champion of civil rights measures. He was against almost every bill Congress passed that would have assisted the black poor. He was antagonistic to the use of busing as a means of achieving school desegregation. Indeed, he was criticized by the U.S. Civil Rights Commission for accelerating the trend toward resegregation through his resistance to open housing and school desegregation. On the other hand, the new president reversed his opposition to amnesty for Vietnam War draft evaders and introduced a modestly successful clemency plan known as the Vietnam Era Reconciliation Program.

One of the problems Ford inherited was the precarious state of the economy, which soon entered a severe recession plagued by rising unemployment, soaring inflation, and a shortage of energy. A drastic increase in energy prices in 1973 and 1974, combined with the abolition of price and wage controls and a decline in world food production, contributed to inflation and slowed economic activity. The president

President Ford and Secretary-General Leonid Brezhnev begin their private talks in Vladivostok. *Courtesy the White House, photograph by David Hume Kennerly.*

adopted a conservative approach to these problems, calling for a cut in federal spending, a tight money policy, and voluntary action to hold down the cost of living. In September 1974 he held a series of meetings with experts from various sectors of the economy, followed by a big conference in Washington on approaches to the nation's economic difficulties. Little came of these efforts, although Ford tried for a time to promote a rather droll voluntary program he called Whip Inflation Now (WIN). He also recommended a tax increase to combat inflation. But his party's dismal showing in the congressional elections of 1974 and the deteriorating economy brought a change in Ford's position. When the first session of the Ninety-fourth Congress convened in January 1975, he proposed a modest tax cut, along with a 50 percent reduction in the rate of growth in federal expenditures. The Democrats, enjoying large majorities in both houses, pressed for a massive tax cut, emergency jobs for the unemployed, housing construction subsidies for an industry hard hit by the economic downturn, and a number of tax reforms. The Republican president and the Democratic-controlled Congress were frequently at loggerheads during the months that followed.

The economic crisis deepened early in 1975, and President Ford was eventually forced to accept both an increase in federal spending and a tax cut. Congress passed a number of other significant bills in 1975, including an extension of the Voting Rights Act of 1965, a compromise energy bill, and a $4-billion public works act. During the previous year, the lawmakers had increased Social Security benefits, raised the minimum wage, and appropriated sizable amounts of money for highways, mass transit, and public service jobs. In 1976 Congress passed a tax revision bill that included several provisions promoted by "tax reformers." The measure extended the personal and corporate tax cuts of 1975. In general Congress rejected Ford's proposals for cutbacks in domestic programs and concentrated new federal spending on several jobs programs. Meanwhile, the economy had begun to recover by mid-1975, the rate of unemployment decreased, and the increase in the cost of living fell from 11 percent in 1974 to 5.8 percent in 1976.

Ford managed to head off some liberal measures by making extensive use of his veto power. He vetoed no fewer than seventeen major bills in 1975, and Congress overrode only four of those executive interdictions. Democratic leaders denounced Ford as "the most veto-prone Republican president in the twentieth century." The Democrats failed to pass the controversial Humphrey-Hawkins bill, which would have required the federal government to become the "employer of last resort" for adults who could not otherwise find jobs. Ford achieved several minor legislative successes. After initially opposing a federal "bailout" of New York City, which stood on the brink of bankruptcy, he helped work out a compromise that Congress approved. And early in 1976, the administration got a bill through Congress that authorized some deregulation of the stagnant railroad industry.

The president's major setback on the domestic front was his failure to formulate and establish a comprehensive energy policy. As the Ninety-fourth Congress began its work in January 1975, the Ford administration had two main objectives in the energy field: to raise petroleum prices enough to limit consumption and to provide producers with economic incentives to seek new sources of supply. Congressional Democrats endeavored to develop their own plan to encourage conservation and increase supply. Ford, a strong advocate of deregulating oil and gas, was unable to get his proposals through Congress. After wrangling for months, the two sides finally agreed on the Energy Policy and Conservation Act, which Ford signed in December 1975. The act rolled back the price of domestic oil to a maximum of $7.66 a barrel, well under current market prices, and continued price controls and the mandatory allocation of domestic petroleum. But it also gave the president authority to implement gradual decontrol over a forty-month period. The administration was unsuccessful during the following year in getting congressional action for the decontrol of natural gas. The new legislation helped relieve the energy crisis involving gasoline and home heating fuel but did little to solve the basic problems underlying the crisis.

In its foreign policy the Ford administration had to adjust to the relative decline of American power in the 1970s. This decline reflected economic problems at home, a weakening dollar abroad, the end of U.S. superiority in nuclear arms and the rapid development of new Soviet strategic weapons systems, strains in the American alliance system, and the recent crisis in the United States presidency. Ford, who assumed office without a firm grasp of either the substance or the procedures of foreign policy, leaned heavily on Secretary of State Kissinger. On the whole, the foreign affairs initiatives of Ford and Kissinger were not very successful. Relations with the Soviet Union, however, remained reasonably good, and Ford forcefully affirmed the American commitment to détente. In November 1974 Ford met with Leonid Brezhnev in Vladivostok, where they negotiated a modest arms-control agreement. Under this rudimentary SALT II, each side would be limited to 2,400 delivery vehicles and could not place multiple warheads on more than 1,320 of its missiles. Ford and Brezhnev, along with the heads of all major European states, met again at the end of July 1975 at a summit in Helsinki, Finland, where the conferees signed a declaration on European security that recognized existing frontiers. The United States thereby accepted the postwar Soviet annexations in Eastern Europe. Although the question of nuclear arms was also discussed at Helsinki, complex technical issues prevented further agreement on the terms of SALT II.

During the spring of 1975, the Indochina peace suddenly fell apart. In April the Khmer Rouge (the Cambodian [Kampuchean] Communists) captured the capital of Phnom Penh and brought on the collapse of the Cambodian government, despite American efforts to save Lon Nol's regime. About the same time, a North Vietnamese offensive moved rapidly to take control of South Vietnam. While this was happening, President Ford asked Congress to provide the beleaguered South Vietnamese with $722 million in military assistance and $250 million in economic and humanitarian aid. Congress was willing to appropriate only $327 million for humanitarian aid and evacuation purposes, although it later approved the president's request for $507 million in refugee assistance. The United States evacuated more than 40,000 Americans and South Vietnamese before the last helicopter left the roof of the U.S. Embassy in Saigon on April 30. The defeat, while long expected, was humiliating for Americans. In all, 58,268 Americans had died in Vietnam, more than 300,000 others had been wounded in battle, and the war had cost a staggering $150 billion. Two weeks after the fall of Saigon, a final Indochina incident captured U.S. headlines. When the new Cambodian government seized an American merchant ship, the *Mayaguez*, off the mainland, Ford authorized the use of force to reclaim the vessel and its crew. Though a number of Americans lost their lives in the rescue operation, the mission was successful. Within a few months, however, foreign policy was once again focused on a crisis in the Middle East.

Kissinger, with Ford's approval, continued his search for a formula that would forge a peace between Israel and the Arab states. After arranging a disengagement of Israeli forces from those of Egypt and Syria, the secretary of state was able to work out an interim agreement between Egypt and Israel in September 1975. The United States basically guaranteed this settlement, in part by providing Israel with a large amount of military equipment, including sophisticated weapons. This agreement was only a beginning, however, no more than a step along the tortuous path to peace in the Middle East.

In Africa, the scene of Third World competition between the Soviet Union and the United States, another American venture turned out badly. The United States provided covert assistance in the mid-1970s to an anti-Marxist faction in a three-way struggle for control of newly independent Angola. The U.S.-backed faction lost out in the struggle.

In the meantime, Congress was demonstrating a new assertiveness in dealing with international issues. The legislators insisted on a thorough examination of Kissinger's request for authority to station American civilians in the Sinai Peninsula as part of the agreement between Egypt and Israel. They imposed a ban on arms shipments to Turkey.

Senators who ran for president shown on the Capitol steps in 1976 (left to right): Strom Thurmond (1948), Edmund Muskie (1968), Robert Dole (1976, 1996), Barry Goldwater (1964), George McGovern (1972), and John Sparkman (1952). *Courtesy U.S. Senate Historical Office.*

They forced the administration to modify a sale of missiles to Jordan, delay construction of a proposed U.S. refueling facility on the Indian Ocean island of Diego Garcia, and proceed slowly in negotiations for a new Panama Canal treaty. A thoroughgoing investigation of the CIA conducted by a select committee headed by Senator Frank Church of Idaho contributed to the establishment of formal congressional oversight of intelligence affairs.

Despite the administration's limited success at home and abroad, Gerald Ford brought a measure of calm and a more optimistic outlook to public affairs in the United States. As Americans approached the bicentennial of their independence in 1976, they could face the future with greater confidence following the upheaval of the 1960s and the agony and disillusionment of Vietnam and Watergate. Ford no doubt shared this renewed sense of possibilities. He also looked ahead to the national election of 1976 and a chance to win the presidency in his own right.

Ford's hopes for another term would, however, go unfulfilled. In the aftermath of Watergate, Democratic leaders, heartened by their gains in the midterm elections of 1974, looked expectantly to the presidential campaign of 1976 and the opportunity to recapture control of the executive branch of government. The intense competition for the Democratic presidential nomination produced a new party leader, a one-term governor of Georgia named James Earl Carter, Jr.

THE ELECTION OF JIMMY CARTER

After Senator Edward M. Kennedy, the early favorite, withdrew for personal reasons in September 1974, a large number of candidates entered the contest for the Democratic presidential nomination in 1976. Among these Democratic aspirants were Senator Henry Jackson of Washington, Representative Morris K. Udall of Arizona, Governor George Wallace of Alabama, and former governor Jimmy Carter of Georgia. Carter stressed the innovative character of his governorship, including his approach to race relations. To the surprise of most observers, the Georgian placed first in the Iowa caucuses in January 1976 and led the nine candidates in the party's New Hampshire primary in February. Carter had traveled all over the country for the Democratic national campaign committee in 1974, and by early 1976 he had already been campaigning for more than a year. He had a disarming smile, adopted an earnest and folksy approach, and employed a manner of campaigning that emphasized personal contact with ordinary people. Running as an outsider, he promised to bring a fresh perspective to a beleaguered Washington.

Having established himself as a serious candidate, Carter began to win other primaries, including a key victory in March over Governor Wallace in Florida. He went on to win additional primaries and establish an insurmountable lead in committed delegates, despite late challenges from Senator Frank F. Church of Idaho and Governor Jerry Brown of California. Carter was nominated on the first ballot when the Democratic National Convention assembled in New York City in July. His choice of Senator Walter F. Mondale of Minnesota as his running mate gave the ticket ideological balance and helped unify the party. The former governor's success in capturing the nomination was facilitated by the new Democratic rules for the selection of delegates to the national convention and the publicity he received from the media.

Meanwhile, President Ford and former governor Ronald Reagan of California were locked in a hard-fought struggle for the Republican nomination. Capitalizing on his incumbency and picturing himself as a conciliator and a moderate, Ford defeated Reagan in the first three Republican primaries. But in March Reagan won an upset victory in North Carolina. Reagan's outspoken conservatism attracted many southern sympathizers of George Wallace, and the Californian moved on to defeat the president in several Sunbelt primaries, as well as the one in Indiana. But Ford clung to a narrow lead and was nominated on the first ballot at the GOP convention in Kansas City in August. Senator Robert J. Dole of Kansas was named the party's vice-presidential nominee.

When the formal campaign began late that summer, Carter was far ahead of Ford in the polls. Recognizing how Watergate had changed the public mood, the Democratic leader talked about restoring morality and integrity to the national government. "I will never tell a lie to the American people," he declared. He did not emphasize his party's New Deal and Great Society traditions but instead pledged himself to balance the budget by 1980, streamline existing programs, and dismantle bureaucratic regulations in areas like banking and transportation. Ford sought to take advantage of his position in the White House and identify his presidency with moderation and constructive leadership. The two nominees campaigned vigorously. Although they met in a series of nationally televised "debates," which added some interest to the campaign, it was not a very exciting contest. Starting from far behind, Ford's campaign began to gain momentum, encouraged by some of Carter's candid comments and growing doubts about his capacity for presidential leadership. By election day, the two men were almost even in the polls.

When the votes came in, the Democrat managed to win, but not by much. By contrast, the Democratic Party retained a comfortable lead in congressional seats and governorships. Carter received 40.8 million popular votes (50.1 percent) to 39.1 million (48 percent) for Ford, who actually carried two more states than did his opponent. The electoral vote was 297 to 240. Carter swept the South, except for Virginia, and ran well in the Northeast, while Ford carried most of the western states.

The pollster Louis Harris concluded that the Democratic nominee had won not because of his personal qualities, but because of "the revival of the old coalition that first sent Franklin D. Roosevelt to the White House in 1932." There was a good deal of truth in Harris's analysis, although a majority of southern white voters supported the Republican ticket. Carter did bring together a diverse collection of supporters that included African Americans, southerners, organized labor members, and ethnic groups. Strong black support was a major factor in Carter's victories in the South and in his election. Mondale also made an important contribution to the success of the Democratic ticket, since his urban liberalism attracted many blue-collar workers and low-income city voters. Nor should Watergate be overlooked. As the *New York Times* commented, Carter was "the candidate of the Watergate backlash."

Hearing Carter's name for the first time before the campaign of 1976, many Americans had asked, "Jimmy who?" It was a fair question, given the southerner's obscurity at the time. Carter was born on October 1, 1924, in Plains, a small town in southwest Georgia. His ancestors had lived in Georgia since the late eighteenth century, and his father was a successful businessman, large landowner, and member of the local gentry. After spending a year at the Georgia Institute of Technology, young Carter entered the United States Naval Academy, graduating with distinction in 1946. He spent the next seven years as a naval officer, working part of the time with Admiral Hyman G. Rickover in developing the navy's first nuclear submarines. When Carter's father died in 1953, the young officer returned to Georgia and took charge of the family farm supply and peanut business. He did well in business, involved himself in numerous civic activities, and won election to the state senate in 1962. After being re-elected two years later, he ran unsuccessfully for governor in 1966. Thereafter, he immediately began to perfect an organization and develop more effective techniques for another gubernatorial bid in 1970. He campaigned tirelessly all over the state, projecting an image of social conservatism (though not racism), opposition to established politicians, and sympathy for common people. This time he won. Carter was a successful governor. He carried out an extensive reorganization of the state government, made use of "zero-based budgeting," helped expand state services in areas like education and mental health, led in the passage of an important campaign disclosure law, and supported consumer and environmental causes. No previous governor of his state had gone as far as Carter did in championing racial equality. He was one of a new breed of southern governors elected in the 1970s.

A leader of great energy and driving ambition, "Jimmy" Carter, as he was invariably called, had an analytical mind, a capacity for hard and disciplined work, and an unshakable faith in his own abilities. Carter described himself as a "born-again" Christian, and it would seem that his Southern Baptist religion reinforced his drive and self-confidence. His pietism was joined with a commitment to social activism. His engineering training in college and the navy probably strengthened his concern for organization and efficiency. The new president could not be called a sparkling speaker, and he lacked magnetism as a leader. On the other hand, he was effective in working with small groups and could inspire

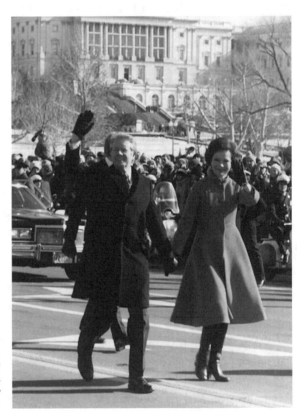

Jimmy and Rosalynn Carter walk down Pennsylvania Avenue on January 20, 1977. *Courtesy the White House.*

loyalty and devotion among his subordinates. In an earlier day he would have been considered a "business progressive," certainly not a Populist redistributionist. He believed in efficiency, preferred a prudent fiscal policy, denounced "special interests," and sought to elevate the nation's moral tone. He viewed himself as a trustee of the public good.

In his inaugural address Carter proclaimed "a new beginning, a new dedication within our government, a new spirit within us all." The Carter administration did seem to represent a new beginning in some respects. For one thing, Carter was the first president from the Deep South in well over a century and the first Georgian ever to hold that office. His election appeared to provide dramatic proof that the southern region had finally been fully integrated into national politics. In staffing the White House, the new chief executive appointed many Georgians who had served in his administration as governor, including Hamilton Jordan as chief of staff, Jody Powell as press secretary, Stuart Eizenstat as head of the Domestic Policy Staff, and Bert Lance as director of the Office of Management and Budget. Carter also appointed many African Americans and women to high-ranking positions in the government. Six women were selected as ambassadors; two women, one of whom was black, were named to the cabinet; and Andrew Young, a black congressman from Georgia, was appointed ambassador to the United Nations. The cabinet as a whole was more conventional; several of its members had served in the Kennedy and Johnson administrations. Cyrus R. Vance, a New York lawyer and former defense official, became secretary of state. Among the other cabinet members were W. Michael Blumenthal as secretary of the treasury, Harold Brown as secretary of defense, and Joseph A. Califano as secretary of health, education, and welfare. Zbigniew Brzezinski, a Columbia University specialist in international affairs, was selected as the president's national security adviser. Apparently, Carter also relied on his wife, Rosalynn, who played an important part as an adviser to the president.

Although many talented people were brought into the new administration, they were not always able to work together as a team. For example, the White House staff—referred to by some journalists as the "Georgia mafia"—tended to be overly protective of the president. Its members were soon involved in quarrels with department heads, and some of the White House functionaries antagonized congressional leaders. Debilitating conflict also developed within the administration over the formulation and conduct of foreign policy, centering in differences between Secretary Vance and the State Department, on one side, and Brzezinski and the National Security Council, on the other. Carter made Vance the sole spokesman for the United States on international questions, but he allowed Brzezinski to control the flow of advice and recommendations to the Oval Office on all matters of national security. The more aggressive and hawkish, Brzezinski became more influential with Carter than Vance, a strong advocate of détente and arms limitation. Carter was unwilling or unable to mend these rifts in the ranks of his advisers.

DEALING WITH PROBLEMS AT HOME

Gerald Ford left his successor a number of unresolved and perplexing problems, including an economy characterized by stagflation, high unemployment, an adverse trade balance, and increasing dependence on foreign sources of energy. Jimmy Carter hoped to respond effectively to these and other national problems. In his first year he sent about eighty legislative proposals to Congress. Seeking to restore confidence in the federal government and mobilize the public behind his programs, the new chief executive portrayed himself as a "people's president" deeply concerned with openness, frugality, compassion, and morality. According to one source, Carter "gave Americans a series of populist symbols—town meetings, fireside chats, and blue jeans—to get his message across, rather than delivering a clearly defined program to Capitol Hill."

In an effort to stimulate the economy and reduce unemployment, the Carter administration pushed for increased federal spending and a sizable tax cut. Carter's first economic stimulus proposal featured a two-year, $31-billion combination of tax cuts and job creation programs. The Democratic-controlled Congress was generally receptive to the president's recommendations, although the legislation it passed was substantially reshaped from its original form. The lawmakers approved federal grants for local public works, appropriated money for public service jobs, and voted to reduce taxes, with incentives for employers who hired additional workers. They also raised the level of farm price supports and approved a phased increase in the minimum wage from $2.30 to $3.35 an hour by 1981. Unemployment declined, whether as a result of these initiatives or other factors, and the rate had fallen from 7.9 percent in December 1976 to 6.4 percent a year later, and to less than 6 percent by mid-1978. As time passed and the economy rebounded, Carter showed less enthusiasm for tax reductions and more concern about federal deficits and the problem of inflation. His recovery plans struck some of his supporters as overly cautious.

The administration was less successful in its efforts to enact social reform legislation. One program demanding attention was the Social Security system, whose funds for old age, disability, and medical benefits were under mounting pressure from rising costs and population changes. In December 1977 Congress acted on the administration's recommendation by increasing payroll taxes in gradual increments and raising the salary limit for such taxes. Secretary of HEW Califano's proposals for more fundamental reforms in the Social Security system, such as raising the minimum retirement age from sixty-two to sixty-five, failed to survive strong opposition within the administration. Though committed to the idea of a national health plan, the president was slow in agreeing to sponsor such a program. In 1978 he finally approved Califano's comprehensive scheme, which would make use of both private and public insurance, in contrast to Senator Edward Kennedy's ambitious plan based on public insurance. By that time it was too late, since Congress was badly divided and other issues had moved to the fore.

President Carter announced, at one of his first presidential press conferences, that his administration planned to reform the widely criticized national welfare system. He had first become concerned about federal welfare programs during his governorship and had been the only southern governor to support President Nixon's Family Assistance Plan. Welfare reform was a key proposal in the domestic agenda he discussed during the campaign of 1976. Carter now boldly set out to tackle the "welfare mess" in Washington and make the system more adequate, efficient, and equitable. Secretary Califano and Secretary of Labor F. Ray Marshall were given the task of developing the administration's legislation. The president unveiled what was called the Program for Better Jobs and Income (PBJI) at a nationally televised press conference on August

6, 1977. The proposed statute represented a comprehensive rather than an incremental approach to welfare reform.

Energy was a major focus of the administration's domestic reform efforts from the outset. In his autobiography Carter wrote that "there was never a moment when I did not consider the creation of a national energy policy equal in importance to any other goal we had." He presented a wide-ranging energy proposal in mid-April 1977 and soon after sent it to Congress. The energy problem, the president asserted in a phrase taken from the philosopher William James, represented "the moral equivalent of war." Referring to the way in which energy costs had multiplied since 1973 and to the fact that the United States was currently importing almost half of the petroleum it used, Carter proposed an energy policy that would end the crisis and meet the nation's future needs. The administration plan, drafted under the supervision of James Schlesinger, a former chairman of the Atomic Energy Commission, emphasized a conservation program designed to improve energy efficiency, reduce the rate of increase in overall energy use, lower gasoline consumption by 10 percent, and cut oil imports to one-eighth of total energy consumption. In all, the plan included dozens of features ranging from taxes and incentives for conservation to alternative energy sources. The administration wanted to retain domestic price controls with a new pricing system and bring supply and demand into balance. Carter also recommended the construction of more nuclear power plants and a two-thirds increase in coal production. Finally, he called for deregulation of natural gas, which would result in higher prices and encourage domestic exploration, and a "windfall profits" tax on the petroleum companies, whose profits would increase following deregulation.

Congress debated Carter's energy bill for eighteen months. After passing the House in August 1977 with relatively few important changes, the measure was torn apart in the Senate, which eventually voted for a bill so different from the House version that it took the conference committee almost a year to work out a compromise. The deregulation of natural gas precipitated a bitter struggle, one aspect of which was a conflict between northeastern consumers and southwestern producers. Special-interest lobbies exerted great weight, party discipline among the Democrats collapsed, and the president found it impossible to mobilize public opinion in support of his plan, since most people were not

convinced that the energy problem was really as serious as the administration claimed. The National Energy Act, which was finally passed in
October 1978, contained many of Carter's original recommendations,
but some of its central provisions were quite different from and much
weaker than those first proposed. The White House lost its fight for the
crude oil equalization tax, a key proposal designed to bring domestic
oil prices up to world levels and thereby reduce U.S. dependence on
imported petroleum; it was forced to accept the gradual deregulation
of natural gas prices over a seven-year period; it also had to abandon a
recommended tax on industrial users of oil and gas.

Most Americans recognized the need for a coherent national energy
policy, but they disagreed about the substance of such a policy. They differed over the best approach to the energy problem—whether to pursue
a supply-stimulus or a demand-reduction solution. Carter's National
Energy Plan had no built-in constituency. Neither the president nor his
aides was very sensitive to the situation in Congress, and the administration's relationship with Capitol Hill on the issue was almost completely
adversarial. More fundamentally, perhaps, the complicated nature of the
energy question represented a conundrum both for U.S. policymakers
and the American people.

By the time the energy legislation was approved in the fall of 1978,
the Carter administration was struggling to solve another economic
problem, the rising rate of inflation. Stimulated by the spending and
tax-cut policies of 1977, as well as more deep-seated pressures, inflation
grew steadily more worrisome. Initially preoccupied with the need for
unemployment, economic growth, and energy policies, Carter found it
difficult to devise a consistent and effective solution to the problem. He
did, however, begin to show more budgetary restraint and resist appropriation bills that threatened to be inflationary, developing, in piecemeal
fashion, an anti-inflation program.

Worsening inflation and a contrary economy clearly had an adverse
effect on President Carter's popularity, which had declined steeply by
the middle of his term. In addition, the administration experienced a
whole other set of difficulties. Businesspeople, labor leaders, and even
African American spokespersons found fault with the president's domestic policies. A long and enervating coal strike in the winter of 1977–
78 forced Carter to resort to an injunction under the Taft-Hartley Act.

President Carter (right) and Vice President Walter Mondale. *Courtesy Jimmy Carter Library.*

His adviser and close friend Bert Lance resigned as budget director in September 1978, following a series of embarrassing allegations of illegal campaign contributions and questionable practices in his earlier banking career. Carter was also dealt several setbacks by Congress. It rejected his proposals for tax reform, a new labor law, and major changes in election procedures. After a long delay, the lawmakers voted against the administration's recommendation that increases in hospital costs be limited to 9 percent a year. Carter's plan for dealing with the swelling volume of illegal aliens in the United States, presented in August 1977, was caught in a congressional cross fire and not enacted. The Georgian had committed himself to federal gun-control legislation as a means of preventing crime, but after eighteen months in office he dropped the issue without making a real effort to secure its adoption. Still, the deteriorating economy overshadowed all of these defeats, as the cost of living skyrocketed and unemployment once again began to increase.

Carter's own limitations were partly to blame for his unimpressive record in the domestic arena. Although he gradually developed better relations with Congress, the chief executive and his lieutenants were too often insensitive and even arrogant in trying to work with congressional leaders. In the spring of 1977, for example, the new president abruptly canceled thirty-two federal water projects Congress had already approved, unnecessarily creating hard feelings and getting his first year off to a bad start. Some observers thought Carter's problems on Capitol Hill were largely the result of poor communication with members of the House and Senate. Congress itself was resistant to executive pressure and eager to defend its prerogatives in the wake of Vietnam and Watergate. There was, moreover, a rising tide of conservatism in the two houses, despite the Democratic majorities, and liberal members could not always be relied on by the administration, since many of them had doubts about the specifics of Carter's programs and had begun to question the desirability of a strong presidency. Another difficulty was that in trying to balance the budget, cut down the size of government, and control inflation, Carter frequently found that he had to deny favors and to say "no" rather than "yes" to individual members of Congress. He was not always familiar with or understanding of traditional Democratic constituencies. In retrospect it is apparent that the thirty-ninth president tried to move on too many fronts at the beginning of his term; he should have adopted a more coherent, focused set of proposals. It is also true that Carter served in a time of deep divisions in Congress and the electorate, multiplying special interests, and the absence of a consensus to facilitate concerted action on most major issues.

Nevertheless, the Carter administration could point to some significant achievements—its recognition of African Americans and women, the creation of cabinet-level departments of education and energy, and its success in reducing unemployment. Carter established a federal task force to deal with draft evaders during the Vietnam War, and amnesty was eventually extended to thousands of American youths who had fled the country or otherwise avoided fighting in the war. The administration successfully sponsored several important conservation measures: controls over strip mining, stronger clean air and clean water laws, a "superfund" to clean up chemical waste sites, and the Alaska lands protection act of 1980 establishing a forest reserve of over 100 million acres. For a brief period, Carter's presidency reasserted federal leadership in antipollution and natural resource protection. Congress also approved other Carter proposals, including the extension of the ratification period for the ERA, legislation reinstating presidential authority to reorganize the executive branch of government, civil service reform, and deregulation of the nation's transportation system and banking industry.

MORALITY AND FOREIGN POLICY

In the realm of foreign policy, Jimmy Carter seemed to challenge his predecessors' preoccupation with the containment of international communism. While inexperienced in foreign policy-making, Carter came to office with a resolve to attack a number of international problems and a commitment to a "Wilsonian" worldview and the importance of peace and human rights. The time had come, he declared in his first major address on foreign affairs, to move beyond the belief "that Soviet expansion was almost inevitable but that it must be contained," beyond "that inordinate fear of communism which once led us to embrace any dictator who joined us in that fear," and beyond the tendency "to adopt the flawed and erroneous principles and tactics of our adversaries, sometimes abandoning our own values for theirs." Carter called for a new American foreign policy "based on constant decency in its values and on optimism in our historical vision." Yet, ironically, this idealistic president eventually fell back on a forceful reassertion of the containment doctrine, urging the development of new strategic weapons, a return to the military draft, and fewer constraints on intelligence collection capabilities.

Perhaps Carter's most striking departure from the foreign policies of recent presidents was his emphasis on human rights. "We can never be indifferent to the fate of freedom elsewhere," he asserted in his inaugural address. "Our commitment to human rights must be absolute." He later described human rights as "the soul of our foreign policy." The administration soon issued statements criticizing the Soviet Union and Czechoslovakia for intimidating citizens who tried to exercise their right to protest, and the president expressed sympathy for prominent Russian dissidents. He also signed the Inter-American Convention on Human Rights, urged Congress to approve the UN Human Rights Covenants of 1966, and expanded American refugee and asylum programs. Critics, of whom there were many, charged that the administration's insistence on human rights abroad was naive and impractical. For one thing, they contended, such a policy would bring the United States into conflict with its own allies—nations such as South Korea and Iran, notorious for having repressive regimes. When the United States accompanied its annual offer of $50 million in military aid to Brazil with a critical report on the status of human rights in that country, the Brazilian government rejected the offer. It became clear that Carter had not fully explored the complex relationship between morality and power in foreign affairs. The consequences were sometimes unfortunate. Thus the president's criticisms of the Russians for human rights violations undermined his efforts to improve relations with the Soviet Union and disrupted negotiations on SALT II.

The Carter administration's sponsorship of the so-called Panama Canal treaties was, by contrast, one of its most signal triumphs. Building on years of earlier negotiations, the United States and the Republic of Panama signed two treaties in September 1977. The heart of the agreements was the promise to give Panama full control of the canal by the year 2000. The treaties also provided for the immediate abolition of the Canal Zone and the transformation of the canal into an international waterway, with Panamanian and U.S. ships having priority of use in times of emergency and war.

A long and acrimonious debate followed the president's submission of the treaties to the Senate for ratification. Led by Carter himself, the administration worked hard to rally support for the agreements, which attracted bipartisan backing in the Senate and the endorsement of Gerald Ford, Henry Kissinger, Senators Howard H. Baker and Robert C. Byrd, and other influential leaders. Carter argued that the treaties would strengthen American security and trade opportunities as well as improve U.S. relations with Latin America. He also made the point that the canal was no longer a vital economic and strategic asset for the United States. Nonetheless, many Americans opposed the agreement; one Gallup poll showed 46 percent of the people opposed and only 39 percent in favor. Conservatives were especially critical, asserting that the treaties would jeopardize American security. For some people the issue seemed less one of control of the Panama Canal than the alleged decline of the United States as a global power. In the end, administration forces prevailed, though not until an amendment had been adopted giving the United States the right to use military force to defend the canal after it was turned over to Panama. The treaties were narrowly ratified in the spring of 1978. Unfortunately, Carter's diplomacy in Latin America as a whole proved to be vacillating and inconsistent. Thus he withdrew support from the repressive regime of Augusto Pinochet in Chile but adopted more traditional methods in dealing with the overthrow of Nicaraguan dictator Anastasio Somoza.

Carter's most celebrated diplomatic achievement came in the Middle East, where efforts to secure a comprehensive peace had been deadlocked for three years following the truce in the October War of 1973. The United States was eager to restore peace and stability to this strategic region, strengthen the position of such allies as Israel and Iran, and safeguard its access to vital sources of petroleum. But the problems were formidable. They included the refusal of the Arab states to recognize the legitimacy of Israel; disposition of Israeli-occupied territories resulting from the wars of 1967 and 1973, particularly the west bank of the Jordan River; and the insistence by the Palestine Liberation Organization (PLO) and other militant groups on the return of all Arab territory and the creation of a permanent homeland for the Palestinian Arabs.

Despite American efforts to follow the course set by Kissinger's Middle East diplomacy, the impasse continued until the fall of 1977, when a ray of hope suddenly altered the gloomy outlook. President Anwar Sadat of Egypt, burdened with economic problems and anxious to strengthen his country's position, announced his willingness to visit Israel and enter into direct negotiations with Prime Minister Menachem Begin. President Carter and Secretary Vance, who had worked hard but without success to help arrange a conference in Geneva on the Middle East conflict, were encouraged. In November 1977 Begin and Sadat held friendly discussions in Tel Aviv, followed by further talks the next year. The discussions eventually broke down, but Carter, assuming the role of mediator, was able to persuade the two leaders to resume their negotiations in the United States.

Meeting at Camp David for almost two weeks in September 1978, Begin and Sadat responded to Carter's patient and persistent efforts by working out a tentative agreement. It appeared to be a momentous breakthrough. "For a few hours," Carter recalled in 1982, "all three of us were flushed with pride and good will toward one another because of our unexpected success. We had no idea at that time how far we still had to go." The two principals agreed to negotiate a separate treaty between their countries and to initiate a "peace process" in which it was hoped other states would later join. Even so, the Camp David accords did not guarantee a fully developed agreement, and it was not until Carter's dramatic journey to the Middle East early in 1979 that a treaty was finally accepted by the two sides. Begin and Sadat then returned to Washington, where they signed the formal treaty on March 26, 1979. The treaty provided for peace between the two nations, Egyptian recognition of Israel, and a phased Israeli withdrawal from the Sinai Peninsula. The agreement was less clear in dealing with the West Bank, calling for gradual self-government for the Palestinians living there, but this part of the treaty soon unraveled. Generally, the entire agreement represented an important advance, but it was only a framework for a comprehensive and definitive settlement of the bitter division in the Middle East. It did little to solve the problem of the displaced Palestinians or suggest how the United States could maintain friendly relations with the Arab states while protecting Israel's security.

In the Far East the Carter administration completed the establishment of diplomatic relations with the People's Republic of China, a process begun by Richard Nixon. Both America and China viewed

Menachem Begin, Jimmy Carter, and Anwar Sadat at Camp David. *Courtesy National Archives.*

the strengthening of their rapprochement as a means of influencing Soviet behavior. An agreement between the United States and the People's Republic was announced in December 1978, following months of secret negotiations. Relations between the two countries would be placed on a normal basis as of January 1, 1979. The United States promised to end diplomatic relations with Taiwan, remove its troops from the island, and abrogate its mutual defense treaty with the Taipei government within a year. While the Americans could continue to provide Taiwan with defensive weapons and maintain cultural and trade relations, they accepted Beijing's claim that Taiwan was a part of mainland China. Conservative critics, led by Senator Barry Goldwater, subjected the agreement to vigorous attack, condemning Carter for his "betrayal" of an American ally. The president was able, nonetheless, to implement the treaty, and the two countries soon signed a number of cultural, economic, and scientific agreements.

The outcome of Carter's approach to the Soviet Union was less satisfactory. During its first year, the Carter administration followed a moderate course with the Russians, hoping to promote détente by developing greater trust, increased trade, and more cultural exchanges between the two nations. Seemingly eager to halt the nuclear arms race, the president ordered the immediate withdrawal of American nuclear weapons from South Korea and delayed approval of the B-1, a new strategic bomber sought by the air force. He later announced a delay in the production of the neutron bomb, an extremely radioactive weapon potentially more dangerous to life than to property. Early in his tenure, Carter decided on a "deep-cut" proposal in the arms-limitation talks, only to have the Soviet Union summarily reject it. Negotiations had not been helped by Carter's human rights policy and the recent normalization of U.S. relations with China. Nevertheless, Secretary Vance and Foreign Minister Andrei Gromyko finally worked out a new strategic arms limitation treaty, which Carter and Brezhnev signed in Vienna in June 1979. SALT II set a limit of 2,400 long-range missiles and bombers on each side, to be reduced to 2,250 by 1981. Each country was limited to 1,320 Multiple independently targetable re-entry vehicle (MIRV) warheads and cruise missiles.

SALT II encountered a barrage of criticism in the United States, and its chances of Senate ratification were uncertain. Many liberals found it overly modest and predicted that it would do nothing to prevent the development of new (and potentially game-changing) weapons systems. Conservatives argued that it would give the Russians a great advantage and that their compliance would be impossible to verify. Carter, who had earlier ordered the construction of the intermediate-range cruise and Pershing II missiles, soon authorized a new missile system—the MX—to be housed in a vast complex of underground tunnels. Carter and Brzezinski were disturbed by the Soviet Union's continuing military buildup, its export of arms and technicians to Third World countries, and the threat it posed in the Middle East and Africa. In Africa, Ambassador Young and other U.S. representatives had attempted to pursue a policy based on more than opposition to the USSR and to encourage the survival of independent black regimes. Yet the Soviet-Cuban presence was both expansive and mischievous, including activities in areas like the Horn of Africa, near the strategic Middle East. The U.S. State Department announced in the spring of 1978, for instance, that Fidel Castro was maintaining 37,000 military personnel in twenty African countries.

Carter gradually adopted a tougher and more aggressive posture toward the Russians. Speaking at the Naval Academy in June 1978, he bluntly declared, "The Soviet Union can choose either confrontation or cooperation. The United States is adequately prepared to meet either choice." One consequence of the president's growing suspicion of and hostility toward the Soviet Union was loss of support for SALT II, the ratification of which appeared increasingly problematic. Meanwhile, Carter called for a significant increase in the military budget for fiscal 1979, the strengthening of NATO forces, and development of the neutron bomb. Notwithstanding its human rights rhetoric, Panama Canal treaties, Camp David accords, and improved relations with the People's Republic of China, the administration had apparently come around to a reaffirmation of the old Cold War strategy of containment.

A SURFEIT OF TROUBLES, 1979–1980

Things went from bad to worse for Jimmy Carter, who was almost overwhelmed by a plethora of perplexing problems in 1979 and 1980. As one magazine remarked, "It was the worst of times, it was the worst of times." Tension mounted between the United States and the Soviet Union. In the spring of 1979 the U.S. index of leading economic indicators dropped more than 3 percent, automobile sales and new housing starts declined, and inflation and interest rates kept climbing. Another energy crisis threatened to paralyze the nation, and before the end of 1979 Carter's renomination was being challenged by a leading Democratic senator. The president tried to respond effectively to these vicissitudes, but his leadership seemed less and less adequate, while his approval rating plunged to 25 percent, lower even than that of Richard Nixon during the height of the controversy over Watergate.

A new energy crisis highlighted the troubles of the Carter administration. This one was precipitated by a worldwide shortfall in oil production, resulting in part from renewed violence in the Middle East and heavy U.S. dependence on foreign sources. Despite the president's earnest efforts to lessen this dependence, the United States was importing about 9 million barrels of petroleum a day by 1979. Declining production led the Organization of Petroleum Exporting Countries (OPEC) to raise prices, and the effect was quickly felt by Americans. Gasoline prices rose sharply, approaching $1 a gallon within a few weeks, and shortages brought long lines of motorists at service stations, along with outbursts of anger and frustration. In April 1979 Carter recommended several long-term measures as a means of hastening the nation's self-sufficiency in energy, but Congress took no immediate action. One of the proposed remedies was greater use of nuclear power, an alternative many Americans had distrusted following a frightening accident in late March 1979 at the nuclear power plant at Three Mile Island, near Harrisburg, Pennsylvania. A catastrophe was averted, but the consequences of a possible meltdown of the reactor core and the emission of large amounts of radioactive gas, endangering the lives of hundreds of thousands of people, were almost too horrible to contemplate.

As the energy crisis deepened, Carter searched for a way to resolve it. He decided to deliver a nationwide television address on energy early in July. Then he canceled that address and spent ten days at his Camp David retreat talking with a cross section of American leaders about the nation's problems. On the evening of July 15, the chief executive attempted to explain his position and inspire support among the mass of his fellow citizens. An estimated 100 million people heard his speech. Acknowledging his own mistakes, Carter made a moving appeal for cooperation and assistance. He quoted a southern governor who had said to him, "Mr. President, you're not leading this nation, you're just managing the government." America's problems, Carter declared, were all rooted in an underlying "crisis of confidence," a malaise that was threatening to destroy the nation's social and political fabric. "For the first time in the history of our country," the president said, "a majority of our people believe that the next five years will be worse than the past five years."

The more substantive part of the address laid out the details of a new energy plan. Carter announced a freeze on imports of petroleum at a maximum level of 8.5 million barrels a day, and he expressed hope that oil imports could be cut in half by 1990. He stressed the need for increased domestic production of energy through the construction of new and safer nuclear plants, a giant "solar energy bank" to promote the use of solar energy in commercial buildings and private homes, and the rapid development of synthetic fuels. Carter renewed his call for deregulation of domestic oil and natural gas and for a windfall profits tax. A few days later he reorganized his cabinet by replacing Blumenthal, Califano, and Secretary of Energy James Schlesinger. While the initial reaction to the president's address was favorable, Congress was slow in responding to his recommendations. Even so, the administration ultimately won several of its energy objectives. Early in 1980, President Carter and legislators reached an agreement through significant compromise with the passage of the Congressional Crude Oil Windfall Profit Tax Act. Many members in Congress had argued that American oil companies were not paying their fair share of federal taxes, and this piece of legislation was aimed at retrieving the allegedly lost funds. But since the tax did not apply to foreign oil, the oil companies largely skirted the tax by stepping up their reliance on importation. In short, the tax generated well below its target range of $250–$400 billion, with revenues estimated at $75–$80 billion in its ten-year existence. Ultimately, Carter's successor, Ronald Reagan, repealed the act in 1988. However, Carter also signed into law the Energy Security Act of 1980, which provided for the establishment of the U.S. Synthetic Fuels Act and the Solar Energy and Energy Conservation Bank. These gave the Carter administration some positive long-term reviews on its energy policies and expanded the nation's attention to clean energy.

Then, in the fall of 1979, an even more frustrating problem suddenly confronted the Carter administration. It began with an abrupt change in the role of Iran as policeman of the Persian Gulf, brought about by the collapse of the regime of the Shah of Iran in January 1979 at the hands of an Islamic revolution led by a holy man named Ayatollah Ruholla Khomeini. The United States had long relied on the shah as a source of stability, an opponent of communism, and a voice of moderation in OPEC. The shah was closely identified with the CIA, which had saved his throne in 1953 and had trained SAVAK, his brutal force of secret police. The Ayatollah Khomeini was virulently hostile to America, which he described as the "great Satan" behind the wicked shah. When President Carter allowed the former Iranian ruler, who suffered from incurable cancer, to enter the United States for surgery in October 1979, it brought disorderly crowds to the streets of Tehran shouting anti-American slogans. On November 4, a large mob of chanting militants overran the U.S. embassy in the Iranian capital, took over the building, and captured more than sixty American diplomatic personnel. The captors demanded that the shah be returned to Iran to stand trial and threatened to hold the American hostages indefinitely or even to try them as spies.

Since the United States was neither willing nor able to force the return of the shah, it found itself in a cruel dilemma, one with few options. The situation dramatized Washington's inability to control events in other parts of the world. The president appealed to the United Nations, protesting the violation of diplomatic immunity and international law in the holding of the American hostages. He suspended arms sales to Iran, froze Iranian assets in U.S. banks, announced an embargo on Iranian oil, and sought without much success to persuade American allies to join him in a trade embargo. He threatened to deport the 50,000 Iranian students in the United States. The chief executive also ordered a contingency plan for military action to rescue the hostages. But nothing worked, in part because of the unstable situation in Iran and the difficulty of finding a responsible party with whom to negotiate. Carter wanted at all costs to avoid sacrificing the lives of the captives.

In December 1979, soon after the beginning of what soon became known as the hostage crisis, the Soviet Union sent an army into the ostensibly neutral state of Afghanistan. This mountainous buffer country between Pakistan and the USSR had been controlled by a pro-Communist government that was threatened by an Islam-based, anti-Communist opposition. Carter, unable to express his wrath publicly over the hostage situation, strongly condemned this Soviet use of military power, which he intemperately described as "the greatest threat to peace since the Second World War." The American leader offered military and economic aid to Pakistan, suspended the shipment of grain to Russia, outlawed the export of high-technology equipment to countries behind the Iron Curtain, and called for a boycott of the summer Olympics in Moscow. He also ordered the Sixth Fleet to the eastern Mediterranean, alerted U.S. units in Turkey, and recommended a crash program to create a Rapid Deployment Force for action in the Persian Gulf. Finally, he decided to withdraw SALT II from further consideration by the Senate. Fearing that the Soviet Union would exploit the unstable situation in Iran by cutting off the flow of Persian Gulf oil to the West, the president enunciated the Carter Doctrine: "An attempt by any outside force to gain control of the Persian Gulf will be regarded as an assault on the vital interests of the United States of America, and such an assault will be repelled by any means necessary, including military force." Carter's mounting suspicion of the Russians was evident earlier in the year when he proposed the largest new nuclear weapons program since the early years of the Cold War. He had become a true convert to anti-Soviet orthodoxy.

The crisis over the American hostages in Iran dominated the foreign affairs agenda during the last fourteen months of the Carter administration, with the president all but consumed by it. He met repeatedly with the families of the hostages and refused to participate in the Democratic preconvention campaign on the ground that he needed to devote full time to the problem. Meanwhile, the American people, daily assaulted by media coverage of the hostage question, were baffled and outraged. It was difficult for the State Department to negotiate with the Iranian government, whose demands seemed to include the return of the shah for trial, the repatriation of his wealth to the Iranian people, admission of guilt and an apology by the United States for its past actions in Iran, and an American promise not to interfere in Iranian affairs in the future. For a moment early in the spring of 1980, the administration thought it had worked out an agreement with President Abol-Hassan Bani-Sadr, but it proved ephemeral. In late April, Carter finally approved a military operation to rescue the hostages. Operation Eagle Claw was launched on April 24 with the intent of establishing a secure zone within Iran, known as Desert One, from which to stage a covert rescue operation that would in a night-time maneuver enter the embassy, secure the hostages, and deliver them via aircraft to the carrier USS *Nimitiz* in the Indian Ocean. It was a brazen plan. Had it succeeded, it surely would have altered Carter's image as a weak and indecisive chief executive. In the early stages of what was supposed to be a two-day mission, an intense sandstorm known as a haboob rendered two of the U.S. helicopters inoperative. Shortly thereafter, a refueling accident at Desert One resulted in the deaths of eight military personnel, and the commanders on the ground gave the order to abort. A shocked and saddened American public perceived the botched rescue attempt as too small, poorly planned, and horribly executed, with the approval rating of a seemingly hapless Carter falling down near 30 percent as the hostage crisis continued day after day, week after week. Not even the shah's death, in July 1980, brought an end to the ordeal. In the meantime, Carter was placed at a great disadvantage in his campaign for re-election. Ultimately, the hostages were released on January 20, 1981, less than thirty minutes after Carter's successor, Ronald Reagan, was sworn into office.

THE REPUDIATION OF A PRESIDENT: 1980

Senator Edward Kennedy announced in November 1979 that he would challenge President Carter's renomination the next year, and at the outset the Massachusetts senator enjoyed a substantial lead over the president in the polls. Kennedy portrayed Carter as a weak and ineffectual leader who had abandoned the Democratic Party's tradition of domestic reformism and was unable to forge a successful foreign policy. The senator won five of the eight Democratic primaries held on "Super Tuesday," June 3, 1980. Meanwhile, Carter had defended his policies but refused to engage in an active preconvention campaign, restricting his public appearances to the White House Rose Garden and fostering the impression of a leader fully preoccupied with urgent national problems. In the end this tactic seemed to work, since many Americans rallied to the support of their president during the Iranian crisis and the growing animosity toward the Soviet Union following their invasion of Afghanistan. Carter won a series of preferential primaries and thus turned back the Kennedy challenge. The Democratic National Convention then re-nominated the Carter-Mondale ticket.

The Republicans, sensing victory, began their search for a presidential nominee with a more open field. Gerald Ford disclaimed interest in the nomination, but several other Republican leaders entered the race. Among these aspirants were two senators, Howard Baker of Tennessee and Robert Dole of Kansas; George Bush of Texas, a former director of the CIA and onetime ambassador to the United Nations; and Ronald Reagan, an ex-governor of California who had come close to winning the GOP nomination in 1976. This time the Californian was successful, and he chose Bush as his running mate. The conservative Reagan provided a sharp contrast to Carter. He urged a reduction in federal spending and promised to "take government off the backs of the people." He blamed the Carter administration for the nation's economic doldrums and accused it of weakening the national defense and allowing the Soviet Union to achieve an advantage in strategic striking power.

At the time of his nomination in mid-July, the opinion polls gave Reagan a 28-percent lead over his Democratic rival. Carter, one scholar has written, was widely perceived as "having gone from blunder to blunder." He remained on the defensive throughout the campaign, buffeted by a faltering economy, deteriorating relations with the Soviet Union, and the humiliating hostage crisis, which seemed to symbolize the bankruptcy of his leadership. The worsening economy also seriously weakened the incumbent's re-election chances. By the first part of 1980, inflation had skyrocketed to a quarterly rate of 20 percent, interest rates were climbing in the wake of the Federal Reserve System's tight-money policy, and unemployment was once again rising, approaching 8 percent before the election. Nevertheless, by the time the campaign began in earnest on Labor Day, Carter's situation appeared to have become stronger than it had been between June and early September.

As might have been expected, the Reagan campaign sought to blame the Carter administration for the nation's ills. Reagan kept referring to the "misery index"—the combined inflation and unemployment rates. Republican speakers also stressed Reagan's record as governor of California and his success in attracting "good people" to work in his administration. Carter's campaign was complicated by the independent candidacy of Representative John B. Anderson of Illinois, an unsuccessful candidate for the Republican nomination earlier in the year. Anderson's campaign threatened to deprive the Democratic president of millions of votes.

Reeling under the attacks of their GOP opponents, the Democrats struck back. Reagan's election, Carter warned, would result in the undoing of hard-won domestic reforms and favor the rich at the expense of the poor and elderly. The Democratic leader accused the Republican nominee of offering simplistic solutions to complex problems, and when provoked he suggested that Reagan was a racist and a warmonger. Republican criticism of the administration's defense policies no doubt influenced Carter's decision to request supplementary appropriations for the Pentagon, announce an agreement with NATO to deploy nearly 600 medium-range cruise and Pershing II missiles in Europe, and issue Presidential Directive 59, introducing greater flexibility in the nation's nuclear-deterrence doctrine. Carter had earlier secured congressional approval of a new military draft registration. Near the end of the campaign, the two major contestants met in a well-publicized television debate. A rather somber and defiant Carter lashed out at his challenger, while a smiling and confident Reagan easily parried his opponent's attacks. Turning to the millions of Americans watching the confrontation, the Republican rhetorically asked, "Are you better off now than you were four years ago?"

The televised debate marked a shift in a close contest and gave greater momentum to the Reagan campaign. The balloting early in November swept Carter from office. In an election that attracted the lowest percentage of voters in the twentieth century, Reagan received 43.9 million popular votes (51 percent) to 35.5 million (41 percent) for Carter. The vote in the Electoral College was an overwhelming 489 to 49, with Carter winning only six states. The president captured 90 percent of the African American ballots and fared better than Reagan with women voters. Anderson received 5.7 million votes, about 7 percent of the total. The Republicans did especially well in the South and West. To their delight, they won control of the Senate for the first time in a quarter-century and made sizable gains in the House of Representatives. Among the defeated Democrats were such prominent liberals as George McGovern (SD), Frank Church (ID), Birch Bayh (IN), and John Brademas (IN).

Reagan proved to be a skillful campaigner. The Republicans conducted a well-organized and united campaign, in contrast to the Democrats' loosely organized and poorly integrated race. Carter's image as a weak and luckless leader played into his challenger's hands, while the state of the economy, particularly the breathtaking acceleration in the cost of living, and the persistence of the hostage crisis seriously damaged the chief executive's chances of re-election. The major obstacle to Carter's bid for a second term was, however, the broad loss of confidence in his leadership. Some observers thought the election signified a realignment of the political parties, the end of the New Deal coalition, and the beginning of a new era of Republican control. In spite of the conservative trend, others questioned this interpretation. A *New York Times*–CBS poll, for example, suggested that the electorate had hardly made "a clear move to the right," noting that there was still "strong public support for a substantial government role in economic matters and for a variety of government programs in health care and education." Much of Carter's difficulty on election day, the historian William E. Leuchtenburg concluded, "came not from being too liberal but from being so little in the image of FDR that millions in the Roosevelt coalition did not go to the polls and many others were so uninspired that they did nothing in the campaign save cast a dutiful vote."

Few American presidents worked harder or sought more exalted objectives than the man from Georgia. He came to office committed to the enactment of an impressive reform program, and his administration made some progress in tackling the nation's most intractable problems. Yet he tried to do too much at once and failed to develop a clear set of priorities. He found himself restrained by a critical press and a dubious public; few of his proposals could claim a public mandate or wide popularity. He was unable to command strong support in an assertive Congress, a body in which his style proved unrewarding. Carter's ability to inspire the people—to educate and to lead—was limited, and his failure to live up to his promises added to his difficulties. Indeed, political scientist Betty Glad believes that his "image problem came from having cast himself in such a heroic mold." Disliking politicking, he and his advisers gave too little attention to political planning. Part of the trouble stemmed from Carter's concept of leadership. The essential responsibility of the president, in his view, was that of a trustee articulating the good of the entire community. This notion encouraged Carter, a man of many admirable qualities, to assume an anti-political outlook and regard bargaining and making deals involving special interests as sordid and even a betrayal of his mandate. Like Herbert Hoover, a president he resembled in many ways, Jimmy Carter was in a sense overtaken by events, one of which was the rising tide of conservatism in America.

———— ★ ————

SUGGESTIONS FOR FURTHER READING

Extraordinary Circumstances: The Presidency of Gerald R. Ford (2007), by David Hume Kennerly, is one of the strongest works on the Ford presidency. Also quite good are John Robert Greene's *The Presidency of Gerald R. Ford* (1995) and Reichley's previously mentioned *Conservatives in an Age of Change*; James Cannon, *Time and Chance: Gerald Ford's Appointment with History* (1994); Richard Reeves, *A Ford, Not a Lincoln* (1975). Kellerman, *The Political Presidency*, and Shogan, *The Riddle of Power*, both mentioned above, contain useful essays on the thirty-eighth president. Other views are provided by Kenneth W. Thompson, ed., *The Ford Presidency: Twenty-Two Intimate Perspectives of Gerald R. Ford* (1988), and Ron Nessen, *It Sure Looks Different from the Inside* (1978). *Gerald R. Ford* (2007), by Douglas Brinkley, is a brief and accessible look at the Ford presidency, and *31 Days: Gerald Ford, the Nixon Pardon and a Government in Crisis* (2007), by Barry Werth, is an engaging scholarly work on Ford's controversial pardon of Richard Nixon.

The presidential election of 1976 is discussed in Jules Witcover, *Marathon: The Pursuit of the Presidency, 1972–1976* (1977); Martin Schram, *Running for President, 1976: The Carter Campaign* (1977); and Patrick Anderson, *Electing Jimmy Carter: The Campaign of 1976* (1994).

The Presidency of James Earl Carter, Jr. (2006), by Burton I. Kaufman and Scott Kaufman, is one of the most balanced examinations of the Carter years. Betty Glad, *Jimmy Carter: In Search of the Great White House* (1980), and Gary M. Fink, *Prelude to the Presidency: The Political Character and Legislative Style of Governor Jimmy Carter* (1980), are helpful for Carter's career before the presidency. See also William Lee Miller, *Yankee from Georgia: The Emergence of Jimmy Carter* (1978), and James T. Wooten, *Dasher: The Roots and the Rising of Jimmy Carter* (1978). For

Carter's religious views, consult Niels C. Nielsen, *The Religion of President Carter* (1977); Burton I. Kaufman, *The Presidency of James Earl Carter, Jr.* (1993); Erwin C. Hargrove, *Jimmy Carter as President: Leadership and the Politics of the Public Good* (1988); and Charles O. Jones, *The Trusteeship Presidency: Jimmy Carter and the United States Congress* (1988). See also Bruce Adams and Kathryn Kavanagh-Baran, *Promise and Performance: Carter Builds a New Administration* (1979); Colin Campbell, *Managing the Presidency: Carter, Reagan, and the Search for Executive Order* (1986); and Robert Shogan, *Promises to Keep: Carter's First Hundred Days* (1977). Other themes are considered in Mark J. Rozell, *The Press and the Carter Presidency* (1989); Garland A. Haas, *Jimmy Carter and the Politics of Frustration* (1992); Haynes Johnson, *In the Absence of Power: Governing America* (1980); and Laurence H. Shoup, *The Carter Presidency and Beyond: Power and Politics in the 1980s* (1980).

Carter's ideas and statements can be found in *Keeping Faith: Memoirs of a President* (1982). Also see Rosalynn Carter, *The First Lady from Plains* (1984); Kenneth W. Thompson, ed., *The Carter Presidency: Fourteen Intimate Perspectives of Jimmy Carter* (1990); and Joseph A. Califano, Jr., *Governing America: An Insider's Report from the White House and the Cabinet* (1981).

The Carter Presidency: Policy Choices in the Post–New Deal Era (2001), by Gary M. Fink and Hugh Davis Graham, is the best work on Carter's domestic policy. Carter's approach to domestic policy-making is discussed in Paul Charles Light, *The President's Agenda: Domestic Policy Choice from Kennedy to Carter (with Notes on Ronald Reagan)* (1982), and M. Glenn Abernathy, Dilys Hill, and Phil Williams, eds., *The Carter Years: The President and Policy Making* (1984). The administration's efforts to reform the welfare system are treated in Laurence E. Lynn, Jr., and David deF. Whitman, *The President as Policymaker: Jimmy Carter and Welfare Reform* (1981), and in two works cited earlier: Patterson, *America's Struggle Against Poverty*, and Berkowitz, *America's Welfare State*. Carter's energy program is analyzed in Vietor, *Energy Policy in America since 1945*, and Melosi, *Coping With Abundance*, cited earlier. For Carter's contributions to environmental regulation, see the works by Shabecott and Hays, both referred to before. Economic issues and policies are dealt with in Stein, *Presidential Economics*, and Calleo, *The Imperious Economy*.

Working in the World: Jimmy Carter and the Making of American Foreign Policy (2006), by Robert A. Strong, is the best work on Carter's foreign policy. A strong study of Carter's foreign policy is Gaddis Smith's incisive *Morality, Reason, and Power: American Diplomacy in the Carter Years* (1986). Also consult Alexander Moens, *Foreign Policy under Carter: Testing Multiple Advocacy Decision Making* (1990), and Joshua Muravchik, *The Uncertain Crusade: Jimmy Carter and the Dilemma of Human Rights* (1986). For the Panama Canal treaties, see Walter LaFeber, *The Panama Canal: The Crisis in Historical Perspective* (1978); J. Michael Hogan, *The Panama*

Canal in American Politics (1986); and Smith, *The Last Years of the Monroe Doctrine,* cited earlier. The Camp David accords are discussed in William B. Quandt, *Camp David: Peacemaking and Politics* (1986), and Moshe Dayan, *Breakthrough: A Personal Account of the Egypt-Israel Peace Negotiations* (1981).

Other aspects of American policy are examined in Garthoff, *Détente and Confrontation,* referred to above; Strobe Talbot, *Endgame: The Inside Story of SALT II* (1979); Gerald J. Bender and others, eds., *African Crisis Areas and U.S. Foreign Policy* (1985); Seth P. Tillman, *The United States in the Middle East: Interests and Obstacles* (1982); and T. G. Fraser, *The USA and the Middle East since World War II* (1989).

The Crisis: The President, the Prophet, and the Shah—1979 and the Coming of Militant Islam (2004), by David Harris, is the definitive work on the Iran hostage crisis. United States relations with Iran and the American response to the Iranian revolution are described in James A. Bill, *The Eagle and the Lion: The Tragedy of American-Iranian Relations* (1988). The hostage crisis is explored in John Stempel, *Inside the Iranian Revolution* (1981), and Warren Christopher and others, *American Hostages in Iran: The Conduct of a Crisis* (1985).

Reagan's Victory: The Presidential Election of 1980 the Rise of the Right (2005), by Andrew Busch, is the best work on the 1980 election. Theodore H. White's *America in Search of Itself: The Making of the President, 1956–1980* (1982) provides interesting background and detail on the election of 1980. Among other useful books are Congressional Quarterly, Inc., *President Carter, 1980* (1981); Thomas Ferguson and Joel Rogers, eds., *The Hidden Election: Politics and Economics in the 1980 Presidential Campaign* (1981); Gerald Pomper, ed., *The Election of 1980* (1981); and Jack W. Germond and Jules Witcover, *Blue Smoke and Mirrors: How Reagan Won and Why Carter Lost the Election of 1980* (1981).

———★———

The Reagan Revolution and Return of Confidence

W
ITH THE ELECTION OF RONALD REAGAN as the nation's fortieth president, the American political landscape began to
undergo a radical change. This was true not merely because
of Reagan's Republicanism but also because of his dedication to conservative principles and overall air of optimism that emanated from his
personality. The new president came to office with a definite agenda,
and he presented Congress with a set of clear alternatives to established
policies. Indeed, he proposed nothing less than a revolution in national
policy—a drastic transformation in the role of government at home and
a sweeping change in its posture abroad.

THE EMERGENCE OF A CONSERVATIVE SPOKESMAN

Ronald Reagan was born in 1911 and reared in a succession of small
northern Illinois towns. He attended Eureka College, a denominational
school near Peoria. Growing up in this environment, he was strongly
influenced by traditional ideas about freedom, hard work, and morality.
His development was also shaped by the modern consumer culture and
especially by what one of his biographers describes as "the new ethos
of entertainment and pleasure." Following his graduation from college,
he began work as a radio broadcaster, spending five years as a sports
announcer for station WHO in Des Moines, Iowa. In 1937 he went

to Hollywood, where initiative and luck gave him an opportunity as an actor. Reagan made a series of grade B movies during the following years, the best of which was probably *King's Row* in 1941. One of his fifty-three films was *Knute Rockne—All American* (1940), in which he played the part of George Gipp and gained modest acclaim as "the Gipper." In 1942 he was commissioned in the Army Air Force, spending most of the war making films for the army.

By the late 1940s, Reagan's acting career appeared to be at a standstill, his marriage to actress Jane Wyman had ended in divorce, and he was becoming increasingly interested in public affairs and politics. He had become active in the Screen Actors Guild, serving several terms as its president and taking the lead in a campaign to prevent alleged Communists from gaining control of the organization. He had not been a conservative in the 1930s and 1940s. In fact, he came from a Democratic family, was a supporter of the New Deal, and greatly admired Franklin D. Roosevelt, for whom he had voted. In 1947 he helped organize the California branch of the Americans for Democratic Action, supported Harry Truman, and in 1950 backed Helen Gahagan Douglas in her campaign against Richard Nixon for the United States Senate. Though not yet an avowed Republican, he voted for Dwight Eisenhower in 1952. Reagan later explained his defection from the Democratic Party by saying, "I didn't desert my party. It deserted me."

The Californian's political orientation changed in the 1950s. His ideological shift was encouraged by his experience in working for the General Electric Corporation, 1954–62. In addition to serving as host of a television program known as the *General Electric Theater*, he traveled widely over the country, promoting the company's interests, meeting with its employees, and making hundreds of speeches. In these talks he increasingly attacked collectivism and centralization in Washington. By the early 1960s, Reagan had become identified as a conservative Republican—as a passionate defender of individual freedom and an aroused critic of governmental intrusion. He became an ardent supporter of Barry Goldwater's nomination and election in 1964, speaking for him in the party's national convention and delivering a national television address in his behalf near the end of the campaign. Reagan soon began to emerge as a new hero of the Republican right. "Although he was as fully committed to the ideas and assumptions that animated Goldwater," historian Robert Dallek writes, "he was a more flexible, accommodating, and ingratiating personality with whom great numbers of middle-class citizens could identify." The actor's ideological position was sharp and polarizing, but his personality and style tended to be "soft and comforting." In 1966 Reagan was elected governor of California, revitalizing the state's Republican Party in the process. He was re-elected in 1970 and compiled a generally successful record as chief executive. While maintaining his commitment to conservative principles, he demonstrated a degree of flexibility and a willingness to compromise his objectives. Governor Reagan made a tentative bid for the GOP presidential nomination as early as 1968, when he showed impressive strength in the South, and in 1976 he almost succeeded in taking the nomination from President Ford.

Just as Jimmy Carter was in large part the product of Watergate, so was Ronald Reagan the beneficiary of a resurgent conservatism in the 1970s and 1980s. This conservative renewal had begun to manifest during the Nixon administration. Meanwhile, other long-term trends were eroding the Democratic majority coalition, among them the decline of organized labor, the shift in the national economy from manufacturing to service industries, the effects of the global economy on the character of domestic production, and the falling turnout of lower-class voters. Racial conflict and the nationalization of the race issue had sapped Democratic strength. Many Americans reacted against the leftward tendencies they identified with the national Democratic Party, and large numbers of them had turned against welfare, "forced busing," affirmative action programs, and rising crime, all of which they associated with an indulgent liberalism. Meanwhile, demographic forces were contributing to the revitalization of conservatism, particularly the large increase in the older population in the 1970s and the growth of the Sunbelt states of the South and West. These developments enhanced the political and economic power of regions that were already hostile to "big government."

The coalescence of the "New Right" owed a good deal to liberalism's left turn in the 1960s and the emergence of a new cultural and political radicalism. Neoconservatives, bolstered by an infusion of intellectuals and the resources of think tanks such as the American Enterprise Institute and the Heritage Foundation, were strongly opposed to the

President Reagan holds a press conference. *Courtesy the White House, photograph by Michael Evans.*

new egalitarianism and the idea of "equality of outcomes." The writer Robert Heilbroner called attention in 1974 to "a recrudescence of an intellectual conservatism that looks askance at the possibilities for large-scale social engineering, stressing the innumerable cases . . . in which the consequences of well-intentioned acts have only given rise to other, sometimes more formidable problems than those they had set out to cure." Conservative resistance to rising taxes, the continuing growth of "big government," and the "rights revolution" attracted increasing support among Americans.

An extraordinary revival of evangelical Christianity in the 1970s also strengthened the conservative movement in the United States. One survey in 1977 revealed that more than 70 million Americans considered themselves "born-again" Christians who had "a direct personal relationship with Jesus." The New Right was able to mobilize many religious conservatives by invoking an array of powerful social issues and appealing to traditional values linked with the family, the church, personal morality, and patriotism. The Moral Majority's Reverend Jerry Falwell, for example, spoke for millions of religious conservatives in his fervent support of free enterprise and opposition to big government and international communism, as well as in his demand for prayer in the public schools, anti-abortion laws, and harsher treatment of criminals. Falwell and other Christian crusaders tried to avoid theological disputes in order to develop an interdenominational political force. After supporting Carter in 1976, a majority of those on the religious right became enthusiastic backers of Reagan.

Ronald Reagan made his own contribution to the conservative revival. He came to Washington after eight years of experience as governor of the nation's most populous state, a position in which he had been adept at focusing on moral and symbolic issues without necessarily being perceived as a right-wing ideologue. Reagan had become the most eloquent and influential spokesperson for the new conservatism. He helped unify the New Right, at least for a time, gave it greater respectability, and provided it with a sounding board in the White House. The Republican Party had found a leader, as journalist Thomas Byrne Edsall remarked, "equipped to bridge divisions between the country club and the fundamentalist church, between the executives of the Fortune 500 and the membership of the National Rifle Association." Reagan's emergence as a successful politician was not solely the result of a resurgent conservatism. His own personal qualities were important. Though at sixty-nine the oldest man ever to be elected president, he was physically fit, charismatic, and had a ready smile and a quick wit. He had a magnetic stage presence and was remarkably effective in projecting himself over radio and television. Throughout his long political career, and in particular during his presidency, Ronald Reagan benefited from his extensive background in the media.

REAGANOMICS

At the outset, the Reagan administration concentrated on the economy. The cost of living had increased by more than 12 percent in 1980, unemployment had risen to 7.4 percent, the prime lending rate was an astonishing 20 percent, and the deficit in Carter's budget for fiscal year 1981 was $78.9 billion. The average family's purchasing power was about $1,000 less than it had been a decade earlier. "In this present crisis," Reagan said in his inaugural address, "government is not the solution to our problem; government is the problem." It was time, the new president declared, "to reawaken this industrial giant, to get government back within its means, and to lighten our punitive tax burden." Reagan's fundamental solution to the nation's economic problems was one he had long urged—the reduction of the power and control of the federal government and the expansion of the freedom of individuals and private enterprise.

Reagan proposed a comprehensive program consisting of a reduction in taxes and domestic spending, elimination of unnecessary federal regulations, and a policy of monetary restraint to slow the rate of inflation. He asked Congress to cut direct federal spending by $41.4 billion in fiscal 1982. Social Security and Medicare payments would not be reduced, and the administration insisted that an adequate "social safety net" would be assured for the "truly needy." The heart of the president's program was a 30 percent reduction in both personal and corporate income taxes over the next three years. This proposal was based on supply-side economics, a set of ideas identified with Professor Arthur Laffer of the University of Southern California. Supply-siders challenged the emphasis of Keynesian economists on strengthening the demand (consumer) side, which they believed encouraged governmental intrusion into the marketplace that resulted in stagflation and budget deficits. The focus of public policy, they argued, should be on producers, the availability of an increasing supply of goods, and incentives to promote work, saving, and investment. Reagan and his advisers reasoned that the proposed tax cuts would greatly stimulate economic growth so that, even with much lower tax rates, revenues would actually rise, deficits would shrink, and a balanced budget could be reached during Reagan's first term. What came to be called "Reaganomics," the economist Herbert Stein remarked, represented a transition from "the old-time religion to the economics of joy."

Many economists were dubious about "Reaganomics," and Howard Baker, the Senate majority leader, who helped get the legislation through the upper house, called it a "riverboat gamble." But public reaction was favorable, and Congress was in no mood to sidetrack the administration's economic proposals. The lawmakers began by considering the Reagan budget, which included large increases for military spending and substantial reductions in social services and welfare benefits. Reagan and his tough-minded budget director, David A. Stockman, pushed hard for these reductions, which were strongly criticized by many liberals. Benjamin Hooks of the NAACP predicted that they would bring new "hardship, havoc, despair, pain, and suffering on blacks and other minorities." Although the chief executive made some concessions and could not get the drastic spending cuts he had demanded, the administration prevailed, with the aid of a large number of conservative southern Democrats in the House of Representatives dubbed "boll weevils." One reason for the administration's success in the negotiations over domestic spending was the Reagan team's decision to move first on tax reduction. This led to the passage of a $280-billion tax-cut bill and an impressive victory for the White House. The Economic Recovery Tax Act provided for a 24 percent across the board tax cut spread over thirty-three months, a drop in maximum tax rates from 70 percent to 50 percent, a reduction in the capital gains tax, and an array of tax incentives.

The legislative branch was less responsive in 1981 to Reagan's recommendations for the strengthening of the Social Security system, whose trust fund reserves were declining at an alarming rate. When Congress refused to go along with the administration's solution, Reagan appointed a bipartisan commission to study the problem. The Social Security Commission, headed by the economist Alan Greenspan, submitted its report late in 1982. The commission recommended a series of reforms but no major changes in the system. Congress approved most of these recommendations in March 1983. Designed to guarantee the solvency of the Social Security trust funds, the legislation provided for the future raising of the basic retirement age from sixty-five to sixty-seven, a six-month delay in the next cost of living increase, and the taxing of benefits paid to the well-to-do.

In his approach to welfare reform, Reagan rejected the guaranteed income strategy of Nixon and Carter. He emphasized the need to "purify" the welfare rolls and force as many welfare recipients as possible to find jobs. His conservative ideas were embodied in the Omnibus Budget Reconciliation Act of 1981 and in reduced expenditures for food stamps, the Aid to Families with Dependent Children program (AFDC), vocational education, unemployment insurance, and federal disability benefits. The administration ended public service employment and eliminated 300,000 jobs under the Comprehensive Employment and Training Act (CETA). In practice it imposed restrictions and limited the rate of growth but not the increase in dollar amounts expended on the welfare system. In 1988 Reagan signed the Family Support bill into law, a reform measure sponsored by the National Governors Association and influenced by the Reagan administration. The act provided for a comprehensive state-managed education and training program, transitional child care and medical assistance benefits, and stronger child-support enforcement.

In his efforts to deregulate the private sector and restrict the federal bureaucracy, Reagan relied on administrative appointments and procedures. He immediately ended all price controls on gasoline and crude oil. The administration sharply reduced spending on energy conservation and renewable energy resources. Indeed, Secretary of Energy James Edwards denied the existence of a fuel crisis and looked toward dismantling his own department. Secretary of Transportation Drew Lewis moved to aid U.S. automobile manufacturers by giving them tax breaks and less regulation. Under Reagan the size and influence of the Department of Education and the Department of Health and Human Services were diminished.

Intent upon economic revival and deregulation, Reagan and his advisers turned against the new environmentalism. The administration's anti-environmental efforts reflected its conservative ideology, its sympathy for business, and its resourceful use of executive power. Reagan cut the budgets of environmental agencies, rescinded earlier orders and relaxed standards, and appointed pro-business administrators to head conservation agencies. Anne Gorsuch Burford, an uncompromising opponent of federal regulation, was selected to administer the Environmental Protection Agency, which housed most of the government's pollution-control activities. Under Burford's leadership, the EPA became a center of deregulation and ultimately the scene of an embarrassing scandal that caused the president to call on William D. Ruckelshaus, the first EPA head, to come back and repair the damage. Secretary of the Interior James G. Watt, who had earlier headed a political lobby that favored exploiting the public domain, was even more controversial. Watt seemed bent on reversing the environmental gains of the past two decades, and he became the symbol of the anti-environmental campaign. He opened federal lands to coal and timber production, narrowed the scope of the wilderness preserves, and sought to make a million acres of offshore land available for oil drilling. Watt's policies and provocative public statements kept him in the middle of controversy until he finally resigned in 1983. Reagan changed the orientation of the presidency on the environmental issue but was unable to repeal protective legislation or dismantle the environmental agencies. Meanwhile, environmentalists found support in Congress and the federal courts, and their cause was strengthened by grassroots vitality, organizational influence, and widespread public approval.

For all its conservative rhetoric, the Reagan administration was not successful in advancing its social philosophy by outlawing busing and affirmative action, providing federal support for private and parochial education, restricting abortions, and permitting prayer in the public schools. Congress and the courts were not as cooperative in this regard as they might have been, and Reagan himself appeared reluctant to wage an all-out battle in areas that might prove divisive and politically dangerous. Still, the administration was not inactive on these fronts. For example, it attacked the Internal Revenue Service's policy of denying tax-exempt status to private schools that discriminated on the basis of race. It was not disposed to support an extension of the 1965 Voting Rights Act, although it finally endorsed a revised version of the law. In 1981 the president enjoyed a notable triumph when he appointed the first woman—the conservative Sandra Day O'Connor—to the Supreme Court, thus bringing together conservative and liberal symbols.

In the meantime, Reagan's economic reforms had not worked, at least in the short run. In fact, a serious recession was in progress by the fall of 1981, brought on by the Federal Reserve Board's tight-money policy, the persistence of inflation, rising interest rates resulting from increasing budget deficits, the drift toward a worldwide recession, and the fact that the Reagan reform measures had not yet become fully effective. In 1982 unemployment rose to more than 10 percent, and the deficit was estimated at $128 billion. The downturn finally induced the president to make a slight reduction in the level of defense spending and approve an increase in business and excise taxes—"a down payment on the deficit." But Reagan continued to insist that his economic policies would work. The recession did bring inflation under control, with the inflation rate dropping from 12 percent in 1980 to 3.5 percent in 1984. However, the process was painful, and a year and a half of recession set in, during which a record number of bankruptcies were filed and unemployment approached 11 percent of the workforce. Recovery began late in 1982, and by the end of 1983 the economy was in a buoyant state. Now inflation hovered around 4 percent, the GNP showed an impressive 4.3 percent gain, domestic investment was rising, and unemployment had declined to 8 percent. The administration naturally took credit for the recovery. The only gloomy aspect of this rosy picture was a projected budget deficit of almost $200 billion and the discovery that federal spending as a percentage of the gross national product had increased substantially since Ronald Reagan became president.

THE ATTEMPTED ASSASSINATION

On March, 30, 1981, just sixty-nine days after taking office, President Reagan and three other individuals, including White House Press Secretary James Brady, were shot outside the entrance to the Washington Hilton Hotel by a psychologically disturbed young man named John Hinckley, Jr. Apparently, Hinckley's motivation for the attempted assassination was his obsession with actress Jody Foster. Hinckley believed that if he were to kill Reagan, it would endear him to Foster. Ultimately Hinckley was found not guilty by reason of insanity and committed to an asylum.

Because of the efficiency of the Secret Service in securing the president and delivering him to nearby George Washington University Hospital, Reagan, who had been critically wounded, survived the ordeal and made a full recovery. The event, covered extensively by the media, also proved to be an emotional rallying point for Americans to stand behind their already popular president. When doctors treating Reagan reported that while he was being prepped for the emergency surgery, the president quipped that he hoped they were "all Republicans," even some of his harshest critics had to admire his charm.

James Brady, however, was not as lucky. Brady, who suffered a traumatic shot to the head, had permanent brain damage. In the years that followed, Brady and his wife, Sarah, became outspoken advocates of gun-control legislation, with their lobbying efforts instrumental in bringing the Brady Handgun Violence Prevention Bill, commonly referred to simply as the Brady Bill, before Congress. The act, which was passed in 1993, placed a five-day wait on the purchase of handguns and also required a background check of the prospective buyer.

One of the controversies that arose out of the attempted assassination involved Secretary of State Alexander Haig. Immediately after the melee, Deputy Press Secretary Larry Speakes held a televised press conference, as Vice President George H. W. Bush was not in D.C. at the time. When asked by a reporter who was in charge, given the circumstances, Speakes responded that he could not answer that question. Immediately after hearing Speakes's comment, Haig rushed into the press room, stood behind the podium, and announced to the national and international audience that he was "in charge." Haig explained: "Constitutionally, gentlemen, you have the president, the vice president, and the secretary of state, in that order, and should the president decide he wants to transfer the helm to the vice president, he will do so. As of now, I am in control here, in the White House, pending the return of the vice president and in close touch with him." Actually, Haig was incorrect, as the secretary of state was not second in line behind the vice president in presidential line of succession but actually fifth, behind the Speaker of the House and the President Pro Tempore of the Senate. Haig was accused of overstepping his authority, which dogged him heavily, leading in part to his resignation the following year.

FOREIGN POLICY: RHETORIC AND CONFRONTATION

Reagan's initial public view of Soviet communism reflected the 1950s' political rhetoric that it was an "evil empire" bent on global domination and the eradication of freedom, capitalism, and religion. However, much of Reagan's hubris would vanish after he began to follow in Richard Nixon's footsteps and attempt to normalize relations with the USSR. Nonetheless, the Californian's obsession with the threat of international communism was genuine and seemed to represent a global extension of his inner fears of government authority and social change, as well as his struggle to defend freedom and morality at home. Initially, in Reagan's eyes, the Soviet Union embodied the evils of overweening government, atheism, and a lack of moral standards. Like the Moral Majority and many other American conservatives, he saw anticommunism as "a crusade to restore traditional assumptions about God, family, and country to a central place in American life." Another goal was to thwart the perceived Soviet determination to export the totalitarian system to all parts of the world. Most of the president's national security and foreign policy advisers shared these attitudes. Secretary of State Alexander Haig, his successor George Shultz, Secretary of Defense Caspar Weinberger, National Security Adviser Richard Allen, and Ambassador to the United Nations Jeane Kirkpatrick all had an exaggerated fear of the power of the USSR.

Reagan and Haig adopted a firm anti-Communist line from the beginning of the new administration; they used tough language in referring to the Soviet Union and demonstrated a taste for confrontation. The president characterized Russian leaders as men who "reserve unto themselves the right to commit any crime, to lie, [and] to cheat." He insisted that the SALT II agreement would have to be revised before it could be ratified. He moved ahead to implement Carter's plans to base cruise and Pershing II missiles in Western Europe. Reagan emphasized, as he had during the campaign of 1980, the imperative need to expand American military forces to meet the Soviet challenge. Charging that the Carter administration had allowed the Soviet Union to gain strategic superiority over the United States, he recommended a military program that would cost $136 billion in 1981–82 and more than a trillion dollars over five years—about 8 percent of the GNP. This massive program would include the development of nuclear weapons, the expansion of the surface fleet and tactical airpower, the creation of a Rapid Deployment Force to defend the Persian Gulf and other Third World areas, and much more. Reagan ordered the controversial (and extremely expensive) B-1 bomber into production and announced his decision to push ahead with construction of the neutron bomb. Although military spending had begun to rise during the Carter years, increasing 5 percent after the Soviet Union invasion of Afghanistan, the buildup under Reagan was unprecedented in the post–World War II era. Congress agreed to virtually all of the president's defense proposals.

In practice, however, the Reagan administration discovered that it frequently had to bow to realities in dealing with the Soviet Union. Even while publicly criticizing SALT II, Reagan observed the limits it imposed, as did his Russian counterpart. American wheat surpluses encouraged the president to lift Carter's embargo on grain shipments to the Soviet Union, and in September 1983 the administration concluded a grain sale to Russia of historic proportions. Indeed, by 1985 Reagan had removed most of Carter's restrictions on the Soviet Union. When Soviet pressure in December 1981 caused Poland's Communist rulers to declare martial law, outlaw the independent trade union Solidarity, and imprison its leader, Lech Walesa, Reagan had to content himself with verbal attacks on the Russians. The American leader's harsh rhetoric was not appreciated by his Western European allies, who were still committed to détente between East and West. West Germany, an active trading partner of the Soviet Union, had negotiated a multibillion-dollar agreement to help the Soviets construct a 3,600-mile pipeline for the delivery of natural gas from Siberia to Western Europe. The United States objected to the arrangement and prohibited the sale of U.S. equipment for the project, but the Reagan administration abandoned this embargo in the face of strong protests by its European allies.

The intensifying arms race between the two superpowers encouraged the development of an antinuclear war movement in Europe and the United States. A nationwide poll in the spring of 1982 showed that 57 percent of the respondents favored an immediate freeze on the production, testing, and deployment of nuclear weapons. A bipartisan resolution in Congress urging such a freeze gathered strong support. Reagan slowly began to respond to the pressure and commit himself to the goal of arms control. After the death of Leonid Brezhnev in November 1982, the president proposed an interim agreement limiting American and Soviet medium-range missiles in Europe to a fixed and equal number of warheads. This ploy was rejected by Yuri Andropov, the new Soviet leader, since it would have forced the destruction of existing Russian SS-20 missiles in exchange for proposed American ones.

Despite evidence from authoritative sources that the United States and the Soviet Union were roughly equal in their possession of land- and sea-based missile warheads and that the United States was ahead if one counted aircraft weapons, the Reagan administration pushed ahead with its military buildup. While the arms-limitation talks languished, the arms race continued. The president succeeded, after a long struggle, in getting congressional approval to begin production of the MX, an abbreviation for Missile-Experimental. The new MX missile, later called the Peacekeeper, was a MIRV capable of releasing ten re-entry missiles in its payload, each with a destructive force over twenty-five times more powerful than the atomic bomb detonated over Hiroshima. This new super weapon was strategically designed to intimidate the Soviets, whom Reagan placed at the center of his international diplomacy concerns. In the spring of 1983 Reagan, citing the continued growth of Soviet military power, called for a 10 percent increase in U.S. defense appropriations for 1984. In a televised address to the nation on March 23, 1983, he dramatically called for a "high-tech" weapons system that would destroy enemy missiles in space. This Strategic Defense Initiative (SDI), controversial and incredibly expensive, became known as the "Star Wars" program. The United States soon launched a $26-billion, five-year program for its development.

Reagan's distrust of the Soviet Union seemed to be confirmed in early September 1983, when a Russian fighter jet shot down a South Korean civil airliner that had strayed over Soviet territory in the western Pacific, killing 269 people, including sixty Americans. Insisting that the plane (KAL-007) was on an American intelligence mission, USSR leaders refused to accept any blame for its loss or to show any remorse. In November 1983 the United States began deploying Pershing and cruise missiles in Great Britain and West Germany, according to the NATO agreement of December 1979. In retaliation the Russians walked out of the arms-control talks, which had been resumed by the two superpowers.

Meanwhile, President Reagan's anti-Communist focus in international affairs found a consuming focus in Central America and particularly in El Salvador and Nicaragua. Jimmy Carter had decided, just before leaving office, to extend military aid to the government of El Salvador, which was being challenged by a leftist insurgency. Reagan and Haig claimed that the rebels in El Salvador were being supplied by the Marxist-Socialist Sandinista radicals in Nicaragua and that the overthrow of the Nicaraguan dictator Anastasio Somoza in 1979 had been supported by the Soviet Union and Cuba. Reagan accused the Sandinista leaders of turning Nicaragua into a "Soviet ally on the American mainland." Haig described a Marxist plot to take over all of Central America. Now Reagan and his supporters feared a new Communist offensive based in Cuba, an offensive that had taken over Nicaragua, was threatening El Salvador, and would ultimately imperil the remainder of Central America. The administration was also alarmed at the possibility that a Communist victory in Central America would lead to an out-pouring of refugees from that region to the United States, exacerbating the problem of illegal immigrants at home.

The Reagan administration sent military advisers, helicopter gun ships, and increasing amounts of combat assistance to the government of El Salvador in its continuing struggle against the rebel forces. Many Americans, remembering Vietnam, questioned the wisdom of U.S. involvement in Central America, and Congress, led by the Democratic-controlled House, forced the secretary of state, as a condition for con-tinuing American aid, to certify every six months that the Salvadoran government was making progress toward democracy and respect for human rights. The administration hailed the holding of elections in El Salvador in March 1982 and was even more optimistic two years later when José Napoleon Duarte, a moderate, won the presidential election. In the meantime, the Reagan government refrained from direct military action in Nicaragua but provided covert assistance to the counterrevo-lutionary "contras," who were fighting to overthrow the established gov-ernment. The Boland Amendment, a measure adopted by the House of Representatives, banned U.S. military support of the contras for several years. Nevertheless, the contras received equipment, training, and finan-cial assistance through the CIA, while Washington applied economic and diplomatic pressure and resorted to other stratagems in its effort to oust the Sandinista regime.

Mounting criticism of his Central American policy—and the bloody atrocities attributed to the "death squads" in El Salvador and the con-tras in Nicaragua—led the president, in the fall of 1983, to appoint a "bipartisan commission on Central America" to investigate the whole question. Henry Kissinger headed the commission, which presented its report in January 1984. The report acknowledged the vital need for long-term social and economic reforms in the region and proposed $8.5 billion in aid over the following three years. It emphasized, how-ever, the necessity of preventing the Soviet Union from consolidating "a hostile foothold" in the western hemisphere and called for a "signifi-cantly larger program of military assistance" to anti-Communist forces in Central America.

In October 1983, the Reagan administration received another boost when it sent a military force to invade and briefly occupy the independent island of Grenada (a member of the British Commonwealth). A left-wing coup resulting in the death of the prime minister and other officials brought the American invasion and a speedy restoration of order. The administration claimed that its gunboat diplomacy was necessary to protect American civilians, including hundreds of medical students on the island, and because Barbados and Jamaica had asked the United States to intervene. Actually, Reagan and his advisers were motivated in large part by anti-Communist considerations. They had become deeply suspicious of the existing government of Grenada since it had permitted Cuban construction workers to build an airfield on the island and had signed military agreements with Communist bloc countries. In any case, the American people, recalling the humiliation of the Iranian hostage ordeal, applauded the "liberation" of the tiny state and the display of military muscle in the Caribbean.

American preoccupation with communism was similarly evident in the Middle East during the early 1980s. Determined to contain the Soviet threat in that region, the Reagan administration attempted to revive the Camp David peace process as a means of stabilizing conditions in the area. It had little success in these efforts. After mid-1982, U.S. policy in the Middle East was dominated by an escalating crisis in Lebanon. The problem in that small nation was that no single force was able to control the country. Christian and Muslim factions struggled for supremacy, while Syrian troops occupied the northern section of the country and the Palestinian Liberation Organization (PLO) was established in the southern portion, facing the Israeli border. This volatile situation led the Israelis to invade Lebanon early in June 1982 in order to crush the PLO. The Israeli troops drove northward and then besieged West Beirut, where refugee camps held thousands of Palestinians and provided a base for PLO soldiers. The United States managed during the next few weeks to work out an agreement for the peaceful evacuation of Yasser Arafat, head of the PLO forces, and Reagan soon announced that he was sending 800 U.S. Marines to Lebanon as part of an international peacekeeping force.

What was originally planned as a thirty-day stay by the marines lasted for a year and a half. The United States tried to arrange agreements among the contending Lebanese factions, but that proved impossible, and it began to seem that the U.S. soldiers were really trying to stabilize the new government led by the Christian Amin Gemayel, which was opposed by Shiite Muslims and several other groups. The peacekeeping forces thus found themselves caught in the cross fire of a civil war. Meanwhile, the United States attempted without success to persuade Israel and Syria to agree to a mutual withdrawal of forces. Back home Reagan was subjected to growing criticism by Congress, which questioned his authority to keep troops in Lebanon, and the public, which was hard put to understand the American purpose in the strife-ridden country. These doubts were heightened on October 23, 1983, when a suicide truck loaded with explosives crashed through a security post and exploded inside the American compound, killing 241 sleeping marines. Reagan refused to get out of Lebanon in spite of the outcry that followed this tragedy. Not until early the next year did he finally order the withdrawal of U.S. troops from Lebanon. The Middle East problem remained as intractable as ever.

As the presidential election of 1984 approached, Ronald Reagan could claim a number of successes in the domestic realm, and he had reversed the post-Watergate decline in presidential power. Although his foreign policies had fared less well, he could point to a dramatic increase in the nation's military strength, a strategic balance with the Soviet Union, and a restoration of confidence and pride in the American people. But in the process he had given renewed impetus to the nuclear arms race. The commitment to the Strategic Defense Initiative, the KAL-007 incident, the American use of force in Lebanon and Grenada, and the deployment of new missiles in Europe all pointed to an escalating level of tension between the United States and the Soviet Union during Reagan's first term. The administration wanted to improve relations with the People's Republic of China, in part to gain leverage with Russia, but that proved difficult, partly because of the president's strong sympathy for the Republic of China on Taiwan. Unlike the successful triangular diplomacy of Nixon and Kissinger, Reagan and his advisers exacerbated relations with both the PRC and the USSR, losing leverage with both nations. Nevertheless, Reagan gradually moved from his early confrontational attitude to a position reflecting containment, "peace through strength," and greater interest in international dialogue and negotiation.

In February 1984 there was talk of resuming Soviet-American arms negotiations and a possible summit meeting, prompted by the accession of a new Soviet leader, Konstantin Chernenko, and the fact that President Reagan would soon be involved in a campaign for re-election.

AN ELECTORAL LANDSLIDE

Reagan's re-election prospects looked good during the early months of 1984. Economic recovery was in full swing and inflation was under control, foreign affairs had assumed a less hazardous outlook, and the president's popularity remained gratifyingly high. Reagan dominated the Republican Party, which was united in support of his re-election. When the GOP convention assembled in Dallas, Reagan and Bush were renominated without opposition.

The road to the Democratic nomination was, by contrast, long and difficult. One of the early developments in the nomination process was the withdrawal of Senator Edward Kennedy, widely regarded as a leading contender. Eight other Democrats eventually sought the nomination, including former vice president Walter Mondale, George McGovern, ex-governor Reubin Askew of Florida, and four U.S. senators. The other candidate was Jesse Jackson, a charismatic black minister based in Chicago and leader of the "Rainbow Coalition" of African Americans, Hispanics, and low-income whites. Mondale seemed to be the strongest candidate, but he was upset in the New Hampshire primary by Senator Gary Hart of Colorado, who identified his candidacy with "new ideas" and attacked Mondale for catering to organized labor and other "special interest groups." The field of competitors gradually shrank as the state caucuses and primaries were held, finally leaving only Mondale, Hart, and Jackson in the race.

Mondale set out to rally the major elements of the Democratic coalition behind his candidacy, while Hart talked about the Democratic Party of the future and the need to streamline social services and defense programs, as well as stressing such "New Politics" themes as environmental reform. Jackson, an eloquent speaker and former associate of Martin Luther King, Jr., represented the forces of black protest and social uplift. Although Hart won a number of primaries in New England and the western states, he had some difficulty in explaining his ideas, and Mon-

The president confers with Secretary of State George Shultz. *Courtesy Ronald Reagan Library.*

dale gradually moved into the lead in the struggle for delegates. Jackson, though a serious candidate and a spirited campaigner, was never a real possibility for the nomination. By the time the Democratic National Convention met in San Francisco, Mondale had won a majority of the delegates, and he was nominated on the first ballot. He then caused quite a stir by selecting Representative Geraldine A. Ferraro of New York for the vice-presidential place on the ticket. Ferraro, an able politician with a strong liberal record, attracted large crowds and proved to be an effective campaigner.

The Democratic preconvention campaign had been a bruising struggle for Walter Mondale, and it left the party in a weakened condition for the main event in the autumn. To win the nomination, one scholar has observed, the former vice president "had to endure an unbelievably grueling delegate selection process, with Gary Hart mobilizing Yuppies against him and Jesse Jackson pre-empting his normal base of support among black voters. Mondale had to go hat in hand, in public, to the labor unions, to 'special' interests, to the National Organization for Women—indeed, to anyone who would listen to his case." Unlike his Democratic challenger, President Reagan began the campaign with several important advantages, including his incumbency. The economy promised to help him, and he had apparently stopped losing ground on foreign policy. He was certainly a popular president, and even people who disagreed with his handling of certain issues found him personally appealing. He also benefited from impressive public approval of his leadership. According to Washington Post/ABC News polls, 72 percent of those asked said Reagan had "strong leadership qualities." Only 49 percent said that about Mondale.

Reagan conducted a very effective campaign. Avoiding specifics, he forecast a continuation of prosperity and a bright future. Mondale, as the underdog, attacked his opponent for the huge increase in the federal deficit and having sponsored domestic policies that favored the well-to-do and penalized the poor and minorities. He promised that if elected he would balance the budget and frankly said that he would raise taxes—and that Reagan would do likewise. Mondale waged a forceful and energetic campaign, but his partisan attacks frequently made him appear somber and mean-spirited. Reagan described the Democratic nominee's platform as a vision of "dreary mediocrity" and talked about his own America as an "opportunity society." In his standard speech the president declared, "I think there's a new feeling of patriotism in our land, a recognition that by any standard America is a decent and generous place, a force for good in the world." Reagan also benefited tremendously from the economic resurgence that took place during his first term, which also elevated the level of optimism within the American society. Mondale, like Reagan, also invoked traditional American values and asserted that he would not desert the beliefs he had always fought for: "I would rather lose a race about decency than win one about self-interest." Mondale's words, however, fell flat.

The polls showed Reagan ahead from beginning to end. As the campaign proceeded, the Democrats' only hope seemed to rest on two televised debates scheduled for October 7 and October 21. Mondale at times got the better of Reagan in the first of those confrontations. Fresh and vigorous, he was on the attack from the opening bell. Reagan, on the other hand, seemed old, tired, and confused; his answers were poorly focused, and he delivered a rambling closing statement. The first debate probably closed the gap between the two men. But in the second discussion Reagan looked refreshed and was ready with his answers. He held his own against his Democratic challenger, which was all his campaign needed. Ronald Reagan interjected humor and consistently demonstrated his quick wit. At one juncture in the debate, and in response to his senior-citizen status, which had received some negative press, Reagan pointed out that he would not hold his opponent's youth and inexperience against him. Reagan reflected this optimism, and he put forth his most powerful charge to the American people during his debates with Mondale and his campaign in general when he asked the voters if they were "better off today than four years ago"; the majority could respond that in fact they were. Reagan, ever the positive booster of American idealism, trounced Mondale in the debate with his dramatic, energized second appearance. Meanwhile, Ferraro and Bush had also engaged in a televised debate, which most voters considered a draw.

It was apparent that Mondale would lose the election, but the extent of his defeat was a surprise. Reagan and Bush won by a landslide, receiving 54.5 million votes (59 percent) to 37.6 million (41 percent) for the Democratic ticket. The Electoral College vote was an overwhelming 525 to 13, with the Republicans carrying every state except Mondale's Minnesota and the District of Columbia. Reagan cut deeply into the traditional Democratic coalition, and he strengthened the Republican hold on the South in presidential elections (70 percent of the region's white voters cast their ballots for the president). Although Reagan did well among almost all groups, he proved less attractive to traditional Democratic elements such as African Americans, Jews, Hispanics, and people with incomes under $10,000 a year. More women voted for Reagan than for Mondale, but there was a "gender gap" of about 8 percent, attributed by some analysts to Ferraro's role in the campaign. In a campaign that placed more emphasis on candidate images than on issues, Reagan's personal popularity was clearly a significant factor in the outcome.

Although Reagan demonstrated his own extraordinary political appeal in the election of 1984, the results of that contest were ambiguous in other respects. Unfortunately for the Republicans, Reagan ran far ahead of his ticket. While the GOP retained control of the Senate, the Democrats gained two seats in that body and lost a net of only fourteen seats in the House. After the Reagan landslide, there were thirty-four Democratic governors to sixteen for the Republicans. Political scientists were divided over the question of whether Reagan's victories in

1980 and 1984 portended a realignment of the political parties—a fundamental shift in voter affiliation that would last through several elections. Despite the decline in party identification and the growth of independent voters, the Democrats were still the majority party in terms of party preference and registration. At the same time, the erosion of the party system since World War II made a national realignment increasingly problematic. Yet by the mid-1980s, the Republicans had become a strong right-of-center party, fashioned in the image of Ronald Reagan. And the election of 1984 had confirmed a developing shift in American politics and social policy.

SECOND TERM: UP THE DOWN STAIRCASE

"Our nation is poised for greatness," Reagan declared in his second inaugural address on January 21, 1985. "There are no limits to growth and human progress when men and women are free to follow their dreams." The president made it clear that he intended to adhere to the conservative principles that had guided his first administration. Once again he condemned big government and vowed to resume his fight to transfer governmental authority from the federal to the state and local levels. He called for a major assault on domestic spending in 1985, a constitutional amendment mandating a balanced budget, and further support of the Star Wars program. In his State of the Union message a few weeks later, Reagan asserted that the budget deficit could be wiped out through "economic growth," not increased taxes. He continued to speak out against abortion, support prayer in the schools, and endorse a tuition tax credit, presumably as a means of injecting competition and choice into a school system under increasing criticism. Reagan's budget recommended an additional increase in military spending and reductions in a wide range of social programs.

The administration enjoyed a number of successes in 1985, particularly involving defense and military aid measures. Congress once again voted its approval of the MX missile program, though not at the level sought by the Pentagon. After voting against further aid to the Nicaraguan contras, the House of Representatives reversed itself and approved "humanitarian" assistance to the guerrillas (which many observers suspected would be used for military purposes). The Senate also approved this assistance. Nevertheless, some of Reagan's proposals encountered stiff resistance. He was forced to compromise on his budget recommendations. The president agreed with most members of Congress on the necessity of reducing the budget deficit, estimated at more than $200 billion in 1985, and he and congressional leaders of both parties accepted a cut of at least $50 billion in the next year's deficit. After a long battle, Reagan finally agreed to a demand by House Democrats that Social Security cost of living adjustments not be tampered with and that other social services receive more money than proposed by the White House. Military spending would increase, though not as much as the chief executive recommended.

Concern over the mounting budget deficit led Congress in December 1985 to pass a measure sponsored by Senators Phil Gramm of Texas and Warren B. Rudman of New Hampshire. The Gramm-Rudman Act, which became effective in March 1986, provided a schedule for balancing the federal budget by 1991. If Congress and the president were unable to agree on annual budget reductions, the act would require automatic cuts in most domestic and military programs. President Reagan endorsed the scheme but was obviously afraid that it would result in substantial reductions in military spending. The Supreme Court intervened by invalidating Gramm-Rudman, and the deficit for 1986 rose to a record height of $226 billion. Congress then revised the law, but the budget procedures worked out by the legislative and executive branches rendered the new act virtually useless.

In the meantime, Reagan had announced, with great fanfare, a tax reform and simplification plan. He and other administration leaders promoted the proposal in a series of speeches. Congress talked about the question for almost two years before approving a comprehensive income-tax overhaul in the fall of 1986. The measure closed some loopholes, lowered rates somewhat, eliminated some deductions, struck at "bracket creep" by reducing the number of brackets from fourteen to three, and exempted many poor Americans from paying any federal income taxes. The Reagan administration could take considerable credit for this reform, along with Senator Robert W. Packwood of Oregon, Representative Daniel D. Rostenkowski of Illinois, and other congressional advocates. Reagan hailed the enactment as historic, saying that it "satisfies my requirements for meaningful tax reform."

Administration leadership was less directly involved in the adoption of a new immigration law, a response to the developing crisis
over millions of illegal aliens in the United States. The administration was concerned about this problem, although it was selective in
implementing the Refugee Act of 1980, a statute designed to protect
those in flight because of a "well-founded fear of persecution" for religious, political, or racial reasons. In the early 1980s, Congress began
to debate new policies to deal with illegal immigration. The lawmakers
were influenced by the recommendations of the Select Commission on
Immigration and Refugee Policy (1978–81) and the development of a
bipartisan proposal by Alan K. Simpson, chairman of the immigration
subcommittee in the Senate, and Romano L. Mazzoli, his counterpart
in the House. In 1986 Congress finally passed the Immigration Reform
and Control Act, a modification of the Simpson-Mazzoli bill. The act
introduced a new program intended to legalize the status of undocumented aliens. It offered amnesty to such immigrants and established
a process for achieving it. The act prohibited employers from know-
ingly hiring or recruiting illegal aliens. It also normalized the status of
certain Cuban and Haitian refugees and broadened admission opportunities for several special immigrant groups. As a result of this act, 1.5
million immigrants were officially admitted to the nation in 1990, an
all-time high at that time.

Efforts to eliminate and otherwise weaken federal regulation of
the economy did not begin with Reagan's presidency. The deregulation movement had begun to gather momentum during the Carter
administration. The initiatives of the independent regulatory commissions and Congress in dealing with industries such as airlines, trucking, and telecommunications were important. But deregulation was a
major objective of the Reagan White House, and its effects were evident
throughout Reagan's presidency. The appointments he made to top positions in the Interior Department, the Federal Communications Commission, the Federal Home Loan Bank Board, and the Securities and
Exchange Commission illustrated the administration's tactics, as did the
cutback in appropriations and staff levels for many federal agencies. The
systematic appointment of conservatives to federal judgeships bolstered
the deregulation movement. Moreover, Reagan and his aides adopted
a permissive attitude toward corporate mergers, antitrust enforcement,

and new forms of financial speculation. The more flagrant attacks on regulatory machinery and standards, notably environmental protection regulation, ran into strong opposition from Congress, environmental advocacy groups, and challenges in the courts, not to mention public outcries and front-page stories about the "dismemberment" of environmental programs. Administration tactics gradually shifted from overt confrontation and assault to a more moderate approach, use of covert attacks, and an interest in incremental change.

One example of deregulation occurred in agencies charged with the protection of worker health and safety. The altered atmosphere in the Occupational Safety and Health Administration (OSHA) brought a reduction in job safety inspections, a drastic cut in hazardous citations, and a sharp decrease in fines for violations of OSHA standards. In a general sense, these changes reflected the declining position of organized labor during the Reagan years. Union membership as a proportion of the labor force dropped to 20 percent in the late 1970s, and in the next decade, labor's attempts to organize nonunion plants were, more often than not, quite unsuccessful. Organized labor's growing impotence was symbolized by President Reagan's handling of a strike in August 1981 by the Professional Air Traffic Controllers Organization (PATCO), which had supported Reagan in 1980. The president, upholding the government's long-standing policy against strikes by federal employees, fired the 12,000 striking controllers and replaced them with substitutes from the military services and elsewhere. He also backed the Federal Aviation Administration in refusing to rehire any striker for any reason, a position approved by the public by a margin of two to one. Reagan's decisive action in firing the air-traffic controllers further endeared him to many Americans as being a strong leader, while critics pointed out that his action was shortsighted, as the nation was actually in need of more air traffic controllers at the time of the strike. The administration's deregulation campaign manifested itself in the decisions of the National Labor Relations Board and that agency's bureaucratic slowdown in responding to labor's appeals. The erosion of labor standards was also encouraged by Reagan's appointments to the federal courts and judicial decisions that often enabled industrial and business firms to cancel or avoid labor contracts through various subterfuges.

Deregulation contributed to a crisis in the savings and loan industry, which became one of the policy's most widely publicized failures. The Federal Home Loan Bank, whose board was charged with overseeing the industry, did its part in easing federal regulations, and in 1982 Congress, with the support of Reagan, eliminated S&L interest ceilings and authorized the "thrifts" to make commercial loans, including investments in nonresidential real estate. Capital reserve requirements were later reduced, and some states were even more liberal in their requirements. With their funds no longer tied up in low-interest mortgages, savings and loan institutions began to boom—and to undertake high-interest, high-risk loans and speculative ventures. Among the more sensational examples was a cautionary tale that unfolded in Orange County, California, where Charles H. Keating gained control of Lincoln Federal Savings and Loan Association. Keating transformed a relatively small company into a multibillion-dollar business, offering high-interest rates, making speculative investments, and selling "junk bonds" through Lincoln Federal's branches. He enjoyed a huge salary and a lavish lifestyle. The end came in 1989, when the company was forced to file for bankruptcy protection and the government took over the institution at a cost of $2.6 billion to the taxpayers. By that time many other S&Ls had collapsed, and when the crisis was over the ultimate cost to the government was estimated to have been about $500 billion.

Economic acquisitiveness, deregulation, and novel forms of speculation were also prominent on Wall Street and in the corporate world during the 1980s. A rash of corporate mergers and takeovers characterized the decade. The fast and easy money of the period brought forth audacious—and sometimes unethical—plungers such as Michael Milken, Ivan Boesky, and Dennis Levine. Many of these Wall Street operators and investment entrepreneurs resorted to insider trading—the use of privileged information to trade in stocks and bonds for personal profit; dealt in "junk bonds"—speculative securities that attracted investors with the promise of high returns; and engaged in risk arbitrage—the purchase of stock in the expectation or hope of profit from later takeovers. Corporate "raiders" engineered what became known as "leveraged buyouts," a technique that leveraged the value of the targeted company by buying out its public stockholders with borrowed money and then using the firm's assets to underwrite large issues of junk bonds, enabling

Colonel Oliver North.
*Courtesy Ronald Reagan
Library.*

the new owners to sell their holdings at inflated prices. The Securities and Exchange Commission finally began to crack down on these practices—Milken, Boesky, and Levine were all prosecuted—and Congress eventually enacted legislation to tighten the regulation of security markets. A wave of selling on Wall Street precipitated a stock market crash on October 19, 1987, with a drop of 508 points in the Dow Jones industrial average. That dramatic event seemed to be a fitting accompaniment to an outbreak of financial scandals in the late 1980s.

In the meantime, the Reagan administration was plagued by scandals of its own. Political appointments and conflict of interest deals in the departments of Interior and Housing and Urban Development became notorious. Michael Deaver, Edwin Meese, and Lyn Nofziger, former White House aides, were all accused of influence peddling after leaving the government. The Wedtech Corporation, a defense contractor in New York, employed Nofziger and other well-placed Washington contacts to secure federal no-bid contracts and loans. When the corporation was forced into bankruptcy in 1986, its illegal activities were revealed and more than two dozen individuals, including Nofzinger and other Washington "friends," were convicted. Wedtech cost the government several hundred million dollars. By 1989, 138 officials and aides in the Reagan administration were reported to have been convicted, indicted, or otherwise caught in legal trouble.

A much more ominous revelation grew out of the administration's support of the Nicaraguan contras. In November 1986, an obscure journal in Beirut reported that the United States had been selling arms to Iran in an effort to secure the release of American hostages held by pro-Iranian terrorists in Lebanon. Such a transfer of arms was illegal, as it was in direct conflict with the Boland Amendment, which severely limited U.S. military assistance for the contras. Named for its chief architect, Congressman Edward Patrick Boland (D-MA), the intent of the legislation, a part of the Defense Appropriations Act of 1983, was expressly to prevent the United States from assisting the contras in an overthrow of the Nicaraguan government. American intelligence sources confirmed the story, and a few days later President Reagan acknowledged that he had known about the sale of arms to Iran. It was gradually learned that Marine Lieutenant Colonel Oliver L. North, an aide to the National Security Council, had illegally diverted profits from the arms deal to support the contras in Nicaragua, with the approval of NSC adviser Robert C. "Bud" McFarlane and others in the administration. This bold scheme might have brought the hostages home, circumvented the Boland Amendment to help defeat the Sandinistas, and strengthened the U.S. position in the Middle East. The president initially denied any wrongdoing and called North "a national hero." The media branded the affair "Irangate."

The Iran-Contra scheme resulted in the most serious crisis of Reagan's presidency. The outlines of a major scandal soon emerged, and damning evidence was unearthed, such as the shredding of incriminating documents by Colonel North, the involvement of the CIA in the affair, and lying to Congress by participants in the venture. Reagan acted by appointing a special review board headed by former senator John G. Tower to investigate the matter. Congressional hearings were also held on the affair in the spring and summer of 1987. Meanwhile, Reagan's popularity fell sharply—by 21 percent in one month—and the administration appeared to lose direction and effectiveness. The Tower Commission submitted its report in late February 1987. While making no attempt to associate the president with the diversion of Iranian arms sale profits to the guerrilla war in Nicaragua, the commission was critical of Reagan's style of management and declared that he must bear "the ultimate responsibility" for the wrongs of his subordinates. The chief executive conceded that serious mistakes had been made and announced changes in the White House staff and in NSC procedures, but he insisted that he had no knowledge of funds illegally diverted to the contras. North, however, later wrote that "Reagan knew everything" about the scheme.

In the end, Reagan's luck held, and the uproar over the Iran-Contra crisis subsided without further damage to the administration. Lawrence E. Walsh, the independent counsel charged with investigating wrongdoing in the case, was convinced that "a cover-up engineered in the White House of one president [Reagan] and completed by his successor [Bush] prevented the rule of law from being applied to the perpetrators of criminal activity of constitutional dimension." What the Democrats called the "Teflon Presidency"—none of Reagan's mistakes seemed

Gorbachev, Reagan, and Bush. *Courtesy Ronald Reagan Library.*

to stick to him—remained intact. Efforts by President Oscar Arias of Costa Rica and other Central American leaders led to a cease-fire in Nicaragua in the spring of 1988 and the introduction of a peace plan by the time Reagan left office in January 1989.

One of Reagan's most notable achievements was an important arms-control agreement with the Soviet Union late in his second administration. Ironically, it was a triumph that came with a remarkable shift in Reagan's approach to an adversary he had darkly characterized as an "evil empire," a shift from confrontation to negotiation and a return to détente. The American leader's attitude toward arms control had begun to change during his first term, in part, it appears, because of criticism his military buildup had provoked in Europe and the United States. In any event, the administration persisted in the arms-control talks, and in a conciliatory statement early in 1984 the president declared the United States was "in its strongest position in years to establish a constructive and realistic working relationship with the Soviet Union." Reagan was no doubt encouraged by the progress of his rearmament campaign, as well as his awareness of worsening problems in the USSR—increasing economic paralysis, a crisis of leadership, a military misadventure in Afghanistan, economic mismanagement in Poland, and declining influence in the Third World. Like many other Americans, he responded favorably to the new Russian leader, Mikhail Gorbachev, who was elected general secretary of the Communist Party in March 1985. Gorbachev was young, well-educated, and politically skillful. His regime promised both internal reform and a more flexible and imaginative approach to relations with the United States and Western Europe.

The change in Russian leadership and the moderation of President Reagan's hard-line attitude toward the Soviet Union paved the way for a meeting in Geneva between Gorbachev and Reagan in November 1985. The two leaders got along well, signed several cultural and scientific agreements, and discussed the need for an arms-control accord. They were unable, however, to agree on arms limitation, given Reagan's refusal to accept any restriction on his SDI (Star Wars) program. Eager for a breakthrough that would strengthen his position in the Kremlin and facilitate his domestic reforms, Gorbachev pushed for a second summit, and one was held, on very short notice, in October 1986 at Reykjavik,

Iceland. Although the conference resulted in few tangible accomplishments, it was of great symbolic importance. The two superpower chiefs considered sweeping proposals for arms control, including the elimination of all nuclear weapons within ten years, and an older American offer, identified with Assistant Secretary of Defense Richard N. Perle, known as the "zero option" plan. That plan would require the Soviet Union to dismantle its SS-20 missiles in exchange for a commitment by the Americans and their European allies to remove (or promise not to deploy) their Pershing and cruise missiles.

Dramatic progress in halting the arms race came at a high-level conference in Washington, D.C., in December 1987, when Gorbachev and Reagan signed the Intermediate Nuclear Force (INF) Treaty. The agreement eliminated all short- and medium-range missiles in Europe and provided for a system of independent, on-site verification and weapons inspection. The INF Treaty served as a prelude to a series of hopeful developments in the Cold War. In Afghanistan the Soviet Union began a phased withdrawal of its troops, while the United States scaled down its aid to the Afghan rebels. The two superpowers joined in a plan for the gradual removal of all foreign troops from Angola and a political effort to settle that country's drawn-out civil war. In the Middle East the Soviet Union and the United States supported a UN-initiated cease-fire in the Iran-Iraq War and the beginning of formal peace talks. Meanwhile, the process of dismantling missiles on both sides proceeded, Gorbachev permitted larger numbers of Soviet Jews to leave the USSR, and Reagan made a successful goodwill trip to Moscow in mid-1988.

Whatever the flaws and shortcomings of his foreign policy, Ronald Reagan restored American self-confidence, negotiated from a position of strength, and eventually encouraged Russian leaders to believe they could reach an accommodation with him that would prove mutually beneficial. Reagan's success in this respect was facilitated by the able stewardship of Secretary of State Shultz. However, Reagan, the fervent Cold Warrior, was a credible president who had first built up the U.S. military supremacy that it held over the U.S.S.R., which prompted the Soviets to enter into negotiations. Reagan, who had previously been viewed as overtly hawkish, in effect was transformed into a dove. That was one reason for the popularity he enjoyed at the end of his presidency.

THE REAGAN LEGACY

Ronald Reagan wanted to change the political landscape of the United States, and his election as president in 1980 marked a major turning point in national politics and domestic policy. When the new president entered the White House, he had three overriding objectives: to reduce the size of the federal government, to bring inflation under control and establish a growth-oriented economy, and to rebuild American defenses. Although he was not uniformly successful in accomplishing these objectives, Reagan revived a sagging economy, intensified the arms buildup begun by Jimmy Carter, and reshaped the national agenda, not only for the 1980s but into the 1990s as well. As the political analyst William Schneider wrote in 1986, Reagan "defines his program in bold, uncompromising terms, and then proceeds to play the cautious, moderate politician, bargaining for the best deal he can get."

The fortieth president's leadership went a long way toward restoring public confidence in the effectiveness of the national government and renewing the authority and prestige of the presidency. One example was his approach to the federal bureaucracy, where he made a more determined effort than any other recent president to bend the permanent government to his will—by mobilizing public support for his policies, using the budget to reorder policy priorities, imposing hiring freezes and reductions in force to shrink the federal government, and deliberately utilizing the power of appointment to fill senior executive positions in departments and agencies with strong advocates of his policies. Reagan's judicial appointments constituted an important legacy, since by the time his tenure ended he had selected almost half of all lower-court judges. His search for conservative jurists had a long-lasting effect on the composition of the federal judiciary and critical areas of legal policy. His rhetorical skill also enabled him to use the symbolism of the presidency to promote leadership and initiatives in the private sector.

Some of Reagan's programs had adverse consequences or enjoyed only limited success. Thus, while his policies stimulated the economy and reined in inflation, they tripled the national debt, kept interest rates high, and weakened the capacity of the United States to compete with European and Asiatic nations in the international market. Reagan shifted certain budget allocations and personnel from domestic to defense agencies, but he failed to reduce the size of the federal government overall. Despite its influence on federal-state-local relationships, the Reagan administration was unable to reverse the historical trend in the expansion of the national government. Hopes for the "new federalism" soon waned. Increasing defense outlays, financial pressure on Medicare and the Social Security system, and record budget deficits placed limits on federal assistance to the states and localities, while the practical difficulty of carrying through the major devolution of programs and revenue Reagan envisaged doomed his reform of federalism, at least in the short run.

In international affairs the president's contributions were ambiguous. His early foreign policies—provocative rhetoric and a posture of confrontation toward the Soviet Union, obsessive anticommunism in Central America, and insensitivity toward Third World conditions and needs—seemed inflexible and counterproductive. The Iran-Contra affair was a scandal that might well have destroyed Reagan's presidency; many Americans, perhaps a majority of them, believed that the chief executive had deliberately broken the law and then lied about it. Yet in dealing with the Russians, in particular, Reagan learned from experience and gradually developed a more coherent and mature policy: negotiating from strength, responding to unexpected opportunities presented by the Soviet situation, and demonstrating a capacity for personal diplomacy in negotiating with Gorbachev. Whatever their provenance, the far-reaching arms control agreement with the USSR and the creation of a new détente in the Cold War provided dramatic evidence of Reagan's achievements and flair as a diplomat. Ultimately, Reagan through his policies proved to be the most significant president in ending the Cold War, and unlike Kennedy, Johnson or Nixon, his approach did not include the prosecution of any long, protracted war fought on the soil of a Third World nation.

As president, Reagan was interested in political change as well as the introduction of broad new policies. The Californian identified himself with the revitalization of the Republican Party, which he dominated in the 1980s, and his leadership more than that of any other politician of his generation made the GOP a thoroughly conservative organization. He worked to strengthen the party at the local and state levels, improve the coordination of policy development and campaign politics, and make Republicanism a more national and programmatic enterprise. He broadened the party's appeal and played a vital role in its assimilation of the religious right, control of presidential politics in the South, and impressive strength in large parts of the urban working class that previously had been closely identified with the Democratic Party. Although a clear-cut realignment of the political parties did not take place during his presidency, Reagan brought the Republicans to a kind of partial realignment.

Republican success in the presidential election of 1988 provided solid evidence of Reagan's continuing influence. The Democrats, invigorated by the knowledge that they would not have to face Reagan in the fall, experienced a spirited struggle before selecting Governor Michael Dukakis of Massachusetts as their presidential nominee and Senator Lloyd M. Bentsen of Texas as his running mate. The Republicans nominated Vice President George Bush to head their ticket and Senator J. Danforth Quayle of Indiana for vice president. Dukakis, who led Bush in the polls from April to August, boasted of his "high-tech" credentials and advocated a liberal program that included compulsory health insurance and a pro-choice position on abortion. Bush, it was said, ran as a carbon copy of Reagan. He and other GOP speakers stressed the nation's economic growth, prosperity, and low inflation rate, and they launched a telling assault on Dukakis's character, judgment, and values. They pictured him as a liberal in the tradition of Teddy Kennedy and George McGovern who opposed gun ownership, the pledge of allegiance, prayer in the schools, and an anticrime program. One feature of the GOP media campaign targeted the Democratic nominee's alleged permissiveness in dealing with crime in Massachusetts. In a blatant appeal to racism, one Republican-sponsored commercial showed a long line of convicts entering and exiting a dreary prison through a revolving door while the voice-over narrative told the story of Willie Horton, a black man convicted of rape and assault who went on to commit rape and assault in Maryland after being furloughed from a Massachusetts state prison. The Massachusetts governor, inexplicably, did not respond to these transparent attacks until it was too late.

Bush and Quayle won a decisive majority, with 53.4 percent of the popular vote and an Electoral College margin of 426 to 112. The Democrats did retain control of Congress. Dukakis and Bentsen carried only ten northern and northwestern states. In the South, where the Republicans ran ahead of their performance in other parts of the country, they won every state. The southern returns revealed a pronounced racial polarization: the Democratic ticket received about 90 percent of the region's African American votes but only 32 percent of its white ballots. Journalist Tom Wicker noted that "white flight into the Republican Party, in all regions of the country but most spectacularly in the South, will be a palpable, continuing, virtually fatal problem for the Democrats as far ahead as a poll-taker can see." There were other factors that had a marked effect on the outcome, including the relative effectiveness of the presidential nominees. Even more important was the fact that Republicans could claim credit for peace, prosperity, and patriotism, identified most conspicuously with Ronald Reagan, the most popular figure in American politics.

———— ★ ————

SUGGESTIONS FOR FURTHER READING

The most satisfactory biography of Ronald Reagan is Lou Cannon's evenhanded *President Reagan: The Role of a Lifetime* (1991). Peggy Noonan's *When Character Was King: A Story of Ronald Reagan* (2002) is an indispensable and revealing look at Reagan's personality. Also of significant note are *Dutch: A Memoir of Ronald Reagan*, by Edmund Morris (1999), Garry Wills, *Reagan's America* (1988), and Stephen Vaughn, *Ronald Reagan in Hollywood: Movies and Politics* (1994). See also Frank Van Der Linden, *The Real Reagan* (1981); Ronald Reagan, with Richard G. Hubler, *Where's the Rest of Me? Ronald Reagan Tells His Own Story* (1965); *An American Life*, by Ronald Reagan (1990); *Ronald Reagan: A Life In Politics*, by Lou Cannon (2004).

One of the best examinations of the Reagan administration's goals and accomplishments in shaping national politics is *The Age of Reagan: The Conservative Counterrevolution, 1980–1989* (2009), by Steven F. Hayward. For the conservative revival, consult William C. Berman, *America's Right Turn: From Nixon to Bush* (1994); Alan Crawford, *Thunder on the Right: The "New Right" and the Politics of Resentment* (1981); Jerome Himmelstein, *To the Right: The Transformation of American Conservatism* (1989); and J. David Hoeveler, Jr., *Watch on the Right: Conservative Intellectuals in the Reagan Era* (1991). The role of conservative Christianity is illuminated in complementary studies by two political scientists: Matthew C. Moen, *The Transformation of the Christian Right* (1991), and Michael Lienesch, *Redeeming America: Piety and Politics in the New Christian Right* (1993). See also Steve

Bruce, *The Rise and Fall of the New Christian Right: Conservative Protestant Politics in America, 1978–1988* (1989); Patrick Allitt, *Catholic Intellectuals and Conservative Politics in America, 1950–1985* (1993); and R. Laurence Moore, *Selling God: American Religion in the Marketplace of Culture* (1994).

The best interpretations of Reagan's presidency include John Patrick Diggins' *Ronald Reagan: Fate, Freedom, and the Making of History* (2007); Michael Schaller, *Reckoning with Reagan: America and Its President in the 1980s* (1992); Robert Dallek, *Ronald Reagan: The Politics of Symbolism* (1984); Martin Anderson, *Revolution: The Reagan Legacy* (rev. ed., 1990); Laurence I. Barrett, *Gambling with History: Ronald Reagan in the White House* (1984); David Mervin, *Ronald Reagan and the American Presidency* (1990); and Haynes Johnson, *Sleepwalking through History: America in the Reagan Years* (1991). Among several collections of essays on the Reagan administration, see Fred I. Greenstein, ed., *The Reagan Presidency: An Early Assessment* (1983); Lester M. Salamon and Michael S. Lund, eds., *The Reagan Presidency and the Governing of America* (1984); Charles O. Jones, ed., *The Reagan Legacy: Promise and Performance* (1988); B. B. Kymlicka and Jean V. Matthews, eds., *The Reagan Revolution* (1988); and Larry Berman, ed., *Looking Back on the Reagan Presidency* (1990). The national political milieu is elucidated in Thomas Byrne Edsall, with Mary D. Edsall, *Chain Reaction: The Impact of Race, Rights, and Taxes on American Politics* (1991), and Stephen Skowronek, *The Politics Presidents Make* (1993).

The Reagan Diaries (2007), by Ronald Reagan, is an edited compilation of a diary that he kept during his presidency. Many of those who served in the Reagan White House have written personal accounts of their experiences. Among these memoirs are David A. Stockman, *The Triumph of Politics: How the Reagan Revolution Failed* (1986); Donald Regan, *For the Record: From Wall Street to Washington* (1988); Caspar W. Weinberger, *Fighting for Peace: Seven Critical Years in the Pentagon* (1990); and Nancy Reagan, with William Novak, *My Turn: The Memoirs of Nancy Reagan* (1989). See also Paul Boyer, ed., *Reagan as President: Contemporary Views of the Man, His Politics, and His Policies* (1990), and Jane Feuer, *Seeing through the Eighties: Television and Reaganism* (1995).

Reagan's domestic agenda and administration of the presidency are discussed in Light, *The President's Agenda*, and Campbell, *Managing the Presidency*, both cited previously. The fortieth president's economic policies are analyzed in Michael J. Boskin, *Reagan and the Economy: The Successes, Failures, and Unfinished Agenda* (1987); Joseph White and Aaron Wildavsky, *The Deficit and the Public Interest: The Search for Responsible Budgeting in the 1980s* (1991); and Stein, *Presidential Economics.* Deregulation and the "new federalism" are explored in Martha Derthick and Paul J. Quirk, *The Politics of Deregulation* (1985), and Richard P. Nathan and others, *Reagan and the States* (1987).

Good overviews of Reagan's foreign policy are available in books by Ambrose, Brands, Garthoff, LaFeber, and McCormick, all mentioned earlier. See also David E.

Kyvig, ed., *Reagan and the World* (1990); John Lewis Gaddis, *The United States and the End of the Cold War: Implications, Reconsiderations, Provocations* (1992); Strobe Talbott, *Reagan and Gorbachev* (1987); and Don Oberdorfer, *The Turn, from Cold War to the New Era: The United States and the Soviet Union, 1983–1990* (1991).

Smith's *The Last Years of the Monroe Doctrine* is indispensable for U.S. involvement in Latin America in the postwar period. Also see Lars Schoultz, *National Security and United States Policy toward Latin America* (1987), and Thomas Carothers, *In the Name of Democracy* (1991). Central America, Nicaragua, and the Iran-Contra affair are explored in Thomas W. Walker, ed., *Reagan versus the Sandinistas: The Undeclared War on Nicaragua* (1987); Theodore Draper, *A Very Thin Line: The Iran-Contra Affairs* (1991); Clifford Krauss, *Inside Central America* (1991); and Jane Mayer and Doyle McManus, *Landslide: The Unmaking of the President, 1984–1988* (1988).

The campaign of 1984 is analyzed in a comprehensive work edited by Michael Nelson, *The Elections of 1984* (1985). Other books on that election include Ellis Sandoz and Cecil V. Crabb, Jr., eds., *Election 84: Landslide Without a Mandate?* (1986), and Steven M. Gillon, *The Democrats' Dilemma: Walter F. Mondale and the Liberal Legacy* (1992). The presidential campaign of 1988 is described by Jack W. Germond and Jules Witcover in *Whose Broad Stripes and Bright Stars: The Trivial Pursuit of the Presidency, 1988* (1989), and Laurence W. Moreland and others, eds., *The 1988 Presidential Election in the South: Continuity Amidst Change in Southern Party Politics* (1991).

———★———

CHAPTER

11

The United States and the New World Order

WITH THE INAUGURATION OF GEORGE BUSH as the nation's forty-first president in January 1989, the United States seemed prepared to continue the Reagan era. Bush himself, despite minor differences with his predecessor, pursued this objective. Although the new administration undertook relatively few major initiatives in domestic affairs, it was forced to deal with a number of serious issues, including the savings and loan scandal and the mounting budget deficit, problems exacerbated by the Reagan revolution. Bush was more confident and surefooted in coping with a series of dramatic events in foreign affairs, the most notable of which was the collapse of the Soviet empire and the end of the Cold War. Meanwhile, the American leader intervened with military force in the Republic of Panama and was instrumental in organizing a coalition that waged a successful war against Iraq following its unprovoked invasion of Kuwait. As a result, Bush's approval rating rose to unprecedented heights.

Nevertheless, by the time of his re-election campaign in 1992, Bush's popularity had declined steeply because of a sluggish economy and growing doubts about his capacity as a leader. He lost the election of 1992, which witnessed the emergence of a new Democratic leader in Bill Clinton, the young governor of Arkansas. Taking office early in 1993, the Clinton administration began with an ambitious reform agenda and high expectations. But over the course of the next four years, the administration was buffeted by one setback after another, some self-inflicted and others resulting from the Republican opposition's increasing strength. These developments appeared to be part of a larger transformation of American politics, a transformation whose beginnings went back to the 1960s.

THE PRESIDENCY OF GEORGE H. W. BUSH

George Herbert Walker Bush came to the White House with impressive credentials. Born on June 12, 1924, in Milton, Massachusetts, he was the son of Prescott S. Bush, a New York investment banker who later became a supporter of Dwight D. Eisenhower and served ten years in the U.S. Senate. The younger Bush grew up in an upper-class suburb of New York City and attended Phillips Andover Academy. Following his graduation in 1942, he enlisted in the navy, moved through the various stages of flight training, flew fifty-nine missions, and was shot down and rescued. An authentic war hero, he was awarded the Distinguished Flying Cross for bravery in combat. When the war ended, Bush entered Yale University, where he majored in economics, was elected a member of the venerable Phi Beta Kappa Society, and captained the baseball team. After completing his degree, he married Barbara Pierce, the daughter of a prominent magazine publisher.

Bush soon decided to move to Texas and enter the oil business. He became a cofounder of the Zapata Oil Company, one of the first and most successful offshore drilling operations in the Gulf of Mexico. At the same time, the young entrepreneur became increasingly interested in politics, and in 1962 he assumed the chairmanship of the Harris County Republican Committee. Two years later, he ran unsuccessfully for the United States Senate and backed Barry Goldwater's campaign for president. In 1966 Bush was elected to the U.S. House of Representatives from a Houston district. He was re-elected in 1968 but lost another bid for the Senate two years later. Bush's political beliefs reflected both the northeastern moderate Republicanism of his father and the more conservative GOP brand of his adopted state; these conflicting influences may help explain a certain blandness and vagueness in his political style. Stephen Hess, an aide in the Nixon White House, remarked that Bush "always emerges as without any sharp edges." The Texan was enthusiastic

President Bush and Vice
President Quayle, June
1989. *Courtesy George
Bush Presidential Library.*

and optimistic, had an ingratiating manner, and was determined to be
liked. He was also very ambitious. His strength lay less in the advocacy
of issues or ideology and more in his ability to project executive qualities,
in particular decisiveness and independent thinking. In the 1970s, Bush
received a series of high-level appointments from Presidents Nixon and
Ford: U.S. ambassador to the United Nations, chairman of the Republican National Committee, chief U.S. emissary to the People's Republic
of China, and director of the Central Intelligence Agency. His efforts
to juggle these various roles may also have contributed to the incorrect
impression that he was an unfocused leader, a man without a compelling
purpose or consuming passion. Nevertheless, in 1980 the well-traveled
George Bush sought his party's presidential nomination.

Though denied the nomination in 1980, Bush ended up as Ronald
Reagan's running mate that year, and after eight years as vice president—
and studied loyalty to the Reagan administration—he finally moved

into the Oval Office. It was an auspicious time for the new president, a time of national calm, continuing economic prosperity, and month after month of favorable news. Less driven by ideological concerns than Reagan, Bush was content to recommend several modest domestic programs in 1989. He seemed eager to foster what he described as a "kinder, gentler" society, in which Americans through cooperation and volunteer work could create "a thousand points of light." The administration presented a plan to rescue the savings and loan industry and to bail out depositors who had suffered losses in its collapse. Congress passed a rescue bill during the following summer that created the Resolution Trust Corporation, an agency charged with liquidating the failed thrifts, and consolidated the insurance fund for S&L deposits with the fund covering banks under the Federal Deposit Insurance Corporation. The cost to the taxpayers was breathtaking—at least $500 billion.

When Bush assumed office, the national debt stood at $2.6 trillion, a great part of it incurred because of the tax cuts and expanded defense spending of the 1980s. The president and the Democratic-controlled Congress agreed that a deficit-reduction measure must be adopted, but they found it almost impossible to work out the details of a tax increase and cutbacks in the appropriations for domestic programs. Neither side trusted the other, and the budget controversy precipitated a long and acrimonious debate. The process almost broke down before a broad agreement was finally reached in the fall of 1990. The result was a budget-reduction package of substantial proportions that promised to cut the deficit by $43 billion in 1991 and to make larger reductions over the next four years. Bush was forced to accept a marginally higher income tax rate and increased excise taxes—breaking his "read my lips, no new taxes" campaign commitment—and he failed to get a cut in the capital gains tax, which remained at 28 percent. The decision to balance the budget may have been prudent fiscally, but it was unpopular socially for the majority of potential Bush supporters, and it did ultimately return to haunt George H. W. Bush. Still, the two branches had managed to act responsibly on a worsening national problem, despite the divided government in Washington.

In April 1990, a large number of Americans joined with millions of other people around the world in celebrating the twentieth anniversary of Earth Day. Environmental consciousness had recently been heightened when, in March 1989, the supertanker *Exxon Valdez* ran into a reef in Prince William Sound, Alaska, resulting in a huge oil spill that devastated miles of coastland and its wildlife. George Bush spoke of becoming "the environmental president," and he made a good beginning toward that end. He strengthened the Environmental Protection Agency, following in the footsteps of Richard Nixon, who had established it. Bush also signed the Clean Air Act of 1990, which raised emission standards for utilities and further increased the powers of the EPA. Automotive industry executives balked at the changes, which they claimed were directed more at U.S. automakers than foreign imports. The auto executives were in one respect correct, as U.S. cars were on average less fuel efficient and did have a higher emission level consequently. Ironically, the push for greater fuel efficiency would quickly fall to the wayside as oil prices consistently fell relative to inflation over the 1990s and American society began a love affair with the suburban utility vehicle (SUV) and other oversized vehicles.

Bush further distanced himself from the oil interests when he endorsed a moratorium on offshore oil-drilling along much of the American coastline. But Bush's zeal for the cause did not last, in part because of a slowdown in the economy and the influence of strong business interests. The Justice Department blocked the EPA's effort to prosecute large corporate polluters, the administration permitted more extensive drilling for petroleum in Alaska and greater commercial development of protected wetlands, and environmental controls frequently encountered opposition from the White House Council on Competitiveness, which emphasized the need for deregulation and economic growth. In 1992 the chief executive's loss of enthusiasm for the environmental movement was reflected in the fact that, ironically, the "environmental president" was the only head of state present who refused to sign a biological diversity treaty presented at the United Nations Earth Summit in Rio de Janeiro.

A telling sign of Bush's pragmatism was reflected in his reversed position in support of labor. After vetoing a measure to raise the minimum wage from $3.35 to $4.55 an hour, Bush signed a revised bill on April 1, 1990, increasing the minimum wage to $3.80 an hour and $4.25 a year later. In reality, the increase was well behind the cost of living increases in the majority of urban centers across the nation. In response, many cities began to legislate change independently of the president's national minimum wages by instituting living-wage regulations. Initially these living-wage levels were criticized by corporate America as well as many "mom and pop" businesses that claimed the wages increases would drive them out of business. In some cases this did, in fact, prove to be true, though the living-wage laws overwhelmingly proved successful.

On another front, the administration intensified the "war" on illegal drugs—a flourishing activity—but without notable success. In no small measure, the antiquated procedures of the Drug Enforcement Agency (DEA) did little to address a recently emerged spike in the national use of methamphetamine, or "crystal meth," a highly addictive stimulant. Over the next two decades, Americans' use of this dangerous and disfiguring drug would continue to escalate. The debate over whether the United States should legalize less powerful and addictive drugs, in particular marijuana, moved in a conservative direction in the wake of the heightened level of hard narcotic use, namely crack and methamphetamine. Small grassroots organizations did continue to push for the legalization of marijuana, which became the base for the medical marijuana movement. Its proponents argued that the perceived medical benefits derived from the plant made it a legitimate health aid for those who suffered from cancer, arthritis, and the effects of HIV-AIDS. While cities and states have passed medical marijuana laws that permit doctors to prescribe marijuana for their patients, the federal government has yet to change its laws concerning the drug, which has created a legal quandary.

In response to the conservative political backlash against the 1989 Supreme Court ruling that burning the American flag as a form of protest represented an expression of opinion protected by the First Amendment to the Constitution, President Bush urged the adoption of a constitutional amendment to permit legislation making desecration of the flag a criminal offense. Congress took a different approach by passing a measure making it illegal to burn or deface the flag. Although the Supreme Court invalidated that enactment, Congress continued to resist pressure for a constitutional amendment dealing with flag-burning.

The administration's conservative bias was also revealed in Bush's selection of Clarence Thomas for a vacancy on the Supreme Court in 1991.

A conservative African American, Thomas had recently been appointed to the federal Court of Appeals after serving as head of the Equal Employment Opportunity Commission. His nomination provoked a rancorous debate, highlighted by Senate hearings in which charges of sexual harassment against the nominee were made by a former associate named Anita Hill. The Thomas hearings were held on national television and drew considerable audiences. The Senate finally confirmed Thomas by the narrow margin of 52 to 48, and Clarence Thomas became the second African American to sit on the Supreme Court bench.

While Bush's presidency began smoothly and enjoyed considerable success, particularly in foreign affairs, it experienced difficult problems in 1991 and 1992. One constraint was Democratic control of the House and Senate, which endangered the administration's domestic program. A more immediate problem was the onset of a recession in the latter part of 1990, marked by slowing business activity and investment, rising unemployment, and declining consumer confidence. While the technology sector was just beginning to rise, the traditional backbone of the American economy, the automotive industry, continued to lose ground to Asian and European imports. Marked by two decades of continued decline in customer satisfaction and overall reliability, the Big Three, Chrysler, Ford and General Motors, had yet to realize a significant turnaround. While genuinely unrelated to his responsibilities as president, this economic downturn resulted in heavy criticism of Bush's leadership. For his part, Bush's public image cast him as being unsure of his major objectives and uncertain about the direction he should take. Furthermore, although a political moderate with a talent for negotiation, Bush provided little cooperative, bipartisan leadership, at least in dealing with domestic issues.

THE END OF THE COLD WAR

International relations absorbed George Bush more fully than domestic questions, and it fell to his lot to preside over a period of extraordinary change in world affairs. He was committed to continuing Reagan's foreign policies and emphasis on national security. Despite pressure to reduce the huge defense appropriations and new weapons systems, Bush was able to maintain the high level of military spending with only modest cuts. He invoked the image of a "new world order," but as a design for international relations the concept remained indistinct and rather abstract. His foreign policy was characterized by continuity, incrementalism, and stability.

One example of the pressure for change in various parts of the world was a protest movement in China, where students were demanding greater freedom, democracy, and a more open government. In the spring of 1989, large demonstrations in Beijing's Tiananmen Square finally resulted in the shooting of hundreds of unarmed protesters and the arrest and execution of student leaders. President Bush deplored this brutal repression by the Chinese government and suspended military sales and high-level exchange agreements with the People's Republic. At the same time, however, Bush endeavored to ease tension between the United States and China, even sending Brent Scowcroft, his national security adviser, to Beijing for secret talks with Chinese authorities. And when Congress passed a bill to protect Chinese students in the United States from punishment by their own government, the president vetoed the measure.

In December 1989, President Bush sent an invading force of 10,000 soldiers to Panama, ostensibly to protect the Panama Canal, defend American citizens, halt an enormous drug traffic through the republic, and apprehend General Manuel Antonio Noriega, head of the Panamanian Defense Forces and the country's strongman. Bush's action followed the administration's launching, in September 1989, of a highly publicized "war on drugs." Noriega had worked for the CIA and played a part in Oliver North's secret activities in Central America. Noriega's relationship with the CIA began in the 1950s, and he officially contracted with the agency in 1967. During George H. W. Bush's tenure as CIA director (1976-77), Noriega continued his CIA contract, which proved an embarrassment once Bush assumed the presidency. Noriega was known to be involved in drug trafficking and money laundering through Panamanian banks. He was also on friendly terms with Fidel Castro. In February 1988, federal grand juries in Miami and Tampa had indicted Noriega and fifteen others on drug charges, and soon afterward U.S. authorities froze Panama's assets in the United States. When Noriega annulled national elections held in May 1989, Bush sharply criticized his action and urged Panamanians to overthrow him.

Bush's decision to invade Panama was no doubt influenced by the death of a U.S. marine who was shot at a military roadblock in Panama. The American forces, eventually numbering about 25,000 troops, struck at various strategic targets on December 20, 1989, and the limited resistance was soon put down. It was obvious that many civilians welcomed the invaders. The "war," reminiscent of Reagan's military adventure in Grenada, had the flavor of a comic opera. General Noriega, who had sought sanctuary with the Vatican's papal nuncio, was subjected to a nonstop blast of rock and roll music at around 150 decibels courtesy of U.S. military personnel: a level of sound considered physically painful. After several days, the psychological tactic broke Noriega's resolve and he surrendered. Soon thereafter he was jailed in Miami to await trial. The fighting had cost the lives of twenty-three U.S. servicemen and several thousand Panamanians, many of them civilians caught in the cross fire of battle. Although Bush did not bother to consult Congress before the invasion, his action was popular with Americans. Nevertheless, his military intervention in the small republic came under fire in the Organization of American States and the United Nations.

In the case of other Central American nations, the Bush administration took a different approach. Taking advantage of the Esquipulas II agreement of 1987 and the preparatory work of Latin American leaders, the administration acted on Secretary of State James Baker's recommendation that the United States dissolve the contras and support an open election in Nicaragua. It was a gamble that paid off. American leaders persuaded Mikhail Gorbachev to stop supplying arms to Nicaragua and influence the Sandinistas to abide by the election results. To the surprise of many observers, the election—held in February 1990—resulted in a defeat for the Sandinistas, victory for a coalition led by Violeta Barros de Chamorro, and a peaceful transfer of power. Early in 1992, a peace treaty brought an end to the civil war in El Salvador, a conflict in which Reagan and Bush had aided the government in fighting left-wing rebels. It was clear that Bush and Baker had begun to encourage the United Nations to play a continuing role as peacemaker in Central America. Meanwhile, the end of the Cold War brought the drying up of Soviet aid to Castro and the growing isolation of Cuba.

As the year 1989 unfolded, it became apparent that the Soviet Union was on its last legs and that the Cold War was rapidly losing its intensity, if not ending, aided considerably by Nixon's détente and Reagan's military spending escalations. Mikhail Gorbachev employed all his political skill in an effort to prevent the deterioration of the USSR economy and to maintain the Soviet empire. His policies of perestroika (restructuring) and glasnost (openness) sought to limit the rigid restraints of central economic planning and censorship, encourage a more harmonious relationship with the West, and lead to a dramatic increase in foreign trade and investments, as well as relief from heavy military costs. In the end the liberal policies Gorbachev proclaimed, his abandonment of the Russian imperial design, and his desire to enter into a rapprochement with the West could not save the Soviet regime. An insurgent spirit moved through Eastern Europe and the Soviet republics. Communist Party rule came to an end in one satellite after another: Poland, Hungary, Czechoslovakia, Bulgaria, and Rumania, sometimes in the midst of violence. In November 1989, the Berlin Wall—symbol of bitter East-West division—was dismantled, with sections of it eventually displayed at the Nixon and Reagan presidential libraries. Finally, the Warsaw Pact was dissolved. Earlier in the year, on April 2, the *New York Times* took note of these developments: "The cold war of poisonous Soviet-American feelings, of domestic political hysteria, of events enlarged and distorted by East-West confrontation, of almost perpetual diplomatic deadlock is over."

How America should respond to these momentous events was not initially clear. It was not easy to determine how best to serve the national interest, especially over the long haul. Bush, like Reagan near the end of his presidency, wanted to encourage the Gorbachev revolution, profit from his initiatives on arms reduction, and bring the Cold War to an end on terms favorable to the West. Yet the American leader was deliberate and prudent, delaying any major commitment while evaluating the course of events in Gorbachev's crumbling empire. Bush first met with Gorbachev at Malta in December 1989, following several overtures from the Soviet leader. Although that conference produced no important agreements, the two men discussed important questions such as the reunification of East and West Germany and the status of the Baltic republics, matters on which they differed. They also considered the feasibility of additional arms-reduction treaties.

Bush and Gorbachev hit it off, and they soon developed a good working relationship. When the Soviet president visited Washington in the spring of 1990, he and Bush signed several significant documents. An arms-control agreement limited the long-range nuclear weapons of the two powers by fixing a ceiling for each side of 1,600 missiles and 6,000 warheads. The conferees also agreed to give up the manufacture of chemical weapons. Another accord was intended to promote trade between the United States and the Soviet Union. In August 1991, Bush and Gorbachev met in Moscow to sign the strategic arms reduction talks (START) treaty, which cut the nuclear arsenals of the two nations by one-fourth. Shortly after the Moscow conference, Communist hardliners tried to overthrow Gorbachev in what proved to be an abortive coup. The coup was foiled by the resistance of Boris Yeltsin, popular president of the Russian Republic, and opposition from the military. Bush moved quickly to give Yeltsin his support and persuade other world leaders to join him. Gorbachev reclaimed the presidency but found it expedient to give up his position as chairman of the Communist Party, which rapidly lost influence. Most of the Soviet republics soon proclaimed their independence. By the end of 1991, eleven of the fifteen former Soviet republics had become members of the Commonwealth of Independent States. Gorbachev's time had passed, and Yeltsin quickly emerged as the new leader of Russia.

Yeltsin needed assistance from the West and was willing to accept further reductions in Russian arms and make other concessions. Like Gorbachev before him, the Russian leader was caught up in the painful transition from a multinational regime to a national state, from a totalitarian to a democratic government, and from a rigid socialist economy to a free-market capitalist system. Bush took advantage of the opportunity. He announced in September 1991, for example, that the United States would destroy all of its tactical nuclear weapons on land and sea in Europe and Asia, take its long-range bombers off twenty-four-hour alert, and begin discussions with the Russians looking toward deeper cuts in the number of ICBMs with multiple warheads. In June 1992, while in Washington in search of economic aid, Yeltsin agreed to give up all of Russia's land-based MIRV missiles in a deal that only required the United States to reduce its submarine missile force by half. Since the Soviet Union officially ceased to exist on December 31, 1991, its former client states could no longer expect military and economic support from Moscow. Suddenly the United States was the only surviving superpower, an outcome that brought Americans satisfaction tinged with a vague apprehension about their nation's future role in world affairs. Though China, with its powerhouse economy, vast military reserves, and global interests, would in the next decade move into the role of superpower, for the time being America stood alone.

It was not long before the United States demonstrated its strength by intervening militarily in the Middle East. The intervention resulted from Iraq's abrupt invasion of its small, oil-rich neighbor, Kuwait, on August 1, 1990. The Iraqi dictator, Saddam Hussein, was frustrated over Kuwait's unilateral decision to increase its oil production—and thereby lower market prices for oil—at a time when Iraq desperately needed money. By annexing Kuwait, Saddam figured he could enhance his own position in determining the fortunes of Middle Eastern petroleum and possibly further his ambitions for a larger role in the Arab world. American leaders were surprised and alarmed by Iraq's aggression, in part because they thought it might threaten Saudi Arabia, a longtime ally. Ironically, the United States had tilted toward Iraq during the war between Iraq and Iran in the 1980s and had secretly provided Saddam with weapons and technology. The United States had a long-standing tradition of ignoring the ever increasing brutal violence demonstrated by Saddam as he held together a splintered Iraq—though subsequently the penchant Saddam had for terror would be exploited by the United States as a reason to go to war. Washington had valued Iraq as a trading partner and a bulwark against Islamic extremism in Tehran; however, loyalty to the Saudi Arabia, the world leader in oil production, won out.

Bush denounced the invasion of Kuwait as "naked aggression" and called the "integrity of Saudi Arabia" a matter of vital interest to America. He appealed to the leaders of other nations for support and welcomed the UN Security Council's 14 to 0 vote in condemning Iraq. In the months that followed, the president proved that he could be an effective leader. As historian Alonzo L. Hamby wrote, "He secured one United Nations resolution after another, orchestrated a largely effective economic embargo against Iraq, built a precarious coalition of Western and Arab states, put a half-million troops into Saudi Arabia, got a UN authorization to use force, and, most remarkably of all, obtained the functional equivalent of a declaration of war from a Democratic Congress." Still, Americans by no means agreed on the need for such decisive action.

A few days after the Iraqis moved into Kuwait, Bush dispatched American planes and troops to Saudi Arabia, a step he characterized as "wholly defensive," and two weeks later the United States began to mobilize its reserve forces for what became known as "Desert Shield." Early in November 1990, the president doubled American troops in the Middle East, from 200,000 to 400,000 men and women. In the meantime, he succeeded in bringing Gorbachev into the coalition against Iraq, even though that required the Russian leader to abandon an Arab ally. Bush, who doubted the effectiveness of economic sanctions against Iraq, pressed for more forceful action by the UN, and on November 29 that organization adopted Resolution 678, authorizing the use of force

Operation Desert Storm: General Colin Powell, chairman of the Joint Chiefs of Staff (second from left); Secretary of Defense Richard B. Cheney, and General Norman Schwarzkopf in the command center, Saudi Arabia. *Courtesy Defense Department, photograph by Master Sgt. Thomas Leigne, Jr..*

and a deadline of January 15, 1991, for Iraq's withdrawal from Kuwait. Public opinion in the United States was effectively shaped and thus was favorable to the Bush administration's arguments, although many questions remained and congressional debate exposed some strong opposition. Congress voted on January 12 to approve the use of American force by a slim margin of 250 to 183 in the House and 52 to 47 in the Senate. By the end of January, twenty-eight nations were committed to Operation Desert Shield, sixteen of which provided ground troops to the allied force.

Even so, "Desert Storm," the name given the allied assault, was in many respects an American war fought under United Nations authorization. The war started on January 17 (Baghdad time), when the first missiles and planes began to hit Iraqi targets. Controlling the air from the beginning, the allies conducted a spectacular air assault that featured precision strikes and the use of "smart bombs" guided by laser beams to their targets: Iraqi cities and the country's infrastructure suffered extensive damage. Saddam Hussein hoped that his soldiers, led by an elite unit called the Republican Guard, could entrench themselves in Kuwait and the southern Iraqi desert, thereby forcing the allies to wage an expensive land struggle. His forces, he promised, would fight the "mother of all battles." But the allied ground attack, which began on February 24, lasted only four days. The invading forces, under the command of U.S. General H. Norman Schwarzkopf, numbered almost 700,000. A contingent of about 200,000 troops—mainly American, British, and French—outflanked the Iraqi army and in a large armored battle routed the enemy in and near Kuwait, capturing thousands of soldiers. The allies were far superior to the Iraqi army in training, technology, and strategy, and they made excellent use of tactical airpower. On February 28, with Saddam's army melting away, President Bush called for a cease-fire, and Iraq agreed to an armistice.

The Gulf War was the focus of intensive media coverage, and Americans followed the action through frequent reports and televised scenes from the front. The nation had reason to savor its diplomatic and military triumph, and the returning soldiers were welcomed home with parades and celebrations. Iraqi aggression had been punished and Kuwait liberated. American casualties were light (only about 450), and the direct financial cost of the war to the United States was limited.

The conflict created an image of overwhelming American power. "By God," the president exclaimed, "we've licked the Vietnam syndrome once and for all"—by which he meant that Americans were no longer afraid to go to war.

Although Bush's leadership was impressive, he made noticeable mistakes in judgment. One was the failure of the president and other allied leaders to announce a clear objective in the war. It was widely understood that the coalition intended to make sure that Saddam Hussein was overthrown, and Bush hoped that the Iraqi people would attend to that. Indeed, Bush had sought to demonize Saddam during the war. At the same time, the Bush administration apparently assumed that preserving Iraq would help stabilize the region, and the Americans may have feared getting trapped in a Vietnam-type mission. In the aftermath of Desert Storm, civil war erupted in Iraq, resulting from the insurgency of a Shiite sect in the south and a large minority of Kurds—Sunni Muslims—in the north. Saddam put down these minorities with ruthless brutality. During this time, the UN was constantly frustrated in its efforts to locate and destroy Iraq's secret military arsenal. These developments contributed to Bush's declining popularity, the remarkable tailspin of which was also propelled downward by the impact of a flailing U.S. economy and a tax increase. In less than a year and a half, the chief executive's approval rating dropped from a spectacular 90 percent to a mere 29 percent. In what would many years hence prove ironic—after Bush's son President George W. Bush authorized a pre-emptive U.S. invasion of Iraq to overthrow Saddam Hussein, both Bush and Dick Cheney, then the secretary of defense, posited that it would have been folly for the U.S. forces to have toppled Hussein, for that would surely lead to a "quagmire," meaning a long and costly U.S. occupation of Iraq.

The United States continued to maintain a military presence in the Persian Gulf and to play a large part in Middle East diplomacy. Secretary Baker arranged a conference to consider the intractable problems that still divided Israel and the Arab states, but the immediate results were disappointing. In 1991 the administration lifted the economic sanctions the United States had adopted against South Africa in 1986. This followed President F. W. de Klerk's release of Nelson Mandela, leader of the African National Congress, from years of imprisonment and de Klerk's decision to abolish the nation's apartheid system. In the wake of their victory in the Gulf War and the knowledge that they had "won" the Cold War, Americans were often disconcerted by the ambiguities and unforeseen consequences of those successes. They discovered how rough the road to capitalism and democracy was in Eastern Europe, the horrors of ethnic and religious strife in Yugoslavia and other regions formerly in the Soviet empire, the challenges of the global recession of the early 1990s, and the difficulties at home stemming from America's relatively poor showing in the competition for international markets and the rising tide of illegal immigration to the United States. These international currents inevitably influenced the course of domestic politics.

RETURN OF THE DEMOCRATS

Although the Democrats maintained control of both houses of Congress in the midterm elections of 1990, the Republicans were confident of retaining possession of the presidency in 1992. George Bush's popularity during and for a time after the Gulf War made him seem invincible, and unfavorable conditions such as the slowdown in the economy did not appear insurmountable. Republicans were encouraged by their auspicious performance in presidential politics in the postwar period: the Grand Old Party had won seven of the eleven presidential elections since 1944 and five of the last six contests.

Yet there were more obstacles to Bush's re-election than he might have anticipated. One of the first was a challenge to his renomination by Patrick J. Buchanan, an ardent conservative and a White House aide during the Nixon and Reagan administrations. Bush won renomination, but in the process he made large concessions on social questions. Meanwhile, competition for the Democratic nomination was spirited, even though Governor Mario Cuomo of New York, Senator Bill Bradley of New Jersey, Jesse Jackson, and other prominent party leaders chose not to run. The contestants were Governors Bill Clinton of Arkansas and L. Douglas Wilder of Virginia, Senators Thomas R. Harkin of Iowa and Robert Kerrey of Nebraska, ex-governor Jerry Brown of California, and former senator Paul Tsongas of Massachusetts. A strong third-party candidate in the person of H. Ross Perot, a wealthy businessman and political maverick from Texas, also entered the race, enlivening the campaign and making its outcome more unpredictable.

In the long and grueling round of Democratic primaries, Governor Clinton soon emerged as the front-runner for the party's nomination. He had much strength as a candidate, most notably his apparent ability to connect with a wide range of voters, but some potential weaknesses included assertions that he was a womanizer. The allegation of the governor's affair with Gennifer Flowers, a state employee in Little Rock, led to national publicity and a crisis in Clinton's campaign. He and his wife, Hillary, fought back. They appeared on CBS' *60 Minutes,* admitting having had marital problems but declaring that they had worked them out. Clinton denied that he had a relationship with Flowers specifically, which then prompted Flowers to disclose that she had recorded conversations with the former Arkansas governor. While some analysts were skeptical of the veracity of the tapes, Clinton was humiliated, though not destroyed, as he managed to sustain his campaign and go on to win the Democratic nomination. Clinton then decided, to the surprise of many observers, on Senator Albert Gore of Tennessee as his running mate. Gore, like Clinton, was a product of the 1960s. He brought significant strength to the ticket: Washington experience, leadership on environmental and arms-control issues, military service, and an attractive family. The Democrats, in the words of one journalist, had a ticket of two "southern progressives without the baggage of liberal excess." And it was significant that both Clinton and Gore were Southerners.

Clinton, in his fight for the nomination, had promised to revive, unify, and reform the Democratic Party. The Arkansan attacked what he called the "trickle down" economic policies of Reagan and Bush, and he sometimes described himself as being in the New Deal tradition. (Democrats associated Bush with Herbert Hoover.) Clinton pointed to the growing disparity between the rich and poor in America, the loss of real income by workers and the middle class, and the Bush administration's seeming indifference to the nation's economic problems. But the governor also portrayed himself as a "new Democrat," a moderate and a man of the center—not a big tax-and-spend Democrat. He returned again and again to his commitment to get the economy moving, create new jobs, and use education and technology as a means of making the nation more productive and more competitive in the global economy. While pledging himself to a determined attack on the budget deficit, he urged the adoption of a comprehensive health care plan and reform of the welfare system. Although the Democratic leader made a special appeal to middle-class Americans, he sought to define himself and his party in still broader terms. He conveyed the idea, journalist Thomas Byrne Edsall notes, of "a more inclusive, less divisive national politics."

Clinton proved exceptionally masterful during the course of the campaign. He not only appeared on the traditional television programs, but also surprised the nation, apparently in a favorable fashion, when he played the saxophone on Arsenio Hall's late night variety show. While Bill Clinton clearly demonstrated a familiarity with the sax, his theatrical skill was considerable: he donned dark sunglasses and played the classic Elvis Presley hit "Heartbreak Hotel." This demonstration of "hipness" endeared him with the nation's youth as well as the baby boomers. On one occasion, however, a Clinton response came across as less than honest. When asked if he had ever smoked marijuana, he responded that he had, though he never inhaled. His response came across as ridiculous to many, though it did not seem to wound his push for the White House too deeply, much in the same way that his infidelity had been relegated to the sidelines. A fairly significant portion of American society seemed willing to accept the flawed but still likeable Bill Clinton.

As the Clinton campaign gathered momentum, George Bush and Ross Perot were waging strenuous campaigns of their own. Emphasizing his foreign policy experience and accomplishments, Bush criticized what he considered the Democrats' fiscal recklessness and refusal to cooperate with him in Congress. He made sly references to Clinton's character and patriotism, raising questions about his opponent's avoidance of the draft during the Vietnam War and a chameleon-like pattern of attitudes and positions that led some observers to call the governor "slick Willy." The Republicans also fought a "culture war" in which Vice President Quayle and his wife Marilyn led the charge against homosexuals, radical feminists, and cultural permissiveness—all of which, they inferred, was somehow related to Democratic liberalism. Meanwhile, Perot began a grassroots campaign to end "political gridlock" in Washington and balance the budget. The Texas billionaire brought an exciting vitality to presidential politics before dropping out of the race, only to return in response to the entreaties of his supporters. Near the end of the election struggle, Bush's attacks on Clinton began to strike home, and the president scored telling points in criticizing the inconsistencies in the Democratic nominee's economic proposals and weaknesses in his governorship of Arkansas. Television played a major role in the election, shaping the campaign and linking the political and the personal. Three presidential debates in which Perot participated were held, and the vice-presidential nominees met in one debate.

While Clinton led in the opinion polls during most of the campaign, Bush's late surge and the effect of Perot's candidacy made the outcome doubtful. In the end, the Democrats recaptured the White House and preserved their majorities in the Senate and House of Representatives. Although Clinton and Gore had a solid electoral majority of 370 to 168, they received only 43 percent of the popular vote to 37.7 percent for Bush and Quayle and an impressive 18.9 percent for Perot. Even though the majority of voters cast their ballot against Bill Clinton, he still captured the White House. The Democratic ticket swept the Northeast, won seven of the eleven western states, divided the Midwest with the Republicans, and made the party competitive again in the South by capturing five of thirteen states. Bush performed best in the South. Women made unprecedented gains in the congressional races. Eleven women won major party nominations for the Senate, and five—all Democrats—were elected, among them Barbara Boxer and Dianne Feinstein of California. Carol Moseley-Braun of Illinois became the first black woman to be elected to the U.S. Senate.

The failure of Bush's bid for re-election represented the first defeat of an elected incumbent Republican since Herbert Hoover in 1932. The flatness of the economy hurt Bush, while, paradoxically, the end of the Cold War effectively eliminated a traditional source of Republican strength with voters. Bush's early complacency and lack of real interest in domestic issues weakened his campaign. Despite the efforts of Bush strategists, the GOP media blitz proved less successful than in 1988, both because electronic journalists displayed greater caution in reporting accusations as straight news and the fact that the Clinton team responded quickly to Republican attacks. The disgust and anger many Americans felt for politicians and government, particularly in Washington, fostered a mood of political insurgency that helps explain Perot's remarkable appeal. The Texan's feisty personality, "let's do it" confidence, and outsider image were equally important.

In the month after his defeat at the polls, on December 24, 1992, President Bush pardoned several of his former colleagues who had been associated with the Iran-Contra scandal. At the top of the list was former secretary of defense Caspar Weinberger, who had been indicted in 1988 on several counts of perjury. Weinberger had also been accused by the media and several Democrats of either gross negligence or outright corruption when it became public knowledge that under his watch, the Defense Department had overpaid for virtually every item it purchased from the public sector. Though Bush's pardons were legal, many felt that he demonstrated a significant lack of ethics and had subverted justice. At the very least, his decision to pardon several high-ranking officials connected with the Iran-Contra scandal cast a shadow over his departure from office and Bush himself as a purveyor of political cronyism and Washington insider.

Bill Clinton actually benefited from being perceived as a candidate from outside the Washington beltway. His success was encouraged by the relative weakness of established liberal groups and the emphasis on individual candidates in the primaries. Following his nomination, the Arkansas governor and his advisers developed an effective campaign organization and devised a good electioneering strategy. Clinton was an articulate and attractive campaigner who dealt skillfully with the issues and conveyed a sense of concern and compassion for the disadvantaged, as well as working people and the middle class. He restored at least a semblance of the old Democratic coalition, including elements of the middle class. Historian Kevin P. Phillips suggests that Clinton tapped the "middle-class anger and fear of the economic future." The question had become whether the return of the Democrats to 1600 Pennsylvania Avenue would make a significant difference.

CLINTON AND THE PERILS OF PRESIDENTIAL LEADERSHIP

The forty-second president of the United States was a southerner, the third chief executive from that region since World War II and the first to begin life in the postwar period. William Jefferson Clinton was born on August 19, 1946, in Hope, Arkansas, a small town in the southwestern part of the state. Clinton's early years were strongly influenced by his mother and his maternal grandparents, Edith and Eldridge Cassidy, with whom he sometimes lived, and by one of his high school teachers. He grew up in Hot Springs, a larger town in west central Arkansas, attending the local schools and graduating from Hot Springs High School in 1964. He was a bright, friendly, and popular lad who had already revealed an aptitude for leadership and an instinct for achievement. During the next few years, the young Arkansan blossomed as his intellectual interests became more focused and his horizons expanded. He managed to attend Georgetown University in Washington, D.C., and to become a part-time aide in the office of Senator J. William Fulbright; his college years gave him a view of the nation's capital and encouraged his study of American politics and government. After Georgetown, he went to Oxford University as a Rhodes Scholar, followed by three years at the Yale Law School and graduation in the class of 1973.

Clinton then returned to Arkansas, where he intended to enter politics. He obtained a position as assistant professor in the University of Arkansas Law School, almost won a seat in Congress in 1974, and was elected attorney general of Arkansas two years later. In 1978 he won the governorship. In the meantime, he was married to Hillary Rodham, a Yale classmate. Although he was defeated for re-election in 1980, a banner year for Ronald Reagan and other Republican candidates, Clinton regained the office in 1982, serving until he was elected president a decade later. He became known as one of the "new" southern Democrats—a moderate, a reformer, a man who could build coalitions and win elections. The governor's national orientation was reflected in his participation in the Democratic Leadership Council, a moderate group in the national party. In July 1992 the Alabama editor Brandt Ayers wrote of Clinton:

> He is a charming, manipulative cultivator of friends who can help him win and govern with a tough, relentless and retentive mind; he is sometimes inconsistent, always energetic and a joyous, optimistic practitioner of the art of politics and an assiduous student of public policy; a man with a life-long fondness for power and a clear understanding of how to get it and use it to achieve results; a warm and passionate man with an intelligent, patient and forgiving wife, a man who is capable of both courage and infidelity.

In the weeks following his election as president, Clinton prepared to take over the White House. He and many other Democrats seemed

The inauguration of the forty-second president, January 20, 1993. *Courtesy the White House.*

to think that the Reagan revolution was over and a new day of Democratic reform was dawning. In his inaugural address on January 20, 1993, Clinton spoke of "American renewal." The incoming administration made plans to stimulate the economy, reduce the deficit, create a national health-care system, and move forward on other reform fronts. Clinton and his team would soon learn that politics inside the Washington beltway was considerably more complex than in Little Rock. Still, the America that Clinton inherited was poised for a period of economic expansion that many historians and economists have viewed as the greatest in the nation's history. While Clinton came to have his challenges in Washington, most Americans enjoyed their prosperity, and a considerable drop in voter participation followed. In effect, the supervision of Washington by the people fell to the wayside at the perilous moment when Washington took on the role of monitoring the world as well as governing the United States.

———— ★ ————

SUGGESTIONS FOR FURTHER READING

The personal memoirs of George H. W. Bush, *All the Best, George Bush: My Life in Letters and Other Writings* (2000), are among the weakest of any former president.

There is neither a good biography of George Bush nor an adequate treatment of his administration, but see Michael Duffy, *Marching in Place: The Status Quo Presidency of George Bush* (1992), and *George H. W. Bush: The American Presidents Series: The 41st President, 1989-1993* (2007), by Timothy Naftali and Arthur M. Schlesinger, Jr. Two useful essays on Bush can be found in Robert A. Wilson, ed., *Character Above All: Ten Presidents from FDR to George Bush* (1995), and Shogan, *The Riddle of Power,* cited before. Colin Campbell and Bert A. Rockman, eds., *The Bush Presidency: First Appraisals* (1991), is an early evaluation by several scholars.

For American diplomacy and the end of the Cold War, consult Gaddis, *The United States and the End of the Cold War,* mentioned earlier; Raymond L. Garthoff, *Deterrence and the Revolution in Soviet Military Doctrine* (1990); James Chace, *The Consequences of the Peace* (1992); and Michael R. Beschloss and Strobe Talbott, *At the Highest Levels: The Inside Story of the End of the Cold War* (1993). The general works cited before also throw light on President Bush's international leadership.

The Gulf War is examined in Alex Roberto Hybel, *Power Over Rationality: The Bush Administration and the Gulf Crisis* (1993); Lawrence Freedman and Efraim Karsh, *The Gulf Conflict, 1990–1991: Diplomacy and War in the New World Order* (1993); and John Mueller, *Policy and Opinion in the Gulf War* (1994). See also Colin L. Powell, with Joseph E. Persico, *My American Journey* (1996); *Crusade: The Untold Story of the Persian Gulf War,* by Rick Atkinson (1994); and *The Generals' War: The Inside Story of the Conflict in the Gulf,* by Michael R. Gordon and General Bernard E. Trainor (1995).

National politics and the presidential election of 1992 are treated in several journalistic accounts: Jack W. Germond and Jules Witcover, *Mad as Hell: Revolt at the Ballot Box, 1992* (1993); Charles F. Allen, *The Comeback Kid: The Life and Career of Bill Clinton* (1992); and Ken Gross, *Ross Perot: The Man Behind the Myth* (1992).

———★———

The Booming Nineties: Clinton, Impeachment, and the High Flying Economy

F OR ALL ITS HIGH HOPES, CLINTON'S PRESIDENCY got off to a wobbly start, one exacerbated by a series of blunders in top-level appointments, a decision to fire the carryover travel personnel in the White House, and a young and inexperienced White House staff. Clinton also encountered stiff opposition in Congress. His $16.3 billion plan to revive a lackluster economy collapsed in a Senate filibuster engineered by minority leader Robert Dole. The incoming president found it necessary to make some hard choices involving economic policy. Notwithstanding his campaign commitments, he decided to attack the budget deficit with a reduction proposal of $500 billion over a five-year period. Clinton and his advisers assumed, correctly as it turned out, that this would bring a fall in interest rates and an increase in investments. Still, it was a painful process, and Congress approved the necessary legislation by the slimmest of margins. Clinton had to jettison his plans for a middle-class tax cut and an appropriation for the development of "human capital," since his budget package provided for a $250-billion tax increase and spending cuts of about the same amount. The burden of the tax hike fell on the well-to-do, and Congress finally agreed to fund some of the domestic programs Clinton wanted.

Another initiative upset the military. During the recent campaign, Clinton had made a commitment to end the ban on gays and lesbians in the armed forces, but his attempt to implement the change aroused controversy and resistance, in and out of Congress. Military authorities generally viewed the proposal as a menace to discipline and order in the ranks, and opponents warned against "feminization" and predatory gay men. According to one marine general, the president's plan "threatens the strong, conservative, moralistic tradition of the troops." Clinton failed to make a strong case for the new policy, tried to placate his opponents, and in the summer of 1993 accepted a "compromise." The result was a "don't ask, don't tell" policy that made little change in the "military closet." Clinton proved far weaker in comparison to Harry S. Truman who, through an executive order, desegregated the military. The Clinton conciliation permitted gays and lesbians to serve in the military, but only by keeping their sexual orientation secret. In effect, the policy encouraged dishonesty.

This setback and others like it revealed the illusion of assuming that Democratic control of the presidency and Congress would lead to concerted reform. Instead, as the historian Alan Brinkley has pointed out, Clinton took office with "no mandate, no war, no party." His election with 43 percent of the popular vote was certainly no mandate, while the end of the Cold War weakened the president vis-à-vis Congress and removed a unifying force among legislators in dealing with national policy. The divided and often clashing elements within the Democratic Party also presented the chief executive with difficult problems. In addition, the new administration, eager to move ahead with its ambitious agenda, failed to establish a clear set of priorities and mobilize maximum support for its most important proposals. In the struggle to save as much of his program as possible in 1993, Clinton abandoned the middle-class tax cut and postponed welfare reform and stronger regulation of campaign finance. Freedom of choice legislation to establish a woman's right to an abortion languished in Congress, while a measure to authorize the funding of abortion for poor women under Medicaid was rejected by both houses. A bill to bar companies from permanently replacing striking workers was stalled in the Senate.

Nonetheless, the administration could point to several congressional successes. Indeed, the *Congressional Quarterly* reported that during the first session of the 103rd Congress the president got his way on

86 percent of 191 roll call votes on which he took a position. Clinton and other Democratic leaders could claim much of the credit for the budget reduction act, and they had a major hand in the passage of the Brady handgun bill, a measure to protect the disabled, and the family leave act. The last of these enactments provided many workers with the right to unpaid leave from work for childbearing, family illness, and other needs. A more significant Clinton victory was congressional approval of the North American Free Trade Agreement (NAFTA), negotiated by the Bush administration in August 1992. The agreement, signed by Canada, Mexico, and the United States, created a single trading bloc with more people and greater production than the European Community. Nonetheless, the passage of NAFTA divided the Democratic Party and faced determined opposition from organized labor and blue-collar workers. Critics charged that it would result in the loss of millions of American jobs as U.S. firms moved south to take advantage of cheap Mexican labor. Clinton and other advocates made a strong case for NAFTA and won a bipartisan vote of approval in both chambers. To this day, however, critics of NAFTA have consistently argued that the alliance has strongly aided Mexico and Canada while negatively affecting the U.S. economy, in particular those in the blue-collar ranks.

The administration later succeeded in lowering trade barriers among members of the General Agreement on Tariffs and Trade (GATT), although GATT was replaced in 1995 by the establishment of the World Trade Organization (WTO). The WTO has more than 150 member nations, and its primary function is to regulate trade on a global level and provide smaller, poorer nations with an equitable opportunity in international trade markets. Much like GATT, there is an emphasis on tariffs. The WTO also serves as a negotiating organization that assists in the development of trade agreements. The WTO has also consistently had its share of critics, who have primarily alleged that rather than achieving its objectives to stimulate global economic growth and encourage free trade, it has eroded the labor class economically while assisting the economic elite.

The popularity of the Clinton administration seemed to improve late in 1993, following favorable congressional action on NAFTA and the Brady bill. The latter, fiercely opposed by the National Rifle Association, provided for a seven-day waiting period in which authorities could check the criminal and mental records of a would-be handgun purchaser. Clinton's own approval rating, after sinking to historic lows for a first-year president, moved up to 60 percent. In 1994 the administration's concentration on national health care, anticrime legislation, and welfare reform became yet another rollercoaster ride. The outcome for each proposal was disappointing, and the major parts of Clinton's program died on the vine during the second session of the 103rd Congress. An overhaul of the welfare system met with delay, and a lobbying disclosure bill, a campaign finance measure, and stronger environmental regulations ran into congressional roadblocks. Clinton and other champions of a comprehensive anticrime bill, stymied by strong bipartisan opposition, were finally able to pass their legislation. The anticrime act of 1994 provided for tougher penalties, additional prisons, prevention programs, and up to 100,000 new police officers on the streets. It also banned nineteen kinds of assault weapons and authorized the expenditure of $30.2 billion. Later in his term, Clinton signed a broad antiterrorist bill and urged a further expansion of federal authority to counter terrorism. His anticrime efforts—and greater emphasis on the victims of crime than on the rights of criminal defendants—enabled him to challenge the longtime Republican monopoly on the crime issue.

In response to the national call to embrace greater diversity, Clinton took pains to strengthen the role of women and minorities at the policy-making level of his administration. His cabinet included three women, two African Americans, and two Hispanic Americans. Women were also selected as ambassador to the United Nations, director of the EPA, and chair of the president's Council of Economic Advisers. Ruth Bader Ginsberg was later appointed by the president to the Supreme Court, and in Clinton's second term, Madeleine Albright became the first female secretary of state.

The centerpiece of Clinton's domestic program in 1994 was national health care. Concerned over the rapidly mounting costs and inadequate coverage of the existing system—Medicare and Medicaid payments rose from $48 billion to $195 billion between 1980 and 1992—Clinton boldly set about establishing a genuine national health-care system. Once in office, he created a task force led by his wife, Hillary Rodham Clinton, and Ira C. Magaziner, a business entrepreneur and public policy consultant, to develop a proposal. The administration's plan, made public in October 1993, precipitated heated controversy, sophisticated lobbying, and powerful opposition.

Designed to provide all Americans with medical and dental coverage and a variety of preventive services, the scheme revolved around the concept of "managed competition." It would control costs by limiting Medicare and Medicaid reimbursements, putting a cap on health insurance premiums, promoting competition among providers, and improving the efficiency of health care in the United States. The proposal would enroll all Americans in large regional purchasing groups—health alliances—created by the states to monitor costs and negotiate with health-care providers. Individuals would join either a fee-for-service plan, under which they could choose their own physicians, or a less expensive health maintenance organization (HMO), under which they would be limited to doctors belonging to that HMO. The self-employed would purchase tax deductible insurance. Medicaid would continue to serve the poor. A seven-member national health board appointed by the president would oversee the operation of the health-care system, monitor the quality of care, and prepare a national health budget. The plan called for about $100 billion in added initial costs, most of which would be paid for by higher taxes on tobacco.

Many members of Congress, Democrats as well as Republicans, found fault with the administration's plan, and the measure's sponsors had to run an intimidating gauntlet of insurance and business lobbies. The administration made almost no effort to attract the support of Republicans, who denounced the proposal as "socialized medicine," and the plan's architects managed to alienate a number of crucial Democrats and interest groups. One of the greatest miscalculations, though, was Bill Clinton's choice of placing First Lady Hillary Clinton in a leadership role for the health care program. As many critics pointed out, Hillary had not been elected to serve in office, nor had she been appointed through the traditional federal procedures. Clinton and his advisers belatedly recognized that the legislation was in trouble, and in late June the president authorized Senator George J. Mitchell and Representative Richard A. Gephardt to make concessions in a search for common ground. By this point, however, it was too late: Mitchell and Gephardt were unable to make progress, even when they presented their own watered down versions of the administration's bill. Neither house ever voted on the Clinton health-reform plan.

Nor did Congress approve a less ambitious scheme, such as a proposal associated with Secretary of the Treasury Lloyd Bentsen. Many observers had assumed that the widespread support for health-care legislation in some form would almost certainly result in the adoption of secondary reforms such as "portability," a guarantee that workers who changed jobs could retain their medical insurance; a ban on refusing to insure those with pre-existing conditions; some kind of across the board pricing to reduce the premium penalty on the self-employed and small entrepreneurs; and a rule to require insurers to offer comparable packages and disclose statistics—enabling health-insurance buyers to make meaningful comparisons among different plans.

Even with more effective leadership and more favorable circumstances, such a sweeping reform would have been very hard to enact, given the formidable array of economic and political obstacles in its path. Clinton and others involved in formulating the plan and devising the tactics for its enactment made mistakes—insisting on too much, being too inflexible, and delaying negotiations for a compromise. By doing most of its work in secret, the task force missed an opportunity to inform the public about a complicated problem and denied itself a chance to find out how the public thought about the issue. Surprisingly, administration leaders misjudged the political environment in which they were operating. They did not seem to recognize the limits on the president's authority imposed by the election returns of 1992. As Thomas Edsall suggests, Clinton's election was a victory for "moderate centrism," not a victory for 1960s liberalism.

The defeat of Clinton's health-care reform had far-reaching consequences for the administration and for national politics. It was a significant factor in the mid-term elections of 1994. Led by Representative Newt Gingrich of Georgia and a ten-point program outlined in their "Contract with America," the Republicans conducted a spirited campaign in the fall, winning control not only of the Senate but of the House of Representatives as well. In January 1995, Republicans assumed control of the House for the first time in forty years. Analysts noted that the Democratic turnout in 1994 was very low, falling a million votes below that of the 1990 election, while GOP candidates attracted 9 million more votes than they had in 1990.

Clinton's audacious attempt to establish universal, affordable health care did stimulate developments in the private sector. By 1996, health maintenance organizations were booming, 58 million Americans were enrolled in prepaid health plans, and three-fourths of the physicians had converted at least part of their practice into work for HMOs and health-care companies. Still, some 41 million Americans had no health insurance whatsoever. A *New York Times* poll in June 1996 revealed that two-thirds of the respondents blamed the Republican Congress more than the Democratic president for the failure to enact national health-care legislation. Ironically, Clinton found reason to defend the system he had tried to make over. As the presidential campaign of 1996 approached, health care seemed to have disappeared as a major issue, and Congress appeared ready to turn Medicaid into a block-grant program under full control of the states.

President Clinton changed course after the Republicans won control of Congress in 1994, using the powers of his office to blunt the far-reaching GOP agenda and striving to make incremental gains of his own. Two domestic concerns illustrate the defensive posture the Clinton administration now assumed. One was the protection of the environment; the other was welfare reform. The administration's early

Professor John Hope Franklin and President Clinton at the White House.

environmental efforts proved disappointing to many environmentalists. Despite the president's commitment to a vigorous federal role in
safeguarding the environment—and the leadership of Vice President
Gore and Secretary of the Interior Bruce Babbitt—few initiatives in
this area succeeded during the first part of Clinton's term. The administration retreated from its proposal to increase grazing fees on public
lands, abandoned the idea of imposing an energy tax, and gave up
on its plan to elevate the EPA to cabinet status. Clinton himself was
uncertain about the best approach, torn between what the *New York
Times* described as "economic forces and ecological imperatives." He
wanted to satisfy both sides, but in seeking consensus he moved from
one confrontation to another. In 1995 he reluctantly signed a bill that
removed some environmental restrictions and permitted increased
logging in national forests. Even so, the administration endeavored to
follow its own course, speeding the cleanup of Superfund toxic waste
sites, employing the Endangered Species Act to negotiate broad compromises that would preserve habitats, and using presidential vetoes
or the threat thereof to prevent the Republican Congress from cutting back the federal role in protecting the environment. After years
of debate, Congress approved a large expansion of the national park
system in California; the lawmakers also passed a new pesticides bill
similar to the one Clinton had proposed three years earlier and legislation to make drinking water safer. Clinton's defensive tactics seemed
to work. Polls showed that most people wanted to protect the environment even if it meant the loss of jobs in their own communities. In
addition, people trusted the president more than they did Congress to
protect the environment—by a margin of nearly two to one.

As a candidate in 1992, Clinton had expressed his determination to
"end welfare as we know it" and "empower people with the education,
training, and child care they need" to break "the cycle of dependency."
As president, he recommended an increase in welfare spending of $10
billion to accomplish these objectives. But Clinton's decision to emphasize health-care reform in 1993 caused him to delay action on welfare
reform, and he did not formally present a reform bill until the summer of
1994. The measure made no progress in that election year, and when the
104th Congress convened early in 1995, the legislature was controlled
by Republicans. Although Clinton seemed to be sympathetic with more

stringent welfare requirements and a larger role for the states in developing their individual welfare systems, he resisted Republican efforts to make drastic cuts in welfare spending and transform the national system. As one commentator said, Clinton borrowed the Republicans' language of values but blocked their most far-reaching plans to reshape the federal government. He vetoed two GOP welfare bills before agreeing in the summer of 1996 to sign a third measure.

In signing the Republicans' welfare bill, the president characterized it as deeply flawed; he was especially critical of the severe cuts in food stamp funds and provisions blocking legal immigrants from receiving an array of social services. The statute provided for a reduction of $56 billion in welfare expenditures over six years, gave the states broad new powers to run their own welfare and work programs with lump sums of federal money, and laid down strict eligibility and work requirements. The law represented one of the most sweeping reversals of social policy since the New Deal. The Clinton administration and its constituencies were divided over this welfare "reform," and some observers predicted that it would lead to a bitter struggle within the Democratic Party. Senator Daniel Patrick Moynihan, one of the Democrats who voted against the measure, remarked, "I wonder if the nation is ready for the profound social change that this legislation will set in motion." While the poorest people in the nation felt keenly the sting of the reduction in welfare spending, for some among that classification, the 1990s brought opportunities for relief.

Native Americans, historically the poorest ethnic group in the United States throughout the twentieth century, were able to become economically self-reliant on an unprecedented scale following the 1987 Supreme Court decision *California* v. *Cabazon Band of Mission Indians,* which upheld Native American rights to operate gaming facilities on their sovereign land if gaming were permitted within their state of residence. Many states, led by California, responded to the successful Indian court case by lobbying Congress for legislation that would place state control over Indian gaming. The result was the passage in 1988 of the Indian Gaming Regulatory Act (IGRA). IGRA established National Indian Gaming Commission and required governors to negotiate compacts with gaming tribes on the modes of gaming permitted and size of casinos allowed. In most cases, revenue sharing by the tribes with local and

A group of Ute drummers at Fort Duchesne, Utah, reflects the desire of many modern Indian communities to maintain their cultural identities. *Courtesy Newberry Library.*

state governments became the central point of negotiation. While perceived by many as a tax on the Indian casinos, the wording of the IGRA specifically refers to the exchange of monies from Indian tribes to state as "shared revenue," as federal law prohibits states from taxing Indian tribal income. (The income of individual American Indians is not, of course, exempt.) Gaming tribes across the nation quickly realized significant economic gains, which they successfully applied to rebuilding their respective communities, providing health care and educational opportunities for their tribal members, in effect beginning a process of rebuilding their sovereign nations.

INTERNATIONAL CHALLENGES

Clinton's handling of defense issues and foreign affairs was shaky and inconsistent during his first years in office, his relationship with the Pentagon and its boosters always shaky. As a president without military experience and one criticized by his political opponents as a "draft dodger," he was condemned in military circles for attempting to remove the ban on homosexuals in the armed forces. The new president had also wanted to reduce military appropriations, and he presented a plan for national service that offered young Americans educational benefits in return for community service. Yet Clinton and Secretary of Defense Leslie Aspin recommended only modest cuts in military spending, made little effort to trim new weapons programs, and later supported an increase in defense funds. Nevertheless, some of Clinton's critics seemed to feel that he was unfit to be commander in chief. Senator Jesse Helms warned that the chief executive had "better have a bodyguard" if he visited North Carolina because he had "serious problems with his record of draft avoidance, with his stand on homosexuals in the military and with the declining defense capability of American's armed forces."

A series of foreign crises, some of which were related to the collapse of the Soviet empire, complicated America's international role in the early 1990s. Clinton's inexperience and the idealistic positions he had taken in his election campaign sometimes resulted in contradiction and confusion. One such example was the African nation of Somalia, caught in the grip of a cruel civil war and a terrible famine. President George H. W. Bush had ordered American troops to participate in a United Nations effort to provide relief and restore order to Somalia, and Clinton continued to support that humanitarian mission. However, the tragic events that took place on October 3–4, 1993, known as the Battle of Mogadishu, shocked the American people. On the first day, two MH-60 Blackhawk helicopters were shot down by Somali rocket-propelled grenades in the city of Mogadishu. Those soldiers who survived the crash landings soon found themselves surrounded by a swarm of hostile Somali militiamen. Over the course of the night, a few thousand Somali militiamen had gathered in repeated attempts to overtake the stranded soldiers, who, through intrepid use of salvaged materials, were able to build makeshift fortifications that saved many of their lives. In the early morning hours of the fourth, a rescue taskforce managed to extract most of the stranded men, but one of the pilots, Michael Durant, remained in the hands of his Somali captors for two weeks. Ultimately, all of the bodies of the fallen U.S. military personnel were recovered through diplomatic channels, although their remains had been grossly disfigured. All told during the incident, U.S. forces suffered nineteen fatalities and more than eighty wounded, while the

Somali casualty figure is believed to lie somewhere between 700 and 2,000 killed in action and in excess of 1,000 wounded. The commanding American officer, General William F. Garrison, accepted responsibility for the tragedy, one that had a powerful influence on the shaping of U.S. foreign policy. Clinton later refused to commit U.S. troops to help halt an outbreak of violence and genocide in the African state of Rwanda, asserting that American interests were not at stake there. In the meantime, the president retreated from his bold call for the protection of human rights in the People's Republic of China; he decided, instead, that American interests, including trade opportunities, would be better served by continuing China's most favored nation status.

Early in April 1993, Clinton met with his Russian counterpart, Boris Yeltsin, in Vancouver, Canada. The two leaders got along well, and the American became convinced of the need to support Yeltsin's plans for Russia's transition to a new era. Clinton led the West in a program of economic aid and technical assistance to promote democracy and a market economy in Russia.

He was uncertain, however, about a policy to address the protracted civil war in Yugoslavia, once dominated by the Soviet Union and now the source of a major crisis in Europe. The forces caught up in that conflict shifted, but at its heart lay Croatian and Bosnian resistance to Serbian determination to maintain control over the former federation of Yugoslav republics. In the campaign of 1992, Clinton had criticized Bush for not doing more to relieve the beleaguered Bosnians, but once in the White House the Arkansan appeared unable to devise a firm policy, probably because he could not figure out how to influence the war's outcome without risking American lives. He seemed to think that the war was basically a European problem. As for the Europeans, they waited and watched, debating the pros and cons of diplomatic mediation, economic sanctions, and military intervention—and whether the United Nations, the European Union (successor to the European Community), or the American-dominated NATO should lead. The Clinton administration finally took a more positive step in the spring of 1994 by joining an international effort to limit the war with the threatened use of NATO air power. Bosnia, more than any other international problem, would dominate Clinton's foreign policy and define its character.

The Clinton administration was less restrained in responding to a festering sore nearer home. The West Indies republic of Haiti, a onetime protectorate of the United States, replaced its repressive government in 1990 by electing as president a charismatic Catholic priest and reformer named Jean-Bertrand Aristide. When Aristide was overthrown by the Haitian army in October 1991, the United States and eventually the UN Security Council imposed an economic blockade on the military regime in an effort to restore Aristide to power. Clinton increased the pressure on the Haitian government, deflected a congressional move to ban the use of U.S. troops in Haiti, and intervened with military force in the fall of 1994, acting under a United Nations resolution. He created a situation in which American casualties would be limited, and the military regime departed the scene quietly. Aristide resumed his office, American troops remained temporarily to guarantee the transition and train the police, and the United States provided the new government with economic assistance. Clinton—and most other Americans—wanted democracy to work in Haiti, but the overriding reason for intervention was the growing stream of Haitian emigrants heading northwest. The success of the Aristide government could stanch a flow of unwanted immigrants to the United States.

Perhaps Clinton thought that bold initiatives abroad would compensate for the failure of his principal domestic reforms. He undoubtedly counted Haiti as an important accomplishment. It is also clear that the frustration of the administration's health-care legislation and the smashing Republican victory in the elections of 1994 ended any chance Clinton had of carrying through his broad domestic reform program, at least before the election of 1996. Republicans in the House, led by a confident and energetic Speaker Gingrich, moved forward to enact their Contract with America, supported by the GOP-controlled Senate. They passed a resolution calling for a balanced budget by 2002. They made radical changes in the welfare system and came close to transforming the federal role in health care. They were unable to complete their so-called revolution, however, because of Democratic opposition in Congress and particularly in the White House, as Clinton began to use his veto power more freely. In December 1995, for instance, he vetoed a budget reconciliation bill that would have slashed federal spending by $894 billion over seven years, including $270 billion from Medicare and

$175 billion from various entitlement programs, while calling for $245 billion in tax cuts. In January 1996, he vetoed a harshly restrictive welfare "reform" measure.

If Clinton had become more combative in dealing with the Republican-controlled Congress, he had also, some observers suggested, begun to refashion himself as a diplomatic and military leader. By the middle of his term, he had developed a more pragmatic, better organized, and politically astute approach to foreign affairs. He had become his own foreign policy spokesman. The president, Secretary of State Warren Christopher, and other administration leaders worked resourcefully to resolve or allay a number of difficult conflicts around the world. In the Middle East, Clinton was a key player in the reconciliation of Israel and the Palestine Liberation Organization, although he made little progress in improving relations between Israel and Syria. The administration eased the threat of nuclear proliferation in North Korea and appeared to make headway in resolving the struggle over Northern Ireland. Clinton tried to link American foreign policy and the domestic economy, and he created the National Economic Council to coordinate foreign economic and domestic policy. In addition to securing the ratification of NAFTA, he obtained financing to save the Russian and Mexican economies and confronted China on its piracy of American intellectual property such as movies, music, and software. Clinton pressed Japan more aggressively to open its markets to American exports, and he forced changes in the trade policy of China as well as Japan.

In 1995 Clinton adopted a bolder and more coherent policy on the war in Yugoslavia. He was impelled to act by a series of developments, including a successful Croatian offensive against the Serbs and the adoption of congressional resolutions demanding the lifting of the arms embargo on Bosnia. Realizing that he would inevitably have to send American soldiers to Yugoslavia, the president became a vital participant in the renewed search for peace. Assistant Secretary of State Richard C. Holbrooke, representing the United States, was a tireless mediator in arranging a peace conference, which was held in Dayton, Ohio, in November 1995. The conference worked out the details of a peace accord that provided for an Implementation Force (IFOR), made up of NATO peacekeeping troops, and national elections to be held in September 1996. The United States contributed 20,000 soldiers to the occupying force. Though imperfect, the peace offered at least some hope for an end to the years of fierce conflict, terrible atrocities, and "ethnic cleansing" in the Balkans. It was, moreover, a significant feature of Clinton's revamped foreign policy in 1995 and 1996.

In 1996, in response to Saddam Hussein's blatant violation of the terms of the peace treaty following Desert Storm, Bill Clinton sent in cruise missile strikes. As the tensions between Taiwan and China escalated in that same year, Clinton indicated his support of a sovereign and independent Taiwan by sending the U.S. Navy's *Independence* aircraft carrier battle group into the Taiwan Straits. While his response to Saddam's arrogance had merit, the carrier group alone could not have prevented a Chinese invasion of Taiwan.

CHALLENGES AT HOME

Additionally, President Clinton seemed to relish serving as the nation's "commander in chief" for domestic disasters and violence—and his rising popularity suggested that millions of his fellow-citizens liked his performance in that role. This attitude was evident not only in his leadership in the passage of crime legislation and a gun-control law but also in his handling of federal relief efforts following the domestic act of terrorism that came to be known as the Oklahoma City bombing.

On April 19, 1995, a psychologically disturbed man, Timothy McVeigh, parked a rented Ryder truck filled with more than five tons of explosive materials consisting of ammonium nitrate and nitro methane in front of a child-care facility located in the Alfred P. Murrah Federal Building. The truck had been rigged with time-delay fuses, which allowed McVeigh to get nearly a mile away by the time it exploded at 9:22 A.M. The blast, which did damage to more than 300 nearby buildings, destroyed the entire north side of the Murrah Building and claimed the lives of 169 innocent persons, nineteen of them children. Three unborn fetuses were also killed in the wretched and senseless act of brutality. McVeigh, a veteran of the first Gulf War and a Bronze Star recipient, had been honorably discharged from the U.S. Army in 1992. Unable to lead a productive and rewarding life, he harbored a festering anger, which some say had started following his failure to qualify for the Special Forces in 1991. McVeigh had acted along with three co-conspirators, Terry Nichols and Michael and Lori Fortier, with McVeigh playing the principal role. McVeigh and Nichols had first met while they were both serving in the army, though they became closer upon becoming reacquainted following their respective discharges. The bonding agent of their friendship was a hatred of the federal government, which the two men blamed for all of their own personal failings. Nichols helped McVeigh gather the necessary materials and assemble the truck bomb, though McVeigh alone delivered the truck to the scene of the explosion. He was pulled over by a police officer less than two hours after the bombing for driving a vehicle without a license plate and was subsequently arrested for illegally possessing a firearm. While in jail, McVeigh was identified as the suspect in the bombing. Within two days, the nationwide investigation uncovered considerable evidence that led federal agents directly to Terry Nichols, who, having learned of the manhunt, had decided to turn himself in. During the course of the investigation, the fringe roles that Michael and Lori Fortier played in the plot came to light; the two had helped McVeigh acquire small material parts through theft and legal purchase. The husband and wife cooperated with authorities, and in return for their testimony against McVeigh, they were granted immunity deals. McVeigh, who never denied his actions, was convicted, sentenced to death, and executed by lethal injection. Nichols was given a life sentence without the possibility of parole. While both McVeigh and Nichols named several motivating factors that lay behind their heinous act of terror and mass murder, one event more than any other, according to McVeigh, had pushed him over the edge, the 1993 tragedy in Waco, Texas.

From February 28 to April 19, 1993, agents of the federal Bureau of Alcohol, Tobacco, and Firearms (ATF) besieged a compound housing the members of a separatist religious cult, the so-called Branch Davidians, led by a man named David Koresh (born Vernon Howell) who had built the cult around the notion that he was a divine leader. Significant aspects of the Branch Davidians gathered at Waco included their cloistered and secretive communal structure and their stockpiling of weapons, which had captured the attention of the ATF. Once authorities began their investigation of the group, evidence pointed to the deeply disturbing possibility that Koresh had been fathering children with several of female Davidians under his leadership, some of whom were minors themselves. ATF agents attempted to serve a search warrant at the Branch Davidian compound on February 28, but Koresh refused to allow the agents to enter and ordered his followers to use deadly force to defend the compound. After two hours of gunfire exchanges, four federal agents and six Davidians lay dead. Remarkably, during this first day of the incident, CNN broadcast a live phone interview with Koresh. In response to the aggressive militaristic display by Koresh and his followers—and citing concern for the children whom she believed might be being abused by Koresh—Attorney General Janet Reno, the first woman to head the Department of Justice, authorized a major offensive against the compound, a force that included several armored army vehicles. The action played out for days, with the majority of the Davidians refusing to surrender, and culminated in a barrage of CS gas grenades being fired into the Davidian buildings. By noon on April 19, several fires had begun to rage inside the buildings—to this day, some say the fires were started by the gas canisters the agents had shot in, some speculate that the cult's cache of ammunition had ignited, while still others claim that Koresh had started the fires to martyr himself and his followers. In any case, Americans had watched the "Siege of Waco" play out over the course of days on national television, and the fact that the fires claimed the lives of seventy-six persons, including twenty children and two unborn fetuses, shocked the nation. Regardless of how the fires how started, few could deny that the operation to take Koresh into custody and seize the cult's cache of weapons had been conducted ineptly. The inexcusable deaths of the children led many to question Reno's judgment in the decision to use deadly force in the operation and, by extension, the ability of the Clinton administration when it came to handling a domestic crisis. While Americans overwhelmingly viewed Koresh as a bigamist, a child molester, even a lunatic, the deaths of the innocent children and unborn babies resulting from the battle plan was interpreted as an unacceptable blunder.

Nevertheless, Clinton had reasons to be optimistic about his prospects for re-election in 1996. He pressured Congress into raising the minimum wage and cooperated with the lawmakers in the enactment of a telecommunications law that promised to generate many new jobs. He resisted basic changes in Medicare and could take satisfaction in action by Congress to make health insurance portable from job to job and curtail certain exclusions based on pre-existing medical conditions.

THE NEW ECONOMY

By 1996 the economy offered a pleasing contrast to its condition in the fall of 1992. Although the economic growth rate during the Clinton years was only a modest 2.4 percent, it increased to a robust 4.2 percent in the second quarter of 1996. Unemployment was low (5.4 percent, compared with 7.1 percent when Clinton took office), the stock market was booming, and inflation was under control. There had been no recession during Clinton's presidency, over 10 million new jobs had been created, foreign trade had expanded, and the federal deficit had been cut in half. Public opinion polls revealed that in the summer of 1996, 60 percent of those interviewed considered the economy to be in good shape, compared with only 23 percent in October 1992.

One of the driving catalysts of what many economists and historians came to refer to as the New Economy was the dramatic expansion of the technology industries. While personal computer ownership had been growing since the 1970s, the 1990s ushered in a new era, aided by the rapidly evolving Internet. Corporations that built computers, software, and hardware witnessed their value skyrocket at an unprecedented rate, and overwhelmingly their stock prices spiked. What had been the upstart stock exchange, NASDAQ (National Association of Securities Dealers Automated Quotations), founded in 1971, had witnessed a rise in stock values from 1995 through 1999, as the trading relied heavily on technology corporations. CDs (compact disks) replaced floppy disks in information storage, though CDs were soon eclipsed by MP3s and flash drives. Home video format welcomed the DVDs (digital video disk), which replaced the VHS video tapes that had long been the staple of the video industry. The shift to DVDs also spawned the home delivery of movies, and Internet-based businesses such as Netflix quickly challenged industry giants like Blockbuster. The digital surge also changed the photography industry as digital cameras replaced the traditional 35mm film cameras. The telecommunications industry also shifted away from so-called landlines as Americans developed a love affair with cellular phones. Each technological change ushered in a purchasing rush, which further stimulated the economy.

The New Economy also witnessed a change in the consumer culture, with many corporations shifting their previously exclusive marketing focus on bringing the customers into the stores and begining to pay considerable attention to the development of their direct sales websites. As more and more purchases were made via an Internet website as opposed to consumers entering into the traditional stores, the latter came to be referred to as the old "brick and mortars." This shift in purchasing procedure also stimulated growth in the parcel delivery industries, with corporations such as UPS and FedEx expanding at unprecedented rates. Unfortunately, as consumerism expanded, consumer debt climbed—then soared. Not coincidentally, credit card corporations and lending institutions expanded as well and began to book immense profits. Another significant shift in consumerism was the fantastic growth of the "big box" discount retailers such as WalMart and Target. While these new businesses were structured on the model of Kmart, they expanded the products on their shelves to include foodstuffs and a far greater choice of brand-name and their own store-brand goods. Their greatest appeal were their deep discounts they offered, which were plainly visible to the consumer; what was not so transparent was that they were able to price their wares so low because they paid their employees low wages and gave them minimal or no benefits. By the end of the 1990s many Americans began to view the discount big box retailers negatively, blaming them for driving their competition, such as the smaller "mom and pop" concerns of traditional downtowns, as well as mid-size companies, out of business. Indeed, in many small towns the arrival of a big box retailer nearby turned the traditional downtown into a ghost town. But for all of the public hyperbole surrounding the aggressive expansion of the discount big boxes, people continued to go to them and their sales only continued to grow.

In the automotive industry, a shift in purchasing preferences from the smaller, economical vehicles to the larger sport utility vehicles (SUVs) breathed new life into the flagging American automobile industry. The decline in U.S. auto sales since the 1960s had previously reached its low mark during the 1980s, when consumer confidence in the mechanical reliability of Japanese and European cars, as well as notable missteps in styles by Ford, GM, and Chrysler, the so-called "big three," resulted in exceptional marketplace gains for the foreign automakers. When the American consumer began to demand increasingly larger

SUVs, Ford and GM launched model after new model, and Americans rekindled their dormant love affair with American-made autos. The low and stable average gas price, $1.12 a gallon, that lingered throughout the 1990s also helped, for the SUVs' average in-city mileage sank to below ten miles per gallon. The sales of American SUVs and oversize pickup trucks even witnessed expanding sales abroad as the entire global economy expanded throughout the decade. But the refreshed American automotive industry did not simply rely on building bigger; it also built better vehicles, replete with innovative gadgets. This near re-invention of the car, though exceptionally detrimental to the environment, moved the U.S. automakers back into the black. In no small measure, it was the rebirth of an industry that many analysts had felt was beyond repair in the decades prior.

The wedding of unprecedented technological advancement and consumerism in all markets produced a rise in stock values, which posted record gains. More and more Americans put their retirement savings—in financial vehicles such as 401ks and IRAs—in mutual funds and stocks. By 1999, the economy had the appearance of an unstoppable juggernaut. However, when the so-called dot.com bubble burst at the dawn of the twenty-first century, which resulted in the disintegration of hundreds of tech firms and related companies, the NASDAQ dropped from its peak of over 5,000 down to barely over 1,000, and the once seemingly infallible New Economy appeared to be a paper tiger in many regards. The NYSE (New York Stock Exchange) had also reached record gains, though a much broader array of stocks traded on its floor. Therefore, its decline was considerably less of a collapse, and it soon was able to continue the breathtaking bull market that began in 1992. When the 1990s began, the Dow Jones Industrial Average stood at 2,810; it breached the 10,000 mark on March 29, 1999, and by the end of the decade it was above 11,000. While the economic contraction that began in 2000 affected the dot.com businesses, the banks and lending institutions continued to surge in value—for the time being. Throughout the 1990s, the economy steamrolled ahead, and consumer confidence reached new highs each year.

While Clinton benefited tremendously from the economic growth—which was reflected by a consistently high public approval rating that hovered near 60 percent on average—he faced a distinct challenge politically. By the autumn of 1995, the main currents of national politics and policy were moving into the channel of the 1996 presidential election, when frustrated voters would have their chance to end the deadlock in Washington. Even though Clinton faced no challengers from his own party, the "character" issue continued to plague him, perhaps the most persistent issue being the so-called Whitewater affair. In 1992, a *New York Times* article outlined Bill and Hillary Clinton's investment in the development of real estate into upscale retirement and vacation homes along the White River in the Ozark Mountains in Arkansas. The development project was the brainchild of Jim and Susan McDougal, who in 1979 formed a partnership, the Whitewater Development Corporation, with the Clintons, whom they had known for several years. Due to poor planning, skyrocketing interest rates, and a brutally stagnant economy, the Clintons and McDougals were unable to build the enclave of homes, and ultimately both couples lost the majority of what had been a joint investment in the range of $200,000. Their failed business venture came under scrutiny because Jim McDougal was under investigation by federal officials for his alleged criminal activities relating to two small savings and loans (S&Ls), businesses that he had purchased and whose assets he subsequently used to secure illegal loans for other real estate development ventures, all of which collapsed during the S&L crisis in the late 1980s. In the course of the investigation, the Whitewater venture came to light, and while the Clintons were never charged with any crimes, Hillary had served as legal counsel to the McDougals in the purchase of said S&Ls as well as later failed attempts at real estate development. Conservative Republicans and others among Clinton's detractors refused to let the Whitewater "scandal," as they continuously referred to it, go. While both McDougals were convicted of several felonies, including fraud, the Clintons were—eventually—fully exonerated. Nonetheless, the guilt by association dogged Bill and Hillary throughout the Clinton administration and drew the attention of the independent counsel's office.

The nature of the campaign for the election of 1996 became fairly clear by that spring. In contrast to the Democrats, the Republicans had a crowded primary field of contestants. Before the primary season advanced very far, however, Senator Robert Dole of Kansas won enough delegates to assure him the GOP nomination. Thus the contest would pit Clinton, who in addition to the brewing Whitewater investigation had to fend off prior allegations of sexual misconduct, against Bob Dole, with Ross Perot and Ralph Nader as third-party candidates.

When the campaign began, Clinton and Gore got off to a fast start, taking advantage of the strong economy, the creation of millions of new jobs, and favorable conditions abroad. They fashioned an effective campaign appeal out of the budget battle, challenging the Republicans' proprietary claim to a balanced budget and presenting their own plan while emphasizing Medicare, Medicaid, education, and the environment. The president seemed to be running as much against Speaker Gingrich and the "extremist" Republican Congress as against Senator Dole. Clinton's response to the bombing of the federal building in Oklahoma City and other disasters caused many Americans to see their young chief executive in a new and more appreciative light. Dole and his running mate, former congressman Jack F. Kemp, conducted an exhaustive and

President Clinton (center) and Vice President Gore (left) emphasize education initiatives at Vanderbuilt University's sixth annual Family Re-Union, June 1997. *Courtesy Vanderbuilt University News and Public Affairs, photograph by Billy Kingsley.*

hard-hitting campaign. They tried everything they could, invoking the Contract with America, promising a 15 percent tax cut, and attacking Clinton's character and ethical standards. But nothing worked, and the polls had the Democrats leading throughout the campaign. The president's popularity with women and his position on social policy issues ranging from abortion to welfare apparently accounted for much of this lead. In particular, Clinton's Family and Medical Leave Act, passed in 1993, which allowed employees to take unpaid leaves of absence from work, proved quite popular. And, in a nod to social conservatives, Clinton also signed the Defense of Marriage Act in 1996, which weakened the prospects of federally recognized same-sex marriages as it defined a legal marriage as that between a man and a woman. One poll near the end of the race gave Clinton a margin over Dole of 61 to 29 percent among women. The Republicans also made mistakes: failing to exploit television in their accustomed fashion, having earlier forced two government shutdowns over the national budget, and selecting a nominee unable to articulate a compelling message. Meanwhile, Perot attracted a good deal of attention and considerable support, while Nader played little part in the campaign.

In one of the lowest voter turnouts in twentieth-century American history for a presidential election—about 50 percent of the voting-age population—Bill Clinton decisively defeated Bob Dole, once again owing much to Perot's campaign. As in 1992, Clinton was again a president elected by a minority. The Democratic ticket received 45.7 million popular votes (slightly less than 50 percent) to 38 million (41 percent) for Dole and 7.9 million (something over 8 percent) for Perot. Clinton carried thirty-one states and 379 electoral votes, while Dole won nineteen states and 159 electoral votes. Perot received no votes in the Electoral College. Clinton and Gore carried every northeastern state, all of the Midwest except Indiana, the West Coast plus Nevada, Arizona, and New Mexico, and five southern states. The Republicans performed best in the South, winning eight of the region's states and an impressive majority of its congressional and gubernatorial contests. They also carried most of the plains and mountain states. The congressional results told a different story: the Republican Party retained control of both houses of Congress. The GOP gained two seats in the Senate, while losing only a handful of its House seats. Thus the voters chose to continue

divided government in Washington and possibly a somewhat different
equilibrium in national politics. At the same time, Clinton moved the
Democratic Party toward the new political center.

Exhilarated by his solid victory over Senator Dole, President Clinton prepared for his second term. He made a number of high-level
changes, including the appointment of Madeleine Albright, former
ambassador to the United Nations, as secretary of state and Senator William S. Cohen of Maine as secretary of defense. Having held
his own with the Republican-controlled 104th Congress, Clinton
staked out a position in the political center and confidently assumed
an incremental approach for his administration in dealing with the
new Congress. Writing in the wake of the November election, Todd
S. Purdum of the *New York Times* observed that, in the president's
"effusive view, it is possible to both balance the budget and provide
new tax breaks for college education, to force families off welfare and
find new jobs for them, to expand the federal role in everything from
encouraging school uniforms to deterring violence on television—all
the while declaring that 'the era of big government is over.'" Yet as
his second term advanced, Clinton continued to face dangerous challenges in Congress and the courts. The independent counsel probing
the Whitewater land development allegations was still at work, apparently focusing on a cover-up of wide-ranging illegality. In the summer
of 1997, a special Senate committee under the chairmanship of Fred
Thompson of Tennessee began hearings on illegal campaign contributions in the recent election; some of the charges involved abuses by
the president and vice president. Then there was the Paula Jones case,
in which Clinton was accused of sexual harassment while governor of
Arkansas and in which the Supreme Court had recently ruled that the
president was not immune from civil suits while in office. It was in this
last matter that President Bill Clinton found himself not only utterly
humiliated, but quite nearly removed from office.

IMPEACHMENT

While the American people were well-accustomed to Bill Clinton's dal-
liances, whether involving Gennifer Flowers or the highly questionable
Arkansas "Troopergate" scandal, wherein two Arkansas state troopers

claimed to have arranged sexual encounters for then Governor Clinton, the Paula Jones sexual harassment lawsuit ultimately reached its climax by fueling the impeachment of President Clinton.

In 1994, Kenneth Starr replaced Robert Fiske as independent counsel in investigating the Whitewater matter. The main criticism levied against Fiske was that he lacked the level of aggression needed in order to prove effective in the position once held by Archibald Cox and Leon Jaworski. No one would ever accuse his successor of lacking aggression. Starr pressured one of the key witnesses of Whitewater, Susan McDougal, into testifying against the Clintons in exchange for full immunity. When McDougal refused to give in to Starr and betray her friends, she was found in contempt of court. McDougal was subsequently imprisoned, though later pardoned by Bill Clinton before he left office. While the Whitewater investigation proved an impenetrable brick wall for Starr, while conducting it, he developed an interest in the ongoing *Clinton* v. *Jones* lawsuit, suspecting that Bill Clinton may have been guilty of criminal acts.

Attorneys for Paula Jones attempted to establish that Bill Clinton had demonstrated a pattern of extramarital affairs that he did not abandon during his presidency. This pattern, they later argued, substantiated their client's claim that Clinton, based on his overall success at seducing women, had repeatedly made unwanted sexual advances against her. Jones' attorneys had been informed that Clinton had in fact been involved with a White House intern, Monica Lewinski. After graduating from Lewis & Clark College in Portland, Oregon, Lewinski secured a summer internship at the White House working in the office of White House Chief of Staff Leon Panetta (who would later be appointed to lead the CIA by President Obama). Following completion of her unpaid White House internship, Lewinski secured a position with the White House Office of Legislative Affairs in December 1995. The month prior, Lewinski and President Clinton began their sexual affair, which they continued into early 1997. When Clinton was asked during his deposition if he ever had sexual relations with Lewinski, he flatly denied any such relationship. In reaction to the persistent allegations that the president in fact had an affair with Lewinski, Clinton appeared on national television and repeated his denials. Looking directly into the camera, the president told the American people, "I did not have sexual

Monica Lewinski. *Courtesy*
Defense Department, photograph
by Helene C. Stikkel, May 1997.

relations with that woman" and further asserted "these allegations are false." Subsequently, taped conversations between Lewinski and Linda Tripp, a federal employee and confidant of Lewinski, were brought to light. In these conversations, Lewinski discussed her affair with Clinton. Linda Tripp, a holdover White House employee from the George H. W. Bush administration, had met Lewinski on the job. Early in 1994, Clinton White House staffers realized that Tripp held the president in low regard, and they successfully maneuvered her out of the White House by securing for her a Pentagon staff position that came with a substantial increase in salary. But even after Tripp was out of the Clinton White House, she maintained her "friendship" with Lewinski. While the taped conversation invigorated Starr's investigation, by far the most damaging evidence was a blue dress owned by Monica Lewinski that was soiled with President Clinton's semen. Following the revelation that physical evidence of his illicit affair with Lewinski existed, Clinton apologized for misleading the public as well as his family. After Lewinski told Tripp about the dress, Tripp encouraged her to hold on to it and not have the semen stain removed in case Monica might later have to produce that particular irrefutable evidence as leverage to protect herself from any possible threats that might emerge from the Clinton team. Clinton's acknowledgment was also tantamount to an admission of perjury, which led to his impeachment.

On September 14, 1998, Ken Starr released the final report of the independent counsel, known as the Starr Report, which, like the Watergate Special Prosecution Force's final report, became a bestseller. Although the findings did not contain any evidence of criminal activity on the part of the Clintons in the Whitewater matter, the Starr Report contained extensive, lurid discussions certain of President Clinton's sexual transgressions. Some Americans commented that Starr and his team had gone too far in chronicling the acts in far too much detail; others could not get enough. The national media flocked to carry the X-rated portions of the reports: newspapers printed full-text excerpts and television pundits read aloud some of the raciest sentences. While Bill Clinton's presidency survived Starr's findings, Ken Starr successfully tarred Clinton's legacy by cementing his errors in judgment in the annals of history. Ultimately, the American taxpayers footed the bill for Starr's unrelenting report, as the investigation and impeachment process ending up costing a whopping $87–$100 million.

On December 19, 1998, Bill Clinton became the second president impeached in U.S. history (Andrew Johnson had been the first in 1868). The House impeached Clinton on two articles: committing perjury by lying to a grand jury and obstruction of justice. Unlike the Watergate scandal, which exposed widespread criminal activities in the Nixon administration, the Clinton impeachment proceeding was overwhelmingly a political operation that focused strictly on the president's actions. Ultimately, Clinton escaped removal from office and a guilty verdict when the Senate did not reach the necessary 67 votes to convict on either charge. While no Democratic Senators voted guilty on either charge, several Republicans did find President Clinton not guilty. Although he survived the impeachment proceedings and his trial before the Senate, Clinton's legal woes did not end there.

Two months after the close of the impeachment trial, Bill Clinton was found in contempt of court for having willfully failed to testify truthfully in regard to the Paula Jones sexual harassment lawsuit. Clinton and Jones later settled out of court, and Clinton agreed to pay Jones $850,000. The day before he left the presidency, Bill Clinton, a lawyer by training, accepted without contention a five-year suspension of his Arkansas law license in agreement with the independent counsel to end the investigations. Clinton was also suspended from the United States

Supreme Court bar. While the Clinton impeachment did achieve one of the goals of its proponents, to leave an indelible mark on Clinton's otherwise impressive legacy as president, the proceedings disrupted federal legislation and only added to the growing rift between the Democrats and Republicans that had started with Watergate. Clinton's impeachment would later have an impact on the 2000 presidential race between Vice President Al Gore and Texas governor George W. Bush.

While Bill Clinton may have been bruised by his legislative defeats and his impeachment, the president consistently pushed ahead, encouraged by month after month of good times, high employment, low inflation, and a roaring bull market on Wall Street. He worked out an agreement with Republican leaders that would balance the budget by 2002, and the two sides talked about compromises on other major issues. The president had become more active and self-assured in dealing with international problems, such as the decision to expand the North Atlantic Treaty Organization. He identified educational reform as the central theme of his second administration and began a national effort to combat racial intolerance in America. Even though Congress had impeached President Clinton, as he left office he enjoyed a favorable level of public support.

THE 2000 ELECTION

The Democratic primaries witnessed the development of only two serious campaigns, those of Vice President Al Gore and former Senator Bill Bradley from New Jersey. Once the primaries began, Al Gore proved to be an unstoppable force, and he was nominated unanimously at the Democratic National Convention. Gore quickly made history by selecting Senator Joe Lieberman of Connecticut as his vice-presidential running mate, making Lieberman the first Jewish candidate on the presidential ballot. While the Democrats appeared poised and focused early on in the presidential campaign, the Republican race for the nomination was heated, and the growing shift to neoconservative domination was in some respects splintering the party, as moderates and "Neocons" did not appear to share many common ideas.

Several prominent Republicans eagerly launched exploratory committees and subsequent primary campaigns, with the potential nominees forming a diverse lot. Former secretary of labor Elizabeth Dole, spouse of former Kansas senator and failed presidential and vice-presidential candidate Bob Dole, became the first woman to contend seriously for the Republican nomination. Alan Keyes, a radical conservative, became the first African American to draw significant national attention as a Republican presidential candidate. Steve Forbes, the most moderate of the major candidates, campaigned hard on his 10 percent flat tax platform. Former Vice President Dan Quayle, who had been widely lampooned by journalists for his gaffes while he served under George H. W. Bush, surprised many when he entered the race. Senator John McCain from Arizona, who fostered his image as an independent, "maverick" Republican, became one of the early favorites. Then, George W. Bush, the former governor of Texas and son of President George H. W. Bush, launched one of the most aggressive primary campaigns in recent history, and the Republican primaries quickly became a two-man race between McCain and Bush.

The contentious and populist-flavored Republican primary drew much greater news coverage than did the tranquil, if not placid, Democratic race. Many McCain loyalists were shocked when the Bush campaign engaged in dirty politics, such as the push poll suggestion that McCain's Bangladesh-born adopted daughter was actually an illegitimate daughter that he fathered in an affair with an African American woman. In this case, the pollster asked, "Would you be less likely to vote for John McCain if you knew that he had fathered a daughter out of wedlock with a black woman?" In return, McCain's campaign suggested Bush was a racist for not having condemned Bob Jones University, at which he spoke, for banning interracial dating among its students. Ultimately, George Bush's solid support from the conservative evangelical Christians pushed him over the top, and he received the Republican nomination. Bush later chose Dick Cheney, former Wyoming congressman and secretary of defense under George H. W. Bush, as his running mate.

While candidates George W. Bush and Al Gore shared the similarity of being born into well-established political families, the two men shared little else. Gore was an articulate, progressive Democrat whose central political platform had been environmental reform while he served in the Senate. Gore was widely considered a man of signifi-

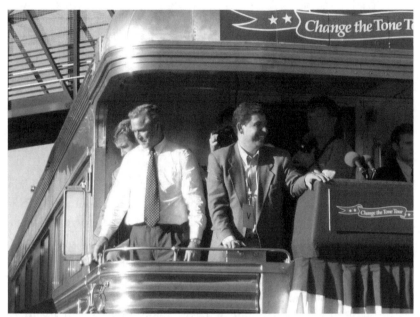

Candidate George W. Bush (left) on a whistle stop tour of the West Coast, August 2000.
Photographer: D. Fitzsimmons, denfitz@yahoo.com.

cant intelligence with a penchant for public policy. As vice president,
Al Gore had a distinguished record and was well respected, though
he was wounded politically when he adamantly supported Bill Clinton as being "truthful" shortly after the president looked the American
people straight in the eye and denied that he had ever had an affair with
Monica Lewinski. Bush's campaign would consistently exploit what
Republicans referred to as the "sleaze factor," a not so subtle reminder
of Clinton's infidelities, and they promised Americans that their presidential administration would be wholly moral and thus a clean break
from the past.

George W. Bush may have been the less articulate of the two candidates, but his self-deprecating humor endeared him with many voters,
even as Al Gore's professionalism and formality gave him the impression of being stiff, at times robotic. During his two-term tenure as
governor of Texas, Bush benefited from a strong state economy and
was regarded as a successful chief executive. While he never promoted
himself as a policy expert, he adroitly referred to himself as a "Reagan
Republican" and a "compassionate conservative." Bush was, however,

plagued by the allegations that had surfaced during the primaries that he had used illicit drugs earlier in his life. Although he never admitted or denied that he had done so, Bush did take the high road and openly discussed that he was a reformed alcoholic and that through his conversion to evangelical Christianity he had successfully closed that unfortunate chapter in his life.

The general campaign issues that both sides debated fell along the traditional lines of taxation, Social Security and Medicare, international affairs, and the federal budget. Perhaps the greatest distinguishing characteristic between the two campaigns were their respective management strategies. Karl Rove, George Bush's campaign architect, pulled no punches. In one memorable television attack ad against Gore, the word "rats" flashed across the screen. Gore's campaign accused Bush of attempting to plant a subversive subliminal message in the minds of voters. But the strongest attribute of Rove's campaign design was its relentless drive and ability to exploit the weaknesses of Gore's campaign, which was headed by Donna Brazile, an African American political analyst. While Bush's campaign was full of energy, at times Gore's campaign seemed listless and complacent. One particular gross miscalculation by Brazile was that Gore could not lose his home state of Tennessee to his opponent, and she reduced his campaign there to a shadow presence. Rove seized on the political blunder, made it a campaign issue, and in the general election Bush captured the Volunteer State.

The election results were some of the closest in United States history. The Deep South and most of the interior states went for Bush. The Northeast and West Coast went for Gore. But before either candidate could be called the winner, the state of Florida's returns, which were extremely close, had to be certified, and the entire process took longer than a month. Both candidates needed Florida in order to reach the 270 delegates necessary to prevail. Initially, Al Gore, following the news reports that picked Bush the winner in Florida, called George W. Bush and conceded. Within a few hours of Gore's concession, the Florida returns began to indicate that no clear victor existed. Gore then called Bush, rescinded his concession, and insisted that the two men wait until Florida had finished its count. Bush attempted to convince Gore that Florida had voted for the Bush-Cheney ticket. As Bush explained to Gore, his brother, Florida governor Jeb Bush, had told him that he had defeated Al Gore in that state. Gore did not back down, and he retorted that George's "little brother" did not have the last word on the outcome of the election. Eventually, the Republican secretary of state of Florida, Katherine Harris, certified Bush the winner. When Gore contested the results, the two candidates turned to the courts to decide. Eventually, on December 12, the United States Supreme Court decided 5–4 (along strict party lines) to end the recount and accept Harris's initial certified count. In his concession speech, Al Gore stated that he disagreed with the Supreme Court's decision, though he accepted it. With the final election results in, Al Gore won 48.38 percent of the popular vote and 266 electoral votes. George Bush garnered 47.87 percent of the popular vote and 271 votes in the Electoral College.

While many allegations of fraud were made by people and organizations sympathetic to either Bush or Gore, political analysts pointed to Green Party candidate Ralph Nader's tally of more than 2.8 million Florida votes as the most significant determining factor that sent Florida into the Bush column. Nader, a far-left liberal whose campaign platform focused heavily on environmental reform, most probably pulled votes from Gore rather than Bush. Had the 2.7 percent of Florida voters who cast their ballots for Nader chosen Gore instead, the 2000 presidential election would have had a different outcome. Consequently, Ralph Nader became the spoiler in the minds of many Al Gore supporters. Others concluded that Bill Clinton's indiscretions and Gore's initial attempts to vouch for the president's honesty had cost Gore the election. Additionally, instances of incredible irregularities, such as the nearly 60,000 African Americans in Florida whom the state erroneously classified as convicted felons and thus rescinded their right to vote, removed a considerable number of likely Gore supporters from the contest. This case was considered a highly suspicious move by political analysts: naturally, it only added to the frustration millions of Americans felt following the election. Indeed, the election had a polarizing effect on American politics and society in general, which would be evidenced in the growing and radicalized division between liberals and conservatives. Across the nation, debates centered on the dismantling of the Electoral College sprang up on college campuses and in the media, as George W. Bush prepared to take office as the first president since Rutherford B. Hayes (R-OH) to enter the

Oval Office having lost the popular vote but having won the vote in the Electoral College. A stark contrast between the two outcomes was that Hayes became president following a political compromise between the Democrats and Republicans in Congress, which led to the end of Reconstruction, among other points, and Bush became president following a 5–4 U.S. Supreme Court decision. As Americans began the new millennium, they did so as a people deeply divided politically.

SUGGESTIONS FOR FURTHER READING

My Life (2004), by Bill Clinton, is a satisfactory presidential memoir. *First in His Class: A Biography of Bill Clinton* (1995), by the journalist David Maraniss, is a well-written, extensively researched, and revealing portrait that takes its subject to the threshold of the White House. Roger Morris, *Partners in Power: The Clintons and Their America* (1996), is a critical and provocative but inadequately documented treatment of the Clintons before they entered the White House. Helpful for the Clinton administration are James L. Sundquist, ed., *Beyond Gridlock: The Prospects for Governance in the Clinton Years—and After* (1993); Haynes Johnson and David S. Broder, *The System: The American Way of Politics at the Breaking Point* (1996); Michael S. Sherry, *In the Shadow of War: The United States Since the 1930s* (1995); and Robert D. Kaplan, *Balkan Ghosts: A Journey Through History* (1993). A fine post-presidency assessment is *The Survivor: Bill Clinton in the White House* (2006), by John F. Harris, as is *Clinton in Exile: A President Out of the White House* (2008), by Carol Felsenthal.

Congress, the president, the Supreme Court, and a number of contemporary issues are considered in C. Lawrence Evans and Walter J. Oleszek, *Congress Under Fire: Reform Politics and the Republican Majority* (1997); John H. Aldrich, *The Origin and Transformation of Party Politics in America* (1995); John David Skrenthy, *The Ironies of Affirmative Action: Politics, Culture, and Justice in America* (1996); Neal Devins, *Shaping Constitutional Values: Elected Government, the Supreme Court, and the Abortion Debate* (1996); Robert Justin Goldstein, *Burning the Flag: The Great 1989–1990 American Flag Desecration Controversy* (1996); and Kenneth S. Stern, *A Force Upon the Plain: The American Militia Movement and the Politics of Hate* (1996). *The Pact: Bill Clinton, Newt Gingrich, and the Rivalry that Defined a Generation* (2008), by Steven M. Gillon, is a fascinating study that should not be overlooked.

On the historic Clinton impeachment, an intelligent legal analysis is *An Affair of State: The Investigation, Impeachment, and Trial of President Clinton* (2000), by Richard A. Posner; Peter Baker's *The Breach: Inside Impeachment and Trial of William Jefferson Clinton* (2001), is a highly accessible read on the proceedings. A fine scholarly and accessible work is *The Impeachment and Trial of President Clinton* (1999), by Merrill McLoughlin and Michael R. Beschloss.

The historical economic growth is treated well by *After the New Economy: The Binge and the Hangover That Won't Go Away* (2005) by Doug Henwood; an insightful look into the changing job markets of the New Economy is *Service America!: Doing Business in the New Economy* (2008), by Karl Albrecht. A fine journalistic take on the role of Alan Greenspan is *Maestro: Greenspan's Fed and The American Boom* (2000), by Bob Woodward. Subsequent, post-collapse criticisms of note include *Greenspan's Bubbles: The Age of Ignorance at the Federal Reserve* (2008) by William Fleckenstein and Fred Sheehan and *Greenspan's Fraud: How Two Decades of His Policies Have Undermined the Global Economy* (2005) by Ravi Batra. Greenspan penned his own reflections on the downturn, *The Age of Turbulence: Adventures in a New World* (2008).

Broad interpretive themes are emphasized in a number of notable books, several of which have been referred to before. Among these are Fraser and Gerstle, eds., *The Rise and Fall of the New Deal Order*; Hamby, *Liberalism and Its Challengers*; Kellerman, *The Political Presidency*; Edsall, *Chain Reaction*; E. J. Dionne, Jr., *Why Americans Hate Politics* (1991); and Susan J. Tolchin, *The Angry American: How Voter Rage Is Changing the Nation* (1996).

———★———

Time of Tragedy:
George W. Bush, 9/11, Two Wars,
and the Great Recession

A   T THE START OF GEORGE W. BUSH's presidential administration, no one could have imagined the incredible course of
events that would soon unfold and dramatically alter life in the
United States and around the world. Coming into office, Bush declared
that, as a compassionate conservative, he would ensure all citizens access
to the American dream and his policies would reflect his strong belief in
a free-market economy, a small government, and strict fiscal responsibility. One of the keys to achieving these goals, the new president declared,
was a reduction of income tax. Over the course of his first three years in
office, Bush obtained congressional approval on three separate occasions
for a historic series of tax reductions. Based in part on Reaganomics,
the Bush economic policies were aimed at increased domestic consumer
spending that would, in theory, expand the greater American economy.
In reality, the economic challenges proved too complex and diverse for
a simple tax-reduction plan to solve. While the economy rode a roller
coaster throughout Bush's tenure in office, the issue of national security
dominated the headlines; not until the end of his administration, following the dawn of the Great Recession in 2007, would financial matters
return to the fore. The enormity of the challenges that the nation faced
in the eight years that George W. Bush occupied the Oval Office were

eclipsed only by the Civil War years and those of the Great Depression and World War II.

GEORGE W. BUSH

George Walker Bush, the nation's forty-third chief executive, was born on July 6, 1946, in New Haven, Connecticut—making him the second baby-boomer U.S. president in a row. His father, George H. W. Bush, was, as mentioned, the forty-first president, and his paternal grandfather, Prescott Bush, was a U.S. senator from Connecticut. While not born into incredible wealth, George W. Bush was of the privileged class. Young George began his elementary education in the public schools of Midland and Houston, Texas, although he ultimately graduated high school from Phillips Academy in Andover, Massachusetts. In 1964 he entered Yale, graduating in 1968 with a degree in history. While critics would later point out that his academic record was less than stellar, George W. Bush passed all of his classes in a satisfactory manner. Where Bush did succeed in college was socially. Each term he participated in a range of activities, was eventually elected president of his fraternity, Delta Kappa Epsilon, and like his father and paternal grandfather became a member of the Skull and Bones society. With the Vietnam War at its peak, George W. Bush enlisted in the Texas Air National Guard in 1968 until being moved to inactive duty in 1973. In that same year, Bush enrolled in Harvard Business School, where he earned his MBA; he was the first person elected president to hold that degree.

In the business world, George W. Bush experienced many failures and a few notable successes. Early attempts at striking it rich in the oil industry proved fruitless, though subsequent investments, in particular his tenure as managing partner of the Major League Baseball team the Texas Rangers, made George W. Bush a multimillionaire in his own right. Bush's foray into politics mirrored his business career. In 1978 he made a run for a seat in the U.S. House of Representatives and lost by more than a 6-percent margin to the politically savvy Democrat, Kent Hance, who cast his opponent as a member of the eastern establishment—and not a genuine Texan. This would be the last election that George W. Bush would ever lose. In 1988, Bush again found himself in the political arena as he worked as a campaign adviser for his father's successful presidential bid. George W., known simply as "W" to many, would also serve in his father's unsuccessful re-election campaign in 1992. During the senior Bush's presidency, George W. Bush began seriously to consider a return to politics, and in 1994 he declared his candidacy for the Texas governorship.

Bush sailed through the Republican state primary, but he faced a significant uphill battle in his quest to unseat the popular incumbent Democratic governor, Ann Richards. The campaign quickly became a rough-and-tumble affair centered on the issues of concealed gun permits, public education, crime, and state welfare reform. Bush's primary campaign advisers, Karen Hughes, Karl Rove, and Joe Allbaugh, portrayed him as a successful businessman and a "regular Joe," regardless of the fact that he was the son of a former president. Mudslinging was a part of the process, though rather than launch a full frontal assault on Governor Richards, a whisper campaign developed that accused her of being a lesbian. While no senior members of the Bush campaign were ever directly blamed, Karl Rove was suspected by many of being behind the untrue accusation. Texas Democrats faulted Richards for not having taken Bush, whom she dubbed "the Shrub," seriously enough and running a lethargic campaign. In any event, Bush went on to win the election with nearly 54 percent of the vote, while Richards received slightly less than 46 percent. George W. Bush would win re-election by a landslide four years later, when nearly 70 percent of eligible Texans cast their ballots for their popular incumbent.

During his governorship, George W. enjoyed a strong, robust Texas economy that permitted him to reduce state taxes to near historic lows. Bush also passed a series of incentives that increased the salaries of Texas school teachers, and he expanded state social programs that provided assistance to recovering alcoholics and drug addicts. Making good on one of his campaign pledges, he also signed a controversial state law that made the acquisition of a concealed weapon permit much easier. Influenced by his strong born again Christian beliefs, Governor Bush issued the statewide proclamation making June 10, 2000, "Jesus Day." With his star on the rise, many individuals within the Republican Party began floating George W. Bush as a strong presidential candidate, and in 1999, he announced his candidacy for the White House.

One aspect of the Bush administration stood out early in stark contrast to all previous ones: the role and significance of his vice president. Originally, George W. had tapped Richard "Dick" Cheney to serve on his campaign and also lead the search for an acceptable vice-presidential candidate. When Cheney failed to find a prospect whom Bush liked, the governor simply asked Cheney himself to take the number-two slot, which he eventually did, and in no small measure: Dick Cheney transformed the office of the vice president.

Before his vice-presidential years, Cheney had built an impressive resume. Beginning in 1969, he entered the political arena with a congressional internship, followed by a job in the Nixon administration's Office of Economic Opportunity that lasted until 1970. Cheney then segued into the Nixon White House as a low-level staffer, but soon thereafter (1971) he emerged as the assistant director of the Cost of Living Council. Following Gerald Ford's move into the Oval Office after Nixon's resignation, Cheney became deputy assistant to the president in 1974. The next year, Dick Cheney rose to White House chief of staff, a post he held for the remainder of the Ford administration. It was during his initial time in Washington in the wake of Watergate that the young Dick Cheney developed his lasting political view that the office of the president should hold greater power than Congress or the Supreme Court.

Dick Cheney successfully ran in 1978 for a seat in the House and was re-elected on five occasions. His tenure in the House featured his rapid rise within his party, and he eventually became House Minority Whip and served as the ranking minority member of the Iran-Contra investigation. During his time in Congress, Cheney impressed others in Washington with his intelligence and doggedness. After President George H. W. Bush failed to secure Senate confirmation for his secretary of defense nominee, John Tower, Cheney received the nomination and was confirmed by a vote of 92–0. While heading the Defense Department, Cheney oversaw Operation Desert Storm in 1991 as well as the U.S. invasion of Panama in 1989. For his management of these two successful and brief military actions, President Bush decorated him with the Presidential Medal of Freedom, the nation's highest award for a civilian. Following his initial two decades in government, Cheney became CEO of the international energy corporation Halliburton and founding member of the conservative think tank Project for a New American Century. By the time he became vice-president, Dick Cheney was a seasoned politico and connected Washington insider, one who could guide and advise President Bush in both domestic and international affairs. And during his first term, Bush would lean heavily on Cheney.

The Bush cabinet contained an impressive bevy of intelligent, experienced individuals along with the typical spoils-system political appointees. Former chairman of the Joint Chiefs of Staff under George H. W. Bush and potential presidential candidate in his own right, Colin Powell became the first African American secretary of state. Powell's years of experience in the military, including having overseen Operation Desert Storm, and his natural ability to convey honesty, sincerity, vision and intelligence made him popular not only at home but abroad. Powell was a natural to head the State Department. Donald Rumsfeld, who served the first President Bush as secretary of defense, returned to his former post. During his tenure in the Nixon administration, President Nixon noted that Rumsfeld was "tough," characterizing him as a "ruthless little bastard." Rumsfeld would at least prove his toughness while he ran the Defense Department.

Diversity of ethnicity and gender marked the Bush cabinet. Some of the notables include the following. Elaine Chao became the first Chinese and first Asian American woman cabinet member in U.S. history when she took over the Department of Labor. Rod Paige, former superintendent of Houston Independent School District, took over as secretary of education, the first African American to fill that position. Ann Veneman became the first woman to serve as secretary of agriculture. Bush's secretary of housing and urban development, Mel Martínez, a Cuban American, would later become the first Latino to serve as chairman for a major national party when he was named chair of the Republican Party. Although not a member of the cabinet, National Security Advisor Condoleezza Rice, the first woman to hold that post, emerged early on as one of President Bush's primary advisers. Rice, formerly a Soviet and Russian affairs adviser in President George H. W. Bush's administration, was a gifted academic who rose to post of provost at Stanford University. A most notable intellectual on international affairs, Rice was also a highly effective communicator who adroitly articulated the administration's goals. Rice would later become the first African American woman to serve as secretary of state.

Even though George W. Bush had to contend with lingering bad sentiments related to the outcome of the contentious 2000 election and the sinking of the NASDAQ in the bursting of the dot.com bubble at the end of his first 100 days in office, the personable, yet untested, president enjoyed high approval ratings. According to a CNN/*USA Today*/ Gallup Poll taken from April 20–22, 2001, Bush carried an approval rating of 62, seven points higher than Clinton had at the 100-day mark and four points higher than his own father at the same juncture. One of the strongest attributes that Bush demonstrated was a keen understanding of how to win over many of his critics, during extensive travel across the nation, with his down-home, self-deprecating humor that typically acknowledged his penchant for mangling the English language.

The first significant diplomatic crisis that Bush faced during this early leg of his presidency involved the collision of a U.S. reconnaissance aircraft with a Chinese fighter jet on April 1, 2001. The Chinese pilot perished in the accident and the American crew, which had to make an emergency landing on a Chinese island, were held by the Chinese government for eleven days. Rather than launching into a round of hard-line rhetoric, Bush expressed regret for the death of the Chinese pilot. After the release of the Americans, Bush ramped up his tone, though it never reached a full rattling of the sabers. The American people overwhelmingly supported the president's diplomatic path, which seemed both prudent and effective. Still, he was not without his critics. Surprisingly, one of Vice President Dick Cheney's contemporaries from the Project for the New American Century and editor/publisher of the *Weekly Standard*, William Kristol, cast the president's response to the incident as weak. Regardless, Bush's approval rating shot up above 70 percent after the Americans arrived home, and in his own self-analysis, George W. Bush stated that he "felt pretty darn good" about how he was carrying out his executive duties.

9/11

Economic uncertainties stemming from the burst of the dot.com bubble dominated the news cycle for the first few months of the Bush administration, but as Americans went to work on the morning of September 11, 2001, they witnessed the greatest attack by terrorists on U.S. soil in history. Not since December 7, 1941, when the Empire of Japan bombed the U.S. naval installation at Pearl Harbor, had the United States been successfully attacked by a foreign aggressor. But the events that unfolded on that fateful fall day, termed 9/11, would radically alter the course of American history.

As the workday began on the East Coast, four commercial passenger jets were hijacked by members of the radical Islamic terrorist organization al-Qaeda. The nineteen hijackers took control of two American Airlines and two United Airlines flights from Boston, Newark, and D.C. that were bound for San Francisco and Los Angeles. At 8:46 A.M., American Airlines flight 11 crashed into the New York City's World Trade Center (WTC) North Tower at about 450 mph, and at 9:03 A.M., United Airlines flight 175 slammed into the South Tower at about 540 mph. Just over thirty minutes later, at 9:37 A.M., American Airlines flight 77, moving faster than 525 mph, crashed into the west wall of the Pentagon. The fourth aircraft, United Airlines flight 93, crashed outside of Shanksville, Pennsylvania, at 10:03 A.M. Believed to have targeted either the U.S. Capitol or the White House, Flight 93 was the only one of the four hijacked aircraft not to reach the terrorists' objective. This was the case due to the insight and bravery of the passengers aboard the doomed plane. Shortly after realizing that a hijacking had taken place, several of the passengers made cell phone calls. After being informed by spouses and loved ones of the attacks on the World Trade Center, the passengers realized their hijackers were taking them on a suicide mission. A team led by Tod Beamer, Tom Burnett, and Mark Bingham refused to submit to the terrorists and tried to retake control of the plane from the four men. After subduing the two terrorists in the passenger compartment, they attempted to gain access to the locked cockpit, which was under the control of two others. Once the terrorists flying the jet realized what had transpired in the passenger compartment, they decided to crash the plane rather than allow the passengers to overtake them and attempt to land the plane safely. All thirty-three of the brave passengers and seven crew members died in the crash along with the four hijackers. While this alone was a horribly tragic event, the passengers who fought back prevented what surely would have been an even greater disaster had the

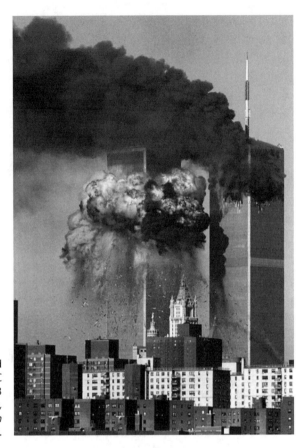

The moment the second plane crashes into WTC South Tower at 9:03 am. *Library of Congress, Photo: Tamara Beckwith (LC-DIG-ppmsca-01810).*

hijackers been able to reach their final objective. As Americans in the western time zones began their day, they faced the horrible realization that their nation had come under attack.

Within minutes of the first crash into the WTC, which by happenstance was captured by local news agencies on assignment as well as camera-toting tourists in the Big Apple, international news services began to carry the events live as they unfolded. Initial reports varied and several incorrect stories peppered the news cycle. The one certainty was that the attacks had clearly caught America off guard. CNN captured the crash of American Airlines flight 11 and broadcast it live around the globe. Within minutes of the attack on the South Tower, the U.S. military was on full alert, but nothing could have prevented the third strike against the Pentagon.

The damage to the Pentagon resulting from the hijackers crashing American Airlines 77. *Courtesy Defense Department, photograph by TSGT Cedric H. Rudisill, USAF.*

More than 400 first response emergency workers, fire fighters, police officers, and paramedics rushed into the smoldering towers in a valiant effort to save lives. Many of these brave souls ended up losing their own lives. As the world watched the images of the smashed and burning towers and the frantic evacuation efforts there and at the Pentagon, the unthinkable happened before their eyes on live television: just before 10:00 A.M., the towers began to collapse. The first to fall was the South Tower, followed in slightly less than thirty minutes by the North Tower. Rather than falling to one side or another, the collapse of these once magnificent structures mirrored the movement of an accordion. In a manner of seconds, an immense and fast-moving cloud of dust and debris enveloped lower Manhattan. Several other buildings in the WTC complex and the immediate vicinity were either damaged or destroyed by the collapse of the twin towers. Other hauntingly horrific images beyond the collapse began to fill television screens. People trapped above the points of impact, with no way to escape via the elevators or emergency stairs, hurled themselves to the sidewalk one hundred stories below just before the buildings fell.

At the time of the attacks, President Bush, along with Secretary of Education Rod Paige, was visiting Emma Booker Elementary School in Sarasota, Florida. When the president addressed the nation, he did so with a backdrop of bright-eyed elementary students, a surreal image given the content of his address. Within the next two days, the American people learned the identity of the attackers, al-Qaeda, and their leader, Osama bin Laden. Within a week, the world watched videotaped images of bin Laden celebrating the level of destruction in the attack. Americans also learned that this had not been al-Qaeda's first attempt at taking down the WTC. Followers of Khaled Shaikh Mohammed, the architect of the 2001 attacks, had received funding from Mohammed to build and deploy a 1,500-pound nitrate and hydrogen car bomb, which they had detonated in the subterranean parking structure at the WTC North Tower back on February 26, 1993. Six people were killed in the blast, which left a crater nearly 100 feet across, and more than 1,000 others suffered minor injuries in the explosion and subsequent evacuation. That time, however, the tower did not fall.

Over the ensuing weeks after 9/11, the massive search and rescue efforts gave way to a grisly, filthy, and monumental cleanup. The casualty count would eventually eclipse 3,000. Thousands of volunteers from across the nation arrived in New York City in the weeks following the attack and joined in the effort of searching for survivors and the long term clean-up. Millions of people sent economic aid to help in this massive effort as well as to assist the more than 2,500 children who lost a parent on that tragic day. While the majority of the people, an estimated 11,000, below the points of impact escaped, the majority of those above the point of impact lost their lives. President Bush addressed the nation from the WTC wreckage site, dubbed Ground Zero, and promised the American people that the United States would bring the culprits behind the horrific deeds to justice.

While the president, intelligence agencies, and the military pored over their retaliatory options, the national economy, already on shaky ground, began to stumble. In the wake of the attacks, no one could be certain when or if another round of hijackings or other acts of terrorism would occur. In a preventive measure, all commercial air traffic was grounded for three days, including parcel delivery. The NASDAQ and the NYSE remained closed until September 17, and in the week that the exchanges reopened, the Dow Jones dropped more than 14 percent, a dollar-value decline in excess of $1.4 billion. New York City witnessed a loss of over 400,000 jobs, and its tourist industry, one of the strongest in the world, plunged by nearly 20 percent. The decline in travel and tourism was not limited to New York, as all Americans-became more cautious and hotels and airlines across the nation took a hit to the bottom line.

One of the first measures taken by the federal government at preventing a reoccurrence of another such catastrophe was a complete overhaul of the intelligence community and intelligence-gathering techniques. On November 25, 2002, Congress passed and President Bush signed into law the Homeland Security Act, which established the new agency bearing the act's name. This transition away from the National Security Act of 1947 was a restructuring of massive proportion. The Department of Homeland Security was headed by a cabinet-level appointee, the first of whom was the former governor of Pennsylvania, Tom Ridge. By the close of its first year of operation, Homeland Security had authority over twenty-two federal agencies, including the Coast Guard, Boarder Patrol, Secret Service, and Federal Emergency Management Agency (FEMA). In effect, the establishment of Homeland Security was the greatest restructuring to the federal bureaucracy since the establishment of the New Deal or the sweeping changes that came after the implementation of NSC68. The general intent behind the formation of Homeland Security was to streamline intelligence operations and enhance national security. While Homeland Security was not without its critics, another White House initiative, the Patriot Act, generated great controversy.

On October 26, 2001, President Bush signed into law the Uniting and Strengthening America by Providing Appropriate Tools Required to Intercept and Obstruct Terrorism Act of 2001, which instantly became known simply as the Patriot Act. Introduced in Congress by Representative Frank James (Jim) Sensenbrenner, Jr. (R-WI) just three days earlier, its meteoric passage was a reflection of the state of perceived national crisis in which the legislators worked. Indeed, in marked contrast to most bills, the rocket ride this act took through the legislative process resulted in few debates, fewer changes, and virtually no discussion of alternatives. While the majority of the people clearly had wanted a more efficient and effective form of national security, after the media began to dissect the complex array of codicils that comprised the Patriot Act, critics began to suggest that certain parts of the radical plan con-

Secretary of Defense, Donald H. Rumsfeld. *Courtesy Defense Department, photograph by U.S. Navy Petty Officer 1st Class Chad J. McNeeley.*

flicted with the most fundamental civil rights and civil liberties afforded Americans by the U.S. Constitution.

At the heart of the backlash against the Patriot Act was the codicil that permitted law enforcement agencies to wiretap American citizens, including a search of voicemail, without having to go through the long-standing procedure of obtaining a court order from a judge. Perhaps the strangest aspect, which puzzled most Americans and infuriated others, was that it authorized law enforcement to obtain the library records of patrons who checked out literature or archival materials deemed potentially connected to any threat to national security. Possibly the greatest irony associated with the Patriot Act was that, on a base level, it was a modern version of the thwarted Huston Plan put forth during the Nixon administration. Designed by a conservative young Nixon White House staffer, Tom Charles Huston, the plan called for domestic surveillance and the use of broad investigative tactics on individuals and organizations that administration officials suspected of being subversive radicals who stood against the Vietnam War and, by extension, against President Nixon. The Huston Plan had also called for a unified effort in domestic intelligence-gathering by the CIA, NSA, and FBI. (The CIA, by its charter, is barred from conducting domestic intelligence gathering.) Somewhat ironically, it was none other than the long-time director of the FBI, J. Edgar Hoover—a man who in a career that spanned nearly half a century had ordered the surveillance of Americans from all walks of life—who disapproved the plan. The aged Hoover approached Attorney General John Mitchell and convinced him to persuade Nixon to abandon it. Nixon followed Mitchell's advice, and the Huston Plan never saw the light of day. While most scholars of the Patriot Act and Homeland Security agree the new agency and national security act have proved successful in gathering domestic intelligence, the one component that has overwhelmingly been a boondoggle concerned securing the borders, as the flood of illegal immigrants actually increased since the act's inception and later led to a significant backlash against undocumented aliens across the nation.

One of the most regrettable early reactions domestically to 9/11 was the aggressive and widespread hostility that Muslim and Arab Americans experienced in the wake of the tragedies. Mosques were vandalized and sometimes set on fire. In other cases, Americans who were perceived to be of Middle Eastern heritage experienced discrimination and violent attacks that in a few tragic instances resulted in death. Unlike the unjust internment of Japanese Americans after the attack on Pearl Harbor, however, this time the federal government and the greater American society refrained from making any judiciously expedient and unconstitutional maneuvers such as widespread arrests and incarcerations of "suspects" on the basis of their ethnicity.

The international response to 9/11 was overwhelmingly supportive of the United States and its citizenry. Condemnation of the terrorist acts echoed across the globe, including the vast majority of Arab and Muslim nations. One noted exception was Saddam Hussein, president of Iraq, who initially stated that Americans had been justly rewarded for their repeated crimes against humanity. (Later, Hussein would extend his sympathies to those who lost family members and loved ones in the tragedy.) On the domestic front, televangelist Jerry Falwell, known for making outlandish and offensive comments on contemporary events, suggested that gays, lesbians, and others whom his church condemned as immoral bore the responsibility for bringing down God's wrath upon the American people. Falwell, who previously suggested that the children's program *Teletubbies* promoted homosexuality because one of its amorphous characters carried something resembling a purse, soon recanted and apologized for his errant remarks regarding the causes of 9/11.

WAR IN AFGHANISTAN AND IRAQ

In the aftermath of 9/11, President Bush's approval ratings soared to 90 percent as Americans rallied around their leader and the flag, though they were anything but content to lick their wounds: rather, they wanted to find and eradicate the terrorists and their organization, al-Qaeda, with swift military actions. The president and Washington were further compelled to take action after a series of parcels laced with anthrax spores began to surface on September 18, 2001. These anthrax attacks resulted in five deaths and over a dozen infections in the metropolitan regions of New York City, D.C., and other cities. Americans wanted retaliatory actions that would prevent any further acts of terrorism. In less than a month, the nation made its first military response, focused on the suspected hideout of Osama bin Laden in Afghanistan, on October 7, 2001.

The initial military strikes against the Taliban regime of Afghanistan, which was giving safe harbor to bin Laden and al-Qaeda, were centered on the capital city of Kabul, the city of Jalalabad, and the military centers in Kandahar. Joining the United States in this military action was the United Kingdom, and together the two nations launched a series of Tomahawk cruise missile strikes from naval vessels, followed by multiple aerial bombings. American and global television audiences were able to view the offensive the same day via CNN. Also covering the military strikes was the Arab international news broadcasting corporation Al Jazeera, which released a video of Osama bin Laden condemning any military aggression against Afghanistan. Bin Laden claimed that this U.S.-led campaign would end in failure, just as the occupation of Afghanistan by the USSR had some two generations earlier. By November 12, U.S.-led ground forces had taken control of Kabul and deposed the Taliban regime, although those insurgents who survived and eluded capture fled into the nearly impenetrable mountain regions of Afghanistan and continued to fight the American-led forces, launching a significant round of counteroffensives from 2003 through 2005. Additionally, the U.S. military and intelligence agencies rounded up many terrorist suspects in Afghanistan and shipped them off for interrogation at the U.S. Marine base in Guantánamo Bay, Cuba, commonly referred to as "Gitmo," rather than bringing them into the United States.

The United States did not, however, just focus its attention on al-Qaeda and bin Laden after 9/11. Since the successful conclusion of the Gulf War in 1991, Iraqi president Saddam Hussein had consistently failed to adhere to the agreements he made with the United Nations during the course of his surrender. The particular point of contention that came to a boiling point in the wake of 9/11 was Iraq's perceived failure to disarm its chemical weapons, nuclear weapons capabilities, and conventional weapons of mass destruction in compliance with the peace treaty. In 2003–04, Hussein frequently and consistently denied UN weapons inspectors access to several key locations in Iraq known to have previously been centers for nuclear weapon development and assembly. The CIA, under Director George Tenet, conducted intelligence operations that yielded no evidence of forbidden weapon development, specifically weapons of mass destruction (WMDs). One particular component of the CIA investigation was the report of the former ambassador to Iraq, Joseph Wilson, which directly addressed whether Iraq had re-initiated its stockpiling of the low-grade nuclear material known as yellowcake uranium. Wilson found no evidence of such activities in Iraq or in Niger, the nation that had allegedly sold yellowcake to Hussein. High officials in the Bush administration, such as Deputy Secretary of Defense Paul Wolfowitz, balked at Wilson's report. Wilson countered the rebuke by publishing an open letter in the *New York Times* that outlined his findings. In the bizarre series of political intrigues that followed the publication of the letter, Wilson's wife, Valerie Plame, was outed by Bush White House officials as being an undercover CIA agent. Subsequent Justice Department investigations of Plame's outing, which naturally ended her career as an agent and possibly placed her in harm's way, indicated that someone or some people in the Bush administration had illegally retaliated due to their strong disdain for Wilson following his public rebuttal of the White House's insistence that Hussein did in fact have WMDs, including the banned yellowcake. The highest Bush administration official eventually found guilty of disclosing the identity of Valarie Plame was Vice President Dick Cheney's chief of staff, Lewis "Scooter" Libby.

As the Bush administration stepped up its effort to force Saddam Hussein to comply with the UN resolutions and give UN weapons inspectors unbridled access in their investigation of disarmament compliance, longtime television news personality Dan Rather secured a personal one-on-one interview with Hussein inside the Iraq presidential palace, which was broadcast internationally. The interview, taped on February 24, 2003, by Iraqi camera technicians, brought Saddam Hussein into living rooms all across America. While the interview was a political gambit, Hussein was reacting to the ever-increasing hard-line rhetoric of President Bush, who had recently begun to state that the use of military force might be necessary in order for Iraq to reach full compliance with the UN resolution. In response to Dan Rather's questions concerning the forbidden long-range al-Samoud missiles, Hussein, through his interpreters, insisted that he had destroyed Iraq's entire cache in utter compliance. When questioned about his concerns regarding a possible U.S.-led invasion of Iraq, Hussein replied that he hoped such a military action would not be forthcoming, but that he and his fellow Iraqis stood ready to respond to such an offensive to the best of their ability. Rather probed Hussein on the issue of whether Iraq had a relationship with Osama bin Laden because the Bush administration had speculated that Hussein had aided and abetted bin Laden's efforts, including the 9/11 tragedy. Saddam Hussein categorically denied having any connection with bin Laden: "We have never had any relationship with Mr. Osama bin Laden, and Iraq has never had any relationship with al-Qaeda. And I think that Mr. Bin Laden himself has recently, in one of his speeches, given such an answer—that we have no relation with him." Saddam Hussein's assurances had no effect on the formulation of U.S. foreign policy. Less than one month after the interview, the United States began its military assault on Iraq.

The legal preparation for a U.S. invasion of Iraq had begun back in October 2002, when Congress passed the Authorization for Use of Military Force Against Iraq Resolution, which authorized the president to use the military in order to ensure Iraq's full compliance. George W. Bush first presented this option as a viable and necessary plan before the UN General Assembly on September 12, 2002. The resolution was cosponsored by Senators Tom Daschle (D-SD) and Trent Lott (R-MS) and by Representatives Dennis Hastert (R-IL) and Richard Gephardt (D-MO) and passed in the House by a vote of 297 to 133 and in the Senate 77 to 23. The United States also ramped up its attempts at securing international support for a military invasion of Iraq, an entreaty that many of the leading industrial nations rallied strongly against. Those who overtly demonstrated full and unconditional opposition to a U.S.-led invasion of Iraq included Russia, France, and Germany, with each nation stating that only through open diplomacy, without the use of military force, should the United States seek a resolution with Iraq. In response to the opposition, President Bush established the "coalition of the willing," which included the United Kingdom, Australia, and Poland. Ultimately, on March 20, 2003, the U.S.-led coalition began its assault on Iraq under the military leadership of U.S. Army General Tommy Franks. The vastly superior military forces of the allied coalition were able to sweep aside the Iraqi army in a matter of weeks. On April 9, 2003, the defense of Baghdad collapsed, bringing Saddam Hussein's twenty-four-year rule to an abrupt and dramatic end.

In response to the general surrender of conventional Iraq military forces, President George W. Bush held a press conference aboard the flight deck of the USS *Abraham Lincoln*, thirty miles from its port in San Diego. He delivered a well-choreographed entry by landing on the aircraft carrier in a Lockheed S-3 Viking jet aircraft instead of the traditional presidential arrival via helicopter. Bush disembarked from the jet in a naval flight suit and after several photo ops, he stood before the television cameras with a large banner that carried the message "Mission Accomplished" unfurled behind him. In his national address, President Bush in no uncertain terms declared victory in Iraq. While it was true that the conventional military forces had been defeated, attacks by Iraqi resistance fighters, termed "insurgents," increased immediately after Bush's speech. As insurgent attacks continued to escalate, the president pressed his military leaders to find Hussein, who had gone into hiding immediately before the military offensive began. Finally, on December 13, 2003, Saddam Hussein was located and captured by the U.S. military outside the town of Tikrit. The images of a bearded and disheveled Hussein being dragged out of a "spider hole"

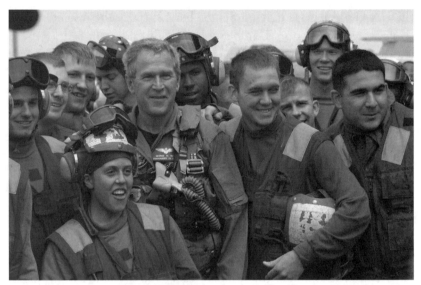

President George W. Bush aboard the USS Abraham Lincoln delivering his "Mission Accomplished" speech, May 1, 2003. *Courtesy Defense Department, photograph by Tyler J. Clements, USN.*

were broadcast across the globe on television and the Internet. But rather than quell the insurgents, Hussein's capture only inspired them to continue and increase their resistance over the succeeding months. Then, the following spring, revelations of abuse of Iraqi and al-Qaeda prisoners at the hands of American soldiers would result in even more insurgent attacks and an international outcry.

THE ABU GHRAIB SCANDAL

In an effort to capture and interrogate terrorist suspects on Iraqi soil, the United States began to utilize the abandoned and formerly infamous Abu Ghraib prison that Saddam Hussein had for years filled with suspected dissidents. On April 28, 2004, the television news journal *60 Minutes II* broadcast a story that claimed U.S. soldiers in the 320th Military Police Battalion had committed widespread illegal abuses of its prisoners. With incriminating pictures of U.S. soldiers humiliating and physically abusing detainees, *60 Minutes II* presented the U.S.-controlled Abu Ghraib prison as a torture chamber. Initially, Americans met the story with skepticism. Within a few days, famed U.S. journalist

Seymour Hersh, who won a Pulitzer Prize in 1970 for exposing the My Lai massacre in Vietnam and the subsequent U.S. cover-up, published an online article with *The New Yorker* magazine that supported the *60 Minutes II* claim. Within a week, more and more images of U.S. soldiers committing acts of torture or humiliation continued to surface. One of the female soldiers, Private Lynndie England, became famous overnight when a photograph of her standing, smoking a cigarette in front of a line of naked Iraqi prisoners, and pointing to one of them being forced to masturbate, was published. With pressure mounting, the U.S. Army expanded its investigation of alleged prison abuse, which had actually begun before the exposés in 2003.

Court martial hearings that took place from 2004 to 2005 resulted in the conviction of seven enlisted soldiers, including England; no officers were convicted. In addition to dishonorable discharges, each of the convicted soldiers received prison sentences that ranged from three to ten years. Brigadier General Janis Karpinski, the commanding officer of the 800th Military Police Brigade, was demoted to the rank of colonel. Karpinski claimed to have no knowledge of American soldiers committing acts of prisoner abuse and later published her memoirs, *One Woman's Army*, in which she placed the blame for prisoner abuse on private military contractors the federal government hired (in this case as additional prison guards or security staff) to supplement U.S. regular and reserve forces.

The official U.S. government responses, delivered by President Bush and Secretary of Defense Rumsfeld, condemned the actions, though Rumsfeld insisted that the abuses did not qualify as forms of torture. One of the strongest critics of the Bush administration's handling of the affair was former vice president Al Gore, who referred to President Bush as the most dishonest president since Richard Nixon. Gore also called, unsuccessfully, for the resignations of Rumsfeld and other senior-level administration officials. Criticisms levied against Rumsfeld continued to escalate following Gore's strong words. Even Republican Senators John McCain and Trent Lott offered their shared opinion that Rumsfeld was not competent for the position of secretary of defense. Nevertheless, President Bush supported Rumsfeld and refused to call for his resignation. Later, in 2006, former General Karpinski stated that she had actually seen a letter signed by Rumsfeld that authorized private contractors to abuse prisoners. Ultimately, the treatment of prisoners at Abu Ghraib humiliated the United States, and in 2006 the Bush administration transferred control of the prison to the Iraqi government.

INCONVENIENT ENVIRONMENTAL REALITIES

By the beginning of the twenty-first century, the vast majority of scientists in the United States had concluded that global warming was not simply a theory but a fact. While there is no consensus on all of the possible outcomes of warmer climates in many places on Earth, on a few points most scientists agree: the oceans will rise; much of the glaciers and polar ice will melt; ocean life will suffer drastic reductions; and deserts will expand. With these drastic changes, many have speculated that human survival everywhere on the planet will pose an increasingly greater challenge. Global warming is overwhelmingly attributed to the rise of greenhouse gases, in particular carbon dioxide, one of the most common byproducts of human activities such as transportation and manufacturing. During the first decade of the twenty-first century, the United States has on average produced 23 percent of global carbon-dioxide emissions.

Since the dawn of the Industrial Revolution, carbon emissions have risen because of the continual growth of modern manufacturing techniques. The inventions of the diesel, internal combustion, and jet and rocket engines, which burn fuels that release a highly toxic waste product, have compounded pollution issues. While Congress has passed and presidents have signed into law legislative acts aimed at lowering emissions, due to consumer demand for larger and less fuel efficient vehicles and an expansion of the airline industry and international shipping since the 1980s, the United States has actually gotten farther away from having a cleaner environment.

The first significant attempt at curtailing air pollution came in 1955 with the passage of the Air Pollution Control Act, but since no government agency existed that could effectively develop policy and enforce regulatory legislation, this act proved to be a paper tiger. For that matter, both the Clean Air Act of 1963 and the Air Quality Act of 1967 proved to be nothing more than political pandering, as neither one had any practical effect in cleaning up the environment. In fact, during this period, all forms of pollution, including those associated with nuclear weapons testing, grew at an accelerated rate. In 1970, the issue of cleaning up and protecting the environment finally gained the legitimate support of the White House and Congress when, as mentioned, Richard Nixon established the Environmental Protection Agency and signed into law the Clean Air Act. While Nixon rightfully receives significant credit for this turning point, Senator Edmund Muskie (D-ME) was the clean environment's greatest ally within Congress, where the Clean Air Act originated.

Following the federal model, by the end of the 1970s many state legislatures and local agencies began to pass measures aimed at protecting the environment. Most of these restrictive laws focused on two distinct areas: automobile emissions and so-called smokestack emissions. But even in the face of consistently more aggressive legislation, for decades the rate of carbon dioxide and other greenhouse gas emissions continued to rise due to a willingness of corporations to pay relatively affordable emission and pollution penalties (and continue to pollute more or less freely) and the overall growth of human population within the nation. Simply put, more people translates into more pollution.

In response to growing concerns and criticisms about having an archaic environmental policy, President George W. Bush proposed the Clean Skies Initiative in 2002. This new approach to cleaning up the environment was based on the assumption that corporations and individuals understood that economic growth was the foundation upon which environmental progress would be built. Carbon-dioxide, sulfur-dioxide, nitrogen-dioxide, and mercury emissions were targeted for reduction by this initiative. The theory that anchored this premise held that if corporations were assessed a surcharge based on their respective rates of emission, they would attempt to become more "green" in order to save money. Thus, the environment would become cleaner as companies sought ways in which to expand their profits. Additionally, the free-market concept of being able to sell one's unused emission allowances, commonly referred to as "cap and trade," would help the power companies' bottom lines and allow consumers to enjoy lower prices. Members of Congress attempted to develop and pass additional regulatory acts, most notably the Clean Skies Act of 2003.

According to the EPA, the Clean Skies Act "would dramatically reduce and cap emissions of sulfur dioxide (SO^2), nitrogen oxides

(NOX), and mercury from electric power generation to approximately 70 percent below 2000 levels" if passed and signed into law. While utilizing the cap and trade system and establishing lower benchmarks for emissions, this platform was a more aggressive response to the environmental woes than President Bush's initiative. Senators James Inhofe (R-OK) and George Voinovich (R-OH) sponsored the bill and from the House; Representatives Billy Tauzin (R-LA) and Joe Barton (R-TX), developed their own version. While many pundits expected the passage of the bill to be smooth, partisan politics created a deadlock in committee, and it never came to the open floor of Congress.

Another significant failure at environmental cleanup and control was the U.S. rejection of the Kyoto Protocol, an initiative named after the Japanese city in which it was delivered to the nations of the world. While not without its legitimate flaws, the Kyoto Protocol was the first significant global attempt to counter the ill effects of global warming. The protocol accepts the theory of global warming as set forth by the Intergovernmental Panel on Climate Change that between 2000 and 2100, the average surface temperature of the earth will rise by more than 10 percent, which many experts have argued would make life impossible in nearly 80 percent of the earth's land regions. In practical terms, the protocol seeks to reduce greenhouse gases and reverse global warming through technological advances and cap-and-trade incentive programs. From the start, the United States has been cold to the idea of joining the Kyoto Protocol.

In 1997, ninety-five members of the U.S. Senate voted unanimously to reject the Kyoto Accords on the grounds that it did not include all industrial nations and would harm the U.S. economy. This uncommon bipartisan rejection is commonly referred to as the Byrd-Hagel resolution, due to the leadership roles of Senators Robert Byrd (D-WV) and Chuck Hagel (R-NE) in blocking U.S. adoption of the Kyoto standards. For his part, President George W. Bush consistently rejected U.S. acceptance of the Kyoto Protocol by pointing out that countries such as China, the second largest producer of greenhouse gases after the United States, was not included on the list of potential signatories.

The only American politician who signed the Kyoto Protocol was Vice President Al Gore, who did so in 1998. Gore had long been a leading environmental advocate, and when he published his first book, *Earth in the Balance*, in 1992, Gore became the first U.S. senator to publish a best seller since John F. Kennedy released *Profiles in Courage*. Gore continued his one-man crusade at cleaning up the environment in his post-political career. In 2006, he wrote and starred in the critically acclaimed motion picture documentary on the environmental concerns centering on global warming, *An Inconvenient Truth*. The film won the Academy Award for best documentary, and in the following year Gore won the Nobel Prize for Peace for his global environmental activism. Eventually, Al Gore's former running mate from the 2000 presidential race, Joe Lieberman, became one of the most outspoken environmental advocates in the Senate.

Motivated by the growth in popular support for improving the environment and slowing the rate of global warming among voters nationwide, members of the Senate debated the America's Climate Security Act of 2007, known as the Lieberman-Warner bill. Senators Joe Lieberman (I-CT) and John Warner (R-VA) introduced the

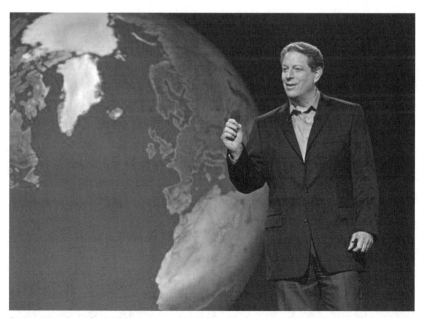

Former Vice President Al Gore appearing in the Academy Award winning environmental documentary, "An Inconvenient Truth." *Credit: © Eric Lee/Paramount Classics, a division of Paramount Pictures. All rights reserved.*

bill, which would have required corporations to lower their emissions progressively through 2050. The key components of the bill focused on capping green house emissions, a financial allowance for "transition assistance" to low- to middle-income families to help them weatherize their homes (and in the process reduce their dependence on utilities) and financial incentives to the developers of low- to zero-carbon emitting technologies. While conservative in comparison to other such initiatives, the bill was killed by Republican senators in the wake of a spike in oil prices that sent the price of a gallon of gasoline above $4 on average across the nation. The lawmakers argued the Lieberman-Warner Bill would effectively propel the price of gas and electric power beyond the reach of the average American.

So, while Al Gore significantly elevated the nation's consciousness on pressing environmental issues, serious action remained somewhat elusive. As the first decade of the twenty-first century came to a close, the U.S. response to global warming was, by almost any measure, completely ineffective.

THE 2004 PRESIDENTIAL RACE

President George W. Bush's popularity rose during his first term in office, partly because he was a wartime president and partly because the economy did not appear to be headed towards collapse. Consequently, Bush did not face any significant challenges to his renomination within the Republican Party. On the Democratic Party front, several strong contenders vied for the nomination. The four leading candidates were Senator John Kerry from Massachusetts, former Vermont governor Howard Dean, North Carolina senator John Edwards, and the retired four-star general Wesley Clark. Though there was much discussion about Al Gore attempting a second run for the White House, the popular former senator and vice president quickly put such speculation to rest when he announced that he had no intention of re-entering the political arena.

Howard Dean was the first to begin his campaign when he formed his exploratory committee in May 2002. Coming from Vermont, one of the least populated states, Dean understood that he was anything but a national figure in the Democratic Party. John Kerry, a longtime senator, became the second major political figure to announce his candidacy, which he did in December 2002. With the issue of national security lying at the core of the race—in the wake of 9/11 and with the United States engaged in wars in Iraq and Afghanistan—Kerry's status as a veteran of the Vietnam War who had been awarded three Purple Hearts gave the Democrats a legitimate candidate who understood the military as well as how Washington worked. John Edwards quickly emerged as one of the most adept campaigners. Handsome, youthful in appearance, articulate, and empathetic, Edwards drew comparisons to Jack and Bobby Kennedy. Wesley Clark stood in contrast to his fellow candidates as the lone U.S. Army general in the race. As a career military officer and leader, Clark had a demeanor of strength, though he also exuded intelligence, patience, and natural diplomacy.

Just before the start of the 2004 campaign year, U.S. troops captured Saddam Hussein, almost giving a false sense of security that the war in Iraq was headed toward a successful conclusion, and, in effect, lowering national concerns surrounding the war. Though it remained a campaign issue, Iraq fell well below two other issues, the economy and health care. The typical pandering to voters' personal financial concerns brought in the usual hollow promises to keep Social Security intact as well as to give a tax break to the largest voting bloc, the broadly defined "middle class." No candidate offered any legitimate, detailed plan for how he would achieve these two goals, beyond a reversal of the tax-relief plan of George W. Bush, which had resulted in lower taxes across the board while favoring the wealthiest Americans.

The Internet played an even more significant role in 2004 than it had in 2000. A greater portion of fund-raising took place online, as did more sophisticated campaigning. Additionally, political action groups found the Internet to be a most effective venue for their advertising. The emergence of MoveOn.org, a self-defined "nonprofit, progressive, liberal public policy advocacy group," attracted millions of constituents and was initially organized in response to the impeachment of President Clinton, which MoveOn claimed had been a political witch hunt. There was some truth to MoveOn's contentions regarding the political motivations behind the Clinton impeachment. Founded by technology entrepreneurs Wes Boyd and Joan Blades, MoveOn made its central goal in 2004 the defeat of George W. Bush, though it offended many of its liberal supporters when it launched an ad that drew parallels between Bush and Adolf Hitler. Following a removal of the Bush-Hitler ads,

MoveOn continued its aggressive anti-Bush campaigning, though in a more subdued fashion.

In the Iowa caucus, the first testing ground in the campaign, Howard Dean and one of the outside candidates, Congressman Dick Gephardt (D-MO), bombarded each other with a series of heavy, negative campaign ads. At this stage, Dean was viewed as the front-runner, for which he drew the heaviest counter-campaign attack ads. Gephardt believed his best chance to become a genuine contender was to beat Dean. The caucus results produced a surprise, as Dean plummeted along with Gephardt, and John Kerry emerged as the victor, followed by John Edwards. Super Tuesday on March 2 produced the same results, Kerry in first and Edwards in second; John Kerry won all ten states in the primary, which included California, Georgia, New York, and Ohio. With his impressive sweep, Senator Kerry was all but assured the Democratic nomination. Less than two weeks later, Kerry secured enough delegates, and for the first time in history the Democratic Party announced Kerry as its candidate online and four months before its national convention. Attempting to create a ticket that balanced youth and experience and northern and southern voters, Kerry selected John Edwards as his running mate. Edwards was clearly the most popular vice-presidential candidate, one whom the Democratic Party also hoped to groom into presidential material. During the meeting of the Democratic National Convention in July, the nation was also introduced to a young, handsome, and articulate candidate for the U.S. Senate, Barack Obama of Illinois, who delivered the keynote speech. Clearly, this was a star on the rise.

To the surprise of no one, the general election campaigning quickly became a heated and controversial affair. Both lead candidates were seasoned political veterans. Further adding to the level of intensity were the political "527" groups: tax-exempt, independent political organizations that are not regulated by federal or state election commissions. In addition to MoveOn, Swift Boat Veterans for Truth was one of the most prominent and successful of the 527s. While MoveOn focused its political attacks on President Bush, the mission of Swift Boat Veterans for Truth was the destruction of the Kerry campaign. From the earliest moments of his run for the White House, John Kerry flaunted his veteran status and challenged President Bush's handling of the war on terror. When accepting the nomination of his party, Kerry stated, "I am John Kerry and I am reporting for duty," a not so subtle reference to his military service, though his words fell flat as Kerry came across as lacking sincerity. Further exacerbating John Kerry's attempt to create the strong veteran image he sought, some of the men who had served with him in Vietnam came forward and challenged the veracity of his statements in regard to his combat service. These men became the foundation for the Swift Boat Veterans for Truth. As in 2000, Bush saw his record of service in the Texas Air National Guard come under scrutiny. However, a blunder committed by the CBS *60 Minutes* production team and its anchor, Dan Rather, actually changed a negative into a positive for President Bush.

For several years Dan Rather, along with several other journalists, had been investigating George W. Bush's military record, attempting to find evidence that he received special treatment in getting into the Texas Air National Guard and thereby avoiding service in Vietnam. When the CBS producer Mary Mapes presented Rather with documents she had been given that supported the long-standing contention that something had been amiss in Bush's service record, Rather and his team believed they had been handed the "smoking gun." After a cursory verification of the authenticity of the alleged military documents, which showed that Bush had failed more than once to perform his duties satisfactorily in accordance with military regulations, the *60 Minutes* segment was aired. Within hours of the broadcast several Internet websites dedicated to exposing fraud began to challenge the alleged memos. Within a week CBS executives began their attempts to distance their company from the memos as more and more evidence came to light that demonstrated either a hoax or outright fraud had taken place. Within two weeks it was clear that the memos had been fabricated; in an attempt to limit the damage, those most directly associated with the memos at CBS were fired, including the *60 Minutes* producer Mary Mapes. Rather, who publicly apologized for not fully verifying the memos' authenticity before airing the show, resigned a year before the end of his contract with CBS. Instead of wounding President Bush, the outcome of the botched exposé added merit to the charge that the nagging hints that he had somehow been afforded privileges during his stint in the Texas Air National Guard were baseless.

The weaknesses in Bush's record that Kerry attempted to exploit were the growing sentiment that the president had mismanaged the war in Iraq and that his fiscal policies would undermine America's future. In return, the Bush campaign blasted Kerry for "flip-flopping" following Kerry's statement regarding his vote on an increase of funds for the Iraq war—"I actually did vote for the $87 billion before I voted against it." Additionally, the Bush people pushed the notion that John Kerry was a "Massachusetts liberal," in effect insinuating he was an elitist unable to understand the issues important to the majority of Americans.

The presidential candidates held three televised debates, the first of which was watched in over 60 million American households and had a few notable points of controversy. In the first debate, no one could help but notice the bulge in the back of President Bush's jacket, just above the waistline. Rumors quickly circulated that Bush was "wired," ostensibly to be fed answers by a third party, which was against the memorandum of understanding between the two candidates. When confronted with the accusation that the president had been using an electronic receiver, his campaign flatly denied the charge and insisted that the bulge was simply a "wrinkle." John Kerry grilled the president about why only two other nations, the United Kingdom and Australia, joined the United States in the invasion of Iraq, but he was mistaken, as he had left Poland off the list. President Bush pointed that out, beginning his rebuttal with "well, actually he forgot Poland," which drew some laughs and embarassed Kerry. Nonetheless, one of the lasting impressions of first debate was President Bush's scowling face, which he made whenever John Kerry criticized his administration. For his part, Kerry came across as an angry man who genuinely lacked optimism. Overall, neither candidate had clearly won.

In the two remaining debates, each candidate attempted to soften his perceived rigidness. In this regard, Bush clearly outperformed Kerry. The president even joked about his previous scowling, easily reverting to his well-known self-deprecating humor. In comparison, Kerry could not shake his "angry man" image. While the debates gave Americans the chance to view and compare the two candidates, polls demonstrated that the perceived outcomes had little effect on who voters supported. The sole vice-presidential debate drew over 40 million viewers, though neither candidate clearly outperformed the other.

Come November 2, more than 122 million voters cast their ballot, with President George W. Bush receiving 62,040,610 to Senator John

Kerry's 59,028,444. In the Electoral College, Bush won 286 to Kerry's 251. Though not a landslide by any standard, unlike the 2000 presidential election, George W. Bush was the clear victor. Nevertheless, during his acceptance speech, the re-elected President Bush virtually suggested it was a landslide when he referred to the results as having given him "political capital." A notable outcome of the election was regionalism. Bush captured the Rocky Mountain states, the Great Plains, the South, and over half of the Midwest, while Kerry secured the entire Northeast and the Pacific states.

The Republicans continued to hold the majority in the House, increasing their numbers from 229 to 232, while the Democrats dropped from 204 to 202 seats. The Republicans also expanded their controlling numbers in the Senate, improving from 51 to 55 members, while the Democrats dropped from 49 to 45. For the next two years, President Bush would enjoy a Republican Congress, though the erosion of confidence in Republican leadership across the nation would bring about a reversal in the next midterm election.

THE SECOND TERM OF GEORGE W. BUSH

One of the primary goals of the Bush administration at the start of the second term was the overhaul of Social Security, a New Deal holdover long considered the "third rail" in American politics, as President Bush quickly learned. First mentioned in his 2005 State of the Union address, the new Bush formula called for a significant privatization of Social Security by permitting individual Americans to decide for themselves where and how they would invest their forced contributions to the Social Security system, similar to the IRA formula, rather than relying on a federal agency to control the entire process. The reason for the overhaul was the Republican assumption that the Social Security Trust Fund would run out before 2020 if no changes were enacted. This view conflicted with the projection favored by most Democrats that the funds would be exhausted slightly after 2050. The majority of Americans over the past two generations had come to doubt the integrity of Social Security, a view that the Bush proposal further complicated with its seemingly blind faith that the U.S. economy would only grow stronger over time, particularly in the realm of stocks and real estate, a necessary component if the Bush plan were to succeed. The vitriolic response by the American people to privatizing Social Security quickly led to the plan's demise.

Turning to one of his stated commitments, bettering education, President Bush and Congress escalated the funding for No Child Left Behind (NCLB). The act, originally passed in 2001 and authored by Senator Ted Kennedy (D-MA) and Representative John Boehner (R-OH) among others, required states to develop standardized tests that measured "adequate yearly progress" in reading and math. Within a year, NCLB had become controversial due to the nature of the individual, state-designed, standards-based testing systems, which many critics claimed would lead to "teaching to the test," instead of encouraging critical analytical skills or independent intellectual thought, because federal funding was directly linked to test-score averages. One of the great motivating factors behind this focus on testing was the great economic incentive for schools that demonstrated improvement. Another point of controversy was the requirement that secondary schools receiving NCLB funding had to permit military recruiters access to their campuses. While no overall consensus was ever reached on the effectiveness of the program, by the end of President Bush's second term, schools across the nation were in obvious need of the financial assistance and NCLB provided them with more than $100 billion. Thus while NCLB did not achieve all of its core objectives, it was one of the largest investments in public education by the federal government in fifty years.

Following in the tradition he established as governor of Texas, Bush reached outside of government for the administration of social programs. Beginning in 2001 and considerably expanded in 2005, the White House Office of Faith-Based and Community Initiatives (OFBCI) provided grants to non-governmental, faith-based agencies. While one of the stipulations for receiving the funds was that the monies could not be used for proselytizing, the American Civil Liberties Union has consistently been opposed to OFBCI on the grounds that it violates the establishment clause of the First Amendment in that it gives tax dollars to religious organizations. As controversies continued to mount, eventually lawsuits developed and court cases followed, leading all the way to the Supreme Court. Finally, on June 25, 2007, the high court decided 5–4 that President Bush's executive order establishing the OFBCI did not violate the establishment clause. While many critics continued to contend that the OFBCI stood in direct violation of the founding fathers' concept of the separation of church and state, agreement on the effectiveness of the grant-based social programs consistently grew each year.

In the first summer of his second term in office, President Bush began to witness what would become a consistent decline in his approval rating for the remainder of his presidency. While this decline, which would eventually lead to historically low levels of public support, was predicated heavily on economic issues and the continued deployment of American soldiers in Iraq and Afghanistan, the weather played a significant role. Technological advances in meteorology had by the start of the twenty-first century enabled scientists to predict with greater accuracy the formation, pattern, and strength of tropical depressions and hurricanes. On August 23, 2005, the National Weather Service reported a significant tropical depression that quickly grew in strength to become a storm over the Bahamas and appeared to be headed for the Gulf of Mexico. Due in part to unusually warm water in the gulf, the storm became a hurricane as it passed over Florida, and upon re-entering the gulf its potency increased again, catapulting it from a category 3 to a category 5. With winds up to 175 mph and an ocean swell of 14 to 16 feet, Hurricane Katrina hit the American Gulf Coast. Two aspects of the storm that distinguished it from other hurricanes were its physical size and the length of time that it sustained hurricane force winds. At the moment it reached its peak, Katrina stretched from the Florida Panhandle through most of Louisiana.

Two days before Katrina reached the shoreline of Louisiana, President Bush, on recommendations by the National Hurricane Center (NHC), declared a state of emergency. The NHC also predicted catastrophic destruction in the city of New Orleans because of the damage that the levees would sustain when the hurricane reached the shore or perhaps even before then. (Some sections of New Orleans actually lie below sea level and are protected by a series of levees.) According to the NHC's prediction, many of these low-lying areas would be uninhabitable for weeks. While these predictions proved to be conservative, they were nonetheless prophetic. On August 29, Hurricane Katrina's storm surge breached more than fifty levees. Hardest hit was the state of Louisiana and the city of New Orleans, the latter all but obliterated. From

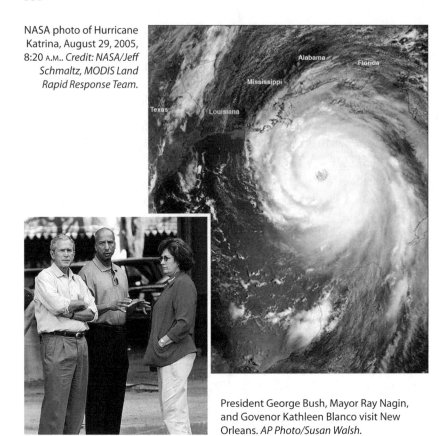

NASA photo of Hurricane Katrina, August 29, 2005, 8:20 A.M.. *Credit: NASA/Jeff Schmaltz, MODIS Land Rapid Response Team.*

President George Bush, Mayor Ray Nagin, and Govenor Kathleen Blanco visit New Orleans. *AP Photo/Susan Walsh.*

the earliest moments of news reporting, it became clear that the ordered evacuation had not fully achieved its goals. Ultimately, more than 1,800 deaths would be attributed to Katrina, with more than 1,500 of those in Louisiana alone. The federal disaster area comprised more than 90,000 square miles, and the property damage would reach over $80 billion. While many observers could have projected the physical impact of the massive hurricane, none had predicted the political fallout.

The pleas emanating from the terrified New Orleans mayor, Ray Nagin, began to hit the national and international news cycle on the day the hurricane ripped apart his city. In his moment of emotional duress, Mayor Nagin was unable to curb his anger, alleging that anti–African American racism had played a role in the perceived lack of response by the federal government. For example, Mayor Nagin stated that "little

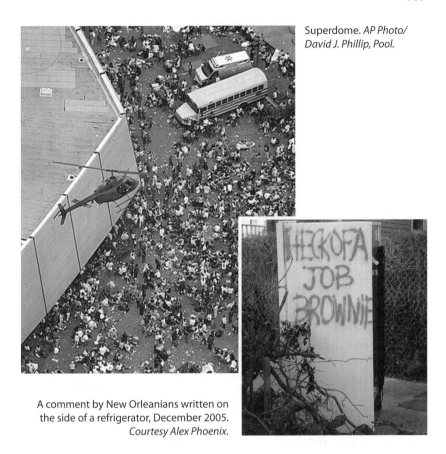

Superdome. *AP Photo/ David J. Phillip, Pool.*

A comment by New Orleanians written on the side of a refrigerator, December 2005. *Courtesy Alex Phoenix.*

babies" were being raped in the Superdome (in which a makeshift shelter had been set up) and that the bodies of the dead in that facility were piling up. Nagin wildly guessed that the death toll might reach 10,000. The media also published and aired stories that African Americans died in disproportionate numbers to whites. In fact, the total death toll in Louisiana included a slightly higher percentage of white citizens than their percentage of the population. Over the ensuing days and weeks, aid did indeed seem slow in coming, which resulted in growing criticisms of President Bush's handling of the crisis. Images of thousands of evacuees taking refuge in the New Orleans Superdome (the bathroom facilities of which were quickly overwhelmed and all but unusable) blanketed the news reports, as did the gruesome images of floating corpses in the persistent floodwaters. As more days passed, more and more Americans began to question why not only the federal government but also the state and local governments, had not put greater effort into evacuating the region. Many pundits suggested that if the hurricane had ripped apart a city that was not predominantly poor and African American, the response would have been much stronger. When President Bush was photographed aboard Air Force One looking down at the devastation caused by Katrina, rather than actually viewing the effects on the ground, the criticism only grew.

During the initial rescue and cleanup, widespread looting took place in New Orleans and the surrounding areas hit hard by Katrina. In some cases, the local police themselves were seen committing the crimes. On August 30, Director of Homeland Security Michael Chertoff had stated that his department would take over all operations. However, Louisiana governor Kathleen Blanco initially blocked the federal agency, insisting that the state's National Guard handle the affair. Eventually, aid began to pour in from the federal government and private citizens across the nation as well as from international sources, though the view that Bush had moved too slowly in his response would dog him for the remainder of his tenure in office. Also politically wounded beyond repair was Governor Blanco, who was viewed as not only inept but also driven by partisan politics that led to a lack of effort in securing federal assistance. Just before Katrina hit Louisiana's shores, Blanco stated in an interview that she was able to "brag about" how prepared she had made the state, referencing the $9 million in aid that she had procured from Washington, D.C., well below the amount needed to cover the eventual damage. Blanco was voted out of office in the next election.

President Bush not only failed to comprehend the enormity of the disaster, but he also gave the impression of someone unequal to copping with the task at hand. Even after the storm struck, he maintained his rather leisurely schedule and remained on vacation on his ranch in Texas instead of flying directly to New Orleans and the Gulf Coast. Then, nearly a week after Katrina, Bush publicly congratulated FEMA Director Brown on doing a "heck of a job"—a gesture that stunned a nation indignant over Brown's obvious incompetence. Governor Blanco also appeared helpless in the wake of the storm. Although she made an appearance at the Superdome and tried to reassure anxious crowds that they would soon receiver help, she failed to provide the transportation the evacuees needed. Mayor Nagin also appeared to be all but overwhelmed. Even though his headquarters were located in the Hyatt-Regency Hotel next to the Superdome, not once did he even appear before the people stranded there. He, too, failed to take necessary actions to assist people. For example, the city's fleet of school buses remained in a parking lot in New Orleans East, where more than 400 of them were flooded. The same thing happened to the city's public transportation buses.

Accusations of neglect were hurled at President Bush, Governor Blanco, and Mayor Nagin, but the most intense criticism was directed at Michael Brown, the FEMA director. Even though FEMA's primary responsibility was to provide immediate assistance to victims of natural disasters, the agency appeared helpless in the face of the monumental resources needed in the aftermath of Katrina. The agency failed to provide transportation to evacuate the victims or to transport the necessary supplies to those in need; and it suffered from a nearly total breakdown in communications. Brown would later claim that he did not even know about the seriousness of the flooding until the day after the storm, when the dire images were already being broadcast on television. FEMA also failed to coordinate relief efforts with the Red Cross, Salvation Army, and countless other agencies that had been available to lend assistance. Although individual men and women employed by FEMA made heroic efforts to save lives and provide aid, the overall impression the agency presented was one of utter incompetence.

QUAGMIRES BOTH: IRAQ AND AFGHANISTAN

On January 31, 2005, Iraq held an election to establish its transitional government. Since 2004, insurgent attacks against coalition forces had been on the rise. Following the historic election, there was a new spike in military assaults committed by dissident Iraqis who viewed the new government as a puppet of the United States. In an effort to pacify the insurgents, American troops who had been scheduled to rotate out of Iraq were left in country. As 2006 began, it became obvious that it would be yet another year in which the U.S. plan for Iraq seemed inadequate, as violence continued. In reaction to growing discontent at home and abroad with the U.S. handling of the war in Iraq, Congress appointed a ten-person panel of experts, the Iraq Study Group, to examine the failings and offer their suggestions. Co-chaired by Republican James Baker and Democrat Lee Hamilton, the bipartisan committee concluded that the overall situation in Iraq had actually deteriorated since the fall of Baghdad and had reached a point where the outlook for Iraq was poor and the country was in grave danger of complete collapse. In their suggestions for bringing about a reversal, the Iraq Study Group advised that the most essential change would be an increased number of Iraqi military personnel. However, understanding that the process of recruiting and training Iraqis would be long and arduous, the group made an immediate call for an increased number of U.S. soldiers on the ground. This point proved unpopular on the American home front, and just as unpopular was the group's caveat that no end date for the U.S. occupation of Iraq should be established. The reasoning on this final point was that insurgents would simply go into hiding and wait for the specified date of U.S. departure before mounting a new wave of assaults. The majority of American people were not persuaded by the group's findings, which were published in book form in early December 2006 and became an instant bestseller. Later that month, Saddam Hussein was hanged by the Iraqi Special Tribunal, which had investigated his domestic crimes against humanity and found him guilty of having murdered more than a hundred people, a rather paltry figure considering his well-known murderous rampages against Shiites, Kurds, and anyone suspected of acts of dissidence. His victims probably numbered in excess of 100,000.

The lack of public support notwithstanding, President Bush accepted the group's findings, and on January 10, 2007, he suggested that a "surge" of over 20,000 additional U.S. troops would help achieve victory, a position he reiterated during the State of the Union speech. Americans, who had turned Republicans out of Congress during the 2006 midterm elections, had anticipated the newly Democratic-controlled House and Senate would not only block such a course but push the president to pull out U.S. troops already in Iraq. One of the most outspoken critics of a troop surge in Congress had been Representative Nancy Pelosi (D-CA), who had recently been elected the first female Speaker of the House. While she, like many other Democrats, continued to stress her goal of ending the U.S. military presence in the Iraq and Afghanistan, when the surge was implemented, Congress had little choice but to support the new strategy, as it did not want to seem unsupportive of the troops. Democrats and Republicans who opposed the military strategy were, however, appeased somewhat when Secretary of Defense Donald Rumsfeld resigned from office on December 18, 2006. Rumsfeld, never popular with Democrats, had lost virtually all of his support from Republicans as well by mid-2006. While President Bush never directly stated that removing Rumsfeld from office was a quid pro quo for supporting the surge, very few Democrats attempted to block the new direction in Iraq during its implementation, January through May 2007. Rumsfeld's replacement, Robert Gates, was not the only change in top-level management: General David Petraeus replaced General George Casey as commanding general of all troops in Iraq. By mid-June, over 28,000 more U.S. troops were on the ground, and by September, Petraeus reported to Congress that the goals of the surge were being met.

Public response to the surge was mixed. According to a CNN poll in spring 2008, 52 percent of the respondents believed the surge was effective and would lead to a quicker conclusion. Additionally, the Pew Research Center released polls that showed that American support for the military effort in Iraq and Afghanistan had actually risen by nearly 30 percent following the perceived success of the surge. Ultimately, the intent of the surge was to bring about greater stability in Iraq in order to shift more responsibility for security and governance to the Iraqi military and government. By the close of 2008, these objectives appeared to be conceivable. Still, achieving stability in Afghanistan and locating Osama bin Laden proved elusive for the remainder of the Bush administration. An additional blemish on President Bush's record would be repeated reports of prisoner abuse at the U.S. military base at Guantánamo Bay, Cuba, which dogged the remainder of his administration.

As more and more detainees were released from the Guantánamo prison, allegations of abuse—ranging from physical, sexual, religious, and mental—were levied against the U.S. Military for conducting what became known as "enhanced interrogation techniques." In 2008, the U.S. Supreme Court ruled against President Bush and his contention that the detainees at Guantánamo were not entitled to the due process of law afforded to American citizens under the Constitution. This ruling proved a significant blow to the Bush legacy, and the controversy surrounding the legality of the treatment of persons in U.S. custody at

Guantánamo under George W. Bush would only escalate during the next presidential administration.

THE GREAT RECESSION BEGINS

The initial negative impact of 9/11 on the U.S. economy was but one of the phenomena that made an already shaky situation even more unstable. Large-scale corporate fraud, gross expansion of consumer credit, and the virtually unchecked home mortgage industry were some of the leading causes that over an eight-year period created a boom-to-bust cycle unprecedented in American history. By no means, however, were the economic woes confined to the United States; rather the crisis was a global one from the start, a fact that further compounded and exacerbated the situation. By the start of 2007, the United States had entered into its greatest economic crisis since the Great Depression.

While many critics have correctly pointed to the two decades of continuing corporate deregulation by the federal government as one of the prime culprits for the collapse of many U.S. businesses during the first decade of the twenty-first century, outright criminal fraud at the executive level lay at the epicenter of some of the greatest corporate failures in history. The complex financial sheets of multibillion-dollar companies with assets, and in some cases distinct markets, around the globe enabled some executives to commit fraud and embezzle funds. Additionally, these white-collar criminals were aided and abetted by banks, law firms, and accounting firms that were paid quite well for their help in either fictionalizing financial records or signing off on those they knew to be misleading. Although several high-profile companies fell apart for these reasons, the two quintessential examples of corporate fraud at the dawn of the new millenium were Enron and WorldCom.

In 1985 the ambitious son of a Baptist preacher and former federal energy regulator, Ken Lay, masterminded the merger of InterNorth and Houston Natural Gas. The outcome of the merger of these two natural gas companies was the establishment of Enron, which operated not simply as an energy company specializing in natural gas but also as a broker for dozens of products and services ranging from freight shipping to electricity. Throughout the 1990s, Enron expanded its interests and holdings, eventually owning nearly forty power stations around the globe. At this point it attempted to break into the burgeoning Internet market with ambitious plans to broker bandwidth and offer on-demand movies, schemes that never fully materialized. But due to creative accounting formulas known as "mark to market," an Enron business venture's failure was hidden from the balance sheet, as the company only presented its shareholders with a financial statement that showed projected future earnings—without identifying them as such. In reality, Enron falsely reported profits that it never earned through this same form of accounting, which Arthur Anderson, the nation's oldest accounting firm, endorsed. Regardless, Enron stock climbed each year, and it was named "America's Most Innovative Company" six years in a row (from 1996 to 2001) by *Fortune* magazine.

Unable to continue its fraudulent business practices when creditors refused to extend any more loans, Enron declared bankruptcy in early December 2001. According to its Chapter 11 filing, Enron had assets of nearly $64 billion, which made it the largest corporation ever to go bankrupt in U.S. history up to that point. During the course of the bankruptcy proceedings, it was revealed that massive fraud had taken place for at least a decade at Enron. Among the many acts of malfeasance that came to light were the establishment of phony holding companies that existed only as temporary holders of Enron debt. Chairman of the board Ken Lay, CEO Jeffery Skilling, CFO Andrew Fastow, and other high-level executives began selling off massive quantities of their personal holdings of Enron stock, which reached a combined worth of more than $1 billion. However, mid- to low-level employees of the Enron Corporation were unable to liquidate any of their company stock, as the corporate officers had instituted a restriction on internal Enron stock trading that literally prevented the workers from accessing their retirement accounts, which in many cases were comprised wholly of shares in Enron. Before the account-access restriction had been put in place, Lay and Skilling had strongly encouraged their employees to purchase as much Enron stock as they could afford. The consistently strong demand for it naturally helped drive up share prices, which Lay, Skilling, and other corporate officers benefited from as they routinely cashed in thousands of shares. By the time the company collapsed, tens of thousands of Enron employees witnessed the implosion of their Enron stock–based retirement accounts. Additionally, Americans learned of Enron's role in generating the fraudulent energy crises in the state of California from 2000 to 2001, which resulted in "rolling blackouts" that raised the price of power to exorbitant levels and ultimately led to the 2003 recall of Governor Gray Davis. Ultimately, several key Enron executives, including Lay, Skilling, and Fastow, were indicted on over fifty criminal charges. In return for a limited immunity agreement with prosecutors, Fastow became a witness against his former bosses. Lay and Skilling were both found guilty of more than a dozen overt criminal acts, though just before his sentencing on July 5, 2006, Ken Lay died. Jeff Skilling was sentenced to prison for twenty-four years; Andrew Fastow received ten years.

While Enron's collapse shocked the nation and sent destructive ripples throughout the American economy, it was not the last major U.S. corporation to fall apart in a short period of time. In 1997, two of the largest telecommunications corporations in the world, MCI and WorldCom, announced their merger, in the process creating MCI WorldCom. Two years later, this company and Sprint announced their intent to merge their holdings. The deal was blocked, however, by the Department of Justice in 2000, when it announced it would investigate whether the merger violated monopoly laws. In the next year rumors of accounting irregularities began to surface, eventually leading to an investigation by the Securities and Exchange Commission (SEC). During the course of the SEC investigation, WorldCom (which had dropped MCI from its corporate name) filed for Chapter 11 bankruptcy with $107 billion in assets, thus eclipsing Enron as the greatest corporate failure in U.S. history. In the ensuing investigation, prosecutors found significant acts of accounting fraud that resulted in the trial and conviction of several high-level WorldCom executives, including CEO Bernard Ebbers, who received a twenty-five-year prison sentence. Unlike Enron, WorldCom was able to escape the grave and emerged from bankruptcy in 2004. In the following year another communications giant, Verizon, purchased WorldCom, which again changed its name to MCI, for more than $7.5 billion.

While the Enron and MCI WorldCom disasters garnered a significant amount of attention from the press, another segment of the economy on thin ice went virtually ignored. The unprecedented expansion of the credit card industry, which relied on the nearly insatiable desire of Americans to live well beyond their means, was generating billions of dollars in profits for the lending institutions. But their greed, which saw them lower their lending standards and issue card after card, even to debt-laden customers, eventually led to an unprecedented level of default that played a central role in a nearly catastrophic collapse in U.S. banking.

Easy access to unsecured credit had consistently increased since the end of the 1950s, when American Express (1958) and BankAmericard (1959), which later changed its name to Visa, began to offer the first widely accepted plastic charge cards, affording people the opportunity to charge their purchases at various stores on a single account. Each successive decade saw more and more lending institutions offer their own charge cards, as did a successively higher number of retailers. In addition to the number of Americans simply holding charge cards, the number of accounts in default rose each year, resulting in higher interest rates and fees as lending institutions attempted not only to cover their loses but also to boost their profits. Advances in technology, in particular electronic communications, streamlined credit purchases by the dawn of the 1980s, and the arrival and growth of the Internet in 1990s offered consumers a new and more convenient realm of spending opportunities that relied heavily on credit card usage. Not coincidentally, credit card debt expanded, even skyrocketed. According to a Nilson Report in April 2009, by the end of 2008, 91.1 million households in the United States had more than one credit card, with the average American carrying 5.4 charge cards. The overall tally of open credit cards in the nation, according to the United States Census Bureau, was an astronomical 1.5 billion in 2008, with an average per capita credit card debt of nearly $11,000. Americans also held an additional eight lines of open credit with other agencies for debt related to car loans, home mortgages, and student loans, among others. The average overall American household debt in 2008, not including home mortgages, was a staggering $18,500, according to the Federal Reserve (also known as the Fed). Perhaps the most significant figure related to personal debt is that by 2008, 43 percent of American families spent more money than they earned each year. As early as 2007, credit card corporations began to report historically higher default rates with each successive quarter. Seemingly over night, lending institutions of all kinds witnessed their once record profits turn into record losses. The skewed spending habits of the American consumers that crushed the unsecured loan industry quickly spread into all areas of the economy, though the first to feel the crunch was the home loan industry, as the collapse of consumer spending sent the economy into a tailspin resulting in higher unemployment rates with each passing month.

One of the mechanisms implemented by Federal Reserve chairman Alan Greenspan to jumpstart the U.S. economy in the wake of 9/11 was to lower the benchmark interest rate at near quarterly intervals beginning in 2002. While many Americans continued to perceive the stock market as risky after the dot.com collapse in 2001, real estate appeared to be a safe haven, as already high home prices began to climb higher, an ascent that continued without interruption through late 2006. But the conditions presented by the bursting bubble in unsecured credit, a rising unemployment rate, and the unsafe mortgage practices eventually led to the formation of a perfect storm in the financial industry. Within the home loan industry itself, there were two specific practices that guaranteed a decline even if all other areas of the economy had remained intact—the dominance of adjustable rate mortgages (ARMs) and subprime lending. These weaknesses in lending were only exacerbated by the growing trend of Americans to spend more than they earned, alongside their virtual refusal to grow their personal savings.

A subprime mortgage package gave many Americans who could not traditionally qualify for a home loan an opportunity to purchase their own home. Over 75 percent of the subprime home loans were ARMs tethered to a benchmark interest rate that was consistently lowered from 2002 through 2008, coupled with interest-only payments for periods of three to ten years. To many, such mortgages appeared to be the only means of obtaining a house that would otherwise be beyond their financial ability. Once monthly mortgage payments came to include a portion of the principal, however, a sharp spike in the monthly mortgage bill resulted, typically placing the actualized monthly mortgage payments suddenly well beyond what the mortgage holder could afford. Why, then, did millions of Americans agree to terms that they knew they simply could not meet? Ironically, the people who took out such high-risk, speculative home loans were gambling in virtually the same fashion as the people who purchased stock on a 10 percent margin dur-

Entrepreneurial minded real estate agents reacting to the record foreclosure rate in San Diego, CA. *Photographer: Cory Doctorow.*

ing the 1920s—they believed the value of their investment would go up forever and that they would be able sell the real estate with ease before having to pay full price; in the process, they would turn a tidy profit. For some Americans, this dream did become reality, but for the vast majority who gambled, failure, foreclosure, and brutal financial hardship resulted. Not only could they not find a buyer in the weakened economy, but the market value of their homes plummeted well below their purchase price, in effect placing their mortgage "under water." Even if they could sell the home they no longer could afford, they could not retrieve enough in the sale to cover their mortgage debt. Many facing this disheartening and seemingly hopeless situation simply opted for foreclosure and bankruptcy. While those who took out loans were certainly responsible for their actions, they were aided and abetted and in many cases coerced by loan officers who had been given virtual carte blanche to offer home loans to individuals without the financial resources to make their payments.

Former Federal Reserve Chairman Alan Greenspan testifying before the House Committee of Government Oversight and Reform in October 2008 on the role of the Fed in relation to the Great Recession. Greenspan concluded his statement with "This crisis will pass, and America will reemerge with a far sounder financial system. *FinancialServices.house.gov.*

As the foreclosure rate escalated beginning in 2006, it sent shockwaves through the financial sector, and the value of homes in the United States, which had risen by more than 125 percent since 2001, began to drop precipitously. Lending and financial institutions that had purchased subprime mortgage–backed securities quickly witnessed a sharp decline in their holdings. Several once prominent financial corporations, such as the nation's largest home loan lending institution, New Century Financial, began to file for bankruptcy protection, while others, such as Ameriquest, one of the largest subprime lending institutions, simply went out of business (in 2007). While 2007 proved to be a dreadful year for the banking industry, 2008 was catastrophic, as the stock market continued to slide, then took a nosedive—further exacerbating the overall economic decline. As they watched the U.S. economy stumble, then fall hard, President Bush and Congress scrambled to find quick solutions to the nation's financial woes. On July

30, 2008, President Bush signed into law the Housing and Economic Recovery Act, which authorized the Federal Housing Administration (FHA) to guarantee $300 billion in home loans if lenders would agree to convert ARMs into traditional thirty-year mortgages and also refinance the loans to represent 90 percent of the houses' current market value. While the proposal prevented many home foreclosures, it failed to halt the skid. In September of the same year, the U.S. Treasury took over two of the largest mortgage lenders, Fannie Mae and Freddie Mac, after the government-sponsored enterprises posted combined losses of nearly $15 billion in one year.

Clearly influenced by the memory of President Herbert Hoover's lack of swift action at the start of the Great Depression, President Bush and Congress continued to expand the government relief programs in 2008. The Emergency Economic Stabilization Act of 2008, signed into law on October 3, aimed at halting the growing number of bank failures. Critics of the plan argued that it rewarded Wall Street investments bankers for gross incompetence and unethical, and in some cases illegal, lending and investment practices. Regardless, the unfathomable sum of $700 billion of taxpayers' money was earmarked for the Troubled Asset Relief Program (TARP), which would identify and purchase "troubled" assets from lenders. In addition to the goal of preventing bank failures, TARP also strongly encouraged banks to continue to lend money for home mortgages to qualified applicants. Nevertheless, the federal government quickly realized that after receiving the bailout money, many banks simply held onto the funds. Over the course of the next few months, Congress had to revamp the rules associated with the receipt of TARP funds in order to compel the lenders to use significant portions of the bailout money to issue new or renegotiated mortgages. For the next few years, temporary government receivership would become the working means through which Washington would attempt to stabilize the economy.

FOREIGN RELATIONS

When campaigning for office in 2000, George W. Bush emphasized that his administration's approach to international relations would involve assisting the developing nations grow their respective economies and that he would depart from the long-standing American tradition of nation building, which involved military support for threatened governments. In the wake of 9/11, however, these goals never materialized, as the United States was forced to re-examine its role in global diplomacy and security.

One of the new, post-9/11 objectives that did materialize was actually based on the Reagan administration's concept of safety through the development of high-tech nuclear weapons and missile-defense shields. While nuclear proliferation remained highly unpopular abroad, on the home front Americans clearly started to warm to the idea, influenced by the al-Qaeda attacks. A little over one month after 9/11, President Bush formally withdrew the United States from President Nixon's historic 1972 Anti-Ballistic Missile Treaty. In justifying the drastic move, Bush explained that in order to protect Americans from "terrorists" or "rogue" nations, the nation needed an extensive arsenal of ICBMs ready to use at a moment's notice. Critics pointed out that the real threats to American security did not come so much from rogue nations with nuclear weapons as from terrorist organizations that operated in cells across many borders; therefore, they posited that revamping the Cold War strategy of nuclear domination would have a negative impact on international relations, which it did from the earliest moments.

In 2002, the United States began to implement its new strategic ballistic weapons program, which included extensive research, development, and testing of ground-, sea- and air-based missiles. The same year, the United States began to negotiate with Poland to place mid- and long-range ballistic weapons on its soil; the other strategic point was Alaska. While the Polish government expressed mild agreement, Russia, not surprisingly, was the strongest opponent of any such U.S. weapons stations so close to its borders. Negotiations between the United States and Poland continued until 2008, when the two nations reached an accord that the military installation would be built. The Russian response was a virtual threat indicating that the United States could anticipate punishment if any such facility were in fact built. Additionally, Russia informed Poland that if the United States were to place any missiles on Polish soil, then it too would face military action, including a possible nuclear strike. Indeed, the rhetoric reached levels of vitriol reminiscent of the Cuban Missile Crisis. The strained relations between the United State and Russia were a sharp departure from those of previous administrations dating back to Richard Nixon, and the acrimony rendered the United States virtually impotent when Russia invaded the sovereign nation of Georgia, a former Soviet satellite, in August 2008 and occupied the South Ossetia region for nearly two weeks. Relations with Russia were not, however, the only diplomatic challenge facing the Bush administration.

Normalized relations with North Korea and Iran also proved elusive, as both nations consistently rebuffed the United States. The main issue that President Bush wanted resolved with each of the two nations, which he had referred to as the "Axis of Evil" in his 2002 State of the Union Address, was their nuclear power and nuclear weapons programs, which Bush claimed posed a real threat to U.S. national security. While North Korea periodically staged pseudo-negotiations with the United States on the matter of developing or abandoning its nuclear research program when the cash-strapped nation sought economic aid, Iran remained steadfast in its refusal to limit or halt its nuclear program. Iranian President Mahmoud Ahmadinejad, following the direction of the religious leaders of his country, flatly refused to curtail any nuclear research and consistently denied that Iran had any intention of developing nuclear weapons, maintaining that nuclear power was the only focus of his nation's program. Before concluding his second term in office, President Bush failed to resolve the tensions between the United States and Iran and North Korea on the issue of their respective nuclear development.

While most areas of U.S. foreign affairs received consistently sharp criticism from both the domestic and international press during the Bush administration, relations with African nations proved to be the one area of positive achievement. Of particular note was President Bush's commitment to assisting African nations in combating the spread of HIV/AIDS; the President's Emergency Plan for AIDS Relief (PEPFAR) allocated over $15 billion in financial assistance beginning in 2003. The administration also imposed harsh economic sanctions against Sudan following the Sudanese Janjaweed genocidal atrocities against the people of Darfur, which involved nearly 500,000 murders and perhaps as many rapes. Additionally, the Bush administration focused a significant amount of spending on the construction of schools throughout Africa, as access to education has proven to be one of the lasting challenges facing nations throughout the continent.

THE 2008 ELECTION

The presidential primaries were hard fought in both parties, although the Democrats clearly experienced the more contentious and controversial of the two contests for nomination. Several leading members of the Democratic Party sensed that due to the record low approval ratings of President Bush and the continued decline in Republican membership, the presidency would be theirs to lose and they aggressively entered the race. The initial front-runner by all accounts was former first lady, Senator Hillary Clinton (NY). Joining Clinton at the top of the list out of the gate was the junior U.S. senator from Illinois, Barack Obama. While there was widespread speculation that former vice president Al Gore would capitalize on his rising star, he emphatically declared, once again, that he had no intention of re-entering politics. Three other significant candidates were New Mexico governor Bill Richardson, former senator and vice-presidential hopeful John Edwards, and longtime member of Congress, Joe Biden (DE).

In the first stage of the long run for the nomination, the Iowa caucus, Senator Obama campaigned relentlessly and, in contrast to his fellow candidates, pointed out that he had very little prior experience in Washington politics, which he insisted was a virtue. Barack Obama campaigned on the promise of change, which was clearly what the majority of the American voters had wanted for nearly four years. Obama's strategy paid off, as he placed first in Iowa, surprising many pundits who believed that because he was African American and the majority of Iowans were of European ancestry, they would not choose the Illinois senator. Perhaps just as surprising, Hillary Clinton, who had been campaigning as though her nomination was virtually inevitable, actually came in third behind Obama and Edwards. Clinton adjusted, presented herself more humbly, and held off Obama to win the New Hampshire primary by a little more than 2 percent of the vote. John Edwards, who had entered the race even though his wife recently had been diagnosed with cancer, now announced that he would be suspending his campaign.

Two of the most populous states, Florida and Michigan, had previously announced that their primaries would be moved to an earlier date.

Their reason for doing so was that by the time their primaries were traditionally held, the nomination process was typically over and therefore the candidates would virtually ignore issues of importance to them. The response of the Democratic National Committee (DNC) was severe: it declared that the results in the Florida and Michigan primaries would not be counted, though a compromise was later reached that permitted a portion of those states' delegates to vote. Both states held their primaries regardless of the DNC's decision, and both produced heavy victories for Hillary Clinton.

The main event in the primary was Super Tuesday on February 4, as twenty-three states, including California, New York, and Illinois, all held their primaries. Clinton won a total of ten to Obama's thirteen states, although she won the overall popular vote by 1 percent, as she took California and New York. The delegate tally was exceptionally close as well, with Obama securing 847 to Clinton's 837. The two candidates would fight on, exchanging victories, through the end of May and into the last day of the primaries, June 3, when Obama not only won the last two states, South Dakota and Montana, but also the 2,117 delegates necessary to secure the nomination. Four days later, Hillary Clinton announced her support of Barack Obama, who eventually selected Joe Biden as his running mate. For the first time in U.S. history, an African American had received the presidential nomination of a major party.

The Republican primaries were not nearly as contentious, though much jockeying for the lead took place between several candidates during the early stages. One of the first candidates to withdraw from the contest was one of the big stars of the Republican Party, former New York City mayor Rudy Giuliani. The former prosecuting attorney garnered national and international acclaim for his management of the city during the 9/11 crisis and its aftermath. But while most people considered Giuliani an adept crisis manager, his presidential nomination campaign lacked direction, and he dropped sharply in the polls before ultimately withdrawing from the race. Former Tennessee senator and contemporary television and silver screen actor Fred Thompson's campaign was even weaker than that of Giuliani, and for months into the election year it remained unclear whether he was actually going to make a bid for the office. By the time he officially entered the race, no one considered him a serious contender, so Thompson withdrew. By January, the three leading candidates were former Massachusetts governor

Mitt Romney, former Arkansas governor Mike Huckabee, and Arizona senator John McCain, who was in his second bid for the Republican nomination, having lost to George W. Bush in 2000.

Each candidate attempted to gain the support of the conservative evangelical base that had remained nearly steadfast in its support of George W. Bush. In this quest, Mike Huckabee, a former evangelical Southern Baptist minister, proved a nearly indomitable adversary. At the same time, Mitt Romney's membership in the Church of Latter Day Saints became a serious obstacle, as many Christians did not have a clear understanding of the Mormon faith and considered it, incorrectly, a non-Christian denomination. Romney repeatedly attempted to put this fear to rest, though ultimately he was unsuccessful on Super Tuesday and in early February pulled out of the race. While John McCain took a significant lead over Mike Huckabee on Super Tuesday, nearly all of the California and New York delegates, the former Arkansas governor stayed in the race. Within a week, many media news agencies began to refer to McCain as the "presumptive" Republican candidate. By that point, McCain's campaign began to focus almost exclusively on the Democrats, and on March 4 he officially clinched his party's nomination. In contrast, Hillary Clinton and Barack Obama would, as mentioned, continue to fight it out until June.

By gaining his party's nomination early in the process, McCain began the campaign with a significant edge on his potential Democratic opponent that allowed him to conduct a search for a vice-presidential candidate who would genuinely aid the ticket. Most analysts had projected either Mitt Romney or Mike Huckabee as the top choice, but remaining true to his maverick reputation, on August 29 John McCain announced Alaska governor Sarah Palin as his running mate. Palin, who became the first female Republican vice-presidential candidate, had been elected governor in 2006. Her prior political experience was two terms as mayor and two terms on the city council of Wasilla, Alaska, a city with a population of less than 10,000. Still, Palin was youthful and attractive—and a seemingly spunky and energetic counterbalance to the elderly, dignified McCain. In the two months leading up to the general election, however, Sarah Palin's weaknesses became apparent. In responding to questions, she often appeared confused and less than articulate. At times she went on long rambles, some of which were nearly incoherent. In short, the

Vice presidential candidates, Sen. Joe Biden (D-DE) an Gov. Sarah Palin (R-AK) squaring off in a debate. *AP Photo/J. Scott Applewhite.*

better acquainted the American public became with Sarah Palin, the more their enthusiasm for her waned, something the McCain campaign realized but was reluctant to remedy.

The issues in the general campaign were the ongoing Iraq War, the fragile state of the U.S. economy, the present administration's unpopularity, Barack Obama's lack of experience compared with McCain's lengthy political career, and Americans' pressing desire for a change of direction in political leadership (which favored Obama). Over the course of their three presidential debates, each candidate demonstrated strong communication skills and the ability to draw empathy from members of the viewing audience. With each successive debate, however, Barack Obama consistently distanced himself from John McCain in the national polls. In the one vice-presidential debate, Joe Biden and Sarah Palin drew a television audience that exceeded 70 million: the vast majority of polls results reported Biden the winner.

One of the biggest stories during the election was fundraising. Barack Obama's campaign produced astonishing figures throughout the primaries and general election. According to the Federal Election Commission, Obama's campaign eventually raised more than $500 million. Senator McCain, who had serious financial issues early in the primary, eventually raised over $375 million. Once again, the significance of the Internet in political fundraising continued to grow, as the Obama campaign was clearly much more adept at using the medium than were McCain's people. McCain even remarked during the campaign that he had trouble using a computer. This gaffe raised some concerns, as the vast majority of Americans, regardless of age, is able to use a computer and does so daily.

On November 4, Barack Obama and Joe Biden won the election convincingly, as more than 69 million people cast their ballot for the Democratic candidates, while fewer than 60 million voted for McCain-Palin. The distance in the Electoral College was greater than the 7 percent divide in the popular vote, as Obama bested McCain 365–173. An estimated 56 to 58 percent of those eligible to vote did so, the highest turnout since the 1960s, when it averaged 60 percent. This strong showing continued a trend of greater voter participation in presidential election years that began in 2000, when 51.5 percent of eligible voters cast ballots, and 2004, when 55 percent did so. The election of 1996 had marked a low point, when only 49 percent of the voters turned out in the contest for the presidency. The overall results in Obama's 2008 victory, though it was not a landslide, indicated that a clear and strong majority wanted a change in political leadership; in the process, the United States elected its first African American president.

The Democratic resurgence in Congress that began in the midterm elections of 2006 continued in the 2008 general election. In the Senate, Democrats picked up eight seats, following the certification of the Minnesota race between incumbent Republican Norm Coleman and humorist Al Franken, one of the closest in recent history. Franken ultimately was awarded the seat by the Minnesota State Supreme Court, having won the contest by less than .5 percent. After the election, Democrats held 59 seats, one shy of the required number to block filibusters. Then, when longtime Pennsylvania senator Arlen Specter defected from the Republican Party and joined the Democrats, the latter suddenly had the necessary 60 seats. Harry Reid of Nevada continued to serve as Senate majority leader, and Mitch McConnell of Kentucky as Senate minority leader. In the House, the Democrats added 21 seats for a total of 257 to the Republican tally of 178. Nancy Pelosi continued in her historic role as the first female Speaker of the House, though she had faced significant criticism from within her own constituency in San Francisco for the perceived weakness in her attempts to end the wars in Iraq and Afghanistan. John Boehner of Ohio maintained his position as House minority leader.

LEGACY OF THE GEORGE W. BUSH YEARS

Throughout his two terms as president, George W. Bush faced challenges that few other presidents ever had, and one characteristic of his leadership that he demonstrated repeatedly was the ability to make difficult decisions quickly and forcefully. While many of his critics routinely cast his aggressive style as haphazard or worse, none doubted his resolve. Bush proved to be one of the most controversial presidents in the post–Civil War era. A good deal of the controversy was linked to the perception that the Bush administration operated in a clandestine fashion and skirted the Constitution in a way that was reminiscent of Nixon years. This view was not completely unfounded. Former Nixon White House counsel John Dean composed a best-selling book, *Worse than Watergate*, that chronicled abuses of presidential power warranting impeachment that he believed the Bush-Cheney White House had committed during its first term. Dean was not alone in his negative interpretation of the administration. In 2006, Sean Wilentz of Princeton, one of the nation's leading historians, composed an article for *Rolling Stone* that discussed not simply whether Bush was a failed president but rather whether he was the worst president in history; Wilentz found no evidence to contradict his failed presidency thesis. National support for Bush consistently declined from his 90 percent approval rating in the immediate aftermath of 9/11 to the abysmal 25 percent during his last days in office. Only two other post–World War II presidents had comparably low approval ratings in the last year in office: Harry Truman and Richard Nixon. In time, the historical view of both Truman and Nixon was rehabilitated, more so for Truman than for Nixon.

While he did not alter the political makeup of the Supreme Court with his two successful nominees, Bush's selections nonetheless guaranteed that a consistently partisan 5–4 vote (with Republican justices in the majority) on most matters would be forthcoming for many years. Following Sandra Day O'Connor's retirement announcement, Bush nominated conservative federal appellate court judge John Roberts. Then, following the death of Supreme Court Chief Justice William Rehnquist, Bush renominated Roberts for chief justice. Roberts was confirmed by a 78–22 vote; all the dissenting senators were Democrats. The second candidate to replace O'Connor was White House counsel Harriet Miers. After facing extreme criticism from both Democrats and Republicans for what was perceived as an overt act of cronyism, Bush withdrew the nomination at Miers' request. His third nominee was Samuel Alito, a conservative federal appellate court judge widely regarded to be in the mold of conservative Supreme Court justice Antonin Scalia, the only other Italian American to serve on the Supreme Court. The Senate ultimately confirmed Alito 58–42. Both Roberts and Alito had received the American Bar Association's highest consideration for the Supreme Court; it found both candidates "well qualified." Still, the American Civil Liberties Union (ACLU) opposed Alito's nomination on the grounds that his opinion on civil liberties might lead him to "abridge individual freedoms," making Alito the first Supreme Court nominee since Robert Bork (nominated by President Reagan) to be opposed by the ACLU. While neither Roberts nor Alito indicated that he would vote for the overturn of *Roe* v. *Wade*, most anti-abortion activists view their seats on the bench as victories.

The two actions for which Bush was most criticized were his decision to have the United States enter a pre-emptive war in Iraq and his handling of the developing economic crisis at home. Concerning Iraq, the most significant impediment to his potential future rehabilitation lies in the controversy about why his administration called for an invasion. The consistent rationale of the Bush administration had been Saddam Hussein's development of WMDs and Iraq's link to the 9/11 attacks. But according to the 9/11 Commission's investigation, no link between Hussein and al-Qaeda existed. Further exacerbating the credibility of the administration was that no WMDs were ever found in Iraq. Compounding the question was the CIA's final report on the matter, which concluded that no WMDs had been in Iraq at the time Bush, his cabinet, and his closest advisers made their case for an invasion—including when Secretary of State Colin Powell went before the UN with what he claimed was compelling evidence. During his last press conference as president, Bush himself admitted that

President George W. Bush announcing his nominee for the U.S. Supreme Court, John Roberts. *White House photo by Eric Draper.*

he had been mistaken about the WMDs. Additionally, most critics claim that the Iraq War destabilized an already volatile Middle East, giving terrorists even more anti-American propaganda to use in their recruitment efforts.

As for the domestic economy, the primary critics from 2001 through 2007 were liberals and moderates, but in 2008 conservatives also began to rail against President Bush's rapid push for massive bailouts of banks and other corporations to the tune of $700 billion. Some of these critics went so far as to declare President Bush a socialist. In response to those who did not agree with his 2008 bailout plan, Bush said that he had inherited a recession on entering office and was later dogged by a second recession as he left Washington, though he pointed out that in between the two downturns were fifty-two months of job growth. While he was basically correct, a great deal of the job growth was based on the expansion of individual debt. Regardless, as Bush left office, the nation lay in the throes of the worst economic crisis since the Great Depression.

The most significant social issues with which society grappled during the Bush years included stem-cell research and gay marriage. On the question of providing federal funds for stem-cell research to combat a list of debilitating diseases including cancer, diabetes, multiple sclerosis, and spinal-cord injuries, President Bush issued his first veto in 2005. He vetoed a second legislative attempt by Congress to authorize federal funding in 2007. While most polls demonstrated that nearly 70 percent of Americans favored stem-cell research, even that which utilizes embryonic cells obtained primarily from aborted fetuses, Bush stayed true to his base of support, the conservative evangelicals, who overwhelmingly stood against the research programs. On the issue of the right of gays and lesbians to a legal marriage with each spouse entitled to the benefits thereof, President Bush never deviated from his open opposition, which dated back to his Texas governorship. He therefore supported the Republican-led Federal Marriage Amendment, which would insert a ban on gay marriage into the Constitution, but he did indicate that he would support state-enacted legislation permitting same-sex civil unions.

In the final weeks of his presidency, historians and political scientists echoed repeatedly that, overall, George W. Bush had not been an effective president. Julian Zelizer of Princeton University's Woodrow Wilson School stated in a CNN interview after the 2008 election that most historians see Bush "as incompetent in terms of how he handled domestic and foreign policy. He is seen as pushing for an agenda to the right of the nation and doing so through executive power that ignored the popular will." As Harvard University professor of political science Barbara Kellerman argued after the start of the Obama administration, Bush may come to be viewed in a softer light. According to Kellerman, he had been "a quite unlucky president," and she cited 9/11, Hurricane Katrina, and the financial crisis as three examples. The potential legacy of George W. Bush has been most often compared to that of Harry Truman, who also left the presidency tied to an unpopular war and during a financial downturn. Ultimately, it will be for future historians to decide on the true legacy of George W. Bush after sufficient time has passed and the true value of his policies and decisions can be weighed against their long-term effects.

---★---

SUGGESTIONS FOR FURTHER READING

To date, no thorough scholarly examination that assesses George W. Bush's presidency has appeared. President Bush's memoir, *Decision Points* (2010), does, however, provide readers with insight on his policy-making rationale as well as into his personal life and is well worth a read. *Courage and Consequences: My Life as a Conservative in the Fight* (2010), by Karl Rove, certainly contains a strong bias, but it also sheds significant light on the political strategies of the Bush administration. During his time in office, the literature published on the Bush presidency tended to be either strongly negative or exceptionally biased in favor of the president, with the majority of the serious works tending to lean toward sharp criticism. Former Nixon White House counsel John W. Dean published a trilogy of best sellers highly critical of both the Bush administration and the Neocons within the Republican Party: *Worse Than Watergate* (2004) examined the administration's obsession with secrecy; *Conservatives Without Conscience* (2006) outlined the rise of the Neocons; and *Broken Government* (2007) argued that the Bush-Cheney administration was responsible for inflicting more damage on the system of Constitutional checks and balances than any other in history. Before entering the 2000 race, George W. Bush and Karen Hughes, one of his chief advisers, collaborated on *A Charge to Keep* (1999), which, although light in overall content, covers the primary political objectives Bush carried from his governorship into the White House. One can find key selections from public statements and speeches from Bush's first term in office in *George W. Bush on God and Country* (2004), edited by Thomas Freiling. For an understanding of the philosophical and religious beliefs that played a central role in Bush's decision making, *The Faith of George W. Bush*, by Stephen Mansfield (2004), offers the best insight.

Former chief counter-terrorism adviser to the National Security Council Richard Clarke composed an insider account on the U.S. response to 9/11 and the war on terror in *Against All Enemies* (2004). Clarke later published a follow-up, *Your Government Failed You* (2009), which drew upon his thirty years in national security. Former Bush administration press secretary Scott McClellan published his memoir, *What Happened: Inside the Bush White House and Washington's Culture of Deception* (2008), which was staunchly critical of President Bush, after leaving government.

On the topic of 9/11 and the wars in Iraq and Afghanistan, the 9/11 Commission published its findings, *9/11 Commission Report: Final Report of the National Commission on Terrorist Attacks upon the United States* (2004). Also the Iraq Study Group published its findings and suggestions in *The Iraq Study Group Report: The Way Forward—A New Approach* (2006). *Washington Post* writer Thomas Ricks, who spent five tours reporting in Iraq, published a harsh criticism of military policy in *Fiasco: The American Military Adventure in Iraq* (2006). The most nuanced and thoughtful memoir by an Iraq War veteran is *The Unforgiving Minute: A Soldier's Education* (2009), by Craig Mullaney. Rand Corporation political scientist Seth Jones has published the best analysis of the war in Afghanistan in *In the Graveyard of Empires: America's War in Afghanistan* (2009).

The eminent historian Douglas Brinkley has composed the best comprehensive work on Hurricane Katrina, *The Great Deluge: Hurricane Katrina, New Orleans, and the Mississippi Gulf Coast* (2006). Jed Horne's analysis of the impact of the storm and its aftermath on New Orleans, *Breach of Faith: Hurricane Katrina and the*

Near Death of a Great American City (2006), is noteworthy. *Come Hell or High Water: Hurricane Katrina and the Color of Disaster* (2006), by Michael Eric Dyson, examines the role that race and ethnicity played in the hurricane and its aftermath.

The Great Recession has received significant attention from scholars, though as the end of it has yet to come as of this writing, no complete study has been published. The strongest work on the subject to date is *Meltdown* (2009), by Thomas Woods. Former Fed chairman Alan Greenspan published his early thoughts as the economy plummeted after 2006 in *The Age of Turbulence: Adventures in a New World* (2007). Billionaire activist George Soros offered his insight on the credit crisis in *The New Paradigm for Financial Markets: The Credit Crisis of 2008 and What It Means* (2008). An early critique of the initial failings of Wall Street that is worth a look is Roger Lowenstein's *When Genius Failed: The Rise and Fall of Long-Term Capital Management* (2000). Bethany McClean and Peter Elkind's investigative account, *Enron: The Smartest Guys in the Room* (2003), is one of the best works on corporate fraud in the past generation.

———★———

CHAPTER

14

Changing America

W HILE A GREAT DEAL OF UNCERTAINTY permeated American society in the wake of the ever-worsening economic collapse and the continuation and escalation of the wars in Iraq and Afghanistan, the desire for change clearly dominated the nation. For most Americans, the young and optimistic president, Barack Hussein Obama, offered the hope for which they were searching. Obama had campaigned on the themes of "hope" and "change," but once in Washington he quickly found out the change he promised would be immensely difficult to achieve. The economy continued to tumble, seemingly beyond control, as Wall Street plummeted and major corporations failed one after another. Even General Motors, once considered the shining example of American manufacturing prowess, filed for bankruptcy. All that had once made the U.S. economy great and the American Dream a reality began to resemble a house of cards.

BARACK OBAMA

In 2008, the United States elected its first African American president in Barack Obama. Born in 1961 in Honolulu, Hawaii, to an American mother and a Kenyan father who divorced three years after his birth, Obama had a transient youth. He spent four years of his childhood in Jakarta, where his mother remarried an Indonesian man. By his eleventh birthday, young Barack was back in the states, though instead of living with his mother, he resided with his maternal grandparents and remained under their care through his high school graduation. While Obama's mother returned from Indonesia in 1972, she only remained in Hawaii until 1977, when she went back to Indonesia to conduct field-work in anthropology. Barack excelled in athletics as well as academics, although he succumbed to substance abuse during his teen years. Rec-ognizing that he had clearly made some poor choices, for which he felt great shame, the young Obama swore off narcotics and quickly rebuilt his life and looked forward to higher education.

Obama matriculated at Occidental College in Southern California, though for his junior and senior years he transferred to Columbia University, where he majored in political science and graduated in 1983. For four years, he tried his hand in the business world of New York City and then changed direction by moving to Chicago and entering the field of community organizing. Hired as director of the Developing Communities Project, Obama proved quite successful in his new position, increasing the size of the staff from one to more than a dozen and its annual budget from just over $60,000 to nearly $500,000. Additionally, Obama established programs in college preparation and career training. After three years at this post, he once again sought a life transition. In 1988, Obama entered Harvard Law School and, remarkably, became one of the editors of the *Harvard Law Review* in his first year. In his second year of law school Obama was named president of the journal, the first African American ever to hold that prestigious post. During the summer of 1989, Obama worked as a summer associate in the Chicago office of the international law firm Sidley Austin, where he met his future wife, Michelle Robinson, who was also a summer associate. After obtaining his J.D., Obama returned to Chicago, practiced law, and entered the world of politics.

Back in Chicago, in 1993 Obama organized and directed Project Vote, which registered nearly half a million previously unregistered African Americans. At this time he also wrote his memoirs, *Dreams from My Father* (1995). Before the end of 1993, Obama joined the law firm Davis, Miner, Barnhill & Galland, where he rose from associate to counsel in three years. Supplementing his already busy professional calendar, he taught constitutional law at the University of Chicago. In 1996, Obama entered the world of electoral politics, winning three successive terms as an Illinois state senator. He suffered his first and only defeat at the polls in 2002 when he lost a primary race for the U.S. House of Representatives to the popular incumbent, Bobby Rush. Undeterred by the loss, Obama boldly set his sights on the U.S. Senate race in 2004.

The March 2004 Democratic primary proved a great success as Obama won over 25 percent more votes than any other candidate in capturing more than 50 percent of the ballots. At the 2004 Democratic National Convention, he was, as mentioned, awarded the opportunity to deliver the keynote address, which he did with poise and eloquence. In the regular election, Obama had a stroke of good luck when Republican candidate Jack Ryan pulled out of the race after it was revealed that he and his former wife, the actress Jeri Ryan, had an unusual sex life. The Republican Party scrambled to find a contender to replace Ryan and ultimately settled on Alan Keyes, a conservative African American who had never lived in Illinois but scrambled to meet the residency requirements before the election. Obama trounced Keyes, besting him by a 40 percent margin, a record in Illinois politics.

In the Senate, Obama proved a loyal and liberal Democrat. In addition to sitting on the Senate Foreign Relations Committee, he worked with his future rival presidential candidate, John McCain, on immigration reform. The *National Journal* in 2007 declared Obama the most liberal member of the Senate, according to its analysis of his voting record. That same year, Obama announced his candidacy for the Oval Office, and after his successful election in 2008 he resigned his seat in the Senate as he prepared his transition to the White House.

THE OBAMA ADMINISTRATION

On a bone-chilling January 20, 2009, Barack Obama took the oath of office and became the forty-fourth president of the United States. The turnout for the inauguration was the greatest in history, with the entire National Mall opened up to accommodate all those physically in attendance. Additionally, the event was one of the most highly viewed broadcasts around the globe in history. Indeed, President Obama's celebrity was on the order that very few presidents entering their first term had ever known. His relative youth, optimism, personal charm, and beautiful wife and daughters projected an image similar to that of John F. Kennedy. While the massive crowds entered and exited the Mall without

Left to right, Secretary of Education Arne Duncan, President Obama, Secretary of the Interior Ken Salazar, Attorney General Eric Holder, and Secretary of Defense Robert Gates. *Official White House Photo by Pete Souza.*

incident and the incredible array of broadcast media carried the historic event without even the slightest error, John Roberts, the Chief Justice of the U.S. Supreme Court, misspoke the oath of office as the world watched and listened. The following day, upon President Obama's request, Roberts administered the oath a second time in the White House Map Room, this time without error.

President Obama assembled diverse, experienced, and well-regarded experts to serve in his cabinet and as his chief advisers. Former political rival Hillary Clinton had been considered by many political analysts a natural fit for the vice presidency. Obama, as mentioned, selected Joe Biden to serve in that capacity, but he did tap Clinton for the highly visible post of secretary of state. Joe Biden's long tenure in Congress would allow him to assist President Obama in federal policy development, and the high level of respect that Biden enjoyed in both houses would serve Obama well as he developed his Oval Office relations with Capitol Hill. For her part, Clinton, along with her husband Bill Clinton, enjoyed popularity, respect, and good standing around the globe. In taking up the nation's financial woes, Obama placed wunderkind

Timothy Geithner at the helm of the Treasury Department. Soon after Geithner's nomination it was revealed that he had not paid his full federal income tax and Social Security bills while employed at the International Monetary Fund. Geithner apologized and quickly paid his debts, though his oversights fueled some pointed criticisms. Due to the economic crises, Geithner would have the highest level of public visibility following President Obama. The only holdover in the cabinet from the Bush administration was Secretary of Defense Robert Gates, in whom President Obama had very high confidence. As Gates had only headed defense since December 2006, Obama reasoned that to appoint a third secretary in less than three years in this crucial area made little sense. Eric Holder became the first African American to serve as the U.S. Attorney General following his confirmation in the Senate, and Steven Chu became the first cabinet official to have previously won a Nobel Prize when he took over the post of secretary of energy. Janet Napolitano became the first woman to head the recently developed Department of Homeland Security. Susan Rice, a former assistant secretary of state for President Bill Clinton, became the first African American U.S. ambassador to the UN and the third woman to hold that post. Perhaps Obama's most controversial cabinet level appointment was his selection of Representative Rahm Emanuel (D-IL) as his chief of staff. Emanuel had developed a reputation for hard-nosed partisan politics, a severe temper, and a proclivity for profanity during his political career. Many critics argued that Emanuel was not properly suited to serve as the gatekeeper to the Oval Office, but, as former Nixon chief of staff H. R. Haldeman had not so delicately put it, the White House chief of staff needed to be the president's "SOB," and Rahm Emanuel fit that job description well. Additionally, President Obama changed the makeup of the Supreme Court in his first two years in office. In 2009, Obama's first nominee, Sonia Sotomayor, became the first Hispanic and third female member of the high court. In 2010, Obama successfully nominated Elena Kagan, and for the first time in United States history, three of the sitting members of the Supreme Court were women.

The first legislative item President Obama signed into law reflected his longstanding concern for individual rights. The Lilly Ledbetter Fair Pay Act of 2009 is an amendment to the 1964 Civil Rights Act and the Discrimination in Employment Act of 1967 that changes the previ-

The United States Supreme Court, the highest court in the United States, in 2010. Top row (left to right): Associate Justice Sonia Sotomayor, Associate Justice Stephen G. Breyer, Associate Justice Samuel A. Alito, and Associate Justice Elena Kagan. Bottom row (left to right): Associate Justice Clarence Thomas, Associate Justice Atonin Scalia, Chief Justice John G. Roberts, Associate Justice Anthony Kennedy, and Associate Justice Ruth Bader Ginsburg. *Courtesy: Steve Petteway, Collection of the Supreme Court of the United States.*

ous statute of limitations for filing a discrimination suit against one's employer. Previously the limit had been set at 180 days following a salary agreement, while the new provision reset the 180-day limit successively with the issuance of each paycheck. The new law grew out of a discrimination lawsuit filed by Lilly Ledbetter against Goodyear Tire and Rubber Company after Ledbetter had discovered that she had been paid less than her male counterparts. In 2007 the Supreme Court had, in a 5–4 decision, found on behalf of Goodyear because Ledbetter had filed her suit after the 180-day limit. While the act came too late to assist Ms. Ledbetter, the individual rights of current and future Americans were clearly enhanced by the new statute.

One of President Obama's campaign promises, the quick closure of Guantánamo Bay prison camp, proved elusive. This prison had become an international embarrassment for the United States after the brutal and unconstitutional activities of the interrogators and prison guards were revealed. However, soon after Obama became president, White House officials found that prosecuting the detainees in accordance with the law would take several months. Rather than begin the closure immediately, Obama issued an executive order for closure within a year. While not considered a political failure, the president's inability to close the prison camp did reveal a certain naivete. However, Obama did issue an executive order that required the military to follow the Army Field manual strictly when interrogating detainees, thus prohibiting the use of torture, including the controversial "waterboarding" techniques implemented during the previous administration.

Arguably the most significant action taken in President Obama's first 100 days was the American Recovery and Reinvestment Act of 2009, which he signed into law on February 17. After more than one month of political wrangling in the House and Senate, this economic stimulus package came in at over $787 billion. The provisions of the package were wide-ranging, including tax cuts for the middle class and below, an $8,000 tax credit for first-time homebuyers (aimed at stabilizing the

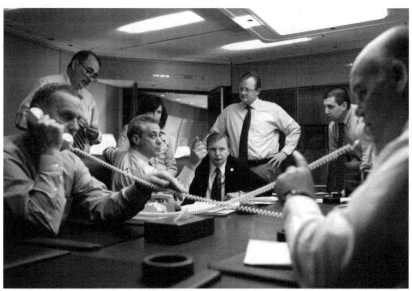

Former Chief of Staff, Rahm Emanuel (pointing finger) running a strategy session. *Official White House Photo by Pete Souza.*

volatile real estate and mortgage market), significant tax credits for the purchase of a new automobile in response to the remarkable decline in car purchases, and, among other incentives, a tax credit for the installation of more energy-efficient appliances and weatherproofing in residences. The act also allocated billions to stabilize Medicare.

Reactions to the stimulus package by economists were mixed and reflected the divisions in Congress, which had passed its versions of the plan 246–183 in the House and 61–37 in the Senate. Public reaction was even more critical. According to a February 4, 2009, *USA Today*/Gallup poll, only 52 percent of the American people supported the president's plan. Not surprisingly, 70 percent of self-identified Democrats favored the plan, while 72 percent of Republicans did not. One feature of the plan that none could dispute was its broad approach, which sought to inject capital across a wide range of the economy.

The high regard in which the international community held the new president was exemplified when, on October 9, 2009, Obama became the fourth U.S. president to be awarded the Nobel Peace Prize: Theodore Roosevelt for his management of the peace accords for the Russo-Japanese War in 1906; Woodrow Wilson for the Fourteen Points he presented at the Paris Peace Conference after the end of World War I; and Jimmy Carter (after he had left office) for "his decades of untiring effort to find peaceful solutions to international conflicts, to advance democracy and human rights, and to promote economic and social development." The decision to award Obama the prize, according to the Nobel committee, was to recognize his "extraordinary efforts to strengthen international diplomacy and cooperation between peoples." The president's critics quickly assailed the Nobel committee for attempting to influence a president who had yet to complete his first year in office. Others noted that Obama had received the nomination just twelve days after he had taken the oath of office. With tongue-in-cheek, conservative political commentator George Will quipped: "The Nobel Prize committee would with this decision have forfeited its reputation for seriousness if it had a reputation for seriousness." Under normal circumstances, winning a Nobel Prize is viewed in a positive light, but President Obama found himself defending his acceptance of the honor. In his own words, he was "surprised and deeply humbled." Although the president accepted the award, he donated the monetary component, $1.4 million, to ten distinct charitable organizations. In his eloquent Nobel lecture, Obama also noted the irony that "the most profound issue surrounding my receipt of this prize is the fact that I am the Commander-in-Chief of the military of a nation in the midst of two wars."

Obama, however, was not without error in judgment. Appearing on the *Tonight Show*, the president responded to a question by host Jay Leno concerning a horrible bowling score Obama had gotten while at a campaign stop. In an attempt at humor, Obama admitted that his score would probably qualify him for the Special Olympics. Obama quickly apologized for the comment, though the insensitive gaffe was a surprise given the president's typically careful choice of words. Within a few months, however, President Obama once again came under fire, this time in response to a hot news item concerning the arrest of Harvard professor Henry Louis Gates Jr., an African American, at his house in Cambridge for disorderly conduct. When asked for his opinion during a press conference, President Obama explained that although he did not have all of the facts, in his opinion the arresting officer (who had been called to the Gates residence by a neighbor who suspected a burglary was in progress) had acted "stupidly." Immediately Obama faced the ire of law enforcement officials and police unions. The arresting officer, Sgt. James Crowley, who had taught a class in racial profiling at a police academy and claimed that he supported the president "110 percent," said that he resented the president's assessment. While Obama did not apologize for his word selection, he did recant. Within a few days, President Obama and Vice President Biden had beers with Gates and Crowley at the White House and managed to put the unfortunate episode to rest. While the real issue at hand, racial profiling by police, has witnessed a decline, this unfortunate practice that overwhelmingly targets men of color persists.

The greatest legislative challenge for the Obama administration was its oft-stated goal of health care reform. Obama experienced early success on this front when he signed the State Children's Health Insurance Program (SCHIP) in early February 2009. SCHIP provides health care for more than 10 million children nationwide. Additionally, the president's stimulus package provided a subsidy for Americans who lost their jobs and consequently had to purchase their own health insurance through COBRA (see below). Then, in March 2010, President

Obama realized one of his greatest legislative successes when Congress passed and he signed into law the Patient Protection and Affordable Health Care Act. The multifaceted legislation expanded Medicaid, offered small businesses incentives for providing health care insurance to employees, and imposed a penalty on individuals who do not have health insurance, though the legislation also provides a subsidy to help lower-income individuals and households purchase health insurance. One of the more controversial components of the new legislation was an amendment to it known as the Health Care and Education Reconciliation Act, which called for a 40 percent tax on so-called "Cadillac" health care plans—it is slated to go into effect in 2018. A Cadillac plan is an expensive one with good coverage that an employer provides to an employee. Nearly universally unpopular with unions, who had fought hard for increases in health care benefits for laborers in exchange for begrudgingly accepting smaller wage increases, the Cadillac tax was designed to help fund the increase in federal spending required by the new universal health care plan. On the other hand, one of the most popular components of the new legislation is the one that prohibits health insurance companies from denying coverage to individuals with pre-existing conditions (including chronic diseases) as well as from dropping individuals once they become become ill. Overall, the passage of these combined legislative acts constituted the greatest and most sweeping change in health care in United States history since the establishment of the Medicare program in 1965 under President Lyndon Johnson's Great Society, which proved health insurance to more than 60 million Americans, and the most significant change since the Consolidated Omnibus Budget Reconciliation Act of 1985 (COBRA), which provided for the continuation of medical benefits at the expense of the individual upon separation from his or her employer.

On April 20, 2010, right on the heels of the Obama administration's hard-won triumph on health care reform, came an explosion on the British Petroleum (BP) Deepwater Horizon oil rig in the Gulf of Mexico—an event that resulted in the worst marine oil-spill disaster in the nation's history. When the explosion occurred, Deepwater Horizon was actively engaged in exploratory drilling about a mile underwater. A buildup of methane shot up the drill columns; once the highly pressurized and flammable gas reached the surface of the

Fire boat response crews battle the blazing remnants of the offshore oil rig Deepwater Horizon, April 21, 2010. *U.S. Coast Guard photo.*

rig, it triggered a massive explosion that sent up a towering column of fire. All but eleven of those working on the rig survived the explosion; the bodies of the deceased were never recovered. Many of those who survived sustained serious wounds and burns. During and immediately after the rescue efforts, the containment of the colossal fire, visible from more than thirty miles away, was the top priority. By late in the second day, however, the gushing hole on the ocean floor that the explosion had unleashed took precedence. Initially, BP executives grossly underestimated the amount of oil leaking daily into the gulf from the shattered wellhead. Just one day after the explosion, both BP and the United States Coast Guard reported the gusher as a leak in the range of 1,000 barrels a day. Subsequent estimates, which were revised nearly daily, only escalated. Over the course of the eighty-six days that the well remained uncapped, more than 200 million gallons of crude shot into the Gulf of Mexico.

Ultimately, a team of diligent workers and scientists managed to seal off the well, but the damage done by the spilled oil—to the marine and coastal wildlife and to people in the the Gulf Coast states whose livelihoods depend on the gulf—was incalculable. Oil sludge and tar balls washed up on the shorelines of several islands and the Gulf Coast states, including areas that had been hit hard by Hurricane Katrina, and Mexico. Observers recorded underwater plumes of oil more than a hundred miles from the point of the well. The severe impact on marine life directly affected the fishing industries. Litigation against BP, which the federal government named as the party responsible for the disaster, resulted in over 20,000 claims. Small businesses in the tourist industry likewise were devastated, as petroleum contamination mandated the closure of hundreds of miles of beaches. Many, though hardly all, of the men and women in the fishing industries who either temporarily or permanently lost their businesses due to the catastrophe were employed by BP in the cleanup process; sadly, a number of them came to suffer significant health problems due to their (unprotected) exposure to the petroleum. BP initially set up a fund that it had promised would fully compensate all of those who had been harmed financially by the disaster. After a July 20, 2010, meeting with President Obama, BP executives agreed to back said fund with a $20-billion trust.

Naturally, the disaster completely undid BP's public image, but the fallout was political, too. In the weeks just prior to the explosion, President Obama had moved in the direction of expanding offshore drilling permits in an effort to make the United States less dependent on foreign oil. Shortly after the disaster, however, the Department of the Interior issued a six-month moratorium on any offshore drilling proposals of 500 feet or deeper. Additionally, the Obama White House received a great deal of blame for not having acted quickly or decisively enough—in effect leaving the great majority of the capping and cleanup efforts up to BP—and some right-wing pundits began to refer to the Deepwater Horizon incident as President Obama's Hurricane Katrina. No one, however, could fairly say that the accident had been the president's fault, and following the successful capping of the sea-floor gusher, the political fallout from the incident quickly evaporated.

THE EVOLVING AMERICAN DEMOGRAPHY AND CULTURE

The population of the United States reached the 300-million mark in 2006, though that particular milestone was not the only one to make headlines in the first decade of the twenty-first century. The U.S. Census

Bureau reported that due to high birthrates and high rates of immigration, Hispanics displaced African Americans as the second largest ethnic group behind whites by the close of 2002. Census Bureau projections, which can only be hypothetical, speculate that by 2035, Hispanics will constitute 25 percent of the total U.S. population. The number of Asian Americans nearly doubled from 1980 to 2010, and they currently represent over 5 percent of the population. While non-Hispanic European Americans make up 65 percent of the nation in 2010, it is anticipated that by 2040 whites will no longer comprise a majority.

While these shifts illustrate a greater global movement and also are reflected in similar fashion in most other nations, the Census Bureau operates under certain difficulties, the first being the most obvious: there is currently no widely acceptable mechanism of accounting for the increasingly multiethnic makeup of Americans as individuals. According to the 2000 U.S. Census, only 6.8 million Americans, roughly 2.5 percent of the population, self-identified as being of two or more "races." Additionally, interracial marriages have risen with each successive decade following the 1967 Supreme Court decision *Loving* v. *Virginia*, which found all state laws prohibiting such unions to be unconstitutional. According to the Census Bureau, the most common interracial marriage is between a white male and an Asian woman. Another distinguishable flaw with the census is the high percentage of Hispanics who are biracial or multiethnic, with some demographers estimating that at least 50 percent of them have more than one categorized line of ancestry. Yet, the U.S. Census Bureau recognizes *all* ethnic groups from Hispanic nations simply as *Hispanic*, even if their ancestry is predominantly African, Asian, or Native American. Perhaps the recent leaps forward in DNA and MDNA testing might conceivably lead to a different process of ethnicity reporting.

Internal migration patterns from the 1980s to the present continued to follow those from the 1960s and 1970s. Americans tended to move out of the Great Lakes region, once known as the nation's industrial hub but now referred to disparagingly as the Rust Belt, and into the Sunbelt in the South and Southwest. By 1980, Los Angeles had displaced Chicago as the second largest city, and Detroit, the big city that once boasted having the highest percentage of middle-class residents in the country, became the textbook example of urban decay. With the decline

An example of urban decay in the former manufacturing belt turned rust belt city of Detroit. Michigan Central Station. *Photo courtesy of Gretchen Wasper - Mason, Michigan*

of the American automotive industry dealing its economy blow after blow in each successive decade, Detroit, the fourth largest city in nation with a peak population of nearly 1.9 million in the 1950s, had dropped to barely over 900,000 residents by 2010. At the same time, states such as California, Arizona, Texas, and Florida consistently drew significant numbers of emigrants. Phoenix, Arizona, and San Diego emerged as two of the top ten largest cities in 1980, with populations in excess of 750,000 each. By 2010, Phoenix had more than doubled in size and San Diego had gone beyond 1.25 million residents.

The Carolinas and Virginia successfully recruited mid- to large-size companies from the Midwest and Northeast with tax-incentive packages, temperate climates, clean, well-conceived suburbs, and strong educational systems, including outstanding colleges and universities. One of the most innovative efforts has been the New South's drive to bring in technology- and research-based companies. Research Triangle Park in North Carolina, designed in 1959, has emerged as one of the most significant research-oriented business parks in the nation. The 7,000-acre facility is strategically located near Duke University, the University of North Carolina, Wake Forest University, and North Carolina State University. In addition to having local major research universities in its backyard, Triangle Park also offers employers and employees a variety of quaint, upscale, college towns with amenities and cultural offerings that rival those of any similar community in the nation, including northern California's Silicon Valley.

The process of gentrification (with upwardly mobile people moving into renovated urban neighborhoods from which poor people were displaced—literally "priced out" of their own homes and apartments) in most of the large cities continued apace with the historic bull run on Wall Street from the 1980s and into the 2000s, as real estate investors and developers sought out low cost "brownstones" in former industrial zones that they turned into mixed-use centers. Lower floors typically housed businesses of various kinds, with residential units above. Cities such as Los Angeles, New York, San Diego, Chicago, San Francisco, Seattle, and Portland realized significant brownstone gentrification projects throughout their respective business districts and saw young urban professionals, the primary target group of this urban-redesign model, move into environments they deemed more exiting than the suburbs. While large cities continued to be more ethnically diverse on average than the bedroom community suburbs, cultural diversity made significant gains throughout the towns and cities once founded by the so-called white-flight movement. A new "flight" emerged in the 1980s and continues as a growing trend nationally, the so-called black flight. Growing numbers of Hispanics and Asians began to settle in traditional African American communities. In response, many African Americans followed the pattern established by whites, moving out of the city centers and into the suburbs. By 2000, major cities such as New York, Boston, and Los Angeles witnessed a greater percentage drop in their African American population than in their white one. In effect, these dramatic migration patterns have resulted in a much more ethnically integrated urban America.

Fine Arts

Movements in fine arts from the 1970s through the first decade of the twenty-first century reflected the greater, overarching changes in American society and culture. Women and minorities came to constitute an ever-increasing percentage of the most successful artists. Meanwhile, a broader array of genres within the nation's fine arts represented the pluralism as well as the openness to experiment with new forms and mediums in contemporary society. One of the most notable new forms is installation art. While one can trace installation art in the modern sense back to the first modern art movement at the dawn of the twentieth century, contemporary artists experimented with dynamic new modes, including a conceptual movement born in the 1960s. Installation artists create three-dimensional works that often incorporate new media, including sound and video. At times, large-scale installations occupy entire gallery rooms and strive to challenge spatial perceptions. Increasingly, museums and commercial galleries have incorporated installations into their holdings as the public demand for such pieces has steadily increased over the past forty years. Artists such as Andrea Zittel, Michael Joo, Tara Donovan, and Renee Green have been at the fore of the movement.

Sculptors, too, have become increasingly diverse in their respective approaches as artists seek original forms and a wider range of materials

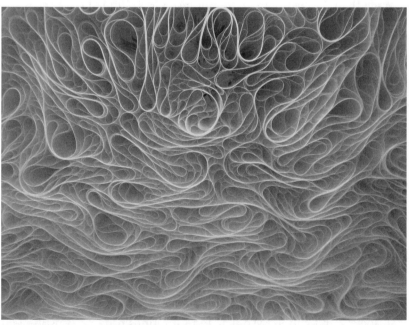

An untitled work of contemporary installation artist Tara Donovan. *Photo courtesy Ryan Dickey.*

with which to work. One of the most commercially successful artists has been Dale Chihuly, whose work is generally recognized as the premiere glass sculpture in the world. Other highly notable individuals are Chakaia Booker, Margaret Swan, Alison Saar, and Renee Stout. Maya Lin, whose best-known work is the controversial Vietnam War Veterans Memorial in Washington, D.C., has also created some of the most significant exhibits with her *2 x 4 Landscape* at the San Francisco De Young Memorial Museum, the Civil Rights Memorial in Montgomery, Alabama, and her Woman's Table at Yale University.

Large-scale exterior art, commonly referred to as "land art," also has become more widely accepted as legitimate throughout the art community. Clearly influenced by ancient indigenous societies, land artists have developed a wide array of work aimed at both captivating the imagination of the viewer as well as provoking emotional and intellectual responses. Some of the most distinguished land artists in the past two generations have been Alice Aycock, James Turrell, Dennis Oppenheim, Michael Heizer, and Alan Sonfist. One of the best-known works of land

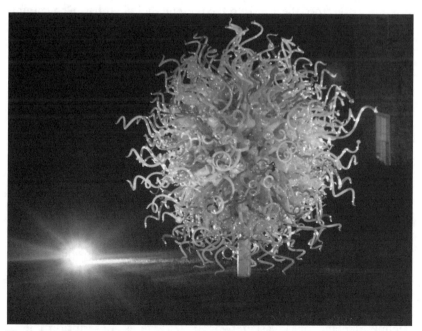

Work of world renowned contemporary glass sculptor Dale Chihuly entitled "The Sun".
Courtesy, Keith Hinkle.

art and also perhaps the largest singular piece is James Turrell's *Roden Crater* a "work in progress" outside Flagstaff, Arizona. Turrell purchased Roden Crater, an extinct volcanic crater nearly 500,000 years old, which he is painstakingly transforming into a naked-eye observatory. Another compelling artist, Michael Heizer, has produced works including *Double Negative,* a 1,500-foot trench that he carved out of a desert mesa in Nevada. One of the most controversial works has been Dennis Oppenheim's Device to Root Out Evil, a one-half scale New England–style Christian church turned upside down, with its steeple serving as the anchor point to the ground.

As the development of improved digital technologies transformed television, film, and photography, artists with specific foci in digital art emerged, expanded, and carved out one of the most economically successful contemporary art genres. The term *digital art* represents a broad array of forms, though it is essentially defined as that which has been created on a computer or digitally enhanced by one. When digital art first emerged in the late 1970s, the limits of the technology did not allow an expansive or sophisticated genre. But with the explosive technological advances consistently made from the 1990s to the present, digital art has been gaining an increasingly wider acceptance in the art world as well as a significantly larger patronage. Leaders in the field include Sid Armstrong, Benjamin Fry, Mary Flanagan, Lisa Jevbratt, and Josh On.

Television

The expansion of subscription television through cable, satellites, and digital fiberoptic networks has transformed the industry. Rather than being limited to a few local or regional channels, depending on the subscription service, households can choose from more than 1,000 options. An ancillary component of this change in home entertainment has been the growth of specialty channels that offer genre-specific programming, which has brought an unprecedented array of selections for the contemporary American viewer, quite a difference from the traditional networks, each of which offered a wide range of programs. A growing trend in television viewership in American homes has been a decline of major broadcast network patronage as subscription television services offered a cornucopia of specialty channels, including those that broadcast commercial-free and uncensored programs. Technological advances also presented consumers with the option of on-demand programming, further enhancing the home-entertainment experience while eroding the significance of the traditional networks in American lives. The form and quality of the television set also evolved dramatically beginning in the 1990s. Digital and high-definition televisions that offered larger screens, a cleaner image, higher quality sound, and a more stylish physical design replaced the formerly ubiquitous analog sets. Additionally, the United States switched all television broadcasting from analog to digital format in 2009.

In 1986 Fox Broadcasting, the fourth major broadcast network, was launched. While it was not at the time considered a major challenge to the Big Three, CBS, NBC and ABC, by 2008 it had become the most viewed network in the nation. Early on, Fox distinguished itself from the other three major networks by taking risks, such as placing animated series in the most coveted timeslots and demonstrating a willingness to broadcast bawdy productions that tested the limits of the censors. Fox shows such as animated series *The Simpsons* and the sitcom *Married with Children* proved popular for several years, with *The Simpsons* exceeding twenty years of production and becoming the longest running prime-time series to date.

Popular television programming from the 1980s to the present retained many of the staple forms of decades past, with situation comedies, serial dramas, game shows, news magazines, live sports, and game shows dominating the timeslots. The first program to draw over 30 million viewers per night was *The Cosby Show*, starring longtime television actor and comedian Bill Cosby. While a few other other highly rated prime-time programs prior to *The Cosby Show*, such as *The Jeffersons, Sanford and Son, Chico and the Man*, showcased actors of color, *The Cosby Show* became the first such program to win the top spot, which it held from 1985 through 1989. The popularity of this program played a significant role in the expansion of minority-based shows on the major networks—as well as the launch of the BET (Black Entertainment Television) channel on cable.

From the end of the 1990s and continuing up to the present, prime-time "reality shows," most of which involved contests of one form or another, have only gained in popularity. The first such program was *Who*

Media magnate
and international
philanthropist Oprah
Winfrey on her 50th
birthday. *Photo by
Alan Light.*

Comedienne and
talk show host, Ellen
DeGeneres accepting an
Emmy in 1997. *Photo by
Alan Light.*

Wants to be a Millionaire?, which actually took the top ratings spot on three different nights in 1999–2000. Subsequent reality hits include *Survivor* and *American Idol*.

Other distinguishable changes in television that reflect America's growing acceptance of its diversity include the broad viewing audience of Oprah Winfrey's morning talk show, *Oprah*, and Ellen DeGeneres' talk and variety show, *Ellen*. Oprah Winfrey, an African American, has for more than a generation been one of the most powerful people in the entire entertainment industry. A self-made billionaire, Oprah not only dominates her morning timeslot but has become such a reputable public figure that literally upon her endorsement, a product becomes a best seller and a person a household name. For example, Oprah's Book Club has had a greater impact on the publishing industry than has any other such forum in the past fifty years. While Oprah has tended to shy away from strong political endorsements, all of the politicians who have appeared on her show have enjoyed popularity boosts. In 2008 Oprah strongly endorsed Barack Obama. Ellen DeGeneres made history when she became the first person to reveal her homosexuality on a sitcom, *Ellen*, in 1997. ABC subsequently cancelled that program, despite its strong ratings. Undeterred, Ellen continued to perform and eventually found her way back to the top of the ratings.

Literature

Americans demonstrated their diverse interests in the world of literature from the 1980s to the present. Landmark publications from generations past, such as Harper Lee's *To Kill A Mockingbird* and J. D. Salinger's *Catcher in the Rye* continued to maintain their presence on the bestseller lists, while the work of British author J. K. Rowling, the Harry Potter fantasy series, has outsold every other publication series in the United States since its arrival in 1997. Dan Brown has also had considerable success with his works *The Da Vinci Code* and *Angels and Demons*. America's longstanding and apparently growing interest in vampires is evidenced in the success of Anne Rice's work as well as that of the young author Stephanie Meyer with her *Twilight* series. Most literary critics recognize the works of Thomas Pynchon, Toni Morrison, Joyce Carol Oates, and Amy Tan as truly visionary. One of the most significant authors to emerge in the past forty years has been Don DeLillo, whose work takes a hard look at American life in the post–Word War II era. While he received notable praise for his first novel, *Americana* (1971), DeLillo's work, though moderately successful over the next decade, did not garner national attention until his release of *White Noise* (1985), for which he won the National Book Award. His next work, *Libra* (1988), a fictional-ized biography of Lee Harvey Oswald, drew a wide range of responses from critics and became an international best seller, one that DeLillo followed up with an epic look at postwar America entitled *Underworld*. Another contemporary master of the "great American novel" is Philip Roth, whose impressive body of work includes *American Pastoral* and *The Plot Against America*. As the American novel continued to move into many divergent directions, a more aggressive style of character develop-ment that clearly stepped beyond the post modernists emerged and has been referred to as transgressive. One of the most controversial of these writers has been Bret Easton Ellis, who drew the ire of many women's rights organization with his novel *American Psycho*. Other transgressives of note include Chuck Palahniuk and Jay McInerney.

The genre of historical literature evolved as it became more inclusive and innovative. Master historian David McCullough continued to pro-duce landmark works that enjoyed wide readership. Newcomer Laura Hillenbrand found instant success with her work *Seabiscuit: An Ameri-can Legend*. The emergence of Big History in the mid-1980s has made a significant impact in American literature. A cross-disciplinary field that generally traces a theme across great spans of time, American Big His-tory notables include Isaac Asimov, Jared Diamond, Eric Roston, and Bill Bryson. Another landmark Big History author is David Christian, who has even developed college coursework on the emerging field.

One of the most noticeable changes in American literature has actu-ally been how Americans purchase and read books. Owing much to the technological advances associated with digital media and the Internet, readers could draw from a greater range of literary materials than ever before. Amazon.com, which started as an Internet-only bookstore in 1995 but quickly evolved into the largest online retailer, began to offer the greatest selection of publications of any bookstore in history. Addi-tionally, Amazon.com innovated in reader participation, as it afforded readers the opportunity to post their own book reviews and literary opinions on its website. While the concept of creating a digital library began in 1971 with the launch of Project Guttenberg, Amazon.com's e-book reader, the Kindle, has proven the most successful digital reader, with more than 250,000 titles available after its first two years in the marketplace. This hand-held unit, roughly the size of a traditional hardcover book, affords readers the opportunity of purchasing and downloading digital versions of titles at a discounted price. On January 27, 2010, Silicon Valley–based Apple, Inc., introduced the iPad, a tablet computer that promises to take the e-book to the next level, making the reading experience Internet linked and truly interactive.

Movies

Beginning with director Stephen Spielberg's film *Jaws* in 1975, Hollywood began a formula for releasing big-budget, action-oriented films with the intent of generating hundreds of millions of dollars in returns over the course of just a few months. This broadly defined genre quickly became known as the "summer blockbuster." Subsequent films, such as the initial *Star Wars* trilogy and *Close Encounters of the Third Kind*, proved that audiences appreciated and anticipated technological innovations that allowed for increasingly more realistic portrayals of science fiction. By the 1980s, audiences came to expect the big Hollywood studios to offer multiple big-budget, action-oriented summer films from which they could choose. In response, movie studios developed an economic reliance on their summer blockbuster, often tying the entire fiscal year's success to the box office returns of the summer films. As the American film industry began to evolve in this seasonal fashion, film critics typically argued that the depth of storylines and character development suffered as a result of the constant drive for bigger and more profitable blockbusters, and the critics saved their praises for the early winter release films that studios projected to be potential Academy Award winners.

Computer-generated imagery (CGI), first introduced in the 1970s, came into its own in the early 1990s. Now filmmakers were able to give audiences realistic, 3D animation that looked as real as the live actors. Films such as *Terminator 2: Judgment Day* and *Jurassic Park* wowed audiences with morphing cyborgs and seemingly real dinosaurs interacting with flesh-and-blood human actors. The first fully computer-animated feature film, *Toy Story*, opened in 1995 and proved immensely popular

Actor and California
Govenor, Arnold
Schwarzenegger in
Terminator 2: Judgment
Day (1991). *Courtesy
Photofest.*

with audiences and critics. The first film to break the $500-million box-office barrier, director James Cameron's *Titanic*, showed that blockbusters could also be released in December and need not rely exclusively on technological gimmicks. Still, by the end of the first decade of the twenty-first century, CGI-heavy films dominated the top all-time box office returns chart.

Once limited to the color print pages of comic books, superheroes found their way onto the big screen with greater regularity as CGI allowed filmmakers the opportunity to bring to life X-Men and Spiderman in a manner that sophisticated audiences would accept. While superhero films such as *Superman* (1978) had made their way to the big screen before the development of CGI, the digital advance truly enhanced the experience of moviegoers, who responded with record-breaking attendance. Cross-marketing practices, first introduced by

George Lucas with his *Star Wars* line of action figures and toys, became an expected and important feature of the action films and helped raise profits for the ever-increasing budgets of the blockbusters. Advance in RealD 3D and IMAX 3D technology permitted director James Cameron to introduce a cinematic experience moviegoers had never before experienced with his 2009 release of *Avatar*. In this first film to earn $2 billion in history, audiences thrilled to a theatrical experience that seemed to leap out from the screen at them. Within a year, over a dozen wide-release films gained great success by employing the same 3D technology.

Ethnic minorities and women witnessed a period of significant movement toward equality as actors and actresses in Hollywood from the 1980s to the present. African American comedian and actor Eddie Murphy was one of the top box-office draws throughout the 1980s as well as one of the highest paid movie stars. Will Smith, who had experienced success first as a rapper and then a television actor, became the first African American actor considered a dominant action star as well as an outstanding dramatic actor. Smith is also the only movie star to have had more than seven films open number-one at the box office. Denzel Washington became the second African American to win a Best Actor Academy Award (following Sidney Poitier); Washington also won the Best Supporting Actor Academy Award. In 2001, Halle Berry became the first African American to win the Academy Award for Best Actress. While African Americans enjoyed a greater range of roles in motion pictures, other ethnic minorities, such as Hispanics and Asian Americans, did not. Female actors nearly reached economic parity with their male counterparts by the early 1990s, as individuals such as Julia Roberts, Halle Berry, and Angelina Jolie commanded per-film compensation in the range of $20 million. Still, films with females playing the central lead role continued to lag well behind those with males in the central lead.

Music

Rock and roll continued to enjoy great success throughout the 1980s and into the present. Though a relatively few distinctive changes in style occurred in the 1990s, the introduction of the "grunge" sound, predominantly growing out of the club scene in Seattle, was the most significant. Grunge effectively replaced the 1980s "alternative" form, as bands such as Pearl Jam, Nirvana, Soundgarden, and Alice in Chains introduced angst-ridden lyrics that railed against corporate America and conformity. An instant sensation with the youth through college age, grunge was viewed by many parents as a threat. The grunge artists quite often appeared disheveled on stage and in their publicity shots, and their rebellious nature struck the same chord with American youth as had bands in the 1960s hippie era. The grunge generation was quickly labeled Generation X by social scientists, who claimed that this new generation was politically apathetic, obsessed with computer games, and self-absorbed. While those opinions are highly debatable, there is one certainty about Generation X; it is the first post–Great Depression generation to enjoy less real earning power than its parents. Prevalent

Grunge band Nirvana, left to right Krist Novoselic, Kurt Cobain, Dave Grohl. *Courtesy Photofest.*

among the grunge artists was excessive drug use, which also permeated their Generation X fan base. In addition to heroin and marijuana, other narcotics of choice included ecstasy and methamphetamine. Use of the latter subsequently reached crisis levels in the United States. But for all of the finger wagging of older Americans, the popularity of grunge began to decline significantly in the late 1990s, and by the early 2000s it had become all but a memory.

Another new form of American music that enjoyed tremendous popularity was hip hop. In the early 1980s hip hop, also commonly referred to as rap music, first began to attract primarily African Americans as both artists and listeners, but a much broader audience quickly emerged, as a highly diverse audience had embraced hip hop (in its many forms) by the late 1980s. One of the distinctive changes in Hip Hop occurred at the same time as its audience was diversifying, the emergence of the so-called gansta rap and West Coast sound, which introduced listeners to an angrier, more violent, and more rebellious style. The work of groups such as N.W.A. featured lyrics that many considered as verging on indecent and inflammatory, resulting in a limited and highly censored airplay on the radio stations. Nevertheless, demand for the music grew with each successive year. The 1990s was the most commercially successful decade hip hop had yet seen, and while demand for the genre did see a decline in the 2000s, it has maintained a significant market share and continues to evolve.

Country music also made significant gains throughout the 1990s and into the 2000s, as many of its artists began to fuse pop music stylistics with those of the traditional country sounds. Casting aside the previous generation's "outlaw" style of country, the contemporary artists offered a relatively conservative style more in harmony with the social and political leanings of the listeners to which country music appealed. Artists such as Garth Brooks, Clint Black, Trisha Yearwood, and Carrie Underwood realized tremendous record sales that exceeded those of many of the rock and roll and hip hop recording artists. While other music genres witnessed declines in record sales by the mid 2000s, many country recording artists realized increases in patronage. By far the most economically successful genre, however, continued to be the broadly defined "popular" music, which included variations of country, hip hop, and rock and roll.

Rap group N.W.A. with rappers the D.O.C. and Laylaw from Above the Law. Left to right, standing: Laylaw, DJ Yella, Dr. Dre and The D.O.C. Left to right, seated: Ice Cube, Easy-E, and MC Ren. From the N.W.A. tour "Straight Outta Compton" in Kansas City, Missouri, June, 1989. *Photo by Raymond Boyd/Michael Ochs Archives/Getty Images.*

The impact of technology arguably redefined the music industry more than it did any other entertainment medium. In the late 1990s "file sharing" on the Internet led to a vast amount of illegally downloaded music in the MP3 format. Initially, the music industry was devastated economically, as fewer and fewer people purchased the traditional CDs (which, of course, had started to replace vinyl records in the 1980s). Corporations such as Napster were sued by recording companies and artists alike. Ultimately, technological advances were made and music pirating was greatly curbed, although a significant change in how consumers purchased their music had become permanent.

In 2001, Apple launched the best-selling digital listening unit in history, the iPod. By 2009, nearly 200 million iPods had been sold to consumers worldwide. Adding to Apple's bottom line, even beyond the sale of its iPod has been iTunes, established two years after the iPod's introduction. A website, iTunes allows consumers to purchase songs, one at a time or more, for a nominal charge in the range of $1. Artists and music

Country music star Carrie Underwood in 2010. *Courtesy Keith Hinkle.*

corporations received their royalties, which, although small on a per unit basis, became their greatest source of revenues in many cases thanks to the volume of purchases. The real economic winner in the shakeup of the American music industry, however, was clearly Apple, as the symbiotic relationship of iTunes and iPod drove sales.

Sports

By the end of the first decade of the new millennia, professional sports in America had reached a new zenith in terms of patronage and net worth, with some franchises valued at over $1 billion. In Major League Baseball (MLB), the New York Yankees topped the list with a *Forbes* magazine–estimated value of $1.5 billion. In the National Basketball Association (NBA), *Forbes* recognized the Los Angeles Lakers, with a net worth of over $600 million, as the top-valued franchise. The average net worth of each NFL team, according to *Forbes*, tops the big-three professional sports leagues at $1.02 billion, the most valuable being the Dallas Cowboys with an estimated value of $1.8 billion—making it the most valuable sports franchise in the nation.

As professional sports became mega-big business, the salaries of professional athletes also skyrocketed from 2000 to 2010. In the NBA, more than ten players earned more than $20 million per year in 2010. The top 25 NFL player salaries for 2010 ranged from $15 to $25 million per season. Product endorsements by professional athletes have netted the superstars among them incredible sums in addition to their salaries. One such example is the NBA's LeBron James (who shocked Cleveland fans by leaving the Cavaliers for the Miami Heat in 2010), whose estimated annual income from endorsements in 2010 topped $30 million. While most sports franchises net considerable profits annually, the Great Recession did affect the bottom line of teams throughout the leagues. In response, team owners have consistently attempted to lower the percentage of the revenue shared with the athletes. Nonetheless, viewership and overall gate receipts increased with steady regularity each year from 2000 to 2010. Viewership in homes across the nation has also steadily risen, bringing added revenues to the leagues as well as the networks. A dramatic change in broadcast television during the past twenty years has been the expansion of the most dominant sports broadcasting corporation, ESPN.

Entertainment Sports Broadcasting Network was launched in 1979 by the father and son team of Bill and Scott Rasmussen, bringing the United States its first twenty-four-hour sports broadcasting channel. By 2010, ESPN had expanded it programming reach with over twenty television networks around the globe as well as over a dozen Internet and radio broadcasts. The tremendous success that ESPN has achieved reflects the growing attention that Americans have given sports, both professional and collegiate, from 1980 to the present. The longstanding professional sports leagues, such as the NFL, NBA, MLB, and the National Hockey League (NHL), have also developed their own broadcasting networks, as have some of the premiere collegiate athletic conferences, such as the Big Ten. Not all of the developments in the sporting world have been as positive as sports networks. In particular, the use of so-called performance-enhancing drugs among professional, college, and Olympic athletes stands out perhaps the most negative development.

As the financial incentives for excellence in sports have spiked, the use of performance-enhancing drugs became the single greatest problem in professional sports by the late 1990s. While some athletes had been taking performance-enhancing drugs like steroids as early as the 1970s, by the end of the 1980s usage became more widespread, in particular in the NFL. Soon thereafter, former star athletes, such as Lyle Alzado—who came forward after he contracted cancer due to, he contended, his years of excessive steroid use—began to open up about their use of performance enhancers. The NFL implemented a ban on steroid use in 1987 and has since expanded its list of banned substances, a policy it enforces with random testing and sharp penalties: repeat offenders can find themselves permanently banished from the league. While it is believed that NFL drug use has declined, each year several players are caught using banned substances. In addition to the NFL, MLB has been plagued with performance-enhancing drug use, a situation that reached a crescendo in the late 1990s and into the early 2000s, as evidenced not simply by the testing results but also by an unprecedented surge in home-run hitting.

For nearly forty years, Roger Maris' single-season home run record of sixty-one (while on the New York Yankees) stood as an achievement of monumental proportion. That changed in 1998, when two sluggers, Sammy Sosa of the Chicago Cubs and Mark McGwire of the St. Louis Cardinals, were locked in a two-man race to establish a new single-season home run record. The media coverage of the two men in their quest was unparalleled in sports history, and at the close of the 162-game regular season, McGwire stood atop the home-run pantheon with a new record of 70. Sosa fell short of McGwire's achievement that year with 66 homers but still beat Maris' old record. The Sosa/McGwire rivalry continued in 1999, when Sosa belted 63 homers, though once again McGwire bested him by hitting 65. In 2001, Sosa became the first player in MLB history to record three seasons with 60 or more home runs. In that same year, however, the longtime great slugger Barry Bonds broke McGwire's record by hitting 73 home runs. While the achievements of Sosa, McGwire, and Bonds captured the lion's share of the attention, home-run totals and batting percentages were moving up across MLB, a phenomenon that continued throughout the first decade of the twenty-first century.

With so many baseballs flying out of so many parks on a daily basis, many fans and baseball experts had no choice but to conclude that something fishy was going on in "America's pastime." After Congress held publicly televised hearings on steroid use in MLB in 2005, the league began policing itself more aggressively, which resulted in a sharp decline in the usage of performance-enhancing drugs as well as an increase in confessions and finger-pointing by current and former players. One notable change that occurred in 2010, the season believed to be the freest of drug use in over a decade, was a sharp decline in batting averages and home runs across the league. Consequently, this relatively "clean" year came to be known as the "year of the pitcher." Unfortunately, sluggers were not the only players accused of doping to improve their statistics; on August 19, 2010, Congress indicted star pitcher and seven-time Cy Young Award winner Roger Clemens for perjury related to voluntary testimony he gave before the House Oversight and Government Reform Committee in 2008 insisting that he had never used performance-enhancing drugs, a position that he adamantly maintained.

Athletes in the NFL and MLB were not alone in their performance-enhancing drug use, for Track and Field superstars such as Olympic gold medalists Marion Jones and Tim Montgomery were stripped of their medals after their use of illegal substances during competition came to light. Jones was later found guilty of committing perjury before a grand jury investigating Bay Area Laboratory Cooperative (BALCO), one of the most notorious performance-enhancing drug suppliers. BALCO has been linked to dozens of professional athletes. Professional cyclists also have used performance-enhancing drugs, including 2006 Tour de France winner Floyd Landis, who was stripped of his victory after testing positive. Landis, a teammate of perhaps the most famous American cyclist, Lance Armstrong, who won the Tour de France a stunning seven consecutive times, charged that Armstrong had been a long-time user of banned substances. Armstrong has denied using any such substances, though the accusations have tainted the image of the champion and noted cancer survivor. The one professional and collegiate sport that has avoided the taint of performance-enhancing drug scandals has been the NBA.

Changing American News Media

As a direct result of Americans utilizing the Internet and twenty-four-hour news programming on television as their primary source for news, a drastic decline in newspaper subscriptions and subsequent advertising revenue losses began at the dawn of the 1990s, and by 2009, many major newspapers could no longer continue production. The papers holding on to the greatest circulations, *USA Today*, the *New York Times*, the *Wall Street Journal*, and the *Washington Post*, each noted declines, though due to their national readerships (something regional and local newspapers never had), they managed to maintain viable market shares. Following the sharp economic decline beginning in 2007, many of the stalwart dailies, such as the *Cincinnati Post*, Denver's *Colorado Rocky Mountain News*, and the *Albuquerque Tribune*, began to disappear.

Newsmagazines such as *Time, US News and World Report*, and *Newsweek* began offering deep subscription discounts, while simultaneously revamping their websites as they attempted to hold onto their readership. Further compounding the economic challenges the traditional news media faced, innovative corporations such as Twitter offered free and direct news sourcing transmission of 140 words or less from organizations, individuals, and celebrities to their subscribers, which further eroded viewership of traditional news media.

The ability of Americans to get their news immediately, with better graphics, streaming video, and the opportunity literally to interact via blogs and poll surveys, made the Internet the most popular choice for news-seekers by the start of the twenty-first century. Further adding to the appeal of Internet news sources was the ability of the consumer to access the information free of cost and to filter out news not of interest. Television broadcasters also turned their attention to the Internet, as all major broadcasters as well as twenty-four-hour news channels offered online versions of their news programming. Even local television stations joined the Internet expansion of news on demand.

AMERICANS MOVE TO RIGHT OF CENTER

The American political universe in the early twenty-first century had a very different appearance from the way it looked at mid-century. A political transformation was evident in the emergence of new attitudes and assumptions about the role of politics in national life, in the presence of powerful new forces in the conduct of political campaigns and the adoption of public policies, and in a slow but extensive alteration in the American party system. Following the great party realignment of the 1930s, the New Deal Democratic coalition dominated the political scene for a long time before beginning to splinter and losing its competitive edge, at first in presidential elections. The revitalization of the Republican Party in the late 1960s and the rise of a dynamic conservative movement in the 1970s brought a dramatic GOP breakthrough with the election of Ronald Reagan in 1980 and the arrival of a strong right-of-center American populace that lasted through the administration of George W. Bush and seemed poised to complete a long-awaited realignment of the party system. And while many political analysts predicted that George W. Bush's low popularity ratings at the end of his presidency might spark a decided move to the left, Americans maintained a right-of-center stance on most issues well into the Obama administration.

Developments in the 1960s and early 1970s threatened Democrats with the loss of another key constituency, one made up of working-class and lower-middle-class whites outside the South, often Catholic and of European ethnic background, who were hard-working, self-reliant, patriotic, and committed to authority and social order. The conflict over social and cultural values in the 1960s undermined the salience of older economic loyalties to the Democratic Party. These Americans tended to associate urban riots, rising crime rates, school busing, open housing, and preferential treatment of minorities with Democratic liberalism. They were, in Nixon's phrase, the "silent majority," slow to turn against the Vietnam War, angry over student protests, and part of the backlash against the counterculture and liberal permissiveness. Such attitudes lay at the heart of Governor Wallace's extraordinary appeal to working-class Americans, in and out of the South. They were concerned about a "social issue" that Nixon and other Republicans exploited with telling effect. Presidents Ronald Reagan and George W. Bush continued in this tradition, though in different manner than Nixon. Reagan and Bush, who cast himself as a "Reagan Republican," emphasized a return to "normal" and "traditional" American values. While Reagan demonstrated restraint in this area of perceived social reform, George W. Bush plowed forward with earnest zeal.

If the "social issue" began to displace the economic and class interests that accounted for the Democratic fidelity of many workers and lower-middle-class Americans, economic prosperity in the 1950s and 1960s influenced others—members of the swelling middle class, profession-als, and suburban dwellers—to adopt more conservative economic and social views and to vote Republican, especially in presidential elections. In a sense, as one commentator remarked, the Democrats were "running out of poor people." There were other disaffected elements in the years of Democratic dominance, including the New Left and the counterculture on the left and a number of influential intellectuals on the right. Origi-nally liberals (mostly Democrats) and hard-line anti-Communists, this small but diverse group became disenchanted with Democratic liberal-ism and what it regarded as the party's dangerous turn to the left in the 1960s and 1970s. These "neoconservatives" found a more comfortable niche in the conservative movement and a role in Republican politics.

The disarray in the Democratic Party and the alienation of many of its traditional constituents was apparent in the election of 1972, in which George McGovern, the Democratic presidential nominee, car-ried only Massachusetts and the District of Columbia and President Nixon won re-election by an overwhelming majority as a centrist con-servative candidate. Even so, the Democratic Party had not disappeared from the political landscape. It continued to control Congress, remained competitive in many state and local contests, and even in the South managed to create successful black-and-white coalitions. Then, in the aftermath of Watergate, Jimmy Carter led the Democrats back to the White House. This Democratic revival soon ended, hastened by a series of difficult problems that demoralized the Carter administration and by the reorientation and resurgence of the Republican Party.

Social and racial issues in the second half of the 1970s, along with increasing opposition to burdensome taxes and an economic downturn associated with the Democrats, gave impetus to the coalescence and growth of political conservatism in the United States and to the election of Ronald Reagan as president and a Republican Senate in 1980. The prime mover in this success and in refashioning the Republican Party was Reagan, who spoke for those who wanted to limit what they consid-ered an irresponsible and spendthrift federal government and to provide tax relief and significant changes in civil rights policies.

The South was a driving force in the realignment of presidential poli-tics beginning in 1968. With deep-seated conservative predilections and a large share of delegates to Republican national conventions, southern

Republicans assumed a leading role in moving the party to the right. Many white southern Democrats had shifted to the Republican Party following the civil rights legislation enacted during the administration of Lyndon Johnson in the mid-1960s. Nixon, appealing to Wallace supporters, was careful to make clear his conservative principles. As Dan T. Carter writes, when Wallace "had played his fiddle, the President of the United States had danced Jim Crow." No other region provided greater support for Republican presidential candidates than the South or was more influential in shaping its conservative philosophy. Between 1976 and 1988, an estimated 54 percent of the region's white conservative Democrats voted Republican in presidential elections. By the 1980s, the South had become a Republican stronghold in national politics and a base for a more competitive GOP in state and local campaigns. Later, the presidency of George W. Bush would continue to solidify this movement, as evidenced in the 2008 election, in which Obama lost all but Florida to his opponent, John McCain.

Another source of the rising tide of political conservatism was the Christian Right, which became a major force in national politics in the late 1970s and early 1980s. Religious conservatives had earlier joined the anti-Communist crusade and opposed liberal economic and social policies. Now they moved more forthrightly into politics, supported organizations like the Moral Majority and the Religious Roundtable, and frequently identified themselves with eloquent televangelists and other ministers. The Christian Right was motivated by several concerns, especially the decline of what it deemed traditional values and morality and a suspicion of secular, scientific norms in modern society. Its spokespersons made skillful use of the media, registered hundreds of thousands, perhaps millions, of new voters, and raised large amounts of money for their political causes. As a rule, these conservative church groups were allied with but separate from the Republican Party. No other president appealed to this voting bloc more effectively than George W. Bush, with the Christian Right becoming his stanchest supporter, even during the final days of his presidency when his approval ratings reached historic lows. Understanding the strength of the Christian Right, Barack Obama deftly reached out to this powerful voting bloc. For example, Southern Californian conservative Christian pastor Rick Warren delivered the invocation at Obama's inauguration. Additionally, even though gays and lesbians were among Obama's strongest supporters, once he became president he made his opinion known repeatedly that he viewed marriage as a union between a man and a woman, mirroring the view of a strong majority of Americans.

Strong support among the affluent and religious conservatives gave Republicans a decided advantage in low-turnout elections in which big money had become essential. The Democrats could no longer rely on the solid support of blue-collar workers and the lower middle class, given the effectiveness of racial fears and other social issues among white working-class Americans. In fact, changes in the old adversarial relationship between workers and management enabled Republicans to create a cross-class alliance of supporters. Meanwhile, the Democratic Party felt the effects of a shrinking manufacturing sector, the growth of service industries, and the relative decline of organized labor. More than 3.5 million workers in manufacturing enterprises lost their jobs between 1980 and 1993. Moreover, millions of working- and middle-class Americans in the late 1970s tended to link rampant inflation, stagnating incomes, increasing costs of welfare, and heavier taxes with Democratic control in Washington.

By the mid-1980s, the Reagan Revolution seemed to have accomplished its major objectives—ending runaway inflation, reducing taxes, and increasing military spending, with rhetorical salvos at an overextended federal government. Whatever the failures and adverse consequences of the Reagan presidency, it restored the confidence of Americans, revitalized the Republican Party, strengthened the appeal of political conservatism, and probably sounded the death knell of Democratic liberalism. Still, the future of American politics was by no means clear when Reagan left office. Writing in 1991, the journalist E. J. Dionne observed that the new conservative majority in presidential politics "is inherently unstable, since it unites upper-income groups, whose main interest is in smaller government and lower taxes, and middle- to lower-income groups, who are culturally conservative but still support most of the New Deal and a lot of the Great Society." The Democrats, regaining a Senate majority in 1986, once again controlled Congress, and in 1992 they recaptured the presidency as well. They scored political points by calling attention to Reagan's reliance on the role of the market, reducing public services, and providing selective tax cuts and expenditures for favored groups. Democratic candidates also cited the growing disparity of income between rich and poor in the United States, as well as the loss of real income by millions of middle-class and professional Americans. Economic issues again seemed to offer the Democrats an opening in contemporary party battles, as did the advantage they appeared to have in the "gender gap." George W. Bush and Barack Obama both advocated lower income taxes. In fact, Barack Obama actually lowered taxes further than his predecessor in an attempt at stimulating the economy, a move reminiscent of traditional Reagan Republican standards.

The tendency of the average American to be "right of center," which began in 1968, did not falter, even though the 2008 general election brought in a wave of Democrats at all political levels nationwide. The heart of this right-leaning American society tends to be fiscally conservative and socially moderate. While the vast majority of Americans favored equal rights for all citizens, the issue of gay marriage continued to be opposed by a strong majority. In both a CNN and *U.S. News & World Report* poll in the summer of 2009, an average of 65 percent of the respondents strongly opposed gay marriage. Americans also overwhelmingly opposed the establishment of a public health care plan to be run by a government agency after its introduction by Democrats in Congress in 2009.

The areas that have witnessed the greatest liberalization in American society have been ethnic inclusiveness and the equality of men and women. Culturally, American views of racism and sexism changed radically from the 1970s to the 2000s. Clearly impacted by the evolution of U.S. society into a more plural one, racism and sexism became viewed as abhorrent and unacceptable by the dawn of the twenty-first century. The one area of contemporary life in which these gains are most obvious is corporate America. Minorities and women have fared well in the business world, much more so than in politics, for example. Clayton Rose of the Columbia University Council of the Graduate School of Business studied the shift in executive leadership from 1980 to 2000 and found that a dramatic increase in nonwhite top executives had taken place. According to Rose, in 1980 only 2.4 percent of top-level executives were minorities, but in 2000, the percentage had increased to 13.5 percent. And of all the minority groups, Rose found that African Americans had the greatest level of success. Women as well increasingly reached the top spots in major corporations. Nonetheless, as *Forbes* reported in 2008 about the 100 most highly paid female executives, while women such as Meg Whitman of eBay, who reported an annual income of over $120 million, had great success in climbing the ladder, women had yet to achieve full earning parity with men overall. This so-called earning gap also exists between whites and minorities in general and continues to be a social issue that the United States has yet to fully resolve.

THE GREAT RECESSION WORSENS

As most economists had predicted, the economy continued to crumble throughout 2009. Home prices consistently dropped with each passing month. Unemployment reached double-digit levels nationally, with some states, such as Michigan, California, Nevada, Rhode Island, Oregon, and Kentucky, going above 10 percent and up to 15 percent unemployment. After reaching an all-time high of over 14,000 in October 2008, the Dow Jones Industrial Average plummeted to 6,547 in March 2009—the first time since 1997 that the Dow closed below the 7,000 mark. Although the market did recover much of its losses by the end of 2010, confidence was slow to return, and Americans probably will never again view stocks simply as a "buy and hold" investment. While housing losses, high unemployment, and a weak stock market plagued the American economy, the continued bankruptcies and collapses of many of the largest U.S. corporations, including several banks, were stark indicators that relief and recovery could not happen overnight. While Americans had hoped that the economy had reached its lowest ebb at the close of George W. Bush's administration, it proved to be wishful thinking.

In June 2009 the American automotive industry witnessed what had always been considered the unthinkable. General Motors (GM), which at its peak in the late 1970s employed more than 500,000 workers, filed for bankruptcy. In many respects, since the end of World War II GM had been the weather vane for the national economy: as the old saying went, "what's good for General Motors is good for the country." Even though that saying by GM president Charlie Wilson (1890–1961) was, according to him, a misquotation, no one was singing GM's praises now. When first faced with the crisis the federal government poured nearly $20 billion into GM in an attempt to fend off bankruptcy, but

Clever advertising during the "Cash for Clunkers" federal rebate incentive program in 2009. *Photographer: David Blalock, www.DavidBlalockJr.com.*

this first bailout proved fruitless. Following its bankruptcy, GM received another $30 billion from Congress as the mega-corporation began a painful restructuring that resulted in the loss of tens of thousands of jobs through layoffs and plant closures. One of the demands set forth by the federal government was that GM become more streamlined, which, in part, resulted in fewer brand names, with Hummer being sold off and Saturn and Pontiac, long one of the most popular brands nationwide, simply eliminated. Additionally, the number of dealerships across the country was trimmed from nearly 6,000 to fewer than 4,000. The job loss tally exceeded 150,000 by the end of 2009. Following the bankruptcy, the American tax payer effectively held a 60 percent stake in the company. Chrysler too had filed for bankruptcy protection a little over one month before GM did so. Chrysler restructured in much of the same manner, though the former relied much more heavily on foreign investments, as it forged a partnership with Italian automaker Fiat. Unlike GM or Chrysler, Ford Motor Company did not file for bankruptcy, even though it, too, had witnessed weak sales. In 2009, Ford's rebound proved nothing short of remarkable, as it reported profits in excess of $1 billion.

One of the most controversial aspects of Bush and Obama stimulus packages were the bailouts of many of so-called "too big to fail" corporations in the insurance and financial sectors. Popular attitudes toward these specific bailout programs was mixed. And when some of the bailed-out companies appeared to abuse their TARP funds, sharp public backlash came swiftly. The pre-eminent instances occurred when American International Group (AIG) announced in March 2009 that it handed out bonuses of more than $150 million to its sales and executive employees—this after the federal government had recently used over $160 billion of the taxpayers' money to prop up the failing corporation. Understandably, shock and anger shot across the country. Perhaps the most remarkable feature of the AIG bonus scandal was that the company had actually reported a 2008 fourth quarter loss of over $60 billion. Members of Congress condemned AIG for its actions; while their rhetoric often appeared hollow, both houses of Congress agreed to tax the bonuses AIG executives received by upwards of 70 percent.

Bank failures continued to pile up through 2009 and reached all levels of the financial industry. When rumors began to surface that some of the nation's largest, such as Washington Mutual, BankUnited, Guaranty Bank, and IndyMac, were poised for collapse, Americans across the country relived scenes reminiscent of the Great Depression: long lines of people intent on withdrawing their deposits before it was too late. The majority of the failed banks were small to midsize institutions, but from large to small, the common denominators that dragged the banks under were the rising rates of unemployment and failed mortgages. While many of the failed banks were purchased by other, healthy financial institutions, a massive bailout by the Federal Deposit Insurance Corporation (FDIC) cost the taxpayers billions of dollars. By summer 2009, the number of failed banks was 300 percent greater than in 2008, and by the end of 2009, more than 100 banks had failed. The states with the greatest number of bank failures were California, Texas, Illinois, Georgia, and Florida.

The operating budgets of states, counties, cities, and towns dropped dramatically from 2007 through 2009, as revenue sources, particularly sales and real estate taxes, dried up. By early 2009, some states, especially California, Michigan, Nevada, and Illinois, began to report record budget deficits that required dramatic changes in spending. The trickle-down effect of empty state coffers was felt immediately by local governments. Further exacerbating matters, many government workers and government contractors across the nation were hit with salary cuts or mandatory days off without pay. In addition, many government agencies were required to cut back their operating hours, at times up to 20 percent, in an attempt to save personnel and other operating costs. This gross reduction in salaries by the largest employers in the country further exacerbated the economic misery of those businesses that relied on the direct spending of state and local government employees. Public higher education across the nation witnessed a spike in tuition and fees, as colleges and universities scrambled to make up for the loss of financial assistance from their respective state governments. An additional means of curbing costs in state-supported colleges and universities was lowering the number of students admitted, thus reducing overall enrollment. Historically, when unemployment rates rise, more people decide to improve their personal economic opportunities by training in a new professional field or simply increasing their educational level. This time, however, with cutbacks in enrollments at colleges and universities, many wishful thinkers were left with fewer opportunities.

By the close of the 2000s, the American economy continued to appear shaky. While the credit crisis seemed to have bottomed out and credit markets began to move in a positive direction, bank failures continued to rise. The stock market also gave many investors the impression that it to had hit its low mark in March 2009, and although it consistently climbed in the months that followed, it remained adrift on a sea of volatility. The perceived passing of the housing bubble inspired many economists to theorize that the Great Recession was winding down, but when unemployment rates continued to climb towards double digits nationwide as 2010 began, their optimism seemed out of touch with the realities many Americans faced in their daily lives.

THE QUAGMIRES IN IRAQ AND AFGHANISTAN

In early 2009, the United States turned over the Green Zone, a nearly four-square-mile fortified section of central Baghdad where the coalition military command was headquartered, to the Iraqi government and President Obama pledged to withdraw all U.S. troops by the end of

2011. And while U.S. troops formally turned over security to Iraqi forces and pulled out of urban areas in June 2009, American troops continued to work directly with Iraqi military personnel. Though the number of U.S. casualties consistently dropped in Iraq from 2008 through 2010, violence there continued, as car bombs and suicide bombers ravaged the nation. The central cause behind the violence was the continuation of the civil war between the Shiite and Sunni populations. While the troop surge proved effective in protecting American lives and establishing a legitimate Iraqi government, it did next to nothing to mollify the conflicts between the warring Iraqi factions. On August 22, 2010, the last U.S. combat troops left Iraq. However, more than 50,000 military personnel remained in country. These residual members of the military, referred to by the Obama administration as "advisory and assistance brigades," were considered a task force whose purpose was to provide support to the fragile Iraqi government.

The incredible sacrifice that American men and women in the armed forces made (and continue to make) in Iraq and Afghanistan was—unlike in World War II though not unlike in the Vietnam War—a hardship

Secretary of State Hillary Clinton meeting with Chairman of the Joint Chiefs of Staff Admiral Mullen, Secretary of Defense Robert Gates and Senator John Kerry (D-MA) *Department of Defense photo by Mass Communication Specialist Chad J. McNeeley/Released.*

and burden not shared by the vast majority of their fellow Americans. Whether facing brutal "improvised explosive devices" (IEDs) with which the insurgents and Taliban mined roads and strategic transportation routes or being charged with the nearly impossible task of trying to win the hearts and minds of a people whose country they were occupying with extensive military power, the soldiers and marines experienced levels of constant stress that—stunningly and tragically—led to a suicide rate among them that surpassed the combat death rate. While the U.S. occupation of Iraq seemingly had neared a conclusion, the situation in Afghanistan proved a wholly different situation.

The escalation in U.S. troop strength in Afghanistan began in response to the growing perception not only that the American forces were having exceptional difficulty in locating insurgents, but also that the number of insurgents had actually been increasing since 2005. In addition to the increase of military personnel, the United States also continued to escalate the number of private contractors in Afghanistan. Remarkably, in September 2009, the *New York Times* reported that even with the steady increase of U.S. military personnel in Afghanistan, private military contract forces outnumbered regular military personnel by at least 7 percent. U.S. troop strength in Afghanistan exceeded 30,000 by the end of 2008, and it surpassed 100,000 by late 2010, according to President Obama. A significant pending issue in Afghanistan is whether or not the United States will install a semi-permanent military presence within its borders. While Iraq appeared to be headed towards the development of a strong central government by late 2008, the U.S.-backed government of President Hamid Karzai of Afghanistan remained mired in corruption and controversy, and it looked to many observers as if it might become a failed state susceptible to a takeover, once again, by the Taliban regime, which had been particularly friendly towards al-Qaeda. A potent ground-troop surge would be aimed at rooting out members of both al-Qaeda and the remaining insurgent Taliban members.

The comparisons between the Vietnam War and the long, protracted wars in Afghanistan and Iraq were unavoidable by the start of 2010. The absence of a military draft, a much lower military personnel casualty rate, and the misery of the Great Recession weighing on the minds of Americans has meant that protest against the contemporary military actions is virtually nonexistent in comparison to the Vietnam years from

U.S. Army troops from the 450th Civil Affairs Battalion moving through the Afghanistan village of HeydarKheyl, ensuring that humanitarian conditions are being met. *U.S. Department of Defense, U.S. Army photo by Sgt. Russell Gilchrest.*

1964 through 1973. Additionally, Vietnam never attacked the United States domestically, while agents of al-Qaeda, with the assistance of the Taliban, clearly had. One similarity among these wars is the considerable length of time that the U.S. military has been engaged on foreign soil. In addition, the U.S. military presence in Afghanistan was limited during the first seven years of the conflict, reminiscent of the first few years of American involvement in Vietnam. Military historians also point to the relatively limited initial war effort by the United States in Iraq prior to the surge as comparable to the Vietnam experience. Finally, both Iraq and Afghanistan have been engaged in an internal civil war, as had been the case in Vietnam. The greatest difference between the Vietnam conflict and the contemporary actions in Iraq and Afghanistan is that in the latter two the United States is warring against an adversary that observes no national borders; rather, the conflict is against insurgents and terrorists, persons who have everything to gain and nothing to lose. This last point has tremendously deepened the quagmires that Iraq and Afghanistan have become. By 2010, U.S. combat fatalities in Iraq eclipsed 4,725, with those in Afghanistan passing 2,025. Calendar year 2007 marked the deadliest year in Iraq, with 961 fatalities, with each subsequent year witnessing a dramatic decline. Also by 2010, more than 30,000 U.S. military personnel had been wounded in Iraq. Conversely, as the fighting intensified along with a significant increase in personnel strength, the combat troop fatalities in Afghanistan steadily increased each year from 2004 forward. The number of wounded personnel there passed 2,500 in 2010. The total number of amputees from both theaters of war surpassed 600 in 2010, and the combined estimated number of service members who suffered traumatic brain injuries exceeded 500,000. In that same year, the financial cost to the United States of both wars swelled beyond $1 trillion.

BACK TO THE FUTURE?

The midterm elections of 2010 saw the political pendulum swing yet again. The results of those contests restored Republican control of the House of Representatives and near parity between the two major parties in the Senate. The Republicans gained 60 House seats, bringing their total to 239 versus 196 for the Democrats; in the Senate the Democrats maintained a slight majority, with 53 seats to the 47 held by Republicans, who gained 6 seats. Commenting a day after the November elections, a clearly disappointed President Obama admitted that his party had taken a "shellacking" and lamented that his administration had "lost track of the ways we connected with the folks who got us here in the first place." While midterm elections historically effect a shift in congressional majorities, the unique feature of the 2010 elections was the establishment shortly before and the impact therein of a new political movement.

Beginning in 2009, a grassroots organization known as the Tea Party, so named after the Boston Tea Party, formed in protest to the American Recovery and Reinvestment Act of 2009, which the so-called Tea Partiers decried as excessive and wasteful government spending bound to create a massive and wholly uncontrollable national deficit. Soon, the protest movement came to stand against other acts of legislation its members regarded as gross expansions of the power of the federal government and, as such, infringements upon their individual liberty. In particular the Patient Protection and Affordable Care Act (PPACA), commonly referred to as "Obamacare," drew their considerable ire. In general, members of the populist Tea Party tended to be libertarian and strongly opposed to tax increases. While no one has emerged as their principal spokesperson, significant figures whom the Tea Party endorses and who deem themselves as active within the organization include Senator Rand Paul (R-KY), Governor Nimrata "Nikki" Randhawa Haley (R-SC) and former vice presidential candidate and Alaska governor Sarah Palin (R).

As we have seen, steady, even dynamic, change—in political power domestically, in the emergence of new political and social movements, and even in the power of the United States relative to that of the other nations of the world—has been one of the only constants in United States history since the end of World War II. Recent America, then, is a nation of change—and stark challenges. While the national mood has gone from one of optimism and pride to one of pessimism and disillusionment several times since the end of World War II, as the first decade of the twenty-first century closed, for the first time in their history, the American people began to question whether their children could look forward to a better life than they had known. The way in which we as a diverse people face and handle the many challenges as they emerge will determine not only our fate, but that of generations to come. Scholars have said that United States history since 1945 has been quite a ride; if the pages herein are any sort of guide, we had better fasten our seatbelts.

———— ★ ————

SUGGESTIONS FOR FURTHER READING

The three books authored by Barack Obama, *Dreams from My Father: A Story of Race and Inheritance* (2004), *The Audacity of Hope: Thoughts on Reclaiming the American Dream* (2008), and *Change We Can Believe In: Barack Obama's Plan to Renew America's Promise* (2008), together offer significant insight into President Obama's life and politics. While no scholarly study of the politics of Barack Obama has yet been published, there has been a wave of critical publications as well as the typical laudatory works; most of both types are primarily propaganda, at best. For contemporary American politics the following offer a variety of views: George Will's *One Man's America: The Pleasures and Provocations of Our Singular Nation* (2008); Paul Krugman's *The Conscience of a Liberal* (2007); Ludvig Beckman's *The Liberal State and the Politics of Virtue* (2001); and *The Battle for America 2008: The Story of an Extraordinary Election* (2009), by Dan Balz and Haynes Johnson

One way to understand the transformation of American politics since World War II is to follow the changes that have occurred in the attitudes and behavior of the major groups that make up the electorate. See, for example, Krickus, *Pursuing the American Dream*; Berman, *America's Right Turn*; Gillon, *The Democrats' Dilemma* (all mentioned above); Robert Boston, *The Most Dangerous Man in America: Pat Robertson and the Christian Coalition* (1996); and Linda Witt, Karen M. Paget, and Glenna Matthews, *Running as a Woman: Gender and Power in American Politics* (1994). The dramatic changes in southern politics are discussed in Earl Black and Merle Black, *Politics and Society in the South* (1987); Black and Black, *The Vital South: How Presidents Are Elected* (1992); Richard Scher, *Politics in the New South: Republicanism, Race, and Leadership in the Twentieth Century* (1992); Chandler Davidson and Bernard Grofman, eds., *Quiet Revolution: The Impact of the Voting Rights Act in the South, 1965–1990* (1993); and previously cited studies by Applebome, *Dixie Rising*, and Carter, *The Politics of Rage*. John W. Dean's *Broken Government* (2007) is a most insightful analysis of the transformations led by the Republican Party and conservatives.

The shifting demographics of the United States have long been a particularly popular topic for social scientists. Some of the most notable works include *Generation Me: Why Today's Young Americans Are More Confident, Assertive, Entitled—and More Miserable Than Ever Before* (2007), by Jean Twenge; *The Disuniting of America: Reflections on a Multicultural Society* (1998), by Arthur Schlesinger; *A Hope in the Unseen: An American Odyssey from the Inner City to the Ivy League* (1999), by Ron Suskind; and *On Being Different: Diversity and Multiculturalism in the North American Mainstream* (2007), by Conrad Kottak and Kathryn Kozaitis. For the changing realities for women in the United States, *No Turning Back: The History of Feminism and the Future of Women* (2002), by Estelle Freedman, explores a variety of issues. *The World Split Open: How the Modern Women's Movement Changed America* (2006), by Ruth Rosen is a strong scholarly examination of the groundwork laid in the mid-twentieth century in the women's rights movements.

Recent works on the economy that offer fine analysis and commentary include Frank Cross and Roger Miller's *The Legal Environment of Business: Text and Cases, Ethical, Regulatory, Global, and E-Commerce Issues* (2008); *Catastrophe* (2009), by Dick Morris; Paul Krugman's *The Return of Depression Economics and the Crisis of 2008* (2008); *The Age of Turbulence: Adventures in a New World* (2008), by Alan Greenspan; *Greenspan's Bubbles: The Age of Ignorance at the Federal Reserve* (2008), by Bill Fleckenstein, Fred Sheehan, and William Fleckenstein; *Bernanke's Test: Ben Bernanke, Alan Greenspan, and the Drama of the Central Banker* (2009), by Johan Van Overtveldt; *Too Big to Fail: The Inside Story of How Wall Street and Washington Fought to Save the Financial System from Crisis and Lost* (2009), by Andrew Ross Sorkin; *The Housing Boom and Bust* (2009), by Thomas Sowell; *Street Fighters: The Last 72 Hours of Bear Stearns, the Toughest Firm on Wall Street* (2009), by Kate Kelly;

A Failure of Capitalism: The Crisis of '08 and the Descent into Depression (2009), by Richard A. Posner; *Why GM Matters: Inside the Race to Transform an American Icon* (2009), by William Holstein; *Changing Corporate America from Inside Out: Lesbian and Gay Workplace Rights* (2004), by Nicole Raeburn.

On the topic of the Iraq War, a good starting point are two books by Bing West (whose 1972 landmark publication *The Village* first opened American's eyes to the horrors of the conflict in Vietnam), *No True Glory: A Frontline Account of the Battle for Fallujah* (2005) and T*he Strongest Tribe: War, Politics, and the Endgame in Iraq* (2009). *The Forever War* (2008), by war correspondent Dexter Filkins, is as nonpolitical as one might consider possible and offers readers a strong sense of daily life in the war zones. *The Graveyard of Empires: America's War in Afghanistan* (2009), by Seth Jones, is a strong scholarly publication on the Afghanistan War. Also of note is Jones' *Counterinsurgency in Afghanistan: RAND Counterinsurgency Study—Volume 4* (2008). Pakistani journalist Ahmed Rashid contextualizes the political and social problems the United States faces in the region with *Descent into Chaos: The United States and the Failure of Nation Building in Pakistan, Afghanistan, and Central Asia* (2008). For a consideration of one of the military contractors in Iraq, see *Blackwater: The Rise of the World's Most Powerful Mercenary Army* (2008), by Jeremy Scahill; *From Mercenaries to Market: The Rise and Regulation of Private Military Companies* (2007), edited by Simon Chesterman and Chia Lehnardt; and *Licensed to Kill: Hired Guns in the War on Terror* (2007), by Robert Young Pelton.

———— ★ ————

Index

background and personal information, 451–452; and domestic policies, 453–456; and election of 1988, 446; and foreign affairs, 456–465; as Vice President, 423, 430, 433, 446
Bush, George W., 507, 510–512, 515–516, 525–527, 550, 555–556, 559–563, 569, 598, 600, 602, 603, 605; background and personal informatiom, 508 509; and domestic policies, 517–519, 528, 535, 536, 551; and election of 2000, 500, 505; and election of 2004, 530–535; and foreign affairs, 520–524, 541, 544, 551–554; and second term, 535–541; and terrorist attacks, 512–520
Bush, Jeb, 503
Bush, Prescott S., 451, 508
Butterfield, Paul, 245
Buzhardt, J. Fred, 355
Byrd, Harry Flood, 208
Byrd, Robert C., 397, 528
Byrne, W. Matthew, 354
Byrnes, James F., 23, 26, 43, 83

Califano, Joseph A., 389, 391, 403
California v. *Cabazon Band of Mission Indians,* 481
Calley, Jr., William, 301, 330
Cambodia, 115–116, 326–330, 351, 382–383
Cameron, James, 588–589
Canada, 36, 38, 190, 306, 475, 484
Canadian Royal Commission, 74
Capehart, Homer, 76
Capote, Truman, 257
Carmichael, Stokely, 170–171
Carnegie Endowment for International Peace, 74
Carson, Rachel, 284, 362
Carswell, G. Harrold, 333
Carter Doctrine, 405
Carter, Dan T., 600
Carter, Elliott, 249
Carter, James Earl "Jimmy", Jr., 385–410, 415, 417, 419, 424–426, 436, 444, 572, 599–600

Carter, Rosalynn, 389
Casey, George, 543
Cassidy, Edith, 469
Cassidy, Eldridge, 469
Castro, Fidel, 123–124, 183, 190–191, 193, 290–291, 349, 401, 457, 458
Castroism, 199, 289
Catholic issue, in U.S. politics, 58, 83, 182–184, 186, 208
Cellar, Emanuel, 235, 268
Celler-Kefauver Act (1950), 144
Central Intelligence Agency (CIA), 16, 123, 128, 131, 132, 191, 217, 224, 304, 349, 356, 373, 384, 404, 407, 427, 440, 452, 457, 497, 518, 521, 560
Chamberlain, Neville, 26
Chambers, Whittaker, 74
Chaney, James, 270
Chao, Elaine, 511
Chávez, César, 174
Cheever, John, 254
Cheney, Dick, 464, 501, 503, 510–512, 522, 559
Chernenko, Konstanin, 430
Chertoff, Michael, 540
Chian Kai-shek, 23, 62, 69, 72, 114, 117
Chihuly, Dale, 581
Chile, 123, 289, 342, 398
China, 17; Nationalist China, 41, 62–63, 113, 119; People's Republic of China (PRC), 62, 107, 116, 119, 124, 197–198, 200, 293, 321–322, 328, 342, 399, 401, 429, 452, 484. *See also* Taiwan
Chisholm, Shirley J., 347
Christian Anti-Communist Crusade, 219
Christian Right, 237, 600
Christian, David, 586
Christopher, Warren, 486
Chu, Steven, 569
Church, Frank, 329, 384–385, 409
Churches, in U.S., *see* Religion
Churchill, Winston, 21–23, 30, 201
Citizens' Council, 103, 213, 219
Civil Rights Act (1964), 269–270, 274, 280, 310, 366, 569; Title 6, 280; Title 7, 366
Civil Rights Act (1968), 274

Cosby, Bill, 583
Council for Mutual Economic
　Assistance, 33
Council of Foreign Ministers, 22, 30, 34
Cox, Archibald, 355, 357–358, 369, 497
Coxe, Louis O., 258
Cozzens, John Gould, 254
Crosby, Bing, 246
Crowley, James, 573
Crude Oil Windfall Profit Tax Act
　(1980), 403
Crump, Edward H., 81
Cuba, 123–124, 130, 184, 190–191, 289,
　342, 401, 426, 458
Cuban Missile Crisis, 193–197, 201, 203,
　552
Culture, *see* Popular culture
cummings, e.e., 258
Cuomo, Mario, 465
Czechoslovakia, 22, 31–33, 41, 119, 123,
　286, 396, 459

Dai, Bao, 115, 117
Daley, Richard J., 312
Dallek, Robert, 415
Daschle, Tom, 523
Davies, Richard O., 61, 85
Davis, Bette, 243
Davis, Elmer, 58
Davis, Gray, 546
Dayton conference, and Implementation
　Force (IFOR), 486
de Chamorro, Violeta Barros, 458
de Gaulle, Charles, 203, 287
de Klerk, F.W., 464–465
de Kooning, Willem, 251
De La Beckwith, Byron, 214
Dean, Howard, 530, 532
Dean III, John W., 354–356, 371, 559
Deaver, Michael, 439
"Declaration on Liberated Europe", 24
Defense Appropriations Act (1983), 440
Defense of Marriage Act (1996), 495
Defense Production Act (1950), 71
Defense Reorganization Acts (1953 and
　1958), 110
DeGeneres, Ellen, 585

DeLillo, Don, 586
Deloria, Vine, 175
Democratic coalition, 57, 83, 151, 310,
　350, 430, 433, 469, 598
Democratic Party, 6, 51–54, 215, 220,
　299, 309–312, 314–316, 347–349,
　386, 406, 414–415, 430, 446, 466,
　474–475, 481, 496, 530, 532, 554,
　598–599, 601; as an instrument of
　change, 45–46
Demographic trends, 155–162, 173–174,
　232, 576, 579
Demonstration Cities and Metropolitan
　Area Redevelopment Act (1966), 282
Department of Agriculture, 59
Department of Health, Education and
　Welfare (HEW), 307
Department of Labor, 90, 511
Department of Urban and Housing
　Affairs, 209
Deregulation, federal, 381, 392–393, 396,
　403, 420, 436–438, 454, 544
"Desert Shield", 462–463
"Desert Storm", 463–464, 487, 510–511
Developing Communities Project, 566
Development Loan Fund, 189
Dewey, Thomas E., 52, 54–57, 79, 85,
　179, 220
Diamond, Jared, 586
Diem, Ngo Dinh, 115, 117, 118, 201–202
Dionne, E.J., 601
Dirksen, Everett M., 268–269
Discrimination in Employment Act
　(1967), 569
Displaced Persons Act (1950), 60
Divine, Robert A., 125
Dixiecrats, States' Rights Democratic
　Party, 54
Dixon, Edgar H., 94
Dixon-Yates contract, 94
Dobrynin, Anatoly, 197
Doctrine of "massive retaliation", 110,
　115, 188
Dole, Elizabeth, 501
Dole, Robert J., 386, 407, 473, 493–496,
　501
Dominican Republic, 290–291

Council, 17, 39, 41, 64, 66, 120, 123–124, 190, 485
Updike, John, 255
Upward Bound, 276
Urban Mass Transportation Act (1966), 283
Urbanization, U.S., 157–160, 161–162, 364

van der Rohe, Ludwig Mies, 249–250
Van Doren, Charles, 240
Vance, Cyrus R., 389–390, 398, 400
Vandenberg resolution, 36
Vandenberg, Arthur H., 14, 28, 43
Vaughan, Harry H., 60
Veneman, Ann, 511
Veterans Administration, 10
Vietcong, 118, 202, 292–293, 297–298, 330–331
Vietminh, 114–115, 200
Vietnam Era Reconciliation Program, 379
Vietnam War, 176, 231, 296–299, 307–316, 322, 329, 332–336, 340–341, 346, 348, 351, 379, 395, 467, 508, 518, 531, 581, 598, 607–608; and antiwar protest, 299–306; and peace negotiations, 351; and Vietnamization, 326, 328, 330–331
Voinovich, George, 528
Volunteers in Service to America (VISTA), 276
Vonnegut, Kurt, 255
Voorhis, Jerry, 323
Voting Rights Act (1965), 169, 271, 334, 381, 421

Wagner Act (1935), 49
Wakeman, Frederic, 147
Walesa, Lech, 425
Walker, Alice, 257
Wallace, George C., 214, 270, 314–316, 318, 334, 336, 347, 349, 385–386, 598, 600
Wallace, Henry A., 26, 40, 48, 51, 54, 76
Walsh, Lawrence E., 441
War Assets Administration, 10

War in Afghanistan, 520–524
"war on drugs", 457
War Powers Act, 351, 373
War Production Board, 8, 10
Warhol, Andy, 252
Warren Commission, 216
Warren Court, 332–333
Warren, Earl, 52, 103, 216, 332
Warren, Robert Penn, 256
Warsaw Pact (1955), 112, 203, 341, 459
Washington, Denzel, 589
Washington, Kenny, 165
Water Quality Act (1965), 284
Watergate scandal, 304, 321, 349, 351, 353–359, 369–374, 379, 384–387, 395, 402, 415, 429, 499–500, 510, 559, 599
Watkins, Arthur V., 98
Watt, James G., 420
Watts riot, of 1965, 169–170
Wayne, John, 243
Weapons of mass destruction (WMD), 521, 560–561
Weathermen, the, 303–304, 331
Weaver, Robert C., 271
Wedemeyer, Albert C., 62
Weeks, Sinclair E., 91
Weill, Kurt, 249
Weinberger, Caspar, 424, 469
Weisgall, Hugo, 249
Welch, Joseph N., 97
Welty, Eudora, 256
Wesberry v. *Sanders,* 222
Wesselmann, Tom, 252
Western Europe, and the Cold War, 111–113
Western European Union, 111
Westmoreland, William C., 296–298
Whip Inflation Now (WIN), 380
White "backlash", 168, 171, 215, 221, 272
White House Special Investigations Unit "plumbers", 354
White Paper, U.S., on China, 63
White, Clifton F., 220
White, Paul Dudley, 99
White, William S., 220

Recent America: The United States Since 1945, Third Edition
Developmental and copy editor: Andrew J. Davidson
Production editor: Linda Gaio
Proofreader: Catherine Cocks
Typesetter and text designer: Bruce Leckie
Indexer: Cherity Bacon
Printer: McNaughton & Gunn, Inc.